# Rules and Guidance for Pharmaceutical Manufacturers and Distributors 2015

Compiled by the Inspection, Enforcement and Standards Division of MHRA

Medicines and Healthcare Products Regulatory Agency

Pharmaceutical Press

**Published by Pharmaceutical Press**

1 Lambeth High Street, London SE1 7JN, UK

© Crown Copyright 2015

MHRA, a center of the Medicines and Healthcare Products Regulatory Agency
151 Buckingham Palace Road
Victoria
London SW1W 9SZ
Information on re-use of crown copyright information can be found on the MHRA
website: www.mhra.gov.uk

Designed and published by Pharmaceutical Press 2015

(**P.P**) is a trade mark of Pharmaceutical Press

Pharmaceutical Press is the publishing division of the Royal Pharmaceutical Society

First edition published in 1971 as the *Guide to Good Pharmaceutical Manufacturing
Practice*, second edition in 1977, third edition 1983, fourth edition as the *Rules and
Guidance for Pharmaceutical Manufacturers* in 1993, fifth edition as the *Rules and
Guidance for Pharmaceutical Manufacturers and Distributors* in 1997, sixth edition in
2002, seventh edition in 2007, eight edition in 2014, ninth edition in 2015.

Typeset by OKS Group, Chennai, India
Printed in Great Britain by Advent Colour, Andover, UK
Index Provided by Indexing Specialists, Hove, UK.

ISBN 978 0 85711 171 5 (print)
ISBN 978 0 85711 196 8 (ePDF)
ISBN 978 0 85711 197 5 (ePub)
ISBN 978 0 85711 198 2 (Mobi)

# Contents

# Preface to the 2015 edition

This 2015 edition of Rules and Guidance for Pharmaceutical Manufacturers and Distributors (the "Orange Guide") has been updated to incorporate changes made to Chapters 3, 5, 6 and 8 of the detailed European Community guidelines on Good Manufacturing Practice (GMP) and the revised EU Guidelines on Good Distribution Practice (GDP). In addition to these updates there are also new sections on:

- the Gold Standard for Responsible Persons;
- MHRA Innovation Office;
- the application and inspection process for new licences "what to expect";
- MHRA Compliance Management and Inspection Action Group;
- MHRA risk-based inspection programme; and
- naming contract Quality Control (QC) laboratories.

There is also a new flow chart on registration requirements for UK companies involved in the sourcing and supply of active substances (ASs) to be used in the manufacture of licensed human medicines.

## GMP Directive

The principles and guidelines of GMP are adopted by the European Commission under powers conferred by Council Directive 2001/83/EC. This is to ensure that all medicinal products for human use manufactured or imported into the Community, including medicinal products intended for export, are to be manufactured in accordance with the principles and guidelines of GMP. The objective of GMP is to ensure that products are consistently produced and controlled to particular quality standards. Commission Directive 2003/94/EC (the "GMP Directive") sets out the requirements relating to the implementation of GMP for medicinal products for human use (currently including investigational medicinal products (IMPs)).

## Changes to the Community Code

The Falsified Medicines Directive 2011/62/EU amends Directive 2001/83/EC in a number of places. The first tranche of these changes in relation to manufacturing, wholesale dealing, supervision and sanctions came into force from 2 January 2013 with others relating to the importation of active substances from countries outside of the European Economic Area (EEA) taking effect from the 2 July 2013. These provisions are implemented in the UK by Regulations amending the Human Medicines Regulations 2012. Several other requirements, such as matters relating to safety features, are still to be transposed as they rely on additional regulations and guidance from the European Commission which are being developed.

The headline changes are as follows:

- The current regulatory expectation for the manufacturer of the medicinal product to have audited their suppliers of active substances for compliance with the relevant GMP has been formalised, as is the requirement for the written confirmation of audit (the "QP Declaration", currently required as part of the marketing authorisation application). This audit may be undertaken by the manufacturer of the medicinal product, or by a suitable and appropriately experienced third party under contract to the manufacturer of the medicinal product.
- In addition a formal requirement for manufacturers of medicinal products (or a third party acting under contract) to audit their suppliers of active substances for compliance with the requirements of Good Distribution Practice (GDP) particular to active substances has also been introduced.
- A new requirement for manufacturers, importers and distributors of active substances to be registered with the competent authority of the Member State in which they are established (in the UK this is MHRA). Registrations will be entered onto a database operated by the European Medicines Agency, in a similar manner to the EudraGMDP database. The manufacturer of the medicinal product must verify that their suppliers of active substances are registered.
- The regulatory expectation that manufacturers of the medicinal product will verify the authenticity and quality of the active substances and excipients they use has been formalised.
- The manufacture of active substances for use in a licensed medicinal product must be in compliance with the relevant GMP. These standards are currently described in Part II of the EU Guidelines on GMP.
- Active substances imported from outside of the EEA must have been manufactured in accordance with standards of GMP, at least equivalent to those in the EU and from the 2 July 2013 must be accompanied by a written confirmation that equivalent GMP standards and supervision

apply in the exporting country, unless the active substance is sourced from a country, listed by the European Commission or exceptionally and where necessary, to ensure availability of medicinal products an EU GMP certificate for the site of manufacture is available.

- Manufacturers of medicinal products are required to assess the risk to product quality presented by any excipients they use, by way of a formalised documented risk assessment, and ascertain the appropriate good manufacturing practices necessary to assure their safety and quality. There is no explicit obligation for the medicinal product manufacturer to audit their suppliers of excipients, but it does require the manufacturer to assure themselves that the appropriate good manufacturing practices are being applied.

- In support of the above changes the European Commission is to adopt the following by means of delegated acts and guidelines:
  - principles and guidelines for GMP for active substances;
  - GDP guidelines for active substances; and
  - guidelines for the formal risk assessment process for excipients.

- New obligations on medicinal product manufacturers, wholesale distributors and brokers to inform the competent authority and the marketing authorisation holder (MAH) should information be obtained that products either manufactured under the scope of the manufacturing authorisation or received or offered may be falsified, whether those products are being distributed through the legitimate supply chain, or by illegal means.

- The introduction of the concept of brokering for finished medicinal products and associated obligations to comply with the applicable aspects of GDP.

- A new requirement for persons undertaking the wholesale distribution of medicinal products to third countries to hold an authorisation and to check that their customers are authorised to receive medicines. Where the medicinal products for export have been imported from a third country checks must also be made to ensure the supplier is authorised to supply medicines.

- An extension of the requirement to notify MHRA and the MAH where a wholesale dealer imports from another EEA Member State into the UK a medicinal product which is the subject of a marketing authorisation, and the importer is not the MAH or acting on the MAH's behalf, to centrally authorised products (those holding a marketing authorisation granted by the European Medicines Agency), and the introduction of the option for the competent authority to charge a fee for processing the notification. For products imported into the UK the competent authority would be either the European Medicines Agency or MHRA, depending on whether the product is centrally authorised or not.

## UK legislation

The Human Medicines Regulations 2012 [SI 2012/1916] which came into force on 14 August 2012 modernises the UK's medicines legislation. It replaces most of the 1968 Medicines Act and over 200 statutory instruments, which had been cluttering up the statute book and complicating the law. This consolidated medicines legislation conjoins the statutory provisions for all licences, authorisations and registrations for human medicines.

## Changes to the EU Guide to GMP

Following earlier restructuring of the GMP Guide publication to create Part II (Basic Requirements for Active Substances used as Starting Materials), in December 2010 a new Part III to the EC GMP Guide was created containing a collection of GMP related documents, which are not detailed guidelines on the principles of GMP laid down in Directives 2003/94/EC and 91/412/EC. The aim of Part III is to clarify regulatory expectations and it should be viewed as a source of information on current best practices. Details on the applicability will be described separately in each document. Part III contains five documents: ICH Q9, ICH Q10, Explanatory Notes on the Preparation of a Site Master File, Internationally Harmonised Requirements for Batch Certification and a Template for the "written confirmation" for active substances exported to the EU.

## New/revised chapters

Chapters 3 and 5 have been revised to improve guidance on the prevention of cross contamination ("dedicated facilities") and include reference to a new complementary toxicological assessment guidance. These revisions come into operation 1 March 2015.

Chapter 5 (in addition to the above) has also been revised to add a new section on the qualification of suppliers in order to reflect the legal obligation of manufacturing authorisation holders to ensure that active substances are produced in accordance with GMP. The changes include supply chain traceability. In addition a new section is inserted to clarify and harmonise expectations of manufacturers regarding the testing of starting materials while a further new section introduces guidance on notification of restrictions in supply. This revised Chapter comes into operation 1 March 2015.

Chapter 6 has been updated and has a new section on technical transfer of testing methods and other items such as Out Of Specification results. This revised Chapter came into operation 1 October 2014.

Chapter 8 has been revised to: reflect Quality Risk Management principles to be applied when investigating quality defects/complaints and when making decisions in relation to product recalls or other risk-mitigating actions; emphasise the need for the cause(s) of quality defects/complaints to be investigated and determined, and that appropriate preventative actions are put in place to guard against a recurrence of the issue and clarify expectations and responsibilities in relation to the reporting of quality defects to the Supervisory Authority. This revised Chapter comes into operation 1 March 2015.

Finally Part II of the GMP guide has been amended. A revision has been made to section 1.2 to take into consideration the completed revision of various Annexes to the GMP guide and hence Part I can no longer be followed for active substances used at starting materials. Furthermore, clarification of the relationship between section 17 of Part II and the forthcoming guidelines on Good Distribution Practices for active substances for medicinal products for human use has been added to section 1.2. An obsolete reference to Annex 20 in section 2.21 has been amended. These revisions came into operation 1 September 2014.

## New/revised annexes

Currently there are no new or revised annexes to report on.

## Changes on the horizon

Further new sections and revisions to the EC Guide to GMP are planned and are currently under discussion. These include:

- Annex 1 is being considered for full revision pending further discussion with PIC/S.
- Annex 15 is at consultation at the Concept Paper stage to align with the concepts of ICH Q9 and Q10, with changes to other chapters and annexes in the GMP Guidelines, the Quality Working Party's revision of its guideline on process validation and there has been advancement in manufacturing technology through the introduction of process analytical technology and the continuous manufacture concept.
- Annex 16 is being revised to reflect the globalisation of the pharmaceutical supply chain and the introduction of new control strategies, changes arising from Directive 2011/62/EU amending Directive 2001/83/EC as regards the prevention of the entry into the legal supply chain of falsified medicinal products, and to align with the concepts and terminology of ICH Q8, Q9 and Q10.
- Annex 17 is being considered for amendment to address the changes from parametric release with a focus on the release of terminally

sterilised medicinal products to align with the concepts of ICH Q8, Q9 Q10 and Q11 guidelines and the Quality Working Party's guideline on real-time release testing.

- New guidelines, based on requirements in Directive 2011/62/EU on the formalised risk assessment for ascertaining the appropriate GMP for excipients of medicinal products for human use.
- New guidelines, based on requirements in 2011/62/EU, on the principles of GDP for active substances for medicinal products for human use.
- The new requirements introduced by the Falsified Medicines Directive for medicinal products to bear safety features (set out below) are to be the subject of a separate delegated act from the European Commission, and any standards for the use of them are still to be defined.
  - the Qualified Person to ensure that they have been affixed.
  - safety features not to be removed or covered unless the manufacturing authorisation holder verifies that the medicinal product is authentic and has not been tampered with and that replacement safety features are equivalent and are applied in accordance with GMP.
  - wholesale dealers to verify that any medicinal products they receive are not falsified, by checking that any "safety features" used on the outer packaging of a product are intact.
  - brokers and wholesale dealers to record the batch numbers of, as a minimum, those products with safety features attached and for wholesale dealers to provide a record of batch numbers when supplying those products to their customers.

## The Orange Guide 2015

The 2014 edition reported that, going forward, to keep up with changes to EU text and national provisions, the print version of the "Rules & Guidance for Pharmaceutical Manufacturers and Distributors" known as the Orange Guide will be revised and published annually.

I am pleased to report that this is the first annual update of the Orange Guide and is the ninth edition of the "Rules & Guidance for Pharmaceutical Manufacturers and Distributors" issued by MHRA. This revised edition continues to bring together existing and revised Commission written material concerning the manufacture, importation, distribution and brokering of human medicines and matters relating to the manufacture, importation and distribution of active substances.

Although it is UK legislation, implementing the directives, that bears directly on activities in the UK, it is often helpful for manufacturers and wholesalers to be aware of the original EU obligations. This is particularly so when trading across boundaries of Member States. Therefore, the "Titles" or sections of Directive 2001/83/EC, as amended, dealing with manufacture and wholesale distribution of products for human use, brokering finished medicinal products and provisions relating to the manufacture, importation and distribution of active substances remain in this edition.

There are revised chapters in GMP (3, 5, 6 and 8) and an amended Part II of GMP. There are new sections covering MHRA's Innovation Office, Compliance Management and Inspection Action Group, and Risk-based inspection programme. There are also new sections on "what to expect" from the application and inspection process for new licences and the naming of contract Quality Control (QC) laboratories on licences.

Following extensive discussion with pharmaceutical companies and MHRA, Cogent (the national skills body for the science industries) has published a new Gold Standard role profile for the Responsible Person. This is included in this edition.

UK guidance and legislation for the brokering of finished medicinal products and the manufacture, importation and distribution of active substances remain and a new flow chart has been included for registration to manufacture, import and distribute active substances.

Although much of the text in this book is available in its original form in other places, including various websites, I am pleased that the Orange Guide continues to satisfy a demand for information in one authoritative and convenient place. In particular, the detailed Index to the Orange Guide at the end of the book, which conjoins the index created by MHRA for the EU GMP guide at readers' request, adds value and simplifies the navigation of these complex documents. Readers are invited to suggest to MHRA further updates to the Index, for future improvements in navigation and cross-referencing.

For the 2015 version, we continue to have the entire Orange Guide available online, as part of "Medicines Complete" – a subscription-based database of leading medicines and healthcare references and in other electronic formats including other E-reader formats. Also available is a separate updated GDP booklet for the wholesale dealing market. I hope that this revised edition in its existing formats will continue to be useful.

**Gerald Heddell**
**Director, Inspection, Enforcement and Standards Division**
September 2014

# Acknowledgements

To the European Commission for permission to reproduce the rules governing medicinal products in the EC. Vol IV. Good Manufacturing Practice for medicinal products (http://ec.europa.eu/health/documents/eudralex/vol-4/index_en.htm) © European Union, 1995–2014 text of the Directives, (Only European Union legislation printed in the paper edition of the *Official Journal of the European Union* [OJ] is deemed authentic) and the guidelines on Good Distribution Practice.

To the Society of Biology, the Royal Pharmaceutical Society and the Royal Society of Chemistry for permission to reproduce the texts of the Code of Practice for Qualified Persons.

To the Heads of Medicines Agencies for permission to reproduce the names and addresses of other human and veterinary medicines authorities in Europe.

To Cogent for permission to reproduce the new Gold Standard role profile for the Responsible Person.

# Feedback

Comments on the content or presentation of the Orange Guide are encouraged and will be used to develop further editions. Your views are valued and both MHRA and Pharmaceutical Press would appreciate you taking the time to contact us. Please visit the feedback page at http://www.pharmpress.com/orangeguide-feedback or send your feedback to the address below:

"The Orange Guide"
Customer Services
Medicines and Healthcare products Regulatory Agency
151 Buckingham Palace Road
Victoria
London SW1W 9SZ
UK
Tel.: +44 (0)20 3080 6000
Fax: +44 (0)20 3118 9803
E-mail: orange.guide@mhra.gsi.gov.uk

# Introduction

This publication brings together the main pharmaceutical regulations, directives and guidance which manufacturers, wholesalers and brokers of human medicines are expected to follow when making, distributing or involved in the supply of medicinal products in the European Union (EU) and European Economic Area (EEA).[1] It also covers the main directive and guidance which affect manufacturers, importers and distributors of active substances. It is of particular relevance to all holders of manufacturer's licences and wholesale dealer's licences and to their Qualified Persons (QPs) and Responsible Persons (RPs), and persons registered to broker finished medicinal products or manufacture, import or distribute active substances within the Community. All these players have a responsibility for ensuring compliance with many of these regulatory requirements.

The obligation on governments of all Member States of the EU to ensure that pharmaceutical manufacturers are authorised is stated in Title IV of Directive 2001/83/EC, as amended (products for human use) and of Directive 2001/82/EC (veterinary products). These titles, or sections, are also the source of requirements for compliance with Good Manufacturing Practice (GMP), employment of QPs and repeated inspections by the regulatory authorities. Title IV also requires importers, manufacturers and distributors of active substances who are established in the Union to register their activity with the competent authority of the Member State in which they are established.

Title VII of the Directive 2001/83/EC requires all wholesale distributors to be authorised, to have available RPs and comply with the guidelines on Good Distribution Practice (GDP). Title VII also requires brokers of medicines within the Community to be registered with their competent authority and to comply with appropriate GDP requirements.

The principles and guidelines of GMP are set out in two Commission Directives: 2003/94/EC for medicinal products for human use (replacing Directive 91/356/EEC) and 91/412/EEC for veterinary medicinal products. In the UK, the provisions for manufacturers and wholesale dealers have

---

[1] The member states of the European Community plus Iceland, Liechtenstein and Norway.

been implemented by requirements and undertakings incorporated in the Human Medicines Regulations 2012 [SI 2012/1916]. Compliance with the principles and guidelines of GMP is a statutory requirement. The European Community (EC) Guide to GMP[2] (including its annexes) provides detailed guidance which interprets and expands on the statutory principles and guidelines. Changes in technical knowledge and in regulations are reflected by additional and revised annexes.

GMP includes elements of the International Standard for Quality Management Systems ISO 9001:2000 with additional requirements specific to medicines. The UK first produced a national guide to GMP (known traditionally as the Orange Guide) in 1971. Guidance on good pharmaceutical wholesaling practice was added in the 1977 edition and a further edition was produced in 1983. The EC guidance, first issued for GMP in 1989 and for GDP in 1993, supersedes this and all other national guides of Member States, although much that was familiar in the old UK Guide can still be recognised in the EC guidance. The Pharmaceutical Inspection Co-operation Scheme has adopted the text of the EC Guide to GMP ensuring harmonisation of guidelines by its member inspectorates throughout the world. Mutual Recognition Agreements between the EC and several third countries have recognised the equivalence of GMP requirements of the parties concerned.

Manufacturers are required to name a QP on their manufacturer's licence. No batch of medicinal product may be released to the market within the EU unless a nominated QP has certified that it has been manufactured and checked in compliance with the laws in force. Guidance to QPs in fulfilling their responsibilities is given in the EC Guide to GMP and in the Code of Practice[3] for Qualified Persons which they are expected to follow. In similar spirit, wholesalers are required to appoint a RP who has the knowledge and responsibility to ensure that correct procedures are followed during distribution. Notes on the qualifications and duties of RPs are given to assist this.

The distribution network for medicinal products has become complex and involves many players. Revised guidelines for GDP assist wholesale distributors in conducting their activities and to prevent falsified medicines from entering the legal supply chain. The guidance also provides specific rules for persons involved in activities in relation to the sale or purchase of

---

[2] Commission of the European Communities. The rules governing medicinal products in the European Community. Vol IV. Good Manufacturing Practice for medicinal products.

[3] The Society of Biology, The Royal Pharmaceutical Society, The Royal Society of Chemistry. Code of Practice for Qualified Persons. In: Register of Qualified Persons. London: The Society of Biology, The Royal Pharmaceutical Society, The Royal Society of Chemistry 2009, Revised February 2013.

medicinal products whilst not conducting a wholesale activity i.e. brokers of licensed human medicines.

The manufacture of active substances for use in a licensed medicinal product must be in compliance with the relevant GMP. These standards are currently described in Part II of EU GMP. Active substances imported from outside of the EEA must have been manufactured in accordance with standards of GMP at least equivalent to those in the EU. From the 2 July 2013 they must be accompanied by a written confirmation that equivalent GMP standards and supervision apply in the exporting country, unless the active substance is sourced from a country listed by the European Commission or exceptionally and where necessary to ensure availability of medicinal products an EU GMP certificate for the site of manufacture is available.

The European Commission will be adopting principles and guidelines for GMP for active substances, GDP guidelines for active substances, guidelines for the formal risk assessment process for excipients by means of delegated acts and guidelines.

The aim of GMP and GDP is to assure the quality of the medicinal product for the safety, well-being and protection of the patient. In achieving this aim it is impossible to over-emphasise the importance of people, at all levels, in the assurance of the quality of medicinal products. This is emphasised in the first principle in the EC Guide to GMP.

The great majority of reported defective medicinal products has resulted from human error or carelessness, not from failures in technology. All the people involved with the production, Quality Control or distribution of medicinal products, whether key personnel, production or control or warehouse staff, inspectors of a regulatory authority or others involved in the many activities which lead to a patient taking a medicine, should bear this constantly in mind when performing their duties.

# MHRA

# 1

# MHRA: Licensing, Inspection and Enforcement for Human Medicines

## Contents

## Overview of the Medicines and Healthcare Products Regulatory Agency Group

In 2002, Ministers announced that the Medicines Control Agency and the Medical Devices Agency would be merged to form the Medicines and Healthcare products Regulatory Agency (MHRA). MHRA is responsible for regulating all medicines and medical devices in the UK by ensuring they work and are acceptably safe.

On the 1 April 2013 the National Institute for Biological Standards and Control (NIBSC), previously part of the Health Protection Agency (HPA), became a new centre of the Medicines and Healthcare Products Regulatory Agency Group alongside the Clinical Practice Research Datalink (CPRD).

MHRA and NIBSC have worked closely together for many years and have common interests in managing risks associated with biological medicines, facilitating development of new medicines safely and effectively, and maintaining UK expertise and ability to contribute to assuring the quality and safety of medicines in Europe and beyond.

These developments have created a new organisation that is a world leader in supporting science and research and the regulation of medicines and medical devices, strengthening the support provided to the UK's medicine's industry. The new Medicines and Healthcare Products Regulatory Agency group consists of:

- **MHRA Regulatory,** who protect health and improve lives by ensuring that medicines and medical devices work, and are acceptably safe; focusing on the core activities of product licensing, inspection and enforcement, and pharmacovigilance.
- **The Clinical Practice Research Datalink** (CPRD), which gives access to an unparalleled resource for conducting observational research and improving the efficiency of interventional research, across all areas of health, medicines and devices. CPRD joined the MHRA in 2012.
- **The National Institute for Biological Standards and Control,** world leaders in assuring the quality of biological medicines through product testing, developing standards and reference materials and carrying out applied research.

### Medicines and Healthcare Products Regulatory Agency

| MHRA | National Institute for Biological Standards Board (NIBSC) | Clinical Practice Research Datalink (CPRD) |
|---|---|---|
| • Operating a system of licensing, classification, monitoring (post-marketing surveillance) and enforcement for medicines. | • Devising and drawing up standards for the purity and potency of biological substances and designing appropriate test procedures. | • Managing and designing CPRD services to maximise the way anonymised NHS clinical data can be linked to enables many types of observational research and deliver research outputs that are beneficial to improving and safeguarding public health. |
| • Discharging statutory obligations for medical devices, including designating and monitoring the performance of notified bodies. | • Preparing, approving, holding and distributing standard preparations of biological substances. | |
| • Ensuring statutory compliance in medicines clinical trials and assessing medical device clinical trials proposals. | • Providing, or arranging for, the provision of laboratory testing facilities for the testing of biological substances, carrying out such testing, examining records of manufacture and quality control and reporting on the results. | |
| • Promulgating good practice in the safe use of medicines and medical devices. | • Carrying out or arranging for the carrying out of research in connection with biological standards and control functions. | |
| • Regulating the safety and quality of blood and blood components. | | |
| • Discharging the functions of the UK Good Laboratory Practice Monitoring Authority (GLPMA). | | |
| • Managing the activities of the British Pharmacopoeia (BP). | | |

## Overview of MHRA

All licensed human medicines available in the UK are subject to rigorous scrutiny by MHRA before they can be used by patients. This ensures that human medicines meet acceptable standards on safety, quality and efficacy. It is the responsibility of MHRA and the expert advisory bodies set up by the Human Medicines Regulations 2012 [SI 2012/1916] (previously under the 1968 Medicines Act) to ensure that the sometimes difficult balance between safety and effectiveness is achieved. MHRA experts assess all applications for new human medicines to ensure they meet the required standards. This is followed up by a system of inspection and testing which continues throughout the lifetime of the medicine.

As the UK government's public health body which brings together the regulation of human medicines and medical devices, science and research the roles of MHRA are to:

- license medicines, manufacturers and distributors;
- register brokers of finished medicines and manufacturers, importers and distributors of active substances;
- regulate medical devices;
- approve UK clinical trials;
- monitor medicines and medical devices after licensing;
- ensure the safety and quality of blood;
- tackle illegal activity involving medicines, medical devices and blood;
- promote an understanding of the benefits and risks;
- facilitate the development of new medicines;
- support innovation in medicines and medical devices;
- be a leading provider of data and data services for healthcare research;
- work with international partners on issues; and
- provide a national voice for the benefits and risks of medicines, medical devices and medical technologies.

MHRA also hosts and supports a number of expert advisory bodies, including the Commission on Human Medicines (which replaced the Committee on the Safety of Medicines in 2005), and the British Pharmacopoeia Commission. In addition, as part of the European system of medicines approval, MHRA or other national bodies may be the Rapporteur or Co-rapporteur for any given pharmaceutical application, taking on the bulk of the verification work on behalf of all members, while the documents are still sent to other members as and where requested.

## MHRA Innovation Office

One of the key objectives of MHRA is to support greater access to safe and effective medicinal products and medical devices. The timely introduction of innovative products benefits both patients and the public. This section provides information about MHRA's Innovation Office and highlights how you can get scientific and regulatory advice to support the development of innovational products.

MHRA's Innovation Office helps organisations that are developing innovative medicines, medical devices or using novel manufacturing processes to navigate the regulatory processes in order to be able to progress their products or technologies. Examples of innovative products include Advanced Therapy Medicinal Products (ATMPs), nanotechnology, stratified medicines, novel drug/device combinations and advanced manufacturing.

If you are a pharmaceutical researcher, developer, manufacturer, etc. and you have a question about an innovative medicine, device or novel manufacturing process, contact the MHRA Innovation Office using one of the routes below.

After contacting the office you will receive a response within 20 working days. Depending on the nature of the query, your response will consist of either a simple answer or a recommended course of action, which may involve regulatory or scientific advice.

### SCIENTIFIC AND REGULATORY ADVICE

MHRA offers regulatory and scientific advice. For medicines, we currently carry out over 250 scientific advice meetings a year. Joint meetings can be held with the National Institute for Health and Care Excellence (NICE) to consider health technology assessment issues at the same time.

### SCIENTIFIC ADVICE FROM THE EU

The European Medicines Agency (EMA) offers a comprehensive scientific advice service, available to provide assistance during the initial development of a medicine and during the post-authorisation phase. The advice is provided by the EMA's Committee for Medicinal Products for Human Use (CHMP),[1] based on recommendations of the Scientific Advice Working Party (SAWP).[2] Further advice on accessing scientific advice can be obtained from the EMA.[3]

---

[1] http://www.ema.europa.eu/ema/index.jsp?curl=pages/about_us/general/general_content_000094.jsp&mid=WC0b01ac0580028c79

[2] http://www.ema.europa.eu/ema/index.jsp?curl=pages/contacts/CHMP/people_listing_000022.jsp&mid=WC0b01ac0580028d94

[3] http://www.ema.europa.eu/ema/index.jsp?curl=pages/regulation/general/general_content_000049.jsp&mid=WC0b01ac05800229b9&jsenabled=true

## SCIENTIFIC ADVICE FROM THE UK

MHRA offers a comprehensive scientific advice service which can assist companies in making decisions about a range of scientific and regulatory issues. Scientific advice can be requested at any stage of the initial development of a medicine and also during the pre-submission period. Please see MHRA webpages on 'Scientific Advice'.[4]

## MHRA supporting innovation in medicines

MHRA supports innovation through:

Medicines

- membership on European committees (Commission on Human Medicinal Products (CHMP), CAT, COMP, PDCO) and CHMP Working Parties;[5]
- membership of European Good Distribution Practice (GDP)/Good Manufacturing Practice (GMP) Inspectors Working Group;
- advice given to EMA Innovation Task Force on a wide range of innovative technologies and products;
- working within the ICH network;
- writing regulatory and scientific guidance documents via the ICH and CHMP; and
- membership of European GDP/GMP Inspectors Working Group

Devices sector

- membership of European committees such as the Medical Devices Expert group (MDEG), Borderlines and Classification Group, New and Emerging Technologies Working Group (NET); and
- part of the International Medical Device Regulators Forum.

## Inspection, Enforcement and Standards Division

MHRA's Inspection, Enforcement and Standards Division is responsible for ensuring compliance with the regulations and standards that apply to the manufacture, control and supply of medicines on the UK market.

---

[4] http://www.mhra.gov.uk/Howweregulate/Medicines/Licensingofmedicines/
Informationforlicenceapplicants/Otherusefulservicesandinformation/Scientific
adviceforlicenceapplicants/index.htm

[5] http://www.ema.europa.eu/ema/index.jsp?curl=pages/about_us/general/general_
content_000217.jsp&mid=

## Inspectorate

The Inspectorate Group in MHRA's Inspection, Enforcement and Standards Division is comprised of dedicated units for Good Manufacturing Practice (GMP), Good Distribution Practice (GDP), Good Laboratory Practice (GLP), Good Clinical Practice (GCP) and Good Pharmacovigilance Practice (GPvP).

## Good Manufacturing Practice (GMP)

GMP Inspectors conduct inspections of pharmaceutical manufacturers and other organisations to assess compliance with EC guidance on Good Manufacturing Practice (GMP) and the relevant details contained in marketing authorisations and Clinical Trials Authorisations. They ensure that medicines supplied in the UK and wider EU meet consistent high standards of quality, safety and efficacy. Overseas manufacturing sites to be named on UK or EU marketing authorisations are also required to pass an inspection prior to approval of the marketing authorisation application. Following approval, a risk-based inspection programme maintains on-going surveillance of UK and overseas manufacturing site compliance with EC GMP.

GMP Inspectors are responsible for inspecting and authorising a range of manufacturers of sterile and non-sterile dosage forms, biological products, investigational medicinal products, herbal products and active pharmaceutical ingredients, in addition to certain analytical laboratories. The manufacture of unlicensed medicines by holders of Manufacturer "Specials" Licences in the UK NHS and commercial sector is also inspected on a routine basis to assess compliance with relevant legislation and GMP.

The safety and quality of human blood for transfusion, or for further manufacture into blood-derived medicines, is ensured through inspections of relevant collection, processing, testing and storage activities at Blood Establishments and UK Hospital Blood Banks. These inspections assess compliance with specific UK and EU regulatory requirements, which take into account the detailed principles of GMP.

GMP Inspectors serve on a number of UK, EU and international technical and standards committees and provide help and advice to senior managers, Ministers and colleagues across the Agency, as necessary. Support and expertise is also provided to the inspection programmes of the European Medicines Agency (EMA), European Directorate for Quality of Medicines (EDQM), and the World Health Organization (WHO).

## Good Distribution Practice (GDP)

GDP Inspectors conduct inspections of sites of wholesale dealers to assess compliance with EU Guidelines on Good Distribution Practice (GDP) and the conditions of a wholesale dealer's licence.

Inspectors will ensure that medicinal products are handled, stored and transported under conditions as prescribed by the marketing authorisation or product specification.

Inspections are undertaken of new applicants and then subsequently on a routine schedule based on a risk assessment of the site.

There are a number of developments that had an impact on GDP during 2013 and going forward including:

- the Human Medicines Regulations 2012 [SI 2012/1916] which came into force in August 2012, replacing the majority of the Medicines Act 1968 and its supporting legislation;
- the transposition of the Falsified Medicines Directive 2011/62/EU into UK medicines legislation which extends GDP to any person or entity who procures, stores or supplies medicinal products, for export to countries outside of the EEA and to brokers of finished medicines within the EEA.
- the application of the revised EU Guidelines on GDP of the 5 November, which entered into force on 24 November 2013. This version replaced the earlier version, which entered into force on 8 September 2013, and introduced the following changes:
  - the maintenance of a quality system setting out responsibilities, processes and risk management principles in relation to wholesale activities;
  - suitable documentation which prevents errors from spoken communication;
  - sufficient competent personnel to carry out all the tasks for which the wholesale distributor is responsible;
  - adequate premises, installations and equipment so as to ensure proper storage and distribution of medicinal products;
  - appropriate management of complaints, returns, suspected falsified medicinal products and recalls;
  - outsourced activities correctly defined to avoid misunderstandings;
  - rules for transport in particular to protect medicinal products against breakage, adulteration and theft, and to ensure that temperature conditions are maintained within acceptable limits during transport;
  - specific rules for brokers (person involved in activities in relation to the sale or purchase of medicinal products, except for wholesale distribution, that do not include physical handling the products).

The revised EU Guidelines on GDP have been included in this publication.

terminations, cancellations, suspensions and revocations making extensive use of computer technology to do so.

## Export Certificates

The Data Processing team are also responsible for issuing certificates in support of the World Health Organization (WHO) scheme on the quality of pharmaceutical products moving in international commerce (often referred to as export certificates):

- Certificate of a pharmaceutical product (CPP). This certificate complies with the WHO format.
- Certificate of licensing status (CLS). This certificate complies with the WHO format.
- Certificate of manufacturing status (CMS).
- Certificate for the importation of a pharmaceutical constituent (CPC).
- Statement of licensing status of a pharmaceutical product(s).

## Importing unlicensed medicines – import notifications

Under regulation 46 of the Human Medicines Regulations 2012 [SI 2012/1916] a medicine must have a marketing authorisation (includes Product Licences) unless exempt. One of these exemptions, which is in regulation 167 to these regulations, is for the supply of unlicensed medicinal products for the special needs of individual patients, commonly, but incorrectly called "named patients". Prospective importers must hold a relevant licence and must notify MHRA of their intention to import:

- for import from within the European Economic Area (EEA), a Wholesale Dealer's Licence valid for import and handling unlicensed relevant medicinal products;
- for import from outside of the EEA, a Manufacturer's 'Specials' Licence valid for import.

The Data Processing team makes use of a bespoke computer system (INS) to enter the information, refer flagged requests to Pharmaceutical Assessors for assessment as required and issue confirmation letters authorising or rejecting importation.

## Defective Medicines Report Centre (DMRC)

MHRA's Defective Medicines Report Centre (DMRC) plays a major part in the protection of public health by minimising the hazard to patients arising from the distribution of defective medicinal products. It does this by providing an emergency assessment and communications system between suppliers of medicinal products, the regulatory authorities and the users. It achieves this by receiving and assessing reports of suspected defective medicines, monitoring and as necessary advising and directing appropriate actions by the responsible authorisation holder and communicating the details of this action as necessary and with appropriate urgency to recipients of the products and other interested parties in the UK and elsewhere by means of drug alerts.

Manufacturers and importers are obliged to report to the licensing authority (MHRA) any quality defect in a medicinal product which could result in a recall or restriction on supply. Other users and distributors of medicinal products are encouraged to do this.

Where a defective medicine is considered to present a risk to public health, the marketing authorisation holder, or the manufacturer as appropriate, is responsible for recalling the affected batch(es) or, in extreme cases, removing all batches of the product from the market. The DMRC will normally support this action by the issue of a drug alert notification to healthcare professionals. Drug alerts are classed from 1 to 4 according to their criticality and the speed with which action must be taken to remove the defective medicine from the distribution chain and, where necessary, from the point of dispensing and use. This varies from immediate action for a Class 1 alert, to action within five days for a Class 3 alert. In some low-risk circumstances the product may be allowed to remain in the supply chain when the DMRC will issue a Class 4 "caution in use" alert.

The DMRC is also part of the European Rapid Alert System, and in the case of Class 1 and Class 2 will notify regulators in other countries using the European Rapid Alert System.

## Enforcement Group

Medicines legislation contains statutory provisions to enforce the requirements of the Human Medicines Regulations 2012 [SI 2012/1916] and the remaining provisions of the 1968 Medicines Act.

This enforcement role is carried out by MHRA's Enforcement Group which is comprised of a Case Referrals Team, Intelligence Analysts, Investigations Team, Prosecution Unit and Policy/Relationships management.

The legislation confers certain powers, including rights of entry, powers of inspection, seizure, sampling and production of documents. Duly authorised Investigation Officers investigate cases using these powers and, where appropriate, criminal prosecutions are brought by the Crown Prosecution Service (CPS). MHRA investigators also investigate offences

- at least one member of the IAG Secretariat;
- any inspector making a referral to the IAG;
- a representative from Enforcement Operations (if required); and
- members of MHRA staff may also attend for training purposes.

In addition, the following will attend IAG1:

- an expert/senior GMP inspector;
- an expert/senior GDP inspector;
- if required a representative from the Veterinary Medicines Directorate (external link); and
- an expert in blood and blood products (if required).

In addition, the following will attend IAG2:

- an expert/senior GCP inspector;
- an expert/senior GPvP inspector;
- the Clinical Trials Unit manager or deputy; and
- the Pharmacovigilance Risk Management Group manager or deputy.

## REASONS FOR REFERRAL

This will usually happen if, during the inspection process, the inspector has identified one or more critical "deficiencies" as a result of a Good Practice Standards (GxP) inspection. However, a referral may also be made as a result of a licence variation, the failure to contact an organisation, the refusal of an organisation to accept an inspection, the outcome of enforcement activity, the outcome of a product recall or from an issue raised by another Member State.

The company will be informed during the closing meeting of an inspection that a referral to IAG will be made. This will be further confirmed in the post-inspection letter. From that point, correspondence between the company and the Agency should go via the IAG Secretariat.

How the process works:

(1) Inspection reveals serious (critical) deficiencies and informs company of IAG referral.
(2) Post-inspection letter is issued to company signed by responsible operations manager/lead inspector.
(3) IAG discusses the case at its next available meeting (if necessary an emergency meeting can be called).
(4) IAG proposes its action to the divisional director for approval.
(5) The referred company is informed of IAG action and next steps.
(6) Actions are followed up at subsequent meetings until the situation is resolved.
(7) The matter is kept on the agenda until IAG is satisfied that the referral can be closed.

## IAG POSSIBLE ACTIONS

### IAG1 (GMP/GDP/BEA)

- refusal to grant a licence or a variation;
- proposal to suspend the licence for a stated period;
- notification of immediate suspension of the licence for a stated period (no longer than three months);
- proposal to revoke the licence;
- action to remove a Qualified Person/Responsible Person (QP/RP) from the licence;
- issue a Cease and Desist order in relation to a Blood Establishment Authorisation;
- issue a warning letter to the company/individual;
- request a written justification for actions of a QP/RP;
- referral of a QP to his/her professional body;
- increased inspection frequency;
- request the company/individual attend a meeting at the Agency; or
- refer to the Enforcement Group for further consideration.

### IAG2 (GCP/GPvP)

- issue an infringement notice in relation to a clinical trial;
- suspend or revoke a clinical trial authorisation;
- further follow-up inspections, or triggered inspections at related organisations (e.g. issues in GCP may trigger a GMP inspection);
- referral to CHMP (Committee for Medicinal Products for Human Use) for consideration for against a marketing authorisation (eg suspended, varied or revoked);
- liaison and coordinated action with EMA (European Medicines Agency) and other Member States regarding concerns;
- refer the case to the EMA for consideration of the use of the EU Infringement Regulation (which could result in a fine);
- request a written justification for action of a QPPV (Qualified Person responsible for pharmacovigilance);
- request the company/individual attend a meeting at the Agency; or
- refer to the Enforcement Group for further consideration.

In the case of inspections in third countries:

- a refusal to name a site on a marketing authorisation;
- a recommendation that a site be removed from a marketing authorisation;
- the issuing of a GMP non-compliance statement;
- in the case of an adverse (voluntary or triggered) active pharmaceutical ingredients (API) inspection, this could result in the removal of the API site from the marketing authorisation; or

● in the case of an adverse (voluntary or triggered) investigational medicinal products (IMP) inspection, this could result in the suspension of a clinical trial.

In all cases, an action could result in the withdrawal of product (API, IMP medicinal product, etc.) from the market. This specific action is, however, handled by the Defective Medicines Reporting Centre (DMRC) rather than directly by IAG.

## LEGAL BASIS FOR THIS ACTION

The legal basis for licensing action is contained in:

● The Human Medicines Regulations 2012;
● The Medicines for Human Use (Clinical Trials) Regulations 2004; and
● The Blood Safety and Quality Regulations 2005.

## WHAT A LICENCE HOLDER SHOULD DO IF REFERRED TO IAG

In the first instance, a referral should be treated as a requirement to immediately correct the deficiencies identified during the inspection and report completed actions to the IAG Secretariat/Inspectorate as soon as possible.

If the referral results in an immediate suspension of a manufacturing/ wholesale dealer's licence, there are no rights of appeal for the immediate suspension (which can last no longer than three months). During this time a company should be focused on correcting the inspection deficiencies.

If the referral results in a proposed suspension, variation or revocation of a licence a company will have the following appeal options prior to a decision being made:

● may make written representations to the licensing authority (MHRA); or
● may appear before and be heard by a person appointed for the purpose by the licensing authority (a fee of £10,000 will be charged for a person appointed request).

If a company submits written representations, the licensing authority shall take those representations into account before determining the matter. In practice, this means that any proposed action will not be progressed until the written representations have been reviewed and considered by IAG and a recommendation made to the Divisional Director on whether to proceed with the action or not.

If a company submits a request for a Person Appointed Hearing, this will be taken forward by the Panel Secretariat, which sits within the MHRA's Policy Division. Any proposed action will not be progressed until the Person Appointed Hearing has taken place.

It should be noted that a Person Appointed Hearing will only offer its opinion into whether a licence condition has been contravened. A final decision on whether to suspend or revoke a licence will still rest with the licensing authority, who will take the report of the Person Appointed Hearing into account.

Follow up actions that may be taken:

- a re-inspection to ensure corrective actions implemented;
- request for regular updates on the corrective action plan;
- the issue of a short dated GMP certificate;
- recommended increase of inspection frequency;
- continued monitoring of the company by IAG via inspectorate updates; or
- if serious and persistent non-compliance continues referral for consideration of criminal prosecution.

Contact for further information: IAGSecretariat@mhra.gsi.gov.uk

## Advice

MHRA publishes a series of Guidance Notes relating to its statutory functions. Those of particular interest to manufacturers and wholesale dealers include:

GN 5   Notes for applicants and holders of a manufacturer's licence
GN 6   Notes for applicants and holders of a wholesale dealer's licence (WDA(H)) or broker registration
GN 8   A guide to what is a medicinal product
GN 14  The supply of unlicensed medicinal products "Specials"

These Guidance Notes and a list of others available may be obtained from MHRA's website or from MHRA's Customer Services Team.

Contact details are as follows:

**Address:**
Customer Services, Medicines and Healthcare products Regulatory Agency, 151 Buckingham Palace Road, Victoria, London SW1W 9SZ, UK
**Telephone:** +44 (0)20 3080 6000 (weekdays 0900–1700)
**Fax:** +44 (0)20 3118 9803
**E-mail:** info@mhra.gsi.gov.uk
**Website:** www.mhra.gov.uk

# Guidance on Good Manufacturing Practice (GMP)

# EU Guidance on Good Manufacturing Practice

## PART I: Basic Requirements for Medicinal Products

> **Editor's note** The Introduction (below) to the EU Guidance on GMP which was written by the Commission makes reference to a "glossary" of some terms used in the Guide for GMP. This glossary appears immediately after the annexes.
>
> In addition to this glossary a number of the annexes themselves also contain a glossary of some of the terms used in the particular annex to which they are attached. Part II of the EU Guidance on GMP contains a further glossary of terms used in that Part.
>
> In this publication the Introduction (below) to the EU Guidance on GMP, the annexes, glossaries and Parts II and III have been presented as the Commission intended.

## Contents of Part I

Contents continued

Contents continued

EU GMP GUIDE

Contents continued

Contents continued

EU GMP GUIDE

Contents continued

Contents continued

EU GMP GUIDE INTRODUCTION

# Introduction

The pharmaceutical industry of the EU maintains high standards of Quality Management in the development, manufacture and control of medicinal products. A system of marketing authorisations ensures that all medicinal products are assessed by a competent authority to ensure compliance with contemporary requirements of safety, quality and efficacy. A system of manufacturing authorisations ensures that all products authorised on the European market are manufactured/imported only by authorised manufacturers, whose activities are regularly inspected by the competent authorities, using Quality Risk Management principles. Manufacturing authorisations are required by all pharmaceutical manufacturers in the EU whether the products are sold within or outside of the Union.

Two directives laying down principles and guidelines of good manufacturing practice (GMP) for medicinal products were adopted by the Commission. Directive 2003/94/EC applies to medicinal products for human use and Directive 91/412/EEC for veterinary use. Detailed guidelines in accordance with those principles are published in the Guide to Good Manufacturing Practice which will be used in assessing applications for manufacturing authorisations and as a basis for inspection of manufacturers of medicinal products.

The principles of GMP and the detailed guidelines are applicable to all operations which require the authorisations referred to in Article 40 of Directive 2001/83/EC, in Article 44 of Directive 2001/82/EC and Article 13 of Directive 2001/20/EC, as amended. They are also relevant for pharmaceutical manufacturing processes, such as that undertaken in hospitals.

All Member States and the industry agreed that the GMP requirements applicable to the manufacture of veterinary medicinal products are the same as those applicable to the manufacture of medicinal products for human use. Certain detailed adjustments to the GMP guidelines are set out in two annexes specific to veterinary medicinal products and to immunological veterinary medicinal products.

The Guide is presented in three parts and supplemented by a series of annexes. Part I covers GMP principles for the manufacture of medicinal products. Part II covers GMP for active substances used as starting materials. Part III contains GMP related documents, which clarify regulatory expectations.

Chapters of Part I on "basic requirements" are headed by principles as defined in Directives 2003/94/EC and 91/412/EEC. Chapter 1 on Quality Management outlines the fundamental concept of quality management as applied to the manufacture of medicinal products. Thereafter, each chapter has a principle outlining the quality management objectives of that chapter and a text which provides sufficient detail for manufacturers to be made aware of the essential matters to be considered when implementing the principle.

According to the revised Article 47 and Article 51, respectively, of the Directive 2001/83/EC and Directive 2001/82/EC, as amended, detailed guidelines on the principles of GMP for active substances used as starting materials shall be adopted and published by the Commission.

Part II was established on the basis of a guideline developed on the level of ICH and published as ICH Q7A on "active pharmaceutical ingredients". It has an extended application both for the human and the veterinary sector.

In addition to the general matters of Good Manufacturing Practice outlined in Parts I and II, a series of annexes providing detail about specific areas of activity is included. For some manufacturing processes, different annexes will apply simultaneously (e.g. annex on sterile preparations and on radiopharmaceuticals and/or on biological medicinal products).

A glossary of some terms used in the Guide has been incorporated after the annexes. Part III is intended to host a collection of GMP related documents, which are not detailed guidelines on the principles of GMP laid down in Directives 2003/94/EC and 91/412/EC. The aim of Part III is to clarify regulatory expectations and it should be viewed as a source of information on current best practices. Details on the applicability will be described separately in each document.

The Guide is not intended to cover safety aspects for the personnel engaged in manufacture. This may be particularly important in the manufacture of certain medicinal products such as highly active, biological and radioactive medicinal products. However, those aspects are governed by other provisions of Union or national law.

Throughout the Guide, it is assumed that the requirements of the Marketing Authorisation relating to the safety, quality and efficacy of the products are systematically incorporated into all the manufacturing, control and release for sale arrangements of the holder of the Manufacturing Authorisation.

For many years, the manufacture of medicinal products has taken place in accordance with guidelines for Good Manufacturing Practice and the manufacture of medicinal products is not governed by CEN/ISO standards. The CEN/ISO standards have been considered but the terminology of these standards has not been implemented in this edition.

It is recognised that there are acceptable methods, other than those described in the Guide, which are capable of achieving the principles of Quality Management. The Guide is not intended to place any restraint upon the development of any new concepts or new technologies which have been validated and which provide a level of Quality Management at least equivalent to those set out in this Guide.

The GMP Guide will be regularly revised in order to reflect continual improvement of best practices in the field of Quality. Revisions will be made publicly available on the website of the European Commission: (http://ec.europa.eu/health/documents/eudralex/vol-4/index_en.htm).

EU GMP GUIDE INTRODUCTION

## 1  PHARMACEUTICAL QUALITY SYSTEM

### Principle

The holder of a Manufacturing Authorisation must manufacture medicinal products so as to ensure that they are fit for their intended use, comply with the requirements of the Marketing Authorisation or Clinical Trial Authorisation, as appropriate and do not place patients at risk due to inadequate safety, quality or efficacy. The attainment of this quality objective is the responsibility of senior management and requires the participation and commitment by staff in many different departments and at all levels within the company, by the company's suppliers and by its distributors. To achieve this quality objective reliably there must be a comprehensively designed and correctly implemented Pharmaceutical Quality System[1] incorporating Good Manufacturing Practice and Quality Risk Management. It should be fully documented and its effectiveness monitored. All parts of the Pharmaceutical Quality System should be adequately resourced with competent personnel, and suitable and sufficient premises, equipment and facilities. There are additional legal responsibilities for the holder of the Manufacturing Authorisation and for the Qualified Person(s).

The basic concepts of Quality Management, Good Manufacturing Practice and Quality Risk Management are inter-related. They are described here in order to emphasise their relationships and their fundamental importance to the production and control of medicinal products.

### Pharmaceutical Quality System[1]

1.1  Quality Management is a wide-ranging concept, which covers all matters, which individually or collectively influence the quality of a product. It is the sum total of the organised arrangements made with the objective of ensuring that medicinal products are of the quality required for their intended use. Quality Management therefore incorporates Good Manufacturing Practice.

1.2  GMP applies to the lifecycle stages from the manufacture of investigational medicinal products, technology transfer, commercial manufacturing through to product discontinuation. However the Pharmaceutical Quality System can extend to the pharmaceutical development lifecycle stage as

---

[1] Art 6 of Directives 2003/94/EC and 91/412/EEC require manufacturers to establish and implement an effective pharmaceutical quality assurance system. The term Pharmaceutical Quality System is used in this chapter in the interests of consistency with ICH Q10 terminology. For the purposes of this chapter these terms can be considered interchangeable.

described in ICH Q10, which while optional, should facilitate innovation and continual improvement and strengthen the link between pharmaceutical development and manufacturing activities. ICH Q10 is reproduced in Part III of the Guide and can be used to supplement the contents of this chapter.

1.3   The size and complexity of the company's activities should be taken into consideration when developing a new Pharmaceutical Quality System or modifying an existing one. The design of the system should incorporate appropriate risk management principles including the use of appropriate tools. While some aspects of the system can be company-wide and others site-specific, the effectiveness of the system is normally demonstrated at the site level.

1.4   A Pharmaceutical Quality System appropriate for the manufacture of medicinal products should ensure that:

(i)     Product realisation is achieved by designing, planning, implementing, maintaining and continuously improving a system that allows the consistent delivery of products with appropriate quality attributes;

(ii)    Product and process knowledge is managed throughout all lifecycle stages;

(iii)   Medicinal products are designed and developed in a way that takes account of the requirements of Good Manufacturing Practice;

(iv)   Production and control operations are clearly specified and Good Manufacturing Practice adopted;

(v)    Managerial responsibilities are clearly specified;

(vi)   Arrangements are made for the manufacture, supply and use of the correct starting and packaging materials, the selection and monitoring of suppliers and for verifying that each delivery is from the approved supply chain;

(vii)  Processes are in place to assure the management of outsourced activities.

(viii) A state of control is established and maintained by developing and using effective monitoring and control systems for process performance and product quality.

(ix)   The results of product and processes monitoring are taken into account in batch release, in the investigation of deviations, and, with a view to taking preventive action to avoid potential deviations occurring in the future.

(x)    All necessary controls on intermediate products, and any other in-process controls and validations are carried out;

(xi)     Continual improvement is facilitated through the implementation of quality improvements appropriate to the current level of process and product knowledge.

(xii)    Arrangements are in place for the prospective evaluation of planned changes and their approval prior to implementation taking into account regulatory notification and approval where required;

(xiii)   After implementation of any change, an evaluation is undertaken to confirm the quality objectives were achieved and that there was no unintended deleterious impact on product quality;

(xiv)    An appropriate level of root cause analysis should be applied during the investigation of deviations, suspected product defects and other problems. This can be determined using Quality Risk Management principles. In cases where the true root cause(s) of the issue cannot be determined, consideration should be given to identifying the most likely root cause(s) and to addressing those. Where human error is suspected or identified as the cause, this should be justified having taken care to ensure that process, procedural or system-based errors or problems have not been overlooked, if present. Appropriate corrective actions and/or preventative actions (CAPAs) should be identified and taken in response to investigations. The effectiveness of such actions should be monitored and assessed, in line with Quality Risk Management principles.

(xv)     Medicinal products are not sold or supplied before a Qualified Person has certified that each production batch has been produced and controlled in accordance with the requirements of the Marketing Authorisation and any other regulations relevant to the production, control and release of medicinal products;

(xvi)    Satisfactory arrangements exist to ensure, as far as possible, that the medicinal products are stored, distributed and subsequently handled so that quality is maintained throughout their shelf life;

(xvii)   There is a process for self-inspection and/or quality audit, which regularly appraises the effectiveness and applicability of the Pharmaceutical Quality System.

1.5    Senior management has the ultimate responsibility to ensure an effective Pharmaceutical Quality System is in place, adequately resourced and that roles, responsibilities, and authorities are defined, communicated and implemented throughout the organisation. Senior management's leadership and active participation in the Pharmaceutical Quality System is essential. This leadership should ensure the support and commitment of staff at all levels and sites within the organisation to the Pharmaceutical Quality System.

**1.6** There should be periodic management review, with the involvement of senior management, of the operation of the Pharmaceutical Quality System to identify opportunities for continual improvement of products, processes and the system itself.

**1.7** The Pharmaceutical Quality System should be defined and documented. A Quality Manual or equivalent documentation should be established and should contain a description of the quality management system including management responsibilities.

## Good Manufacturing Practice for Medicinal Products

**1.8** Good Manufacturing Practice is that part of Quality Management which ensures that products are consistently produced and controlled to the quality standards appropriate to their intended use and as required by the Marketing Authorisation, Clinical Trial Authorisation or product specification.

Good Manufacturing Practice is concerned with both production and quality control. The basic requirements of GMP are that:

(i) all manufacturing processes are clearly defined, systematically reviewed in the light of experience and shown to be capable of consistently manufacturing medicinal products of the required quality and complying with their specifications;

(ii) critical steps of manufacturing processes and significant changes to the process are validated;

(iii) all necessary facilities for GMP are provided including:
- appropriately qualified and trained personnel;
- adequate premises and space;
- suitable equipment and services;
- correct materials, containers and labels;
- approved procedures and instructions, in accordance with the Pharmaceutical Quality System;
- suitable storage and transport;

(iv) instructions and procedures are written in an instructional form in clear and unambiguous language, specifically applicable to the facilities provided;

(v) procedures are carried out correctly and operators are trained to do so;

(vi) records are made, manually and/or by recording instruments, during manufacture which demonstrate that all the steps required by the defined procedures and instructions were in fact taken and that the quantity and quality of the product was as expected.

(vii) Any significant deviations are fully recorded, investigated with the objective of determining the root cause and appropriate corrective and preventive action implemented;

(viii) records of manufacture including distribution which enable the complete history of a batch to be traced are retained in a comprehensible and accessible form;

(ix) the distribution of the products minimises any risk to their quality and takes account of Good Distribution Practice;

(x) a system is available to recall any batch of product, from sale or supply;

(xi) complaints about products are examined, the causes of quality defects investigated and appropriate measures taken in respect of the defective products and to prevent reoccurrence.

## Quality Control

1.9 Quality Control is that part of Good Manufacturing Practice which is concerned with sampling, specifications and testing, and with the organisation, documentation and release procedures which ensure that the necessary and relevant tests are actually carried out and that materials are not released for use, nor products released for sale or supply, until their quality has been judged to be satisfactory.

The basic requirements of Quality Control are that:

(i) adequate facilities, trained personnel and approved procedures are available for sampling and testing starting materials, packaging materials, intermediate, bulk, and finished products, and where appropriate for monitoring environmental conditions for GMP purposes;

(ii) samples of starting materials, packaging materials, intermediate products, bulk products and finished products are taken by approved personnel and methods;

(iii) test methods are validated;

(iv) records are made, manually and/or by recording instruments, which demonstrate that all the required sampling, inspecting and testing procedures were actually carried out. Any deviations are fully recorded and investigated;

(v) the finished products contain active ingredients complying with the qualitative and quantitative composition of the Marketing Authorisation or Clinical Trial Authorisation, are of the purity required, and are enclosed within their proper containers and correctly labelled;

(vi) records are made of the results of inspection and that testing of materials, intermediate, bulk, and finished products is formally assessed against specification. Product assessment includes a review and evaluation of relevant production documentation and an assessment of deviations from specified procedures;

(vii) no batch of product is released for sale or supply prior to certification by a Qualified Person that it is in accordance with the requirements of the relevant authorisations in accordance with Annex 16;

(viii) sufficient reference samples of starting materials and products are retained in accordance with Annex 19 to permit future examination of the product if necessary and that the sample is retained in the final pack.

## Product Quality Review

1.10   Regular periodic or rolling quality reviews of all authorised medicinal products, including export only products, should be conducted with the objective of verifying the consistency of the existing process, the appropriateness of current specifications for both starting materials and finished product to highlight any trends and to identify product and process improvements. Such reviews should normally be conducted and documented annually, taking into account previous reviews, and should include at least:

   (i)    A review of starting materials including packaging materials used in the product, especially those from new sources and in particular the review of supply chain traceability of active substances;

   (ii)   A review of critical in-process controls and finished product results;

   (iii)  A review of all batches that failed to meet established specification(s) and their investigation;

   (iv)   A review of all significant deviations or non-conformances, their related investigations, and the effectiveness of resultant corrective and preventive actions taken;

   (v)    A review of all changes carried out to the processes or analytical methods;

   (vi)   A review of Marketing Authorisation variations submitted, granted or refused, including those for third country (export only) dossiers;

   (vii)  A review of the results of the stability monitoring programme and any adverse trends;

   (viii) A review of all quality-related returns, complaints and recalls and the investigations performed at the time;

   (ix)   A review of adequacy of any other previous product process or equipment corrective actions;

   (x)    For new marketing authorisations and variations to marketing authorisations, a review of post-marketing commitments;

   (xi)    The qualification status of relevant equipment and utilities, e.g. HVAC, water, compressed gases, etc;

   (xii)    A review of any contractual arrangements as defined in Chapter 7 to ensure that they are up to date.

**1.11**    The manufacturer and, where different, marketing authorisation holder should evaluate the results of the review and an assessment made as to whether corrective and preventive action or any revalidation should be undertaken under the Pharmaceutical Quality System. There should be management procedures for the ongoing management and review of these actions and the effectiveness of these procedures verified during self-inspection. Quality reviews may be grouped by product type, e.g. solid dosage forms, liquid dosage forms, sterile products, etc. where scientifically justified.

    Where the marketing authorisation holder is not the manufacturer, there should be a technical agreement in place between the various parties that defines their respective responsibilities in producing the product quality review.

## Quality Risk Management

**1.12**    Quality risk management is a systematic process for the assessment, control, communication and review of risks to the quality of the medicinal product. It can be applied both proactively and retrospectively.

**1.13**    The principles of quality risk management are that:

   (i)    The evaluation of the risk to quality is based on scientific knowledge, experience with the process and ultimately links to the protection of the patient;

   (ii)    The level of effort, formality and documentation of the quality risk management process is commensurate with the level of risk.

Examples of the processes and applications of quality risk management can be found inter alia in ICH Q9 which is reproduced in Part III of the Guide.

## 2    PERSONNEL

## Principle

The correct manufacture of medicinal products relies upon people. For this reason there must be sufficient qualified personnel to carry out all the tasks which are the responsibility of the manufacturer. Individual responsibilities should be clearly understood by the individuals and recorded. All personnel should be aware of the principles of Good Manufacturing Practice that affect them and receive initial and continuing training, including hygiene instructions, relevant to their needs.

## General

2.1    The manufacturer should have an adequate number of personnel with the necessary qualifications and practical experience. Senior management should determine and provide adequate and appropriate resources (human, financial, materials, facilities and equipment) to implement and maintain the quality management system and continually improve its effectiveness. The responsibilities placed on any one individual should not be so extensive as to present any risk to quality.

2.2    The manufacturer must have an organisation chart in which the relationships between the heads of Production, Quality Control and where applicable Head of Quality Assurance or Quality Unit referred to in point 2.5 and the position of the Qualified Person(s) are clearly shown in the managerial hierarchy.

2.3    People in responsible positions should have specific duties recorded in written job descriptions and adequate authority to carry out their responsibilities. Their duties may be delegated to designated deputies of a satisfactory qualification level. There should be no gaps or unexplained overlaps in the responsibilities of those personnel concerned with the application of Good Manufacturing Practice.

2.4    Senior management has the ultimate responsibility to ensure an effective quality management system is in place to achieve the *quality objectives*, and, that roles, responsibilities, and authorities are defined, communicated and implemented throughout the organisation. Senior management should establish a quality policy that describes the overall intentions and direction of the company related to quality and should ensure continuing suitability and effectiveness of the quality management system and GMP compliance through participation in management review.

## Key Personnel

**2.5** Senior Management should appoint Key Management Personnel including the head of Production, the head of Quality Control, and if at least one of these persons is not responsible for the duties described in Article 51 of Directive 2001/83/EC[1], an adequate number, but at least one, Qualified Person(s) designated for the purpose. Normally, key posts should be occupied by full-time personnel. The heads of Production and Quality Control must be independent from each other. In large organisations, it may be necessary to delegate some of the functions listed in 2.6 and 2.7. Additionally depending on the size and organisational structure of the company, a separate Head of Quality Assurance or Head of the Quality Unit may be appointed. Where such a function exists usually some of the responsibilities described in 2.6, 2.7 and 2.8 are shared with the Head of Quality Control and Head of Production and senior management should therefore take care that roles, responsibilities, and authorities are defined.

**2.6** The duties of the Qualified Person(s) are described in Article 51 of Directive 2001/83/EC, and can be summarised as follows:

(a) for medicinal products manufactured within the European Union, a Qualified Person must ensure that each batch has been manufactured and checked in compliance with the laws in force in that Member State and in accordance with the requirements of the marketing authorisation;[2]

(b) in the case of medicinal products coming from third countries, irrespective of whether the product has been manufactured in the European Union a Qualified Person must ensure that each production batch has undergone in a Member State a full qualitative analysis, a quantitative analysis of at least all the active substances and all the other tests or checks necessary to ensure the quality of medicinal products in accordance with the requirements of the marketing authorisation. The Qualified Person must certify in a register or equivalent document, as operations are carried out and before any release, that each production batch satisfies the provisions of Article 51.

The persons responsible for these duties must meet the qualification requirements laid down in Article 49[3] of the same Directive, they shall be

---

[1] Article 55 of Directive 2001/82/EC.

[2] According to Article 51 paragraph 1 of Directive (2001/83/EC), the batches of medicinal products which have undergone such controls in a Member State shall be exempt from the controls if they are marketed in another Member State, accompanied by the control reports signed by the qualified person.

[3] Article 53 of Directive 2001/82/EC.

permanently and continuously at the disposal of the holder of the Manufacturing Authorisation to carry out their responsibilities.

The responsibilities of a Qualified Person may be delegated, but only to other Qualified Person(s).

Guidance on the role of the Qualified Person is elaborated in Annex 16.

**2.7**   The head of the Production Department generally has the following responsibilities:

(i)   To ensure that products are produced and stored according to the appropriate documentation in order to obtain the required quality;

(ii)   To approve the instructions relating to production operations and to ensure their strict implementation;

(iii)   To ensure that the production records are evaluated and signed by an authorised person;

(iv)   To ensure that the qualification and maintenance of his department, premises and equipment;

(v)   To ensure that the appropriate validations are done;

(vi)   To ensure that the required initial and continuing training of his department personnel is carried out and adapted according to need.

**2.8**   The head of the Quality Control Department generally has the following responsibilities:

(i)   To approve or reject, as he sees fit, starting materials, packaging materials, and intermediate, bulk and finished products;

(ii)   To ensure that all necessary testing is carried out and the associated records evaluated;

(iii)   To approve specifications, sampling instructions, test methods and other Quality Control procedures;

(iv)   To approve and monitor any contract analysts;

(v)   To ensure the qualification and maintenance of his department, premises and equipment;

(vi)   To ensure that the appropriate validations are done;

(vii)   To ensure that the required initial and continuing training of his department personnel is carried out and adapted according to need.

Other duties of the Quality Control Department are summarised in Chapter 6.

**2.9**   The heads of Production and Quality Control and where relevant, Head of Quality Assurance or Head of Quality Unit, generally have some shared, or jointly exercised, responsibilities relating to quality including in particular the design, effective implementation, monitoring and maintenance of the quality management system. These may include, subject to any national regulations:

(i)     The authorisation of written procedures and other documents, including amendments;

(ii)    The monitoring and control of the manufacturing environment;

(iii)   Plant hygiene;

(iv)    Process validation;

(v)     Training;

(vi)    The approval and monitoring of suppliers of materials;

(vii)   The approval and monitoring of contract manufacturers and providers of other GMP related outsourced activities;

(viii)  The designation and monitoring of storage conditions for materials and products;

(ix)    The retention of records;

(x)     The monitoring of compliance with the requirements of Good Manufacturing Practice;

(xi)    The inspection, investigation, and taking of samples, in order to monitor factors which may affect product quality;

(xii)   Participation in management reviews of process performance, product quality and of the quality management system and advocating continual improvement;

(xiii)  Ensuring that a timely and effective communication and escalation process exists to raise quality issues to the appropriate levels of management.

## Training

2.10    The manufacturer should provide training for all the personnel whose duties take them into production and storage areas or into control laboratories (including the technical, maintenance and cleaning personnel), and for other personnel whose activities could affect the quality of the product.

2.11    Besides the basic training on the theory and practice of Good Manufacturing Practice, newly recruited personnel should receive training appropriate to the duties assigned to them. Continuing training should also be given, and its practical effectiveness should be periodically assessed. Training programmes should be available, approved by either the head of Production or the head of Quality Control, as appropriate. Training records should be kept.

2.12    Personnel working in areas where contamination is a hazard, e.g. clean areas or areas where highly active, toxic, infectious or sensitising materials are handled, should be given specific training.

2.13    Visitors or untrained personnel should, preferably, not be taken into the production and quality control areas. If this is unavoidable, they should be given information in advance, particularly about personal hygiene and the prescribed protective clothing. They should be closely supervised.

2.14 The pharmaceutical quality system and all the measures capable of improving its understanding and implementation should be fully discussed during the training sessions.

## Personnel Hygiene

2.15 Detailed hygiene programmes should be established and adapted to the different needs within the factory. They should include procedures relating to the health, hygiene practices and clothing of personnel. These procedures should be understood and followed in a very strict way by every person whose duties take him into the production and control areas. Hygiene programmes should be promoted by management and widely discussed during training sessions.

2.16 All personnel should receive medical examination upon recruitment. It must be the manufacturer's responsibility that there are instructions ensuring that health conditions that can be of relevance to the quality of products come to the manufacturer's knowledge. After the first medical examination, examinations should be carried out when necessary for the work and personal health.

2.17 Steps should be taken to ensure as far as is practicable that no person affected by an infectious disease or having open lesions on the exposed surface of the body is engaged in the manufacture of medicinal products.

2.18 Every person entering the manufacturing areas should wear protective garments appropriate to the operations to be carried out.

2.19 Eating, drinking, chewing or smoking, or the storage of food, drink, smoking materials or personal medication in the production and storage areas should be prohibited. In general, any unhygienic practice within the manufacturing areas or in any other area where the product might be adversely affected should be forbidden.

2.20 Direct contact should be avoided between the operator's hands and the exposed product as well as with any part of the equipment that comes into contact with the products.

2.21 Personnel should be instructed to use the hand-washing facilities.

2.22 Any specific requirements for the manufacture of special groups of products, for example sterile preparations, are covered in the annexes.

## Consultants

2.23    Consultants should have adequate education, training, and experience, or any combination thereof, to advise on the subject for which they are retained. Records should be maintained stating the name, address, qualifications, and type of service provided by these consultants.

## 3   PREMISES AND EQUIPMENT

## Principle

Premises and equipment must be located, designed, constructed, adapted and maintained to suit the operations to be carried out. Their layout and design must aim to minimise the risk of errors and permit effective cleaning and maintenance in order to avoid cross-contamination, build up of dust or dirt and, in general, any adverse effect on the quality of products.

## Premises

### General

3.1   Premises should be situated in an environment which, when considered together with measures to protect the manufacture, presents minimal risk of causing contamination of materials or products.

3.2   Premises should be carefully maintained, ensuring that repair and maintenance operations do not present any hazard to the quality of products. They should be cleaned and, where applicable, disinfected according to detailed written procedures.

3.3   Lighting, temperature, humidity and ventilation should be appropriate and such that they do not adversely affect, directly or indirectly, either the medicinal products during their manufacture and storage, or the accurate functioning of equipment.

3.4   Premises should be designed and equipped so as to afford maximum protection against the entry of insects or other animals.

3.5   Steps should be taken in order to prevent the entry of unauthorised people. Production, storage and quality control areas should not be used as a right of way by personnel who do not work in them.

## Production area

**3.6** Cross-contamination should be prevented for all products by appropriate design and operation of manufacturing facilities. The measures to prevent cross-contamination should be commensurate with the risks. Quality Risk Management principles should be used to assess and control the risks.

Depending of the level of risk, it may be necessary to dedicate premises and equipment for manufacturing and/or packaging operations to control the risk presented by some medicinal products.

Dedicated facilities are required for manufacturing when a medicinal product presents a risk because:

(i) the risk cannot be adequately controlled by operational and/ or technical measures,

(ii) scientific data from the toxicological evaluation does not support a controllable risk (e.g. allergenic potential from highly sensitising materials such as beta lactams) or

(iii) relevant residue limits, derived from the toxicological evaluation, cannot be satisfactorily determined by a validated analytical method.

Further guidance can be found in Chapter 5 and in Annexes 2, 3, 4, 5 & 6.

**3.7** Premises should preferably be laid out in such a way as to allow the production to take place in areas connected in a logical order corresponding to the sequence of the operations and to the requisite cleanliness levels.

**3.8** The adequacy of the working and in-process storage space should permit the orderly and logical positioning of equipment and materials so as to minimise the risk of confusion between different medicinal products or their components, to avoid cross-contamination and to minimise the risk of omission or wrong application of any of the manufacturing or control steps.

**3.9** Where starting and primary packaging materials, intermediate or bulk products are exposed to the environment, interior surfaces (walls, floors and ceilings) should be smooth, free from cracks and open joints, and should not shed particulate matter and should permit easy and effective cleaning and, if necessary, disinfection.

**3.10** Pipework, light fittings, ventilation points and other services should be designed and sited to avoid the creation of recesses which are difficult to clean. As far as possible, for maintenance purposes, they should be accessible from outside the manufacturing areas.

**3.11** Drains should be of adequate size, and have trapped gullies. Open channels should be avoided where possible, but if necessary, they should be shallow to facilitate cleaning and disinfection.

3.12 Production areas should be effectively ventilated, with air control facilities (including temperature and, where necessary, humidity and filtration) appropriate both to the products handled, to the operations undertaken within them and to the external environment.

3.13 Weighing of starting materials usually should be carried out in a separate weighing room designed for such use.

3.14 In cases where dust is generated (e.g. during sampling, weighing, mixing and processing operations, packaging of dry products), specific provisions should be taken to avoid cross-contamination and facilitate cleaning.

3.15 Premises for the packaging of medicinal products should be specifically designed and laid out so as to avoid mix-ups or cross-contamination.

3.16 Production areas should be well lit, particularly where visual on-line controls are carried out.

3.17 In-process controls may be carried out within the production area provided they do not carry any risk to production.

## Storage areas

3.18 Storage areas should be of sufficient capacity to allow orderly storage of the various categories of materials and products: starting and packaging materials, intermediate, bulk and finished products, products in quarantine, released, rejected, returned or recalled.

3.19 Storage areas should be designed or adapted to ensure good storage conditions. In particular, they should be clean and dry and maintained within acceptable temperature limits. Where special storage conditions are required (e.g. temperature, humidity) these should be provided, checked and monitored.

3.20 Receiving and dispatch bays should protect materials and products from the weather. Reception areas should be designed and equipped to allow containers of incoming materials to be cleaned where necessary before storage.

3.21 Where quarantine status is ensured by storage in separate areas, these areas must be clearly marked and their access restricted to authorised personnel. Any system replacing the physical quarantine should give equivalent security.

3.22 There should normally be a separate sampling area for starting materials. If sampling is performed in the storage area, it should be conducted in such a way as to prevent contamination or cross-contamination.

**3.23** Segregated areas should be provided for the storage of rejected, recalled or returned materials or products.

**3.24** Highly active materials or products should be stored in safe and secure areas.

**3.25** Printed packaging materials are considered critical to the conformity of the medicinal product and special attention should be paid to the safe and secure storage of these materials.

## Quality control areas

**3.26** Normally, Quality Control laboratories should be separated from production areas. This is particularly important for laboratories for the control of biologicals, microbiologicals and radioisotopes, which should also be separated from each other.

**3.27** Control laboratories should be designed to suit the operations to be carried out in them. Sufficient space should be given to avoid mix-ups and cross-contamination. There should be adequate suitable storage space for samples and records.

**3.28** Separate rooms may be necessary to protect sensitive instruments from vibration, electrical interference, humidity, etc.

**3.29** Special requirements are needed in laboratories handling particular substances, such as biological or radioactive samples.

## Ancillary areas

**3.30** Rest and refreshment rooms should be separate from other areas.

**3.31** Facilities for changing clothes, and for washing and toilet purposes should be easily accessible and appropriate for the number of users. Toilets should not directly communicate with production or storage areas.

**3.32** Maintenance workshops should as far as possible be separated from production areas. Whenever parts and tools are stored in the production area, they should be kept in rooms or lockers reserved for that use.

**3.33** Animal houses should be well isolated from other areas, with separate entrance (animal access) and air handling facilities.

## Equipment

**3.34**  Manufacturing equipment should be designed, located and maintained to suit its intended purpose.

**3.35**  Repair and maintenance operations should not present any hazard to the quality of the products.

**3.36**  Manufacturing equipment should be designed so that it can be easily and thoroughly cleaned. It should be cleaned according to detailed and written procedures and stored only in a clean and dry condition.

**3.37**  Washing and cleaning equipment should be chosen and used in order not to be a source of contamination.

**3.38**  Equipment should be installed in such a way as to prevent any risk of error or of contamination.

**3.39**  Production equipment should not present any hazard to products. Parts of the production equipment that come into contact with the product must not be reactive, additive or absorptive to such an extent that it will affect the quality of the product and thus present any hazard.

**3.40**  Balances and measuring equipment of an appropriate range and precision should be available for production and control operations.

**3.41**  Measuring, weighing, recording and control equipment should be calibrated and checked at defined intervals by appropriate methods. Adequate records of such tests should be maintained.

**3.42**  Fixed pipework should be clearly labelled to indicate the contents and, where applicable, the direction of flow.

**3.43**  Distilled, deionised and, where appropriate, other water pipes should be sanitised according to written procedures that detail the action limits for microbiological contamination and the measures to be taken.

**3.44**  Defective equipment should, if possible, be removed from production and quality control areas, or at least be clearly labelled as defective.

## 4   DOCUMENTATION

## Principle

Good documentation constitutes an essential part of the quality assurance system and is key to operating in compliance with GMP requirements. The various types of documents and media used should be fully defined in the manufacturer's Quality Management System.

Documentation may exist in a variety of forms, including paper-based, electronic or photographic media. The main objective of the system of documentation utilized must be to establish, control, monitor and record all activities which directly or indirectly impact on all aspects of the quality of medicinal products. The Quality Management System should include sufficient instructional detail to facilitate a common understanding of the requirements, in addition to providing for sufficient recording of the various processes and evaluation of any observations, so that ongoing application of the requirements may be demonstrated.

There are two primary types of documentation used to manage and record GMP compliance: instructions (directions, requirements) and records/reports. Appropriate good documentation practice should be applied with respect to the type of document.

Suitable controls should be implemented to ensure the accuracy, integrity, availability and legibility of documents. Instruction documents should be free from errors and available in writing. The term "written" means recorded, or documented on media from which data may be rendered in a human readable form.

## Required GMP documentation (by type):

*Site Master File:* A document describing the GMP related activities of the manufacturer.

### Instructions (directions, or requirements) type:

*Specifications:* Describe in detail the requirements with which the products or materials used or obtained during manufacture have to conform. They serve as a basis for quality evaluation.

*Manufacturing Formulae, Processing, Packaging and Testing Instructions:* Provide detail all the starting materials, equipment and computerised systems (if any) to be used and specify all processing, packaging, sampling and testing instructions. In-process controls and process analytical technologies to be employed should be specified where relevant, together with acceptance criteria.

*Procedures:* (Otherwise known as Standard Operating Procedures, or SOPs), give directions for performing certain operations.

*Protocols:* Give instructions for performing and recording certain discreet operations.

*Technical Agreements:* Are agreed between contract givers and acceptors for outsourced activities.

**Record/Report type:**

*Records:* Provide evidence of various actions taken to demonstrate compliance with instructions, e.g. activities, events, investigations, and in the case of manufactured batches a history of each batch of product, including its distribution. Records include the raw data which is used to generate other records. For electronic records regulated users should define which data are to be used as raw data. At least, all data on which quality decisions are based should be defined as raw data

*Certificates of Analysis:* Provide a summary of testing results on samples of products or materials[1] together with the evaluation for compliance to a stated specification.

*Reports:* Document the conduct of particular exercises, projects or investigations, together with results, conclusions and recommendations.

## Generation and Control of Documentation

4.1   All types of document should be defined and adhered to. The requirements apply equally to all forms of document media types. Complex systems need to be understood, well documented, validated, and adequate controls should be in place. Many documents (instructions and/or records) may exist in hybrid forms, i.e. some elements as electronic and others as paper based. Relationships and control measures for master documents, official copies, data handling and records need to be stated for both hybrid and homogenous systems. Appropriate controls for electronic documents such as templates, forms, and master documents should be implemented. Appropriate controls should be in place to ensure the integrity of the record throughout the retention period.

4.2   Documents should be designed, prepared, reviewed and distributed with care. They should comply with the relevant parts of Product Specification Files, Manufacturing and Marketing Authorisation dossiers, as appropriate. The reproduction of working documents from master documents should not allow any error to be introduced through the reproduction process.

---

[1] Alternatively the certification may be based, in-whole or in-part, on the assessment of real time data (summaries and exception reports) from batch related process analytical technology (PAT), parameters or metrics as per the approved marketing authorisation dossier.

4.3   Documents containing instructions should be approved, signed and dated by appropriate and authorised persons. Documents should have unambiguous contents and be uniquely identifiable. The effective date should be defined.

4.4   Documents containing instructions should be laid out in an orderly fashion and be easy to check. The style and language of documents should fit with their intended use. Standard Operating Procedures, Work Instructions and Methods should be written in an imperative mandatory style.

4.5   Documents within the Quality Management System should be regularly reviewed and kept up-to-date.

4.6   Documents should not be hand-written; although, where documents require the entry of data, sufficient space should be provided for such entries.

## Good Documentation Practices

4.7   Handwritten entries should be made in clear, legible, indelible way.

4.8   Records should be made or completed at the time each action is taken and in such a way that all significant activities concerning the manufacture of medicinal products are traceable.

4.9   Any alteration made to the entry on a document should be signed and dated; the alteration should permit the reading of the original information. Where appropriate, the reason for the alteration should be recorded.

## Retention of Documents

4.10  It should be clearly defined which record is related to each manufacturing activity and where this record is located. Secure controls must be in place to ensure the integrity of the record throughout the retention period and validated where appropriate.

4.11  Specific requirements apply to batch documentation which must be kept for one year after expiry of the batch to which it relates or at least five years after certification of the batch by the Qualified Person, whichever is the longer. For investigational medicinal products, the batch documentation must be kept for at least five years after the completion or formal discontinuation of the last clinical trial in which the batch was used. Other requirements for retention of documentation may be described in legislation in relation to specific types of product (e.g. Advanced Therapy Medicinal Products) and specify that longer retention periods be applied to certain documents.

**4.12** For other types of documentation, the retention period will depend on the business activity which the documentation supports. Critical documentation, including raw data (for example relating to validation or stability), which supports information in the Marketing Authorisation should be retained whilst the authorization remains in force. It may be considered acceptable to retire certain documentation (e.g. raw data supporting validation reports or stability reports) where the data has been superseded by a full set of new data. Justification for this should be documented and should take into account the requirements for retention of batch documentation; for example, in the case of process validation data, the accompanying raw data should be retained for a period at least as long as the records for all batches whose release has been supported on the basis of that validation exercise.

The following section gives some examples of required documents. The quality management system should describe all documents required to ensure product quality and patient safety.

## Specifications

**4.13** There should be appropriately authorised and dated specifications for starting and packaging materials, and finished products.

### Specifications for starting and packaging materials

**4.14** Specifications for starting and primary or printed packaging materials should include or provide reference to, if applicable:

(a) A description of the materials including:
- The designated name and the internal code reference;
- The reference, if any, to a pharmacopoeial monograph;
- The approved suppliers and, if reasonable, the original producer of the material;
- A specimen of printed materials;
(b) Directions for sampling and testing;
(c) Qualitative and quantitative requirements with acceptance limits;
(d) Storage conditions and precautions;
(e) The maximum period of storage before re-examination.

### Specifications for intermediate and bulk products

**4.15** Specifications for intermediate and bulk products should be available for critical steps or if these are purchased or dispatched. The specifications should be similar to specifications for starting materials or for finished products, as appropriate.

## Specifications for finished products

**4.16**   Specifications for finished products should include or provide reference to:

(a) The designated name of the product and the code reference where applicable;

(b) The formula;

(c) A description of the pharmaceutical form and package details;

(d) Directions for sampling and testing

(e) The qualitative and quantitative requirements, with the acceptance limits;

(f) The storage conditions and any special handling precautions, where applicable;

(g) The shelf-life.

## Manufacturing Formula and Processing Instructions

Approved, written Manufacturing Formula and Processing Instructions should exist for each product and batch size to be manufactured.

**4.17**   The Manufacturing Formula should include:

(a) The name of the product, with a product reference code relating to its specification;

(b) A description of the pharmaceutical form, strength of the product and batch size;

(c) A list of all starting materials to be used, with the amount of each, described; mention should be made of any substance that may disappear in the course of processing;

(d) A statement of the expected final yield with the acceptable limits, and of relevant intermediate yields, where applicable.

**4.18**   The Processing Instructions should include:

(a) A statement of the processing location and the principal equipment to be used;

(b) The methods, or reference to the methods, to be used for preparing the critical equipment (e.g. cleaning, assembling, calibrating, sterilising);

(c) Checks that the equipment and work station are clear of previous products, documents or materials not required for the planned process, and that equipment is clean and suitable for use;

(d) Detailed stepwise processing instructions [e.g. checks on materials, pre-treatments, sequence for adding materials, critical process parameters (time, temp etc)];

(e) The instructions for any in-process controls with their limits;

(f) Where necessary, the requirements for bulk storage of the products; including the container, labeling and special storage conditions where applicable;

(g) Any special precautions to be observed.

## Packaging instructions

4.19    Approved Packaging Instructions for each product, pack size and type should exist. These should include, or have a reference to, the following:

(a) Name of the product; including the batch number of bulk and finished product

(b) Description of its pharmaceutical form, and strength where applicable;

(c) The pack size expressed in terms of the number, weight or volume of the product in the final container;

(d) A complete list of all the packaging materials required, including quantities, sizes and types, with the code or reference number relating to the specifications of each packaging material;

(e) Where appropriate, an example or reproduction of the relevant printed packaging materials, and specimens indicating where to apply batch number references, and shelf life of the product;

(f) Checks that the equipment and work station are clear of previous products, documents or materials not required for the planned packaging operations (line clearance), and that equipment is clean and suitable for use.

(g) Special precautions to be observed, including a careful examination of the area and equipment in order to ascertain the line clearance before operations begin;

(h) A description of the packaging operation, including any significant subsidiary operations, and equipment to be used;

(i) Details of in-process controls with instructions for sampling and acceptance limits.

## Batch processing record

4.20    A Batch Processing Record should be kept for each batch processed. It should be based on the relevant parts of the currently approved

Manufacturing Formula and Processing Instructions, and should contain the following information:

(a) The name and batch number of the product;

(b) Dates and times of commencement, of significant intermediate stages and of completion of production;

(c) Identification (initials) of the operator(s) who performed each significant step of the process and, where appropriate, the name of any person who checked these operations;

(d) The batch number and/or analytical control number as well as the quantities of each starting material actually weighed (including the batch number and amount of any recovered or reprocessed material added);

(e) Any relevant processing operation or event and major equipment used;

(f) A record of the in-process controls and the initials of the person(s) carrying them out, and the results obtained;

(g) The product yield obtained at different and pertinent stages of manufacture;

(h) Notes on special problems including details, with signed authorisation for any deviation from the Manufacturing Formula and Processing Instructions;

(i) Approval by the person responsible for the processing operations.

**Note:** Where a validated process is continuously monitored and controlled, then automatically generated reports may be limited to compliance summaries and exception/ out-of-specification (OOS) data reports.

## Batch packaging record

4.21    A Batch Packaging Record should be kept for each batch or part batch processed. It should be based on the relevant parts of the Packaging Instructions. The batch packaging record should contain the following information:

(a) The name and batch number of the product,

(b) The date(s) and times of the packaging operations;

(c) Identification (initials) of the operator(s) who performed each significant step of the process and, where appropriate, the name of any person who checked these operations;

(d) Records of checks for identity and conformity with the packaging instructions, including the results of in-process controls;

(e) Details of the packaging operations carried out, including references to equipment and the packaging lines used;

(f) Whenever possible, samples of printed packaging materials used, including specimens of the batch coding, expiry dating and any additional overprinting;

(g) Notes on any special problems or unusual events including details, with signed authorisation for any deviation from the Packaging Instructions;

(h) The quantities and reference number or identification of all printed packaging materials and bulk product issued, used, destroyed or returned to stock and the quantities of obtained product, in order to provide for an adequate reconciliation. Where there are there are robust electronic controls in place during packaging there may be justification for not including this information

(i) Approval by the person responsible for the packaging operations

## Procedures and records

### Receipt

4.22 There should be written procedures and records for the receipt of each delivery of each starting material, (including bulk, intermediate or finished goods), primary, secondary and printed packaging materials.

4.23 The records of the receipts should include:

(a) The name of the material on the delivery note and the containers;

(b) The "in-house" name and/or code of material (if different from a);

(c) Date of receipt;

(d) Supplier's name and, manufacturer's name;

(e) Manufacturer's batch or reference number;

(f) Total quantity and number of containers received;

(g) The batch number assigned after receipt;

(h) Any relevant comment.

4.24 There should be written procedures for the internal labeling, quarantine and storage of starting materials, packaging materials and other materials, as appropriate.

### Sampling

4.25 There should be written procedures for sampling, which include the methods and equipment to be used, the amounts to be taken and any precautions to be observed to avoid contamination of the material or any deterioration in its quality.

## Testing

**4.26** There should be written procedures for testing materials and products at different stages of manufacture, describing the methods and equipment to be used. The tests performed should be recorded.

## Other

**4.27** Written release and rejection procedures should be available for materials and products, and in particular for the certification for sale of the finished product by the Qualified Person(s). All records should be available to the Qualified Person. A system should be in place to indicate special observations and any changes to critical data.

**4.28** Records should be maintained for the distribution of each batch of a product in order to facilitate recall of any batch, if necessary.

**4.29** There should be written policies, procedures, protocols, reports and the associated records of actions taken or conclusions reached, where appropriate, for the following examples:

- Validation and qualification of processes, equipment and systems;
- Equipment assembly and calibration;
- Technology transfer;
- Maintenance, cleaning and sanitation;
- Personnel matters including signature lists, training in GMP and technical matters, clothing and hygiene and verification of the effectiveness of training.
- Environmental monitoring;
- Pest control;
- Complaints;
- Recalls;
- Returns;
- Change control;
- Investigations into deviations and non-conformances;
- Internal quality/GMP compliance audits;
- Summaries of records where appropriate (e.g. product quality review);
- Supplier audits.

**4.30** Clear operating procedures should be available for major items of manufacturing and test equipment.

**4.31** Logbooks should be kept for major or critical analytical testing, production equipment, and areas where product has been processed. They should be used to record in chronological order, as appropriate, any use of the area, equipment/method, calibrations, maintenance, cleaning or repair operations, including the dates and identity of people who carried these operations out.

**4.32**  An inventory of documents within the Quality Management System should be maintained.

## 5    PRODUCTION

## Principle

Production operations must follow clearly defined procedures; they must comply with the principles of Good Manufacturing Practice in order to obtain products of the requisite quality and be in accordance with the relevant manufacturing and marketing authorisations.

## General

5.1    Production should be performed and supervised by competent people.

5.2    All handling of materials and products, such as receipt and quarantine, sampling, storage, labelling, dispensing, processing, packaging and distribution should be done in accordance with written procedures or instructions and, where necessary, recorded.

5.3    All incoming materials should be checked to ensure that the consignment corresponds to the order. Containers should be cleaned where necessary and labelled with the prescribed data.

5.4    Damage to containers and any other problem which might adversely affect the quality of a material should be investigated, recorded and reported to the Quality Control Department.

5.5    Incoming materials and finished products should be physically or administratively quarantined immediately after receipt or processing, until they have been released for use or distribution.

5.6     Intermediate and bulk products purchased as such should be handled on receipt as though they were starting materials.

5.7     All materials and products should be stored under the appropriate conditions established by the manufacturer and in an orderly fashion to permit batch segregation and stock rotation.

5.8     Checks on yields, and reconciliation of quantities, should be carried out as necessary to ensure that there are no discrepancies outside acceptable limits.

5.9     Operations on different products should not be carried out simultaneously or consecutively in the same room unless there is no risk of mix-up or cross-contamination.

5.10    At every stage of processing, products and materials should be protected from microbial and other contamination.

5.11    When working with dry materials and products, special precautions should be taken to prevent the generation and dissemination of dust. This applies particularly to the handling of highly active or sensitising materials.

5.12    At all times during processing, all materials, bulk containers, major items of equipment and where appropriate rooms used should be labelled or otherwise identified with an indication of the product or material being processed, its strength (where applicable) and batch number. Where applicable, this indication should also mention the stage of production.

5.13    Labels applied to containers, equipment or premises should be clear, unambiguous and in the company's agreed format. It is often helpful in addition to the wording on the labels to use colours to indicate status (for example, quarantined, accepted, rejected, clean).

5.14    Checks should be carried out to ensure that pipelines and other pieces of equipment used for the transportation of products from one area to another are connected in a correct manner.

5.15    Any deviation from instructions or procedures should be avoided as far as possible. If a deviation occurs, it should be approved in writing by a competent person, with the involvement of the Quality Control Department when appropriate.

5.16    Access to production premises should be restricted to authorised personnel.

## Prevention of Cross-contamination in Production

5.17    Normally, the production of non-medicinal products should be avoided in areas and with equipment destined for the production of medicinal products but, where justified, could be allowed where the measures to prevent cross-contamination with medicinal products described below and in Chapter 3 can be applied. The production and/or storage of technical poisons, such as pesticides (except where these are used for manufacture of medicinal products) and herbicides, should not be allowed in areas used for the manufacture and / or storage of medicinal products.

5.18    Contamination of a starting material or of a product by another material or product should be prevented. This risk of accidental cross-contamination resulting from the uncontrolled release of dust, gases, vapours, aerosols, genetic material or organisms from active substances, other starting materials, and products in process, from residues on equipment, and from operators' clothing should be assessed. The significance of this risk varies with the nature of the contaminant and that of the product being contaminated. Products in which cross-contamination is likely to be most significant are those administered by injection and those given over a long time. However, contamination of all products poses a risk to patient safety dependent on the nature and extent of contamination.

5.19    Cross-contamination should be prevented by attention to design of the premises and equipment as described in Chapter 3. This should be supported by attention to process design and implementation of any relevant technical or organizational measures, including effective and reproducible cleaning processes to control risk of cross-contamination.

5.20    A Quality Risk Management process, which includes a potency and toxicological evaluation, should be used to assess and control the cross-contamination risks presented by the products manufactured. Factors including; facility/equipment design and use, personnel and material flow, microbiological controls, physico-chemical characteristics of the active substance, process characteristics, cleaning processes and analytical capabilities relative to the relevant limits established from the evaluation of the products should also be taken into account. The outcome of the Quality Risk Management process should be the basis for determining the necessity for and extent to which premises and equipment should be dedicated to a particular product or product family. This may include dedicating specific product contact parts or dedication of the entire manufacturing facility. It may be acceptable to confine manufacturing activities to a segregated, self contained production area within a multiproduct facility, where justified.

**5.21**    The outcome of the Quality Risk Management process should be the basis for determining the extent of technical and organisational measures required to control risks for cross-contamination. These could include, but are not limited to, the following:

## Technical Measures

(i)     Dedicated manufacturing facility (premises and equipment);

(ii)    Self-contained production areas having separate processing equipment and separate heating, ventilation and air-conditioning (HVAC) systems. It may also be desirable to isolate certain utilities from those used in other areas;

(iii)   Design of manufacturing process, premises and equipment to minimize opportunities for cross-contamination during processing, maintenance and cleaning;

(iv)    Use of "closed systems" for processing and material/product transfer between equipment;

(v)     Use of physical barrier systems, including isolators, as containment measures;

(vi)    Controlled removal of dust close to source of the contaminant e.g. through localised extraction;

(vii)   Dedication of equipment, dedication of product contact parts or dedication of selected parts which are harder to clean (e.g. filters), dedication of maintenance tools;

(viii)  Use of single use disposable technologies;

(ix)    Use of equipment designed for ease of cleaning;

(x)     Appropriate use of air-locks and pressure cascade to confine potential airborne contaminant within a specified area;

(xi)    Minimising the risk of contamination caused by recirculation or re-entry of untreated or insufficiently treated air;

(xii)   Use of automatic clean in place systems of validated effectiveness;

(xiii)  For common general wash areas, separation of equipment washing, drying and storage areas.

## Organisational Measures

(i)     Dedicating the whole manufacturing facility or a self contained production area on a campaign basis (dedicated by separation in time) followed by a cleaning process of validated effectiveness;

(ii)    Keeping specific protective clothing inside areas where products with high risk of cross-contamination are processed;

(iii) Cleaning verification after each product campaign should be considered as a detectability tool to support effectiveness of the Quality Risk Management approach for products deemed to present higher risk;

(iv) Depending on the contamination risk, verification of cleaning of non product contact surfaces and monitoring of air within the manufacturing area and/or adjoining areas in order to demonstrate effectiveness of control measures against airborne contamination or contamination by mechanical transfer;

(v) Specific measures for waste handling, contaminated rinsing water and soiled gowning;

(vi) Recording of spills, accidental events or deviations from procedures;

(vii) Design of cleaning processes for premises and equipment such that the cleaning processes in themselves do not present a cross-contamination risk;

(viii) Design of detailed records for cleaning processes to assure completion of cleaning in accordance with approved procedures and use of cleaning status labels on equipment and manufacturing areas;

(ix) Use of common general wash areas on a campaign basis;

(x) Supervision of working behaviour to ensure training effectiveness and compliance with the relevant procedural controls.

5.22 Measures to prevent cross-contamination and their effectiveness should be reviewed periodically according to set procedures.

## Validation

5.23 Validation studies should reinforce Good Manufacturing Practice and be conducted in accordance with defined procedures. Results and conclusions should be recorded.

5.24 When any new manufacturing formula or method of preparation is adopted, steps should be taken to demonstrate its suitability for routine processing. The defined process, using the materials and equipment specified, should be shown to yield a product consistently of the required quality.

5.25 Significant amendments to the manufacturing process, including any change in equipment or materials, which may affect product quality and/or the reproducibility of the process should be validated.

5.26 Processes and procedures should undergo periodic critical re-validation to ensure that they remain capable of achieving the intended results.

EU GMP GUIDE PART I CHAPTER 5 PRODUCTION

## Starting Materials

**5.27** The selection, qualification, approval and maintenance of suppliers of starting materials, together with their purchase and acceptance, should be documented as part of the pharmaceutical quality system. The level of supervision should be proportionate to the risks posed by the individual materials, taking account of their source, manufacturing process, supply chain complexity and the final use to which the material is put in the medicinal product. The supporting evidence for each supplier / material approval should be maintained. Staff involved in these activities should have a current knowledge of the suppliers, the supply chain and the associated risks involved. Where possible, starting materials should be purchased directly from the manufacturer of the starting material.

**5.28** The quality requirements established by the manufacturer for the starting materials should be discussed and agreed with the suppliers. Appropriate aspects of the production, testing and control, including handling, labelling, packaging and distribution requirements, complaints, recalls and rejection procedures should be documented in a formal quality agreement or specification.

**5.29** For the approval and maintenance of suppliers of active substances and excipients, the following is required:

## Active substances[1]

Supply chain traceability should be established and the associated risks, from active substance starting materials to the finished medicinal product, should be formally assessed and periodically verified. Appropriate measures should be put in place to reduce risks to the quality of the active substance.

The supply chain and traceability records for each active substance (including active substance starting materials) should be available and be retained by the EEA based manufacturer or importer of the medicinal product.

Audits should be carried out at the manufacturers and distributors of active substances to confirm that they comply with the relevant good manufacturing practice and good distribution practice requirements. The holder of the manufacturing authorisation shall verify such compliance either by himself or through an entity acting on his behalf under a contract. For veterinary medicinal products, audits should be conducted based on risk.

---

[1] Specific requirements apply to the importation of active substances to be used in the manufacture of medicinal products for human use in article 46b of Directive 2001/83/EC.

Audits should be of an appropriate duration and scope to ensure that a full and clear assessment of GMP is made; consideration should be given to potential cross-contamination from other materials on site. The report should fully reflect what was done and seen on the audit with any deficiencies clearly identified. Any required corrective and preventive actions should be implemented.

Further audits should be undertaken at intervals defined by the quality risk management process to ensure the maintenance of standards and continued use of the approved supply chain.

## Excipients

Excipients and excipient suppliers should be controlled appropriately based on the results of a formalised quality risk assessment in accordance with the European Commission 'Guidelines on the formalised risk assessment for ascertaining the appropriate Good Manufacturing Practice for excipients of medicinal products for human use'.

5.30    For each delivery of starting material the containers should be checked for integrity of package, including tamper evident seal where relevant, and for correspondence between the delivery note, the purchase order, the supplier's labels and approved manufacturer and supplier information maintained by the medicinal product manufacturer. The receiving checks on each delivery should be documented.

5.31    If one material delivery is made up of different batches, each batch must be considered as separate for sampling, testing and release.

5.32    Starting materials in the storage area should be appropriately labelled (see section 13). Labels should bear at least the following information:

(i)    The designated name of the product and the internal code reference where applicable;

(ii)   A batch number given at receipt;

(iii)  Where appropriate, the status of the contents (e.g. in quarantine, on test, released, rejected);

(iv)   Where appropriate, an expiry date or a date beyond which retesting is necessary.

When fully computerised storage systems are used, all the above information need not necessarily be in a legible form on the label.

5.33    There should be appropriate procedures or measures to assure the identity of the contents of each container of starting material. Bulk containers from which samples have been drawn should be identified (see Chapter 6).

**5.34**  Only starting materials which have been released by the Quality Control department and which are within their retest period should be used.

**5.35**  Manufacturers of finished products are responsible for any testing of starting materials[2] as described in the marketing authorisation dossier. They can utilise partial or full test results from the approved starting material manufacturer but must, as a minimum, perform identification testing[3] of each batch according to Annex 8.

**5.36**  The rationale for the outsourcing of this testing should be justified and documented and the following requirements should be fulfilled:

(i)   Special attention should be paid to the distribution controls (transport, wholesaling, storage and delivery) in order to maintain the quality characteristics of the starting materials and to ensure that test results remain applicable to the delivered material;

(ii)  The medicinal product manufacturer should perform audits, either itself or via third parties, at appropriate intervals based on risk at the site(s) carrying out the testing (including sampling) of the starting materials in order to assure compliance with Good Manufacturing Practice and with the specifications and testing methods described in the marketing authorisation dossier;

(iii) The certificate of analysis provided by the starting material manufacturer/supplier should be signed by a designated person with appropriate qualifications and experience. The signature assures that each batch has been checked for compliance with the agreed product specification unless this assurance is provided separately;

(iv)  The medicinal product manufacturer should have appropriate experience in dealing with the starting material manufacturer (including experience via a supplier).

**5.37**  Starting materials should only be dispensed by designated persons, following a written procedure, to ensure that the correct materials are accurately weighed or measured into clean and properly labelled containers.

**5.38**  Each dispensed material and its weight or volume should be independently checked and the check recorded.

**5.39**  Materials dispensed for each batch should be kept together and conspicuously labelled as such.

---

[2]  A similar approach should apply to packaging materials as stated in section 5.42.
[3]  Identity testing of starting materials should be performed according to the methods and the specifications of the relevant marketing authorisation dossier.

## Processing Operations: intermediate and bulk products

5.40    Before any processing operation is started, steps should be taken to ensure that the work area and equipment are clean and free from any starting materials, products, product residues or documents not required for the current operation.

5.41    Intermediate and bulk products should be kept under appropriate conditions.

5.42    Critical processes should be validated (see "Validation" in this Chapter).

5.43    Any necessary in-process controls and environmental controls should be carried out and recorded.

5.44    Any significant deviation from the expected yield should be recorded and investigated.

## Packaging Materials

5.45    The selection, qualification, approval and maintenance of suppliers of primary and printed packaging materials shall be accorded attention similar to that given to starting materials.

5.46    Particular attention should be paid to printed materials. They should be stored in adequately secure conditions such as to exclude unauthorised access. Cut labels and other loose printed materials should be stored and transported in separate closed containers so as to avoid mix-ups. Packaging materials should be issued for use only by authorised personnel following an approved and documented procedure.

5.47    Each delivery or batch of printed or primary packaging material should be given a specific reference number or identification mark.

5.48    Outdated or obsolete primary packaging material or printed packaging material should be destroyed and this disposal recorded.

## Packaging Operations

5.49    When setting up a programme for the packaging operations, particular attention should be given to minimising the risk of cross-contamination, mix-ups or substitutions. Different products should not be packaged in close proximity unless there is physical segregation.

5.50    Before packaging operations are begun, steps should be taken to ensure that the work area, packaging lines, printing machines and other equipment are clean and free from any products, materials or documents previously used, if these are not required for the current operation. The line-clearance should be performed according to an appropriate check-list.

5.51    The name and batch number of the product being handled should be displayed at each packaging station or line.

5.52    All products and packaging materials to be used should be checked on delivery to the packaging department for quantity, identity and conformity with the Packaging Instructions.

5.53    Containers for filling should be clean before filling. Attention should be given to avoid and remove any contaminants such as glass fragments and metal particles.

5.54    Normally, filling and sealing should be followed as quickly as possible by labelling. If it is not the case, appropriate procedures should be applied to ensure that no mix-ups or mislabelling can occur.

5.55    The correct performance of any printing operation (for example code numbers, expiry dates) to be done separately or in the course of the packaging should be checked and recorded. Attention should be paid to printing by hand which should be re-checked at regular intervals.

5.56    Special care should be taken when using cut-labels and when over-printing is carried out off-line. Roll-feed labels are normally preferable to cut-labels, in helping to avoid mix-ups.

5.57    Checks should be made to ensure that any electronic code readers, label counters or similar devices are operating correctly.

5.58    Printed and embossed information on packaging materials should be distinct and resistant to fading or erasing.

5.59    On-line control of the product during packaging should include at least checking the following:

(i)     General appearance of the packages;
(ii)    Whether the packages are complete;
(iii)   Whether the correct products and packaging materials are used;
(iv)    Whether any over-printing is correct;
(v)     Correct functioning of line monitors.

Samples taken away from the packaging line should not be returned.

5.60    Products which have been involved in an unusual event should only be reintroduced into the process after special inspection, investigation and approval by authorised personnel. Detailed record should be kept of this operation.

5.61   Any significant or unusual discrepancy observed during reconciliation of the amount of bulk product and printed packaging materials and the number of units produced should be investigated and satisfactorily accounted for before release.

5.62   Upon completion of a packaging operation, any unused batch-coded packaging materials should be destroyed and the destruction recorded. A documented procedure should be followed if un-coded printed materials are returned to stock.

## Finished Products

5.63   Finished products should be held in quarantine until their final release under conditions established by the manufacturer.

5.64   The evaluation of finished products and documentation which is necessary before release of product for sale is described in Chapter 6 (Quality Control).

5.65   After release, finished products should be stored as usable stock under conditions established by the manufacturer.

## Rejected, Recovered and Returned Materials

5.66   Rejected materials and products should be clearly marked as such and stored separately in restricted areas. They should either be returned to the suppliers or, where appropriate, reprocessed or destroyed. Whatever action is taken should be approved and recorded by authorised personnel.

5.67   The reprocessing of rejected products should be exceptional. It is only permitted if the quality of the final product is not affected, if the specifications are met and if it is done in accordance with a defined and authorised procedure after evaluation of the risks involved. Record should be kept of the reprocessing.

5.68   The recovery of all or part of earlier batches which conform to the required quality by incorporation into a batch of the same product at a defined stage of manufacture should be authorised beforehand. This recovery should be carried out in accordance with a defined procedure after evaluation of the risks involved, including any possible effect on shelf life. The recovery should be recorded.

5.69   The need for additional testing of any finished product which has been reprocessed, or into which a recovered product has been incorporated, should be considered by the Quality Control Department.

**5.70**  Products returned from the market and which have left the control of the manufacturer should be destroyed unless without doubt their quality is satisfactory; they may be considered for re-sale, re-labelling or recovery in a subsequent batch only after they have been critically assessed by the Quality Control Department in accordance with a written procedure. The nature of the product, any special storage conditions it requires, its condition and history, and the time elapsed since it was issued should all be taken into account in this assessment. Where any doubt arises over the quality of the product, it should not be considered suitable for re-issue or re-use, although basic chemical reprocessing to recover active ingredient may be possible. Any action taken should be appropriately recorded.

## Product shortage due to manufacturing constraints

**5.71**  The manufacturer should report to the marketing authorisation holder (MAH) any constraints in manufacturing operations which may result in abnormal restriction in the supply. This should be done in a timely manner to facilitate reporting of the restriction in supply by the MAH, to the relevant competent authorities, in accordance with its legal obligations[4].

EU GMP GUIDE PART I CHAPTER 5 PRODUCTION

---

[4]  Articles 23a and 81 of Directive 2001/83/EC.

## 6    QUALITY CONTROL

**Editor's note**    Chapter 6 of Part I of the GMP Guide has been updated and has a new section on technical transfer of testing methods and other items such as Out Of Specification results. This revised Chapter came into operation 1 October 2014.

## Principle

This chapter should be read in conjunction with all relevant sections of the GMP guide.

Quality Control is concerned with sampling, specifications and testing as well as the organisation, documentation and release procedures which ensure that the necessary and relevant tests are carried out, and that materials are not released for use, nor products released for sale or supply, until their quality has been judged satisfactory. Quality Control is not confined to laboratory operations, but must be involved in all decisions which may concern the quality of the product. The independence of Quality Control from Production is considered fundamental to the satisfactory operation of Quality Control.

## General

6.1    Each holder of a manufacturing authorisation should have a Quality Control Department. This department should be independent from other departments, and under the authority of a person with appropriate qualifications and experience, who has one or several control laboratories at his disposal. Adequate resources must be available to ensure that all the Quality Control arrangements are effectively and reliably carried out.

6.2    The principal duties of the head of Quality Control are summarised in Chapter 2. The Quality Control Department as a whole will also have other duties, such as to establish, validate and implement all quality control procedures, oversee the control of the reference and/or retention samples of materials and products when applicable, ensure the correct labelling of containers of materials and products, ensure the monitoring of the stability of the products, participate in the investigation of complaints related to the quality of the product, etc. All these operations should be carried out in accordance with written procedures and, where necessary, recorded.

**6.3** Finished product assessment should embrace all relevant factors, including production conditions, results of in-process testing, a review of manufacturing (including packaging) documentation, compliance with Finished Product Specification and examination of the final finished pack.

**6.4** Quality Control personnel should have access to production areas for sampling and investigation as appropriate.

## Good Quality Control Laboratory Practice

**6.5** Control laboratory premises and equipment should meet the general and specific requirements for Quality Control areas given in Chapter 3. Laboratory equipment should not be routinely moved between high risk areas to avoid accidental cross-contamination. In particular, the micro-biological laboratory should be arranged so as to minimize risk of cross-contamination.

**6.6** The personnel, premises, and equipment in the laboratories should be appropriate to the tasks imposed by the nature and the scale of the manufacturing operations. The use of outside laboratories, in conformity with the principles detailed in Chapter 7, Contract Analysis, can be accepted for particular reasons, but this should be stated in the Quality Control records.

## Documentation

**6.7** Laboratory documentation should follow the principles given in Chapter 4. An important part of this documentation deals with Quality Control and the following details should be readily available to the Quality Control Department:

(i) Specifications;
(ii) Procedures describing sampling, testing, records (including test worksheets and/or laboratory notebooks), recording and verifying;
(iii) Procedures for and records of the calibration/qualification of instruments and maintenance of equipment;
(iv) A procedure for the investigation of Out of Specification and Out Of Trend results;
(v) Testing reports and/or certificates of analysis;
(vi) Data from environmental (air, water and other utilities) monitoring, where required;
(vii) Validation records of test methods, where applicable.

6.8 Any Quality Control documentation relating to a batch record should be retained following the principles given in chapter 4 on retention of batch documentation.

6.9 Some kinds of data (e.g. tests results, yields, environmental controls) should be recorded in a manner permitting trend evaluation. Any out of trend or out of specification data should be addressed and subject to investigation.

6.10 In addition to the information which is part of the batch documentation, other raw data such as laboratory notebooks and/or records should be retained and readily available.

## Sampling

6.11 The sample taking should be done and recorded in accordance with approved written procedures that describe:

(i) The method of sampling;
(ii) The equipment to be used;
(iii) The amount of the sample to be taken;
(iv) Instructions for any required sub-division of the sample;
(v) The type and condition of the sample container to be used;
(vi) The identification of containers sampled;
(vii) Any special precautions to be observed, especially with regard to the sampling of sterile or noxious materials;
(viii) The storage conditions;
(ix) Instructions for the cleaning and storage of sampling equipment.

6.12 Samples should be representative of the batch of materials or products from which they are taken. Other samples may also be taken to monitor the most stressed part of a process (e.g. beginning or end of a process). The sampling plan used should be appropriately justified and based on a risk management approach.

6.13 Sample containers should bear a label indicating the contents, with the batch number, the date of sampling and the containers from which samples have been drawn. They should be managed in a manner to minimize the risk of mix-up and to protect the samples from adverse storage conditions.

6.14 Further guidance on reference and retention samples is given in Annex 19.

## Testing

6.15 Testing methods should be validated. A laboratory that is using a testing method and which did not perform the original validation, should verify the appropriateness of the testing method. All testing operations described in the marketing authorisation or technical dossier should be carried out according to the approved methods.

**6.16** The results obtained should be recorded. Results of parameters identified as quality attribute or as critical should be trended and checked to make sure that they are consistent with each other. Any calculations should be critically examined.

**6.17** The tests performed should be recorded and the records should include at least the following data:

(i) Name of the material or product and, where applicable, dosage form;
(ii) Batch number and, where appropriate, the manufacturer and/or supplier;
(iii) References to the relevant specifications and testing procedures;
(iv) Test results, including observations and calculations, and reference to any certificates of analysis;
(v) Dates of testing;
(vi) Initials of the persons who performed the testing;
(vii) Initials of the persons who verified the testing and the calculations, where appropriate;
(viii) A clear statement of approval or rejection (or other status decision) and the dated signature of the designated responsible person;
(ix) Reference to the equipment used.

**6.18** All the in-process controls, including those made in the production area by production personnel, should be performed according to methods approved by Quality Control and the results recorded.

**6.19** Special attention should be given to the quality of laboratory reagents, solutions, glassware, reference standards and culture media. They should be prepared and controlled in accordance with written procedures. The level of controls should be commensurate to their use and to the available stability data.

**6.20** Reference standards should be established as suitable for their intended use. Their qualification and certification as such should be clearly stated and documented. Whenever compendial reference standards from an officially recognised source exist, these should preferably be used as primary reference standards unless fully justified (the use of secondary standards is permitted once their traceability to primary standards has been demonstrated and is documented). These compendial materials should be used for the purpose described in the appropiate monograph unless otherwise authorised by the National Competent Authority.

6.21   Laboratory reagents, solutions, reference standards and culture media should be marked with the preparation and opening date and the signature of the person who prepared them. The expiry date of reagents and culture media should be indicated on the label, together with specific storage conditions. In addition, for volumetric solutions, the last date of standardisation and the last current factor should be indicated.

6.22   Where necessary, the date of receipt of any substance used for testing operations (e.g. reagents, solutions and reference standards) should be indicated on the container. Instructions for use and storage should be followed. In certain cases it may be necessary to carry out an identification test and/or other testing of reagent materials upon receipt or before use.

6.23   Culture media should be prepared in accordance with the media manufacturer's requirements unless scientifically justified. The performance of all culture media should be verified prior to use.

6.24   Used microbiological media and strains should be decontaminated according to a standard procedure and disposed of in a manner to prevent the cross-contamination and retention of residues. The in-use shelf life of microbiological media should be established, documented and scientifically justified.

6.25   Animals used for testing components, materials or products, should, where appropriate, be quarantined before use. They should be maintained and controlled in a manner that assures their suitability for the intended use. They should be identified, and adequate records should be maintained, showing the history of their use.

## On-going stability programme

6.26   After marketing, the stability of the medicinal product should be monitored according to a continuous appropriate programme that will permit the detection of any stability issue (e.g. changes in levels of impurities or dissolution profile) associated with the formulation in the marketed package.

6.27   The purpose of the on-going stability programme is to monitor the product over its shelf life and to determine that the product remains, and can be expected to remain, within specifications under the labelled storage conditions.

6.28   This mainly applies to the medicinal product in the package in which it is sold, but consideration should also be given to the inclusion in the programme of bulk product. For example, when the bulk product is stored for a long period before being packaged and/or shipped from a manufacturing site to a packaging site, the impact on the stability of the packaged product should be evaluated and studied under ambient conditions. In addition, consideration should be given to intermediates that are stored and used over prolonged periods. Stability studies on reconstituted product are performed during product development and need not be monitored on an on-going basis. However, when relevant, the stability of reconstituted product can also be monitored.

6.29   The on-going stability programme should be described in a written protocol following the general rules of Chapter 4 and results formalised as a report. The equipment used for the ongoing stability programme (stability chambers among others) should be qualified and maintained following the general rules of Chapter 3 and Annex 15.

6.30   The protocol for an on-going stability programme should extend to the end of the shelf life period and should include, but not be limited to, the following parameters:

(i)    Number of batch(es) per strength and different batch sizes, if applicable;

(ii)   Relevant physical, chemical, microbiological and biological test methods;

(iii)  Acceptance criteria;

(iv)   Reference to test methods;

(v)    Description of the container closure system(s);

(vi)   Testing intervals (time points);

(vii)  Description of the conditions of storage (standardised ICH/VICH conditions for long term testing, consistent with the product labelling, should be used);

(viii) Other applicable parameters specific to the medicinal product.

6.31   The protocol for the on-going stability programme can be different from that of the initial long term stability study as submitted in the marketing authorisation dossier provided that this is justified and documented in the protocol (for example the frequency of testing, or when updating to ICH/VICH recommendations).

6.32   The number of batches and frequency of testing should provide a sufficient amount of data to allow for trend analysis. Unless otherwise justified, at least one batch per year of product manufactured in every strength and every primary packaging type, if relevant, should be included in the stability programme (unless none are produced during that year). For products where on-going stability monitoring would normally require testing using animals and no appropriate alternative, validated techniques are available, the frequency of testing may take account of a risk-benefit approach. The principle of bracketing and matrixing designs may be applied if scientifically justified in the protocol.

6.33    In certain situations, additional batches should be included in the on-going stability programme. For example, an on-going stability study should be conducted after any significant change or significant deviation to the process or package. Any reworking, reprocessing or recovery operation should also be considered for inclusion.

6.34    Results of on-going stability studies should be made available to key personnel and, in particular, to the Qualified Person(s). Where on-going stability studies are carried out at a site other than the site of manufacture of the bulk or finished product, there should be a written agreement between the parties concerned. Results of on-going stability studies should be available at the site of manufacture for review by the competent authority.

6.35    Out of specification or significant atypical trends should be investigated. Any confirmed out of specification result, or significant negative trend, affecting product batches released on the market should be reported to the relevant competent authorities. The possible impact on batches on the market should be considered in accordance with Chapter 8 of the GMP Guide and in consultation with the relevant competent authorities.

6.36    A summary of all the data generated, including any interim conclusions on the programme, should be written and maintained. This summary should be subjected to periodic review.

## Technical transfer of testing methods

6.37    Prior to transferring a test method, the transferring site should verify that the test method(s) comply with those as described in the Marketing Authorisation or the relevant technical dossier. The original validation of the test method(s) should be reviewed to ensure compliance with current ICH/VICH requirements. A gap analysis should be performed and documented to identify any supplementary validation that should be performed, prior to commencing the technical transfer process.

6.38    The transfer of testing methods from one laboratory (transferring laboratory) to another laboratory (receiving laboratory) should be described in a detailed protocol.

6.39    The transfer protocol should include, but not be limited to, the following parameters:

(i)    Identification of the testing to be performed and the relevant test method(s) undergoing transfer;

(ii)   Identification of the additional training requirements;

(iii)  Identification of standards and samples to be tested;

(iv)   Identification of any special transport and storage conditions of test items;

(v)    The acceptance criteria which should be based upon the current validation study of the methodology and with respect to ICH/VICH requirements.

**6.40**   Deviations from the protocol should be investigated prior to closure of the technical transfer process. The technical transfer report should document the comparative outcome of the process and should identify areas requiring further test method revalidation, if applicable.

**6.41**   Where appropriate, specific requirements described in others European Guidelines, should be addressed for the transfer of particular testing methods (e.g Near Infrared Spectroscopy).

## 7   OUTSOURCED ACTIVITIES

### Principle

Any activity covered by the GMP Guide that is outsourced should be appropriately defined, agreed and controlled in order to avoid misunder-standings which could result in a product or operation of unsatisfactory quality. There must be a written Contract between the Contract Giver and the Contract Acceptor which clearly establishes the duties of each party. The Quality Management System of the Contract Giver must clearly state the way that the Qualified Person certifying each batch of product for release exercises his full responsibility.

> **Note:** *This chapter deals with the responsibilities of manufacturers towards the Competent Authorities of the Member States with respect to the granting of marketing and manufacturing authorisations. It is not intended in any way to affect the respective liability of Contract Acceptors and Contract Givers to consumers; this is governed by other provisions of Community and national law.*

### General

**7.1**   There should be a written Contract covering the outsourced activities, the products or operations to which they are related and any technical arrangements made in connection with it.

**7.2**   All arrangements for the outsourced activities including any proposed changes in technical or other arrangements should be in accordance with regulations in force, and the Marketing Authorisation for the product concerned, where applicable.

**7.3**   Where the marketing authorization holder and the manufacturer are not the same, appropriate arrangements should be in place, taking into account the principles described in this chapter.

### The Contract Giver

**7.4**   The pharmaceutical quality system of the Contract Giver should include the control and review of any outsourced activities. The Contract Giver is ultimately responsible to ensure processes are in place to assure the control of outsourced activities. These processes should incorporate quality risk management principles and notably include:

7.5     Prior to outsourcing activities, the Contract Giver is responsible for assessing the legality, suitability and the competence of the Contract Acceptor to carry out successfully the outsourced activities. The Contract Giver is also responsible for ensuring by means of the Contract that the principles and guidelines of GMP as interpreted in this Guide are followed.

7.6     The Contract Giver should provide the Contract Acceptor with all the information and knowledge necessary to carry out the contracted operations correctly in accordance with regulations in force, and the Marketing Authorisation for the product concerned. The Contract Giver should ensure that the Contract Acceptor is fully aware of any problems associated with the product or the work which might pose a hazard to his premises, equipment, personnel, other materials or other products.

7.7     The Contract Giver should monitor and review the performance of the Contract Acceptor and the identification and implementation of any needed improvement.

7.8     The Contract Giver should be responsible for reviewing and assessing the records and the results related to the outsourced activities. He should also ensure, either by himself, or based on the confirmation of the Contract Acceptor's Qualified Person, that all products and materials delivered to him by the Contract Acceptor have been processed in accordance with GMP and the marketing authorisation.

## The Contract Acceptor

7.9     The Contract Acceptor must be able to carry out satisfactorily the work ordered by the Contract Giver such as having adequate premises, equipment, knowledge, experience, and competent personnel.

7.10    The Contract Acceptor should ensure that all products, materials and knowledge delivered to him are suitable for their intended purpose.

7.11    The Contract Acceptor should not subcontract to a third party any of the work entrusted to him under the Contract without the Contract Giver's prior evaluation and approval of the arrangements. Arrangements made between the Contract Acceptor and any third party should ensure that information and knowledge, including those from assessments of the suitability of the third party, are made available in the same way as between the original Contract Giver and Contract Acceptor.

**7.12** The Contract Acceptor should not make unauthorized changes outside the terms of the Contract which may adversely affect the quality of the outsourced activities for the Contract Giver.

**7.13** The Contract Acceptor should understand that outsourced activities, including contract analysis, may be subject to inspection by the competent authorities.

## The Contract

**7.14** A Contract should be drawn up between the Contract Giver and the Contract Acceptor which specifies their respective responsibilities and communication processes relating to the outsourced activities. Technical aspects of the Contract should be drawn up by competent persons suitably knowledgeable in related outsourced activities and Good Manufacturing Practice. All arrangements for outsourced activities must be in accordance with regulations in force and the Marketing Authorisation for the product concerned and agreed by both parties.

**7.15** The Contract should describe clearly who undertakes each step of the outsourced activity, e.g. knowledge management, technology transfer, supply chain, subcontracting, quality and purchasing of materials, testing and releasing materials, undertaking production and quality controls (including in-process controls, sampling and analysis).

**7.16** All records related to the outsourced activities, e.g. manufacturing, analytical and distribution records, and reference samples, should be kept by, or be available to, the Contract Giver. Any records relevant to assessing the quality of a product in the event of complaints or a suspected defect or to investigating in the case of a suspected falsified product must be accessible and specified in the relevant procedures of the Contract Giver.

**7.17** The Contract should permit the Contract Giver to audit outsourced activities, performed by the Contract Acceptor or his mutually agreed subcontractors.

# 8 COMPLAINTS, QUALITY DEFECTS AND PRODUCT RECALLS

| | |
|---|---|
| **Editor's note** | Extensive changes have been made to this chapter which now reflect that Quality Risk Management principles should be applied when investigating quality defects or complaints and when making decisions in relation to product recalls or other risk-mitigating actions. It emphasises the need for the cause(s) of quality defects or complaints to be investigated and determined, and that appropriate preventative actions are put in place to guard against a recurrence of the issue and clarifies expectations and responsibilities in relation to the reporting of quality defects to the Competent Authorities.<br>The deadline for coming into operation is 1 March 2015 |

## Principle

In order to protect public and animal health, a system and appropriate procedures should be in place to record, assess, investigate and review complaints including potential quality defects, and if necessary, to effectively and promptly recall medicinal products for human or veterinary use and investigational medicinal products from the distribution network. Quality Risk Management principles should be applied to the investigation and assessment of quality defects and to the decision-making process in relation to product recalls corrective and preventative actions and other risk-reducing actions. Guidance in relation to these principles is provided in Chapter 1.

All concerned competent authorities should be informed in a timely manner in case of a confirmed quality defect (faulty manufacture, product deterioration, detection of falsification, non-compliance with the marketing authorisation or product specification file, or any other serious quality problems) with a medicinal or investigational medicinal product which may result in the recall of the product or an abnormal restriction in the supply. In situations where product on the market is found to be non-compliant with the marketing authorisation, there is no requirement to notify concerned competent authorities provided the degree of non-compliance satisfies the Annex 16 restrictions regarding the handling of unplanned deviations.

In case of outsourced activities, a contract should describe the role and responsibilities of the manufacturer, the marketing authorisation holder and/or sponsor and any other relevant third parties in relation to assessment, decision-making, and dissemination of information and implementation of risk-reducing actions relating to a defective product. Guidance in relation to contracts is provided in Chapter 7. Such contracts should also address how to contact those responsible at each party for the management of quality defect and recall issues.

## Personnel and Organisation

8.1 Appropriately trained and experienced personnel should be responsible for managing complaint and quality defect investigations and for deciding the measures to be taken to manage any potential risk(s) presented by those issues, including recalls. These persons should be independent of the sales and marketing organisation, unless otherwise justified. If these persons do not include the Qualified Person involved in the certification for release of the concerned batch or batches, the latter should be made formally aware of any investigations, any risk-reducing actions and any recall operations, in a timely manner.

8.2 Sufficient trained personnel and resources should be made available for the handling, assessment, investigation and review of complaints and quality defects and for implementing any risk-reducing actions. Sufficient trained personnel and resources should also be available for the management of interactions with competent authorities.

8.3 The use of inter-disciplinary teams should be considered, including appropriately trained Quality Management personnel.

8.4 In situations in which complaint and quality defect handling is managed centrally within an organisation, the relative roles and responsibilities of the concerned parties should be documented. Central management should not, however, result in delays in the investigation and management of the issue.

## Procedures for handling and investigating complaints including possible quality defects

8.5 There should be written procedures describing the actions to be taken upon receipt of a complaint. All complaints should be documented and assessed to establish if they represent a potential quality defect or other issue.

8.6 Special attention should be given to establishing whether a complaint or suspected quality defect relates to falsification.

8.7 As not all complaints received by a company may represent actual quality defects, complaints which do not indicate a potential quality defect should be documented appropriately and communicated to the relevant group or person responsible for the investigation and management of complaints of that nature, such as suspected adverse events.

8.8   There should be procedures in place to facilitate a request to investigate the quality of a batch of a medicinal product in order to support an investigation into a reported suspected adverse event.

8.9   When a quality defect investigation is initiated, procedures should be in place to address at least the following:

(i)     The description of the reported quality defect.

(ii)    The determination of the extent of the quality defect. The checking or testing of reference and/or retention samples should be considered as part of this, and in certain cases, a review of the batch production record, the batch certification record and the batch distribution records (especially for temperature-sensitive products) should be performed.

(iii)   The need to request a sample, or the return, of the defective product from the complainant and, where a sample is provided, the need for an appropriate evaluation to be carried out.

(iv)    The assessment of the risk(s) posed by the quality defect, based on the severity and extent of the quality defect.

(v)     The decision-making process that is to be used concerning the potential need for risk-reducing actions to be taken in the distribution network, such as batch or product recalls, or other actions.

(vi)    The assessment of the impact that any recall action may have on the availability of the medicinal product to patients/animals in any affected market, and the need to notify the relevant authorities of such impact.

(vii)   The internal and external communications that should be made in relation to a quality defect and its investigation.

(viii)  The identification of the potential root cause(s) of the quality defect.

(ix)    The need for appropriate Corrective and Preventative Actions (CAPAs) to be identified and implemented for the issue, and for the assessment of the effectiveness of those CAPAs.

## Investigation and Decision-making

8.10  The information reported in relation to possible quality defects should be recorded, including all the original details. The validity and extent of all reported quality defects should be documented and assessed in accordance with Quality Risk Management principles in order to support decisions regarding the degree of investigation and action taken.

**8.11**  If a quality defect is discovered or suspected in a batch, consideration should be given to checking other batches and in some cases other products, in order to determine whether they are also affected. In particular, other batches which may contain portions of the defective batch or defective components should be investigated.

**8.12**  Quality defect investigations should include a review of previous quality defect reports or any other relevant information for any indication of specific or recurring problems requiring attention and possibly further regulatory action.

**8.13**  The decisions that are made during and following quality defect investigations should reflect the level of risk that is presented by the quality defect as well as the seriousness of any non-compliance with respect to the requirements of the marketing authorisation/product specification file or GMP. Such decisions should be timely to ensure that patient and animal safety is maintained, in a way that is commensurate with the level of risk that is presented by those issues.

**8.14**  As comprehensive information on the nature and extent of the quality defect may not always be available at the early stages of an investigation, the decision-making processes should still ensure that appropriate risk-reducing actions are taken at an appropriate time-point during such investigations. All the decisions and measures taken as a result of a quality defect should be documented.

**8.15**  Quality defects should be reported in a timely manner by the manufacturer to the marketing authorisation holder/sponsor and all concerned Competent Authorities in cases where the quality defect may result in the recall of the product or in an abnormal restriction in the supply of the product.

## Root Cause Analysis and Corrective and Preventative Actions

**8.16**  An appropriate level of root cause analysis work should be applied during the investigation of quality defects. In cases where the true root cause(s) of the quality defect cannot be determined, consideration should be given to identifying the most likely root cause(s) and to addressing those.

**8.17**  Where human error is suspected or identified as the cause of a quality defect, this should be formally justified and care should be exercised so as to ensure that process, procedural or system-based errors or problems are not overlooked, if present.

**8.18**  Appropriate CAPAs should be identified and taken in response to a quality defect. The effectiveness of such actions should be monitored and assessed.

8.19 Quality defect records should be reviewed and trend analyses should be performed regularly for any indication of specific or recurring problems requiring attention.

## Product Recalls and other potential risk-reducing actions

8.20 There should be established written procedures, regularly reviewed and updated when necessary, in order to undertake any recall activity or implement any other risk-reducing actions.

8.21 After a product has been placed on the market, any retrieval of it from the distribution network as a result of a quality defect should be regarded and managed as a recall. (This provision does not apply to the retrieval (or return) of samples of the product from the distribution network to facilitate an investigation into a quality defect issue/report.)

8.22 Recall operations should be capable of being initiated promptly and at any time. In certain cases recall operations may need to be initiated to protect public or animal health prior to establishing the root cause(s) and full extent of the quality defect

8.23 The batch/product distribution records should be readily available to the persons responsible for recalls, and should contain sufficient information on wholesalers and directly supplied customers (with addresses, phone and/or fax numbers inside and outside working hours, batches and amounts delivered), including those for exported products and medical samples.

8.24 In the case of investigational medicinal products, all trial sites should be identified and the countries of destination should be indicated. In the case of an investigational medicinal product for which a marketing authorisation has been issued, the manufacturer of the investigational medicinal product should, in cooperation with the sponsor, inform the marketing authorisation holder of any quality defect that could be related to the authorised medicinal product. The sponsor should implement a procedure for the rapid unblinding of blinded products, where this is necessary for a prompt recall. The sponsor should ensure that the procedure discloses the identity of the blinded product only in so far as is necessary.

8.25 Consideration should be given following consultation with the concerned Competent Authorities, as to how far into the distribution network a recall action should extend, taking into account the potential risk to public or animal health and any impact that the proposed recall action may have. The Competent Authorities should also be informed in situations in which no recall action is being proposed for a defective batch because the batch has expired (such as with short shelf-life products.)

**8.26** All concerned Competent Authorities should be informed in advance in cases where products are intended to be recalled. For very serious issues (i.e. those with the potential to seriously impact upon patient or animal health), rapid risk-reducing actions (such as a product recall) may have to be taken in advance of notifying the Competent Authorities. Wherever possible, attempts should be made to agree these in advance of their execution with the concerned Competent Authorities

**8.27** It should also be considered whether the proposed recall action may affect different markets in different ways, and if this is the case, appropriate market-specific risk-reducing actions should be developed and discussed with the concerned competent authorities. Taking account of its therapeutic use the risk of shortage of a medicinal product which has no authorised alternative should be considered before deciding on a risk-reducing action such as a recall. Any decisions not to execute a risk-reducing action which would otherwise be required should be agreed with the competent authority in advance.

**8.28** Recalled products should be identified and stored separately in a secure area while awaiting a decision on their fate. A formal disposition of all recalled batches should be made and documented. The rationale for any decision to rework recalled products should be documented and discussed with the relevant competent authority. The extent of shelf-life remaining for any reworked batches that are being considered for placement onto the market should also be considered.

**8.29** The progress of the recall process should be recorded until closure and a final report issued, including a reconciliation between the delivered and recovered quantities of the concerned products/batches.

**8.30** The effectiveness of the arrangements in place for recalls should be periodically evaluated to confirm that they remain robust and fit for use. Such evaluations should extend to both within office-hour situations as well as out-of-office hour situations and, when performing such evaluations, consideration should be given as to whether mock-recall actions should be performed. This evaluation should be documented and justified.

**8.31** In addition to recalls, there are other potential risk-reducing actions that may be considered in order to manage the risks presented by quality defects. Such actions may include the issuance of cautionary communications to healthcare professionals in relation to their use of a batch that is potentially defective. These should be considered on a case-by-case basis and discussed with the concerned competent authorities.

## 9   SELF INSPECTION

## Principle

Self inspections should be conducted in order to monitor the implementation and compliance with Good Manufacturing Practice principles and to propose necessary corrective measures.

9.1   Personnel matters, premises, equipment, documentation, production, quality control, distribution of the medicinal products, arrangements for dealing with complaints and recalls, and self inspection, should be examined at intervals following a pre-arranged programme in order to verify their conformity with the principles of Quality Assurance.

9.2   Self inspections should be conducted in an independent and detailed way by designated competent person(s) from the company. Independent audits by external experts may also be useful.

9.3   All self inspections should be recorded. Reports should contain all the observations made during the inspections and, where applicable, proposals for corrective measures. Statements on the actions subsequently taken should also be recorded.

# ANNEX 1 MANUFACTURE OF STERILE MEDICINAL PRODUCTS

## Principle

The manufacture of sterile products is subject to special requirements in order to minimise risks of microbiological contamination, and of particulate and pyrogen contamination. Much depends on the skill, training and attitudes of the personnel involved. Quality Assurance is particularly important, and this type of manufacture must strictly follow carefully established and validated methods of preparation and procedure. Sole reliance for sterility or other quality aspects must not be placed on any terminal process or finished product test.

**Note:** *This guidance does not lay down detailed methods for determining the microbiological and particulate cleanliness of air, surfaces etc. Reference should be made to other documents such as the EN/ISO Standards.*

## General

1   The manufacture of sterile products should be carried out in clean areas entry to which should be through airlocks for personnel and/or for equipment and materials. Clean areas should be maintained to an appropriate cleanliness standard and supplied with air which has passed through filters of an appropriate efficiency.

2   The various operations of component preparation, product preparation and filling should be carried out in separate areas within the clean area. Manufacturing operations are divided into two categories; firstly those where the product is terminally sterilised, and secondly those which are conducted aseptically at some or all stages.

3   Clean areas for the manufacture of sterile products are classified according to the required characteristics of the environment. Each manufacturing operation requires an appropriate environmental cleanliness level in the operational state in order to minimise the risks of particulate or microbial contamination of the product or materials being handled.

   In order to meet "in operation" conditions these areas should be designed to reach certain specified air-cleanliness levels in the "at rest" occupancy state. The "at-rest" state is the condition where the installation is installed and operating, complete with production equipment but with no operating personnel present. The "in operation" state is the condition

EU GMP GUIDE PART I ANNEX 1 MANUFACTURE OF STERILE MEDICINAL PRODUCTS

where the installation is functioning in the defined operating mode with the specified number of personnel working.

The "in operation" and "at rest" states should be defined for each clean room or suite of clean rooms.

For the manufacture of sterile medicinal products 4 grades can be distinguished:

**Grade A:** The local zone for high risk operations, e.g. filling zone, stopper bowls, open ampoules and vials, making aseptic connections. Normally such conditions are provided by a laminar air flow work station. Laminar air flow systems should provide a homogeneous air speed in a range of 0.36–0.54 m/s (guidance value) at the working position in open clean room applications. The maintenance of laminarity should be demonstrated and validated.

A uni-directional air flow and lower velocities may be used in closed isolators and glove boxes.

**Grade B:** For aseptic preparation and filling, this is the background environment for the grade A zone.

**Grade C and D:** Clean areas for carrying out less critical stages in the manufacture of sterile products.

## Clean Room and Clean Air Device Classification

4 Clean rooms and clean air devices should be classified in accordance with EN ISO 14644-1. Classification should be clearly differentiated from operational process and environmental monitoring. The maximum permitted airborne particle concentration for each grade is given in the following table.

| | Maximum permitted number of particles per $m^3$ equal to or greater than the tabulated size. | | | |
| --- | --- | --- | --- | --- |
| | At rest | | In operation | |
| Grade | 0.5 µm | 5.0 µm | 0.5 µm | 5.0 µm |
| A | 3 520 | 20 | 3 520 | 20 |
| B | 3 520 | 29 | 352 000 | 2 900 |
| C | 352 000 | 2 900 | 3 520 000 | 29 000 |
| D | 3 520 000 | 29 000 | Not defined | Not defined |

5 For classification purposes in Grade A zones, a minimum sample volume of 1 $m^3$ should be taken per sample location. For Grade A the airborne

particle classification is ISO 4.8 dictated by the limit for particles $\geq$ 5.0 µm. For Grade B (at rest) the airborne particle classification is ISO 5 for both considered particle sizes. For Grade C (at rest and in operation) the airborne particle classification is ISO 7 and ISO 8 respectively. For Grade D (at rest) the airborne particle classification is ISO 8. For classification purposes EN/ISO 14644-1 methodology defines both the minimum number of sample locations and the sample size based on the class limit of the largest considered particle size and the method of evaluation of the data collected.

6    Portable particle counters with a short length of sample tubing should be used for classification purposes because of the relatively higher rate of precipitation of particles $\geq$ 5.0 µm in remote sampling systems with long lengths of tubing. Isokinetic sample heads shall be used in unidirectional airflow systems.

7    "In operation" classification may be demonstrated during normal operations, simulated operations or during media fills as worst-case simulation is required for this. EN ISO 14644-2 provides information on testing to demonstrate continued compliance with the assigned cleanliness classifications.

## Clean Room and Clean Air Device Monitoring

8    Clean rooms and clean air devices should be routinely monitored in operation and the monitoring locations based on a formal risk analysis study and the results obtained during the classification of rooms and/or clean air devices.

9    For Grade A zones, particle monitoring should be undertaken for the full duration of critical processing, including equipment assembly, except where justified by contaminants in the process that would damage the particle counter or present a hazard, e.g. live organisms and radiological hazards. In such cases monitoring during routine equipment set up operations should be undertaken prior to exposure to the risk. Monitoring during simulated operations should also be performed. The Grade A zone should be monitored at such a frequency and with suitable sample size that all interventions, transient events and any system deterioration would be captured and alarms triggered if alert limits are exceeded. It is accepted that it may not always be possible to demonstrate low levels of $\geq$ 5.0 µm particles at the point of fill when filling is in progress, due to the generation of particles or droplets from the product itself.

**10** It is recommended that a similar system be used for Grade B zones although the sample frequency may be decreased. The importance of the particle monitoring system should be determined by the effectiveness of the segregation between the adjacent Grade A and B zones. The Grade B zone should be monitored at such a frequency and with suitable sample size that changes in levels of contamination and any system deterioration would be captured and alarms triggered if alert limits are exceeded.

**11** Airborne particle monitoring systems may consist of independent particle counters; a network of sequentially accessed sampling points connected by manifold to a single particle counter; or a combination of the two. The system selected must be appropriate for the particle size considered. Where remote sampling systems are used, the length of tubing and the radii of any bends in the tubing must be considered in the context of particle losses in the tubing. The selection of the monitoring system should take account of any risk presented by the materials used in the manufacturing operation, for example those involving live organisms or radiopharmaceuticals.

**12** The sample sizes taken for monitoring purposes using automated systems will usually be a function of the sampling rate of the system used. It is not necessary for the sample volume to be the same as that used for formal classification of clean rooms and clean air devices.

**13** In Grade A and B zones, the monitoring of the $\geq$ 5.0 μm particle concentration count takes on a particular significance as it is an important diagnostic tool for early detection of failure. The occasional indication of $\geq$ 5.0 μm particle counts may be false counts due to electronic noise, stray light, coincidence, etc. However consecutive or regular counting of low levels is an indicator of a possible contamination event and should be investigated. Such events may indicate early failure of the HVAC system, filling equipment failure or may also be diagnostic of poor practices during machine set-up and routine operation.

**14** The particle limits given in the table for the "at rest" state should be achieved after a short "clean up" period of 15–20 minutes (guidance value) in an unmanned state after completion of operations.

**15** The monitoring of Grade C and D areas in operation should be performed in accordance with the principles of quality risk management. The requirements and alert/action limits will depend on the nature of the operations carried out, but the recommended "clean up period" should be attained.

16   Other characteristics such as temperature and relative humidity depend on the product and nature of the operations carried out. These parameters should not interfere with the defined cleanliness standard.

17   Examples of operations to be carried out in the various grades are given in the table below. (see also paragraphs 28 and 35):

| Grade | Examples of operations for terminally sterilised products. (see paragraphs 28–30) |
| --- | --- |
| A | Filling of products, when unusually at risk. |
| C | Preparation of solutions, when unusually at risk. Filling of products. |
| D | Preparation of solutions and components for subsequent filling. |
| Grade | Examples of operations for aseptic preparations. (see paragraphs 31–35) |
| A | Aseptic preparation and filling. |
| C | Preparation of solutions to be filtered. |
| D | Handling of components after washing. |

18   Where aseptic operations are performed monitoring should be frequent using methods such as settle plates, volumetric air and surface sampling (e.g. swabs and contact plates). Sampling methods used in operation should not interfere with zone protection. Results from monitoring should be considered when reviewing batch documentation for finished product release. Surfaces and personnel should be monitored after critical operations. Additional microbiological monitoring is also required outside production operations, e.g. after validation of systems, cleaning and sanitisation.

19   Recommended limits for microbiological monitoring of clean areas during operation:

| Grade | Recommended limits for microbial contamination (a) | | | |
| --- | --- | --- | --- | --- |
| | air sample cfu/m$^3$ | settle plates (diameter 90 mm), cfu/4 hours (b) | contact plates (diameter 55 mm), cfu/plate | glove print 5 fingers cfu/glove |
| A | < 1 | < 1 | < 1 | < 1 |
| B | 10 | 5 | 5 | 5 |
| C | 100 | 50 | 25 | – |
| D | 200 | 100 | 50 | – |

Notes:
(a) These are average values.
(b) Individual settle plates may be exposed for less than 4 hours.

20   Appropriate alert and action limits should be set for the results of particulate and microbiological monitoring. If these limits are exceeded operating procedures should prescribe corrective action.

## Isolator Technology

21   The utilisation of isolator technology to minimise human interventions in processing areas may result in a significant decrease in the risk of microbiological contamination of aseptically manufactured products from the environment. There are many possible designs of isolators and transfer devices. The isolator and the background environment should be designed so that the required air quality for the respective zones can be realised. Isolators are constructed of various materials more or less prone to puncture and leakage. Transfer devices may vary from a single door to double door designs to fully sealed systems incorporating sterilisation mechanisms.

22   The transfer of materials into and out of the unit is one of the greatest potential sources of contamination. In general the area inside the isolator is the local zone for high risk manipulations, although it is recognised that laminar air flow may not exist in the working zone of all such devices.

23   The air classification required for the background environment depends on the design of the isolator and its application. It should be controlled and for aseptic processing it should be at least grade D.

24   Isolators should be introduced only after appropriate validation. Validation should take into account all critical factors of isolator technology, for example the quality of the air inside and outside (background) the isolator, sanitisation of the isolator, the transfer process and isolator integrity.

25   Monitoring should be carried out routinely and should include frequent leak testing of the isolator and glove/sleeve system.

## Blow/Fill/Seal Technology

26   Blow/fill/seal units are purpose built machines in which, in one continuous operation, containers are formed from a thermoplastic granulate, filled and then sealed, all by the one automatic machine. Blow/fill/seal equipment used for aseptic production which is fitted with an effective grade A air shower may be installed in at least a grade C environment, provided that grade A/B clothing is used. The environment should comply with the viable and non viable limits at rest and the viable limit only when in operation.

Blow/fill/seal equipment used for the production of products which are terminally sterilised should be installed in at least a grade D environment.

27    Because of this special technology particular attention should be paid to, at least the following:

- equipment design and qualification
- validation and reproducibility of cleaning-in-place and sterilisation-in-place
- background cleanroom environment in which the equipment is located
- operator training and clothing
- interventions in the critical zone of the equipment including any aseptic assembly prior to the commencement of filling.

## Terminally Sterilised Products

28    Preparation of components and most products should be done in at least a grade D environment in order to give low risk of microbial and particulate contamination, suitable for filtration and sterilisation. Where the product is at a high or unusual risk of microbial contamination, (for example, because the product actively supports microbial growth or must be held for a long period before sterilisation or is necessarily processed not mainly in closed vessels), then preparation should be carried out in a grade C environment.

29    Filling of products for terminal sterilisation should be carried out in at least a grade C environment.

30    Where the product is at unusual risk of contamination from the environment, for example because the filling operation is slow or the containers are wide-necked or are necessarily exposed for more than a few seconds before sealing, the filling should be done in a grade A zone with at least a grade C background. Preparation and filling of ointments, creams, suspensions and emulsions should generally be carried out in a grade C environment before terminal sterilisation.

## Aseptic Preparation

31    Components after washing should be handled in at least a grade D environment. Handling of sterile starting materials and components, unless subjected to sterilisation or filtration through a micro-organism-retaining filter later in the process, should be done in a grade A environment with grade B background.

32    Preparation of solutions which are to be sterile filtered during the process should be done in a grade C environment; if not filtered, the preparation of materials and products should be done in a grade A environment with a grade B background.

33    Handling and filling of aseptically prepared products should be done in a grade A environment with a grade B background.

34    Prior to the completion of stoppering, transfer of partially closed containers, as used in freeze drying should be done either in a grade A environment with grade B background or in sealed transfer trays in a grade B environment.

35    Preparation and filling of sterile ointments, creams, suspensions and emulsions should be done in a grade A environment, with a grade B background, when the product is exposed and is not subsequently filtered.

## Personnel

36    Only the minimum number of personnel required should be present in clean areas; this is particularly important during aseptic processing. Inspections and controls should be conducted outside the clean areas as far as possible.

37    All personnel (including those concerned with cleaning and maintenance) employed in such areas should receive regular training in disciplines relevant to the correct manufacture of sterile products. This training should include reference to hygiene and to the basic elements of microbiology. When outside staff who have not received such training (e.g. building or maintenance contractors) need to be brought in, particular care should be taken over their instruction and supervision.

38    Staff who have been engaged in the processing of animal tissue materials or of cultures of micro-organisms other than those used in the current manufacturing process should not enter sterile-product areas unless rigorous and clearly defined entry procedures have been followed.

39    High standards of personal hygiene and cleanliness are essential. Personnel involved in the manufacture of sterile preparations should be instructed to report any condition which may cause the shedding of abnormal numbers or types of contaminants; periodic health checks for such conditions are desirable. Actions to be taken about personnel who could be introducing undue microbiological hazard should be decided by a designated competent person.

40    Wristwatches, make-up and jewellery should not be worn in clean areas.

41    Changing and washing should follow a written procedure designed to minimise contamination of clean area clothing or carry-through of contaminants to the clean areas.

42    The clothing and its quality should be appropriate for the process and the grade of the working area. It should be worn in such a way as to protect the product from contamination.

43    The description of clothing required for each grade is given below:

- **Grade D.**  Hair and, where relevant, beard should be covered. A general protective suit and appropriate shoes or overshoes should be worn. Appropriate measures should be taken to avoid any contamination coming from outside the clean area.
- **Grade C.**  Hair and where relevant beard and moustache should be covered. A single or two-piece trouser suit, gathered at the wrists and with high neck and appropriate shoes or overshoes should be worn. They should shed virtually no fibres or particulate matter.
- **Grade A/B.**  Headgear should totally enclose hair and, where relevant, beard and moustache; it should be tucked into the neck of the suit; a face mask should be worn to prevent the shedding of droplets. Appropriate sterilised, non-powdered rubber or plastic gloves and sterilised or disinfected footwear should be worn. Trouser-legs should be tucked inside the footwear and garment sleeves into the gloves. The protective clothing should shed virtually no fibres or particulate matter and retain particles shed by the body.

44    Outdoor clothing should not be brought into changing rooms leading to grade B and C rooms. For every worker in a grade A/B area, clean sterile (sterilised or adequately sanitised) protective garments should be provided at each work session. Gloves should be regularly disinfected during operations. Masks and gloves should be changed at least for every working session.

45    Clean area clothing should be cleaned and handled in such a way that it does not gather additional contaminants which can later be shed. These operations should follow written procedures. Separate laundry facilities for such clothing are desirable. Inappropriate treatment of clothing will damage fibres and may increase the risk of shedding of particles.

## Premises

**46** In clean areas, all exposed surfaces should be smooth, impervious and unbroken in order to minimise the shedding or accumulation of particles or micro-organisms and to permit the repeated application of cleaning agents, and disinfectants where used.

**47** To reduce accumulation of dust and to facilitate cleaning there should be no uncleanable recesses and a minimum of projecting ledges, shelves, cupboards and equipment. Doors should be designed to avoid those uncleanable recesses; sliding doors may be undesirable for this reason.

**48** False ceilings should be sealed to prevent contamination from the space above them.

**49** Pipes and ducts and other utilities should be installed so that they do not create recesses, unsealed openings and surfaces which are difficult to clean.

**50** Sinks and drains should be prohibited in grade A/B areas used for aseptic manufacture. In other areas air breaks should be fitted between the machine or sink and the drains. Floor drains in lower grade clean rooms should be fitted with traps or water seals to prevent back-flow.

**51** Changing rooms should be designed as airlocks and used to provide physical separation of the different stages of changing and so minimise microbial and particulate contamination of protective clothing. They should be flushed effectively with filtered air. The final stage of the changing room should, in the at-rest state, be the same grade as the area into which it leads. The use of separate changing rooms for entering and leaving clean areas is sometimes desirable. In general hand washing facilities should be provided only in the first stage of the changing rooms.

**52** Both airlock doors should not be opened simultaneously. An interlocking system or a visual and/or audible warning system should be operated to prevent the opening of more than one door at a time.

**53** A filtered air supply should maintain a positive pressure and an air flow relative to surrounding areas of a lower grade under all operational conditions and should flush the area effectively. Adjacent rooms of different grades should have a pressure differential of 10–15 pascals (guidance values). Particular attention should be paid to the protection of the zone of greatest risk, that is, the immediate environment to which a product and cleaned components which contact the product are exposed. The various recommendations regarding air supplies and pressure differentials may need to be modified where it becomes necessary to contain some materials, e.g. pathogenic, highly toxic, radioactive or live viral or bacterial materials or products. Decontamination of facilities and treatment of air leaving a clean area may be necessary for some operations.

54   It should be demonstrated that air-flow patterns do not present a contamination risk, e.g. care should be taken to ensure that air flows do not distribute particles from a particle-generating person, operation or machine to a zone of higher product risk.

55   A warning system should be provided to indicate failure in the air supply. Indicators of pressure differences should be fitted between areas where these differences are important. These pressure differences should be recorded regularly or otherwise documented.

## Equipment

56   A conveyor belt should not pass through a partition between a grade A or B area and a processing area of lower air cleanliness, unless the belt itself is continually sterilised (e.g. in a sterilising tunnel).

57   As far as practicable equipment, fittings and services should be designed and installed so that operations, maintenance and repairs can be carried out outside the clean area. If sterilisation is required, it should be carried out, wherever possible, after complete reassembly.

58   When equipment maintenance has been carried out within the clean area, the area should be cleaned, disinfected and/or sterilised where appropriate, before processing recommences if the required standards of cleanliness and/or asepsis have not been maintained during the work.

59   Water treatment plants and distribution systems should be designed, constructed and maintained so as to ensure a reliable source of water of an appropriate quality. They should not be operated beyond their designed capacity. Water for injections should be produced, stored and distributed in a manner which prevents microbial growth, for example by constant circulation at a temperature above 70°C.

60   All equipment such as sterilisers, air handling and filtration systems, air vent and gas filters, water treatment, generation, storage and distribution systems should be subject to validation and planned maintenance; their return to use should be approved.

## Sanitation

61   The sanitation of clean areas is particularly important. They should be cleaned thoroughly in accordance with a written programme. Where disinfectants are used, more than one type should be employed.

Monitoring should be undertaken regularly in order to detect the development of resistant strains.

62 Disinfectants and detergents should be monitored for microbial contamination; dilutions should be kept in previously cleaned containers and should only be stored for defined periods unless sterilised. Disinfectants and detergents used in Grades A and B areas should be sterile prior to use.

63 Fumigation of clean areas may be useful for reducing microbiological contamination in inaccessible places.

## Processing

64 Precautions to minimise contamination should be taken during all processing stages including the stages before sterilisation.

65 Preparations of microbiological origin should not be made or filled in areas used for the processing of other medicinal products; however, vaccines of dead organisms or of bacterial extracts may be filled, after inactivation, in the same premises as other sterile medicinal products.

66 Validation of aseptic processing should include a process simulation test using a nutrient medium (media fill). Selection of the nutrient medium should be made based on dosage form of the product and selectivity, clarity, concentration and suitability for sterilisation of the nutrient medium.

67 The process simulation test should imitate as closely as possible the routine aseptic manufacturing process and include all the critical subsequent manufacturing steps. It should also take into account various interventions known to occur during normal production as well as worst-case situations.

68 Process simulation tests should be performed as initial validation with three consecutive satisfactory simulation tests per shift and repeated at defined intervals and after any significant modification to the HVAC-system, equipment, process and number of shifts. Normally process simulation tests should be repeated twice a year per shift and process.

69 The number of containers used for media fills should be sufficient to enable a valid evaluation. For small batches, the number of containers for media fills should at least equal the size of the product batch. The target should be zero growth and the following should apply:

- When filling fewer than 5000 units, no contaminated units should be detected.
- When filling 5,000 to 10,000 units:

   (a) One (1) contaminated unit should result in an investigation, including consideration of a repeat media fill;

   (b) Two (2) contaminated units are considered cause for revalidation, following investigation.

- When filling more than 10,000 units:

   (a) One (1) contaminated unit should result in an investigation;

   (b) Two (2) contaminated units are considered cause for revalidation, following investigation.

70   For any run size, intermittent incidents of microbial contamination may be indicative of low-level contamination that should be investigated. Investigation of gross failures should include the potential impact on the sterility assurance of batches manufactured since the last successful media fill.

71   Care should be taken that any validation does not compromise the processes.

72   Water sources, water treatment equipment and treated water should be monitored regularly for chemical and biological contamination and, as appropriate, for endotoxins. Records should be maintained of the results of the monitoring and of any action taken.

73   Activities in clean areas and especially when aseptic operations are in progress should be kept to a minimum and movement of personnel should be controlled and methodical, to avoid excessive shedding of particles and organisms due to over-vigorous activity. The ambient temperature and humidity should not be uncomfortably high because of the nature of the garments worn.

74   Microbiological contamination of starting materials should be minimal. Specifications should include requirements for microbiological quality when the need for this has been indicated by monitoring.

75   Containers and materials liable to generate fibres should be minimised in clean areas.

76   Where appropriate, measures should be taken to minimise the particulate contamination of the end product.

77   Components, containers and equipment should be handled after the final cleaning process in such a way that they are not recontaminated.

78   The interval between the washing and drying and the sterilisation of components, containers and equipment as well as between their sterilisation and use should be minimised and subject to a time-limit appropriate to the storage conditions.

**79** The time between the start of the preparation of a solution and its sterilisation or filtration through a micro-organism-retaining filter should be minimised. There should be a set maximum permissible time for each product that takes into account its composition and the prescribed method of storage.

**80** The bioburden should be monitored before sterilisation. There should be working limits on contamination immediately before sterilisation, which are related to the efficiency of the method to be used. Bioburden assay should be performed on each batch for both aseptically filled product and terminally sterilised products. Where overkill sterilisation parameters are set for terminally sterilised products, bioburden might be monitored only at suitable scheduled intervals. For parametric release systems, bioburden assay should be performed on each batch and considered as an in-process test. Where appropriate the level of endotoxins should be monitored. All solutions, in particular large volume infusion fluids, should be passed through a micro-organism-retaining filter, if possible sited immediately before filling.

**81** Components, containers, equipment and any other article required in a clean area where aseptic work takes place should be sterilised and passed into the area through double-ended sterilisers sealed into the wall, or by a procedure which achieves the same objective of not introducing contamination. Non-combustible gases should be passed through micro-organism retentive filters.

**82** The efficacy of any new procedure should be validated, and the validation verified at scheduled intervals based on performance history or when any significant change is made in the process or equipment.

## Sterilisation

**83** All sterilisation processes should be validated. Particular attention should be given when the adopted sterilisation method is not described in the current edition of the European Pharmacopoeia, or when it is used for a product which is not a simple aqueous or oily solution. Where possible, heat sterilisation is the method of choice. In any case, the sterilisation process must be in accordance with the marketing and manufacturing authorisations.

**84** Before any sterilisation process is adopted its suitability for the product and its efficacy in achieving the desired sterilising conditions in all parts of each type of load to be processed should be demonstrated by physical measurements and by biological indicators where appropriate. The validity of the process should be verified at scheduled intervals, at least annually, and whenever significant modifications have been made to the equipment. Records should be kept of the results.

85    For effective sterilisation the whole of the material must be subjected to the required treatment and the process should be designed to ensure that this is achieved.

86    Validated loading patterns should be established for all sterilisation processes.

87    Biological indicators should be considered as an additional method for monitoring the sterilisation. They should be stored and used according to the manufacturer's instructions, and their quality checked by positive controls. If biological indicators are used, strict precautions should be taken to avoid transferring microbial contamination from them.

88    There should be a clear means of differentiating products which have not been sterilised from those which have. Each basket, tray or other carrier of products or components should be clearly labelled with the material name, its batch number and an indication of whether or not it has been sterilised. Indicators such as autoclave tape may be used, where appropriate, to indicate whether or not a batch (or sub-batch) has passed through a sterilisation process, but they do not give a reliable indication that the lot is, in fact, sterile.

89    Sterilisation records should be available for each sterilisation run. They should be approved as part of the batch release procedure.

## Sterilisation by Heat

90    Each heat sterilisation cycle should be recorded on a time/temperature chart with a sufficiently large scale or by other appropriate equipment with suitable accuracy and precision. The position of the temperature probes used for controlling and/or recording should have been determined during the validation, and where applicable also checked against a second independent temperature probe located at the same position.

91    Chemical or biological indicators may also be used, but should not take the place of physical measurements.

92    Sufficient time must be allowed for the whole of the load to reach the required temperature before measurement of the sterilising time-period is commenced. This time must be determined for each type of load to be processed.

93    After the high temperature phase of a heat sterilisation cycle, precautions should be taken against contamination of a sterilised load during cooling.

Any cooling fluid or gas in contact with the product should be sterilised unless it can be shown that any leaking container would not be approved for use.

## Moist Heat

94 Both temperature and pressure should be used to monitor the process. Control instrumentation should normally be independent of monitoring instrumentation and recording charts. Where automated control and monitoring systems are used for these applications they should be validated to ensure that critical process requirements are met. System and cycle faults should be registered by the system and observed by the operator. The reading of the independent temperature indicator should be routinely checked against the chart recorder during the sterilisation period. For sterilisers fitted with a drain at the bottom of the chamber, it may also be necessary to record the temperature at this position, throughout the sterilisation period. There should be frequent leak tests on the chamber when a vacuum phase is part of the cycle.

95 The items to be sterilised, other than products in sealed containers, should be wrapped in a material which allows removal of air and penetration of steam but which prevents recontamination after sterilisation. All parts of the load should be in contact with the sterilizing agent at the required temperature for the required time.

96 Care should be taken to ensure that steam used for sterilisation is of suitable quality and does not contain additives at a level which could cause contamination of product or equipment.

## Dry Heat

97 The process used should include air circulation within the chamber and the maintenance of a positive pressure to prevent the entry of non-sterile air. Any air admitted should be passed through a HEPA filter. Where this process is also intended to remove pyrogens, challenge tests using endotoxins should be used as part of the validation.

## Sterilisation by Radiation

98 Radiation sterilisation is used mainly for the sterilisation of heat sensitive materials and products. Many medicinal products and some packaging materials are radiation-sensitive, so this method is permissible only when the absence of deleterious effects on the product has been confirmed

experimentally. Ultraviolet irradiation is not normally an acceptable method of sterilisation.

99    During the sterilisation procedure the radiation dose should be measured. For this purpose, dosimetry indicators which are independent of dose rate should be used, giving a quantitative measurement of the dose received by the product itself. Dosimeters should be inserted in the load in sufficient number and close enough together to ensure that there is always a dosimeter in the irradiator. Where plastic dosimeters are used they should be used within the time-limit of their calibration. Dosimeter absorbances should be read within a short period after exposure to radiation.

100    Biological indicators may be used as an additional control.

101    Validation procedures should ensure that the effects of variations in density of the packages are considered.

102    Materials handling procedures should prevent mix-up between irradiated and non-irradiated materials. Radiation sensitive colour disks should also be used on each package to differentiate between packages which have been subjected to irradiation and those which have not.

103    The total radiation dose should be administered within a predetermined time span.

## Sterilisation with Ethylene Oxide

104    This method should only be used when no other method is practicable. During process validation it should be shown that there is no damaging effect on the product and that the conditions and time allowed for degassing are such as to reduce any residual gas and reaction products to defined acceptable limits for the type of product or material.

105    Direct contact between gas and microbial cells is essential; precautions should be taken to avoid the presence of organisms likely to be enclosed in material such as crystals or dried protein. The nature and quantity of packaging materials can significantly affect the process.

106    Before exposure to the gas, materials should be brought into equilibrium with the humidity and temperature required by the process. The time required for this should be balanced against the opposing need to minimise the time before sterilisation.

107    Each sterilisation cycle should be monitored with suitable biological indicators, using the appropriate number of test pieces distributed throughout the load. The information so obtained should form part of the batch record.

108   For each sterilisation cycle, records should be made of the time taken to complete the cycle, of the pressure, temperature and humidity within the chamber during the process and of the gas concentration and of the total amount of gas used. The pressure and temperature should be recorded throughout the cycle on a chart. The record(s) should form part of the batch record.

109   After sterilisation, the load should be stored in a controlled manner under ventilated conditions to allow residual gas and reaction products to reduce to the defined level. This process should be validated.

## Filtration of Medicinal Products which cannot be Sterilised in their Final Container

110   Filtration alone is not considered sufficient when sterilisation in the final container is possible. With regard to methods currently available, steam sterilisation is to be preferred. If the product cannot be sterilised in the final container, solutions or liquids can be filtered through a sterile filter of nominal pore size of 0.22 micron (or less), or with at least equivalent micro-organism retaining properties, into a previously sterilised container. Such filters can remove most bacteria and moulds, but not all viruses or mycoplasmas. Consideration should be given to complementing the filtration process with some degree of heat treatment.

111   Due to the potential additional risks of the filtration method as compared with other sterilisation processes, a second filtration via a further sterilised micro-organism retaining filter, immediately prior to filling, may be advisable. The final sterile filtration should be carried out as close as possible to the filling point.

112   Fibre-shedding characteristics of filters should be minimal.

113   The integrity of the sterilised filter should be verified before use and should be confirmed immediately after use by an appropriate method such as a bubble point, diffusive flow or pressure hold test. The time taken to filter a known volume of bulk solution and the pressure difference to be used across the filter should be determined during validation and any significant differences from this during routine manufacturing should be noted and investigated. Results of these checks should be included in the batch record. The integrity of critical gas and air vent filters should be confirmed after use. The integrity of other filters should be confirmed at appropriate intervals.

114   The same filter should not be used for more than one working day unless such use has been validated.

115    The filter should not affect the product by removal of ingredients from it or by release of substances into it.

## Finishing of Sterile Products

116    Partially stoppered freeze drying vials should be maintained under Grade A conditions at all times until the stopper is fully inserted.

117    Containers should be closed by appropriately validated methods. Containers closed by fusion, e.g. glass or plastic ampoules should be subject to 100% integrity testing. Samples of other containers should be checked for integrity according to appropriate procedures.

118    The container closure system for aseptically filled vials is not fully integral until the aluminium cap has been crimped into place on the stoppered vial. Crimping of the cap should therefore be performed as soon as possible after stopper insertion.

119    As the equipment used to crimp vial caps can generate large quantities of non-viable particulates, the equipment should be located at a separate station equipped with adequate air extraction.

120    Vial capping can be undertaken as an aseptic process using sterilised caps or as a clean process outside the aseptic core. Where this latter approach is adopted, vials should be protected by Grade A conditions up to the point of leaving the aseptic processing area, and thereafter stoppered vials should be protected with a Grade A air supply until the cap has been crimped.

121    Vials with missing or displaced stoppers should be rejected prior to capping. Where human intervention is required at the capping station, appropriate technology should be used to prevent direct contact with the vials and to minimise microbial contamination.

122    Restricted access barriers and isolators may be beneficial in assuring the required conditions and minimising direct human interventions into the capping operation.

123    Containers sealed under vacuum should be tested for maintenance of that vacuum after an appropriate, pre-determined period.

124    Filled containers of parenteral products should be inspected individually for extraneous contamination or other defects. When inspection is done visually, it should be done under suitable and controlled conditions of illumination and background. Operators doing the inspection should pass regular eye-sight checks, with spectacles if worn, and be allowed frequent

breaks from inspection. Where other methods of inspection are used, the process should be validated and the performance of the equipment checked at intervals. Results should be recorded.

## Quality Control

125   The sterility test applied to the finished product should only be regarded as the last in a series of control measures by which sterility is assured. The test should be validated for the product(s) concerned.

126   In those cases where parametric release has been authorised, special attention should be paid to the validation and the monitoring of the entire manufacturing process.

127   Samples taken for sterility testing should be representative of the whole of the batch, but should in particular include samples taken from parts of the batch considered to be most at risk of contamination, e.g.:

(a) for products which have been filled aseptically, samples should include containers filled at the beginning and end of the batch and after any significant intervention,

(b) or products which have been heat sterilised in their final containers, consideration should be given to taking samples from the potentially coolest part of the load.

# ANNEX 2 MANUFACTURE OF BIOLOGICAL ACTIVE SUBSTANCES AND MEDICINAL PRODUCTS FOR HUMAN USE

## Scope

The methods employed in the manufacture of biological active substances and biological medicinal products for human use ('biological active substances and medicinal products') are a critical factor in shaping the appropriate regulatory control. Biological active substances and medicinal products can be defined therefore largely by reference to their method of manufacture. This annex provides guidance on the full range of active substances and medicinal products defined as biological.

This annex is divided into two main parts:

(a) Part A contains supplementary guidance on the manufacture of biological active substances and medicinal products, from control over seed lots and cell banks through to finishing activities, and testing.
(b) Part B contains further guidance on selected types of biological active substances and medicinal products.

This annex, along with several other annexes of the Guide to GMP in EudraLex Volume 4, provides guidance which supplements that in Part I and in Part II of that Guide. There are two aspects to the scope of this annex:

(a) Stage of manufacture - for biological active substances to the point immediately prior to their being rendered sterile, the primary guidance source is Part II. Guidance for the subsequent manufacturing steps of biological products are covered in Part I.
(b) Type of product - this annex provides guidance on the full range of medicinal products defined as biological.

These two aspects are shown in Table 1, it should be noted that this table is illustrative only and is not meant to describe the precise scope. It should also be understood that in line with the corresponding table in Part II of EudraLex, Volume 4, the level of GMP increases in detail from early to later steps in the manufacture of biological active substances but GMP principles should always be adhered to. The inclusion of some early steps of manufacture within the scope of this Annex does not imply that those steps will be routinely subject to inspection by the authorities.

Antibiotics are not defined as biological medicinal products, however where biological stages of manufacture occur, guidance in this Annex may be used. Guidance for medicinal products derived from fractionated human blood or plasma is covered in Annex 14 of EudraLex, Volume 4, and for non-transgenic plant products in Annex 7.

In certain cases, other legislation is applicable to the starting materials:

(a) Tissue and cells used for industrially manufactured products (such as medicinal products): Directive 2004/23/EC of the European Parliament and of the Council of 31 March 2004 on setting standards of quality and safety for the donation, procurement, testing, processing, preservation, storage and distribution of human tissues and cells,[3] and Commission Directive 2006/17/EC of 8 February 2006 implementing Directive 2004/23/EC of the European Parliament and of the Council as regards certain technical requirements for the donation, procurement and testing of human tissues and cells[4] cover only their donation, procurement and testing. Such tissues and cells become the biological active substances for several biological medicinal product types (e.g when 'engineered'[5]) at which point GMP and other medicinal product legislation requirements apply.

(b) Where blood or blood components are used as starting materials for advanced therapy medicinal products (ATMPs), Directive 2002/98/EC of the European Parliament and of the Council of 27 January 2003 setting standards of quality and safety for the collection, testing, processing, storage and distribution of human blood and blood components and amending Directive 2001/83/EC[6] and its Commission Directives provides the technical requirements[7] for the selection of donors and the collection and testing of blood and blood components.

(c) The manufacture and control of genetically modified organisms needs to comply with local and national requirements. In accordance with Directive 2009/41/EC of the European Parliament and of the Council of 6 May 2009 on the contained use of genetically modified micro-organisms,[8] appropriate containment and other protective measures shall be established and maintained in facilities where any genetically modified micro-organism are handled. Advice should be obtained according to national legislation in order to establish and maintain the appropriate Biological Safety Level. There should be no conflicts with GMP requirements.

---

[3] OJ L 102, 7.4.2004, p. 48.
[4] OJ L 38, 9.2.2006, p. 40.
[5] Details in Article 3.2 and 3.3 of Commission Directive 2009/120/EC
[6] OJ L 33, 8.2.2003, p. 30.
[7] "Good Practice" guidance under development.
[8] OJ L 125, 21.5.2009, p. 75.

## Principle

The manufacture of biological medicinal active substances and products involves certain specific considerations arising from the nature of the products and the processes. The ways in which biological medicinal products are manufactured, controlled and administered make some particular precautions necessary.

Unlike conventional medicinal products, which are manufactured using chemical and physical techniques capable of a high degree of consistency, the manufacture of biological active substances and medicinal products involves biological processes and materials, such as cultivation of cells or extraction from living organisms. These biological processes may display inherent variability, so that the range and nature of by-products may be variable. As a result, quality risk management (QRM) principles are particularly important for this class of materials and should be used to develop the control strategy across all stages of manufacture so as to minimise variability and to reduce the opportunity for contamination and cross-contamination.

Since materials and processing conditions used in cultivation processes are designed to provide conditions for the growth of specific cells and microorganisms, this provides extraneous microbial contaminants the opportunity to grow. In addition, many products are limited in their ability to withstand a wide range of purification techniques particularly those designed to inactivate or remove adventitious viral contaminants. The design of the processes, equipment, facilities, utilities, the conditions of preparation and addition of buffers and reagents, sampling and training of the operators are key considerations to minimise such contamination events.

Specifications related to products (such as those in Pharmacopoeial monographs, Marketing Authorisation (MA), and Clinical Trial Authorisation, (CTA)) will dictate whether and to what stage substances and materials can have a defined level of bioburden or need to be sterile. Similarly, manufacturing must be consistent with other specifications set out in the MA or CTA guidance (e.g. number of generations (doublings, passages) between the seed lot or cell bank).

For biological materials that cannot be sterilized (e.g. by filtration), processing must be conducted aseptically to minimise the introduction of contaminants. Where they exist, CHMP guidance documents should be consulted on the validation of specific manufacturing methods, e.g. virus removal or inactivation. The application of appropriate environmental controls and monitoring and, wherever feasible, in-situ cleaning and sterilization systems together with the use of closed systems can significantly reduce the risk of accidental contamination and cross-contamination.

**Table 1** Illustrative guide to manufacturing activities within the scope of Annex 2.

| Type and source of material | Example product | Application of this guide to manufacturing steps shown in grey | | | |
|---|---|---|---|---|---|
| 1. Animal or plant sources: non-transgenic | Heparins, insulin, enzymes, proteins, allergen extract, ATMPs immunosera | Collection of plant, organ, tissue or fluid[9] | Cutting, mixing, and / or initial processing | Isolation and purification | Formulation, filling |
| 2. Virus or bacteria / fermentation / cell culture | Viral or bacterial vaccines; enzymes, proteins | Establishment & maintenance of MCB[10], WCB, MVS, WVS | Cell culture and/or fermentation | Inactivation when applicable, isolation and purification | Formulation, filling |
| 3. Biotech-nology - fermentation/ cell culture | Recombinant. products, MAb, allergens, vaccines Gene Therapy (viral and non-viral vectors, plasmids) | Establishment & maintenance of MCB, and WCB, MSL, WSL | Cell culture and / or fermentation | Isolation, purification, modification | Formulation, filling |
| 4. Animal sources: transgenic | Recombinant proteins, ATMPs | Master and working transgenic bank | Collection, cutting, mixing, and / or initial processing | Isolation, purification and modification | Formulation, filling |
| 5. Plant sources: transgenic | Recombinant proteins, vaccines, allergen | Master and working transgenic bank | Growing, harvesting[11] | Initial extraction, isolation, purification, modification | Formulation, filling |
| 6. Human sources | Urine derived enzymes, hormones | Collection of fluid[12] | Mixing, and/or initial processing | Isolation and purification | Formulation, filling |
| 7. Human and / or animal sources | Gene therapy: genetically modified cells | Donation, procurement and testing of starting tissue / cells[14] | Manufacture vector[13] and cell purification and processing, | Ex-vivo genetic modification of cells, Establish MCB, WCB or cell stock | Formulation, filling |
| | Somatic cell therapy | Donation, procurement and testing of starting tissue / cells[14] | Establish MCB, WCB or cell stock | Cell isolation, culture purification, combination with noncellular components | Formulation, combination, fill |
| | Tissue engineered products | Donation, procurement and testing of starting tissue / cells[14] | Initial processing, isolation and purification, establish MCB, WCB, primary cell stock | Cell isolation, culture, purification, combination with noncellular components | Formulation, combination, fill |

**Increasing GMP requirements** →

See Glossary for explanation of acronyms.

[9] See section B1 for the extent to which GMP principles apply.

[10] See section on 'Seed lot and cell bank system' for the extent to which GMP applies.

[11] HMPC guideline on Good Agricultural and Collection Practice - EMEA/HMPC/246816/2005 may be applied to growing, harvesting and initial processing in open fields.

[12] Principles of GMP apply, see explanatory text in 'Scope'.

[13] Where these are viral vectors, the main controls are as for virus manufacture (row 2).

[14] Human tissues and cells must comply with Directive 2004/23/EC and implementing Directives at these stages.

Control usually involves biological analytical techniques, which typically have a greater variability than physico-chemical determinations. A robust manufacturing process is therefore crucial and in-process controls take on a particular importance in the manufacture of biological active substances and medicinal products.

Biological medicinal products which incorporate human tissues or cells, such as certain ATMPs must comply with the requirements of Directive 2004/23/EC and Commission Directive 2006/17/EC. In line with Commission Directive 2006/86/EC of 24 October 2006 implementing Directive 2004/23/EC of the European Parliament and of the Council as regards traceability requirements, notification of serious adverse reactions and events and certain technical requirements for the coding, processing, preservation, storage and distribution of human tissues and cells,[15] collection and testing must be done in accordance with an appropriate quality system for which standards and specifications are defined in its Annex[16]. Furthermore, the requirements of Commission Directive 2006/86/EC of 24 October 2006 implementing Directive 2004/23/EC of the European Parliament and of the Council as regards traceability requirements, notification of serious adverse reactions and events and certain technical requirements for the coding, processing, preservation, storage and distribution of human tissues and cells,[17]on traceability apply from the donor (while maintaining donor confidentiality) through stages applicable at the Tissue Establishment and then continue under medicines legislation through to the institution where the product is used.

Biological active substances and medicinal products must comply with the latest version of the Note for Guidance on Minimising the Risk of Transmitting Animal Spongiform Encephalopathy (TSE) Agents via Human and Veterinary Medicinal Products.

## PART A. GENERAL GUIDANCE

## Personnel

1    Personnel (including those concerned with cleaning, maintenance or quality control) employed in areas where biological active substances and products are manufactured and tested should receive training, and periodic retraining, specific to the products manufactured to their work, including any specific security measures to protect product, personnel and the environment.

---

[15] OJ L 294, 25.10.2006, p. 32:
[16] "Good Practice" guidance under development.
[17] OJ L 294, 25.10.2006, p. 32.

2   The health status of personnel should be taken into consideration for product safety. Where necessary, personnel engaged in production, maintenance, testing and animal care (and inspections) should be vaccinated with appropriate specific vaccines and have regular health checks.

3   Any changes in the health status of personnel, which could adversely affect the quality of the product, should preclude work in the production area and appropriate records kept. Production of BCG vaccine and tuberculin products should be restricted to staff who are carefully monitored by regular checks of immunological status or chest X-ray. Health monitoring of staff should be commensurate with the risk, medical advice should be sought for personnel involved with hazardous organisms.

4   Where required to minimise the opportunity for cross-contamination, restrictions on the movement of all personnel (including quality control (QC), maintenance and cleaning staff) should be controlled on the basis of QRM principles. In general, personnel should not pass from areas where exposure to live micro-organisms, genetically modified organisms, toxins or animals to areas where other products, inactivated products or different organisms are handled. If such passage is unavoidable, the contamination control measures should be based on QRM principles.

## Premises and equipment

5   As part of the control strategy, the degree of environmental control of particulate and microbial contamination of the production premises should be adapted to the active substance, intermediate or finished product and the production step, bearing in mind the potential level of contamination of the starting materials and the risks to the product. The environmental monitoring programme should be supplemented by the inclusion of methods to detect the presence of specific microorganisms (i.e. host organism, yeast, moulds, anaerobes, etc) where indicated by the QRM process.

6   Manufacturing and storage facilities, processes and environmental classifications should be designed to prevent the extraneous contamination of products. Prevention of contamination is more appropriate than detection and removal, although contamination is likely to become evident during processes such as fermentation and cell culture. Where processes are not closed and there is therefore exposure of the product to the immediate room environment (e.g. during additions of supplements, media, buffers, gasses, manipulations during the manufacture of ATMPs) control measures should be put in place, including engineering and environmental controls on the basis of QRM principles. These QRM principles should

take into account the principles and guidance from the appropriate sections of Annex 1[18] to EudraLex, Volume 4, when selecting environmental classification cascades and associated controls.

7  Dedicated production areas should be used for the handling of live cells capable of persistence in the manufacturing environment. Dedicated production area should be used for the manufacture of pathogenic organisms (i.e. Biosafety level 3 or 4).

8  Manufacture in a multi-product facility may be acceptable where the following, or equivalent (as appropriate to the product types involved) considerations and measures are part of an effective control strategy to prevent cross-contamination:

(a) Knowledge of key characteristics of all cells, organisms and any adventitious agents (e.g. pathogenicity, detectability, persistence, susceptibility to inactivation) within the same facility.

(b) Where production is characterised by multiple small batches from different starting materials (e.g. cell-based products) factors such as the health status of donors and the risk of total loss of product from or for specific patients should be taken into account when considering the acceptance of concurrent working during development of the control strategy.

(c) Live organisms and spores are prevented from entering non-related areas or equipment by addressing all potential routes of cross-contamination and utilizing single use components and engineering measures such as closed systems.

(d) Control measures to remove the organisms and spores before the subsequent manufacture of other products, these control measures should also take the heating, ventilation and air conditioning (HVAC) system into account. Cleaning and decontamination for the organisms and spores should be validated.

(e) Environmental monitoring specific for the micro-organism being manufactured, where the micro-organisms are capable of persistence in the manufacturing environment and where methods are available, is conducted in adjacent areas during manufacture and after completion of cleaning and decontamination. Attention should also be given to risks arising with use of certain monitoring equipment (e.g. airborne particle monitoring) in areas handling live and/or spore forming organisms.

---

[18] Although the title of Annex 1 refers to the manufacture of sterile medicinal products it is not the intention to force the manufacture of sterile product at a stage when a low bioburden is appropriate and authorised. Its use is because it is the only EU GMP source of guidance on all of the classified manufacturing areas including the lower grades D and C.

(f) Products, equipment, ancillary equipment (e.g. for calibration and validation) and disposable items are only moved within and removed from such areas in a manner that prevents contamination of other areas, other products and different product stages (e.g. prevent contamination of inactivated or toxoided products with non-inactivated products).

(g) Campaign-based manufacturing.

9   For finishing (secondary) operations[19], the need for dedicated facilities will depend on consideration of the above together with additional considerations such as the specific needs of the biological medicinal product and on the characteristics of other products, including any non-biological products, in the same facility. Other control measures for finishing operations may include the need for specific addition sequences, mixing speeds, time and temperature controls, limits on exposure to light and containment and cleaning procedures in the event of spillages.

10  The measures and procedures necessary for containment (i.e. for environment and operator safety) should not conflict with those for product quality.

11  Air handling units should be designed, constructed and maintained to minimise the risk of cross-contamination between different manufacturing areas and may need to be specific for an area. Consideration, based on QRM principles, should be given to the use of single pass air systems.

12  Positive pressure areas should be used to process sterile products but negative pressure in specific areas at the point of exposure of pathogens is acceptable for containment reasons. Where negative pressure areas or safety cabinets are used for aseptic processing of materials with particular risks (e.g. pathogens) they should be surrounded by a positive pressure clean zone of appropriate grade. These pressure cascades should be clearly defined and continuously monitored with appropriate alarm settings.

13  Equipment used during handling of live organisms and cells, including those for sampling, should be designed to prevent any contamination during processing.

14  Primary containment[20] should be designed and periodically tested to ensure the prevention of escape of biological agents into the immediate working environment.

---

[19] Formulation, filling and packaging
[20] See main GMP Glossary on "Containment"

15   The use of "clean in place" and "steam in place" ("sterilisation in place") systems should be used where possible. Valves on fermentation vessels should be completely steam sterilisable.

16   Air vent filters should be hydrophobic and validated for their scheduled life span with integrity testing at appropriate intervals based on appropriate QRM principles.

17   Drainage systems must be designed so that effluents can be effectively neutralised or decontaminated to minimise the risk of cross-contamination. Local regulation must be complied with to minimise the risk of contamination of the external environment according to the risk associated with the biohazardous nature of waste materials.

18   Due to the variability of biological products or manufacturing processes, relevant/critical raw materials (such as culture media and buffers) have to be measured or weighed during the production process. In these cases, small stocks of these raw materials may be kept in the production area for a specified duration based on defined criteria such as for the duration of manufacture of the batch or of the campaign.

## Animals

19   A wide range of animal species are used in the manufacture of a number of biological medicinal products. These can be divided into 2 broad types of sources:

(a) Live groups, herds, flocks: examples include polio vaccine (monkeys), immunosera to snake venoms and tetanus (horses, sheep and goats), allergens (cats), rabies vaccine (rabbits, mice and hamsters), transgenic products (goats, cattle).

(b) Animal tissues and cells derived post-mortem and from establishments such as abattoirs: examples include xenogeneic cells from animal tissues and cells, feeder cells to support the growth of some ATMPs, abattoir sources for enzymes, anticoagulants and hormones (sheep and pigs).

In addition, animals may also be used in quality control either in generic assays, e.g. pyrogenicity, or specific potency assays, e.g. pertussis vaccine (mice), pyrogenicity (rabbits), BCG vaccine (guinea-pigs).

20   In addition to compliance with TSE regulations, other adventitious agents that are of concern (zoonotic diseases, diseases of source animals) should be monitored by an ongoing health programme and recorded. Specialist advice should be obtained in establishing such programmes.

Instances of ill-health occurring in the source/donor animals should be investigated with respect to their suitability and the suitability of in-contact animals for continued use (in manufacture, as sources of starting and raw materials, in quality control and safety testing), the decisions must be documented. A look-back procedure should be in place which informs the decision-making process on the continued suitability of the biological active substance or medicinal product in which the animal sourced starting or raw materials have been used or incorporated. This decision-making process may include the re-testing of retained samples from previous collections from the same donor animal (where applicable) to establish the last negative donation. The withdrawal period of therapeutic agents used to treat source/donor animals must be documented and used to determine the removal of those animals from the programme for defined periods.

21  Particular care should be taken to prevent and monitor infections in the source/donor animals. Measures should include the sourcing, facilities, husbandry, biosecurity procedures, testing regimes, control of bedding and feed materials. This is of special relevance to specified pathogen free animals where PhEur monograph requirements must be met. Housing and health monitoring should be defined for other categories of animals (e.g. healthy flocks or herds).

22  For products manufactured from transgenic animals, traceability should be maintained in the creation of such animals from the source animals.

23  Note should be taken of Council Directive 86/609/EEC on the approximation of laws, regulations and administrative provisions of the Member States regarding the protection of animals used for experimental and other scientific purposes as regards requirements for animal quarters, care and quarantine. Housing for animals used in production and control of biological active substances and medicinal products should be separated from production and control areas.

24  For different animal species, key criteria should be defined, monitored, and recorded. These may include age, weight and health status of the animals.

25  Animals, biological agents, and tests carried out should be the subject of an identification system to prevent any risk of confusion and to control all identified hazards.

## Documentation

26    Starting and raw materials may need additional documentation on the source, origin, distribution chain, method of manufacture, and controls applied, to assure an appropriate level of control including their microbiological quality.

27    Some product types may require specific definition of what materials constitutes a batch, particularly somatic cells in the context of ATMPs. For autologous and donor-matched situations, the manufactured product should be viewed as a batch.

28    Where human cell or tissue donors are used, full traceability is required from starting and raw materials, including all substances coming into contact with the cells or tissues through to confirmation of the receipt of the products at the point of use whilst maintaining the privacy of individuals and confidentiality of health related information[21]. Traceability records[22] must be retained for 30 years after the expiry date of the medicinal product. Particular care should be taken to maintain the traceability of medicinal products for special use cases, such as donor-matched cells. Directives 2002/98/EC and Commission Directive 2005/61/EC of 30 September 2005 implementing Directive 2002/98/EC of the European Parliament and of the Council as regards traceability requirements and notification of serious adverse reactions and events[23] apply to blood components when they are used as starting or raw materials in the manufacturing process of medicinal products. For ATMPs, traceability requirement regarding human cells including haematopoietic cells must comply with the principles laid down in Directives 2004/23/EC and 2006/86/EC. The arrangements necessary to achieve the traceability and retention period should be incorporated into technical agreements between the responsible parties.

## Production

29    Given the variability inherent in many biological active substances and medicinal products, steps to increase process robustness thereby reducing process variability and enhancing reproducibility at the different stages of the product lifecycle such as process design should be reassessed during Product Quality Reviews.

---

[21] Article 15 of Regulation 1394/ 2007

[22] See ENTR/F/2/SF/dn D(2009) 35810, 'Detailed guidelines on good clinical practice specific to advanced therapy medicinal Products' for further information on traceability of investigational ATMPs

[23] OJ L 256, 1.10.2005, p. 32.

30 Since cultivation conditions, media and reagents are designed to promote the growth of cells or microbial organisms, typically in an axenic state, particular attention should be paid in the control strategy to ensure there are robust steps that prevent or minimise the occurrence of unwanted bioburden and associated metabolites and endotoxins. For cell based ATMPs where production batches are frequently small the risk of cross-contamination between cell preparations from different donors with various health status should be controlled under defined procedures and requirements.

## Starting and raw materials

31 The source, origin and suitability of biological starting and raw materials (e.g. cryoprotectants, feeder cells, reagents, culture media, buffers, serum, enzymes, cytokines, growth factors) should be clearly defined. Where the necessary tests take a long time, it may be permissible to process starting materials before the results of the tests are available, the risk of using a potentially failed material and its potential impact on other batches should be clearly understood and assessed under the principles of QRM. In such cases, release of a finished product is conditional on satisfactory results of these tests. The identification of all starting materials should be in compliance with the requirements appropriate to its stage of manufacture. For biological medicinal products further guidance can be found in Part I and Annex 8 and for biological active substances in Part II.

32 The risk of contamination of starting and raw materials during their passage along the supply chain must be assessed, with particular emphasis on TSE. Materials that come into direct contact with manufacturing equipment or the product (such as media used in media fill experiments and lubricants that may contact the product) must also be taken into account.

33 Given that the risks from the introduction of contamination and the consequences to the finished product is the same irrespective of the stage of manufacture, establishment of a control strategy to protect the product and the preparation of solutions, buffers and other additions should be based on the principles and guidance contained in the appropriate sections of Annex 1. The controls required for the quality of starting and raw materials and on the aseptic manufacturing process, particularly for cell-based products, where final sterilisation is generally not possible and the ability to remove microbial by-products is limited, assume greater importance. Where an MA or CTA provides for an allowable type and level of bioburden, for example at active substance stage, the control

strategy should address the means by which this is maintained within the specified limits.

34  Where sterilization of starting and raw materials is required, it should be carried out where possible by heat. Where necessary, other appropriate methods may also be used for inactivation of biological materials (e.g. irradiation and filtration).

35  Reduction in bioburden associated with procurement of living tissues and cells may require the use of other measures such as antibiotics at early manufacturing stages. This should be avoided, but where it is necessary their use should be justified, they should be removed from the manufacturing process at the stage specified in the MA or CTA.

36  For human tissues and cells used as starting materials for biological medicinal products:

(a) Their procurement, donation and testing in the EU is regulated under Directive 2004/23/EC and its implementing Commission directives. Such EU supply sites must hold appropriate approvals from the national competent authority(ies) under this Directive which should be verified as part of starting material supplier management.

(b) Where such human cells or tissues are imported from third countries they must meet equivalent Community standards of quality and safety equivalent to those laid down in Directive 2004/23/EC. The traceability and serious adverse reaction and serious adverse event notification requirements are set out in Directive 2006/86/EC.

(c) There may be some instances where processing of cells and tissues used as starting materials for biological medicinal products will be conducted at tissue establishments, e.g. to derive early cell lines or banks prior to establishing a Master Cell Bank (MCB). Such processing steps, are under the scope of Directive 2004/23/EC, which provides for the need of a Responsible Person (RP).

(d) Tissue and cells are released by the RP in the tissue establishment before shipment to the medicinal product manufacturer, after which normal medicinal product starting material controls apply. The test results of all tissues / cells supplied by the tissue establishment should be available to the manufacturer of the medicinal product. Such information must be used to make appropriate material segregation and storage decisions. In cases where manufacturing must be initiated prior to receiving test results from the tissue establishment, tissue and cells may be shipped to the medicinal product manufacturer provided controls are in place to prevent cross-contamination with tissue and cells that have been released by the RP in the tissue establishment.

(e) The transport of human tissues and cells to the manufacturing site must be controlled by a written agreement between the responsible parties. The manufacturing sites should have documentary evidence of adherence to the specified storage and transport conditions.

(f) Continuation of traceability requirements started at tissue establishments through to the recipient(s), and vice versa, including materials in contact with the cells or tissues, should be maintained.

(g) A technical agreement should be in place between the responsible parties (e.g. manufacturers, tissue establishment, Sponsors, MA Holder) which defines the tasks of each party, including the RP and Qualified Person.

37 With regard to gene therapy[24]:

(a) For products consisting of viral vectors, the starting materials are the components from which the viral vector is obtained, i.e. the master virus seed or the plasmids to transfect the packaging cells and the MCB of the packaging cell line.

(b) For products consisting of plasmids, non-viral vectors and genetically modified micro-organisms other than viruses or viral vectors, the starting materials are the components used to generate the producing cell, i.e. the plasmid, the host bacteria and the MCB of the recombinant microbial cells.

(c) For genetically modified cells, the starting materials are the components used to obtain the genetically modified cells, i.e. the starting materials to manufacture the vector and the human or animal cell preparations.

(d) The principles of GMP apply from the bank system used to manufacture the vector or plasmid used for gene transfer.

38 Where human or animal cells are used in the manufacturing process as feeder cells, appropriate controls over the sourcing, testing, transport and storage should be in place, including control of compliance with Directive 2004/23.

## Seed lot and cell bank system

39 In order to prevent the unwanted drift of properties which might ensue from repeated subcultures or multiple generations, the production of biological medicinal substances and products obtained by microbial culture, cell culture or propagation in embryos and animals should be

---

[24] Details in section 3.2 of Part IV of Annex I to Directive 2001/83/EC.

based on a system of master and working virus seed lots and/or cell banks. Such a system may not be applicable to all types of ATMPs.

40    The number of generations (doublings, passages) between the seed lot or cell bank, the active biological substance and the finished product should be consistent with specifications in the MA or CTA.

41    As part of product lifecycle management, establishment of seed lots and cell banks, including master and working generations, should be performed under circumstances which are demonstrably appropriate. This should include an appropriately controlled environment to protect the seed lot and the cell bank and the personnel handling it. During the establishment of the seed lot and cell bank, no other living or infectious material (e.g. virus, cell lines or cell strains) should be handled simultaneously in the same area or by the same persons. For stages prior to the master seed or cell bank generation, where only the principles of GMP may be applied, documentation should be available to support traceability including issues related to components used during development with potential impact on product safety (e.g. reagents of biological origin) from initial sourcing and genetic development if applicable. For vaccines the requirements of Ph Eur monograph 2005;153 "Vaccines for human use" will apply.

42    Following the establishment of master and working cell banks and master and working seed lots, quarantine and release procedures should be followed. This should include adequate characterization and testing for contaminants. Their on-going suitability for use should be further demonstrated by the consistency of the characteristics and quality of the successive batches of product. Evidence of the stability and recovery of the seeds and banks should be documented and records should be kept in a manner permitting trend evaluation.

43    Seed lots and cell banks should be stored and used in such a way as to minimize the risks of contamination, (e.g. stored in the vapour phase of liquid nitrogen in sealed containers) or alteration. Control measures for the storage of different seeds and/or cells in the same area or equipment should prevent mix-up and take account the infectious nature of the materials to prevent cross contamination.

44    Cell based medicinal products are often generated from a cell stock obtained from limited number of passages. In contrast with the two tiered system of Master and Working cell banks, the number of production runs from a cell stock is limited by the number of aliquots obtained after expansion and does not cover the entire life cycle of the product. Cell stock changes should be covered by a validation protocol."

45 Storage containers should be sealed, clearly labelled and kept at an appropriate temperature. A stock inventory must be kept. The storage temperature should be recorded continuously and, where used, the liquid nitrogen level monitored. Deviation from set limits and corrective and preventive action taken should be recorded.

46 It is desirable to split stocks and to store the split stocks at different locations so as to minimize the risks of total loss. The controls at such locations should provide the assurances outlined in the preceding paragraphs.

47 The storage and handling conditions for stocks should be managed according to the same procedures and parameters. Once containers are removed from the seed lot / cell bank management system, the containers should not be returned to stock.

## Operating principles

48 Change management should, on a periodic basis, take into account the effects, including cumulative effects of changes (e.g. to the process) on the quality, safety and efficacy of the finished product.

49 Critical operational (process) parameters, or other input parameters which affect product quality, need to be identified, validated, documented and be shown to be maintained within requirements.

50 A control strategy for the entry of articles and materials into production areas should be based on QRM principles. For aseptic processes, heat stable articles and materials entering a clean area or clean/contained area should preferably do so through a double-ended autoclave or oven. Heat labile articles and materials should enter through an air lock with interlocked doors where they are subject to effective surface sanitisation procedures. Sterilisation of articles and materials elsewhere is acceptable provided that they are multiple wrappings, as appropriate to the number of stages of entry to the clean area, and enter through an airlock with the appropriate surface sanitisation precautions.

51 The growth promoting properties of culture media should be demonstrated to be suitable for its intended use. If possible, media should be sterilized in situ. In-line sterilizing filters for routine addition of gases, media, acids or alkalis, anti-foaming agents etc. to fermenters should be used where possible.

52 Addition of materials or cultures to fermenters and other vessels and sampling should be carried out under carefully controlled conditions to

prevent contamination. Care should be taken to ensure that vessels are correctly connected when addition or sampling takes place.

53  Continuous monitoring of some production processes (e.g. fermentation) may be necessary, such data should form part of the batch record. Where continuous culture is used, special consideration should be given to the quality control requirements arising from this type of production method.

54  Centrifugation and blending of products can lead to aerosol formation and containment of such activities to minimise cross-contamination is necessary.

55  Accidental spillages, especially of live organisms, must be dealt with quickly and safely. Qualified decontamination measures should be available for each organism or groups of related organisms. Where different strains of single bacteria species or very similar viruses are involved, the decontamination process may be validated with one representative strain, unless there is reason to believe that they may vary significantly in their resistance to the agent(s) involved.

56  If obviously contaminated, such as by spills or aerosols, or if a potentially hazardous organism is involved, production and control materials, including paperwork, must be adequately disinfected, or the information transferred out by other means.

57  In cases where a virus inactivation or removal process is performed during manufacture, measures should be taken to avoid the risk of recontamination of treated products by non-treated products.

58  For products that are inactivated by the addition of a reagent (e.g. micro-organisms in the course of vaccine manufacture) the process should ensure the complete inactivation of live organism. In addition to the thorough mixing of culture and inactivant, consideration should be given to contact of all product-contact surfaces exposed to live culture and, where required, the transfer to a second vessel.

59  A wide variety of equipment is used for chromatography. QRM principles should be used to devise the control strategy on matrices, the housings and associated equipment when used in campaign manufacture and in multi-product environments. The re-use of the same matrix at different stages of processing is discouraged. Acceptance criteria, operating conditions, regeneration methods, life span and sanitization or sterilization methods of columns should be defined.

60  Where irradiated equipment and materials are used, Annex 12 to EudraLex, Volume 4, should be consulted for further guidance.

61 There should be a system to assure the integrity and closure of containers after filling where the final products or intermediates represent a special risk and procedures to deal with any leaks or spillages. Filling and packaging operations need to have procedures in place to maintain the product within any specified limits, e.g. time and/or temperature.

62 Activities in handling vials containing live biological agents must be performed in such a way to prevent the contamination of other products or egress of the live agents into the work environment or the external environment. The viability of such organisms and their biological classification should take into consideration as part of the management of such risks.

63 Care should be taken in the preparation, printing, storage and application of labels, including any specific text for patient-specific products or signifying the use of genetic engineering of the contents on the immediate and outer packaging. In the case of ATMPs used for autologous use, the unique patient identifier and the statement "for autologous use only" should be indicated on the outer packaging or, where there is no outer packaging, on the immediate packaging.[25]

64 The compatibility of labels with ultra-low storage temperatures, where such temperatures are used, should be verified.

65 Where donor (human or animal) health information becomes available after procurement, which affects product quality, it should be taken into account in recall procedures.

## Quality control

66 In-process controls have a greater importance in ensuring the consistency of the quality of biological active substance and medicinal products than for conventional products. In-process control testing should be performed at appropriate stages of production to control those conditions that are important for the quality of the finished product.

67 Where intermediates can be stored for extended periods of time (days, weeks or longer), consideration should be given to the inclusion of finished product batches made from materials held for their maximum in-process periods in the on-going stability programme.

68 Certain types of cells (e.g. autologous cells used in ATMPs) may be available in limited quantities and, where allowed in the MA, a modified testing and sample retention strategy may be developed and documented.

---

[25] Article 11 of Regulation (EC) No 1349/2007.

EU GMP GUIDE PART I ANNEX 2 MANUFACTURE OF BIOLOGICAL ACTIVE SUBSTANCES AND MEDICINAL PRODUCTS FOR HUMAN USE

**69** For cell-based ATMPs, sterility tests should be conducted on antibiotic-free cultures of cells or cell banks to provide evidence for absence of bacterial and fungal contamination and to be able to detect fastidious organisms where appropriate.

**70** For biological medicinal products with a short shelf life, which for the purposes of the annex is taken to mean a period of 14 days or less, and which need batch certification before completion of all end product quality control tests (e.g. sterility tests) a suitable control strategy must be in place. Such controls need to be built on enhanced understanding of product and process performance and take into account the controls and attributes of starting and raw materials. The exact and detailed description of the entire release procedure, including the responsibilities of the different personnel involved in assessment of production and analytical data is essential. A continuous assessment of the effectiveness of the quality assurance system must be in place including records kept in a manner which permit trend evaluation. Where end product tests are not available due to their short shelf life, alternative methods of obtaining equivalent data to permit initial batch certification should be considered (e.g. rapid microbiological methods). The procedure for batch certification and release may be carried out in two or more stages - :

(a) Assessment by designated person(s) of batch processing records, results from environmental monitoring (where available) which should cover production conditions, all deviations from normal procedures and the available analytical results for review in preparation for the initial certification by the Qualified Person.
(b) Assessment of the final analytical tests and other information available for final certification by the Qualified Person.

A procedure should be in place to describe the measures to be taken (including liaison with clinical staff) where out of specification test results are obtained. Such events should be fully investigated and the relevant corrective and preventive actions taken to prevent recurrence documented.

## PART B. SPECIFIC GUIDANCE ON SELECTED PRODUCT TYPES

## B1. ANIMAL SOURCED PRODUCTS[26]

This guidance applies to animal materials which includes materials from establishments such as abattoirs. Since the supply chains can be extensive and complex, controls based on QRM principles need to be applied, see

---

[26] See also PhEur monograph requirements, 0333

also requirements of Ph Eur monographs, including the need for specific tests at defined stages. Documentation to demonstrate the supply chain traceability[27] and clear roles of participants in the supply chain, typically including a sufficiently detailed and current process map, should be in place.

1   Monitoring programmes should be in place for animal disease that are of concern to human health. Organisations should take into account reports from trustworthy sources on national disease prevalence when compiling their assessment of risk and mitigation factors. Such organisations include the World Organisation for Animal Health (OIE, Office International des Epizooties[28]). This should be supplemented by information on health monitoring and control programme(s) at national and local levels, the latter to include the sources (e.g. farm or feedlot) from which the animals are drawn and the control measures in place during transport to the abattoirs.

2   Where abattoirs are used to source animal tissues, they should be shown to operate to standards equivalent to those used in the EU. Account should be taken of reports from organisations such as the Food and Veterinary Office[29] who verify compliance with the requirements of food safety and quality, veterinary and plant health legislation within the EU and in third countries exporting to the EU.

3   Control measures for starting or raw materials at establishments such as abattoirs should include appropriate elements of a Quality Management System to assure a satisfactory level of operator training, materials traceability, control and consistency. These measures may be drawn from sources outside EU GMP but should be shown to provide equivalent levels of control.

4   Control measures for starting or raw materials should be in place which prevent interventions which may affect the quality of materials, or which at least provides evidence of such activities, during their progression through the manufacturing and supply chain. This includes the movement of material between sites of initial collection, partial and final purification(s), storage sites, hubs, consolidators and brokers. Details of such arrangements should be recorded within the traceability system and any breaches recorded, investigated and actions taken.

5   Regular audits of the starting or raw material supplier should be undertaken which verify compliance with controls for materials at the

---

[27] See Chapter 5 in EudraLex, Volume 4.
[28] http://www.oie.int/eng/en_index.htm
[29] http://ec.europa.eu/food/fvo/index_en.htm

different stages of manufacture. Issues must be investigated to a depth appropriate to their significance, for which full documentation should be available. Systems should also be in place to ensure that effective corrective and preventive actions are taken.

6    Cells, tissues and organs intended for the manufacture of xenogeneic cell-based medicinal products should be obtained only from animals that have been bred in captivity (barrier facility) specifically for this purpose and under no circumstances should cells, tissues and organs from wild animals or from abattoirs be used. Tissues of founder animals similarly should not be used. The health status of the animals should be monitored and documented.

7    For xenogeneic cell therapy products appropriate guidance in relation to procurement and testing of animal cells should be followed. Reference is made to the EMA Guideline document[30] on xenogeneic cell-based medicinal products.

## B2. ALLERGEN PRODUCTS

Materials may be manufactured by extraction from natural sources or manufactured by recombinant DNA technology.

1    Source materials should be described in sufficient detail to ensure consistency in their supply, e.g. common and scientific name, origin, nature, contaminant limits, method of collection. Those derived from animals should be from healthy sources. Appropriate biosecurity controls should be in place for colonies (e.g. mites, animals) used for the extraction of allergens. Allergen products should be stored under defined conditions to minimise deterioration.

2    The production process steps including pre-treatment, extraction, filtration, dialysis, concentration or freeze-drying steps should be described in detail and validated.

3    The modification processes to manufacture modified allergen extracts (e.g. allergoids, conjugates) should be described. Intermediates in the manufacturing process should be identified and controlled.

4    Allergen extract mixtures should be prepared from individual extracts from single source materials. Each individual extract should be considered as one active substance.

---

[30] EMEA/CHMP/CPWP/83508/2009.

## B3. ANIMAL IMMUNOSERA PRODUCTS

1    Particular care should be exercised on the control of antigens of biological origin to assure their quality, consistency and freedom from adventitious agents. The preparation of materials used to immunise the source animals (e.g. antigens, hapten carriers, adjuvants, stabilising agents), the storage of such material immediately prior to immunisation should be in accordance with documented procedures.

2    The immunisation, test bleed and harvest bleed schedules should conform to those approved in the CTA or MA.

3    The manufacturing conditions for the preparation of antibody sub-fragments (e.g. Fab or F(ab')2) and any further modifications must be in accordance with validated and approved parameters. Where such enzymes are made up of several components, their consistency should be assured.

## B4. VACCINES

1    Where eggs are used, the health status of all source flocks used in the production of eggs (whether specified pathogen free or healthy flocks) should be assured.

2    The integrity of containers used to store intermediate products and the hold times must be validated.

3    Vessels containing inactivated products should not be opened or sampled in areas containing live biological agents.

4    The sequence of addition of active ingredients, adjuvants and excipients during the formulation of an intermediate or final product must be in compliance with specifications.

5    Where organisms with a higher biological safety level (e.g. pandemic vaccine strains) are to be used in manufacture or testing, appropriate containment arrangements must be in place. The approval of such arrangements should be obtained from the appropriate national authority(ies) and the approval documents be available for verification.

## B5. RECOMBINANT PRODUCTS

1    Process condition during cell growth, protein expression and purification must be maintained within validated parameters to assure a consistent product with a defined range of impurities that is within the capability of the process to reduce to acceptable levels. The type of cell used in production may require increased measures to be taken to assure freedom

from viruses. For production involving multiple harvest, the period of continuous cultivation should be within specified limits.

2    The purification processes to remove unwanted host cell proteins, nucleic acids, carbohydrates, viruses and other impurities should be within defined validated limits.

## B6. MONOCLONAL ANTIBODY PRODUCTS

1    Monoclonal antibodies may be manufactured from murine hybridomas, human hybridomas or by recombinant DNA technology. Control measures appropriate to the different source cells (including feeder cells if used) and materials used to establish the hybridoma / cell line should be in place to assure the safety and quality of the product. It should be verified that these are within approved limits. Freedom from viruses should be given particular emphasis. It should be noted that data originating from products generated by the same manufacturing technology platform may be acceptable to demonstrate suitability.

2    Criteria to be monitored at the end of a production cycle and for early termination of production cycles should be verified that these are within approved limits.

3    The manufacturing conditions for the preparation of antibody sub-fragments (e.g. Fab, F(ab')2, scFv) and any further modifications (e.g. radio labelling, conjugation, chemical linking) must be in accordance with validated parameters.

## B7. TRANSGENIC ANIMAL PRODUCTS

Consistency of starting material from a transgenic source is likely to be more problematic than is normally the case for non-transgenic biotechnology sources. Consequently, there is an increased requirement to demonstrate batch-to-batch consistency of product in all respects.

1    A range of species may be used to produce biological medicinal products, which may be expressed into body fluids (e.g. milk) for collection and purification. Animals should be clearly and uniquely identified and backup arrangements should be put in place in the event of loss of the primary marker.

2    The arrangements for housing and care of the animals should be defined such that they minimise the exposure of the animals to pathogenic and zoonotic agents. Appropriate measures to protect the external environment

should be established. A health-monitoring programme should be established and all results documented, any incident should be investigated and its impact on the continuation of the animal and on previous batches of product should be determined. Care should be taken to ensure that any therapeutic products used to treat the animals do not contaminate the product.

3   The genealogy of the founder animals through to production animals must be documented. Since a transgenic line will be derived from a single genetic founder animal, materials from different transgenic lines should not be mixed.

4   The conditions under which the product is harvested should be in accordance with MA or CTA conditions. The harvest schedule and conditions under which animals may be removed from production should be performed according to approved procedures and acceptance limits.

## B8. TRANSGENIC PLANT PRODUCTS

Consistency of starting material from a transgenic source is likely to be more problematic than is normally the case for non-transgenic biotechnology sources. Consequently, there is an increased requirement to demonstrate batch-to-batch consistency of product in all respects.

1   Additional measures, over and above those given in Part A, may be required to prevent contamination of master and working transgenic banks by extraneous plant materials and relevant adventitious agents. The stability of the gene within defined generation numbers should be monitored.

2   Plants should be clearly and uniquely identified, the presence of key plant features, including health status, across the crop should be verified at defined intervals through the cultivation period to assure consistency of yield between crops.

3   Security arrangements for the protection of crops should be defined, wherever possible, such that they minimise the exposure to contamination by microbiological agents and cross-contamination with non-related plants. Measures should be in place to prevent materials such as pesticides and fertilisers from contaminating the product. A monitoring programme should be established and all results documented, any incident should be investigated and its impact on the continuation of the crop in the production programme should be determined.

4    Conditions under which plants may be removed from production should be defined. Acceptance limits should be set for materials (e.g. host proteins) that may interfere with the purification process. It should be verified that the results are within approved limits.

5    Environmental conditions (temperature, rain), which may affect the quality attributes and yield of the recombinant protein from time of planting, through cultivation to harvest and interim storage of harvested materials should be documented. The principles in documents such as "Guideline on Good Agricultural and Collection Practice for Starting Materials of Herbal origin"[31] of the Committee of Herbal Medicinal Products should be taken into account when drawing up such criteria.

## B9. GENE THERAPY PRODUCTS

Point 2.1. of Part IV of the Annex to Directive 2001/83/EC contains a definition of gene therapy (GT) medicinal products.

There are several types of GT medicinal products (GT products containing recombinant nuceic acid sequence(s) or genetically modified organism(s) or virus(es) and GT medicinal products containing genetically modified cells) and all are within the scope of the guidance in this section. For cell based GT medicinal products, some aspects of guidance in section B10 of Part B may be applicable.

1    Since the cells used in the manufacture of gene therapy products are obtained either from humans (autologous or allogeneic) or animals (xenogeneic), there is a potential risk of contamination by adventitious agents. Particular considerations must be applied to the segregation of autologous materials obtained from infected donors. The robustness of the control and test measures for such starting materials, cryoprotectants, culture media, cells and vectors should be based on QRM principles and in line with the MA or CTA. Established cell lines used for viral vector production and their control and test measures should similarly be based on QRM principles. Virus seed lots and cell banking systems should be used where relevant.

2    Factors such as the nature of the genetic material, type of (viral or non-viral) vector and type of cells have a bearing on the range of potential impurities, adventitious agents and cross-contaminations that should be taken into account as part of the development of an overall strategy to minimise risk. This strategy should be used as a basis for the design of the process, the manufacturing and storage facilities and equipment,

---

[31]  Doc. Ref. EMEA/HMPC/246816/2005.

cleaning and decontamination procedures, packaging, labelling and distribution.

3   The manufacture and testing of GT medicinal products raises specific issues regarding the safety and quality of the final product and safety issues for recipients and staff. A risk based approach for operator, environment and patient safety and the implementation of controls based on the biological hazard class should be applied. Legislated local and, if applicable, international safety measures should be applied.

4   Personnel (including QC and maintenance staff) and material flows, including those for storage and testing (e.g. starting materials, in-process and final product samples and environmental monitoring samples), should be controlled on the basis of QRM principles, where possible utilising unidirectional flows. This should take into account movement between areas containing different genetically modified organisms and areas containing non-genetically-modified organisms.

5   Any special cleaning and decontamination methods required for the range of organisms being handled should be considered in the design of facilities and equipment. Where possible, the environmental monitoring programme should be supplemented by the inclusion of methods to detect the presence of the specific organisms being cultivated.

6   Where replication limited vectors are used, measures should be in place to prevent the introduction of wild-type viruses, which may lead to the formation of replication competent recombinant vectors.

7   An emergency plan for dealing with accidental release of viable organisms should be in place. This should address methods and procedures for containment, protection of operators, cleaning, decontamination and safe return to use. An assessment of impact on the immediate products and any others in the affected area should also be made.

8   Facilities for the manufacture of viral vectors should be separated from other areas by specific measures. The arrangements for separation should be demonstrated to be effective. Closed systems should be used wherever possible, sample collection additions and transfers should prevent the release of viral material.

9   Concurrent manufacture of different viral gene therapy vectors in the same area is not acceptable. Concurrent production of non-viral vectors in the same area should be controlled on the basis of QRM principles. Changeover procedures between campaigns should be demonstrated to be effective.

10  A description of the production of vectors and genetically modified cells should be available in sufficient detail to ensure the traceability of the

products from the starting material (plasmids, gene of interest and regulatory sequences, cell banks, and viral or non viral vector stock) to the finished product.

11   Shipment of products containing or consisting of GMO should conform to appropriate legislation.

12   The following considerations apply to the ex-vivo gene transfer to recipient cells:

(a) These should take place in facilities dedicated to such activities where appropriate containment arrangements exist.

(b) Measures (including considerations outlined under paragraph 10 in Part A) to minimise the potential for cross-contamination and mix-up between cells from different patients are required, this should include the use of validated cleaning procedures. The concurrent use of different viral vectors should be subject to controls based on QRM principles. Some viral vectors (e.g. Retro- or Lenti-viruses) cannot be used in the manufacturing process of genetically modified cells until they have been shown to be devoid of replication-competent contaminating vector.

(c) Traceability requirements must be maintained. There should be a clear definition of a batch, from cell source to final product container(s).

(d) For products that utilise non-biological means to deliver the gene, their physico-chemical properties should be documented and tested.

## B10. SOMATIC AND XENOGENEIC CELL THERAPY PRODUCTS AND TISSUE ENGINEERED PRODUCTS

Point 2.2. of Part IV of Annex I of Directive 2001/83/EC contains the definition of somatic cell therapy (SCT) medicinal products and the definition of a tissue engineered medicinal product is given in Article 2(1)(b) of Regulation (EC) 1394/2007 of the European Parliament and of the Council of 13 November 2007 on advanced therapy medicinal products and amending Directive 2001/83/EC and Regulation (EC) No 726/2004.[32] For genetically modified cell based products that are not classified as GT products, some aspects of guidance in section B9 may be applicable.

1   Where they are available, authorised sources (i.e. authorised medicinal products or CE marked medical devices) of additional substances (such as cellular products, bio-molecules, bio-materials, scaffolds, matrices) should be used in the manufacture of these products.

---

[32] OJ L 324, 10.12.2007, p. 121.

2    Where devices, including custom-made devices, are incorporated as part of the products:

(a) There should be written agreement between the manufacturer of the medicinal product and the manufacturer of the medical device, which should provide enough information on the medical device to avoid alteration of its properties during manufacturing of the ATMP. This should include the requirement to control changes proposed for the medical device.

(b) The technical agreement should also require the exchange of information on deviations in the manufacture of the medical device.

3    Since somatic cells are obtained either from humans (autologous or allogeneic) or animals (xenogeneic), there is a potential risk of contamination by adventitious agents. Special considerations must be applied to the segregation of autologous materials obtained from infected donors. The robustness of the control and test measures put in place for these source materials should be ensured.

4    Manufacturing steps should be conducted aseptically where sterilisation of the finished product cannot be achieved using standard methods such as filtration.

5    Careful attention should be paid to specific requirements at any cryopreservation stages, e.g. the rate of temperature change during freezing or thawing. The type of storage chamber, placement and retrieval process should minimise the risk of cross-contamination, maintain the quality of the products and facilitate their accurate retrieval. Documented procedures should be in place for the secure handling and storage of products with positive serological markers.

6    Sterility tests should be conducted on antibiotic-free cultures of cells or cell banks to provide evidence for absence of bacterial and fungal contamination and consider the detection of fastidious organism.

7    Where relevant, a stability-monitoring programme should be in place together with reference and retain samples in sufficient quantity to permit further examination.

## GLOSSARY TO ANNEX 2

Entries are only included where the terms are used in Annex 2 and require further explanation. Definitions which already exist in legislation or other sources are cross-referenced. In addition to this glossary, the GMP-glossary in EudraLex, Volume 4[33] applies, unless indicated otherwise.

### ACTIVE SUBSTANCE

See Article 1(3a) of Directive 2001/83/EC.

### ADJUVANT

A chemical or biological substance that enhances the immune response against an antigen.

### ALLERGOIDS

Allergens which are chemically modified to reduce IgE reactivity.

### ANTIGENS

Substances (e.g. toxins, foreign proteins, bacteria, tissue cells) capable of inducing specific immune responses.

### ANTIBODY

Proteins produced by the B-lymphocytes that bind to specific antigens. Antibodies may divided into two main types based on key differences in their method of manufacture:

**Monoclonal antibodies (MAb)** – homogenous antibody population obtained from a single clone of lymphocytes or by recombinant technology and which bind to a single epitope.
**Polyclonal antibodies** – derived from a range of lymphocyte clones, produced in human and animals in response to the epitopes on most 'non-self' molecules.

### AREA

A specific set of rooms within a building associated with the manufacturing of any one product or multiple products that has a common air handling unit.

### BIOBURDEN

The level and type (i.e. objectionable or not) of micro-organism present in raw materials, media, biological substances, intermediates or products. Regarded as contamination when the level and/or type exceed specifications.

---

[33] http://ec.europa.eu/health/files/eudralex/vol-4/pdfs-en/glos4en200408_en.pdf

## BIOLOGICAL MEDICINAL PRODUCT

See 3$^{rd}$ paragraph of point 3.2.1.1.b. of Part I of Annex I to Directive 2001/83/EC.

## BIOSAFETY LEVEL (BSL)

The containment conditions required to safely handle organisms of different hazards ranging from BSL1 (lowest risk, unlikely to cause human disease) to BSL4 (highest risk, cause severe disease, likely to spread and no effective prophylaxis or treatment available).

## CAMPAIGNED MANUFACTURE

The manufacture of a series of batches of the same product in sequence in a given period of time followed by strict adherence to accepted control measures before transfer to another product. The products are not run at the same time but may be run on the same equipment.

## CELL BANK

A collection of appropriate containers, whose contents are of uniform composition, stored under defined conditions. Each container represents an aliquot of a single pool of cells.

## CELL STOCK

Primary cells expanded to a given number of cells to be aliquoted and used as starting material for production of a limited number of lots of a cell based medicinal product.

## CLOSED SYSTEM

Where a drug substance or product is not exposed to the immediate room environment during manufacture.

## CONTAINED USE

**See Article 2(c) of Directive 2009/41/EC** for all genetically modified organisms.

## DELIBERATE RELEASE

See Article 2(3) of Directive 2001/18/EC of the European Parliament and of the Council of 12 March 2001 on the deliberate release into the environment of genetically modified organisms and repealing Council Directive 90/220/EEC.[34]

## EXCIPIENT

See Article 1(3b) of Directive 2001/83/EC.

---

[34] OJ L 106, 17.4.2001, p. 1.

## EX-VIVO

Where procedures are conducted on tissues or cells outside the living body and returned to the living body.

## FEEDER CELLS

Cells used in co-culture to maintain pluripotent stem cells. For human embryonic stem cell culture, typical feeder layers include mouse embryonic fibroblasts (MEFs) or human embryonic fibroblasts that have been treated to prevent them from dividing.

## GENE

A sequence of DNA that codes for one (or more) protein(s).

## GENE TRANSFER

A process to transfer a gene in cells, involving an expression system contained in a delivery system known as a vector, which can be of viral, as well as non-viral origin. After gene transfer, genetically modified cells are also termed *transduced cells*.

## GENETICALLY MODIFIED ORGANISM (GMO)

See Article 2(2) of Directive 2001/18/EC.

## HAPTEN

A low molecular weight molecule that is not in itself antigenic unless conjugated to a "carrier" molecule.

## HYBRIDOMA

An immortalised cell line that secrete desired (monoclonal) antibodies and are typically derived by fusing B-lymphocytes with tumour cells.

## INTERMEDIATE PRODUCT

See definitions in GMP Glossary and in Part II.

## IN-VIVO

Procedures conducted in living organisms.

## LOOK-BACK

Documented procedure to trace biological medicinal substances or products which may be adversely affected by the use or incorporation of animal or human materials when either such materials fail release tests due to the presence of contaminating agent(s) or when conditions of concern become apparent in the source animal or human.

## MASTER CELL BANK (MCB)

An aliquot of a single pool of cells which generally has been prepared from the selected cell clone under defined conditions, dispensed into multiple containers and stored under defined conditions. The MCB is used to derive all working cell banks. **Master virus seed (MVS)** – as above, but in relation to viruses; **master transgenic bank** – as above but for transgenic plants or animals.

## MONOSEPSIS (AXENIC)

A single organism in culture which is not contaminated with any other organism.

## MULTI-PRODUCT FACILITY

A facility that manufactures, either concurrently or in campaign mode, a range of different biological medicinal substances and products and within which equipment train(s) may or may not be dedicated to specific substances or products.

## PLASMID

A plasmid is a piece of DNA usually present in a bacterial cell as a circular entity separated from the cell chromosome; it can be modified by molecular biology techniques, purified out of the bacterial cell and used to transfer its DNA to another cell.

## RAW MATERIALS

See 4th paragraph of point 3.2.1.1.b. of Part I of Annex I to Directive 2001/83/EC.

## RESPONSIBLE PERSON (RP)

The person designated in accordance with Article 17 of Directive 2004/23/EC.

## SCAFFOLD

A support, delivery vehicle or matrix that may provided structure for or facilitate the migration, binding or transport of cells and/or bioactive molecules.

## SOMATIC CELLS

Cells, other than reproductive (germ line) cells, which make up the body of a human or animal. These cells may be autologous (from the patient), allogeneic (from another human being) or xenogeneic (from animals) somatic living cells, that have been manipulated or altered ex vivo, to be administered in humans to obtain a therapeutic, diagnostic or preventive effects.

## SPECIFIED PATHOGEN FREE (SPF)

Animal materials (e.g. chickens, embryos or cell cultures) used for the production or quality control of biological medicinal products derived from groups (e.g. flocks or herds) of animals free from specified pathogens. Such flocks or herds are defined as animals sharing a common environment

EU GMP GUIDE PART I ANNEX 2 MANUFACTURE OF
BIOLOGICAL ACTIVE SUBSTANCES AND MEDICINAL
PRODUCTS FOR HUMAN USE

and having their own caretakers who have no contact with non-SPF groups.

## STARTING MATERIALS

See the 1$^{st}$ and 2$^{nd}$ paragraph of point 3.2.1.1.b of Part I of Annex I to Directive 2001/83/EC.

## TRANSGENIC

An organism that contains a foreign gene in its normal genetic component for the expression of biological pharmaceutical materials.

## VECTOR

An agent of transmission, which transmits genetic information from one cell or organism to another, e.g. plasmids, liposomes, viruses.

## VIRAL VECTOR

A vector derived from a virus and modified by means of molecular biology techniques in a way as to retain some, but not all, the parental virus genes; if the genes responsible for virus replication capacity are deleted, the vector is made replication-incompetent.

## WORKING CELL BANK (WCB)

A homogeneous pool of micro-organisms or cells, that are distributed uniformly into a number of containers derived from a MCB that are stored in such a way to ensure stability and for use in production. **Working virus seed** (WVS) – as above but in relation to viruses, **working transgenic bank** – as above but for transgenic plants or animals.

## ZOONOSIS

Animal diseases that can be transmitted to humans.

## ANNEX 3 MANUFACTURE OF RADIOPHARMACEUTICALS

EU GMP GUIDE PART I ANNEX 3 MANUFACTURE OF RADIOPHARMACEUTICALS

> **Editor's note** All radiopharmacies subject to a Manufacturer's 'Specials' Licence will be expected to comply with these requirements.

## Principle

The manufacture of radiopharmaceuticals shall be undertaken in accordance with the principles of Good Manufacturing Practice for Medicinal Products Part I and II. This annex specifically addresses some of the practices, which may be specific for radiopharmaceuticals.

**Note i.** Preparation of radiopharmaceuticals in radiopharmacies (hospitals or certain pharmacies), using Generators and Kits with a marketing authorisation or a national licence, is not covered by this guideline, unless covered by national requirement.

**Note ii.** According to radiation protection regulations it should be ensured that any medical exposure is under the clinical responsibility of a practitioner. In diagnostic and therapeutic nuclear medicine practices a medical physics expert shall be available.

**Note iii.** This annex is also applicable to radiopharmaceuticals used in clinical trials.

**Note iv.** Transport of radiopharmaceuticals is regulated by the International Atomic Energy Association (IAEA) and radiation protection requirements.

**Note v.** It is recognised that there are acceptable methods, other than those described in this annex, which are capable of achieving the principles of Quality Assurance. Other methods should be validated and provide a level of Quality Assurance at least equivalent to those set out in this annex.

## Introduction

1   The manufacturing and handling of radiopharmaceuticals is potentially hazardous. The level of risk depends in particular upon the types of radiation, the energy of radiation and the half-lives of the radioactive isotopes. Particular attention must be paid to the prevention of cross-contamination, to the retention of radionuclide contaminants, and to waste disposal.

2    Due to short shelf-life of their radionuclides, some radiopharmaceuticals may be released before completion of all quality control tests. In this case, the exact and detailed description of the whole release procedure including the responsibilities of the involved personnel and the continuous assessment of the effectiveness of the quality assurance system is essential.

3    This guideline is applicable to manufacturing procedures employed by industrial manufacturers, Nuclear Centres/Institutes and PET Centres for the production and quality control of the following types of products:

● Radiopharmaceuticals
● Positron Emitting (PET) Radiopharmaceuticals
● Radioactive Precursors for radiopharmaceutical production
● Radionuclide Generators

| Type of manufacture | Non - GMP* | GMP part II & I (Increasing) including relevant annexes | | | |
|---|---|---|---|---|---|
| Radiopharmaceuticals PET Radiopharmaceuticals Radioactive Precursors | Reactor/ Cyclotron Production | Chemical synthesis | Purification steps | Processing, formulation and dispensing | Aseptic or final sterilization |
| Radionuclide Generators | Reactor/ Cyclotron Production | Processing | | | |

* Target and transfer system from cyclotron to synthesis rig may be considered as the first step of active substance manufacture.

4    The manufacturer of the final radiopharmaceutical should describe and justify the steps for manufacture of the active substance and the final medicinal product and which GMP (part I or II) applies for the specific process/manufacturing steps.

5    Preparation of radiopharmaceuticals involves adherence to regulations on radiation protection.

6    Radiopharmaceuticals to be administered parenterally should comply with sterility requirements for parenterals and, where relevant, aseptic working conditions for the manufacture of sterile medicinal products, which are covered in Eudralex Volume 4, Annex 1.

7    Specifications and quality control testing procedures for the most commonly used radiopharmaceuticals are specified in the European Pharmacopoeia or in the marketing authorisation.

## Clinical trials

8 Radiopharmaceuticals intended for use in clinical trials as investigational medicinal products should in addition be produced in accordance with the principles in Eudralex Volume 4, annex 13.

## Quality Assurance

9 Quality assurance is of even greater importance in the manufacture of radiopharmaceuticals because of their particular characteristics, low volumes and in some circumstances the need to administer the product before testing is complete.

10 As with all pharmaceuticals, the products must be well protected against contamination and cross-contamination. However, the environment and the operators must also be protected against radiation. This means that the role of an effective quality assurance system is of the utmost importance.

11 It is important that the data generated by the monitoring of premises and processes are rigorously recorded and evaluated as part of the release process.

12 The principles of qualification and validation should be applied to the manufacturing of radiopharmaceuticals and a risk management approach should be used to determine the extent of qualification/validation, focusing on a combination of Good Manufacturing Practice and Radiation Protection.

## Personnel

13 All manufacturing operations should be carried out under the responsibility of personnel with additional competence in radiation protection. Personnel involved in production, analytical control and release of radiopharmaceuticals should be appropriately trained in radiopharmaceutical specific aspects of the quality management system. The QP should have the overall responsibility for release of the products.

14 All personnel (including those concerned with cleaning and maintenance) employed in areas where radioactive products are manufactured should receive appropriate additional training specific to these types of procedures and products.

15 Where production facilities are shared with research institutions, the research personnel must be adequately trained in GMP regulations and the QA function must review and approve the research activities to

ensure that they do not pose any hazard to the manufacturing of radiopharmaceuticals.

## Premises and Equipment

### General

16   Radioactive products should be manufactured in controlled (environmental and radioactive) areas. All manufacturing steps should take place in self-contained facilities dedicated to radiopharmaceuticals.

17   Measures should be established and implemented to prevent cross-contamination from personnel, materials, radionuclides etc. Closed or contained equipment should be used whenever appropriate. Where open equipment is used, or equipment is opened, precautions should be taken to minimize the risk of contamination. The risk assessment should demonstrate that the environmental cleanliness level proposed is suitable for the type of product being manufactured.

18   Access to the manufacturing areas should be via a gowning area and should be restricted to authorised personnel.

19   Workstations and their environment should be monitored with respect to radioactivity, particulate and microbiological quality as established during performance qualification (PQ).

20   Preventive maintenance, calibration and qualification programmes should be operated to ensure that all facilities and equipment used in the manufacture of radiopharmaceutical are suitable and qualified. These activities should be carried out by competent personnel and records and logs should be maintained.

21   Precautions should be taken to avoid radioactive contamination within the facility. Appropriate controls should be in place to detect any radioactive contamination, either directly through the use of radiation detectors or indirectly through a swabbing routine.

22   Equipment should be constructed so that surfaces that come into contact with the product are not reactive, additive or absorptive so as to alter the quality of the radiopharmaceutical.

23   Re-circulation of air extracted from area where radioactive products are handled should be avoided unless justified. Air outlets should be designed to minimize environmental contamination by radioactive particles and gases and appropriate measures should be taken to protect the controlled areas from particulate and microbial contamination.

24    In order to contain radioactive particles, it may be necessary for the air pressure to be lower where products are exposed, compared with the surrounding areas. However, it is still necessary to protect the product from environmental contamination. This may be achieved by, for example, using barrier technology or airlocks, acting as pressure sinks.

## Sterile production

25    Sterile radiopharmaceuticals may be divided into those, which are manufactured aseptically, and those, which are terminally sterilised. The facility should maintain the appropriate level of environmental cleanliness for the type of operation being performed. For manufacture of sterile products the working zone where products or containers may be exposed to the environment, the cleanliness requirements should comply with the requirements described in the Eudralex Volume 4, Annex 1.

26    For manufacture of radiopharmaceuticals a risk assessment may be applied to determine the appropriate pressure differences, air flow direction and air quality.

27    In case of use of closed and automated systems (chemical synthesis, purification, on-line sterile filtration) a grade C environment (usually "Hot-cell") will be suitable. Hot-cells should meet a high degree of air cleanliness, with filtered feed air, when closed. Aseptic activities must be carried out in a grade A area.

28    Prior to the start of manufacturing, assembly of sterilised equipment and consumables (tubing, sterilised filters and sterile closed and sealed vials to a sealed fluid path) must be performed under aseptic conditions.

## Documentation

29    All documents related to the manufacture of radiopharmaceuticals should be prepared, reviewed, approved and distributed according to written procedures.

30    Specifications should be established and documented for raw materials, labelling and packaging materials, critical intermediates and the finished radiopharmaceutical. Specifications should also be in place for any other critical items used in the manufacturing process, such as process aids, gaskets, sterile filtering kits, that could critically impact on quality.

31    Acceptance criteria should be established for the radiopharmaceutical including criteria for release and shelf life specifications (examples:

chemical identity of the isotope, radioactive concentration, purity, and specific activity).

32    Records of major equipment use, cleaning, sanitisation or sterilisation and maintenance should show the product name and batch number, where appropriate, in addition to the date and time and signature for the persons involved in these activities.

33    Records should be retained for at least 3 years unless another timeframe is specified in national requirements.

## Production

34    Production of different radioactive products in the same working area (i.e. hot-cell, LAF unit), at the same time should be avoided in order to minimise the risk of radioactive cross-contamination or mix-up.

35    Special attention should be paid to validation including validation of computerised systems which should be carried out in accordance in compliance with Eudralex Volume 4, annex 11. New manufacturing processes should be validated prospectively.

36    The critical parameters should normally be identified before or during validation and the ranges necessary for reproducible operation should be defined.

37    Integrity testing of the membrane filter should be performed for aseptically filled products, taking into account the need for radiation protection and maintenance of filter sterility.

38    Due to radiation exposure it is accepted that most of the labelling of the direct container, is done prior to manufacturing. Sterile empty closed vials may be labelled with partial information prior to filling providing that this procedure does not compromise sterility or prevent visual control of the filled vial.

## Quality Control

39    Some radiopharmaceuticals may have to be distributed and used on the basis of an assessment of batch documentation and before all chemical and microbiology tests have been completed. Radiopharmaceutical product release may be carried out in two or more stages, before and after full analytical testing:

(a) Assessment by a designated person of batch processing records, which should cover production conditions and analytical testing performed thus far, before allowing transportation of the radiopharmaceutical under quarantine status to the clinical department.

(b) Assessment of the final analytical data, ensuring all deviations from normal procedures are documented, justified and appropriately released prior to documented certification by the Qualified Person. Where certain test results are not available before use of the product, the Qualified Person should conditionally certify the product before it is used and should finally certify the product after all the test results are obtained.

40 Most radiopharmaceuticals are intended for use within a short time and the period of validity with regard to the radioactive shelf-life, must be clearly stated.

41 Radiopharmaceuticals having radionuclides with long half-lives should be tested to show, that they meet all relevant acceptance criteria before release and certification by the QP.

42 Before testing is performed samples can be stored to allow sufficient radioactivity decay. All tests including the sterility test should be performed as soon as possible.

43 A written procedure detailing the assessment of production and analytical data, which should be considered before the batch is dispatched, should be established.

44 Products that fail to meet acceptance criteria should be rejected. If the material is reprocessed, pre-established procedures should be followed and the finished product should meet acceptance criteria before release. Returned products may not be reprocessed and must be stored as radioactive waste.

45 A procedure should also describe the measures to be taken by the Qualified Person if unsatisfactory test results (Out-of-Specification) are obtained after dispatch and before expiry. Such events should be investigated to include the relevant corrective and preventative actions taken to prevent future events. This process must be documented.

46 Information should be given to the clinical responsible persons, if necessary. To facilitate this, a traceability system should be implemented for radiopharmaceuticals.

47 A system to verify the quality of starting materials should be in place. Supplier approval should include an evaluation that provides adequate assurance that the material consistently meets specifications. The starting materials, packaging materials and critical process aids should be purchased from approved suppliers.

## Reference and Retention Samples

48    For radiopharmaceuticals sufficient samples of each batch of bulk formulated product shall be retained for at least six months after expiry of the finished medicinal product unless otherwise justified through risk management.

49    Samples of starting materials, other than solvents gases or water used in the manufacturing process shall be retained for at least two years after the release of the product. That period may be shortened if the period of stability of the material as indicated in the relevant specification is shorter.

50    Other conditions may be defined by agreement with the competent authority, for the sampling and retaining of starting materials and products manufactured individually or in small quantities or when their storage could raise special problems.

## Distribution

51    Distribution of the finished product under controlled conditions, before all appropriate test results are available, is acceptable for radiopharmaceuticals, providing the product is not administered by the receiving institute until satisfactory test results has been received and assessed by a designated person.

## Glossary

### PREPARATION

Handling and radiolabelling of kits with radionuclide eluted from generators or radioactive precursors within a hospital. Kits, generators and precursors should have a marketing authorisation or a national licence.

### MANUFACTURING

Production, quality control and release and delivery of radiopharmaceuticals from the active substance and starting materials.

### HOT–CELLS

Shielded workstations for manufacture and handling of radioactive materials. Hot-cells are not necessarily designed as an isolator.

### QUALIFIED PERSON

QP as described in Directives 2001/83/EC and 2001/82/EC. QP responsibilities are elaborated in Eudralex Volume 4, annex 16.

## ANNEX 4 MANUFACTURE OF VETERINARY MEDICINAL PRODUCTS OTHER THAN IMMUNOLOGICAL VETERINARY MEDICINAL PRODUCTS

**Note:** *This annex applies to all veterinary medicinal products falling within the scope of Directive 2001/82/EC other than immunological veterinary medicinal products, which are the subject of a separate annex.*

## Manufacture of Premixes for Medicated Feedingstuffs

For the purposes of these paragraphs,

- *a medicated feedingstuff* is any mixture of a veterinary medicinal product or products and feed or feeds which is ready prepared for marketing and intended to be fed to animals without further processing because of its curative or preventative properties or other properties as a medicinal product covered by Article 1(2) of Directive 2001/82/EC;
- *a pre-mix for medicated feedingstuffs* is any veterinary medicinal product prepared in advance with a view to the subsequent manufacture of medicated feedingstuffs.

1   The manufacture of premixes for medicated feedingstuffs requires the use of large quantities of vegetable matter which is likely to attract insects and rodents. Premises should be designed, equipped and operated to minimise this risk (point 3.4.) and should also be subject to a regular pest control programme.

2   Because of the large volume of dust generated during the production of bulk material for premixes, specific attention should be given to the need to avoid cross-contamination and facilitate cleaning (point 3.14), for example through the installation of sealed transport systems and dust extraction, whenever possible. The installation of such systems does not, however, eliminate the need for regular cleaning of production areas.

3   Parts of the process likely to have a significant adverse influence on the stability of the active ingredient(s) (e.g. use of steam in pellet manufacture) should be carried out in an uniform manner from batch to batch.

4   Consideration should be given to undertake the manufacture of premixes in dedicated areas which, if at all possible, do not form part of a main manufacturing plant. Alternatively, such dedicated areas should be

surrounded by a buffer zone in order to minimise the risk of contamination of other manufacturing areas.

## Manufacture of Ectoparasiticides

5    In derogation from point 3.6, ectoparasiticides for external application to animals, which are veterinary medicinal products, and subject to marketing authorisation, may be produced and filled on a campaign basis in pesticide specific areas. However other categories of veterinary medicinal products should not be produced in such areas.

6    Adequate validated cleaning procedures should be employed to prevent cross-contamination, and steps should be taken to ensure the secure storage of the veterinary medicinal product in accordance with the guide.

## Manufacture of Veterinary Medicinal Products Containing Penicillins

7    The use of penicillins in veterinary medicine does not present the same risks of hypersensitivity in animals as in humans. Although incidents of hypersensitivity have been recorded in horses and dogs, there are other materials which are toxic to certain species, e.g. the ionophore antibiotics in horses. Although desirable, the requirements that such products be manufactured in dedicated, self-contained facilities (point 3.6) may be dispensed with in the case of facilities dedicated to the manufacture of veterinary medicinal products only. However, all necessary measures should be taken to avoid cross-contamination and any risk to operator safety in accordance with the guide. In such circumstances, penicillin-containing products should be manufactured on a campaign basis and should be followed by appropriate, validated decontamination and cleaning procedures.

## Retention of Samples (point 1.4 viii and point 6.14)

8    It is recognised that because of the large volume of certain veterinary medicinal products in their final packaging, in particular premixes, it may not be feasible for manufacturers to retain samples from each batch in its final packaging. However, manufacturers should ensure that sufficient representative samples of each batch are retained and stored in accordance with the guide.

9    In all cases, the container used for storage should be composed of the same material as the market primary container in which the product is marketed.

## Sterile Veterinary Medicinal Products

10 Where this has been accepted by the competent authorities, terminally sterilised veterinary medicinal products may be manufactured in a clean area of a lower grade than the grade required in the annex on "Sterile preparations", but at least in a grade D environment.

# ANNEX 5 MANUFACTURE OF IMMUNOLOGICAL VETERINARY MEDICINAL PRODUCTS

## Principle

The manufacture of immunological veterinary medicinal products has special characteristics which should be taken into consideration when implementing and assessing the quality assurance system.

Due to the large number of animal species and related pathogenic agents, the variety of products manufactured is very wide and the volume of manufacture is often low; hence, work on a campaign basis is common. Moreover, because of the very nature of this manufacture (cultivation steps, lack of terminal sterilisation, etc.), the products must be particularly well-protected against contamination and cross-contamination. The environment also must be protected especially when the manufacture involves the use of pathogenic or exotic biological agents and the worker must be particularly well-protected when the manufacture involves the use of biological agents pathogenic to man.

These factors, together with the inherent variability of immunological products and the relative inefficiency in particular of final product quality control tests in providing adequate information about products, means that the role of the quality assurance system is of the utmost importance. The need to maintain control over all of the following aspects of GMP, as well as those outlined in this Guide, cannot be overemphasised. In particular, it is important that the data generated by the monitoring of the various aspects of GMP (equipment, premises, product etc.) are rigorously assessed and informed decisions, leading to appropriate action, are made and recorded.

## Personnel

1    All personnel (including those concerned with cleaning and maintenance) employed in areas where immunological products are manufactured should be given training in and information on hygiene and microbiology. They should receive additional training specific to the products with which they work.

2    Responsible personnel should be formally trained in some or all of the following fields: bacteriology, biology, biometry, chemistry, immunology, medicine, parasitology, pharmacy, pharmacology, virology and veterinary medicine and should also have an adequate knowledge of environmental protection measures.

3   Personnel should be protected against possible infection with the biological agents used in manufacture. In the case of biological agents known to cause disease in humans, adequate measures should be taken to prevent infection of personnel working with the agent or with experimental animals.

Where relevant, the personnel should be vaccinated and subject to medical examination.

4   Adequate measures should be taken to prevent biological agents being taken outside the manufacturing plant by personnel acting as a carrier. Dependent on the type of biological agent, such measures may include complete change of clothes and compulsory showering before leaving the production area.

5   For immunological products, the risk of contamination or cross-contamination by personnel is particularly important.

Prevention of *contamination* by personnel should be achieved by a set of measures and procedures to ensure that appropriate protective clothing is used during the different stages of the production process.

Prevention of *cross-contamination* by personnel involved in production should be achieved by a set of measures and procedures to ensure that they do not pass from one area to another unless they have taken appropriate measures to eliminate the risk of contamination. In the course of a working day, personnel should not pass from areas where contamination with live micro-organisms is likely or where animals are housed to premises where other products or organisms are handled. If such passage is unavoidable, clearly defined decontamination procedures, including change of clothing and shoes, and, where necessary, showering, should be followed by staff involved in any such production.

Personnel entering a contained area where organisms had not been handled in open circuit operations in the previous twelve hours to check on cultures in sealed, surface decontaminated flasks would not be regarded as being at risk of contamination, unless the organism involved was an exotic.

## Premises

6   Premises should be designed in such a way as to control both the risk to the product and to the environment.

This can be achieved by the use of containment, clean, clean/contained or controlled areas.

7   Live biological agents should be handled in contained areas. The level of containment should depend on the pathogenicity of the micro-organism

and whether it has been classified as exotic. (Other relevant legislation, such as Directives 90/219/EEC[1] and 90/220/EEC,[2] also applies).

8    Inactivated biological agents should be handled in clean areas. Clean areas should also be used when handling non-infected cells isolated from multicellular organisms and, in some cases, filtration-sterilised media.

9    Open circuit operations involving products or components not subsequently sterilised should be carried out within a laminar air flow work station (grade A) in a grade B area.

10   Other operations where live biological agents are handled (quality control, research and diagnostic services, etc.) should be appropriately contained and separated if production operations are carried out in the same building. The level of containment should depend on the pathogenicity of the biological agent and whether they have been classified as exotic. Whenever diagnostic activities are carried out, there is the risk of introducing highly pathogenic organisms. Therefore, the level of containment should be adequate to cope with all such risks. Containment may also be required if quality control or other activities are carried out in buildings in close proximity to those used for production.

11   Containment premises should be easily disinfected and should have the following characteristics:

(a) the absence of direct venting to the outside;
(b) a ventilation with air at negative pressure. Air should be extracted through HEPA filters and not be re circulated except to the same area, and provided further HEPA filtration is used (normally this condition would be met by routing the re circulated air through the normal supply HEPAs for that area). However, recycling of air between areas may be permissible provided that it passes through two exhaust HEPAs, the first of which is continuously monitored for integrity, and there are adequate measures for safe venting of exhaust air should this filter fail;

---

[1] Council Directive 98/81/EC of 26 October 1998 amending Directive 90/219/EEC on the contained use of genetically modified micro-organisms (OJ L 330, 05.12.1998, p. 13–31).

[2] Directive 2001/18/EC of the European Parliament and of the Council of 12 March 2001 on the deliberate release into the environment of genetically modified organisms and repealing Council Directive 90/220/EEC - Commission Declaration (OJ L 106, 17.04.2001, p. 01–39).

(c) air from manufacturing areas used for the handling of exotic organisms should be vented through 2 sets of HEPA filters in series, and that from production areas not re-circulated;

(d) a system for the collection and disinfection of liquid effluents including contaminated condensate from sterilizers, biogenerators, etc. Solid wastes, including animal carcasses, should be disinfected, sterilized or incinerated as appropriate. Contaminated filters should be removed using a safe method;

(e) changing rooms designed and used as air locks, and equipped with washing and showering facilities if appropriate. Air pressure differentials should be such that there is no flow of air between the work area and the external environment or risk of contamination of outer clothing worn outside the area;

(f) an air lock system for the passage of equipment, which is constructed so that there is no flow of contaminated air between the work area and the external environment or risk of contamination of equipment within the lock. The air lock should be of a size which enables the effective surface decontamination of materials being passed through it. Consideration should be given to having a timing device on the door interlock to allow sufficient time for the decontamination process to be effective.

(g) in many instances, a barrier double-door autoclave for the secure removal of waste materials and introduction of sterile items.

12  Equipment passes and changing rooms should have an interlock mechanism or other appropriate system to prevent the opening of more than one door at a time. Changing rooms should be supplied with air filtered to the same standard as that for the work area, and equipped with air extraction facilities to produce an adequate air circulation independent of that of the work area. Equipment passes should normally be ventilated in the same way, but unventilated passes, or those equipped with supply air only, may be acceptable.

13  Production operations such as cell maintenance, media preparation, virus culture, etc. likely to cause contamination should be performed in separate areas. Animals and animal products should be handled with appropriate precautions.

14  Production areas where biological agents particularly resistant to disinfection (e.g. spore-forming bacteria) are handled should be separated and dedicated to that particular purpose until the biological agents have been inactivated.

15  With the exception of blending and subsequent filling operations, one biological agent only should be handled at a time within an area.

16   Production areas should be designed to permit disinfection between campaigns, using validated methods.

17   Production of biological agents may take place in controlled areas provided it is carried out in totally enclosed and heat sterilised equipment, all connections being also heat sterilised after making and before breaking. It may be acceptable for connections to be made under local laminar air flow provided these are few in number and proper aseptic techniques are used and there is no risk of leakage. The sterilisation parameters used before breaking the connections must be validated for the organisms being used. Different products may be placed in different biogenerators, within the same area, provided that there is no risk of accidental cross-contamination. However, organisms generally subject to special requirements for containment should be in areas dedicated to such products.

18   Animal houses where animals intended or used for production are accommodated, should be provided with the appropriate containment and/or clean area measures, and should be separate from other animal accommodation.

Animal houses where animals used for quality control, involving the use of pathogenic biological agents, are accommodated, should be adequately contained.

19   Access to manufacturing areas should be restricted to authorised personnel. Clear and concise written procedures should be posted as appropriate.

20   Documentation relating to the premises should be readily available in a plant master file.

The manufacturing site and buildings should be described in sufficient detail (by means of plans and written explanations) so that the designation and conditions of use of all the rooms are correctly identified as well as the biological agents which are handled in them. The flow of people and product should also be clearly marked.

The animal species accommodated in the animal houses or otherwise on the site should be identified.

The activities carried out in the vicinity of the site should also be indicated. Plans of contained and/or clean area premises, should describe the ventilation system indicating inlets and outlets, filters and their specifications, the number of air changes per hour, and pressure gradients. They should indicate which pressure gradients are monitored by pressure indicator.

## Equipment

21   The equipment used should be designed and constructed so that it meets the particular requirements for the manufacture of each product.

Before being put into operation the equipment should be qualified and validated and subsequently be regularly maintained and validated.

22 Where appropriate, the equipment should ensure satisfactory primary containment of the biological agents.

Where appropriate, the equipment should be designed and constructed as to allow easy and effective decontamination and/or sterilisation.

23 Closed equipment used for the primary containment of the biological agents should be designed and constructed as to prevent any leakage or the formation of droplets and aerosols.

Inlets and outlets for gases should be protected so as to achieve adequate containment e.g. by the use of sterilising hydrophobic filters.

The introduction or removal of material should take place using a sterilisable closed system, or possibly in an appropriate laminar air flow.

24 Equipment where necessary should be properly sterilised before use, preferably by pressurised dry steam. Other methods can be accepted if steam sterilisation cannot be used because of the nature of the equipment. It is important not to overlook such individual items as bench centrifuges and water baths.

Equipment used for purification, separation or concentration should be sterilised or disinfected at least between use for different products. The effect of the sterilisation methods on the effectiveness and validity of the equipment should be studied in order to determine the life span of the equipment.

All sterilisation procedures should be validated.

25 Equipment should be designed so as to prevent any mix-up between different organisms or products. Pipes, valves and filters should be identified as to their function.

Separate incubators should be used for infected and non infected containers and also generally for different organisms or cells. Incubators containing more than one organism or cell type will only be acceptable if adequate steps are taken to seal, surface decontaminate and segregate the containers. Culture vessels, etc. should be individually labelled. The cleaning and disinfection of the items can be particularly difficult and should receive special attention.

Equipment used for the storage of biological agents or products should be designed and used in such a manner as to prevent any possible mix-up. All stored items should be clearly and unambiguously labelled and in leak-proof containers. Items such as cells and organisms seed stock should be stored in dedicated equipment.

26 Relevant equipment, such as that requiring temperature control, should be fitted with recording and/or alarm systems.

To avoid breakdowns, a system of preventive maintenance, together with trend analysis of recorded data, should be implemented.

27 The loading of freeze dryers requires an appropriate clean/contained area.

Unloading freeze dryers contaminates the immediate environment. Therefore, for single-ended freeze dryers, the clean room should be decontaminated before a further manufacturing batch is introduced into the area, unless this contains the same organisms, and double door freeze dryers should be sterilised after each cycle unless opened in a clean area.

Sterilisation of freeze dryers should be done in accordance with item 24. In case of campaign working, they should at least be sterilised after each campaign.

## Animals and Animal Houses

28 General requirements for animal quarters, care and quarantine are laid down in Directive 86/609/EEC[3].

29 Animal houses should be separated from the other production premises and suitably designed.

30 The sanitary status of the animals used for production should be defined, monitored, and recorded. Some animals should be handled as defined in specific monographs (e.g. Specific Pathogen Free flocks).

31 Animals, biological agents, and tests carried out should be the subject of an identification system so as to prevent any risk of confusion and to control all possible hazards.

## Disinfection–Waste Disposal

32 Disinfection and/or wastes and effluents disposal may be particularly important in the case of manufacture of immunological products. Careful consideration should therefore be given to procedures and equipment aiming at avoiding environmental contamination as well as to their validation or qualification.

---

[3] Directive 2003/65/EC of the European Parliament and of the Council of 22 July 2003 amending Council Directive 86/609/EEC on the approximation of laws, regulations and administrative provisions of the Member States regarding the protection of animals used for experimental and other scientific purposes (OJ L 230, 16.09.2003, p. 32–33).

## Production

**33**  Because of the wide variety of products, the frequently large number of stages involved in the manufacture of immunological veterinary medicinal products and the nature of the biological processes, careful attention must be paid to adherence to validated operating procedures, to the constant monitoring of production at all stages and to in-process controls.

Additionally, special consideration should be given to starting materials, media and the use of a seed lot system.

## Starting Materials

**34**  The suitability of starting materials should be clearly defined in written specifications. These should include details of the supplier, the method of manufacture, the geographical origin and animal species from which the materials are derived. The controls to be applied to starting materials must be included. Microbiological controls are particularly important.

**35**  The results of tests on starting materials must comply with the specifications. Where the tests take a long time (e.g. eggs from SPF flocks) it may be necessary to process starting materials before the results of analytical controls are available. In such cases, the release of a finished product is conditional upon satisfactory results of the tests on starting materials.

**36**  Special attention should be paid to a knowledge of the supplier's quality assurance system in assessing the suitability of a source and the extent of quality control testing required.

**37**  Where possible, heat is the preferred method for sterilising starting materials. If necessary, other validated methods, such as irradiation, may be used.

## Media

**38**  The ability of media to support the desired growth should be properly validated in advance.

**39**  Media should preferably be sterilised in situ or in line. Heat is the preferred method. Gases, media, acids, alkalis, defoaming agents and other materials introduced into sterile biogenerators should themselves be sterile.

## Seed lot and cell bank system

**40**  In order to prevent the unwanted drift of properties which might ensue from repeated subcultures or multiple generations, the production of immunological veterinary medicinal products obtained by microbial, cell or tissue culture, or propagation in embryos and animals, should be based on a system of seed lots or cell banks.

41    The number of generations (doublings, passages) between the seed lot or cell bank and the finished product should be consistent with the dossier of authorisation for marketing.

42    Seed lots and cell banks should be adequately characterised and tested for contaminants. Acceptance criteria for new seed lots should be established. Seed lots and cell banks shall be established, stored and used in such a way as to minimise the risks of contamination, or any alteration. During the establishment of the seed lot and cell bank, no other living or infectious material (e.g. virus or cell lines) shall be handled simultaneously in the same area or by the same person.

43    Establishment of the seed lot and cell bank should be performed in a suitable environment to protect the seed lot and the cell bank and, if applicable, the personnel handling it and the external environment.

44    The origin, form and storage conditions of seed material should be described in full. Evidence of the stability and recovery of the seeds and cells should be provided. Storage containers should be hermetically sealed, clearly labelled and stored at an appropriate temperature. Storage conditions shall be properly monitored. An inventory should be kept and each container accounted for.

45    Only authorised personnel should be allowed to handle the material and this handling should be done under the supervision of a responsible person. Different seed lots or cell banks shall be stored in such a way to avoid confusion or cross-contamination errors. It is desirable to split the seed lots and cell banks and to store the parts at different locations so as to minimise the risk of total loss.

## Operating principles

46    The formation of droplets and the production of foam should be avoided or minimised during manufacturing processes. Centrifugation and blending procedures which can lead to droplet formation should be carried out in appropriate contained or clean/contained areas to prevent transfer of live organisms.

47    Accidental spillages, especially of live organisms, must be dealt with quickly and safely. Validated decontamination measures should be available for each organism. Where different strains of single bacteria species or very similar viruses are involved, the process need be validated

against only one of them, unless there is reason to believe that they may vary significantly in their resistance to the agent(s) involved.

48   Operations involving the transfer of materials such as sterile media, cultures or product should be carried out in pre-sterilised closed systems wherever possible. Where this is not possible, transfer operations must be protected by laminar airflow work stations.

49   Addition of media or cultures to biogenerators and other vessels should be carried out under carefully controlled conditions to ensure that contamination is not introduced. Care must be taken to ensure that vessels are correctly connected when addition of cultures takes place.

50   Where necessary, for instance when two or more fermenters are within a single area, sampling and addition ports, and connectors (after connection, before the flow of product, and again before disconnection) should be sterilised with steam. In other circumstances, chemical disinfection of ports and laminar air flow protection of connections may be acceptable.

51   Equipment, glassware, the external surfaces of product containers and other such materials must be disinfected before transfer from a contained area using a validated method (see item 47 above). Batch documentation can be a particular problem. Only the absolute minimum required to allow operations to GMP standards should enter and leave the area. If obviously contaminated, such as by spills or aerosols, or if the organism involved is an exotic, the paperwork must be adequately disinfected through an equipment pass, or the information transferred out by such means as photocopy or fax.

52   Liquid or solid wastes such as the debris after harvesting eggs, disposable culture bottles, unwanted cultures or biological agents, are best sterilised or disinfected before transfer from a contained area. However, alternatives such as sealed containers or piping may be appropriate in some cases.

53   Articles and materials, including documentation, entering a production room should be carefully controlled to ensure that only articles and materials concerned with production are introduced. There should be a system which ensures that articles and materials entering a room are reconciled with those leaving so that their accumulation within the room does not occur.

54   Heat stable articles and materials entering a clean area or clean/contained area should do so through a double-ended autoclave or oven. Heat labile articles and materials should enter through an air-lock with interlocked doors where they are disinfected. Sterilisation of articles and materials elsewhere is acceptable provided that they are double wrapped and enter through an airlock with the appropriate precautions.

55    Precautions must be taken to avoid contamination or confusion during incubation. There should be a cleaning and disinfection procedure for incubators. Containers in incubators should be carefully and clearly labelled.

56    With the exception of blending and subsequent filling operations (or when totally enclosed systems are used) only one live biological agent may be handled within a production room at any given time. Production rooms must be effectively disinfected between the handling of different live biological agents.

57    Products should be inactivated by the addition of inactivant accompanied by sufficient agitation. The mixture should then be transferred to a second sterile vessel, unless the container is of such a size and shape as to be easily inverted and shaken so as to wet all internal surfaces with the final culture/inactivant mixture.

58    Vessels containing inactivated products should not be opened or sampled in areas containing live biological agents. All subsequent processing of inactivated products should take place in clean areas grade A-B or enclosed equipment dedicated to inactivated products.

59    Careful consideration should be given to the validation of methods for sterilisation, disinfection, virus removal and inactivation.

60    Filling should be carried out as soon as possible following production. Containers of bulk product prior to filling should be sealed, appropriately labelled and stored under specified conditions of temperature.

61    There should be a system to assure the integrity and closure of containers after filling.

62    The capping of vials containing live biological agents must be performed in such a way that ensures that contamination of other products or escape of the live agents into other areas or the external environment does not occur.

63    For various reasons there may be a delay between the filling of final containers and their labelling and packaging. Procedures should be specified for the storage of unlabelled containers in order to prevent confusion and to ensure satisfactory storage conditions. Special attention should be paid to the storage of heat labile or photosensitive products. Storage temperatures should be specified.

64    For each stage of production, the yield of product should be reconciled with that expected from that process. Any significant discrepancies should be investigated.

## Quality Control

**65** In-process controls play a specially important role in ensuring the consistency of the quality of biological medicinal products. Those controls which are crucial for the quality (e.g. virus removal) but which cannot be carried out on the finished product, should be performed at an appropriate stage of production.

**66** It may be necessary to retain samples of intermediate products in sufficient amount and under appropriate storage conditions to allow repetition or confirmation of a batch control.

**67** There may be a requirement for the continuous monitoring of data during a production process, for example monitoring of physical parameters during fermentation.

**68** Continuous culture of biological products is a common practice and special consideration needs to be given to the quality control requirements arising from this type of production method.

# ANNEX 6 MANUFACTURE OF MEDICINAL GASES

## Principle

Gases which fulfil the definition of medicinal product of Directive 2001/83/EC or Directive 2001/82/EC (hereinafter, medicinal gases) are subject to the requirements laid down in these Directives, including the requirements on manufacturing. In this regard, this Annex deals with the manufacture of active substance gases and with the manufacture of medicinal gases.

The delineation between the manufacture of the active substance and the manufacture of the medicinal product should be clearly defined in each Marketing Authorisation dossier. Normally, the production and purification steps of the gas belong to the field of manufacture of active substances. Gases enter the pharmaceutical field from the first storage of gas intended for such use.

Manufacture of active substance gases should comply with the Basic Requirements of this guide (Part II), with the relevant part of this Annex, and with the other Annexes of the guide if relevant.

Manufacture of medicinal gases should comply with the Basic Requirements of this guide (Part I), with the relevant part of this Annex, and with the other Annexes of the guide if relevant.

In the exceptional cases of continuous processes where no intermediate storage of gas between the manufacture of the active substance and the manufacture of the medicinal product is possible, the whole process (from starting materials of active substance to medicinal finished product) should be considered as belonging to the pharmaceutical field. This should be clearly stated in the Marketing Authorisation dossier.

The Annex does not cover the manufacture and handling of medicinal gases in hospitals unless this is considered industrial preparation or manufacturing. However, relevant parts of this Annex may be used as a basis for such activities.

## Manufacture of Active Substance Gases

Active substance gases can be prepared by chemical synthesis or be obtained from natural sources followed by purification steps, if necessary (as for example in an air separation plant).

1   The processes corresponding to these two methods of manufacturing active substance gases should comply with Part II of the Basic Requirements. However:

(a) the requirements regarding starting materials for active substances (Part II Chapter 7) do not apply to the production of active substance gases by air separation (however, the manufacturer should ensure that the quality of ambient air is suitable for the established process and any changes in the quality of ambient air do not affect the quality of the active substance gas);

(b) the requirements regarding on-going stability studies (Part II chapter 11.5), which are used to confirm storage conditions and expiry/retest dates (Part II chapter 11.6), do not apply in case initial stability studies have been replaced by bibliographic data (see Note for Guidance CPMP/QWP/1719/00); and

(c) the requirements regarding reserve/retention samples (Part II chapter 11.7) do not apply to active substance gases, unless otherwise specified.

2 The production of active substance gases through a continuous process (e.g. air separation) should be continuously monitored for quality. The results of this monitoring should be kept in a manner permitting trend evaluation.

3 In addition:

(a) transfers and deliveries of active substance gases in bulk should comply with the same requirements as those mentioned below for the medicinal gases (sections 19 to 21 of this Annex);

(b) filling of active substance gases into cylinders or into mobile cryogenic vessels should comply with the same requirements as those mentioned below for the medicinal gases (sections 22 to 37 of this Annex) as well as Part II Chapter 9.

## Manufacture of Medicinal Gases

Manufacture of medicinal gases is generally carried out in closed equipment. Consequently, environmental contamination of the product is minimal. However, risks of contamination (or cross contamination with other gases) may arise, in particular because of the reuse of containers.

4 Requirements applying to cylinders should also apply to cylinders bundles (except storage and transportation under cover).

## Personnel

5 All personnel involved in manufacture and distribution of medicinal gases should receive an appropriate GMP training specifically applying to this type of products. They should be aware of the critically important aspects and potential hazards for patients from these products. The training programs should include the tanker lorries drivers.

6   Personnel of subcontractors that could influence the quality of medicinal gases (such as personnel in charge of maintenance of cylinders or valves) should be appropriately trained.

## Premises and equipment

PREMISES

7   Cylinders and mobile cryogenic vessels should be checked, prepared, filled and stored in separate areas from non-medicinal gases, and there should be no exchange of cylinders / mobile cryogenic vessels between these areas. However, it could be accepted to check, prepare, fill and store other gases in the same areas, provided they comply with the specifications of medicinal gases and that the manufacturing operations are performed according to GMP standards.

8   Premises should provide sufficient space for manufacturing, testing and storage operations in order to prevent any risk of mix-up. Premises should be designed to provide:

(a) separate marked areas for different gases;
(b) clear identification and segregation of cylinders/mobile cryogenic vessels at various stages of processing (e.g. "waiting checking" "awaiting filling", "quarantine", "certified", "rejected" "prepared deliveries").

The method used to achieve these various levels of segregation will depend on the nature, extent and complexity of the overall operation. Marked-out floor areas, partitions, barriers, signs, labels or other appropriate means could be used.

9   Empty cylinders/home cryogenic vessels after sorting or maintenance, and filled cylinders/home cryogenic vessels should be stored under cover, protected from adverse weather conditions. Filled cylinders/mobile cryogenic vessels should be stored in a manner that ensures that they will be delivered in a clean state, compatible with the environment in which they will be used.

10  Specific storage conditions should be provided as required by the Marketing Authorisation (e.g. for gas mixtures where phase separation occurs on freezing).

EQUIPMENT

11  Equipment should be designed to ensure the correct gas is filled into the correct container. There should normally be no cross connections between pipelines carrying different gases. If cross connections are needed (e.g.

filling equipment of mixtures), qualification should ensure that there is no risk of cross contamination between the different gases. In addition, the manifolds should be equipped with specific connections. These connections may be subject to national or international standards. The use of connections meeting different standards at the same filling site should be carefully controlled, as well as the use of adaptors needed in some situations to bypass the specific fill connection systems.

12   Tanks and tankers should be dedicated to a single and defined quality of gas. However medicinal gases may be stored or transported in the same tanks, other containers used for intermediate storage, or tankers, as the same non-medicinal gas, provided that the quality of the latter is at least equal to the quality of the medicinal gas and that GMP standards are maintained. In such cases, quality risk management should be performed and documented.

13   A common system supplying gas to medicinal and non-medicinal gas manifolds is only acceptable if there is a validated method to prevent backflow from the non-medicinal gas line to the medicinal gas line.

14   Filling manifolds should be dedicated to a single medicinal gas or to a given mixture of medicinal gases. In exceptional cases, filling gases used for other medical purposes on manifolds dedicated to medicinal gases may be acceptable if justified and performed under control. In these cases, the quality of the non-medicinal gas should be at least equal to the required quality of the medicinal gas and GMP standards should be maintained. Filling should then be carried out by campaigns.

15   Repair and maintenance operations (including cleaning and purging) of equipment, should not adversely affect the quality of medicinal gases. In particular, procedures should describe the measures to be taken after repair and maintenance operations involving breaches of the system's integrity. Specifically it should be demonstrated that the equipment is free from any contamination that may adversely affect the quality of the finished product before releasing it for use. Records should be maintained.

16   A procedure should describe the measures to be taken when a tanker is back into medicinal gas service (after transporting non-medicinal gas in the conditions mentioned in section 12, or after a maintenance operation). This should include analytical testing.

## Documentation

17   Data included in the records for each batch of cylinders/mobile cryogenic vessels must ensure that each filled container is traceable to significant

aspects of the relevant filling operations. As appropriate, the following should be entered:

(a) name of the product;

(b) batch number;

(c) date and time of the filling operation;

(d) identification of the person(s) carrying out each significant step (e.g. line clearance, receipt, preparation before filling, filling etc.);

(e) batch(es) reference(s) for the gas(es) used for the filling operation as referred to in section 22, including status;

(f) equipment used (e.g. filling manifold);

(g) quantity of cylinders/mobile cryogenic vessels before filling, including individual identification references and water capacity(ies);

(h) pre-filling operations performed (see section 30);

(i) key parameters that are needed to ensure correct filling at standard conditions;

(j) results of appropriate checks to ensure the cylinders/mobile cryogenic vessels have been filled;

(k) a sample of the batch label;

(l) specification of the finished product and results of quality control tests (including reference to the calibration status of the test equipment);

(m) quantity of rejected cylinders/mobile cryogenic vessels, with individual identification references and reasons for rejections;

(n) details of any problems or unusual events, and signed authorisation for any deviation from filling instructions; and

(o) certification statement by the Qualified Person, date and signature.

18    Records should be maintained for each batch of gas intended to be delivered into hospital tanks. These records should, as appropriate, include the following (items to be recorded may vary depending on local legislation):

(a) name of the product;

(b) batch number;

(c) identification reference for the tank (tanker) in which the batch is certified;

(d) date and time of the filling operation;

(e) identification of the person(s) carrying out the filling of the tank (tanker);

(f) reference to the supplying tanker (tank), reference to the source gas as applicable;

(g) relevant details concerning the filling operation;

(h) specification of the finished product and results of quality control tests (including reference to the calibration status of the test equipment);

(i) details of any problems or unusual events, and signed authorisation for any deviation from filling instructions; and

(j) certification statement by the Qualified Person, date and signature.

## Production

### TRANSFERS AND DELIVERIES OF CRYOGENIC AND LIQUEFIED GAS

19  The transfers of cryogenic or liquefied gases from primary storage, including controls before transfers, should be in accordance with validated procedures designed to avoid the possibility of contamination. Transfer lines should be equipped with non-return valves or other suitable alternatives. Flexible connections, coupling hoses and connectors should be flushed with the relevant gas before use.

20  The transfer hoses used to fill tanks and tankers should be equipped with product-specific connections. The use of adaptors allowing the connection of tanks and tankers not dedicated to the same gases should be adequately controlled.

21  Deliveries of gas may be added to tanks containing the same defined quality of gas provided that a sample is tested to ensure that the quality of the delivered gas is acceptable. This sample may be taken from the gas to be delivered or from the receiving tank after delivery.

   *Note: See specific arrangements in section 42 for filling of tanks retained by customers at the customer's premises.*

### FILLING AND LABELLING OF CYLINDERS AND MOBILE CRYOGENIC VESSELS

22  Before filling cylinders and mobile cryogenic vessels, a batch (batches) of gas(es) should be determined, controlled according to specifications and approved for filling.

23  In the case of continuous processes as those mentioned in 'Principle', there should be adequate in-process controls to ensure that the gas complies with specifications.

24  Cylinders, mobile cryogenic vessels and valves should conform to appropriate technical specifications and any relevant requirements of the Marketing Authorisation. They should be dedicated to a single medicinal gas or to a given mixture of medicinal gases. Cylinders should be colour-coded according to relevant standards. They should preferably be fitted with minimum pressure retention valves with non-return mechanism in order to provide adequate protection against contamination.

25  Cylinders, mobile cryogenic vessels and valves should be checked before first use in production, and should be properly maintained. Where CE marked medical devices are used, the maintenance should address the medical device manufacturer's instructions.

26  Checks and maintenance operations should not affect the quality and the safety of the medicinal product. The water used for the hydrostatic pressure testing carried out on cylinders should be at least of drinking quality.

27  As part of the checks and maintenance operations, cylinders should be subject to an internal visual inspection before fitting the valve, to make sure they are not contaminated with water or other contaminants. This should be done:

- when they are new and initially put into medicinal gas service;
- following any hydrostatic statutory pressure test or equivalent test where the valve is removed;
- whenever the valve is replaced.

After fitting, the valve should be kept closed to prevent any contamination from entering the cylinder. If there is any doubt about the internal condition of the cylinder, the valve should be removed and the cylinder internally inspected to ensure it has not been contaminated.

28  Maintenance and repair operations of cylinders, mobile cryogenic vessels and valves are the responsibility of the manufacturer of the medicinal product. If subcontracted, they should only be carried out by approved subcontractors, and contracts including technical agreements should be established. Subcontractors should be audited to ensure that appropriate standards are maintained.

29  There should be a system to ensure the traceability of cylinders, mobile cryogenic vessels and valves.

30  Checks to be performed before filling should include:

(a) in the case of cylinders, a check, carried out according to defined procedure, to ensure there is a positive residual pressure in each cylinder;
  - if the cylinder is fitted with a minimum pressure retention valve, when there is no signal indicating there is a positive residual pressure, the correct functioning of the valve should be checked, and if the valve is shown not to function properly the cylinder should be sent to maintenance,
  - if the cylinder is not fitted with a minimum pressure retention valve, when there is no positive residual pressure the cylinder should be put aside for additional measures, to make sure it is not contaminated

with water or other contaminants; additional measures could consist of internal visual inspection followed by cleaning using a validated method;

(**b**) a check to ensure that all previous batch labels have been removed;

(**c**) a check that any damaged product labels have been removed and replaced;

(**d**) a visual external inspection of each cylinder, mobile cryogenic vessel and valve for dents, arc burns, debris, other damage and contamination with oil or grease; cleaning should be done if necessary;

(**e**) a check of each cylinder or mobile cryogenic vessel outlet connection to determine that it is the proper type for the particular gas involved;

(**f**) a check of the date of the next test to be performed on the valve (in the case of valves that need to be periodically tested);

(**g**) a check of the cylinders or mobile cryogenic vessels to ensure that any tests required by national or international regulations (e.g. hydrostatic pressure test or equivalent for cylinders) have been conducted and are still valid; and

(**h**) a check to determine that each cylinder is colour-coded as specified in the Marketing Authorisation (colour-coding of the relevant national/international standards).

31   A batch should be defined for filling operations.

32   Cylinders that have been returned for refilling should be prepared with care in order to minimise the risks of contamination, in line with the procedures defined in the Marketing Authorisation. These procedures, which should include evacuation and/or purging operations, should be validated.

*Note: For compressed gases, a maximum theoretical impurity of 500 ppm v/v should be obtained for a filling pressure of 200 bar at 15°C (and equivalent for other filling pressures).*

33   Mobile cryogenic vessels that have been returned for refilling should be prepared with care in order to minimise the risks of contamination, in line with the procedures defined in the Marketing Authorisation. In particular, mobile vessels with no residual pressure should be prepared using a validated method.

34   There should be appropriate checks to ensure that each cylinder/mobile cryogenic vessel has been properly filled.

35   Each filled cylinder should be tested for leaks using an appropriate method, prior to fitting the tamper evident seal (see section 36). The test method should not introduce any contaminant into the valve outlet and, if applicable, should be performed after any quality sample is taken.

36   After filling, cylinders valves should be fitted with covers to protect the outlets from contamination. Cylinders and mobile cryogenic vessels should be fitted with tamper-evident seals.

37   Each cylinder or mobile cryogenic vessel should be labelled. The batch number and the expiry date may be on a separate label.

38   In the case of medicinal gases produced by mixing two or more different gases (in-line before filling or directly into the cylinders); the mixing process should be validated to ensure that the gases are properly mixed in every cylinder and that the mixture is homogeneous.

## Quality control

39   Each batch of medicinal gas (cylinders, mobile cryogenic vessels, hospital tanks) should be tested in accordance with the requirements of the Marketing Authorisation and certified.

40   Unless different provisions are required in the Marketing Authorisation, the sampling plan and the analysis to be performed should comply, in the case of cylinders with the following requirements.

(a) In the case of a single medicinal gas filled into cylinders via a multi-cylinder manifold, the gas from at least one cylinder from each manifold filling cycle should be tested for identity and assay each time the cylinders are changed on the manifold.

(b) In the case of a single medicinal gas filled into cylinders one at a time, the gas from at least one cylinder of each uninterrupted filling cycle should be tested for identity and assay. An example of an uninterrupted filling cycle is one shift's production using the same personnel, equipment, and batch of gas to be filled.

(c) In the case of a medicinal gas produced by mixing two or more gases in a cylinder from the same manifold, the gas from every cylinder should be tested for assay and identity of each component gas. For excipients, if any, testing on identity could be performed on one cylinder per manifold filling cycle (or per uninterrupted filling cycle in case of cylinders filled one at a time). Fewer cylinders may be tested in case of validated automated filling system.

(d) Premixed gases should follow the same principles as single gases when continuous in-line testing of the mixture to be filled is performed.
Premixed gases should follow the same principle as medicinal gases produced by mixing gases in the cylinders when there is no continuous in-line testing of the mixture to be filled.

Testing for water content should be performed unless otherwise justified. Other sampling and testing procedures that provide at least equivalent level of quality assurance may be justified.

41    Unless different provisions are required in the Marketing Authorisation, final testing on mobile cryogenic vessels should include a test for assay and identity on each vessel. Testing by batches should only be carried out if it has been demonstrated that the critical attributes of the gas remaining in each vessel before refilling have been maintained.

42    Cryogenic vessels retained by customers (hospital tanks or home cryogenic vessels), which are refilled in place from dedicated tankers do not need to be sampled after filling provided that a certificate of analysis on the contents of the tanker accompanies the delivery. However, it should be demonstrated that the specification of the gas in the vessels is maintained over the successive refillings.

43    Reference and retention samples are not required, unless otherwise specified.

44    On-going stability studies are not required in case initial stability studies have been replaced by bibliographic data (see Note for Guidance CPMP/ QWP/1719/00).

## Transportation of packaged gases

45    Filled gas cylinders and home cryogenic vessels should be protected during transportation, so that, in particular, they are delivered to customers in a clean state compatible with the environment in which they will be used.

## Glossary

### ACTIVE SUBSTANCE GAS
Any gas intended to be an active substance for a medicinal product.

### AIR SEPARATION
Separation of atmospheric air into its constituent gases using fractional distillation at cryogenic temperatures.

### COMPRESSED GAS
Gas which, when packaged under pressure for transport, is entirely gaseous at all temperatures above −50°C.

### CONTAINER

A container is a cryogenic vessel (tank, tanker or other type of mobile cryogenic vessel) a cylinder, a cylinder bundle or any other package that is in direct contact with the gas.

### CRYOGENIC GAS

A gas which liquefies at 1.013 bar at temperatures below −150°C.

### CYLINDER

Container usually cylindrical suited for compressed, liquefied or dissolved gas, fitted with a device to regulate the spontaneous outflow of gas at atmospheric pressure and room temperature.

### CYLINDER BUNDLE

An assembly of cylinders that are fastened together, interconnected by a manifold and transported and used as a unit.

### EVACUATE

To remove the residual gas from a container / system to a pressure less than 1.013 bar, using a vacuum system.

### GAS

Any substance that is completely gaseous at 1.013 bar and +20°C or has a vapour pressure exceeding 3 bar at +50°C.

### HOME CRYOGENIC VESSEL

Mobile cryogenic vessel designed to hold liquid oxygen and dispense gaseous oxygen at patients' home.

### HYDROSTATIC PRESSURE TEST

Test performed as required by national or international regulations, in order to ensure that pressure containers are able to withstand pressures up to the container's design pressure.

### LIQUEFIED GAS

A gas which, when packaged for transport, is partially liquid (or solid) at a temperature above −50°C.

### MANIFOLD

Equipment or apparatus designed to enable one or more gas containers to be emptied and filled at the same time.

### MAXIMUM THEORETICAL RESIDUAL IMPURITY

Gaseous impurity from a possible backflow that remains after the cylinder pre-treatment process before filling. The calculation of the maximum theoretical residual impurity is only relevant for compressed gases and assumes that the gases behave as perfect gases.

## MEDICINAL GAS

Any gas or mixture of gases classified as a medicinal product (as defined in Directives 2001/83/EC and 2001/82/EC).

## MINIMUM PRESSURE RETENTION VALVE

A cylinder valve, which maintains a positive pressure above atmospheric pressure in a gas cylinder after use, in order to prevent internal contamination of the cylinder.

## MOBILE CRYOGENIC VESSEL

Mobile thermally insulated container designed to maintain the contents in a liquid state. In the Annex, this term does not include the tankers.

## NON-RETURN VALVE

Valve, which permits flow in one direction only.

## PURGE

To remove the residual gas from a container / system by first pressurising and then venting the gas used for purging to 1.013 bar.

## TANK

Static thermally insulated container designed for the storage of liquefied or cryogenic gas. They are also called "Fixed cryogenic vessels".

## TANKER

In the context of the Annex, thermally insulated container fixed on a vehicle for the transport of liquefied or cryogenic gas.

## VALVE

Device for opening and closing containers.

## VENT

To remove the residual gas from a container / system down to 1.013 bar, by opening the container / system to atmosphere.

# ANNEX 7 MANUFACTURE OF HERBAL MEDICINAL PRODUCTS

## Principle

Because of their often complex and variable nature, control of starting materials, storage and processing assume particular importance in the manufacture of herbal medicinal products.

The "starting material" in the manufacture of a herbal medicinal product[1] can be a medicinal plant, a herbal substance[2] or a herbal preparation[1]. The herbal substance shall be of suitable quality and supporting data should be provided to the manufacturer of the herbal preparation/herbal medicinal product. Ensuring consistent quality of the herbal substance may require more detailed information on its agricultural production. The selection of seeds, cultivation and harvesting conditions represent important aspects of the quality of the herbal substance and can influence the consistency of the finished product. Recommendations on an appropriate quality assurance system for good agricultural and collection practice are provided in the HMPC guidance document: "Guideline on Good Agricultural and Collection Practice for starting materials of herbal origin".

This Annex applies to all herbal starting materials: medicinal plants, herbal substances or herbal preparations.

---

[1] Throughout the annex and unless otherwise specified, the term "herbal medicinal product/ preparation" includes "traditional herbal medicinal product/ preparation".

[2] The terms herbal substance and herbal preparation as defined in Directive 2004/24/EC are considered to be equivalent to the Ph. Eur. terms herbal drug and herbal drug preparation respectively.

**Table** Illustrating the application of Good Practices to the manufacture of herbal medicinal products.[3]

| Activity | Good Agricultural and Collection Practice (GACP)[4] | Part II of the GMP Guide[†] | Part I of the GMP Guide[†] |
|---|---|---|---|
| Cultivation, collection and harvesting of plants, algae, fungi and lichens, and collection of exudates | | | |
| Cutting, and drying of plants, algae, fungi, lichens and exudates* | | | |
| Expression from plants and distillation** | | | |
| Comminution, processing of exudates, extraction from plants, fractionation, purification, concentration or fermentation of herbal substances | | | |
| Further processing into a dosage form including packaging as a medicinal product | | | |

†Explanatory Note. The GMP classification of the herbal material is dependent upon the use made of it by the manufacturing authorisation holder. The material may be classified as an active substance, an intermediate or a finished product. It is the responsibility of the manufacturer of the medicinal product to ensure that the appropriate GMP classification is applied.

*Manufacturers should ensure that these steps are carried out in accordance with the marketing authorisation/registration. For those initial steps that take place in the field, as justified in the marketing authorisation/registration, the standards of Good Agricultural and Collection Practice for starting materials of herbal origin (GACP) is applicable. GMP is applicable to further cutting and drying steps.

**Regarding the expression from plants and distillation, if it is necessary for these activities to be an integral part of harvesting to maintain the quality of the product within the approved specifications, it is acceptable that they are performed in the field, provided that the cultivation is in compliance with GACP. These circumstances should be regarded as exceptional and justified in the relevant marketing authorisation/registration documentation. For activities carried out in the field, appropriate documentation, control, and validation according to the GMP principles should be assured. Regulatory authorities may carry out GMP inspections of these activities in order to assess compliance.

---

[3] This table expands in detail the herbal section of Table 1 in part II of the GMP Guide.

[4] As published by the European Medicines Agency EMEA.

EU GMP GUIDE PART I ANNEX 7 MANUFACTURE OF HERBAL MEDICINAL PRODUCTS

## Premises & Equipment

### Storage areas

1    Herbal substances should be stored in separate areas. The storage area should be equipped in such a way as to give protection against the entry of insects or other animals, especially rodents. Effective measures should be taken to prevent the spread of any such animals and micro-organisms brought in with the herbal substance, to prevent fermentation or mould growth and to prevent cross-contamination. Different enclosed areas should be used to quarantine incoming herbal substances and for the approved herbal substances.

2    The storage area should be well aerated and the containers should be located in such a way so as to allow free circulation of air.

3    Special attention should be paid to the cleanliness and maintenance of the storage areas particularly when dust is generated.

4    Storage of herbal substances and herbal preparations may require special conditions of humidity, temperature or light protection; these conditions should be provided and monitored.

### Production area

5    Specific provisions should be made during sampling, weighing, mixing and processing operations of herbal substances and herbal preparations whenever dust is generated, to facilitate cleaning and to avoid cross-contamination, as for example, dust extraction, dedicated premises, etc.

## Equipment

6    The equipment, filtering materials etc. used in the manufacturing process must be compatible with the extraction solvent, in order to prevent any release or undesirable absorption of substance that could affect the product.

## Documentation

### Specifications for starting materials

7    Herbal medicinal product manufacturers must ensure that they use only herbal starting materials manufactured in accordance with GMP and the Marketing Authorisation dossier. Comprehensive documentation on

audits of the herbal starting material suppliers carried out by, or on behalf of the herbal medicinal product manufacturer should be made available. Audit trails for the active substance are fundamental to the quality of the starting material. The manufacturer should ensure that the suppliers of the herbal substance/preparation are in compliance with Good Agricultural and Collection Practice.

8    To fulfil the specification requirements described in the basic requirements of the Guide (chapter 4), documentation for herbal substances/ preparations should include:

- the binomial scientific name of plant (genus, species, subspecies/variety and author (e.g. Linnaeus); other relevant information such as the cultivar name and the chemotype should also be provided, as appropriate;
- details of the source of the plant (country or region of origin, and where applicable, cultivation, time of harvesting, collection procedures, possible pesticides used, possible radioactive contamination etc.);
- which part(s) of the plant is/are used;
- when a dried plant is used, the drying system should be specified;
- a description of the herbal substance and its macro and microscopic examination;
- suitable identification tests including, where appropriate, identification tests for constituents with known therapeutic activity, or markers. Specific distinctive tests are required where an herbal substance is liable to be adulterated/substituted. A reference authentic specimen should be available for identification purposes;
- the water content for herbal substances, determined in accordance with the European Pharmacopoeia;
- assay of constituents of known therapeutic activity or, where appropriate, of markers;
- the methods suitable to determine possible pesticide contamination and limits accepted in accordance with European Pharmacopoeia methods or, in absence thereof, with an appropriate validated method, unless otherwise justified;
- tests to determine fungal and/or microbial contamination, including aflatoxins, other mycotoxins, pest-infestations and limits accepted, as appropriate;
- tests for toxic metals and for likely contaminants and adulterants, as appropriate;
- tests for foreign materials, as appropriate.
- any other additional test according to the European Pharmacopoeia general monograph on herbal substances or to the specific monograph of the herbal substance, as appropriate.

EU GMP GUIDE PART I ANNEX 7 MANUFACTURE OF HERBAL MEDICINAL PRODUCTS

Any treatment used to reduce fungal/microbial contamination or other infestation should be documented. Specifications and procedures should be available and should include details of process, tests and limits for residues.

## Processing Instructions

9   The processing instructions should describe the different operations carried out upon the herbal substance such as cleaning, drying, crushing and sifting, and include drying time and temperatures, and methods used to control cut size or particle size.

10  In particular, there should be written instructions and records, which ensure that each container of herbal substance is carefully examined to detect any adulteration/substitution or presence of foreign matter, such as metal or glass pieces, animal parts or excrement, stones, sand, etc., or rot and signs of decay.

11  The processing instructions should also describe security sieving or other methods of removing foreign materials and appropriate procedures for cleaning/selection of plant material before the storage of the approved herbal substance or before the start of manufacturing.

12  For the production of an herbal preparation, instructions should include details of solvent, time and temperature of extraction, details of any concentration stages and methods used.

## Quality Control

## Sampling

13  Due to the fact that medicinal plant/herbal substances are heterogeneous in nature, their sampling should be carried out with special care by personnel with particular expertise. Each batch should be identified by its own documentation.

14  A reference sample of the plant material is necessary, especially in those cases where the herbal substance is not described in the European Pharmacopoeia or in another Pharmacopoeia of a Member State. Samples of unmilled plant material are required if powders are used.

15  Quality Control personnel should have particular expertise and experience in herbal substances, herbal preparations and/or herbal medicinal products in order to be able to carry out identification tests and recognise adulteration, the presence of fungal growth, infestations, non-uniformity within a delivery of crude material, etc.

**16** The identity and quality of herbal substances, herbal preparations and of herbal medicinal products should be determined in accordance with the relevant current European guidance on quality and specifications of herbal medicinal products and traditional herbal medicinal products and, where relevant, to the specific Ph. Eur. Monographs.

# ANNEX 8 SAMPLING OF STARTING AND PACKAGING MATERIALS

## Principle

Sampling is an important operation in which only a small fraction of a batch is taken. Valid conclusions on the whole cannot be based on tests which have been carried out on non-representative samples. Correct sampling is thus an essential part of a system of Quality Assurance.

> **Note:** *Sampling is dealt with in Chapter 6 of the Guide, items 6.11–6.14. This annex gives additional guidance on the sampling of starting and packaging materials.*

## Personnel

1    Personnel who take samples should receive initial and on-going regular training in the disciplines relevant to correct sampling. This training should include:

- sampling plans;
- written sampling procedures;
- the techniques and equipment for sampling;
- the risks of cross-contamination;
- the precautions to be taken with regard to unstable and/or sterile substances;
- the importance of considering the visual appearance of materials, containers and labels;
- the importance of recording any unexpected or unusual circumstances.

## Starting Materials

2    The identity of a complete batch of starting materials can normally only be ensured if individual samples are taken from all the containers and an identity test performed on each sample. It is permissible to sample only a proportion of the containers where a validated procedure has been established to ensure that no single container of starting material has been incorrectly labelled.

3    This validation should take account of at least the following aspects:

- the nature and status of the manufacturer and of the supplier and their understanding of the GMP requirements of the Pharmaceutical Industry;
- the Quality Assurance system of the manufacturer of the starting material;
- the manufacturing conditions under which the starting material is produced and controlled;
- the nature of the starting material and the medicinal products in which it will be used.

Under such a system, it is possible that a validated procedure exempting identity testing of each incoming container of starting material could be accepted for:

- starting materials coming from a single product manufacturer or plant;
- starting materials coming directly from a manufacturer or in the manufacturer's sealed container where there is a history of reliability and regular audits of the manufacturer's Quality Assurance system are conducted by the purchaser (the manufacturer of the medicinal product) or by an officially accredited body.

It is improbable that a procedure could be satisfactorily validated for:

- starting materials supplied by intermediaries such as brokers where the source of manufacture is unknown or not audited;
- starting materials for use in parenteral products.

4    The quality of a batch of starting materials may be assessed by taking and testing a representative sample. The samples taken for identity testing could be used for this purpose. The number of samples taken for the preparation of a representative sample should be determined statistically and specified in a sampling plan. The number of individual samples which may be blended to form a composite sample should also be defined, taking into account the nature of the material, knowledge of the supplier and the homogeneity of the composite sample.

## Packaging Material

5    The sampling plan for packaging materials should take account of at least the following: the quantity received, the quality required, the nature of the material (e.g. primary packaging materials and/or printed packaging materials), the production methods, and what is known of the Quality Assurance system of the packaging materials manufacturer based on audits. The number of samples taken should be determined statistically and specified in a sampling plan.

EU GMP GUIDE PART I ANNEX 8 SAMPLING OF STARTING AND PACKAGING MATERIALS

## ANNEX 9 MANUFACTURE OF LIQUIDS, CREAMS AND OINTMENTS

### Principle

Liquids, creams and ointments may be particularly susceptible to microbial and other contamination during manufacture. Therefore special measures must be taken to prevent any contamination.

### Premises and Equipment

1   The use of closed systems for processing and transfer is recommended in order to protect the product from contamination. Production areas where the products or open clean containers are exposed should normally be effectively ventilated with filtered air.

2   Tanks, containers, pipework and pumps should be designed and installed so that they may be readily cleaned and if necessary sanitised. In particular, equipment design should include a minimum of dead-legs or sites where residues can accumulate and promote microbial proliferation.

3   The use of glass apparatus should be avoided wherever possible. High quality stainless steel is often the material of choice for parts coming into contact with product.

### Production

4   The chemical and microbiological quality of water used in production should be specified and monitored. Care should be taken in the maintenance of water systems in order to avoid the risk of microbial proliferation. After any chemical sanitisation of the water systems, a validated flushing procedure should be followed to ensure that the sanitising agent has been effectively removed.

5   The quality of materials received in bulk tankers should be checked before they are transferred to bulk storage tanks.

6   Care should be taken when transferring materials via pipelines to ensure that they are delivered to their correct destination.

7   Materials likely to shed fibres or other contaminants, like cardboard or wooden pallets, should not enter the areas where products or clean containers are exposed.

8   Care should be taken to maintain the homogeneity of mixtures, suspensions, etc. during filling. Mixing and filling processes should be

validated. Special care should be taken at the beginning of a filling process, after stoppages and at the end of the process to ensure that homogeneity is maintained.

9   When the finished product is not immediately packaged, the maximum period of storage and the storage conditions should be specified and adhered to.

# ANNEX 10 MANUFACTURE OF PRESSURISED METERED DOSE AEROSOL PREPARATIONS FOR INHALATION

## Principle

The manufacture of pressurised aerosol products for inhalation with metering valves requires special consideration because of the particular nature of this form of product. It should be done under conditions which minimise microbial and particulate contamination. Assurance of the quality of the valve components and, in the case of suspensions, of uniformity is also of particular importance.

## General

1    There are presently two common manufacturing and filling methods as follows:

    (a) Two-shot system (pressure filling). The active ingredient is suspended in a high boiling point propellant, the dose is put into the container, the valve is crimped on and the lower boiling point propellant is injected through the valve stem to make up the finished product. The suspension of active ingredient in propellant is kept cool to reduce evaporation loss.

    (b) One-shot process (cold filling). The active ingredient is suspended in a mixture of propellants and held either under high pressure or at a low temperature, or both. The suspension is then filled directly into the container in one shot.

## Premises and Equipment

2    Manufacture and filling should be carried out as far as possible in a closed system.

3    Where products or clean components are exposed, the area should be fed with filtered air, should comply with the requirements of at least a Grade D environment and should be entered through airlocks.

## Production and Quality Control

4    Metering valves for aerosols are more complex pieces of engineering than most items used in pharmaceutical production. Their specifications, sampling and testing should recognise this. Auditing the Quality Assurance system of the valve manufacturer is of particular importance.

5   All fluids (e.g. liquid or gaseous propellants) should be filtered to remove particles greater than 0.2 micron. An additional filtration where possible immediately before filling is desirable.

6   Containers and valves should be cleaned using a validated procedure appropriate to the use of the product to ensure the absence of any contaminants such as fabrication aids (e.g. lubricants) or undue microbiological contaminants. After cleaning, valves should be kept in clean, closed containers and precautions taken not to introduce contamination during subsequent handling, e.g. taking samples. Containers should be fed to the filling line in a clean condition or cleaned on line immediately before filling.

7   Precautions should be taken to ensure uniformity of suspensions at the point of fill throughout the filling process.

8   When a two-shot filling process is used, it is necessary to ensure that both shots are of the correct weight in order to achieve the correct composition. For this purpose, 100% weight checking at each stage is often desirable.

9   Controls after filling should ensure the absence of undue leakage. Any leakage test should be performed in a way which avoids microbial contamination or residual moisture.

# ANNEX 11 COMPUTERISED SYSTEMS

## Principle

This annex applies to all forms of computerised systems used as part of a GMP regulated activities. A computerised system is a set of software and hardware components which together fulfill certain functionalities.

The application should be validated; IT infrastructure should be qualified.

Where a computerised system replaces a manual operation, there should be no resultant decrease in product quality, process control or quality assurance. There should be no increase in the overall risk of the process.

## General

### 1    Risk Management

Risk management should be applied throughout the lifecycle of the computerised system taking into account patient safety, data integrity and product quality. As part of a risk management system, decisions on the extent of validation and data integrity controls should be based on a justified and documented risk assessment of the computerised system.

### 2    Personnel

There should be close cooperation between all relevant personnel such as Process Owner, System Owner, Qualified Persons and IT. All personnel should have appropriate qualifications, level of access and defined responsibilities to carry out their assigned duties.

### 3    Suppliers and Service Providers

3.1    When third parties (e.g. suppliers, service providers) are used e.g. to provide, install, configure, integrate, validate, maintain (e.g. via remote access), modify or retain a computerised system or related service or for data processing, formal agreements must exist between the manufacturer and any third parties, and these agreements should include clear statements of the responsibilities of the third party. IT-departments should be considered analogous.

3.2    The competence and reliability of a supplier are key factors when selecting a product or service provider. The need for an audit should be based on a risk assessment.

**3.3** Documentation supplied with commercial off-the-shelf products should be reviewed by regulated users to check that user requirements are fulfilled.

**3.4** Quality system and audit information relating to suppliers or developers of software and implemented systems should be made available to inspectors on request.

## Project Phase

### 4    Validation

**4.1** The validation documentation and reports should cover the relevant steps of the life cycle. Manufacturers should be able to justify their standards, protocols, acceptance criteria, procedures and records based on their risk assessment.

**4.2** Validation documentation should include change control records (if applicable) and reports on any deviations observed during the validation process.

**4.3** An up to date listing of all relevant systems and their GMP functionality (inventory) should be available.

For critical systems an up to date system description detailing the physical and logical arrangements, data flows and interfaces with other systems or processes, any hardware and software pre-requisites, and security measures should be available.

**4.4** User Requirements Specifications should describe the required functions of the computerised system and be based on documented risk assessment and GMP impact. User requirements should be traceable throughout the life-cycle.

**4.5** The regulated user should take all reasonable steps, to ensure that the system has been developed in accordance with an appropriate quality management system. The supplier should be assessed appropriately.

**4.6** For the validation of bespoke or customised computerised systems there should be a process in place that ensures the formal assessment and reporting of quality and performance measures for all the life-cycle stages of the system.

**4.7** Evidence of appropriate test methods and test scenarios should be demonstrated. Particularly, system (process) parameter limits, data limits and error handling should be considered. Automated testing tools and test environments should have documented assessments for their adequacy.

**4.8**    If data are transferred to another data format or system, validation should include checks that data are not altered in value and/or meaning during this migration process.

## Operational Phase

### 5    Data

Computerised systems exchanging data electronically with other systems should include appropriate built-in checks for the correct and secure entry and processing of data, in order to minimize the risks.

### 6    Accuracy Checks

For critical data entered manually, there should be an additional check on the accuracy of the data. This check may be done by a second operator or by validated electronic means. The criticality and the potential consequences of erroneous or incorrectly entered data to a system should be covered by risk management.

### 7    Data Storage

**7.1**    Data should be secured by both physical and electronic means against damage. Stored data should be checked for accessibility, readability and accuracy. Access to data should be ensured throughout the retention period.

**7.2**    Regular back-ups of all relevant data should be done. Integrity and accuracy of backup data and the ability to restore the data should be checked during validation and monitored periodically.

### 8    Printouts

**8.1**    It should be possible to obtain clear printed copies of electronically stored data.

**8.2**    For records supporting batch release it should be possible to generate printouts indicating if any of the data has been changed since the original entry.

## 9 Audit Trails

Consideration should be given, based on a risk assessment, to building into the system the creation of a record of all GMP-relevant changes and deletions (a system generated "audit trail"). For change or deletion of GMP-relevant data the reason should be documented. Audit trails need to be available and convertible to a generally intelligible form and regularly reviewed.

## 10 Change and Configuration Management

Any changes to a computerised system including system configurations should only be made in a controlled manner in accordance with a defined procedure.

## 11 Periodic evaluation

Computerised systems should be periodically evaluated to confirm that they remain in a valid state and are compliant with GMP. Such evaluations should include, where appropriate, the current range of functionality, deviation records, incidents, problems, upgrade history, performance, reliability, security and validation status reports.

## 12 Security

12.1 Physical and/or logical controls should be in place to restrict access to computerised system to authorised persons. Suitable methods of preventing unauthorised entry to the system may include the use of keys, pass cards, personal codes with passwords, biometrics, restricted access to computer equipment and data storage areas.

12.2 The extent of security controls depends on the criticality of the computerised system.

12.3 Creation, change, and cancellation of access authorisations should be recorded.

12.4 Management systems for data and for documents should be designed to record the identity of operators entering, changing, confirming or deleting data including date and time.

## 13    Incident Management

All incidents, not only system failures and data errors, should be reported and assessed. The root cause of a critical incident should be identified and should form the basis of corrective and preventive actions.

## 14    Electronic Signature

Electronic records may be signed electronically. Electronic signatures are expected to:

(a) have the same impact as hand-written signatures within the boundaries of the company,
(b) be permanently linked to their respective record,
(c) include the time and date that they were applied.

## 15    Batch release

When a computerised system is used for recording certification and batch release, the system should allow only Qualified Persons to certify the release of the batches and it should clearly identify and record the person releasing or certifying the batches. This should be performed using an electronic signature.

## 16    Business Continuity

For the availability of computerised systems supporting critical processes, provisions should be made to ensure continuity of support for those processes in the event of a system breakdown (e.g. a manual or alternative system). The time required to bring the alternative arrangements into use should be based on risk and appropriate for a particular system and the business process it supports. These arrangements should be adequately documented and tested.

## 17    Archiving

Data may be archived. This data should be checked for accessibility, readability and integrity. If relevant changes are to be made to the system (e.g. computer equipment or programs), then the ability to retrieve the data should be ensured and tested.

## Glossary

### APPLICATION

Software installed on a defined platform/hardware providing specific functionality.

### BESPOKE/CUSTOMIZED COMPUTERISED SYSTEM

A computerised system individually designed to suit a specific business process.

### COMMERCIAL OFF THE SHELF SOFTWARE

Software commercially available, whose fitness for use is demonstrated by a broad spectrum of users.

### IT INFRASTRUCTURE

The hardware and software such as networking software and operation systems, which makes it possible for the application to function.

### LIFE CYCLE

All phases in the life of the system from initial requirements until retirement including design, specification, programming, testing, installation, operation, and maintenance.

### PROCESS OWNER

The person responsible for the business process.

### SYSTEM OWNER

The person responsible for the availability, and maintenance of a computerised system and for the security of the data residing on that system.

### THIRD PARTY

Parties not directly managed by the holder of the manufacturing and/or import authorisation.

# ANNEX 12 USE OF IONISING RADIATION IN THE MANUFACTURE OF MEDICINAL PRODUCTS

**Note:** *The holder of, or applicant for, a marketing authorisation for a product which includes irradiation as part of its processing should also refer to the note produced by the Committee for Proprietary Medicinal Products giving guidance on "Ionising radiation in the manufacture of medicinal products".*

## Introduction

Ionising radiation may be used during the manufacturing process for various purposes including the reduction of bioburden and the sterilisation of starting materials, packaging components or products and the treatment of blood products.

There are two types of irradiation process: Gamma Irradiation from a radioactive source and high energy Electron Irradiation (Beta radiation) from an accelerator.

Gamma Irradiation: two different processing modes may be employed:

(i)   Batch mode: the product is arranged at fixed locations around the radiation source and cannot be loaded or unloaded while the radiation source is exposed.

(ii)  Continuous mode: an automatic system conveys the products into the radiation cell, past the exposed radiation source along a defined path and at an appropriate speed, and out of the cell.

Electron Irradiation: the product is conveyed past a continuous or pulsed beam of high energy electrons (Beta radiation) which is scanned back and forth across the product pathway.

## Responsibilities

1   Treatment by irradiation may be carried out by the pharmaceutical manufacturer or by an operator of a radiation facility under contract (a "contract manufacturer"), both of whom must hold an appropriate manufacturing authorisation.

2   The pharmaceutical manufacturer bears responsibility for the quality of the product including the attainment of the objective of irradiation. The contract operator of the radiation facility bears responsibility for ensuring that the dose of radiation required by the manufacturer is delivered to the

irradiation container (i.e. the outermost container in which the products are irradiated).

3    The required dose including justified limits will be stated in the marketing authorisation for the product.

## Dosimetry

4    Dosimetry is defined as the measurement of the absorbed dose by the use of dosimeters. Both understanding and correct use of the technique is essential for the validation, commissioning and control of the process.

5    The calibration of each batch of routine dosimeters should be traceable to a national or international standard. The period of validity of the calibration should be stated, justified and adhered to.

6    The same instrument should normally be used to establish the calibration curve of the routine dosimeters and to measure the change in their absorbance after irradiation. If a different instrument is used, the absolute absorbance of each instrument should be established.

7    Depending on the type of dosimeter used, due account should be taken of possible causes of inaccuracy including the change in moisture content, change in temperature, time elapsed between irradiation and measurement, and the dose rate.

8    The wavelength of the instrument used to measure the change in absorbance of dosimeters and the instrument used to measure their thickness should be subject to regular checks of calibration at intervals established on the basis of stability, purpose and usage.

## Validation of the Process

9    Validation is the action of proving that the process, i.e. the delivery of the intended absorbed dose to the product, will achieve the expected results. The requirements for validation are given more fully in the note for guidance on "the use of ionising radiation in the manufacture of medicinal products."

10    Validation should include dose mapping to establish the distribution of absorbed dose within the irradiation container when packed with product in a defined configuration.

11    An irradiation process specification should include at least the following:

(a) details of the packaging of the product;

(b) the loading pattern(s) of product within the irradiation container. Particular care needs to be taken, when a mixture of products is allowed in the irradiation container, that there is no under-dosing of dense product or shadowing of other products by dense product. Each mixed product arrangement must be specified and validated;

(c) the loading pattern of irradiation containers around the source (batch mode) or the pathway through the cell (continuous mode);

(d) maximum and minimum limits of absorbed dose to the product (and associated routine dosimetry);

(e) maximum and minimum limits of absorbed dose to the irradiation container and associated routine dosimetry to monitor this absorbed dose;

(f) other process parameters, including dose rate, maximum time of exposure, number of exposures, etc.

When irradiation is supplied under contract at least parts (d) and (e) of the irradiation process specification should form part of that contract.

## Commissioning of the Plant

### General

12    Commissioning is the exercise of obtaining and documenting evidence that the irradiation plant will perform consistently within predetermined limits when operated according to the process specification. In the context of this annex, predetermined limits are the maximum and minimum doses designed to be absorbed by the irradiation container. It must not be possible for variations to occur in the operation of the plant which give a dose to the container outside these limits without the knowledge of the operator.

13    Commissioning should include the following elements:

(a) design;
(b) dose mapping;
(c) documentation;
(d) requirement for re-commissioning.

### Gamma irradiators

DESIGN

14    The absorbed dose received by a particular part of an irradiation container at any specific point in the irradiator depends primarily on the following factors:

(a) the activity and geometry of the source;

(b) the distance from source to container;

(c) the duration of irradiation controlled by the timer setting or conveyor speed;

(d) the composition and density of material, including other products, between the source and the particular part of the container.

15    The total absorbed dose will in addition depend on the path of containers through a continuous irradiator or the loading pattern in a batch irradiator, and on the number of exposure cycles.

16    For a continuous irradiator with a fixed path or a batch irradiator with a fixed loading pattern, and with a given source strength and type of product, the key plant parameter controlled by the operator is conveyor speed or timer setting.

## DOSE MAPPING

17    For the dose mapping procedure, the irradiator should be filled with irradiation containers packed with dummy products or a representative product of uniform density. Dosimeters should be placed throughout a minimum of three loaded irradiation containers which are passed through the irradiator, surrounded by similar containers or dummy products. If the product is not uniformly packed, dosimeters should be placed in a larger number of containers.

18    The positioning of dosimeters will depend on the size of the irradiation container. For example, for containers up to 1 x 1 x 0.5 m, a three-dimensional 20 cm grid throughout the container including the outside surfaces might be suitable. If the expected positions of the minimum and maximum dose are known from a previous irradiator performance characterisation, some dosimeters could be removed from regions of average dose and replaced to form a 10 cm grid in the regions of extreme dose.

19    The results of this procedure will give minimum and maximum absorbed doses in the product and on the container surface for a given set of plant parameters, product density and loading pattern.

20    Ideally, reference dosimeters should be used for the dose mapping exercise because of their greater precision. Routine dosimeters are permissible but it is advisable to place reference dosimeters beside them at the expected positions of minimum and maximum dose and at the routine monitoring position in each of the replicate irradiation containers. The observed values of dose will have an associated random uncertainty which can be estimated from the variations in replicate measurements.

21 The minimum observed dose, as measured by the routine dosimeters, necessary to ensure that all irradiation containers receive the minimum required dose will be set in the knowledge of the random variability of the routine dosimeters used.

22 Irradiator parameters should be kept constant, monitored and recorded during dose mapping. The records, together with the dosimetry results and all other records generated, should be retained.

## Electron beam irradiators

### DESIGN

23 The absorbed dose received by a particular portion of an irradiated product depends primarily on the following factors:

     (a) the characteristics of the beam, which are: electron energy, average beam current, scan width and scan uniformity;

     (b) the conveyor speed;

     (c) the product composition and density;

     (d) the composition, density and thickness of material between the output window and the particular portion of product;

     (e) the output window to container distance.

24 Key parameters controlled by the operator are the characteristics of the beam and the conveyor speed.

### DOSE MAPPING

25 For the dose-mapping procedure, dosimeters should be placed between layers of homogeneous absorber sheets making up a dummy product, or between layers of representative products of uniform density, such that at least ten measurements can be made within the maximum range of the electrons. Reference should also be made to sections 18–21.

26 Irradiator parameters should be kept constant, monitored and recorded during dose mapping. The records, together with the dosimetry results and all other records generated, should be retained.

## Re-commissioning

27 Commissioning should be repeated if there is a change to the process or the irradiator which could affect the dose distribution to the irradiation container (e.g. change of source pencils). The extent to re-commissioning depends on the extent of the change in the irradiator or the load that has taken place. If in doubt, re-commission.

## Premises

28 Premises should be designed and operated to segregate irradiated from non-irradiated containers to avoid their cross-contamination. Where materials are handled within closed irradiation containers, it may not be necessary to segregate pharmaceutical from non-pharmaceutical materials, provided there is no risk of the former being contaminated by the latter.

Any possibility of contamination of the products by radionuclide from the source must be excluded.

## Processing

29 Irradiation containers should be packed in accordance with the specified loading pattern(s) established during validation.

30 During the process, the radiation dose to the irradiation containers should be monitored using validated dosimetry procedures. The relationship between this dose and the dose absorbed by the product inside the container must have been established during process validation and plant commissioning.

31 Radiation indicators should be used as an aid to differentiating irradiated from non-irradiated containers. They should not be used as the sole means of differentiation or as an indication of satisfactory processing.

32 Processing of mixed loads of containers within the irradiation cell should only be done when it is known from commissioning trials or other evidence that the radiation dose received by individual containers remains within the limits specified.

33 When the required radiation dose is by design given during more than one exposure or passage through the plant, this should be with the agreement of the holder of the marketing authorisation and occur within a predetermined time period. Unplanned interruptions during irradiation should be notified to the holder of the marketing authorisation if this extends the irradiation process beyond a previously agreed period.

34 Non-irradiated products must be segregated from irradiated products at all times. Methods of doing this include the use of radiation indicators (item 31) and appropriate design of premises (item 28).

## Gamma irradiators

35 For continuous processing modes, dosimeters should be placed so that at least two are exposed in the irradiation at all times.

36    For batch modes, at least two dosimeters should be exposed in positions related to the minimum dose position.

37    For continuous process modes, there should be a positive indication of the correct position of the source and an interlock between source position and conveyor movement. Conveyor speed should be monitored continuously and recorded.

38    For batch process modes source movement and exposure times for each batch should be monitored and recorded.

39    For a given desired dose, the timer setting or conveyor speed requires adjustment for source decay and source additions. The period of validity of the setting or speed should be recorded and adhered to.

## Electron beam irradiators

40    A dosimeter should be placed on every container.

41    There should be continuous recording of average beam current, electron energy, scan-width and conveyor speed. These variables, other than conveyor speed, need to be controlled within the defined limits established during commissioning since they are liable to instantaneous change.

## Documentation

42    The numbers of containers received, irradiated and dispatched should be reconciled with each other and with the associated documentation. Any discrepancy should be reported and resolved.

43    The irradiation plant operator should certify in writing the range of doses received by each irradiated container within a batch or delivery.

44    Process and control records for each irradiation batch should be checked and signed by a nominated responsible person and retained. The method and place of retention should be agreed between the plant operator and the holder of the marketing authorisation.

45    The documentation associated with the validation and commissioning of the plant should be retained for one year after the expiry date or at least five years after the release of the last product processed by the plant, whichever is the longer.

## Microbiological Monitoring

**46**    Microbiological monitoring is the responsibility of the pharmaceutical manufacturer. It may include environmental monitoring where product is manufactured and pre-irradiation monitoring of the product as specified in the marketing authorisation.

# ANNEX 13 INVESTIGATIONAL MEDICINAL PRODUCTS

## Principle

Investigational medicinal products should be produced in accordance with the principles and the detailed guidelines of Good Manufacturing Practice for Medicinal Products (The Rules Governing Medicinal Products in The European Community, Volume IV). Other guidelines published by the European Commission should be taken into account where relevant and as appropriate to the stage of development of the product. Procedures need to be flexible to provide for changes as knowledge of the process increases, and appropriate to the stage of development of the product.

In clinical trials there may be added risk to participating subjects compared to patients treated with marketed products. The application of GMP to the manufacture of investigational medicinal products is intended to ensure that trial subjects are not placed at risk, and that the results of clinical trials are unaffected by inadequate safety, quality or efficacy arising from unsatisfactory manufacture. Equally, it is intended to ensure that there is consistency between batches of the same investigational medicinal product used in the same or different clinical trials, and that changes during the development of an investigational medicinal product are adequately documented and justified.

The production of investigational medicinal products involves added complexity in comparison to marketed products by virtue of the lack of fixed routines, variety of clinical trial designs, consequent packaging designs, and the need, often, for randomisation and blinding and increased risk of product cross-contamination and mix up. Furthermore, there may be incomplete knowledge of the potency and toxicity of the product and a lack of full process validation, or, marketed products may be used which have been re-packaged or modified in some way. These challenges require personnel with a thorough understanding of, and training in, the application of GMP to investigational medicinal products. Co-operation is required with trial sponsors who undertake the ultimate responsibility for all aspects of the clinical trial including the quality of investigational medicinal products. The increased complexity in manufacturing operations requires a highly effective quality system.

The Annex also includes guidance on ordering, shipping, and returning clinical supplies, which are at the interface with, and complementary to, guidelines on Good Clinical Practice.

## Notes

### NON-INVESTIGATIONAL MEDICINAL PRODUCT[1]

Products other than the test product, placebo or comparator may be supplied to subjects participating in a trial. Such products may be used as support or escape medication for preventative, diagnostic or therapeutic reasons and/or needed to ensure that adequate medical care is provided for the subject. They may also be used in accordance with the protocol to induce a physiological response. These products do not fall within the definition of investigational medicinal products and may be supplied by the sponsor, or the investigator. The sponsor should ensure that they are in accordance with the notification/request for authorisation to conduct the trial and that they are of appropriate quality for the purposes of the trial taking into account the source of the materials, whether or not they are the subject of a marketing authorisation and whether they have been repackaged. The advice and involvement of a Qualified Person is recommended in this task.

### MANUFACTURING AUTHORISATION AND RECONSTITUTION

Both the total and partial manufacture of investigational medicinal products, as well as the various processes of dividing up, packaging or presentation, is subject to the authorisation referred to in Article 13(1) Directive 2001/20/EC, cf. Article 9(1) Directive 2005/28/EC. This authorisation, however, shall not be required for reconstitution under the conditions set out in Article 9(2) Directive 2005/28/EC. For the purpose of this provision, reconstitution shall be understood as a simple process of:

- dissolving or dispersing the investigational medicinal product for administration of the product to a trial subject,
- or, diluting or mixing the investigational medicinal product(s) with some other substance(s) used as a vehicle for the purposes of administering it,

Reconstitution is not mixing several ingredients, including the active substance, together to produce the investigational medicinal product.

An investigational medicinal product must exist before a process can be defined as reconstitution.

The process of reconstitution has to be undertaken as soon as practicable before administration.

This process has to be defined in the clinical trial application / IMP dossier and clinical trial protocol, or related document, available at the site.

---

[1] Further information can be found in the European Commission's Guidance on Investigational Medicinal Products (IMPs) and other Medicinal Products used in Clinical Trials

## Glossary

### BLINDING

A procedure in which one or more parties to the trial are kept unaware of the treatment assignment(s). Single-blinding usually refers to the subject(s) being unaware, and double-blinding usually refers to the subject(s), investigator(s), monitor, and, in some cases, data analyst(s) being unaware of the treatment assignment(s). In relation to an investigational medicinal product, blinding shall mean the deliberate disguising of the identity of the product in accordance with the instructions of the sponsor. Unblinding shall mean the disclosure of the identity of blinded products.

### CLINICAL TRIAL

Any investigation in human subjects intended to discover or verify the clinical, pharmacological and/or other pharmacodynamic effects of an investigational product(s) and/or to identify any adverse reactions to an investigational product(s), and/or to study absorption, distribution, metabolism, and excretion of one or more investigational medicinal product(s) with the object of ascertaining its/their safety and/or efficacy.

### COMPARATOR PRODUCT

An investigational or marketed product (i.e. active control), or placebo, used as a reference in a clinical trial.

### INVESTIGATIONAL MEDICINAL PRODUCT

A pharmaceutical form of an active substance or placebo being tested or used as a reference in a clinical trial, including a product with a marketing authorisation when used or assembled (formulated or packaged) in a way different from the authorised form, or when used for an unauthorised indication, or when used to gain further information about the authorised form.

### INVESTIGATOR

A person responsible for the conduct of the clinical trial at a trial site. If a trial is conducted by a team of individuals at a trial site, the investigator is the responsible leader of the team and may be called the principal investigator.

### MANUFACTURER/IMPORTER OF INVESTIGATIONAL MEDICINAL PRODUCTS

Any person engaged in activities for which the authorisation referred to in Article 13(1) of Directive 2001/20/EC is required.

### ORDER

Instruction to process, package and/or ship a certain number of units of investigational medicinal product(s).

## PRODUCT SPECIFICATION FILE

A reference file containing, or referring to files containing, all the information necessary to draft the detailed written instructions on processing, packaging, quality control testing, batch release and shipping of an investigational medicinal product.

## RANDOMISATION

The process of assigning trial subjects to treatment or control groups using an element of chance to determine the assignments in order to reduce bias.

## RANDOMISATION CODE

A listing in which the treatment assigned to each subject from the randomisation process is identified.

## SHIPPING

The operation of packaging for shipment and sending of ordered medicinal products for clinical trials.

## SPONSOR

An individual, company, institution or organisation which takes responsibility for the initiation, management and/or financing of a clinical trial.

## Quality Management

1   The Quality System, designed, set up and verified by the manufacturer or importer, should be described in written procedures available to the sponsor, taking into account the GMP principles and guidelines applicable to investigational medicinal products.

2   The product specifications and manufacturing instructions may be changed during development but full control and traceability of the changes should be maintained.

## Personnel

3   All personnel involved with investigational medicinal products should be appropriately trained in the requirements specific to these types of product. Even in cases where the number of staff involved is small there should be, for each batch, separate people responsible for production and quality control.

4   The Qualified Person should ensure that there are systems in place that meet the requirements of GMP and should have a broad knowledge of pharmaceutical development and clinical trial processes. Guidance for the

Qualified Person in connection with the certification of investigational medicinal products is given in paragraphs 38 to 41.

## Premises and Equipment

5    The toxicity, potency and sensitising potential may not be fully understood for investigational medicinal products and this reinforces the need to minimise all risks of cross-contamination. The design of equipment and premises, inspection / test methods and acceptance limits to be used after cleaning should reflect the nature of these risks. Consideration should be given to campaign working where appropriate. Account should be taken of the solubility of the product in decisions about the choice of cleaning solvent.

## Documentation

### Specifications and instructions

6    Specifications (for starting materials, primary packaging materials, intermediate, bulk products and finished products), manufacturing formulae and processing and packaging instructions should be as comprehensive as possible given the current state of knowledge. They should be periodically re-assessed during development and updated as necessary. Each new version should take into account the latest data, current technology used, regulatory and pharmacopoeial requirements, and should allow traceability to the previous document. Any changes should be carried out according to a written procedure, which should address any implications for product quality such as stability and bio-equivalence.

7    Rationales for changes should be recorded and the consequences of a change on product quality and on any on-going clinical trials should be investigated and documented.[2]

---

[2] Guidance on changes that require the request of a substantial amendment to the IMP dossier submitted to the Competent Authorities is given in the CHMP guideline on the Requirements to the Chemical and Pharmaceutical Quality Documentation Concerning Investigational Medicinal Products in Clinical Trials

## Order

8　The order should request the processing and/or packaging of a certain number of units and/or their shipping and be given by or on behalf of the sponsor to the manufacturer. It should be in writing (though it may be transmitted by electronic means), and precise enough to avoid any ambiguity. It should be formally authorised and refer to the Product Specification File and the relevant clinical trial protocol as appropriate.

## Product specification file

9　The Product Specification File (see glossary) should be continually updated as development of the product proceeds, ensuring appropriate traceability to the previous versions. It should include, or refer to, the following documents:

- Specifications and analytical methods for starting materials, packaging materials;
- Intermediate, bulk and finished product;
- Manufacturing methods;
- In-process testing and methods;
- Approved label copy;
- Relevant clinical trial protocols and randomisation codes, as appropriate;
- Relevant technical agreements with contract givers, as appropriate;
- Stability data;
- Storage and shipment conditions.

The above listing is not intended to be exclusive or exhaustive. The contents will vary depending on the product and stage of development. The information should form the basis for assessment of the suitability for certification and release of a particular batch by the Qualified Person and should therefore be accessible to him/her. Where different manufacturing steps are carried out at different locations under the responsibility of different Qualified Persons, it is acceptable to maintain separate files limited to information of relevance to the activities at the respective locations.

## Manufacturing formulae and processing instructions

10　For every manufacturing operation or supply there should be clear and adequate written instructions and written records. Where an operation is not repetitive it may not be necessary to produce Master Formulae and Processing Instructions. Records are particularly important for the preparation of the final version of the documents to be used in routine manufacture once the marketing authorisation is granted.

EU GMP GUIDE PART I ANNEX 13 INVESTIGATIONAL MEDICINAL PRODUCTS

11   The information in the Product Specification File should be used to produce the detailed written instructions on processing, packaging, quality control testing, storage conditions and shipping.

## Packaging instructions

12   Investigational medicinal products are normally packed in an individual way for each subject included in the clinical trial. The number of units to be packaged should be specified prior to the start of the packaging operations, including units necessary for carrying out quality control and any retention samples to be kept. Sufficient reconciliations should take place to ensure the correct quantity of each product required has been accounted for at each stage of processing.

## Processing, testing and packaging batch records

13   Batch records should be kept in sufficient detail for the sequence of operations to be accurately determined. These records should contain any relevant remarks which justify the procedures used and any changes made, enhance knowledge of the product and develop the manufacturing operations.

14   Batch manufacturing records should be retained at least for the periods specified in Directive 2003/94/EC.

## Production

### Packaging materials

15   Specifications and quality control checks should include measures to guard against unintentional unblinding due to changes in appearance between different batches of packaging materials.

### Manufacturing operations

16   During development critical parameters should be identified and in-process controls primarily used to control the process. Provisional production parameters and in-process controls may be deduced from prior experience, including that gained from earlier development work. Careful consideration by key personnel is called for in order to formulate the necessary instructions and to adapt them continually to the experience gained in production. Parameters identified and controlled should be justifiable based on knowledge available at the time.

17 Production processes for investigational medicinal products are not expected to be validated to the extent necessary for routine production but premises and equipment are expected to be qualified. For sterile products, the validation of sterilising processes should be of the same standard as for products authorised for marketing. Likewise, when required, virus inactivation/removal and that of other impurities of biological origin should be demonstrated, to assure the safety of biotechnologically derived products, by following the scientific principles and techniques defined in the available guidance in this area.

18 Validation of aseptic processes presents special problems when the batch size is small; in these cases the number of units filled may be the maximum number filled in production. If practicable, and otherwise consistent with simulating the process, a larger number of units should be filled with media to provide greater confidence in the results obtained. Filling and sealing is often a manual or semi-automated operation presenting great challenges to sterility so enhanced attention should be given to operator training, and validating the aseptic technique of individual operators.

## Principles applicable to comparator product

19 If a product is modified, data should be available (e.g. stability, comparative dissolution, bioavailability) to demonstrate that these changes do not significantly alter the original quality characteristics of the product.

20 The expiry date stated for the comparator product in its original packaging might not be applicable to the product where it has been repackaged in a different container that may not offer equivalent protection, or be compatible with the product. A suitable use-by date, taking into account the nature of the product, the characteristics of the container and the storage conditions to which the article may be subjected, should be determined by or on behalf of the sponsor. Such a date should be justified and must not be later than the expiry date of the original package. There should be compatibility of expiry dating and clinical trial duration.

## Blinding operations

21 Where products are blinded, systems should be in place to ensure that the blind is achieved and maintained while allowing for identification of "blinded" products when necessary, including the batch numbers of the products before the blinding operation. Rapid identification of product should also be possible in an emergency.

EU GMP GUIDE PART I ANNEX 13 INVESTIGATIONAL MEDICINAL PRODUCTS

## Randomisation code

22    Procedures should describe the generation, security, distribution, handling and retention of any randomisation code used for packaging investigational products, and code-break mechanisms. Appropriate records should be maintained.

## Packaging

23    During packaging of investigational medicinal products, it may be necessary to handle different products on the same packaging line at the same time. The risk of product mix-up must be minimised by using appropriate procedures and/or, specialised equipment as appropriate and relevant staff training.

24    Packaging and labelling of investigational medicinal products are likely to be more complex and more liable to errors (which are also harder to detect) than for marketed products, particularly when "blinded" products with similar appearance are used. Precautions against mis-labelling such as label reconciliation, line clearance, in-process control checks by appropriately trained staff should accordingly be intensified.

25    The packaging must ensure that the investigational medicinal product remains in good condition during transport and storage at intermediate destinations. Any opening or tampering of the outer packaging during transport should be readily discernible.

## Labelling

26    Table 1 summarises the contents of Articles 26–30 that follow. Labelling should comply with the requirements of Directive 2003/94/EC. The following information should be included on labels, unless its absence can be justified, e.g. use of a centralised electronic randomisation system:

(a) name, address and telephone number of the sponsor, contract research organisation or investigator (the main contact for information on the product, clinical trial and emergency unblinding);

(b) pharmaceutical dosage form, route of administration, quantity of dosage units, and in the case of open trials, the name/identifier and strength/potency;

(c) the batch and/or code number to identify the contents and packaging operation;

(d) a trial reference code allowing identification of the trial, site, investigator and sponsor if not given elsewhere;

(e) the trial subject identification number/treatment number and where relevant, the visit number;

(f) the name of the investigator (if not included in (a) or (d));

(g) directions for use (reference may be made to a leaflet or other explanatory document intended for the trial subject or person administering the product);

(h) "For clinical trial use only" or similar wording;

(i) the storage conditions;

(j) period of use (use-by date, expiry date or re-test date as applicable), in month/year format and in a manner that avoids any ambiguity;

(k) "keep out of reach of children" except when the product is for use in trials where the product is not taken home by subjects.

27   The address and telephone number of the main contact for information on the product, clinical trial and for emergency unblinding need not appear on the label where the subject has been given a leaflet or card which provides these details and has been instructed to keep this in their possession at all times.

28   Particulars should appear in the official language(s) of the country in which the investigational medicinal product is to be used. The particulars listed in Article 26 should appear on the primary packaging and on the secondary packaging (except for the cases described in Articles 29 and 30). The requirements with respect to the contents of the label on the primary and outer packaging are summarised in Table 1. Other languages may be included.

29   When the product is to be provided to the trial subject or the person administering the medication within a primary package together with secondary packaging that is intended to remain together, and the secondary packaging carries the particulars listed in Paragraph 26, the following information shall be included on the label of the primary package (or any sealed dosing device that contains the primary packaging):

(a) name of sponsor, contract research organisation or investigator;

(b) pharmaceutical dosage form, route of administration (may be excluded for oral solid dose forms), quantity of dosage units and in the case of open label trials, the name/identifier and strength/potency;

(c) batch and/or code number to identify the contents and packaging operation;

(d) a trial reference code allowing identification of the trial, site, investigator and sponsor if not given elsewhere;

(e) the trial subject identification number/treatment number and where relevant, the visit number.

**30**  If the primary packaging takes the form of blister packs or small units such as ampoules on which the particulars required in Paragraph 26 cannot be displayed, secondary packaging should be provided bearing a label with those particulars. The primary packaging should nevertheless contain the following:

(a) name of sponsor, contract research organisation or investigator;

(b) route of administration (may be excluded for oral solid dose forms) and in the case of open label trials, the name/identifier and strength/potency;

(c) batch and/or code number to identify the contents and packaging operation;

(d) a trial reference code allowing identification of the trial, site, investigator and sponsor if not given elsewhere;

(e) the trial subject identification number/treatment number and where relevant, the visit number.

**31**  Symbols or pictograms may be included to clarify certain information mentioned above. Additional information, warnings and/or handling instructions may be displayed.

**32**  For clinical trials with the characteristics identified in Article 14 of Directive 2001/20/EC, the following particulars should be added to the original container but should not obscure the original labelling:

(i)   name of sponsor, contract research organisation or investigator;

(ii)  trial reference code allowing identification of the trial site, investigator and trial subject.

**33**  If it becomes necessary to change the use-by date, an additional label should be affixed to the investigational medicinal product. This additional label should state the new use-by date and repeat the batch number. It may be superimposed on the old use-by date, but for quality control reasons, not on the original batch number. This operation should be performed at an appropriately authorised manufacturing site. However, when justified, it may be performed at the investigational site by or under the supervision of the clinical trial site pharmacist, or other health care professional in accordance with national regulations. Where this is not possible, it may be performed by the clinical trial monitor(s) who should be appropriately trained. The operation should be performed in accordance with GMP principles, specific and standard operating procedures and under contract, if applicable, and should be checked by a second person. This additional labelling should be properly documented in both the trial documentation and in the batch records.

## Quality Control

**34** As processes may not be standardised or fully validated, testing takes on more importance in ensuring that each batch meets its specification.

**35** Quality control should be performed in accordance with the Product Specification File and in accordance with the information notified pursuant to Article 9(2) of Directive 2001/20/EC. Verification of the effectiveness of blinding should be performed and recorded.

**36** Samples are retained to fulfill two purposes; firstly to provide a sample for analytical testing and secondly to provide a specimen of the finished product. Samples may therefore fall into two categories:

> *Reference sample*: a sample of a batch of starting material, packaging material, product contained in its primary packaging or finished product which is stored for the purpose of being analysed should the need arise. Where stability permits, reference samples from critical intermediate stages (e.g. those requiring analytical testing and release) or intermediates, which are transported outside of the manufacturer's control, should be kept.
>
> *Retention sample*: a sample of a packaged unit from a batch of finished product for each packaging run/trial period. It is stored for identification purposes. For example, presentation, packaging, labeling, leaflet, batch number, expiry date should the need arise.

In many instances the reference and retention samples will be presented identically, i.e. as fully packaged units. In such circumstances, reference and retention samples may be regarded as interchangeable. Reference and retention samples of investigational medicinal product, including blinded product should be kept for at least two years after completion or formal discontinuation of the last clinical trial in which the batch was used, whichever period is the longer.

Consideration should be given to keeping retention samples until the clinical report has been prepared to enable confirmation of product identity in the event of, and as part of an investigation into inconsistent trial results.

**37** The storage location of Reference and Retention samples should be defined in a Technical Agreement between the sponsor and manufacturer(s) and should allow timely access by the competent authorities.

> *Reference samples* of finished product should be stored within the EEA or in a third country where appropriate arrangements have been made by the Community with the exporting country to ensure that the manufacturer of the investigational medicinal product applies standards of good manufacturing practice at least equivalent to those laid down by

EU GMP GUIDE PART I ANNEX 13 INVESTIGATIONAL MEDICINAL PRODUCTS

the Community. In exceptional circumstances the reference samples of the finished product may be stored by the manufacturer in another third country, in which case this should be justified, and documented in a technical agreement between the sponsor, importer in the EEA and that third country manufacturer.

The reference sample should be of sufficient size to permit the carrying out, on, at least, two occasions, of the full analytical controls on the batch in accordance with the IMP dossier submitted for authorisation to conduct the clinical trial.

In the case of *retention samples*, it is acceptable to store information related to the final packaging as written or electronic records if such records provide sufficient information. In the case of the latter, the system should comply with the requirements of Annex 11.

## Release of Batches

38   Release of investigational medicinal products (see paragraph 43) should not occur until after the Qualified Person has certified that the requirements of Article 13.3 of Directive 2001/20/EC have been met (see paragraph 39). The Qualified Person should take into account the elements listed in paragraph 40 as appropriate.

39   The duties of the Qualified Person in relation to investigational medicinal products are affected by the different circumstances that can arise and are referred to below. Table 2 summarises the elements that need to be considered for the most common circumstances:

(a)(i)   Product manufactured within EU but not subject to an EU marketing authorisation: the duties are laid down in Article 13.3 (a) of Directive 2001/20/EC.

(b)(ii)  Product sourced from the open market within EU in accordance with Article 80(b) of Directive 2001/83/EC and subject to an EU marketing authorisation, regardless of manufacturing origin: the duties are as described above, however, the scope of certification can be limited to assuring that the products are in accordance with the notification/request for authorisation to conduct the trial and any subsequent processing for the purpose of blinding, trial-specific packaging and labelling. The Product Specification File will be similarly restricted in scope (see 9).

(c)      Product imported directly from a 3rd country: the duties are laid down in Article 13.3(b) of Directive 2001/20/EC. Where investigational medicinal products are imported from a 3rd country and they are subject to arrangements concluded between the Community and that country, such as a Mutual Recognition Agreement (MRA), equivalent standards of Good Manufacturing Practice apply provided any such agreement is relevant to the product in question. In the absence of an MRA, the Qualified Person should determine that equivalent standards of Good Manufacturing Practice apply through knowledge of the quality system employed at the manufacturer. This knowledge is normally acquired through audit of the manufacturer's quality systems. In either case, the Qualified Person may then certify on the basis of documentation supplied by the 3rd country manufacturer (see 40).

(d)    For imported comparator products where adequate assurance cannot be obtained in order to certify that each batch has been manufactured to equivalent standards of Good Manufacturing Practice, the duty of the Qualified Person is defined in Article 13.3(c) of Directive 2001/20/EC.

40   Assessment of each batch for certification prior to release may include as appropriate:

- batch records, including control reports, in-process test reports and release reports demonstrating compliance with the product specification file, the order, protocol and randomisation code. These records should include all deviations or planned changes, and any consequent additional checks or tests, and should be completed and endorsed by the staff authorised to do so according to the quality system;
- production conditions;
- the validation status of facilities, processes and methods;
- examination of finished packs;
- where relevant, the results of any analyses or tests performed after importation;
- stability reports;
- the source and verification of conditions of storage and shipment;
- audit reports concerning the quality system of the manufacturer;
- Documents certifying that the manufacturer is authorised to manufacture investigational medicinal products or comparators for export by the appropriate authorities in the country of export;
- where relevant, regulatory requirements for marketing authorisation, GMP standards applicable and any official verification of GMP compliance;
- all other factors of which the QP is aware that are relevant to the quality of the batch.

The relevance of the above elements is affected by the country of origin of the product, the manufacturer, and the marketed status of the product (with or without a marketing authorisation, in the EU or in a third country) and its phase of development. The sponsor should ensure that the elements taken into account by the qualified person when certifying the batch are consistent with the information notified pursuant to Article 9(2) of Directive 2001/20/EC. See also section 44.

41 Where investigational medicinal products are manufactured and packaged at different sites under the supervision of different Qualified Persons, the recommendations listed in Annex 16 to the GMP Guide should be followed as applicable.

42 Where, permitted in accordance with local regulations, packaging or labelling is carried out at the investigator site by, or under the supervision of a clinical trials pharmacist, or other health care professional as allowed in those regulations, the Qualified Person is not required to certify the activity in question. The sponsor is nevertheless responsible for ensuring that the activity is adequately documented and carried out in accordance with the principles of GMP and should seek the advice of the Qualified Person in this regard.

## Shipping

43 Investigational medicinal products should remain under the control of the sponsor until after completion of a two-step procedure: certification by the Qualified Person; and release by the sponsor for use in a clinical trial following fulfillment of the requirements of Article 9 (Commencement of a clinical trial) of Directive 2001/20/EC. Both steps should be recorded[3] and retained in the relevant trial files held by or on behalf of the sponsor. The Sponsor should ensure that the details set out in the clinical trial application and considered by the Qualified Person are consistent with what is finally accepted by the Competent Authorities. Suitable arrangements to meet this requirement should be established. In practical terms, this can best be achieved through a change control process for the Product Specification File and defined in a Technical Agreement between the QP and the Sponsor.

44 Shipping of investigational products should be conducted according to instructions given by or on behalf of the sponsor in the shipping order.

45 De-coding arrangements should be available to the appropriate responsible personnel before investigational medicinal products are shipped to the investigator site.

---

[3] A harmonised format for batch certification to facilitate movement between Member States is provided in attachment 3.

46 A detailed inventory of the shipments made by the manufacturer or importer should be maintained. It should particularly mention the addressees' identification.

47 Transfers of investigational medicinal products from one trial site to another should remain the exception. Such transfers should be covered by standard operating procedures. The product history while outside of the control of the manufacturer, through for example, trial monitoring reports and records of storage conditions at the original trial site should be reviewed as part of the assessment of the product's suitability for transfer and the advice of the Qualified Person should be sought. The product should be returned to the manufacturer, or another authorised manufacturer for re-labelling, if necessary, and certification by a Qualified Person. Records should be retained and full traceability ensured.

## Complaints

48 The conclusions of any investigation carried out in relation to a complaint which could arise from the quality of the product should be discussed between the manufacturer or importer and the sponsor (if different). This should involve the Qualified Person and those responsible for the relevant clinical trial in order to assess any potential impact on the trial, product development and on subjects.

## Recalls and Returns

### Recalls

49 Procedures for retrieving investigational medicinal products and documenting this retrieval should be agreed by the sponsor, in collaboration with the manufacturer or importer where different. The investigator and monitor need to understand their obligations under the retrieval procedure.

50 The Sponsor should ensure that the supplier of any comparator or other medication to be used in a clinical trial has a system for communicating to the Sponsor the need to recall any product supplied.

### Returns

51 Investigational medicinal products should be returned on agreed conditions defined by the sponsor, specified in approved written procedures.

52    Returned investigational medicinal products should be clearly identified and stored in an appropriately controlled, dedicated area. Inventory records of the returned medicinal products should be kept.

## Destruction

53    The Sponsor is responsible for the destruction of unused and/or returned investigational medicinal products. Investigational medicinal products should therefore not be destroyed without prior written authorisation by the Sponsor.

54    The delivered, used and recovered quantities of product should be recorded, reconciled and verified by or on behalf of the Sponsor for each trial site and each trial period. Destruction of unused investigational medicinal products should be carried out for a given trial site or a given trial period only after any discrepancies have been investigated and satisfactorily explained and the reconciliation has been accepted. Recording of destruction operations should be carried out in such a manner that all operations may be accounted for. The records should be kept by the Sponsor.

55    When destruction of investigational medicinal products takes place a dated certificate of, or receipt for destruction, should be provided to the Sponsor. These documents should clearly identify, or allow traceability to, the batches and/or patient numbers involved and the actual quantities destroyed.

## ATTACHMENT 3

[LETTERHEAD OF MANUFACTURER]
   Content of the Batch Certificate
   Referred to in Art. 13.3 Directive 2001/20/EC

(1)    Name(s) of product(s)/product identifier(s) as referred to in the clinical trial application, where applicable.

(2)    EudraCT No(s) and sponsor protocol code number, when available.

(3)    Strength
       *Identity (name) and amount per unit dose for all active substance(s) for each IMP (including placebo). The manner in which this information is provided should not unblind the study.*

(4)    Dosage form (pharmaceutical form)

(5)   Package size (contents of container) and type (e.g. vials, bottles, blisters).

(6)   Lot/batch number

(7)   Expiry/retest/use by date

(8)   Name and address of manufacturer where the Qualified Person issuing the certificate is located.

(9)   Manufacturing Authorisation number for the site listed under item 8.

(10)   Comments/remarks

(11)   Any additional information considered relevant by the QP.

(12)   Certification statement.

(13)   "I hereby certify that this batch complies with the requirements of Article 13.3 of Directive 2001/20/EC"

(14)   Name of the QP signing the certificate

(15)   Signature

(16)   Date of signature

## Explanatory note

Investigational medicinal products may not be used in a clinical trial in a Member State of the EEA until the completion of the two-step procedure referred to in section 43 of this Annex. The first step is the certification of each batch by the Qualified Person of the manufacturer or importer that the provisions of Article 13.3(a), (b) or (c) of Directive 2001/20/EC have been complied with and documented in accordance with Art. 13.4 of the same Directive. According to Directive 2001/20/EC a batch of investigational medicinal product shall not have to undergo further checks in relation to the provisions of article 13.3(a), (b) or (c) of the same directive when it moves between Member States accompanied by batch certification signed by the Qualified Person. In order to facilitate the free movement of investigational medicinal products between Member States the content of these certificates should be in accordance with the above harmonised format. This format may also be used to certify batches destined for use within the Member State of the manufacturer or importer.

**Table 1** Summary of labelling details (§26 to 30)

| | |
|---|---|
| (a) name, address and telephone number of the sponsor, contract research organisation or investigator (the main contact for information on the product, clinical trial and emergency unblinding) | GENERAL CASE<br>For both the primary and secondary packaging (§26) |
| (b) pharmaceutical dosage form, route of administration, quantity of dosage units, and in the case of open trials, the name/identifier and strength/potency; | |
| (c) the batch and/or code number to identify the contents and packaging operation; | Particulars $a^1$ to k |
| (d) a trial reference code allowing identification of the trial, site, investigator and sponsor if not given elsewhere; | |
| (e) the trial subject identification number/treatment number and where relevant, the visit number; | PRIMARY PACKAGE<br>Where primary and secondary packaging remain together throughout (§29)$^5$ |
| (f) the name of the investigator (if not included in (a) or (d)); | |
| (g) directions for use (reference may be made to a leaflet or other explanatory document intended for the trial subject or person administering the product); | $a^2 b^3$ c d e |
| (h) "for clinical trial use only" or similar wording; | |
| (i) the storage conditions; | |
| (j) period of use (use-by date, expiry date or re-test date as applicable), in month/year format and in a manner that avoids any ambiguity; | PRIMARY PACKAGE<br>Blisters or small packaging units (§30)$^5$ |
| (k) "keep out of reach of children" except when the product is for use in trials where the product is not taken home by subjects. | $a^2 b^{3,4}$ c d e |

$^1$ The address and telephone number of the main contact for information on the product, clinical trial and for emergency unblinding need not appear on the label where the subject has been given a leaflet or card which provides these details and has been instructed to keep this in their possession at all times (§27).

$^2$ The address and telephone number of the main contact for information on the product, clinical trial and for emergency unblinding need not be included.

$^3$ Route of administration may be excluded for oral solid dose forms.

$^4$ The pharmaceutical dosage form and quantity of dosage units may be omitted.

$^5$ When the outer packaging carries the particulars listed in Article 26.

## Table 2 Batch release of products

| ELEMENTS TO BE TAKEN INTO ACCOUNT(3) | PRODUCT AVAILABLE IN THE EU | | PRODUCT IMPORTED FROM THIRD COUNTRIES | | |
|---|---|---|---|---|---|
| | Product manufactured in EU without MA | Product with MA and available on EU market | Product without any EU MA | Product with a EU MA | Comparator where documentation certifying that each batch has been manufactured in conditions at least equivalent to those laid down in Directive 2003/94/EC cannot be obtained |
| **BEFORE CLINICAL TRIAL PROCESSING** | | | | | |
| a) Shipping and storage conditions | Yes | | | | |
| b) All relevant factors (1) showing that each batch has been manufactured and released in accordance with: | | | | | |
| Directive 2003/94/EC. | Yes | | Yes (2) | | |
| GMP standards at least equivalent to those laid down in Directive 2003/94/EC. | – | | | | |
| c) Documentation showing that each batch has been released within the EU according to EU GMP requirements (see Directive 2001/83/EC, article 51), or documentation showing that the product is available on the EU market and has been procured in accordance with article 80(b) of Directive 2001/83/EC. | | Yes | | | |
| d) Documentation showing that the product is available on the local market and documentation to establish confidence in the local regulatory requirements for marketing authorisation and release for local use. | | | | | Yes |
| e) Results of all analysis, tests and checks performed to assess the quality of the imported batch according to: | | | | | |
| the requirements of the MA (see Directive 2001/83/EC, article 51b), or | | | – | Yes | – |
| the Product Specification File, the Order, article 9.2 submission to the regulatory authorities. | | | Yes | – | Yes |
| Where these analyses and tests are not performed in the EU, this should be justified and the QP must certify that they have been carried out in accordance with GMP standards at least equivalent to those laid down in Directive 2003/94/EC. | | | Yes | Yes | Yes |
| **AFTER CLINICAL TRIAL PROCESSING** | | | | | |
| f) In addition to the assessment before clinical trial processing, all further relevant factors (1) showing that each batch has been processed for the purposes of blinding, trial-specific packaging, labelling and testing in accordance with: | | | | | |
| Directive 2003/94/EC, or | Yes | | Yes (2) | | |
| GMP standards at least equivalent to those laid down in Directive 2003/94/EC. | – | | | | |

(1) These factors are summarised in paragraph 40.

(2) Where an MRA or similar arrangements are in place covering the products in question, equivalent standards of GMP apply.

(3) In all cases the information notified pursuant to Article 9(2) of Directive 2001/20/EC should be consistent with the elements actually taken into account by the QP who certifies the batch prior to release.

EU GMP GUIDE PART I ANNEX 13 INVESTIGATIONAL MEDICINAL PRODUCTS

# ANNEX 14 MANUFACTURE OF MEDICINAL PRODUCTS DERIVED FROM HUMAN BLOOD OR PLASMA

## Glossary

**BLOOD**

Blood, as referred to in Directive 2002/98/EC (Art. 3a), means whole blood collected from a donor and processed either for transfusion or for further manufacturing.

**BLOOD COMPONENT**

A blood component, as referred to in Directive 2002/98/EC (Art. 3b), means a therapeutic constituent of blood (red cells, white cells, platelets and plasma) that can be prepared by various methods.

**BLOOD ESTABLISHMENT**

A blood establishment, as referred to in Directive 2002/98/EC (Art. 3e), is any structure or body that is responsible for any aspect of the collection and testing of human blood and blood components, whatever their intended purpose, and their processing, storage and distribution when intended for transfusion. While this definition does not include hospital blood banks, it is understood to include centres where apheresis of plasma is performed.

**BLOOD PRODUCTS**

A blood product, as referred to in Directive 2002/98/EC (Art. 3c), means any therapeutic product derived from human blood or plasma.

**FRACTIONATION, FRACTIONATION PLANT**

Fractionation is the manufacturing process in a plant (fractionation plant) during which plasma components are separated/purified by various physical and chemical methods such as e.g. precipitation, chromatography.

**GOOD PRACTICE GUIDELINES**

Good practice guidelines give interpretation on the Community standards and specifications defined for quality systems in blood establishments established in the Annex of Directive 2005/62/EC.[1]

**MEDICINAL PRODUCTS DERIVED FROM HUMAN BLOOD OR HUMAN PLASMA**

Medicinal products derived from human blood or human plasma, as referred to in Directive 2001/83/EC (Art. 1 No. 10), are medicinal products based on blood constituents which are prepared industrially by public or private establishments.

---

[1] At the time of publication of this Annex adoption of the Good Practice guidelines by the European Commission was still pending.

## PLASMA FOR FRACTIONATION

Plasma for fractionation is the liquid part of human blood remaining after separation of the cellular elements from blood collected in a container containing an anticoagulant, or separated by continuous filtration or centrifugation of anti-coagulated blood in an apheresis procedure; it is intended for the manufacture of plasma derived medicinal products, in particular albumin, coagulation factors and immunoglobulins of human origin and specified in the European Pharmacopoeia (Ph. Eur.) monograph "Human Plasma for fractionation" (0853).

## PLASMA MASTER FILE (PMF)

A Plasma Master File, as referred to in Directive 2001/83/EC (Annex I, Part III, No. 1.1.a), is a stand-alone document, which is separate from the dossier for marketing authorisation. It provides all relevant detailed information on the characteristics of the entire human plasma used as a starting material and/or a raw material for the manufacture of sub/intermediate fractions, constituents of the excipients and active substances, which are part of plasma, derived medicinal products or medical devices.

## PROCESSING

According to the terminology of Directive 2005/62/EC, "processing means any step in the preparation of blood component that is carried out between the collection of blood and the issuing of a blood component", e.g. separation and freezing of blood components. In this Annex, processing in addition refers to those operations performed at the blood establishment that are specific to plasma to be used for fractionation.

## QUALIFIED PERSON (QP)

The qualified person is the person referred to in Directive 2001/83/EC (Art. 48).

## RESPONSIBLE PERSON (RP)

The responsible person is the person referred to in Directive 2002/98/EC (Art. 9).

## THIRD COUNTRIES CONTRACT FRACTIONATION PROGRAM

This is a contract fractionation in a plant of a fractionator/manufacturer in the EU/EEA, using starting material from third countries and manufacturing products not intended for the EU/EEA market.

## 1    Scope

1.1    The provisions of this Annex apply to medicinal products derived from human blood or plasma, fractionated in or imported into the EU/EEA. The Annex applies also to the starting material (e.g. human plasma) for these products. In line with the conditions set out in Directive 2003/63/EC, the requirements apply also for stable derivatives of human blood or human plasma (e.g. Albumin) incorporated into medical devices.

1.2    This Annex defines specific Good Manufacturing Practices (GMP) requirements for processing, storage and transport of human plasma used for fractionation and for the manufacture of medicinal products derived from human blood or plasma.

1.3    The Annex addresses specific provisions for when starting material is imported from third countries and for contract fractionation programs for third countries.

1.4    The Annex does not apply to blood components intended for transfusion.

## 2    Principles

2.1    Medicinal products derived from human blood or plasma (and their active substances which are used as starting materials) must comply with the principles and guidelines of Good Manufacturing Practice (as laid down in Commission Directive 2003/94/EC and the EU Guidelines on GMP published by the European Commission) as well as the relevant marketing authorisation (Directive 2001/83/EC, Art. 46, 51). They are considered to be biological medicinal products and the starting materials include biological substances, such as cells or fluids (including blood or plasma) of human origin (Directive 2001/83/EC Annex I Part I, No.3.2.1.1.b). Certain special features arise from the biological nature of the source material. For example, disease-transmitting agents, especially viruses, may contaminate the source material. The quality and safety of these products relies therefore on the control of source materials and their origin as well as on the subsequent manufacturing procedures, including infectious marker testing, virus removal and virus inactivation.

2.2    In principle active substances used as starting material for medicinal products must comply with the principles and guidelines of Good Manufacturing Practice (see 2.1). For starting materials derived from human blood and plasma the requirements for the collection and testing defined in Directive 2002/98/EC are to be followed. Collection and testing must be performed in accordance with an appropriate quality system for which standards and specifications are defined in the Annex of Directive

2005/62/EC and interpreted in the Good Practice guidelines referred to in Article 2 (2) of Directive 2005/62/EC. Furthermore, the requirements of Directive 2005/61/EC on traceability and serious adverse reactions and serious adverse event notifications from the donor to the recipient apply. In addition the monographs of the European Pharmacopoeia are to be observed (Directive 2001/83/EC, Annex 1, Part III No. 1.1.b).

2.3     Starting material for the manufacture of medicinal products derived from human blood or plasma imported from third countries and intended for use or distribution in the EU/EEA must meet standards which are equivalent to Community Standards and specifications relating to a quality system for blood establishments as set out in Commission Directive 2005/62/EC (Recital 6; Article 2(3)), the traceability and serious adverse reaction and serious adverse event notification requirements as set out in Commission Directive 2005/61/EC (Recital 5; Article 7), and the technical requirements for blood and blood components as set out in Commission Directive 2004/33/EC (Recital 4; point 2.3 of Annex V)

2.4     In the case of third country contract fractionation programs the starting material imported from third countries must be in compliance with the quality and safety requirements as laid down in Directive 2002/98/EC and in Annex V of Directive 2004/33/EC. The activities conducted within the EU/EEA must fully comply with GMP. Consideration should be given to the Community standards and specifications relating to a quality system for blood establishments set out in Commission Directive 2005/62/EC, the traceability requirements and notification of serious adverse reactions and events set out in Commission Directive 2005/61/EC and the relevant WHO guidelines and recommendations as listed in the addendum

2.5     For all subsequent steps after collection and testing (e.g. processing (including separation), freezing, storage and transport to the manufacturer) the requirements of Directive 2001/83/EC apply and must therefore be done in accordance with the principles and guidelines of Good Manufacturing Practice. Normally, these activities would be carried out under the responsibility of a Qualified Person in an establishment with a manufacturing authorisation. Where specific processing steps in relation to plasma for fractionation take place in a blood establishment, the specific appointment of a Qualified Person may, however, not be proportionate given the presence and responsibility of a Responsible Person. To address this particular situation and to ensure the legal responsibilities of the Qualified Person are properly addressed, the fractionation plant/manufacturer should establish a contract in accordance with Chapter 7 of the GMP Guide with the blood establishment that defines respective responsibilities and the detailed requirements in order to ensure compliance. The Responsible Person of the blood establishment and the

Qualified Person of the fractionation/manufacturing plant (see 3.5) should be involved in drawing up this contract. The Qualified Person should ensure that audits are performed to confirm that the blood establishment complies with the contract.

**2.6** Specific requirements for documentation and other arrangements relating to the starting material of plasma-derived medicinal products are defined in the Plasma Master File.

## 3    Quality Management

**3.1** Quality management should govern all stages from donor selection to delivery of the finished product. Reference is made to Directive 2005/61/EC for traceability up to and including the delivery of plasma to the fractionation plant, and to Directive 2005/62/EC for all stages concerning collection and testing of human blood and human plasma to be used for the manufacture of medicinal products.

**3.2** Blood or plasma used as source material for the manufacture of medicinal products must be collected by blood establishments and be tested in laboratories which apply quality systems in accordance with Directive 2005/62/EC, are authorised by a national competent authority and are subject to regular inspections as referred to in Directive 2002/98/EC. Third country contract fractionation programs have to be notified to the competent EU authority by the manufacturer as referred to in Directive 2001/83/EC.

**3.3** If plasma is imported from third countries it should only be purchased from approved suppliers (e.g. blood establishments, including external ware-houses). They should be named in the specifications for starting materials as defined by the fractionation plant/manufacturer, and be accepted by an EU/EEA competent authority (e.g. following an inspection) and by the Qualified Person of the fractionation plant in the EU/EEA. Certification and release of plasma (plasma for fractionation) as starting material is mentioned in section 6.8.

**3.4** Supplier qualification, including audits, should be performed by the fractionation plant/manufacturer of the finished product according to written procedures. Re-qualification of suppliers should be performed at regular intervals taking a risk-based approach into account.

**3.5** The fractionation plant/manufacturer of the finished product should establish written contracts with the supplying blood establishments. As a minimum the following key aspects should be addressed:

- definition of duties and respective responsibilities
- quality system and documentation requirements

- donor selection criteria and testing
- requirements for the separation of blood into blood components/plasma
- freezing of plasma
- storage and transport of plasma
- traceability and post donation / collection information (including adverse events).

The test results of all units supplied by the blood establishment should be available to the fractionation plant/manufacturer of the medicinal product. In addition, any fractionation step subcontracted should be defined in a written contract.

**3.6** A formal change control system should be in place to plan, evaluate and document all changes that may affect the quality or safety of the products, or traceability. The potential impact of proposed changes should be evaluated. The need for additional testing and validation, especially viral inactivation and removal steps, should be determined.

**3.7** An adequate safety strategy should be in place to minimise the risk from infectious agents and emerging infectious agents. This strategy should involve a risk assessment that:

- defines an inventory holding time (internal quarantine time) before processing the plasma i.e. to remove look back units[2]
- considers all aspects of virus reduction and/or testing for infectious agents or surrogates.
- considers the virus reduction capabilities, the pool size and other relevant aspects of the manufacturing processes.

## 4 Traceability and Post Collection Measures

**4.1** There must be a system in place that enables each donation to be traced, from the donor and the donation via the blood establishment through to the batch of medicinal product and vice versa.

**4.2** Responsibilities for traceability of the product should be defined (there should be no gaps):

- from the donor and the donation in the blood establishment to the fractionation plant (this is the responsibility of the RP at the blood establishment),

---

[2] Plasma units donated by donors during a defined period (as defined on a national / EU basis) before it is found that a donation from a high-risk donor should have been excluded from processing, e.g. due to a positive test result.

- from the fractionation plant to the manufacturer of the medicinal product and any secondary facility, whether a manufacturer of a medicinal product or of a medical device (this is the responsibility of the QP).

4.3   Data needed for full traceability must be stored for at least 30 years, according to Article 4 of Directive 2005/61/EC and Article 14 of Directive 2002/98/EC[3].

4.4   The contracts (as mentioned in 3.5) between the blood establishments (including testing laboratories) and the fractionation plant/manufacturer should ensure that traceability and post collection measures cover the complete chain from the collection of the plasma to all manufacturers responsible for release of the final products.

4.5   The blood establishments should notify the fractionating plant/manufacturer of any event which may affect the quality or safety of the product including events listed in Annex II part A and Annex III part A of Directive 2005/61/EC, and other relevant information found subsequent to donor acceptance or release of the plasma, e.g. look back information[4] (post-collection information). Where the fractionation plant/manufacturer is located in a third country, the information should be forwarded to the manufacturer responsible for release in the EU/EEA of any product manufactured from the plasma concerned. In both cases, if relevant for the quality or safety of the final product, this information should be forwarded to the competent authority[5] responsible for the fractionation plant/manufacturer.

4.6   The notification procedure as described in 4.5 also applies when an inspection of a blood establishment by a competent authority leads to a withdrawal of an existing licence/certificate/ approval.

4.7   The management of post-collection information should be described in standard operating procedures and taking into account obligations and procedures for informing the competent authorities. Post-collection measures should be available as defined in the "Note for Guidance on Plasma Derived Medicinal Products" in its current version as adopted by the Committee for Medicinal Products for Human Use (CHMP) and published by the European Medicines Agency.[6]

---

[3] Both Directives are linked to Article 109 of Directive 2001/83/EC by defining specific rules for medicinal products derived from human blood or plasma.

[4] Information that appears if a subsequent donation from a donor previously found negative for viral markers is found positive for any of the viral markers or any other risk factors which may induce a viral infection.

[5] as referred to in Directive 2001/83/EC

[6] Current version at date of publication: CPMP/BWP/269/95

## 5 Premises and Equipment

5.1 In order to minimise microbiological contamination or the introduction of foreign material into the plasma pool, thawing and pooling of plasma units should be performed in an area conforming at least to the Grade D requirements defined in Annex 1 of the EU-GMP Guide. Appropriate clothing should be worn including face masks and gloves. All other open manipulations during the manufacturing process should be done under conditions conforming to the appropriate requirements of Annex 1 of the EU-GMP Guide.

5.2 Environmental monitoring should be performed regularly, especially during the 'opening' of plasma containers, and during subsequent thawing and pooling processes in accordance with Annex 1 of the EU-GMP Guide. Acceptance limits should be specified.

5.3 In the production of plasma-derived medicinal products, appropriate viral inactivation or removal procedures are used and steps should be taken to prevent cross contamination of treated with untreated products. Dedicated and distinct premises and equipment should be used for manufacturing steps after viral inactivation treatment.

5.4 To avoid placing routine manufacture at risk of contamination from viruses used during validation studies, the validation of methods for virus reduction should not be conducted in production facilities. Validation should be performed according to the "Note for Guidance on Virus Validation Studies: The Design, Contribution and Interpretation of Studies validating the Inactivation and Removal of Viruses" in its current version as adopted by the Committee for Medicinal Products for Human Use (CHMP) and published by the European Medicines Agency[7].

## 6 Manufacturing

### Starting material

6.1 The starting material should comply with the requirements of all relevant monographs of the European Pharmacopoeia and of the conditions laid down in the respective marketing authorisation dossier including the Plasma Master File. These requirements should be defined in the written contract (see 3.5) between the blood establishment and the fractionating plant/manufacturer and controlled through the quality system.

EU GMP GUIDE PART I ANNEX 14 MANUFACTURE OF MEDICINAL PRODUCTS DERIVED FROM HUMAN BLOOD OR PLASMA

---

[7] Current version at date of publication: CHMP/BWP/268/95

**6.2** Starting material for third country contract fractionation programs should comply with the requirements as specified in 2.4.

**6.3** Depending on the type of collection (i.e. either whole blood collection or automated apheresis) different processing steps may be required. All processing steps (e.g. centrifugation and/or separation, sampling, labelling, freezing) should be defined in written procedures.

**6.4** Any mix-ups of units and of samples, especially during labelling, as well as any contamination, e.g. when cutting the tube segments/sealing the containers, must be avoided.

**6.5** Freezing is a critical step for the recovery of proteins that are labile in plasma, e.g. clotting factors. Freezing should therefore be performed as soon as possible after collection (see the European Pharmacopoeia monograph No 0853 "*Human Plasma for Fractionation*" and where relevant, monograph No 1646 "*Human Plasma pooled and treated for virus inactivation*"), following a validated method.

**6.6** The storage and transport of blood or plasma at any stage in the transport chain to the fractionation plant should be defined and recorded. Any deviation from the defined temperature should be notified to the fractionation plant. Qualified equipment and validated procedures should be used.

## Certification/release of plasma for fractionation as starting material

**6.7** Plasma for fractionation should only be released, i.e. from a quarantine status, through systems and procedures that assure the quality needed for the manufacture of the finished product. It should only be distributed to the plasma fractionation plant/manufacturer after it has been documented by the Responsible Person (or in case of blood/plasma collection in third countries by a person with equivalent responsibilities and qualifications) that the plasma for fractionation does comply with the requirements and specifications defined in the respective written contracts and that all steps have been performed in accordance with Good Practice and GMP Guidelines, as appropriate.

**6.8** On entering the fractionation plant, the plasma units should be released for fractionation under the responsibility of the Qualified Person. The Qualified Person should confirm that the plasma complies with the requirements of all relevant monographs and the conditions laid down in the respective marketing authorisation dossier including the Plasma Master File or, in case of plasma to be used for third country contract fractionation programs, with the requirements as specified in 2.4.

## Processing of plasma for fractionation

**6.9** The steps used in the fractionation process vary according to product and manufacturer and usually include several fractionation/purification procedures, some of which may contribute to the inactivation and/or removal of potential contamination.

**6.10** Requirements for the processes of pooling, pool sampling and fractionation/purification and virus inactivation/removal should be defined and followed thoroughly.

**6.11** The methods used in the viral inactivation process should be undertaken with strict adherence to validated procedures and in compliance with the methods used in the virus validation studies. Detailed investigation of failures in virus inactivation procedures should be performed. Adherence to the validated production process is especially important in the virus reduction procedures as any deviation could result in a safety risk for the final product. Procedures should be in place, that take this risk into consideration.

**6.12** Any reprocessing or reworking may only be performed after a quality risk management exercise has been performed and using processing steps as defined in the relevant marketing authorisation.

**6.13** A system for clearly segregating/distinguishing between products or intermediates which have undergone a process of virus reduction, from those which have not, should be in place.

**6.14** Depending on the outcome of a thorough risk management process (taking into consideration possible differences in epidemiology) production in campaigns including clear segregation and defined validated cleaning procedures should be adopted when plasma/intermediates of different origins is processed at the same plant. The requirement for such measures should be based on the recommendations of the Guideline on Epidemiological Data on Blood Transmissible Infections[8]. The risk management process should consider whether it is necessary to use dedicated equipment in the case of third country contract fractionation programs.

**6.15** For intermediate products intended to be stored, a shelf-life should be defined based on stability data.

**6.16** The storage and transport of intermediate and finished medicinal products at any stage of the transport chain should be specified and recorded. Qualified equipment and validated procedures should be used.

EU GMP GUIDE PART I ANNEX 14 MANUFACTURE OF MEDICINAL PRODUCTS DERIVED FROM HUMAN BLOOD OR PLASMA

---

[8] EMEA/CPMP/BWP/125/04

## 7    Quality Control

**7.1**    Testing requirements for viruses or other infectious agents should be considered in the light of knowledge emerging on infectious agents and on the availability of appropriate, validated test methods.

**7.2**    The first homogeneous plasma pool (e.g. after separation of the cryoprecipitate from the plasma pool) should be tested using validated test methods of suitable sensitivity and specificity, according to the relevant European Pharmacopoeia monographs (e.g. No. 0853).

## 8    Release of intermediate and finished products

**8.1**    Only batches derived from plasma pools tested and found negative for virus markers/ antibodies and found in compliance with the relevant European Pharmacopoeia monographs, including any specific virus cut-off limits, and with the approved specifications (e.g. Plasma Master File), should be released.

**8.2**    The release of intermediates intended for further in-house processing or delivery to a different site, and, the release of finished products should be performed by the Qualified Person and in accordance with the approved marketing authorisation.

**8.3.**    The release of intermediates and final products used in third country contract fractionation programs should be performed by the Qualified Person on the basis of standards agreed with the contract giver, and compliance with EU GMP standards. Compliance with relevant European Pharmacopoeia monographs may not be applicable, as these products are not intended for the use on the European market.

## 9    Retention of plasma pool samples

One plasma pool may be used to manufacture more than one batch and/or product. Retention samples and corresponding records from every pool should be kept for at least one year after the expiry date of the finished medicinal product with the longest shelf-life derived from the pool.

## 10    Disposal of waste

There should be written procedures for the safe and documented storage and disposal of waste, disposable and rejected items (e.g. contaminated units, units from infected donors, out of date blood, plasma, intermediate or finished products).

# Addendum

**(A)** Member States should implement the following Directives and guidelines:

**(1)** for collection and testing of blood and blood components:

| Directive/Guidelines | Title | Scope |
|---|---|---|
| Directive 2002/98/EC of the European Parliament and of the Council | Setting standards of quality and safety for the collection, testing, processing, storage and distribution of human blood and blood components, amending Directive 2001/83/EC. | Art.2 Defines standards of quality and safety for the collection and testing of human blood and blood components, whatever their intended purpose, and for their processing, storage and distribution when intended for transfusion. |
| Commission Directive 2004/33/EC | Implementing Directive 2002/98/EC of the European Parliament and of the Council as regards certain technical requirements for blood and blood components | Defines the provision of information to prospective donors and information required from donors (Part A and B, Annex II), eligibility of donors (Annex III), storage, transport and distribution conditions for blood and blood components (Annex IV), as well as quality and safety requirements for blood and blood components (Annex V). |
| Commission Directive 2005/61/EC | Implementing Directive 2002/98/EC of the European Parliament and of the Council as regards traceability requirements and notification of serious adverse reactions and events. | Defines traceability requirements for blood establishments, donors, blood and blood components, and for the final destination of each unit, whatever the intended purpose. It further defines the reporting requirements in the event of serious adverse events and reactions. |

EU GMP GUIDE PART I ANNEX 14 MANUFACTURE OF MEDICINAL PRODUCTS DERIVED FROM HUMAN BLOOD OR PLASMA

| Directive/Guidelines | Title | Scope |
|---|---|---|
| Commission Directive 2005/62/EC | Implementing Directive 2002/98/EC of the European Parliament and of the Council as regards Community standards and specifications relating to a quality system for blood establishments. | Defines the implementation of quality system standards and specifications as referred to in article 47 of Directive 2001/83/EC. |

(2)    for collection and regulatory submission of data/information for plasma for fractionation:

| Directive/Guidelines | Title | Scope |
|---|---|---|
| Directive 2001/83/EC of the European Parliament and the Council | On the Community Code relating to medicinal products for human use. | Art. 2 Medicinal products for human use intended to be placed on the market in Member States and either prepared industrially or manufactured by a method involving an industrial process, covering medicinal products derived from human blood or human plasma. |
| Commission Directive 2003/63/EC | Amending Directive 2001/83/EC of the European Parliament and of the Council on the Community code relating to medicinal products for human use; Amending the Annex on documentation of medicinal products | |
| Commission Directive 2003/94/EC | Laying down the principles and guidelines of good manufacturing practice in respect of medicinal products for human use and investigational medicinal products for human use | Art. 1 Principles and guidelines of good manufacturing practice in respect of medicinal products for human use and investigational medicinal products for human use |
| EU Guidelines on Good Manufacturing Practice | Giving interpretation on the principles and guidelines on GMP | |

| Directive/Guidelines | Title | Scope |
|---|---|---|
| EMEA/CHMP/ BWP/3794/03 Rev.1, 15. Nov. 2006 | Guideline on the Scientific data requirements for a Plasma Master File (PMF) Revision 1 | |
| EMEA/CHMP/ BWP/548524/2008 EMEA Guideline | Guideline on Epidemiological Data on Blood Transmissible Infections | |

**(B)** Other relevant documents:

| Document | Title | Scope |
|---|---|---|
| Recommendation No. R (95) 15 (Council of Europe) | Guide to the Preparation, use and quality assurance of blood components | |
| WHO Recommendations for the production, control and regulation of human plasma for fractination. Annex 4 in: WHO Expert Committee on Biological Standardization. Fifty-sixth report. Geneva, World Health Organization,2007 (WHO Technical Report Series, No.941) | WHO Recommendations for the production, control and regulation of human plasma for fractionation | Guidance on the production, control and regulation of human plasma for fractionation |
| WHO guidelines on Good Manufacturing Practices for blood establishments | | |

Reference should be made to the latest revisions of these documents for current guidance.

EU GMP GUIDE PART I ANNEX 14 MANUFACTURE OF MEDICINAL PRODUCTS DERIVED FROM HUMAN BLOOD OR PLASMA

## ANNEX 15 QUALIFICATION AND VALIDATION

### Principle

1 This Annex describes the principles of qualification and validation which are applicable to the manufacture of medicinal products. It is a requirement of GMP that manufacturers identify what validation work is needed to prove control of the critical aspects of their particular operations. Significant changes to the facilities, the equipment and the processes, which may affect the quality of the product, should be validated. A risk assessment approach should be used to determine the scope and extent of validation.

### Planning for Validation

2 All validation activities should be planned. The key elements of a validation programme should be clearly defined and documented in a validation master plan (VMP) or equivalent documents.

3 The VMP should be a summary document which is brief, concise and clear.

4 The VMP should contain data on at least the following:

(a) validation policy;
(b) organisational structure of validation activities;
(c) summary of facilities, systems, equipment and processes to be validated;
(d) documentation format: the format to be used for protocols and reports;
(e) planning and scheduling;
(f) change control;
(g) reference to existing documents.

5 In case of large projects, it may be necessary to create separate validation master plans.

### Documentation

6 A written protocol should be established that specifies how qualification and validation will be conducted. The protocol should be reviewed and approved. The protocol should specify critical steps and acceptance criteria.

7 A report that cross-references the qualification and/or validation protocol should be prepared, summarising the results obtained, commenting on any deviations observed, and drawing the necessary conclusions, including

recommending changes necessary to correct deficiencies. Any changes to the plan as defined in the protocol should be documented with appropriate justification.

8  After completion of a satisfactory qualification, a formal release for the next step in qualification and validation should be made as a written authorisation.

## Qualification

### Design qualification

9  The first element of the validation of new facilities, systems or equipment could be design qualification (DQ).

10  The compliance of the design with GMP should be demonstrated and documented.

### Installation qualification

11  Installation qualification (IQ) should be performed on new or modified facilities, systems and equipment.

12  IQ should include, but not be limited to the following:

(a) installation of equipment, piping, services and instrumentation checked to current engineering drawings and specifications;
(b) collection and collation of supplier operating and working instructions and maintenance requirements;
(c) calibration requirements;
(d) verification of materials of construction.

### Operational qualification

13  Operational qualification (OQ) should follow Installation qualification.

14  OQ should include, but not be limited to the following:

(a) tests that have been developed from knowledge of processes, systems and equipment;
(b) tests to include a condition or a set of conditions encompassing upper and lower operating limits, sometimes referred to as "worst case" conditions.

15  The completion of a successful Operational qualification should allow the finalisation of calibration, operating and cleaning procedures, operator

training and preventative maintenance requirements. It should permit a formal "release" of the facilities, systems and equipment.

## Performance qualification

16  Performance qualification (PQ) should follow successful completion of Installation qualification and Operational qualification.

17  PQ should include, but not be limited to the following:

(a) tests, using production materials, qualified substitutes or simulated product, that have been developed from knowledge of the process and the facilities, systems or equipment;

(b) tests to include a condition or set of conditions encompassing upper and lower operating limits.

18  Although PQ is described as a separate activity, it may in some cases be appropriate to perform it in conjunction with OQ.

## Qualification of established (in-use) facilities, systems and equipment

19  Evidence should be available to support and verify the operating parameters and limits for the critical variables of the operating equipment. Additionally, the calibration, cleaning, preventative maintenance, operating procedures and operator training procedures and records should be documented.

## Process Validation

### General

20  The requirements and principles outlined in this chapter are applicable to the manufacture of pharmaceutical dosage forms. They cover the initial validation of new processes, subsequent validation of modified processes and re-validation.

21  Process validation should normally be completed prior to the distribution and sale of the medicinal product (prospective validation). In exceptional circumstances, where this is not possible, it may be necessary to validate processes during routine production (concurrent validation). Processes in use for some time should also be validated (retrospective validation).

22  Facilities, systems and equipment to be used should have been qualified and analytical testing methods should be validated. Staff taking part in the validation work should have been appropriately trained.

23   Facilities, systems, equipment and processes should be periodically evaluated to verify that they are still operating in a valid manner.

## Prospective validation

24   Prospective validation should include, but not be limited to the following:

(a) short description of the process;
(b) summary of the critical processing steps to be investigated;
(c) list of the equipment/facilities to be used (including measuring/monitoring/recording equipment) together with its calibration status;
(d) finished product specifications for release;
(e) list of analytical methods, as appropriate;
(f) proposed in-process controls with acceptance criteria;
(g) additional testing to be carried out, with acceptance criteria and analytical validation, as appropriate;
(h) sampling plan;
(i) methods for recording and evaluating results;
(j) functions and responsibilities;
(k) proposed timetable.

25   Using this defined process (including specified components) a series of batches of the final product may be produced under routine conditions. In theory the number of process runs carried out and observations made should be sufficient to allow the normal extent of variation and trends to be established and to provide sufficient data for evaluation. It is generally considered acceptable that three consecutive batches/runs within the finally agreed parameters, would constitute a validation of the process.

26   Batches made for process validation should be the same size as the intended industrial scale batches.

27   If it is intended that validation batches be sold or supplied, the conditions under which they are produced should comply fully with the requirements of Good Manufacturing Practice, including the satisfactory outcome of the validation exercise, and with the marketing authorisation.

## Concurrent validation

28   In exceptional circumstances it may be acceptable not to complete a validation programme before routine production starts.

29   The decision to carry out concurrent validation must be justified, documented and approved by authorised personnel.

EU GMP GUIDE PART I ANNEX 15 QUALIFICATION AND VALIDATION

30  Documentation requirements for concurrent validation are the same as specified for prospective validation.

## Retrospective validation

31  Retrospective validation is only acceptable for well-established processes and will be inappropriate where there have been recent changes in the composition of the product, operating procedures or equipment.

32  Validation of such processes should be based on historical data. The steps involved require the preparation of a specific protocol and the reporting of the results of the data review, leading to a conclusion and a recommendation.

33  The source of data for this validation should include, but not be limited to batch processing and packaging records, process control charts, maintenance log books, records of personnel changes, process capability studies, finished product data, including trend cards and storage stability results.

34  Batches selected for retrospective validation should be representative of all batches made during the review period, including any batches that failed to meet specifications, and should be sufficient in number to demonstrate process consistency. Additional testing of retained samples may be needed to obtain the necessary amount or type of data to retrospectively validate the process.

35  For retrospective validation, generally data from ten to thirty consecutive batches should be examined to assess process consistency, but fewer batches may be examined if justified.

## Cleaning Validation

36  Cleaning validation should be performed in order to confirm the effectiveness of a cleaning procedure. The rationale for selecting limits of carry over of product residues, cleaning agents and microbial contamination should be logically based on the materials involved. The limits should be achievable and verifiable.

37  Validated analytical methods having sensitivity to detect residues or contaminants should be used. The detection limit for each analytical method should be sufficiently sensitive to detect the established acceptable level of the residue or contaminant.

38  Normally only cleaning procedures for product contact surfaces of the equipment need to be validated. Consideration should be given to non-contact parts. The intervals between use and cleaning as well as cleaning

and reuse should be validated. Cleaning intervals and methods should be determined.

39    For cleaning procedures for products and processes which are similar, it is considered acceptable to select a representative range of similar products and processes. A single validation study utilising a "worst case" approach can be carried out which takes account of the critical issues.

40    Typically three consecutive applications of the cleaning procedure should be performed and shown to be successful in order to prove that the method is validated.

41    "Test until clean" is not considered an appropriate alternative to cleaning validation.

42    Products which simulate the physicochemical properties of the substances to be removed may exceptionally be used instead of the substances themselves, where such substances are either toxic or hazardous.

## Change Control

43    Written procedures should be in place to describe the actions to be taken if a change is proposed to a starting material, product component, process equipment, process environment (or site), method of production or testing or any other change that may affect product quality or reproducibility of the process. Change control procedures should ensure that sufficient supporting data are generated to demonstrate that the revised process will result in a product of the desired quality, consistent with the approved specifications.

44    All changes that may affect product quality or reproducibility of the process should be formally requested, documented and accepted. The likely impact of the change of facilities, systems and equipment on the product should be evaluated, including risk analysis. The need for, and the extent of, re-qualification and re-validation should be determined.

## Revalidation

45    Facilities, systems, equipment and processes, including cleaning, should be periodically evaluated to confirm that they remain valid. Where no significant changes have been made to the validated status, a review with evidence that facilities, systems, equipment and processes meet the prescribed requirements fulfils the need for revalidation.

## Glossary

Definitions of terms relating to qualification and validation which are not given in the glossary of the current EC Guide to GMP, but which are used in this Annex, are given below.

### CHANGE CONTROL

A formal system by which qualified representatives of appropriate disciplines review proposed or actual changes that might affect the validated status of facilities, systems, equipment or processes. The intent is to determine the need for action that would ensure and document that the system is maintained in a validated state.

### CLEANING VALIDATION

Cleaning validation is documented evidence that an approved cleaning procedure will provide equipment which is suitable for processing medicinal products.

### CONCURRENT VALIDATION

Validation carried out during routine production of products intended for sale.

### DESIGN QUALIFICATION (DQ)

The documented verification that the proposed design of the facilities, systems and equipment is suitable for the intended purpose.

### INSTALLATION QUALIFICATION (IQ)

The documented verification that the facilities, systems and equipment, as installed or modified, comply with the approved design and the manufacturer's recommendations.

### OPERATIONAL QUALIFICATION (OQ)

The documented verification that the facilities, systems and equipment, as installed or modified, perform as intended throughout the anticipated operating ranges.

### PERFORMANCE QUALIFICATION (PQ)

The documented verification that the facilities, systems and equipment, as connected together, can perform effectively and reproducibly, based on the approved process method and product specification.

### PROCESS VALIDATION

The documented evidence that the process, operated within established parameters, can perform effectively and reproducibly to produce a medicinal product meeting its predetermined specifications and quality attributes.

## PROSPECTIVE VALIDATION

Validation carried out before routine production of products intended for sale.

## RETROSPECTIVE VALIDATION

Validation of a process for a product which has been marketed based upon accumulated manufacturing, testing and control batch data.

## RE-VALIDATION

A repeat of the process validation to provide an assurance that changes in the process/equipment introduced in accordance with change control procedures do not adversely affect process characteristics and product quality.

## RISK ANALYSIS

Method to assess and characterise the critical parameters in the functionality of an equipment or process.

## SIMULATED PRODUCT

A material that closely approximates the physical and, where practical, the chemical characteristics (e.g. viscosity, particle size, pH etc.) of the product under validation. In many cases, these characteristics may be satisfied by a placebo product batch.

## SYSTEM

A group of equipment with a common purpose.

## WORST CASE

A condition or set of conditions encompassing upper and lower processing limits and circumstances, within standard operating procedures, which pose the greatest chance of product or process failure when compared to ideal conditions. Such conditions do not necessarily induce product or process failure.

## ANNEX 16 CERTIFICATION BY A QUALIFIED PERSON AND BATCH RELEASE

### 1 Scope

1.1 This annex to the Guide to Good Manufacturing Practice for Medicinal Products ("the Guide") gives guidance on the certification by a Qualified Person (Q.P.) and batch release within the European Community (EC) or European Economic Area (EEA) of medicinal products holding a marketing authorisation or made for export. The relevant legislative requirements are contained in Article 51 of Directive 2001/83/EC or Article 55 of Directive 2001/82/EC.

1.2 The annex covers in particular those cases where a batch has had different stages of production or testing conducted at different locations or by different manufacturers, and where an intermediate or bulk production batch is divided into more than one finished product batch. It also covers the release of batches which have been imported to the EC/EEA both when there is and is not a mutual recognition agreement between the Community and the third country. The guidance may also be applied to investigational medicinal products, subject to any difference in the legal provisions and more specific guidance in Annex 13 to the Guide.

1.3 This annex does not, of course, describe all possible arrangements which are legally acceptable. Neither does it address the official control authority batch release which may be specified for certain blood and immunological products in accordance with Article 11 point 5.4 and Articles 109[1] and 110 of Directive 2001/83/EC.

1.4 The basic arrangements for batch release for a product are defined by its Marketing Authorisation. Nothing in this Annex should be taken as overriding those arrangements.

### 2 Principle

2.1 Each batch of finished product must be certified by a Q.P. within the EC/EEA before being released for sale or supply in the EC/EEA or for export.

2.2 The purpose of controlling batch release in this way is:

---

[1] As amended by Directive 2002/98/EC of the European Parliament and of the Council of 27 January 2003 setting standards of quality and safety for the collection, testing, processing, storage and distribution of human blood and blood components and amending Directive 2001/83/EC (OJ L 33, 8.2.2003, p. 30).

● to ensure that the batch has been manufactured and checked in accordance with the requirements of its marketing authorisation, the principles and guidelines of EC Good Manufacturing Practice or the good manufacturing practice of a third country recognised as equivalent under a mutual recognition agreement and any other relevant legal requirement before it is placed on the market, and

● in the event that a defect needs to be investigated or a batch recalled, to ensure that the Q.P. who certified the batch and the relevant records are readily identifiable.

## 3   Introduction

**3.1**   Manufacture, including quality control testing, of a batch of medicinal products takes place in stages which may be conducted at different sites and by different manufacturers. Each stage should be conducted in accordance with the relevant marketing authorisation, Good Manufacturing Practice and the laws of the Member State concerned and should be taken into account by the Q.P. who certifies the finished product batch before release to the market.

**3.2**   However in an industrial situation it is usually not possible for a single Q.P. to be closely involved with every stage of manufacture. The Q.P. who certifies a finished product batch may need therefore to rely in part on the advice and decisions of others. Before doing so he should ensure that this reliance is well founded, either from personal knowledge or from the confirmation by other Q.P.s within a quality system which he has accepted.

**3.3**   When some stages of manufacture occur in a third country it is still a requirement that production and testing are in accordance with the marketing authorisation, that the manufacturer is authorised according to the laws of the country concerned and that manufacture follows good manufacturing practices at least equivalent to those of the EC.

**3.4**   Certain words used in this annex have particular meanings attributed to them, as defined in the glossary [to Annex 16].

## 4   General

**4.1**   One batch of finished product may have different stages of manufacture, importation, testing and storage before release conducted at different sites. Each site should be approved under one or more manufacturing authorisations and should have at its disposal the services of at least one Q.P. However the correct manufacture of a particular batch of product, regardless of how many sites are involved, should be the overall concern of the Q.P. who certifies that finished product batch before release.

4.2    Different batches of a product may be manufactured or imported and released at different sites in the EC/EEA. For example a Community marketing authorisation may name batch release sites in more than one Member State, and a national authorisation may also name more than one release site. In this situation the holder of the marketing authorisation and each site authorised to release batches of the product should be able to identify the site at which any particular batch has been released and the Q.P. who was responsible for certifying that batch.

4.3    The Q.P. who certifies a finished product batch before release may do so based on his personal knowledge of all the facilities and procedures employed, the expertise of the persons concerned and of the quality system within which they operate. Alternatively he may rely on the confirmation by one or more other Q.P.s of the compliance of intermediate stages of manufacture within a quality system which he has accepted.

This confirmation by other Q.P.s should be documented and should identify clearly the matters which have been confirmed. The systematic arrangements to achieve this should be defined in a written agreement.

4.4    The agreement mentioned above is required whenever a Q.P. wishes to rely on the confirmation by another Q.P. The agreement should be in general accordance with Chapter 7 of the Guide. The Q.P. who certifies the finished product batch should ensure the arrangements in the agreement are verified. The form of such an agreement should be appropriate to the relationship between the parties; for example a standard operating procedure within a company or a formal contract between different companies even if within the same group.

4.5    The agreement should include an obligation on the part of the provider of a bulk or intermediate product to notify the recipient(s) of any deviations, out-of-specification results, non-compliance with GMP, investigations, complaints or other matters which should be taken into account by the Q.P. who is responsible for certifying the finished product batch.

4.6    When a computerised system is used for recording certification and batch release, particular note should be taken of the guidance in Annex 11 to this Guide.

4.7    Certification of a finished product batch against a relevant marketing authorisation by a Q.P. in the EC/EEA need not be repeated on the same batch provided the batch has remained within the EC/EEA.

4.8    Whatever particular arrangements are made for certification and release of batches, it should always be possible to identify and recall without delay all products which could be rendered hazardous by a quality defect in the batch.

## 5 Batch Testing and Release of Products Manufactured in EC/EEA

5.1 *When all manufacture occurs at a single authorised site.*

When all production and control stages are carried out at a single site, the conduct of certain checks and controls may be delegated to others but the Q.P. at this site who certifies the finished product batch normally retains personal responsibility for these within a defined quality system. However he may, alternatively, take account of the confirmation of the intermediate stages by other Q.Ps on the site who are responsible for those stages.

5.2 *Different stages of manufacture are conducted at different sites within the same company.*

When different stages of the manufacture of a batch are carried out at different sites within the same company (which may or may not be covered by the same manufacturing authorisation) a Q.P. should be responsible for each stage. Certification of the finished product batch should be performed by a Q.P. of the manufacturing authorisation holder responsible for releasing the batch to the market, who may take personal responsibility for all stages or may take account of the confirmation of the earlier stages by the relevant Q.P.s responsible for those stages.

5.3 *Some intermediate stages of manufacture are contracted to a different company.*

One or more intermediate production and control stages may be contracted to a holder of a manufacturing authorisation in another company. A Q.P. of the contract giver may take account of the confirmation of the relevant stage by a Q.P. of the contract acceptor but is responsible for ensuring that this work is conducted within the terms of a written agreement. The finished product batch should be certified by a Q.P. of the manufacturing authorisation holder responsible for releasing the batch to the market.

5.4 *A bulk production batch is assembled at different sites into several finished product batches which are released under a single marketing authorisation. This could occur, for example, under a national marketing authorisation when the assembly sites are all within one member state or under a Community marketing authorisation when the sites are in more than one member state.*

**5.4.1** One alternative is for a Q.P. of the manufacturing authorisation holder making the bulk production batch to certify all the finished product batches before release to the market. In doing so he may either take personal responsibility for all manufacturing stages or take account of the confirmation of assembly by the Q.P.s of the assembly sites.

**5.4.2** Another alternative is for the certification of each finished product batch before release to the market to be performed by a Q.P of the manufacturer who has conducted the final assembly operation. In doing so he may either take personal responsibility for all manufacturing stages or take account of the confirmation of the bulk production batch by a Q.P. of the manufacturer of the bulk batch.

**5.4.3** In all cases of assembly at different sites under a single marketing authorisation, there should be one person, normally a Q.P. of the manufacturer of the bulk production batch, who has an overall responsibility for all released finished product batches which are derived from one bulk production batch. The duty of this person is to be aware of any quality problems reported on any of the finished product batches and to co-ordinate any necessary action arising from a problem with the bulk batch. While the batch numbers of the bulk and finished product batches are not necessarily the same, there should be a documented link between the two numbers so that an audit trail can be established.

**5.5** *A bulk production batch is assembled at different sites into several finished product batches which are released under different marketing authorisations. This could occur, for example, when a multi-national organisation holds national marketing authorisations for a product in several member states or when a generic manufacturer purchases bulk products and assembles and releases them for sale under his own marketing authorisation.*

**5.5.1** A Q.P. of the manufacturer doing the assembly who certifies the finished product batch may either take personal responsibility for all manufacturing stages or may take account of the confirmation of the bulk production batch by a Q.P. of the bulk product manufacturer.

**5.5.2** Any problem identified in any of the finished product batches which may have arisen in the bulk production batch should be communicated to the Q.P. responsible for confirming the bulk production batch, who should then take any necessary action in respect of all finished product batches produced from the suspected bulk production batch. This arrangement should be defined in a written agreement.

**5.6** *A finished product batch is purchased and released to the market by a manufacturing authorisation holder in accordance with his own marketing authorisation. This could occur, for example, when a company supplying generic products holds a marketing authorisation for products made by another company, purchases finished products which have not been certified against his marketing authorisation and releases them under his own manufacturing authorisation in accordance with his own marketing authorisation.*

In this situation a Q.P. of the purchaser should certify the finished product batch before release. In doing so he may either take personal responsibility for all manufacturing stages or may take account of the confirmation of the batch by a Q.P. of the vendor manufacturer.

**5.7** *The quality control laboratory and the production site are authorised under different manufacturing authorisations.*

A Q.P. certifying a finished product batch may either take personal responsibility for the laboratory testing or may take account of the confirmation by another Q.P. of the testing and results. The other laboratory and Q.P. need not be in the same member state as the manufacturing authorisation holder releasing the batch. In the absence of such confirmation the Q.P. should himself have personal knowledge of the laboratory and its procedures relevant to the finished product to be certified.

## 6   Batch Testing and Release of Products Imported from a Third Country

**6.1** *General*

**6.1.1** Importation of finished products should be conducted by an importer as defined in the glossary to this annex.

**6.1.2** Each batch of imported finished product should be certified by a Q.P. of the importer before release for sale in the EC/EEA.

**6.1.3** Unless a mutual recognition agreement is in operation between the Community and the third country (see Section 7 [of Annex 16]), samples from each batch should be tested in the EC/EEA before certification of the finished product batch by a Q.P. Importation and testing need not necessarily be performed in the same member state.

**6.1.4** The guidance in this section should also be applied as appropriate to the importation of partially manufactured products.

**6.2**   *A complete batch or the first part of a batch of a medicinal product is imported.*

The batch or part batch should be certified by a Q.P of the importer before release. This Q.P. may take account of the confirmation of the checking, sampling or testing of the imported batch by a Q.P. of another manufacturing authorisation holder (i.e. within EC/EEA).

**6.3**   *Part of a finished product batch is imported after another part of the same batch has previously been imported to the same or a different site.*

**6.3.1** A Q.P. of the importer receiving a subsequent part of the batch may take account of the testing and certification by a Q.P. of the first part of the batch. If this is done, the Q.P. should ensure, based on evidence, that the two parts do indeed come from the same batch, that the subsequent part has been transported under the same conditions as the first part and that the samples that were tested are representative of the whole batch.

**6.3.2** The conditions in paragraph 6.3.1 is most likely to be met when the manufacturer in the third country and the importer(s) in the EC/EEA belong to the same organisation operating under a corporate system of quality assurance. If the Q.P. cannot ensure that the conditions in paragraph 6.3.1 are met, each part of the batch should be treated as a separate batch.

**6.3.3** When different parts of the batch are released under the same marketing authorisation, one person, normally a Q.P. of the importer of the first part of a batch, should take overall responsibility for ensuring that records are kept of the importation of all parts of the batch and that the distribution of all parts of the batch is traceable within the EC/EEA. He should be made aware of any quality problems reported on any part of the batch and should co-ordinate any necessary action concerning these problems and their resolution.

This should be ensured by a written agreement between all the importers concerned.

**6.4**   *Location of sampling for testing in EC/EEA.*

**6.4.1** Samples should be representative of the batch and be tested in the EC/EEA. In order to represent the batch it may be preferable to take some samples during processing in the third country. For example, samples for sterility testing may best be taken throughout the filling operation. However in order to represent the batch after storage and transportation some samples should also be taken after receipt of the batch in the EC/EEA.

**6.4.2** When any samples are taken in a third country, they should either be shipped with and under the same conditions as the batch which they represent, or if sent separately it should be demonstrated that the samples are still representative of the batch, for example by defining and monitoring the conditions of storage and shipment. When the Q.P. wishes to rely on testing of samples taken in a third country, this should be justified on technical grounds.

## 7 Batch Testing and Release of Products Imported from a Third Country with which the EC has a Mutual Recognition Agreement (MRA)

**7.1** Unless otherwise specified in the agreement, an MRA does not remove the requirement for a Q.P. within the EC/EEA to certify a batch before it is released for sale or supply within the EC/EEA. However, subject to details of the particular agreement, the Q.P. of the importer may rely on the manufacturer's confirmation that the batch has been made and tested in accordance with its marketing authorisation and the GMP of the third country and need not repeat the full testing. The Q.P. may certify the batch for release when he is satisfied with this confirmation and that the batch has been transported under the required conditions and has been received and stored in the EC/EEA by an importer as defined in Section 8 [Annex 16].

**7.2** Other procedures, including those for receipt and certification of part batches at different times and/or at different sites, should be the same as in Section 6 [Annex 16].

## 8 Routine Duties of a Qualified Person

**8.1** Before certifying a batch prior to release the Q.P. doing so should ensure, with reference to the guidance above, that at least the following requirements have been met:

(a) the batch and its manufacture comply with the provisions of the marketing authorisation (including the authorisation required for importation where relevant);

(b) manufacture has been carried out in accordance with Good Manufacturing Practice or, in the case of a batch imported from a third country, in accordance with good manufacturing practice standards at least equivalent to EC GMP;

(c) the principal manufacturing and testing processes have been validated; account has been taken of the actual production conditions and manufacturing records;

(d) any deviations or planned changes in production or quality control have been authorised by the persons responsible in accordance with a defined system. Any changes requiring variation to the marketing or manufacturing authorisation have been notified to and authorised by the relevant authority;

(e) all the necessary checks and tests have been performed, including any additional sampling, inspection, tests or checks initiated because of deviations or planned changes;

(f) all necessary production and quality control documentation has been completed and endorsed by the staff authorised to do so;

(g) all audits have been carried out as required by the quality assurance system;

(h) the QP should in addition take into account any other factors of which he is aware which are relevant to the quality of the batch.

A Q.P. may have additional duties in accordance with national legislation or administrative procedures.

8.2    A Q.P. who confirms the compliance of an intermediate stage of manufacture, as described in paragraph 4.3, has the same obligations as above in relation to that stage unless specified otherwise in the agreement between the Q.P.s.

8.3    A Q.P. should maintain his knowledge and experience up to date in the light of technical and scientific progress and changes in quality management relevant to the products which he is required to certify.

8.4    If a Q.P. is called upon to certify a batch of a product type with which he is unfamiliar, for example because the manufacturer for whom he works introduces a new product range or because he starts to work for a different manufacturer, he should first ensure that he has gained the relevant knowledge and experience necessary to fulfil this duty.

In accordance with national requirements the Q.P. may be required to notify the authorities of such a change and may be subject to renewed authorisation.

## 9  Glossary

Certain words and phrases in this annex are used with the particular meanings defined below. Reference should also be made to the Glossary in the main part of the Guide.

### BULK PRODUCTION BATCH

A batch of product, of a size described in the application for a marketing authorisation, either ready for assembly into final containers or in individual containers ready for assembly to final packs. (A bulk production batch may, for example, consist of a bulk quantity of liquid product, of solid dosage forms such as tablets or capsules, or of filled ampoules.)

## CERTIFICATION OF THE FINISHED PRODUCT BATCH

The certification in a register or equivalent document by a Q.P., as defined in Article 51 of Directive 2001/83/EC and Article 55 of Directive 2001/82/EC, before a batch is released for sale or distribution.

## CONFIRMATION

A signed statement that a process or test has been conducted in accordance with GMP and the relevant marketing authorisation, as agreed in writing with the Q.P. responsible for certifying the finished product batch before release. *Confirm* and *confirmed* have equivalent meanings.

## FINISHED PRODUCT BATCH

With reference to the control of the finished product, a finished product batch is defined in Part 1 Module 3 point 3.2.2.5 of Directive 2001/83/EC[2] and in Part 2 Section F 1 of Directive 2001/82/EC. In the context of this annex the term in particular denotes the batch of product in its final pack for release to the market.

## IMPORTER

The holder of the authorisation required by Article 40.3 of Directive 2001/83/EC and Article 44.3 of Directive 2001/82/EC for importing medicinal products from third countries.

## MUTUAL RECOGNITION AGREEMENT (MRA)

The "appropriate arrangement" between the Community and an exporting third country mentioned in Article 51(2) of Directive 2001/83/EC and Article 55(2) of Directive 2001/82/EC.

## QUALIFIED PERSON (Q.P.)

The person defined in Article 48 of Directive 2001/83/EC and Article 52 of Directive 2001/82/EC.

EU GMP GUIDE PART I ANNEX 16 CERTIFICATION BY A QUALIFIED PERSON AND BATCH RELEASE

---

[2] Amended by Commission Directive 2003/63/EC of 25 June 2003 amending Directive 2001/83/EC of the European Parliament and of the Council on the Community code relating to medicinal products for human use (OJ L 159, 27. 06.2003, p.46).

# ANNEX 17 PARAMETRIC RELEASE

## 1 Principle

**1.1** The definition of Parametric Release used in this Annex is based on that proposed by the European Organization for Quality: "A system of release that gives the assurance that the product is of the intended quality based on information collected during the manufacturing process and on the compliance with specific GMP requirements related to Parametric Release".

**1.2** Parametric release should comply with the basic requirements of GMP, with applicable annexes and the following guidelines.

## 2 Parametric Release

**2.1** It is recognised that a comprehensive set of in-process tests and controls may provide greater assurance of the finished product meeting specification than finished product testing.

**2.2** Parametric release may be authorised for certain specific parameters as an alternative to routine testing of finished products. Authorisation for parametric release should be given, refused or withdrawn jointly by those responsible for assessing products together with the GMP inspectors.

## 3 Parametric Release for Sterile Products

**3.1** This section is only concerned with that part of Parametric Release which deals with the routine release of finished products without carrying out a sterility test. Elimination of the sterility test is only valid on the basis of successful demonstration that predetermined, validated sterilising conditions have been achieved.

**3.2** A sterility test only provides an opportunity to detect a major failure of the sterility assurance system due to statistical limitations of the method.

**3.3** Parametric Release can be authorised if the data demonstrating correct processing of the batch provides sufficient assurance, on its own, that the process designed and validated to ensure the sterility of the product has been delivered.

**3.4** At present Parametric release can only be approved for products terminally sterilized in their final container.

**3.5**   Sterilization methods according to European Pharmacopeia requirements using steam, dry heat and ionising radiation may be considered for parametric release.

**3.6**   It is unlikely that a completely new product would be considered as suitable for Parametric Release because a period of satisfactory sterility test results will form part of the acceptance criteria. There may be cases when a new product is only a minor variation, from the sterility assurance point of view, and existing sterility test data from other products could be considered as relevant.

**3.7**   A risk analysis of the sterility assurance system focused on an evaluation of releasing non-sterilised products should be performed.

**3.8**   The manufacturer should have a history of good compliance with GMP.

**3.9**   The history of non-sterility of products and of results of sterility tests carried out on the product in question together with products processed through the same or a similar sterility assurance system should be taken into consideration when evaluating GMP compliance.

**3.10**   A qualified experienced sterility assurance engineer and a qualified microbiologist should normally be present on the site of production and sterilization.

**3.11**   The design and original validation of the product should ensure that integrity can be maintained under all relevant conditions.

**3.12**   The change control system should require review of change by sterility assurance personnel.

**3.13**   There should be a system to control microbiological contamination in the product before sterilisation.

**3.14**   There should be no possibility for mix ups between sterilised and non-sterilised products. Physical barriers or validated electronic systems may provide such assurance.

**3.15**   The sterilization records should be checked for compliance to specification by at least two independent systems. These systems may consist of two people or a validated computer system plus a person.

**3.16**   The following additional items should be confirmed prior to release of each batch of product.

- All planned maintenance and routine checks have been completed in the sterilizer used.
- All repairs and modifications have been approved by the sterility assurance engineer and microbiologist.
- All instrumentation was in calibration.

● The sterilizer had a current validation for the product load processed.

**3.17**    Once parametric release has been granted, decisions for release or rejection of a batch should be based on the approved specifications. Non-compliance with the specification for parametric release cannot be overruled by a pass of a sterility test.

## 4    Glossary

### PARAMETRIC RELEASE

A system of release that gives the assurance that the product is of the intended quality based on information collected during the manufacturing process and on the compliance with specific GMP requirements related to Parametric Release.

### STERILITY ASSURANCE SYSTEM

The sum total of the arrangements made to assure the sterility of products. For terminally sterilized products these typically include the following stages:

(a) Product design.
(b) Knowledge of and, if possible, control of the microbiological condition of starting materials and process aids (e.g. gases and lubricants).
(c) Control of the contamination of the process of manufacture to avoid the ingress of microorganisms and their multiplication in the product. This is usually accomplished by cleaning and sanitization of product contact surfaces, prevention of aerial contamination by handling in clean rooms, use of process control time limits and, if applicable, filtration stages.
(d) Prevention of mix up between sterile and non-sterile product streams.
(e) Maintenance of product integrity.
(f) The sterilization process.
(g) The totality of the Quality System that contains the Sterility Assurance System e.g. change control, training, written procedures, release checks, planned preventative maintenance, failure mode analysis, prevention of human error, validation calibration, etc.

# ANNEX 18 GOOD MANUFACTURING PRACTICE FOR ACTIVE PHARMACEUTICAL INGREDIENTS

**Editor's note** Requirements for active substances used as starting materials from October 2005 are now covered in Part II.

## ANNEX 19 REFERENCE AND RETENTION SAMPLES

## 1   Scope

**1.1**   This Annex to the Guide to Good Manufacturing Practice for Medicinal Products ("the GMP Guide") gives guidance on the taking and holding of reference samples of starting materials, packaging materials or finished products and retention samples of finished products.

**1.2**   Specific requirements for investigational medicinal products are given in Annex 13 to the Guide.

**1.3**   This annex also includes guidance on the taking of retention samples for parallel imported/ distributed medicinal products.

## 2   Principle

**2.1**   Samples are retained to fulfil two purposes; firstly to provide a sample for analytical testing and secondly to provide a specimen of the fully finished product. Samples may therefore fall into two categories:

*Reference sample*: a sample of a batch of starting material, packaging material or finished product which is stored for the purpose of being analysed should the need arise during the shelf life of the batch concerned. Where stability permits, reference samples from critical intermediate stages (e.g. those requiring analytical testing and release) or intermediates, that are transported outside of the manufacturer's control, should be kept.

*Retention sample*: a sample of a fully packaged unit from a batch of finished product. It is stored for identification purposes. For example, presentation, packaging, labelling, patient information leaflet, batch number, expiry date should the need arise during the shelf life of the batch concerned. There may be exceptional circumstances where this requirement can be met without retention of duplicate samples e.g. where small amounts of a batch are packaged for different markets or in the production of very expensive medicinal products.

For finished products, in many instances the reference and retention samples will be presented identically, i.e. as fully packaged units. In such circumstances, reference and retention samples may be regarded as interchangeable.

**2.2**   It is necessary for the manufacturer, importer or site of batch release, as specified under Sections 7 and 8, to keep reference and/or retention samples from each batch of finished product and, for the manufacturer to keep a reference sample from a batch of starting material (subject to certain exceptions – see Section 3.2 below) and/or intermediate product. Each packaging site should keep reference samples of each batch of primary and printed packaging materials. Availability of printed materials as part of the reference and/or retention sample of the finished product can be accepted.

**2.3** The reference and/or retention samples serve as a record of the batch of finished product or starting material and can be assessed in the event of, for example, a dosage form quality complaint, a query relating to compliance with the marketing authorisation, a labelling/packaging query or a pharmacovigilance report.

**2.4** Records of traceability of samples should be maintained and be available for review by competent authorities.

## 3  Duration of Storage

**3.1** Reference and retention samples from each batch of finished product should be retained for at least one year after the expiry date. The reference sample should be contained in its finished primary packaging or in packaging composed of the same material as the primary container in which the product is marketed (for veterinary medicinal products other than immunologicals, see also Annex 4, paragraphs 8 & 9).

**3.2** Unless a longer period is required under the law of the Member State of manufacture, samples of starting materials (other than solvents, gases or water used in the manufacturing process) shall be retained for at least two years after the release of product. That period may be shortened if the period of stability of the material, as indicated in the relevant specification, is shorter. Packaging materials should be retained for the duration of the shelf life of the finished product concerned.

## 4  Size of Reference and Retention Samples

**4.1** The reference sample should be of sufficient size to permit the carrying out, on, at least, two occasions, of the full analytical controls on the batch in accordance with the Marketing Authorisation File which has been assessed and approved by the relevant Competent Authority/Authorities. Where it is necessary to do so, unopened packs should be used when carrying out each set of analytical controls. Any proposed exception to this should be justified to, and agreed with, the relevant competent authority.

**4.2** Where applicable, national requirements relating to the size of reference samples and, if necessary, retention samples, should be followed.

**4.3**    Reference samples should be representative of the batch of starting material, intermediate product or finished product from which they are taken. Other samples may also be taken to monitor the most stressed part of a process (e.g. beginning or end of a process). Where a batch is packaged in two, or more, distinct packaging operations, at least one retention sample should be taken from each individual packaging operation. Any proposed exception to this should be justified to, and agreed with, the relevant competent authority.

**4.4**    It should be ensured that all necessary analytical materials and equipment are still available, or are readily obtainable, in order to carry out all tests given in the specification until one year after expiry of the last batch manufactured.

## 5    Storage Conditions

**5.1**    Storage of reference samples of finished products and active substances should be in accordance with the current version of the Note for Guidance on Declaration of Storage Conditions for Medicinal Products and Active Substances.

**5.2**    Storage conditions should be in accordance with the marketing authorisation (e.g. refrigerated storage where relevant).

## 6    Written Agreements

**6.1**    Where the marketing authorisation holder is not the same legal entity as the site(s) responsible for batch release within the EEA, the responsibility for taking and storage of reference/retention samples should be defined in a written agreement between the two parties in accordance with Chapter 7 of the EC Guide to Good Manufacturing Practice. This applies also where any manufacturing or batch release activity is carried out at a site other than that with overall responsibility for the batch on the EEA market and the arrangements between each different site for the taking and keeping of reference and retention samples should be defined in a written agreement.

**6.2**    The Qualified Person who certifies a batch for sale should ensure that all relevant reference and retention samples are accessible at all reasonable times. Where necessary, the arrangements for such access should be defined in a written agreement.

**6.3**    Where more than one site is involved in the manufacture of a finished product, the availability of written agreements is key to controlling the taking and location of reference and retention samples.

## 7   Reference Samples – General Points

**7.1**   Reference samples are for the purpose of analysis and, therefore, should be conveniently available to a laboratory with validated methodology. For starting materials used for medicinal products manufactured within the EEA, this is the original site of manufacture of the finished product. For finished products manufactured within the EEA, this is the original site of manufacture.

**7.2**   For finished products manufactured by a manufacturer in a country outside the EEA;

**7.2.1** where an operational Mutual Recognition Agreement (MRA) is in place, the reference samples may be taken and stored at the site of manufacture. This should be covered in a written agreement (as referred to in Section 6 above) between the importer/site of batch release and the manufacturer located outside the EEA.

**7.2.2** where an operational MRA is not in place, reference samples of the finished medicinal product should be taken and stored at an authorised manufacturer located within the EEA. These samples should be taken in accordance with written agreement(s) between all of the parties concerned. The samples should, preferably, be stored at the location where testing on importation has been performed.

**7.2.3** reference samples of starting materials and packaging materials should be kept at the original site at which they were used in the manufacture of the medicinal product.

## 8   Retention Samples – General Points

**8.1**   A retention sample should represent a batch of finished products as distributed in the EEA and may need to be examined in order to confirm non-technical attributes for compliance with the marketing authorisation or EU legislation. Therefore, retention samples should in all cases be located within the EEA. These should preferably be stored at the site where the Qualified Person (QP) certifying the finished product batch is located.

**8.2**   In accordance with Section 8.1 above, where an operational MRA is in place and reference samples are retained at a manufacturer located in a country outside the EEA (Section 7.2.2 above), separate retention samples should be kept within the EEA.

**8.3**   Retention samples should be stored at the premises of an authorised manufacturer in order to permit ready access by the Competent Authority.

**8.4**    Where more than one manufacturing site within the EEA is involved in the manufacture importation/packaging/testing/batch release, as appropriate of a product, the responsibility for taking and storage of retention samples should be defined in a written agreement(s) between the parties concerned.

## 9    Reference and Retention Samples for Parallel Imported/ Parallel Distributed Products

**9.1**    Where the secondary packaging is not opened, only the packaging material used needs to be retained, as there is no, or little, risk of product mix up.

**9.2**    Where the secondary packaging is opened, for example, to replace the carton or patient information leaflet, then one retention sample, per packaging operation, containing the product should be taken, as there is a risk of product mix-up during the assembly process. It is important to be able to identify quickly who is responsible in the event of a mix-up (original manufacturer or parallel import assembler), as it would affect the extent of any resulting recall.

## 10    Reference and Retention Samples in the Case of Closedown of a Manufacturer

**10.1**    Where a manufacturer closes down and the manufacturing authorisation is surrendered, revoked, or ceases to exist, it is probable that many unexpired batches of medicinal products manufactured by that manufacturer remain on the market. In order for those batches to remain on the market, the manufacturer should make detailed arrangements for transfer of reference and retention samples (and relevant GMP documentation) to an authorised storage site. The manufacturer should satisfy the Competent Authority that the arrangements for storage are satisfactory and that the samples can, if necessary, be readily accessed and analysed.

**10.2**    If the manufacturer is not in a position to make the necessary arrangements this may be delegated to another manufacturer. The Marketing Authorisation holder (MAH) is responsible for such delegation and for the provision of all necessary information to the Competent Authority. In addition, the MAH should, in relation to the suitability of the proposed arrangements for storage of reference and retention samples, consult with the competent authority of each Member State in which any unexpired batch has been placed on the market.

**10.3**   These requirements apply also in the event of the closedown of a manufacture located outside the EEA. In such instances, the importer has a particular responsibility to ensure that satisfactory arrangements are put in place and that the competent authority/authorities is/are consulted.

## GLOSSARY OF TERMS USED IN THE EU GUIDE TO GMP

**Note:** *Definitions given below apply to the words as used in this guide. They may have different meanings in other contexts.*

### AIR-LOCK

An enclosed space with two or more doors, and which is interposed between two or more rooms, e.g. of differing class of cleanliness, for the purpose of controlling the air-flow between those rooms when they need to be entered. An air-lock is designed for and used by either people or goods.

### BATCH (OR LOT)

A defined quantity of starting material, packaging material or product processed in one process or series of processes so that it could be expected to be homogeneous.

**Note:** *To complete certain stages of manufacture, it may be necessary to divide a batch into a number of sub-batches, which are later brought together to form a final homogeneous batch. In the case of continuous manufacture, the batch must correspond to a defined fraction of the production, characterised by its intended homogeneity.*

For control of the finished product, the following definition has been given in Annex 1 of Directive 2001/83/EC as amended by Directive 2003/63/EC "For the control of the finished product, a batch of a proprietary medicinal product comprises all the units of a pharmaceutical form which are made from the same initial mass of material and have undergone a single series of manufacturing operations or a single sterilisation operation or, in the case of a continuous production process, all the units manufactured in a given period of time."

### BATCH NUMBER (OR LOT NUMBER)

A distinctive combination of numbers and/or letters which specifically identifies a batch.

### BIOGENERATOR

A contained system, such as a fermenter, into which biological agents are introduced along with other materials so as to effect their multiplication or their production of other substances by reaction with the other materials.

Biogenerators are generally fitted with devices for regulation, control, connection, material addition and material withdrawal.

## BIOLOGICAL AGENTS

Micro-organisms, including genetically engineered micro-organisms, cell cultures and endoparasites, whether pathogenic or not.

## BULK PRODUCT

Any product which has completed all processing stages up to, but not including, final packaging.

## CALIBRATION

The set of operations which establish, under specified conditions, the relationship between values indicated by a measuring instrument or measuring system, or values represented by a material measure, and the corresponding known values of a reference standard.

## CELL BANK

*Cell bank system*: A cell bank system is a system whereby successive batches of a product are manufactured by culture in cells derived from the same master cell bank. A number of containers from the master cell bank are used to prepare a working cell bank. The cell bank system is validated for a passage level or number of population doublings beyond that achieved during routine production.

*Master cell bank*: A culture of [fully characterised] cells distributed into containers in a single operation, processed together in such a manner as to ensure uniformity and stored in such a manner as to ensure stability. A master cell bank is usually stored at −70°C or lower.

*Working cell bank*: A culture of cells derived from the master cell bank and intended for use in the preparation of production cell cultures. The working cell bank is usually stored at −70°C or lower.

## CELL CULTURE

The result from the in-vitro growth of cells isolated from multicellular organisms.

## CLEAN AREA

An area with defined environmental control of particulate and microbial contamination, constructed and used in such a way as to reduce the introduction, generation and retention of contaminants within the area.

**Note:** *The different degrees of environmental control are defined in the Supplementary Guidelines for the Manufacture of sterile medicinal products.*

## CLEAN/CONTAINED AREA

An area constructed and operated in such a manner that will achieve the aims of both a clean area and a contained area at the same time.

## CONTAINMENT

The action of confining a biological agent or other entity within a defined space.

*Primary containment*: A system of containment which prevents the escape of a biological agent into the immediate working environment. It involves the use of closed containers or safety biological cabinets along with secure operating procedures.

*Secondary containment*: A system of containment which prevents the escape of a biological agent into the external environment or into other working areas. It involves the use of rooms with specially designed air handling, the existence of airlocks and/or sterilisers for the exit of materials and secure operating procedures. In many cases it may add to the effectiveness of primary containment.

## CONTAINED AREA

An area constructed and operated in such a manner (and equipped with appropriate air handling and filtration) so as to prevent contamination of the external environment by biological agents from within the area.

## CONTROLLED AREA

An area constructed and operated in such a manner that some attempt is made to control the introduction of potential contamination (an air supply approximating to grade D may be appropriate), and the consequences of accidental release of living organisms. The level of control exercised should reflect the nature of the organism employed in the process. At a minimum, the area should be maintained at a pressure negative to the immediate external environment and allow for the efficient removal of small quantities of airborne contaminants.

## COMPUTERISED SYSTEM

A system including the input of data, electronic processing and the output of information to be used either for reporting or automatic control.

## CROSS-CONTAMINATION

Contamination of a material or of a product with another material or product.

## CRUDE PLANT (VEGETABLE DRUG)

Fresh or dried medicinal plant or parts thereof.

## CRYOGENIC VESSEL

A container designed to contain liquefied gas at extremely low temperature.

## CYLINDER

A container designed to contain gas at a high pressure.

## EXOTIC ORGANISM

A biological agent where either the corresponding disease does not exist in a given country or geographical area, or where the disease is the subject of prophylactic measures or an eradication programme undertaken in the given country or geographical area.

## FINISHED PRODUCT

A medicinal product which has undergone all stages of production, including packaging in its final container.

## HERBAL MEDICINAL PRODUCT

Medicinal product containing, as active ingredients, exclusively plant material and/or vegetable drug preparations.

## INFECTED

Contaminated with extraneous biological agents and therefore capable of spreading infection.

## IN-PROCESS CONTROL

Checks performed during production in order to monitor and if necessary to adjust the process to ensure that the product conforms its specification. The control of the environment or equipment may also be regarded as a part of in-process control.

## INTERMEDIATE PRODUCT

Partly processed material which must undergo further manufacturing steps before it becomes a bulk product.

## LIQUIFIABLE GASES

Those which, at the normal filling temperature and pressure, remain as a liquid in the cylinder.

## MANIFOLD

Equipment or apparatus designed to enable one or more gas containers to be filled simultaneously from the same source.

## MANUFACTURE

All operations of purchase of materials and products, Production, Quality Control, release, storage, distribution of medicinal products and the related controls.

## MANUFACTURER

Holder of a Manufacturing Authorisation as described in Article 40 of Directive 2001/83/EC.[1]

## MEDICINAL PLANT

Plant the whole or part of which is used for medicinal purpose.

## MEDICINAL PRODUCT

Any substance or combination of substances presented for treating or preventing disease in human beings or animals. Any substance or combination of substances which may be administered to human beings or animals with a view to making a medical diagnosis or to restoring, correcting or modifying physiological functions in human beings or in animals is likewise considered a medicinal product.

## PACKAGING

All operations, including filling and labelling, which a bulk product has to undergo in order to become a finished product.

**Note:** *Sterile filling would not normally be regarded as part of packaging, the bulk product being the filled, but not finally packaged, primary containers.*

## PACKAGING MATERIAL

Any material employed in the packaging of a medicinal product, excluding any outer packaging used for transportation or shipment. Packaging materials are referred to as primary or secondary according to whether or not they are intended to be in direct contact with the product.

## PROCEDURES

Description of the operations to be carried out, the precautions to be taken and measures to be applied directly or indirectly related to the manufacture of a medicinal product.

---

[1] Article 44 of Directive 2001/82/EC.

## PRODUCTION

All operations involved in the preparation of a medicinal product, from receipt of materials, through processing and packaging, to its completion as a finished product.

## QUALIFICATION

Action of proving that any equipment works correctly and actually leads to the expected results. The word *validation* is sometimes widened to incorporate the concept of qualification.

## QUALITY CONTROL

See GMP Guide, Chapter 1.

## QUARANTINE

The status of starting or packaging materials, intermediate, bulk or finished products isolated physically or by other effective means whilst awaiting a decision on their release or refusal.

## RADIOPHARMACEUTICAL

"Radiopharmaceutical" shall mean any medicinal product which, when ready for use, contains one or more radionuclides (radioactive isotopes) included for a medicinal purpose (Article 1(6) of Directive 2001/83/EC).

## RECONCILIATION

A comparison, making due allowance for normal variation, between the amount of product or materials theoretically and actually produced or used.

## RECORD

See GMP Guide, Chapter 4.

## RECOVERY

The introduction of all or part of previous batches of the required quality into another batch at a defined stage of manufacture.

## REPROCESSING

The reworking of all or part of a batch of product of an unacceptable quality from a defined stage of production so that its quality may be rendered acceptable by one or more additional operations.

## RETURN

Sending back to the manufacturer or distributor of a medicinal product which may or may not present a quality defect.

## SEED LOT

*Seed lot system*: A seed lot system is a system according to which successive batches of a product are derived from the same master seed lot at a given passage level. For routine production, a working seed lot is prepared from the master seed lot. The final product is derived from the working seed lot and has not undergone more passages from the master seed lot than the vaccine shown in clinical studies to be satisfactory with respect to safety and efficacy. The origin and the passage history of the master seed lot and the working seed lot are recorded.

*Master seed lot*: A culture of a micro-organism distributed from a single bulk into containers in a single operation in such a manner as to ensure uniformity, to prevent contamination and to ensure stability. A master seed lot in liquid form is usually stored at or below −70°C. A freeze-dried master seed lot is stored at a temperature known to ensure stability.

*Working seed lot*: A culture of a micro-organism derived from the master seed lot and intended for use in production. Working seed lots are distributed into containers and stored as described above for master seed lots.

## SPECIFICATION

See GMP Guide, Chapter 4.

## STARTING MATERIAL

Any substance used in the production of a medicinal product, but excluding packaging materials.

## STERILITY

Sterility is the absence of living organisms. The conditions of the sterility test are given in the European Pharmacopoeia.

## SYSTEM

Is used in the sense of a regulated pattern of interacting activities and techniques which are united to form an organised whole.

## VALIDATION

Action of proving, in accordance with the principles of Good Manufacturing Practice, that any procedure, process, equipment, material, activity or system actually leads to the expected results (see also qualification).

# PART II: Basic Requirements for Active Substances Used as Starting Materials

## Contents of Part II

Contents continued

Contents continued

> **Editor's note** Part II of the GMP guide has been amended. A revision has been made to section 1.2 to take into consideration the completed revision of various Annexes to the GMP guide and hence Part I can no longer be followed for active substances used at starting materials. Furthermore, clarification of the relationship between section 17 of this Part II and the forthcoming guidelines on Good Distribution Practices for active substances for medicinal products for human use has been added to section 1.2. An obsolete reference to Annex 20 in section 2.21 has been amended.
> Came into operation 1 September 2014.

# 1 Introduction

This guideline was published in November 2000 as Annex 18 to the GMP Guide reflecting the EU's agreement to ICH Q7A and has been used by manufacturers and GMP inspectorates on a voluntary basis. Article 46 (f) of Directive 2001/83/EC and Article 50 (f) of Directive 2001/82/EC; as amended by Directives 2004/27/EC and 2004/28/EC respectively, place new obligations on manufacturing authorisation holders to use only active substances that have been manufactured in accordance with Good Manufacturing Practice for starting materials. The directives go on to say that the principles of Good Manufacturing Practice for active substances are to be adopted as detailed guidelines. Member States have agreed that the text of former Annex 18 should form the basis of the detailed guidelines to create Part II of the GMP Guide.

## 1.1 Objective

These guidelines are intended to provide guidance regarding Good Manufacturing Practice (GMP) for the manufacture of active substances under an appropriate system for managing quality. It is also intended to help ensure that active substances meet the requirements for quality and purity that they purport or are represented to possess.

In these guidelines "manufacturing" includes all operations of receipt of materials, production, packaging, repackaging, labeling, relabelling, quality control, release, storage and distribution of active substances and the related controls. The term "should" indicates recommendations that are expected to apply unless shown to be inapplicable, modified in any relevant annexes to the GMP Guide, or replaced by an alternative demonstrated to provide at least an equivalent level of quality assurance.

The GMP Guide as a whole does not cover safety aspects for the personnel engaged in manufacture, nor aspects of protection of the environment. These controls are inherent responsibilities of the manufacturer and are governed by other parts of the legislation.

These guidelines are not intended to define registration requirements or modify pharmacopoeial requirements and do not affect the ability of the responsible competent authority to establish specific registration requirements regarding active substances within the context of marketing/manufacturing authorisations. All commitments in registration documents must be met.

## 1.2   Scope

These guidelines apply to the manufacture of active substances for medicinal products for both human and veterinary use. They apply to the manufacture of sterile active substances only up to the point immediately prior to the active substance being rendered sterile. The sterilisation and aseptic processing of sterile active substances are not covered, but should be performed in accordance with the principles and guidelines of GMP as laid down in Directive 2003/94/EC and interpreted in the GMP Guide including its Annex 1.

In the case of ectoparasiticides for veterinary use, other standards than these guidelines, that ensure that the material is of appropriate quality, may be used.

These guidelines exclude whole blood and plasma, as Directive 2002/98/EC and the technical requirements supporting that directive lay down the detailed requirements for the collection and testing of blood, however, it does include active substances that are produced using blood or plasma as raw materials.

Finally, these guidelines do not apply to bulk-packaged medicinal products. They apply to all other active starting materials subject to any derogations described in the annexes to the GMP Guide, in particular Annexes 2 to 7 where supplementary guidance for certain types of active substance may be found.

Section 17 gives guidance to parties who, among others, distribute or store an active substance or intermediate. This guidance is expanded in the guideline on the principles of good distribution practices for active substances for medicinal products for human use referred to in Article 47 of Directive 2001/83/EC.

Section 19 contains guidance that only applies to the manufacture of active substances used in the production of investigational medicinal products although it should be noted that its application in this case, although recommended, is not required by Community legislation.

An "Active Substance Starting Material" is a raw material, intermediate, or an active substance that is used in the production of an active substance and that is incorporated as a significant structural fragment into the structure of the active substance. An Active Substance Starting Material can be an article of commerce, a material purchased from one or more suppliers under contract or commercial agreement, or produced in-house. Active Substance Starting Materials normally have defined chemical properties and structure.

The manufacturer should designate and document the rationale for the point at which production of the active substance begins. For synthetic processes, this is known as the point at which "Active Substance Starting Materials" are entered into the process. For other processes (e.g. fermentation, extraction, purification, etc), this rationale should be established on a case-by-case basis. Table 1 gives guidance on the point at which the Active Substance Starting Material is normally introduced into the process. From this point on, appropriate GMP as defined in these guidelines should be applied to these intermediate and/or active substance manufacturing steps. This would include the validation of critical process steps determined to impact the quality of the active substance. However, it should be noted that the fact that a manufacturer chooses to validate a process step does not necessarily define that step as critical. The guidance in this document would normally be applied to the steps shown in grey in Table 1. It does not imply that all steps shown should be completed. The stringency of GMP in active substance manufacturing should increase as the process proceeds from early steps to final steps, purification, and packaging. Physical processing of active substances, such as granulation, coating or physical manipulation of particle size (e.g. milling, micronising), should be conducted at least to the standards of these guidelines. These guidelines do not apply to steps prior to the first introduction of the defined "Active Substance Starting Material".

In the remainder of this guideline the term Active Pharmaceutical Ingredient (API) is used repeatedly and should be considered interchangeable with the term "Active Substance". The glossary in section 20 of Part II should only be applied in the context of Part II. Some of the same terms are already defined in Part I of the GMP guide and these therefore should only be applied in the context of Part I.

EU GMP GUIDE PART II SECTION 1 INTRODUCTION

## 2    Quality Management

### 2.1    Principles

**2.10**    Quality should be the responsibility of all persons involved in manufacturing.

**2.11**    Each manufacturer should establish, document, and implement an effective system for managing quality that involves the active participation of management and appropriate manufacturing personnel.

**2.12**    The system for managing quality should encompass the organisational structure, procedures, processes and resources, as well as activities necessary to ensure confidence that the API will meet its intended specifications for quality and purity. All quality related activities should be defined and documented.

**2.13**    There should be a quality unit(s) that is independent of production and that fulfills both quality assurance (QA) and quality control (QC) responsibilities. This can be in the form of separate QA and QC units or a single individual or group, depending upon the size and structure of the organization.

**2.14**    The persons authorised to release intermediates and APIs should be specified.

**2.15**    All quality related activities should be recorded at the time they are performed.

**2.16**    Any deviation from established procedures should be documented and explained. Critical deviations should be investigated, and the investigation and its conclusions should be documented.

**2.17**    No materials should be released or used before the satisfactory completion of evaluation by the quality unit(s) unless there are appropriate systems in place to allow for such use (e.g. release under quarantine as described in Section 10.20 or the use of raw materials or intermediates pending completion of evaluation).

**2.18**    Procedures should exist for notifying responsible management in a timely manner of regulatory inspections, serious GMP deficiencies, product defects and related actions (e.g. quality related complaints, recalls, regulatory actions, etc.).

**2.19**    To achieve the quality objective reliably there must be a comprehensively designed and correctly implemented quality system incorporating Good Manufacturing Practice, Quality Control and Quality Risk Management.

**Table 1** Application of this Guide to API Manufacturing

| Type of Manufacturing | Application of this Guide to steps (shown in grey) used in this type of manufacturing | | | | |
|---|---|---|---|---|---|
| Chemical Manufacturing | Production of the API Starting Material | Introduction of the API Starting Material into process | Production of Intermediate(s) | Isolation and purification | Physical processing, and packaging |
| API derived from animal sources | Collection of organ, fluid, or tissue | Cutting, mixing, and/or initial processing | Introduction of the API Starting Material into process | Isolation and purification | Physical processing, and packaging |
| API extracted from plant sources | Collection of plant | Cutting and initial extraction(s) | Introduction of the API Starting Material into process | Isolation and purification | Physical processing, and packaging |
| Herbal extracts used as API | Collection of plants | Cutting and initial extraction | | Further extraction | Physical processing, and packaging |
| API consisting of comminuted or powdered herbs | Collection of plants and/or cultivation and harvesting | Cutting/ comminuting | | | Physical processing, and packaging |
| Biotechnology: fermentation/ cell culture | Establishment of master cell bank and working cell bank | Maintenance of working cell bank | Cell culture and/or fermentation | Isolation and purification | Physical processing, and packaging |
| "Classical" Fermentation to produce an API | Establishment of cell bank | Maintenance of the cell bank | Introduction of the cells into fermentation | Isolation and purification | Physical processing, and packaging |

**Increasing GMP requirements**

→

EU GMP GUIDE PART II SECTION 2 QUALITY MANAGEMENT

## 2.2  Quality risk management

**2.20**  Quality risk management is a systematic process for the assessment, control, communication and review of risks to the quality of the active substance. It can be applied both proactively and retrospectively.

**2.21**  The quality risk management system should ensure that:

- the evaluation of the risk to quality is based on scientific knowledge, experience with the process and ultimately links to the protection of the patient through communication with the user of the active substance
- the level of effort, formality and documentation of the quality risk management process is commensurate with the level of risk

Examples of the processes and applications of quality risk management can be found, inter alia, in Part III of the GMP guide.

## 2.3   Responsibilities of the quality unit(s)

**2.30**   The quality unit(s) should be involved in all quality-related matters.

**2.31**   The quality unit(s) should review and approve all appropriate quality-related documents.

**2.32**   The main responsibilities of the independent quality unit(s) should not be delegated. These responsibilities should be described in writing and should include but not necessarily be limited to:

(1)   Releasing or rejecting all APIs. Releasing or rejecting intermediates for use outside the control of the manufacturing company;

(2)   Establishing a system to release or reject raw materials, intermediates, packaging and labelling materials;

(3)   Reviewing completed batch production and laboratory control records of critical process steps before release of the API for distribution;

(4)   Making sure that critical deviations are investigated and resolved;

(5)   Approving all specifications and master production instructions;

(6)   Approving all procedures impacting the quality of intermediates or APIs;

(7)   Making sure that internal audits (self-inspections) are performed;

(8)   Approving intermediate and API contract manufacturers;

(9)   Approving changes that potentially impact intermediate or API quality;

(10)   Reviewing and approving validation protocols and reports;

(11)   Making sure that quality related complaints are investigated and resolved;

(12)   Making sure that effective systems are used for maintaining and calibrating critical equipment;

(13)   Making sure that materials are appropriately tested and the results are reported;

(14)   Making sure that there is stability data to support retest or expiry dates and storage conditions on APIs and/or intermediates where appropriate; and

(15)   Performing product quality reviews (as defined in Section 2.5).

## 2.4    Responsibility for production activities

The responsibility for production activities should be described in writing, and should include but not necessarily be limited to:

(1)    Preparing, reviewing, approving and distributing the instructions for the production of intermediates or APIs according to written procedures;

(2)    Producing APIs and, when appropriate, intermediates according to pre-approved instructions;

(3)    Reviewing all production batch records and ensuring that these are completed and signed;

(4)    Making sure that all production deviations are reported and evaluated and that critical deviations are investigated and the conclusions are recorded;

(5)    Making sure that production facilities are clean and when appropriate disinfected;

(6)    Making sure that the necessary calibrations are performed and records kept;

(7)    Making sure that the premises and equipment are maintained and records kept;

(8)    Making sure that validation protocols and reports are reviewed and approved;

(9)    Evaluating proposed changes in product, process or equipment; and

(10)  Making sure that new and, when appropriate, modified facilities and equipment are qualified.

## 2.5    Internal audits (self inspection)

**2.50**    In order to verify compliance with the principles of GMP for APIs, regular internal audits should be performed in accordance with an approved schedule.

**2.51**    Audit findings and corrective actions should be documented and brought to the attention of responsible management of the firm. Agreed corrective actions should be completed in a timely and effective manner.

## 2.6    Product quality review

**2.60**    Regular quality reviews of APIs should be conducted with the objective of verifying the consistency of the process. Such reviews should normally be conducted and documented annually and should include at least:

• A review of critical in-process control and critical API test results;
• A review of all batches that failed to meet established specification(s);

- A review of all critical deviations or non-conformances and related investigations;
- A review of any changes carried out to the processes or analytical methods;
- A review of results of the stability monitoring program;
- A review of all quality-related returns, complaints and recalls; and
- A review of adequacy of corrective actions.

2.61    The results of this review should be evaluated and an assessment made of whether corrective action or any revalidation should be undertaken.

Reasons for such corrective action should be documented. Agreed corrective actions should be completed in a timely and effective manner.

## 3    Personnel

### 3.1    Personnel qualifications

3.10    There should be an adequate number of personnel qualified by appropriate education, training and/or experience to perform and supervise the manufacture of intermediates and APIs.

3.11    The responsibilities of all personnel engaged in the manufacture of intermediates and APIs should be specified in writing.

3.12    Training should be regularly conducted by qualified individuals and should cover, at a minimum, the particular operations that the employee performs and GMP as it relates to the employee's functions. Records of training should be maintained. Training should be periodically assessed.

### 3.2    Personnel hygiene

3.20    Personnel should practice good sanitation and health habits.

3.21    Personnel should wear clean clothing suitable for the manufacturing activity with which they are involved and this clothing should be changed when appropriate. Additional protective apparel, such as head, face, hand, and arm coverings, should be worn when necessary, to protect intermediates and APIs from contamination.

3.22    Personnel should avoid direct contact with intermediates or APIs.

3.23    Smoking, eating, drinking, chewing and the storage of food should be restricted to certain designated areas separate from the manufacturing areas.

3.24    Personnel suffering from an infectious disease or having open lesions on the exposed surface of the body should not engage in activities that could result in compromising the quality of APIs. Any person shown at any time (either by medical examination or supervisory observation) to have an apparent illness or open lesions should be excluded from activities where the health condition could adversely affect the quality of the APIs until the condition is corrected or qualified medical personnel determine that the person's inclusion would not jeopardize the safety or quality of the APIs.

## 3.3 Consultants

**3.30** Consultants advising on the manufacture and control of intermediates or APIs should have sufficient education, training, and experience, or any combination thereof, to advise on the subject for which they are retained.

**3.31** Records should be maintained stating the name, address, qualifications, and type of service provided by these consultants.

## 4 Buildings and Facilities

### 4.1 Design and construction

**4.10** Buildings and facilities used in the manufacture of intermediates and APIs should be located, designed, and constructed to facilitate cleaning, maintenance, and operations as appropriate to the type and stage of manufacture. Facilities should also be designed to minimize potential contamination. Where microbiological specifications have been established for the intermediate or API, facilities should also be designed to limit exposure to objectionable microbiological contaminants as appropriate.

**4.11** Buildings and facilities should have adequate space for the orderly placement of equipment and materials to prevent mix-ups and contamination.

**4.12** Where the equipment itself (e.g., closed or contained systems) provides adequate protection of the material, such equipment can be located outdoors.

**4.13** The flow of materials and personnel through the building or facilities should be designed to prevent mix-ups or contamination.

**4.14** There should be defined areas or other control systems for the following activities:

- Receipt, identification, sampling, and quarantine of incoming materials, pending release or rejection;
- Quarantine before release or rejection of intermediates and APIs;
- Sampling of intermediates and APIs;

- Holding rejected materials before further disposition (e.g., return, reprocessing or destruction)
- Storage of released materials;
- Production operations;
- Packaging and labelling operations; and
- Laboratory operations.

4.15    Adequate, clean washing and toilet facilities should be provided for personnel. These washing facilities should be equipped with hot and cold water as appropriate, soap or detergent, air driers or single service towels. The washing and toilet facilities should be separate from, but easily accessible to, manufacturing areas. Adequate facilities for showering and/or changing clothes should be provided, when appropriate.

4.16    Laboratory areas/operations should normally be separated from production areas. Some laboratory areas, in particular those used for in-process controls, can be located in production areas, provided the operations of the production process do not adversely affect the accuracy of the laboratory measurements, and the laboratory and its operations do not adversely affect the production process or intermediate or API.

## 4.2    Utilities

4.20    All utilities that could impact on product quality (e.g. steam, gases, compressed air, and heating, ventilation and air conditioning) should be qualified and appropriately monitored and action should be taken when limits are exceeded. Drawings for these utility systems should be available.

4.21    Adequate ventilation, air filtration and exhaust systems should be provided, where appropriate. These systems should be designed and constructed to minimise risks of contamination and cross-contamination and should include equipment for control of air pressure, microorganisms (if appropriate), dust, humidity, and temperature, as appropriate to the stage of manufacture. Particular attention should be given to areas where APIs are exposed to the environment.

4.22    If air is recirculated to production areas, appropriate measures should be taken to control risks of contamination and cross-contamination.

4.23    Permanently installed pipework should be appropriately identified. This can be accomplished by identifying individual lines, documentation, computer control systems, or alternative means. Pipework should be located to avoid risks of contamination of the intermediate or API.

4.24    Drains should be of adequate size and should be provided with an air break or a suitable device to prevent back-siphonage, when appropriate.

## 4.3  Water

**4.30**  Water used in the manufacture of APIs should be demonstrated to be suitable for its intended use.

**4.31**  Unless otherwise justified, process water should, at a minimum, meet World Health Organization (WHO) guidelines for drinking (potable) water quality.

**4.32**  If drinking (potable) water is insufficient to assure API quality, and tighter chemical and/or microbiological water quality specifications are called for, appropriate specifications for physical/chemical attributes, total microbial counts, objectionable organisms and/or endotoxins should be established.

**4.33**  Where water used in the process is treated by the manufacturer to achieve a defined quality, the treatment process should be validated and monitored with appropriate action limits.

**4.34**  Where the manufacturer of a non-sterile API either intends or claims that it is suitable for use in further processing to produce a sterile drug (medicinal) product, water used in the final isolation and purification steps should be monitored and controlled for total microbial counts, objectionable organisms, and endotoxins.

## 4.4  Containment

**4.40**  Dedicated production areas, which can include facilities, air handling equipment and/or process equipment, should be employed in the production of highly sensitizing materials, such as penicillins or cephalosporins.

**4.41**  Dedicated production areas should also be considered when material of an infectious nature or high pharmacological activity or toxicity is involved (e.g., certain steroids or cytotoxic anti-cancer agents) unless validated inactivation and/or cleaning procedures are established and maintained.

**4.42**  Appropriate measures should be established and implemented to prevent cross-contamination from personnel, materials, etc. moving from one dedicated area to another.

**4.43**  Any production activities (including weighing, milling, or packaging) of highly toxic non-pharmaceutical materials such as herbicides and pesticides should not be conducted using the buildings and/or equipment being used for the production of APIs. Handling and storage of these highly toxic non-pharmaceutical materials should be separate from APIs.

## 4.5  Lighting

4.50  Adequate lighting should be provided in all areas to facilitate cleaning, maintenance, and proper operations.

## 4.6  Sewage and refuse

4.60  Sewage, refuse, and other waste (e.g., solids, liquids, or gaseous by-products from manufacturing) in and from buildings and the immediate surrounding area should be disposed of in a safe, timely, and sanitary manner. Containers and/or pipes for waste material should be clearly identified.

## 4.7  Sanitation and maintenance

4.70  Buildings used in the manufacture of intermediates and APIs should be properly maintained and repaired and kept in a clean condition.

4.71  Written procedures should be established assigning responsibility for sanitation and describing the cleaning schedules, methods, equipment, and materials to be used in cleaning buildings and facilities.

4.72  When necessary, written procedures should also be established for the use of suitable rodenticides, insecticides, fungicides, fumigating agents, and cleaning and sanitizing agents to prevent the contamination of equipment, raw materials, packaging/labelling materials, intermediates, and APIs.

## 5  Process Equipment

### 5.1  Design and construction

5.10  Equipment used in the manufacture of intermediates and APIs should be of appropriate design and adequate size, and suitably located for its intended use, cleaning, sanitization (where appropriate), and maintenance.

5.11  Equipment should be constructed so that surfaces that contact raw materials, intermediates, or APIs do not alter the quality of the intermediates and APIs beyond the official or other established specifications.

5.12  Production equipment should only be used within its qualified operating range.

5.13  Major equipment (e.g., reactors, storage containers) and permanently installed processing lines used during the production of an intermediate or API should be appropriately identified.

**5.14** Any substances associated with the operation of equipment, such as lubricants, heating fluids or coolants, should not contact intermediates or APIs so as to alter their quality beyond the official or other established specifications. Any deviations from this should be evaluated to ensure that there are no detrimental effects upon the fitness for purpose of the material. Wherever possible, food grade lubricants and oils should be used.

**5.15** Closed or contained equipment should be used whenever appropriate. Where open equipment is used, or equipment is opened, appropriate precautions should be taken to minimize the risk of contamination.

**5.16** A set of current drawings should be maintained for equipment and critical installations (e.g., instrumentation and utility systems).

## 5.2   Equipment maintenance and cleaning

**5.20** Schedules and procedures (including assignment of responsibility) should be established for the preventative maintenance of equipment.

**5.21** Written procedures should be established for cleaning of equipment and its subsequent release for use in the manufacture of intermediates and APIs. Cleaning procedures should contain sufficient details to enable operators to clean each type of equipment in a reproducible and effective manner. These procedures should include:

- Assignment of responsibility for cleaning of equipment;
- Cleaning schedules, including, where appropriate, sanitizing schedules;
- A complete description of the methods and materials, including dilution of cleaning agents used to clean equipment;
- When appropriate, instructions for disassembling and reassembling each article of equipment to ensure proper cleaning;
- Instructions for the removal or obliteration of previous batch identification;
- Instructions for the protection of clean equipment from contamination prior to use;
- Inspection of equipment for cleanliness immediately before use, if practical; and
- Establishing the maximum time that may elapse between the completion of processing and equipment cleaning, when appropriate.

**5.22** Equipment and utensils should be cleaned, stored, and, where appropriate, sanitized or sterilized to prevent contamination or carry-over of a material that would alter the quality of the intermediate or API beyond the official or other established specifications.

5.23    Where equipment is assigned to continuous production or campaign production of successive batches of the same intermediate or API, equipment should be cleaned at appropriate intervals to prevent build-up and carry-over of contaminants (e.g. degradants or objectionable levels of micro-organisms).

5.24    Non-dedicated equipment should be cleaned between production of different materials to prevent cross-contamination.

5.25    Acceptance criteria for residues and the choice of cleaning procedures and cleaning agents should be defined and justified.

5.26    Equipment should be identified as to its contents and its cleanliness status by appropriate means.

## 5.3    Calibration

5.30    Control, weighing, measuring, monitoring and test equipment that is critical for assuring the quality of intermediates or APIs should be calibrated according to written procedures and an established schedule.

5.31    Equipment calibrations should be performed using standards traceable to certified standards, if existing.

5.32    Records of these calibrations should be maintained.

5.33    The current calibration status of critical equipment should be known and verifiable.

5.34    Instruments that do not meet calibration criteria should not be used.

5.35    Deviations from approved standards of calibration on critical instruments should be investigated to determine if these could have had an impact on the quality of the intermediate(s) or API(s) manufactured using this equipment since the last successful calibration.

## 5.4    Computerized systems

5.40    GMP related computerized systems should be validated. The depth and scope of validation depends on the diversity, complexity and criticality of the computerized application.

5.41    Appropriate installation qualification and operational qualification should demonstrate the suitability of computer hardware and software to perform assigned tasks.

5.42    Commercially available software that has been qualified does not require the same level of testing. If an existing system was not validated at time of installation, a retrospective validation could be conducted if appropriate documentation is available.

**5.43** Computerized systems should have sufficient controls to prevent unauthorized access or changes to data. There should be controls to prevent omissions in data (e.g. system turned off and data not captured). There should be a record of any data change made, the previous entry, who made the change, and when the change was made.

**5.44** Written procedures should be available for the operation and maintenance of computerized systems.

**5.45** Where critical data are being entered manually, there should be an additional check on the accuracy of the entry. This can be done by a second operator or by the system itself.

**5.46** Incidents related to computerized systems that could affect the quality of intermediates or APIs or the reliability of records or test results should be recorded and investigated.

**5.47** Changes to the computerized system should be made according to a change procedure and should be formally authorized, documented and tested. Records should be kept of all changes, including modifications and enhancements made to the hardware, software and any other critical component of the system. These records should demonstrate that the system is maintained in a validated state.

**5.48** If system breakdowns or failures would result in the permanent loss of records, a back-up system should be provided. A means of ensuring data protection should be established for all computerized systems.

**5.49** Data can be recorded by a second means in addition to the computer system.

## 6 Documentation and Records

### 6.1 Documentation system and specifications

**6.10** All documents related to the manufacture of intermediates or APIs should be prepared, reviewed, approved and distributed according to written procedures. Such documents can be in paper or electronic form.

**6.11** The issuance, revision, superseding and withdrawal of all documents should be controlled with maintenance of revision histories.

**6.12** A procedure should be established for retaining all appropriate documents (e.g., development history reports, scale-up reports, technical transfer reports, process validation reports, training records, production records, control records, and distribution records). The retention periods for these documents should be specified.

**6.13**   All production, control, and distribution records should be retained for at least 1 year after the expiry date of the batch. For APIs with retest dates, records should be retained for at least 3 years after the batch is completely distributed.

**6.14**   When entries are made in records, these should be made indelibly in spaces provided for such entries, directly after performing the activities, and should identify the person making the entry. Corrections to entries should be dated and signed and leave the original entry still readable.

**6.15**   During the retention period, originals or copies of records should be readily available at the establishment where the activities described in such records occurred. Records that can be promptly retrieved from another location by electronic or other means are acceptable.

**6.16**   Specifications, instructions, procedures, and records can be retained either as originals or as true copies such as photocopies, microfilm, microfiche, or other accurate reproductions of the original records. Where reduction techniques such as microfilming or electronic records are used, suitable retrieval equipment and a means to produce a hard copy should be readily available.

**6.17**   Specifications should be established and documented for raw materials, intermediates where necessary, APIs, and labelling and packaging materials. In addition, specifications may be appropriate for certain other materials, such as process aids, gaskets, or other materials used during the production of intermediates or APIs that could critically impact on quality. Acceptance criteria should be established and documented for in-process controls.

**6.18**   If electronic signatures are used on documents, they should be authenticated and secure.

## 6.2   Equipment cleaning and use record

**6.20**   Records of major equipment use, cleaning, sanitization and/or sterilization and maintenance should show the date, time (if appropriate), product, and batch number of each batch processed in the equipment, and the person who performed the cleaning and maintenance.

**6.21**   If equipment is dedicated to manufacturing one intermediate or API, then individual equipment records are not necessary if batches of the intermediate or API follow in traceable sequence. In cases where dedicated equipment is employed, the records of cleaning, maintenance, and use can be part of the batch record or maintained separately.

### 6.3 Records of raw materials, intermediates, API labelling and packaging materials

**6.30** Records should be maintained including:

- The name of the manufacturer, identity and quantity of each shipment of each batch of raw materials, intermediates or labelling and packaging materials for API's; the name of the supplier; the supplier's control number(s), if known, or other identification number; the number allocated on receipt; and the date of receipt;
- The results of any test or examination performed and the conclusions derived from this;
- Records tracing the use of materials;
- Documentation of the examination and review of API labelling and packaging materials for conformity with established specifications; and
- The final decision regarding rejected raw materials, intermediates or API labeling and packaging materials.

**6.31** Master (approved) labels should be maintained for comparison to issued labels.

### 6.4 Master production instructions (master production and control records)

**6.40** To ensure uniformity from batch to batch, master production instructions for each intermediate and API should be prepared, dated, and signed by one person and independently checked, dated, and signed by a person in the quality unit(s).

**6.41** Master production instructions should include:

- The name of the intermediate or API being manufactured and an identifying document reference code, if applicable;
- A complete list of raw materials and intermediates designated by names or codes sufficiently specific to identify any special quality characteristics;
- An accurate statement of the quantity or ratio of each raw material or intermediate to be used, including the unit of measure. Where the quantity is not fixed, the calculation for each batch size or rate of production should be included. Variations to quantities should be included where they are justified;
- The production location and major production equipment to be used;
- Detailed production instructions, including the:

— sequences to be followed,

— ranges of process parameters to be used,

- sampling instructions and in-process controls with their acceptance criteria, where appropriate,
- time limits for completion of individual processing steps and/or the total process, where appropriate; and
- expected yield ranges at appropriate phases of processing or time;
- Where appropriate, special notations and precautions to be followed, or cross references to these; and
- The instructions for storage of the intermediate or API to assure its suitability for use, including the labelling and packaging materials and special storage conditions with time limits, where appropriate.

## 6.5    Batch production records (Batch production and control records)

**6.50**    Batch production records should be prepared for each intermediate and API and should include complete information relating to the production and control of each batch. The batch production record should be checked before issuance to assure that it is the correct version and a legible accurate reproduction of the appropriate master production instruction. If the batch production record is produced from a separate part of the master document, that document should include a reference to the current master production instruction being used.

**6.51**    These records should be numbered with a unique batch or identification number, dated and signed when issued. In continuous production, the product code together with the date and time can serve as the unique identifier until the final number is allocated.

**6.52**    Documentation of completion of each significant step in the batch production records (batch production and control records) should include:

- Dates and, when appropriate, times;
- Identity of major equipment (e.g., reactors, driers, mills, etc.) used;
- Specific identification of each batch, including weights, measures, and batch numbers of raw materials, intermediates, or any reprocessed materials used during manufacturing;
- Actual results recorded for critical process parameters;
- Any sampling performed;
- Signatures of the persons performing and directly supervising or checking each critical step in the operation;
- In-process and laboratory test results;
- Actual yield at appropriate phases or times;

- Description of packaging and label for intermediate or API;
- Representative label of API or intermediate if made commercially available;
- Any deviation noted, its evaluation, investigation conducted (if appropriate) or reference to that investigation if stored separately; and
- Results of release testing.

**6.53** Written procedures should be established and followed for investigating critical deviations or the failure of a batch of intermediate or API to meet specifications. The investigation should extend to other batches that may have been associated with the specific failure or deviation.

## 6.6 Laboratory control records

**6.60** Laboratory control records should include complete data derived from all tests conducted to ensure compliance with established specifications and standards, including examinations and assays, as follows:

- A description of samples received for testing, including the material name or source, batch number or other distinctive code, date sample was taken, and, where appropriate, the quantity and date the sample was received for testing;
- A statement of or reference to each test method used;
- A statement of the weight or measure of sample used for each test as described by the method; data on or cross-reference to the preparation and testing of reference standards, reagents and standard solutions,
- A complete record of all raw data generated during each test, in addition to graphs, charts, and spectra from laboratory instrumentation, properly identified to show the specific material and batch tested;
- A record of all calculations performed in connection with the test, including, for example, units of measure, conversion factors, and equivalency factors;
- A statement of the test results and how they compare with established acceptance criteria;
- The signature of the person who performed each test and the date(s) the tests were performed; and
- The date and signature of a second person showing that the original records have been reviewed for accuracy, completeness, and compliance with established standards.

**6.61** Complete records should also be maintained for:

- Any modifications to an established analytical method,
- Periodic calibration of laboratory instruments, apparatus, gauges, and recording devices;

- All stability testing performed on APIs; and
- Out-of-specification (OOS) investigations.

## 6.7   Batch production record review

**6.70**   Written procedures should be established and followed for the review and approval of batch production and laboratory control records, including packaging and labelling, to determine compliance of the intermediate or API with established specifications before a batch is released or distributed.

**6.71**   Batch production and laboratory control records of critical process steps should be reviewed and approved by the quality unit(s) before an API batch is released or distributed. Production and laboratory control records of non-critical process steps can be reviewed by qualified production personnel or other units following procedures approved by the quality unit(s).

**6.72**   All deviation, investigation, and OOS reports should be reviewed as part of the batch record review before the batch is released.

**6.73**   The quality unit(s) can delegate to the production unit the responsibility and authority for release of intermediates, except for those shipped outside the control of the manufacturing company.

## 7   Materials Management

### 7.1   General controls

**7.10**   There should be written procedures describing the receipt, identification, quarantine, storage, handling, sampling, testing, and approval or rejection of materials.

**7.11**   Manufacturers of intermediates and/or APIs should have a system for evaluating the suppliers of critical materials.

**7.12**   Materials should be purchased against an agreed specification, from a supplier or suppliers approved by the quality unit(s).

**7.13**   If the supplier of a critical material is not the manufacturer of that material, the name and address of that manufacturer should be known by the intermediate and/or API manufacturer.

**7.14**   Changing the source of supply of critical raw materials should be treated according to Section 13, Change Control.

## 7.2 Receipt and quarantine

**7.20**  Upon receipt and before acceptance, each container or grouping of containers of materials should be examined visually for correct labelling (including correlation between the name used by the supplier and the in-house name, if these are different), container damage, broken seals and evidence of tampering or contamination. Materials should be held under quarantine until they have been sampled, examined or tested as appropriate, and released for use.

**7.21**  Before incoming materials are mixed with existing stocks (e.g., solvents or stocks in silos), they should be identified as correct, tested, if appropriate, and released. Procedures should be available to prevent discharging incoming materials wrongly into the existing stock.

**7.22**  If bulk deliveries are made in non-dedicated tankers, there should be assurance of no cross-contamination from the tanker. Means of providing this assurance could include one or more of the following:

- certificate of cleaning
- testing for trace impurities
- audit of the supplier.

**7.23**  Large storage containers, and their attendant manifolds, filling and discharge lines should be appropriately identified.

**7.24**  Each container or grouping of containers (batches) of materials should be assigned and identified with a distinctive code, batch, or receipt number. This number should be used in recording the disposition of each batch. A system should be in place to identify the status of each batch.

## 7.3 Sampling and testing of incoming production materials

**7.30**  At least one test to verify the identity of each batch of material should be conducted, with the exception of the materials described below in 7.32. A supplier's Certificate of Analysis can be used in place of performing other tests, provided that the manufacturer has a system in place to evaluate suppliers.

**7.31**  Supplier approval should include an evaluation that provides adequate evidence (e.g., past quality history) that the manufacturer can consistently provide material meeting specifications. Full analyses should be conducted on at least three batches before reducing in-house testing. However, as a minimum, a full analysis should be performed at appropriate intervals and compared with the Certificates of Analysis. Reliability of Certificates of Analysis should be checked at regular intervals.

**7.32** Processing aids, hazardous or highly toxic raw materials, other special materials, or materials transferred to another unit within the company's control do not need to be tested if the manufacturer's Certificate of Analysis is obtained, showing that these raw materials conform to established specifications. Visual examination of containers, labels, and recording of batch numbers should help in establishing the identity of these materials. The lack of on-site testing for these materials should be justified and documented.

**7.33** Samples should be representative of the batch of material from which they are taken. Sampling methods should specify the number of containers to be sampled, which part of the container to sample, and the amount of material to be taken from each container. The number of containers to sample and the sample size should be based upon a sampling plan that takes into consideration the criticality of the material, material variability, past quality history of the supplier, and the quantity needed for analysis.

**7.34** Sampling should be conducted at defined locations and by procedures designed to prevent contamination of the material sampled and contamination of other materials.

**7.35** Containers from which samples are withdrawn should be opened carefully and subsequently reclosed. They should be marked to indicate that a sample has been taken.

## 7.4  Storage

**7.40** Materials should be handled and stored in a manner to prevent degradation, contamination, and cross-contamination.

**7.41** Materials stored in fiber drums, bags, or boxes should be stored off the floor and, when appropriate, suitably spaced to permit cleaning and inspection.

**7.42** Materials should be stored under conditions and for a period that have no adverse affect on their quality, and should normally be controlled so that the oldest stock is used first.

**7.43** Certain materials in suitable containers can be stored outdoors, provided identifying labels remain legible and containers are appropriately cleaned before opening and use.

**7.44** Rejected materials should be identified and controlled under a quarantine system designed to prevent their unauthorised use in manufacturing.

## 7.5 Re-evaluation

**7.50** Materials should be re-evaluated as appropriate to determine their suitability for use (e.g., after prolonged storage or exposure to heat or humidity).

## 8  Production and In-Process Controls

### 8.1  Production operations

**8.10** Raw materials for intermediate and API manufacturing should be weighed or measured under appropriate conditions that do not affect their suitability for use. Weighing and measuring devices should be of suitable accuracy for the intended use.

**8.11** If a material is subdivided for later use in production operations, the container receiving the material should be suitable and should be so identified that the following information is available:

- Material name and/or item code;
- Receiving or control number;
- Weight or measure of material in the new container; and
- Re-evaluation or retest date if appropriate.

**8.12** Critical weighing, measuring, or subdividing operations should be witnessed or subjected to an equivalent control. Prior to use, production personnel should verify that the materials are those specified in the batch record for the intended intermediate or API.

**8.13** Other critical activities should be witnessed or subjected to an equivalent control.

**8.14** Actual yields should be compared with expected yields at designated steps in the production process. Expected yields with appropriate ranges should be established based on previous laboratory, pilot scale, or manufacturing data. Deviations in yield associated with critical process steps should be investigated to determine their impact or potential impact on the resulting quality of affected batches.

**8.15** Any deviation should be documented and explained. Any critical deviation should be investigated.

**8.16** The processing status of major units of equipment should be indicated either on the individual units of equipment or by appropriate documentation, computer control systems, or alternative means.

**8.17** Materials to be reprocessed or reworked should be appropriately controlled to prevent unauthorized use.

## 8.2    Time limits

8.20    If time limits are specified in the master production instruction (see 6.41), these time limits should be met to ensure the quality of intermediates and APIs. Deviations should be documented and evaluated. Time limits may be inappropriate when processing to a target value (e.g., pH adjustment, hydrogenation, drying to predetermined specification) because completion of reactions or processing steps are determined by in-process sampling and testing.

8.21    Intermediates held for further processing should be stored under appropriate conditions to ensure their suitability for use.

## 8.3    In-process sampling and controls

8.30    Written procedures should be established to monitor the progress and control the performance of processing steps that cause variability in the quality characteristics of intermediates and APIs. In-process controls and their acceptance criteria should be defined based on the information gained during the development stage or historical data.

8.31    The acceptance criteria and type and extent of testing can depend on the nature of the intermediate or API being manufactured, the reaction or process step being conducted, and the degree to which the process introduces variability in the product's quality. Less stringent in-process controls may be appropriate in early processing steps, whereas tighter controls may be appropriate for later processing steps (e.g., isolation and purification steps).

8.32    Critical in-process controls (and critical process monitoring), including the control points and methods, should be stated in writing and approved by the quality unit(s).

8.33    In-process controls can be performed by qualified production department personnel and the process adjusted without prior quality unit(s) approval if the adjustments are made within pre-established limits approved by the quality unit(s). All tests and results should be fully documented as part of the batch record.

8.34    Written procedures should describe the sampling methods for in-process materials, intermediates, and APIs. Sampling plans and procedures should be based on scientifically sound sampling practices.

8.35    In-process sampling should be conducted using procedures designed to prevent contamination of the sampled material and other intermediates or APIs. Procedures should be established to ensure the integrity of samples after collection.

8.36   Out-of-specification (OOS) investigations are not normally needed for in-process tests that are performed for the purpose of monitoring and/or adjusting the process.

## 8.4   Blending batches of intermediates or APIs

8.40   For the purpose of this document, blending is defined as the process of combining materials within the same specification to produce a homogeneous intermediate or API. In-process mixing of fractions from single batches (e.g., collecting several centrifuge loads from a single crystallization batch) or combining fractions from several batches for further processing is considered to be part of the production process and is not considered to be blending.

8.41   Out-Of-Specification batches should not be blended with other batches for the purpose of meeting specifications. Each batch incorporated into the blend should have been manufactured using an established process and should have been individually tested and found to meet appropriate specifications prior to blending.

8.42   Acceptable blending operations include but are not limited to:

- Blending of small batches to increase batch size
- Blending of tailings (i.e., relatively small quantities of isolated material) from batches of the same intermediate or API to form a single batch.

8.43   Blending processes should be adequately controlled and documented and the blended batch should be tested for conformance to established specifications where appropriate.

8.44   The batch record of the blending process should allow traceability back to the individual batches that make up the blend.

8.45   Where physical attributes of the API are critical (e.g., APIs intended for use in solid oral dosage forms or suspensions), blending operations should be validated to show homogeneity of the combined batch. Validation should include testing of critical attributes (e.g., particle size distribution, bulk density, and tap density) that may be affected by the blending process.

8.46   If the blending could adversely affect stability, stability testing of the final blended batches should be performed.

8.47   The expiry or retest date of the blended batch should be based on the manufacturing date of the oldest tailings or batch in the blend.

## 8.5   Contamination control

8.50   Residual materials can be carried over into successive batches of the same intermediate or API if there is adequate control. Examples include residue adhering to the wall of a micronizer, residual layer of damp crystals remaining in a centrifuge bowl after discharge, and incomplete discharge of fluids or crystals from a processing vessel upon transfer of the material to the next step in the process. Such carryover should not result in the carryover of degradants or microbial contamination that may adversely alter the established API impurity profile.

8.51   Production operations should be conducted in a manner that will prevent contamination of intermediates or APIs by other materials.

8.52   Precautions to avoid contamination should be taken when APIs are handled after purification.

## 9   Packaging and Identification Labelling of APIs and Intermediates

### 9.1   General

9.10   There should be written procedures describing the receipt, identification, quarantine, sampling, examination and/or testing and release, and handling of packaging and labelling materials.

9.11   Packaging and labelling materials should conform to established specifications. Those that do not comply with such specifications should be rejected to prevent their use in operations for which they are unsuitable.

9.12   Records should be maintained for each shipment of labels and packaging materials showing receipt, examination, or testing, and whether accepted or rejected.

### 9.2   Packaging materials

9.20   Containers should provide adequate protection against deterioration or contamination of the intermediate or API that may occur during transportation and recommended storage.

9.21   Containers should be clean and, where indicated by the nature of the intermediate or API, sanitized to ensure that they are suitable for their intended use. These containers should not be reactive, additive, or absorptive so as to alter the quality of the intermediate or API beyond the specified limits.

**9.22** If containers are re-used, they should be cleaned in accordance with documented procedures and all previous labels should be removed or defaced.

## 9.3 Label issuance and control

**9.30** Access to the label storage areas should be limited to authorised personnel.

**9.31** Procedures should be used to reconcile the quantities of labels issued, used, and returned and to evaluate discrepancies found between the number of containers labelled and the number of labels issued. Such discrepancies should be investigated, and the investigation should be approved by the quality unit(s).

**9.32** All excess labels bearing batch numbers or other batch-related printing should be destroyed. Returned labels should be maintained and stored in a manner that prevents mix-ups and provides proper identification.

**9.33** Obsolete and out-dated labels should be destroyed.

**9.34** Printing devices used to print labels for packaging operations should be controlled to ensure that all imprinting conforms to the print specified in the batch production record.

**9.35** Printed labels issued for a batch should be carefully examined for proper identity and conformity to specifications in the master production record. The results of this examination should be documented.

**9.36** A printed label representative of those used should be included in the batch production record.

## 9.4 Packaging and labelling operations

**9.40** There should be documented procedures designed to ensure that correct packaging materials and labels are used.

**9.41** Labelling operations should be designed to prevent mix-ups. There should be physical or spatial separation from operations involving other intermediates or APIs.

**9.42** Labels used on containers of intermediates or APIs should indicate the name or identifying code, the batch number of the product, and storage conditions, when such information is critical to assure the quality of intermediate or API.

**9.43** If the intermediate or API is intended to be transferred outside the control of the manufacturer's material management system, the name and address of the manufacturer, quantity of contents, and special transport conditions and any special legal requirements should also be included on the label. For intermediates or APIs with an expiry date, the expiry date should be indicated on the label and Certificate of Analysis. For intermediates or APIs with a retest date, the retest date should be indicated on the label and/or Certificate of Analysis.

9.44 Packaging and labelling facilities should be inspected immediately before use to ensure that all materials not needed for the next packaging operation have been removed. This examination should be documented in the batch production records, the facility log, or other documentation system.

9.45 Packaged and labelled intermediates or APIs should be examined to ensure that containers and packages in the batch have the correct label. This examination should be part of the packaging operation. Results of these examinations should be recorded in the batch production or control records.

9.46 Intermediate or API containers that are transported outside of the manufacturer's control should be sealed in a manner such that, if the seal is breached or missing, the recipient will be alerted to the possibility that the contents may have been altered.

## 10 Storage and Distribution

### 10.1 Warehousing procedures

10.10 Facilities should be available for the storage of all materials under appropriate conditions (e.g. controlled temperature and humidity when necessary). Records should be maintained of these conditions if they are critical for the maintenance of material characteristics.

10.11 Unless there is an alternative system to prevent the unintentional or unauthorised use of quarantined, rejected, returned, or recalled materials, separate storage areas should be assigned for their temporary storage until the decision as to their future use has been taken.

### 10.2 Distribution procedures

10.20 APIs and intermediates should only be released for distribution to third parties after they have been released by the quality unit(s). APIs and intermediates can be transferred under quarantine to another unit under the company's control when authorized by the quality unit(s) and if appropriate controls and documentation are in place.

**10.21** APIs and intermediates should be transported in a manner that does not adversely affect their quality.

**10.22** Special transport or storage conditions for an API or intermediate should be stated on the label.

**10.23** The manufacturer should ensure that the contract acceptor (contractor) for transportation of the API or intermediate knows and follows the appropriate transport and storage conditions.

**10.24** A system should be in place by which the distribution of each batch of intermediate and/or API can be readily determined to permit its recall.

## 11 Laboratory Controls

### 11.1 General controls

**11.10** The independent quality unit(s) should have at its disposal adequate laboratory facilities.

**11.11** There should be documented procedures describing sampling, testing, approval or rejection of materials, and recording and storage of laboratory data. Laboratory records should be maintained in accordance with Section 6.6.

**11.12** All specifications, sampling plans, and test procedures should be scientifically sound and appropriate to ensure that raw materials, intermediates, APIs, and labels and packaging materials conform to established standards of quality and/or purity. Specifications and test procedures should be consistent with those included in the registration/filing. There can be specifications in addition to those in the registration/filing. Specifications, sampling plans, and test procedures, including changes to them, should be drafted by the appropriate organizational unit and reviewed and approved by the quality unit(s).

**11.13** Appropriate specifications should be established for APIs in accordance with accepted standards and consistent with the manufacturing process. The specifications should include a control of the impurities (e.g. organic impurities, inorganic impurities, and residual solvents). If the API has a specification for microbiological purity, appropriate action limits for total microbial counts and objectionable organisms should be established and met. If the API has a specification for endotoxins, appropriate action limits should be established and met.

**11.14** Laboratory controls should be followed and documented at the time of performance. Any departures from the above described procedures should be documented and explained.

**11.15**    Any out-of-specification result obtained should be investigated and documented according to a procedure. This procedure should require analysis of the data, assessment of whether a significant problem exists, allocation of the tasks for corrective actions, and conclusions. Any re-sampling and/or retesting after OOS results should be performed according to a documented procedure.

**11.16**    Reagents and standard solutions should be prepared and labelled following written procedures. "Use by" dates should be applied as appropriate for analytical reagents or standard solutions.

**11.17**    Primary reference standards should be obtained as appropriate for the manufacture of APIs. The source of each primary reference standard should be documented. Records should be maintained of each primary reference standard's storage and use in accordance with the supplier's recommendations. Primary reference standards obtained from an officially recognised source are normally used without testing if stored under conditions consistent with the supplier's recommendations.

**11.18**    Where a primary reference standard is not available from an officially recognized source, an "in-house primary standard" should be established. Appropriate testing should be performed to establish fully the identity and purity of the primary reference standard. Appropriate documentation of this testing should be maintained.

**11.19**    Secondary reference standards should be appropriately prepared, identified, tested, approved, and stored. The suitability of each batch of secondary reference standard should be determined prior to first use by comparing against a primary reference standard. Each batch of secondary reference standard should be periodically requalified in accordance with a written protocol.

## 11.2    Testing of intermediates and APIs

**11.20**    For each batch of intermediate and API, appropriate laboratory tests should be conducted to determine conformance to specifications.

**11.21**    An impurity profile describing the identified and unidentified impurities present in a typical batch produced by a specific controlled production process should normally be established for each API. The impurity profile should include the identity or some qualitative analytical designation (e.g. retention time), the range of each impurity observed, and classification of each identified impurity (e.g. inorganic, organic, solvent). The impurity profile is normally dependent upon the production process and origin of the API. Impurity profiles are normally not necessary for APIs from herbal or animal tissue origin. Biotechnology considerations are covered in ICH Guideline Q6B.

**11.22**  The impurity profile should be compared at appropriate intervals against the impurity profile in the regulatory submission or compared against historical data in order to detect changes to the API resulting from modifications in raw materials, equipment operating parameters, or the production process.

**11.23**  Appropriate microbiological tests should be conducted on each batch of intermediate and API where microbial quality is specified.

## 11.3   Validation of analytical procedures

See Section 12.

## 11.4   Certificates of analysis

**11.40**  Authentic Certificates of Analysis should be issued for each batch of intermediate or API on request.

**11.41**  Information on the name of the intermediate or API including where appropriate its grade, the batch number, and the date of release should be provided on the Certificate of Analysis. For intermediates or APIs with an expiry date, the expiry date should be provided on the label and Certificate of Analysis. For intermediates or APIs with a retest date, the retest date should be indicated on the label and/or Certificate of Analysis.

**11.42**  The Certificate should list each test performed in accordance with compendial or customer requirements, including the acceptance limits, and the numerical results obtained (if test results are numerical).

**11.43**  Certificates should be dated and signed by authorised personnel of the quality unit(s) and should show the name, address and telephone number of the original manufacturer. Where the analysis has been carried out by a repacker or reprocessor, the Certificate of Analysis should show the name, address and telephone number of the repacker/ reprocessor and a reference to the name of the original manufacturer.

**11.44**  If new Certificates are issued by or on behalf of repackers/ reprocessors, agents or brokers, these Certificates should show the name, address and telephone number of the laboratory that performed the analysis. They should also contain a reference to the name and address of the original manufacturer and to the original batch Certificate, a copy of which should be attached.

## 11.5    Stability monitoring of APIs

11.50    A documented, on-going testing program should be designed to monitor the stability characteristics of APIs, and the results should be used to confirm appropriate storage conditions and retest or expiry dates.

11.51    The test procedures used in stability testing should be validated and be stability indicating.

11.52    Stability samples should be stored in containers that simulate the market container. For example, if the API is marketed in bags within fiber drums, stability samples can be packaged in bags of the same material and in smaller-scale drums of similar or identical material composition to the market drums.

11.53    Normally the first three commercial production batches should be placed on the stability monitoring program to confirm the retest or expiry date. However, where data from previous studies show that the API is expected to remain stable for at least two years, fewer than three batches can be used.

11.54    Thereafter, at least one batch per year of API manufactured (unless none is produced that year) should be added to the stability monitoring program and tested at least annually to confirm the stability.

11.55    For APIs with short shelf-lives, testing should be done more frequently. For example, for those biotechnological/biologic and other APIs with shelf-lives of one year or less, stability samples should be obtained and should be tested monthly for the first three months, and at three month intervals after that. When data exist that confirm that the stability of the API is not compromised, elimination of specific test intervals (e.g. 9 month testing) can be considered.

11.56    Where appropriate, the stability storage conditions should be consistent with the ICH guidelines on stability.

## 11.6    Expiry and retest dating

11.60    When an intermediate is intended to be transferred outside the control of the manufacturer's material management system and an expiry or retest date is assigned, supporting stability information should be available (e.g. published data, test results).

11.61    An API expiry or retest date should be based on an evaluation of data derived from stability studies. Common practice is to use a retest date, not an expiration date.

11.62    Preliminary API expiry or retest dates can be based on pilot scale batches if (1) the pilot batches employ a method of manufacture and procedure that simulates the final process to be used on a commercial manufacturing scale; and (2) the quality of the API represents the material to be made on a commercial scale.

**11.63** A representative sample should be taken for the purpose of performing a retest.

## 11.7 Reserve/retention samples

**11.70** The packaging and holding of reserve samples is for the purpose of potential future evaluation of the quality of batches of API and not for future stability testing purposes.

**11.71** Appropriately identified reserve samples of each API batch should be retained for one year after the expiry date of the batch assigned by the manufacturer, or for three years after distribution of the batch, whichever is the longer. For APIs with retest dates, similar reserve samples should be retained for three years after the batch is completely distributed by the manufacturer.

**11.72** The reserve sample should be stored in the same packaging system in which the API is stored or in one that is equivalent to or more protective than the marketed packaging system. Sufficient quantities should be retained to conduct at least two full compendial analyses or, when there is no pharmacopoeial monograph, two full specification analyses.

## 12 Validation

### 12.1 Validation policy

**12.10** The company's overall policy, intentions, and approach to validation, including the validation of production processes, cleaning procedures, analytical methods, in-process control test procedures, computerized systems, and persons responsible for design, review, approval and documentation of each validation phase, should be documented.

**12.11** The critical parameters/attributes should normally be identified during the development stage or from historical data, and the ranges necessary for the reproducible operation should be defined. This should include:

- Defining the API in terms of its critical product attributes;
- Identifying process parameters that could affect the critical quality attributes of the API;
- Determining the range for each critical process parameter expected to be used during routine manufacturing and process control.

**12.12** Validation should extend to those operations determined to be critical to the quality and purity of the API.

## 12.2  Validation documentation

**12.20** A written validation protocol should be established that specifies how validation of a particular process will be conducted. The protocol should be reviewed and approved by the quality unit(s) and other designated units.

**12.21** The validation protocol should specify critical process steps and acceptance criteria as well as the type of validation to be conducted (e.g. retrospective, prospective, concurrent) and the number of process runs.

**12.22** A validation report that cross-references the validation protocol should be prepared, summarising the results obtained, commenting on any deviations observed, and drawing the appropriate conclusions, including recommending changes to correct deficiencies.

**12.23** Any variations from the validation protocol should be documented with appropriate justification.

## 12.3  Qualification

**12.30** Before starting process validation activities, appropriate qualification of critical equipment and ancillary systems should be completed. Qualification is usually carried out by conducting the following activities, individually or combined:

- Design Qualification (DQ): documented verification that the proposed design of the facilities, equipment, or systems is suitable for the intended purpose.
- Installation Qualification (IQ): documented verification that the equipment or systems, as installed or modified, comply with the approved design, the manufacturer's recommendations and/or user requirements.
- Operational Qualification (OQ): documented verification that the equipment or systems, as installed or modified, perform as intended throughout the anticipated operating ranges.
- Performance Qualification (PQ): documented verification that the equipment and ancillary systems, as connected together, can perform effectively and reproducibly based on the approved process method and specifications.

## 12.4 Approaches to process validation

**12.40** Process Validation (PV) is the documented evidence that the process, operated within established parameters, can perform effectively and reproducibly to produce an intermediate or API meeting its predetermined specifications and quality attributes.

**12.41** There are three approaches to validation. Prospective validation is the preferred approach, but there are exceptions where the other approaches can be used. These approaches and their applicability are listed below.

**12.42** Prospective validation should normally be performed for all API processes as defined in 12.12. Prospective validation performed on an API process should be completed before the commercial distribution of the final drug product manufactured from that API.

**12.43** Concurrent validation can be conducted when data from replicate production runs are unavailable because only a limited number of API batches have been produced, API batches are produced infrequently, or API batches are produced by a validated process that has been modified. Prior to the completion of concurrent validation, batches can be released and used in final drug product for commercial distribution based on thorough monitoring and testing of the API batches.

**12.44** An exception can be made for retrospective validation for well established processes that have been used without significant changes to API quality due to changes in raw materials, equipment, systems, facilities, or the production process. This validation approach may be used where:

(1) Critical quality attributes and critical process parameters have been identified;
(2) Appropriate in-process acceptance criteria and controls have been established;
(3) There have not been significant process/product failures attributable to causes other than operator error or equipment failures unrelated to equipment suitability; and,
(4) Impurity profiles have been established for the existing API.

**12.45** Batches selected for retrospective validation should be representative of all batches made during the review period, including any batches that failed to meet specifications, and should be sufficient in number to demonstrate process consistency. Retained samples can be tested to obtain data to retrospectively validate the process.

## 12.5    Process validation program

**12.50**    The number of process runs for validation should depend on the complexity of the process or the magnitude of the process change being considered. For prospective and concurrent validation, three consecutive successful production batches should be used as a guide, but there may be situations where additional process runs are warranted to prove consistency of the process (e.g., complex API processes or API processes with prolonged completion times). For retrospective validation, generally data from ten to thirty consecutive batches should be examined to assess process consistency, but fewer batches can be examined if justified.

**12.51**    Critical process parameters should be controlled and monitored during process validation studies. Process parameters unrelated to quality, such as variables controlled to minimize energy consumption or equipment use, need not be included in the process validation.

**12.52**    Process validation should confirm that the impurity profile for each API is within the limits specified. The impurity profile should be comparable to or better than historical data and, where applicable, the profile determined during process development or for batches used for pivotal clinical and toxicological studies.

## 12.6    Periodic review of validated systems

**12.60**    Systems and processes should be periodically evaluated to verify that they are still operating in a valid manner. Where no significant changes have been made to the system or process, and a quality review confirms that the system or process is consistently producing material meeting its specifications, there is normally no need for revalidation.

## 12.7    Cleaning validation

**12.70**    Cleaning procedures should normally be validated. In general, cleaning validation should be directed to situations or process steps where contamination or carryover of materials poses the greatest risk to API quality. For example, in early production it may be unnecessary to validate equipment cleaning procedures where residues are removed by subsequent purification steps.

**12.71**    Validation of cleaning procedures should reflect actual equipment usage patterns. If various APIs or intermediates are manufactured in the same equipment and the equipment is cleaned by the same process, a representative intermediate or API can be selected for cleaning validation. This selection should be based on the solubility and difficulty of cleaning and the calculation of residue limits based on potency, toxicity, and stability.

**12.72** The cleaning validation protocol should describe the equipment to be cleaned, procedures, materials, acceptable cleaning levels, parameters to be monitored and controlled, and analytical methods. The protocol should also indicate the type of samples to be obtained and how they are collected and labelled.

**12.73** Sampling should include swabbing, rinsing, or alternative methods (e.g., direct extraction), as appropriate, to detect both insoluble and soluble residues. The sampling methods used should be capable of quantitatively measuring levels of residues remaining on the equipment surfaces after cleaning. Swab sampling may be impractical when product contact surfaces are not easily accessible due to equipment design and/or process limitations (e.g., inner surfaces of hoses, transfer pipes, reactor tanks with small ports or handling toxic materials, and small intricate equipment such as micronizers and microfluidizers).

**12.74** Validated analytical methods having sensitivity to detect residues or contaminants should be used. The detection limit for each analytical method should be sufficiently sensitive to detect the established acceptable level of the residue or contaminant. The method's attainable recovery level should be established. Residue limits should be practical, achievable, verifiable and based on the most deleterious residue. Limits can be established based on the minimum known pharmacological, toxicological, or physiological activity of the API or its most deleterious component.

**12.75** Equipment cleaning/sanitization studies should address microbiological and endotoxin contamination for those processes where there is a need to reduce total microbiological count or endotoxins in the API, or other processes where such contamination could be of concern (e.g., non-sterile APIs used to manufacture sterile products).

**12.76** Cleaning procedures should be monitored at appropriate intervals after validation to ensure that these procedures are effective when used during routine production. Equipment cleanliness can be monitored by analytical testing and visual examination, where feasible. Visual inspection can allow detection of gross contamination concentrated in small areas that could otherwise go undetected by sampling and/or analysis.

## 12.8 Validation of analytical methods

**12.80** Analytical methods should be validated unless the method employed is included in the relevant pharmacopoeia or other recognised standard reference. The suitability of all testing methods used should nonetheless be verified under actual conditions of use and documented.

**12.81**   Methods should be validated to include consideration of characteristics included within the ICH guidelines on validation of analytical methods. The degree of analytical validation performed should reflect the purpose of the analysis and the stage of the API production process.

**12.82**   Appropriate qualification of analytical equipment should be considered before starting validation of analytical methods.

**12.83**   Complete records should be maintained of any modification of a validated analytical method. Such records should include the reason for the modification and appropriate data to verify that the modification produces results that are as accurate and reliable as the established method.

## 13    Change Control

**13.10**   A formal change control system should be established to evaluate all changes that may affect the production and control of the intermediate or API.

**13.11**   Written procedures should provide for the identification, documentation, appropriate review, and approval of changes in raw materials, specifications, analytical methods, facilities, support systems, equipment (including computer hardware), processing steps, labelling and packaging materials, and computer software.

**13.12**   Any proposals for GMP relevant changes should be drafted, reviewed, and approved by the appropriate organisational units, and reviewed and approved by the quality unit(s).

**13.13**   The potential impact of the proposed change on the quality of the intermediate or API should be evaluated. A classification procedure may help in determining the level of testing, validation, and documentation needed to justify changes to a validated process. Changes can be classified (e.g. as minor or major) depending on the nature and extent of the changes, and the effects these changes may impart on the process. Scientific judgment should determine what additional testing and validation studies are appropriate to justify a change in a validated process.

**13.14**   When implementing approved changes, measures should be taken to ensure that all documents affected by the changes are revised.

**13.15**   After the change has been implemented, there should be an evaluation of the first batches produced or tested under the change.

**13.16**   The potential for critical changes to affect established retest or expiry dates should be evaluated. If necessary, samples of the intermediate or API produced by the modified process can be placed on an accelerated stability program and/or can be added to the stability monitoring program.

**13.17**    Current dosage form manufacturers should be notified of changes from established production and process control procedures that can impact the quality of the API.

## 14    Rejection and Re-Use of Materials

### 14.1    Rejection

**14.10**    Intermediates and APIs failing to meet established specifications should be identified as such and quarantined. These intermediates or APIs can be reprocessed or reworked as described below. The final disposition of rejected materials should be recorded.

### 14.2    Reprocessing

**14.20**    Introducing an intermediate or API, including one that does not conform to standards or specifications, back into the process and reprocessing by repeating a crystallization step or other appropriate chemical or physical manipulation steps (e.g., distillation, filtration, chromatography, milling) that are part of the established manufacturing process is generally considered acceptable. However, if such reprocessing is used for a majority of batches, such reprocessing should be included as part of the standard manufacturing process.

**14.21**    Continuation of a process step after an in-process control test has shown that the step is incomplete is considered to be part of the normal process. This is not considered to be reprocessing.

**14.22**    Introducing unreacted material back into a process and repeating a chemical reaction is considered to be reprocessing unless it is part of the established process. Such reprocessing should be preceded by careful evaluation to ensure that the quality of the intermediate or API is not adversely impacted due to the potential formation of by-products and over-reacted materials.

### 14.3    Reworking

**14.30**    Before a decision is taken to rework batches that do not conform to established standards or specifications, an investigation into the reason for non-conformance should be performed.

**14.31**    Batches that have been reworked should be subjected to appropriate evaluation, testing, stability testing if warranted, and documentation to show that the reworked product is of equivalent quality to that produced by the original process. Concurrent validation is often the appropriate validation approach for rework procedures. This allows a protocol to define the rework procedure, how it will be carried out, and the expected results. If there is only one batch to be reworked, then a report can be written and the batch released once it is found to be acceptable.

**14.32**    Procedures should provide for comparing the impurity profile of each reworked batch against batches manufactured by the established process. Where routine analytical methods are inadequate to characterize the reworked batch, additional methods should be used.

## 14.4    Recovery of materials and solvents

**14.40**    Recovery (e.g. from mother liquor or filtrates) of reactants, intermediates, or the API is considered acceptable, provided that approved procedures exist for the recovery and the recovered materials meet specifications suitable for their intended use.

**14.41**    Solvents can be recovered and reused in the same processes or in different processes, provided that the recovery procedures are controlled and monitored to ensure that solvents meet appropriate standards before reuse or co-mingling with other approved materials.

**14.42**    Fresh and recovered solvents and reagents can be combined if adequate testing has shown their suitability for all manufacturing processes in which they may be used.

**14.43**    The use of recovered solvents, mother liquors, and other recovered materials should be adequately documented.

## 14.5    Returns

**14.50**    Returned intermediates or APIs should be identified as such and quarantined.

**14.51**    If the conditions under which returned intermediates or APIs have been stored or shipped before or during their return or the condition of their containers casts doubt on their quality, the returned intermediates or APIs should be reprocessed, reworked, or destroyed, as appropriate.

**14.52**    Records of returned intermediates or APIs should be maintained. For each return, documentation should include:

- Name and address of the consignee
- Intermediate or API, batch number, and quantity returned
- Reason for return
- Use or disposal of the returned intermediate or API

## 15   Complaints and Recalls

**15.10**   All quality related complaints, whether received orally or in writing, should be recorded and investigated according to a written procedure.

**15.11**   Complaint records should include:

- Name and address of complainant;
- Name (and, where appropriate, title) and phone number of person submitting the complaint;
- Complaint nature (including name and batch number of the API);
- Date complaint is received;
- Action initially taken (including dates and identity of person taking the action);
- Any follow-up action taken;
- Response provided to the originator of complaint (including date response sent); and
- Final decision on intermediate or API batch or lot.

**15.12**   Records of complaints should be retained in order to evaluate trends, product-related frequencies, and severity with a view to taking additional, and if appropriate, immediate corrective action.

**15.13**   There should be a written procedure that defines the circumstances under which a recall of an intermediate or API should be considered.

**15.14**   The recall procedure should designate who should be involved in evaluating the information, how a recall should be initiated, who should be informed about the recall, and how the recalled material should be treated.

**15.15**   In the event of a serious or potentially life-threatening situation, local, national, and/or international authorities should be informed and their advice sought.

## 16   Contract Manufacturers (including Laboratories)

**16.10**   All contract manufacturers (including laboratories) should comply with the GMP defined in this Guide. Special consideration should be given to the prevention of cross-contamination and to maintaining traceability.

**16.11**  Contract manufacturers (including laboratories) should be evaluated by the contract giver to ensure GMP compliance of the specific operations occurring at the contract sites.

**16.12**  There should be a written and approved contract or formal agreement between the contract giver and the contract acceptor that defines in detail the GMP responsibilities, including the quality measures, of each party.

**16.13**  The contract should permit the contract giver to audit the contract acceptor's facilities for compliance with GMP.

**16.14**  Where subcontracting is allowed, the contract acceptor should not pass to a third party any of the work entrusted to him under the contract without the contract giver's prior evaluation and approval of the arrangements.

**16.15**  Manufacturing and laboratory records should be kept at the site where the activity occurs and be readily available.

**16.16**  Changes in the process, equipment, test methods, specifications, or other contractual requirements should not be made unless the contract giver is informed and approves the changes.

## 17    Agents, Brokers, Traders, Distributors, Repackers, and Relabellers

### 17.1    Applicability

**17.10**  This section applies to any party other than the original manufacturer who may trade and/or take possession, repack, relabel, manipulate, distribute or store an API or intermediate.

**17.11**  All agents, brokers, traders, distributors, repackers, and relabellers should comply with GMP as defined in this Guide.

### 17.2    Traceability of distributed APIs and intermediates

**17.20**  Agents, brokers, traders, distributors, repackers, or relabellers should maintain complete traceability of APIs and intermediates that they distribute. Documents that should be retained and available include:

- Identity of original manufacturer
- Address of original manufacturer
- Purchase orders
- Bills of lading (transportation documentation)
- Receipt documents
- Name or designation of API or intermediate

- Manufacturer's batch number
- Transportation and distribution records
- All authentic Certificates of Analysis, including those of the original manufacturer
- Retest or expiry date

## 17.3 Quality management

17.30 Agents, brokers, traders, distributors, repackers, or relabellers should establish, document and implement an effective system of managing quality, as specified in Section 2.

## 17.4 Repackaging, relabelling and holding of APIs and intermediates

17.40 Repackaging, relabelling and holding of APIs and intermediates should be performed under appropriate GMP controls, as stipulated in this Guide, to avoid mix-ups and loss of API or intermediate identity or purity.

17.41 Repackaging should be conducted under appropriate environmental conditions to avoid contamination and cross-contamination.

## 17.5 Stability

17.50 Stability studies to justify assigned expiration or retest dates should be conducted if the API or intermediate is repackaged in a different type of container than that used by the API or intermediate manufacturer.

## 17.6 Transfer of information

17.60 Agents, brokers, distributors, repackers, or relabellers should transfer all quality or regulatory information received from an API or intermediate manufacturer to the customer, and from the customer to the API or intermediate manufacturer.

17.61 The agent, broker, trader, distributor, repacker, or relabeller who supplies the API or intermediate to the customer should provide the name of the original API or intermediate manufacturer and the batch number(s) supplied.

17.62 The agent should also provide the identity of the original API or intermediate manufacturer to regulatory authorities upon request. The original manufacturer can respond to the regulatory authority directly or through its authorized agents, depending on the legal relationship between the authorized agents and the original API or intermediate manufacturer. (In this context "authorized" refers to authorized by the manufacturer.)

17.63    The specific guidance for Certificates of Analysis included in Section 11.4 should be met.

## 17.7   Handling of complaints and recalls

17.70    Agents, brokers, traders, distributors, repackers, or relabellers should maintain records of complaints and recalls, as specified in Section 15, for all complaints and recalls that come to their attention.

17.71    If the situation warrants, the agents, brokers, traders, distributors, repackers, or relabellers should review the complaint with the original API or intermediate manufacturer in order to determine whether any further action, either with other customers who may have received this API or intermediate or with the regulatory authority, or both, should be initiated. The investigation into the cause for the complaint or recall should be conducted and documented by the appropriate party.

17.72    Where a complaint is referred to the original API or intermediate manufacturer, the record maintained by the agents, brokers, traders, distributors, repackers, or relabellers should include any response received from the original API or intermediate manufacturer (including date and information provided).

## 17.8   Handling of returns

17.80    Returns should be handled as specified in Section 14.52. The agents, brokers, traders, distributors, repackers, or relabellers should maintain documentation of returned APIs and intermediates.

## 18   Specific Guidance for APIs Manufactured by Cell Culture/ Fermentation

### 18.1   General

18.10    Section 18 is intended to address specific controls for APIs or intermediates manufactured by cell culture or fermentation using natural or recombinant organisms and that have not been covered adequately in the previous sections. It is not intended to be a stand-alone Section. In general, the GMP principles in the other sections of this document apply. Note that the principles of fermentation for "classical" processes for production of small molecules and for processes using recombinant and non-recombinant organisms for production of proteins and/or polypeptides are the same, although the degree of control will differ. Where practical, this section will address these differences. In general, the degree of control for biotechnological processes used to produce proteins and polypeptides is greater than that for classical fermentation processes.

18.11 The term "biotechnological process" (biotech) refers to the use of cells or organisms that have been generated or modified by recombinant DNA, hybridoma or other technology to produce APIs. The APIs produced by biotechnological processes normally consist of high molecular weight substances, such as proteins and polypeptides, for which specific guidance is given in this Section. Certain APIs of low molecular weight, such as antibiotics, amino acids, vitamins, and carbohydrates, can also be produced by recombinant DNA technology. The level of control for these types of APIs is similar to that employed for classical fermentation.

18.12 The term "classical fermentation" refers to processes that use microorganisms existing in nature and/or modified by conventional methods (e.g. irradiation or chemical mutagenesis) to produce APIs. APIs produced by "classical fermentation" are normally low molecular weight products such as antibiotics, amino acids, vitamins, and carbohydrates.

18.13 Production of APIs or intermediates from cell culture or fermentation involves biological processes such as cultivation of cells or extraction and purification of material from living organisms. Note that there may be additional process steps, such as physicochemical modification, that are part of the manufacturing process. The raw materials used (media, buffer components) may provide the potential for growth of microbiological contaminants. Depending on the source, method of preparation, and the intended use of the API or intermediate, control of bioburden, viral contamination, and/or endotoxins during manufacturing and monitoring of the process at appropriate stages may be necessary.

18.14 Appropriate controls should be established at all stages of manufacturing to assure intermediate and/or API quality. While this Guide starts at the cell culture/fermentation step, prior steps (e.g. cell banking) should be performed under appropriate process controls. This Guide covers cell culture/fermentation from the point at which a vial of the cell bank is retrieved for use in manufacturing.

18.15 Appropriate equipment and environmental controls should be used to minimize the risk of contamination. The acceptance criteria for quality of the environment and the frequency of monitoring should depend on the step in production and the production conditions (open, closed, or contained systems).

18.16 In general, process controls should take into account:

- Maintenance of the Working Cell Bank (where appropriate);
- Proper inoculation and expansion of the culture;
- Control of the critical operating parameters during fermentation/cell culture;
- Monitoring of the process for cell growth, viability (for most cell culture processes) and productivity where appropriate;
- Harvest and purification procedures that remove cells, cellular debris and media components while protecting the intermediate or API from contamination (particularly of a microbiological nature) and from loss of quality;
- Monitoring of bioburden and, where needed, endotoxin levels at appropriate stages of production; and
- Viral safety concerns as described in ICH Guideline Q5A *Quality of Biotechnological Products: Viral Safety Evaluation of Biotechnology Products Derived from Cell Lines of Human or Animal Origin.*

18.17    Where appropriate, the removal of media components, host cell proteins, other process-related impurities, product-related impurities and contaminants should be demonstrated.

## 18.2    Cell bank maintenance and record keeping

18.20    Access to cell banks should be limited to authorized personnel.

18.21    Cell banks should be maintained under storage conditions designed to maintain viability and prevent contamination.

18.22    Records of the use of the vials from the cell banks and storage conditions should be maintained.

18.23    Where appropriate, cell banks should be periodically monitored to determine suitability for use.

18.24    See ICH Guideline Q5D *Quality of Biotechnological Products: Derivation and Characterization of Cell Substrates Used for Production of Biotechnological/Biological Products* for a more complete discussion of cell banking.

## 18.3    Cell culture fermentation

18.30    Where aseptic addition of cell substrates, media, buffers, and gases is needed, closed or contained systems should be used where possible. If the inoculation of the initial vessel or subsequent transfers or additions (media, buffers) are performed in open vessels, there should be controls and procedures in place to minimize the risk of contamination.

**18.31** Where the quality of the API can be affected by microbial contamination, manipulations using open vessels should be performed in a biosafety cabinet or similarly controlled environment.

**18.32** Personnel should be appropriately gowned and take special precautions handling the cultures.

**18.33** Critical operating parameters (for example temperature, pH, agitation rates, addition of gases, pressure) should be monitored to ensure consistency with the established process. Cell growth, viability (for most cell culture processes), and, where appropriate, productivity should also be monitored. Critical parameters will vary from one process to another, and for classical fermentation, certain parameters (cell viability, for example) may not need to be monitored.

**18.34** Cell culture equipment should be cleaned and sterilized after use. As appropriate, fermentation equipment should be cleaned, and sanitized or sterilized.

**18.35** Culture media should be sterilized before use when appropriate to protect the quality of the API.

**18.36** There should be appropriate procedures in place to detect contamination and determine the course of action to be taken. This should include procedures to determine the impact of the contamination on the product and those to decontaminate the equipment and return it to a condition to be used in subsequent batches. Foreign organisms observed during fermentation processes should be identified as appropriate and the effect of their presence on product quality should be assessed, if necessary. The results of such assessments should be taken into consideration in the disposition of the material produced.

**18.37** Records of contamination events should be maintained.

**18.38** Shared (multi-product) equipment may warrant additional testing after cleaning between product campaigns, as appropriate, to minimize the risk of cross-contamination.

## 18.4   Harvesting, isolation and purification

**18.40** Harvesting steps, either to remove cells or cellular components or to collect cellular components after disruption, should be performed in equipment and areas designed to minimize the risk of contamination.

**18.41** Harvest and purification procedures that remove or inactivate the producing organism, cellular debris and media components (while minimizing degradation, contamination, and loss of quality) should be adequate to ensure that the intermediate or API is recovered with consistent quality.

18.42    All equipment should be properly cleaned and, as appropriate, sanitized after use. Multiple successive batching without cleaning can be used if intermediate or API quality is not compromised.

18.43    If open systems are used, purification should be performed under environmental conditions appropriate for the preservation of product quality.

18.44    Additional controls, such as the use of dedicated chromatography resins or additional testing, may be appropriate if equipment is to be used for multiple products.

## 18.5    Viral removal/inactivation steps

18.50    See the ICH Guideline Q5A *Quality of Biotechnological Products: Viral Safety Evaluation of Biotechnology Products Derived from Cell Lines of Human or Animal Origin* for more specific information.

18.51    Viral removal and viral inactivation steps are critical processing steps for some processes and should be performed within their validated parameters.

18.52    Appropriate precautions should be taken to prevent potential viral contamination from pre-viral to post-viral removal/inactivation steps. Therefore, open processing should be performed in areas that are separate from other processing activities and have separate air handling units.

18.53    The same equipment is not normally used for different purification steps. However, if the same equipment is to be used, the equipment should be appropriately cleaned and sanitized before reuse. Appropriate precautions should be taken to prevent potential virus carry-over (e.g. through equipment or environment) from previous steps.

## 19    APIs for Use in Clinical Trials

### 19.1    General

19.10    Not all the controls in the previous sections of this Guide are appropriate for the manufacture of a new API for investigational use during its development. Section 19 provides specific guidance unique to these circumstances.

19.11    The controls used in the manufacture of APIs for use in clinical trials should be consistent with the stage of development of the drug product incorporating the API. Process and test procedures should be flexible to provide for changes as knowledge of the process increases and clinical testing of a drug product progresses from pre-clinical stages through clinical stages. Once drug development reaches the stage where the API is produced for use in drug products intended for clinical trials, manufacturers should ensure that APIs are manufactured in suitable facilities using appropriate production and control procedures to ensure the quality of the API.

## 19.2  Quality

19.20  Appropriate GMP concepts should be applied in the production of APIs for use in clinical trials with a suitable mechanism of approval of each batch.

19.21  A quality unit(s) independent from production should be established for the approval or rejection of each batch of API for use in clinical trials.

19.22  Some of the testing functions commonly performed by the quality unit(s) can be performed within other organizational units.

19.23  Quality measures should include a system for testing of raw materials, packaging materials, intermediates, and APIs.

19.24  Process and quality problems should be evaluated.

19.25  Labelling for APIs intended for use in clinical trials should be appropriately controlled and should identify the material as being for investigational use.

## 19.3  Equipment and facilities

19.30  During all phases of clinical development, including the use of small-scale facilities or laboratories to manufacture batches of APIs for use in clinical trials, procedures should be in place to ensure that equipment is calibrated, clean and suitable for its intended use.

19.31  Procedures for the use of facilities should ensure that materials are handled in a manner that minimizes the risk of contamination and cross-contamination.

## 19.4  Control of raw materials

19.40  Raw materials used in production of APIs for use in clinical trials should be evaluated by testing, or received with a supplier's analysis and subjected to identity testing. When a material is considered hazardous, a supplier's analysis should suffice.

**19.41** In some instances, the suitability of a raw material can be determined before use based on acceptability in small-scale reactions (i.e., use testing) rather than on analytical testing alone.

## 19.5  Production

**19.50** The production of APIs for use in clinical trials should be documented in laboratory notebooks, batch records, or by other appropriate means. These documents should include information on the use of production materials, equipment, processing, and scientific observations.

**19.51** Expected yields can be more variable and less defined than the expected yields used in commercial processes. Investigations into yield variations are not expected.

## 19.6  Validation

**19.60** Process validation for the production of APIs for use in clinical trials is normally inappropriate, where a single API batch is produced or where process changes during API development make batch replication difficult or inexact. The combination of controls, calibration, and, where appropriate, equipment qualification assures API quality during this development phase.

**19.61** Process validation should be conducted in accordance with Section 12 when batches are produced for commercial use, even when such batches are produced on a pilot or small scale.

## 19.7  Changes

**19.70** Changes are expected during development, as knowledge is gained and the production is scaled up. Every change in the production, specifications, or test procedures should be adequately recorded.

## 19.8  Laboratory controls

**19.80** While analytical methods performed to evaluate a batch of API for clinical trials may not yet be validated, they should be scientifically sound.

**19.81** A system for retaining reserve samples of all batches should be in place. This system should ensure that a sufficient quantity of each reserve sample is retained for an appropriate length of time after approval, termination, or discontinuation of an application.

**19.82** Expiry and retest dating as defined in Section 11.6 applies to existing APIs used in clinical trials. For new APIs, Section 11.6 does not normally apply in early stages of clinical trials.

## 19.9  Documentation

**19.90** A system should be in place to ensure that information gained during the development and the manufacture of APIs for use in clinical trials is documented and available.

**19.91** The development and implementation of the analytical methods used to support the release of a batch of API for use in clinical trials should be appropriately documented.

**19.92** A system for retaining production and control records and documents should be used. This system should ensure that records and documents are retained for an appropriate length of time after the approval, termination, or discontinuation of an application.

## 20  Glossary

**ACCEPTANCE CRITERIA**

Numerical limits, ranges, or other suitable measures for acceptance of test results.

**ACTIVE PHARMACEUTICAL INGREDIENT (API)** *(OR DRUG SUBSTANCE)*

Any substance or mixture of substances intended to be used in the manufacture of a drug (medicinal) product and that, when used in the production of a drug, becomes an active ingredient of the drug product. Such substances are intended to furnish pharmacological activity or other direct effect in the diagnosis, cure, mitigation, treatment, or prevention of disease or to affect the structure and function of the body.

**API STARTING MATERIAL**

A raw material, intermediate, or an API that is used in the production of an API and that is incorporated as a significant structural fragment into the structure of the API. An API Starting Material can be an article of commerce, a material purchased from one or more suppliers under contract or commercial agreement, or produced in-house. API Starting Materials are normally of defined chemical properties and structure.

**BATCH (OR LOT)**

A specific quantity of material produced in a process or series of processes so that it is expected to be homogeneous within specified limits. In the case of continuous production, a batch may correspond to a defined fraction of the production. The batch size can be defined either by a fixed quantity or by the amount produced in a fixed time interval.

## BATCH NUMBER (OR LOT NUMBER)

A unique combination of numbers, letters, and/or symbols that identifies a batch (or lot) and from which the production and distribution history can be determined.

## BIOBURDEN

The level and type (e.g. objectionable or not) of micro-organisms that can be present in raw materials, API starting materials, intermediates or APIs. Bioburden should not be considered contamination unless the levels have been exceeded or defined objectionable organisms have been detected.

## CALIBRATION

The demonstration that a particular instrument or device produces results within specified limits by comparison with those produced by a reference or traceable standard over an appropriate range of measurements.

## COMPUTER SYSTEM

A group of hardware components and associated software, designed and assembled to perform a specific function or group of functions.

## COMPUTERIZED SYSTEM

A process or operation integrated with a computer system.

## CONTAMINATION

The undesired introduction of impurities of a chemical or microbiological nature, or of foreign matter, into or onto a raw material, intermediate, or API during production, sampling, packaging or repackaging, storage or transport.

## CONTRACT MANUFACTURER

A manufacturer performing some aspect of manufacturing on behalf of the original manufacturer.

## CRITICAL

Describes a process step, process condition, test requirement, or other relevant parameter or item that must be controlled within predetermined criteria to ensure that the API meets its specification.

## CROSS-CONTAMINATION

Contamination of a material or product with another material or product.

## DEVIATION

Departure from an approved instruction or established standard.

## DRUG (MEDICINAL) PRODUCT

The dosage form in the final immediate packaging intended for marketing. (Reference Q1A).

## DRUG SUBSTANCE

See Active Pharmaceutical Ingredient

## EXPIRY DATE (OR EXPIRATION DATE)

The date placed on the container/labels of an API designating the time during which the API is expected to remain within established shelf life specifications if stored under defined conditions, and after which it should not be used.

## IMPURITY

Any component present in the intermediate or API that is not the desired entity.

## IMPURITY PROFILE

A description of the identified and unidentified impurities present in an API.

## IN-PROCESS CONTROL (OR PROCESS CONTROL)

Checks performed during production in order to monitor and, if appropriate, to adjust the process and/or to ensure that the intermediate or API conforms to its specifications.

## INTERMEDIATE

A material produced during steps of the processing of an API that undergoes further molecular change or purification before it becomes an API. Intermediates may or may not be isolated. (Note: this Guide only addresses those intermediates produced after the point that the company has defined as the point at which the production of the API begins.)

## LOT

See Batch

## LOT NUMBER

See Batch Number

## MANUFACTURE

All operations of receipt of materials, production, packaging, repackaging, labelling, relabelling, quality control, release, storage, and distribution of APIs and related controls.

## MATERIAL

A general term used to denote raw materials (starting materials, reagents, solvents), process aids, intermediates, APIs and packaging and labelling materials.

## MOTHER LIQUOR

The residual liquid which remains after the crystallization or isolation processes. A mother liquor may contain unreacted materials, intermediates, levels of the API and/or impurities. It may be used for further processing.

## PACKAGING MATERIAL

Any material intended to protect an intermediate or API during storage and transport.

## PROCEDURE

A documented description of the operations to be performed, the precautions to be taken and measures to be applied directly or indirectly related to the manufacture of an intermediate or API.

## PROCESS AIDS

Materials, excluding solvents, used as an aid in the manufacture of an intermediate or API that do not themselves participate in a chemical or biological reaction (e.g. filter aid, activated carbon, etc).

## PROCESS CONTROL

See In-Process Control.

## PRODUCTION

All operations involved in the preparation of an API from receipt of materials through processing and packaging of the API.

## QUALIFICATION

Action of proving and documenting that equipment or ancillary systems are properly installed, work correctly, and actually lead to the expected results. Qualification is part of validation, but the individual qualification steps alone do not constitute process validation.

## QUALITY ASSURANCE (QA)

The sum total of the organised arrangements made with the object of ensuring that all APIs are of the quality required for their intended use and that quality systems are maintained.

## QUALITY CONTROL (QC)

Checking or testing that specifications are met.

## QUALITY UNIT(S)

An organizational unit independent of production which fulfills both Quality Assurance and Quality Control responsibilities. This can be in the form of separate QA and QC units or a single individual or group, depending upon the size and structure of the organization.

## QUARANTINE

The status of materials isolated physically or by other effective means pending a decision on their subsequent approval or rejection.

## RAW MATERIAL

A general term used to denote starting materials, reagents, and solvents intended for use in the production of intermediates or APIs.

## REFERENCE STANDARD, PRIMARY

A substance that has been shown by an extensive set of analytical tests to be authentic material that should be of high purity. This standard can be: (1) obtained from an officially recognised source, or (2) prepared by independent synthesis, or (3) obtained from existing production material of high purity, or (4) prepared by further purification of existing production material.

## REFERENCE STANDARD, SECONDARY

A substance of established quality and purity, as shown by comparison to a primary reference standard, used as a reference standard for routine laboratory analysis.

## REPROCESSING

Introducing an intermediate or API, including one that does not conform to standards or specifications, back into the process and repeating a crystallization step or other appropriate chemical or physical manipulation steps (e.g., distillation, filtration, chromatography, milling) that are part of the established manufacturing process. Continuation of a process step after an in-process control test has shown that the step is incomplete is considered to be part of the normal process, and not reprocessing.

## RETEST DATE

The date when a material should be re-examined to ensure that it is still suitable for use.

## REWORKING

Subjecting an intermediate or API that does not conform to standards or specifications to one or more processing steps that are different from the established manufacturing process to obtain acceptable quality intermediate or API (e.g., recrystallizing with a different solvent).

## SIGNATURE (SIGNED)

See definition for signed

## SIGNED (SIGNATURE)

The record of the individual who performed a particular action or review. This record can be initials, full handwritten signature, personal seal, or authenticated and secure electronic signature.

## SOLVENT

An inorganic or organic liquid used as a vehicle for the preparation of solutions or suspensions in the manufacture of an intermediate or API.

## SPECIFICATION

A list of tests, references to analytical procedures, and appropriate acceptance criteria that are numerical limits, ranges, or other criteria for the test described. It establishes the set of criteria to which a material should conform to be considered acceptable for its intended use. "Conformance to specification" means that the material, when tested according to the listed analytical procedures, will meet the listed acceptance criteria.

## VALIDATION

A documented program that provides a high degree of assurance that a specific process, method, or system will consistently produce a result meeting pre-determined acceptance criteria.

## VALIDATION PROTOCOL

A written plan stating how validation will be conducted and defining acceptance criteria. For example, the protocol for a manufacturing process identifies processing equipment, critical process parameters/operating ranges, product characteristics, sampling, test data to be collected, number of validation runs, and acceptable test results.

## YIELD, EXPECTED

The quantity of material or the percentage of theoretical yield anticipated at any appropriate phase of production based on previous laboratory, pilot scale, or manufacturing data.

## YIELD, THEORETICAL

The quantity that would be produced at any appropriate phase of production, based upon the quantity of material to be used, in the absence of any loss or error in actual production.

# PART III: GMP Related Documents

## Contents of Part III

Contents continued

## SITE MASTER FILE – EXPLANATORY NOTES ON THE PREPARATION OF A SITE MASTER FILE

These notes are intended to provide guidance on the recommended content of the Site Master File. A requirement for a Site Master File is referred to in Chapter 4 of the GMP Guide.

## 1   Introduction

1.1   The Site Master File is prepared by the pharmaceutical manufacturer and should contain specific information about the quality management policies and activities of the site, the production and/or quality control of pharmaceutical manufacturing operations carried out at the named site and any closely integrated operations at adjacent and nearby buildings. If only part of a pharmaceutical operation is carried out on the site, a Site Master File need only describe those operations, e.g. analysis, packaging, etc.

1.2   When submitted to a regulatory authority, the Site Master File should provide clear information on the manufacturer's GMP related activities that can be useful in general supervision and in the efficient planning and undertaking of GMP inspections.

1.3   A Site Master File should contain adequate information but, as far as possible, not exceed 25–30 pages plus appendices. Simple plans outline drawings or schematic layouts are preferred instead of narratives. The Site Master File, including appendices, should be readable when printed on A4 paper sheets.

1.4   The Site Master File should be a part of documentation belonging to the quality management system of the manufacturer and kept updated accordingly. The Site Master File should have an edition number, the date it becomes effective and the date by which it has to be reviewed. It should be subject to regular review to ensure that it is up to date and representative of current activities. Each Appendix can have an individual effective date, allowing for independent updating.

## 2   Purpose

The aim of these Explanatory Notes is to guide the manufacturer of medicinal products in the preparation of a Site Master File that is useful to the regulatory authority in planning and conducting GMP inspections.

## 3   Scope

These Explanatory Notes apply to the preparation and content of the Site Master File.

Manufacturers should refer to regional / national regulatory requirements to establish whether it is mandatory for manufacturers of medicinal products to prepare a Site Master File.

These Explanatory Notes apply for all kind of manufacturing operations such as production, packaging and labelling, testing, relabeling and repackaging of all types of medicinal products. The outlines of this guide could also be used in the preparation of a Site Master File or corresponding document by Blood and Tissue Establishments and manufacturers of Active Pharmaceutical Ingredients.

## 4   Content of Site Master File

Refer to the Annex for the format to be used.

# ANNEX CONTENT OF SITE MASTER FILE

## 1 General Information on the Manufacturer

**1.1** Contact information on the manufacturer

- Name and official address of the manufacturer;
- Names and street addresses of the site, buildings and production units located on the site;
- Contact information of the manufacturer including 24 hrs telephone number of the contact personnel in the case of product defects or recalls.
- Identification number of the site as e.g. GPS details, or any other geographic location system, D-U-N-S (Data Universal Numbering System) Number (a unique identification number provided by Dun & Bradstreet) of the site[1]

**1.2** Authorised pharmaceutical manufacturing activities of the site.

- Copy of the valid manufacturing authorisation issued by the relevant
- Competent Authority in Appendix 1; or when applicable, reference to the
- EudraGMP database. If the Competent Authority does not issue manufacturing authorizations, this should be stated.
- Brief description of manufacture, import, export, distribution and other activities as authorized by the relevant Competent Authorities including foreign authorities with authorized dosage forms/activities, respectively;
- where not covered by the manufacturing authorization;
- Type of products currently manufactured on-site (list in Appendix 2) where not covered by Appendix 1 or EudraGMP entry;
- List of GMP inspections of the site within the last 5 years; including dates and name/country of the Competent Authority having performed the inspection. A copy of current GMP certificate (Appendix 3) or reference to the EudraGMP database, should be included, if available.

**1.3** Any other manufacturing activities carried out on the site

- Description of non-pharmaceutical activities on-site, if any.

## 2 Quality Management System of the Manufacturer

**2.1** The quality management system of the manufacturer

- Brief description of the quality management systems run by the company and reference to the standards used;

---

[1] A D-U-N-S reference is required for Site Master Files submitted to EU/EEA authorities for manufacturing sites located outside of the EU/EEA.

- Responsibilities related to the maintaining of quality system including senior management;
- Information of activities for which the site is accredited and certified, including dates and contents of accreditations, names of accrediting bodies.

**2.2**    Release procedure of finished products

- Detailed description of qualification requirements (education and work experience) of the Authorised Person(s) / Qualified Person(s) responsible for batch certification and releasing procedures;
- General description of batch certification and releasing procedure;
- Role of Authorised Person / Qualified Person in quarantine and release of finished products and in assessment of compliance with the Marketing Authorisation;
- The arrangements between Authorised Persons / Qualified Persons when several Authorised Persons / Qualified Persons are involved;
- Statement on whether the control strategy employs Process Analytical Technology (PAT) and/or Real Time Release or Parametric Release;

**2.3**    Management of suppliers and contractors

- A brief summary of the establishment/knowledge of supply chain and the external audit program;
- Brief description of the qualification system of contractors, manufacturers of active pharmaceutical ingredients (API) and other critical materials suppliers;
- Measures taken to ensure that products manufactured are compliant with TSE (Transmitting animal spongiform encephalopathy) guidelines.
- Measures adopted where counterfeit/falsified products, bulk products (i.e. unpacked tablets), active pharmaceutical ingredients or excipients are suspected or identified.
- Use of outside scientific, analytical or other technical assistance in relation to manufacture and analysis;
- List of contract manufacturers and laboratories including the addresses and contact information and flow charts of supply-chains for outsourced manufacturing and Quality Control activities; e.g. sterilization of primary packaging material for aseptic processes, testing of starting raw-materials etc, should be presented in Appendix 4;
- Brief overview of the responsibility sharing between the contract giver and acceptor with respect to compliance with the Marketing Authorization (where not included under 2.2).

**2.4**    Quality Risk Management (QRM)

- Brief description of QRM methodologies used by the manufacturer;

- Scope and focus of QRM including brief description of any activities which are performed at corporate level, and those which are performed locally. Any application of the QRM system to assess continuity of supply should be mentioned;

**2.5**    Product Quality Reviews

- Brief description of methodologies used

## 3   Personnel

- Organisation chart showing the arrangements for quality management, production and quality control positions/titles in Appendix 5, including senior management and Qualified Person(s);
- Number of employees engaged in the quality management, production, quality control, storage and distribution respectively;

## 4   Premises and Equipment

**4.1**    Premises

- Short description of plant; size of the site and list of buildings. If the production for different markets, i.e. for local, EU, USA etc. takes place in different buildings on the site, the buildings should be listed with destined markets identified (if not identified under 1.1);
- Simple plan or description of manufacturing areas with indication of scale (architectural or engineering drawings are not required);
- Lay outs and flow charts of the production areas (in Appendix 6) showing the room classification and pressure differentials between adjoining areas and indicating the production activities (i.e. compounding, filling, storage, packaging, etc.) in the rooms.;
- Lay-outs of warehouses and storage areas, with special areas for the storage and handling of highly toxic, hazardous and sensitising materials indicated, if applicable;
- Brief description of specific storage conditions if applicable, but not indicated on the lay-outs;

**4.1.1** Brief description of heating, ventilation and air conditioning (HVAC) systems

- Principles for defining the air supply, temperature, humidity, pressure differentials and air change rates, policy of air recirculation (%);

**4.1.2** Brief description of water systems

- Quality references of water produced
- Schematic drawings of the systems in Appendix 7

**4.1.3** Brief description of other relevant utilities, such as steam, compressed air, nitrogen, etc.

**4.2** Equipment

**4.2.1** Listing of major production and control laboratory equipment with critical pieces of equipment identified should be provided in Appendix 8.

**4.2.2 Cleaning and sanitation**

- Brief description of cleaning and sanitation methods of product contact surfaces (i.e. manual cleaning, automatic Clean-in-Place, etc).

**4.2.3 GMP critical computerised systems**

- Description of GMP critical computerised systems (excluding equipment specific Programmable Logic Controllers (PLCs)

## 5  Documentation

- Description of documentation system (i.e. electronic, manual);
- When documents and records are stored or archived off-site (including pharmacovigilance data, when applicable): List of types of documents/ records; Name and address of storage site and an estimate of time required retrieving documents from the off-site archive.

## 6  Production

**6.1** Type of products

- (References to Appendix 1 or 2 can be made):
- Type of products manufactured including
  — list of dosage forms of both human and veterinary products which are manufactured on the site
  — list of dosage forms of investigational medicinal products (IMP) manufactured for any clinical trials on the site, and when different from the commercial manufacturing, information of production areas and personnel
- Toxic or hazardous substances handled (e.g. with high pharmacological activity and/or with sensitising properties);

- Product types manufactured in a dedicated facility or on a campaign basis, if applicable;
- Process Analytical Technology (PAT) applications, if applicable: general statement of the relevant technology, and associated computerized systems;

6.2 Process validation

- Brief description of general policy for process validation;
- Policy for reprocessing or reworking;

6.3 Material management and warehousing

- Arrangements for the handling of starting materials, packaging materials, bulk and finished products including sampling, quarantine, release and storage
- Arrangements for the handling of rejected materials and products

## 7 Quality Control (QC)

Description of the Quality Control activities carried out on the site in terms of physical, chemical, and microbiological and biological testing.

## 8 Distribution, Complaints, Product Defects and Recalls

8.1 Distribution (to the part under the responsibility of the manufacturer)

- Types (wholesale licence holders, manufacturing licence holders, etc) and locations (EU/EEA, USA, etc) of the companies to which the products are shipped from the site;
- Description of the system used to verify that each customer / recipient is legally entitled to receive medicinal products from the manufacturer
- Brief description of the system to ensure appropriate environmental conditions during transit, e.g. temperature monitoring/ control;
- Arrangements for product distribution and methods by which product traceability is maintained;
- Measures taken to prevent manufacturers' products to fall in the illegal supply chain.

8.2 Complaints, product defects and recalls

- Brief description of the system for handling complains, product defects and recalls

## 9 Self Inspections

Short description of the self inspection system with focus on criteria used for selection of the areas to be covered during planned inspections, practical arrangements and follow-up activities

Appendix 1  Copy of valid manufacturing authorisation
Appendix 2  List of dosage forms manufactured including the INN-names or common name (as available) of active pharmaceutical ingredients (API) used
Appendix 3  Copy of valid GMP Certificate
Appendix 4  List of contract manufacturers and laboratories including the addresses and contact information, and flow-charts of the supply-chains for these outsourced activities
Appendix 5  Organisational charts
Appendix 6  Lay outs of production areas including material and personnel flows, general flow charts of manufacturing processes of each product type (dosage form)
Appendix 7  Schematic drawings of water systems
Appendix 8  List of major production and laboratory equipment

## QUALITY RISK MANAGEMENT (ICH Q9)

The ICH Q9 document on Quality Risk Management was adopted at step 4 at the ICH Steering Committee meeting on 9 November 2005.

Quality Risk Management can be applied not only in the manufacturing environment, but also in connection with pharmaceutical development and preparation of the quality part of marketing authorisation dossiers. The guideline applies also to the regulatory authorities in the fields of pharmaceutical assessment of the quality part of the marketing authorisation dossier, GMP inspections and the handling of suspected quality defects. Nevertheless for coherence the text was included within the GMP Guide as Annex 20 in March 2008. Since the creation of Part III of the GMP Guide it has been recognised that Part III is a more appropriate location for its publication.

As part of the EU implementation of ICH Q9, an amendment to Chapter 1 of the GMP Guide (Quality Management) was published in February 2008 which came into force in July 2008. This amendment incorporated the principles of Quality Risk Management into the Chapter.

The text of this document, formerly Annex 20, remains optional and provides examples of the processes and applications of Quality Risk Management.

## 1   Introduction

Risk management principles are effectively utilized in many areas of business and government including finance, insurance, occupational safety, public health, pharmacovigilance, and by agencies regulating these industries. Although there are some examples of the use of quality risk management in the pharmaceutical industry today, they are limited and do not represent the full contributions that risk management has to offer. In addition, the importance of quality systems has been recognized in the pharmaceutical industry and it is becoming evident that quality risk management is a valuable component of an effective quality system.

It is commonly understood that risk is defined as the combination of the probability of occurrence of harm and the severity of that harm. However, achieving a shared understanding of the application of risk management among diverse stakeholders is difficult because each stakeholder might perceive different potential harms, place a different probability on each harm occurring and attribute different severities to each harm. In relation to pharmaceuticals, although there are a variety of stakeholders, including patients and medical practitioners as well as government and industry, the protection of the patient by managing the risk to quality should be considered of prime importance.

The manufacturing and use of a drug (medicinal) product, including its components, necessarily entail some degree of risk. The risk to its quality is just one component of the overall risk. It is important to understand that product quality should be maintained throughout the product lifecycle such that the attributes that are important to the quality of the drug (medicinal) product remain consistent with those used in the clinical studies. An effective quality risk management approach can further ensure the high quality of the drug (medicinal) product to the patient by providing a proactive means to identify and control potential quality issues during development and manufacturing. Additionally, use of quality risk management can improve the decision making if a quality problem arises. Effective quality risk management can facilitate better and more informed decisions, can provide regulators with greater assurance of a company's ability to deal with potential risks and can beneficially affect the extent and level of direct regulatory oversight.

The purpose of this document is to offer a systematic approach to quality risk management. It serves as a foundation or resource document that is independent of, yet supports, other ICH Quality documents and complements existing quality practices, requirements, standards, and guidelines within the pharmaceutical industry and regulatory environment. It specifically provides guidance on the principles and some of the tools of quality risk management that can enable more effective and consistent risk based decisions, both by regulators and industry, regarding the quality of drug substances and drug (medicinal) products across the product lifecycle. It is not intended to create any new expectations beyond the current regulatory requirements.

It is neither always appropriate nor always necessary to use a formal risk management process (using recognized tools and/ or internal procedures e.g. standard operating procedures). The use of informal risk management processes (using empirical tools and/ or internal procedures) can also be considered acceptable. Appropriate use of quality risk management can facilitate but does not obviate industry's obligation to comply with regulatory requirements and does not replace appropriate communications between industry and regulators.

## 2  Scope

This guideline provides principles and examples of tools for quality risk management that can be applied to different aspects of pharmaceutical quality. These aspects include development, manufacturing, distribution, and the inspection and submission/review processes throughout the lifecycle of drug substances, drug (medicinal) products, biological and biotechnological products (including the use of raw materials, solvents, excipients, packaging and labelling materials in drug (medicinal) products, biological and biotechnological products).

## 3 Principles of Quality Risk Management

Two primary principles of quality risk management are:

- The evaluation of the risk to quality should be based on scientific knowledge and ultimately link to the protection of the patient; and
- The level of effort, formality and documentation of the quality risk management process should be commensurate with the level of risk.

## 4 General Quality Risk Management Process

Quality risk management is a systematic process for the assessment, control, communication and review of risks to the quality of the drug (medicinal) product across the product lifecycle. A model for quality risk

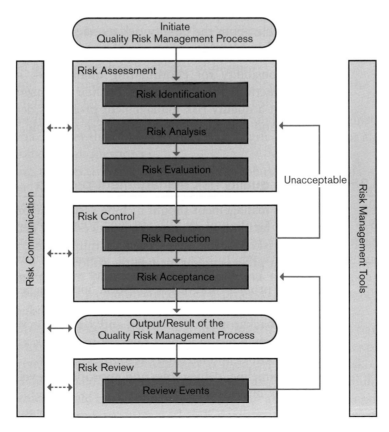

**Figure 1** Overview of a typical Quality risk management process.

specific consequence, given a set of risk-generating circumstances. Thus, quantitative risk estimation is useful for one particular consequence at a time. Alternatively, some risk management tools use a relative risk measure to combine multiple levels of severity and probability into an overall estimate of relative risk. The intermediate steps within a scoring process can sometimes employ quantitative risk estimation.

## 4.4  Risk control

*Risk control* includes decision making to reduce and/or accept risks. The purpose of risk control is to reduce the risk to an acceptable level. The amount of effort used for risk control should be proportional to the significance of the risk. Decision makers might use different processes, including benefit-cost analysis, for understanding the optimal level of risk control.

Risk control might focus on the following questions:

- Is the risk above an acceptable level?
- What can be done to reduce or eliminate risks?
- What is the appropriate balance among benefits, risks and resources?
- Are new risks introduced as a result of the identified risks being controlled?

*Risk reduction* focuses on processes for mitigation or avoidance of quality risk when it exceeds a specified (acceptable) level (see Fig. 1). Risk reduction might include actions taken to mitigate the severity and probability of harm. Processes that improve the detectability of hazards and quality risks might also be used as part of a risk control strategy. The implementation of risk reduction measures can introduce new risks into the system or increase the significance of other existing risks. Hence, it might be appropriate to revisit the risk assessment to identify and evaluate any possible change in risk after implementing a risk reduction process.

*Risk acceptance* is a decision to accept risk. Risk acceptance can be a formal decision to accept the residual risk or it can be a passive decision in which residual risks are not specified. For some types of harms, even the best quality risk management practices might not entirely eliminate risk. In these circumstances, it might be agreed that an appropriate quality risk management strategy has been applied and that quality risk is reduced to a specified (acceptable) level. This (specified) acceptable level will depend on many parameters and should be decided on a case-by-case basis.

## 4.5  Risk communication

*Risk communication* is the sharing of information about risk and risk management between the decision makers and others. Parties can communicate at any stage of the risk management process (see Fig. 1: dashed arrows).

The output/result of the quality risk management process should be appropriately communicated and documented (see Fig. 1: solid arrows). Communications might include those among interested parties; e.g., regulators and industry, industry and the patient, within a company, industry or regulatory authority, etc. The included information might relate to the existence, nature, form, probability, severity, acceptability, control, treatment, detectability or other aspects of risks to quality. Communication need not be carried out for each and every risk acceptance. Between the industry and regulatory authorities, communication concerning quality risk management decisions might be effected through existing channels as specified in regulations and guidances.

## 4.6  Risk review

Risk management should be an ongoing part of the quality management process. A mechanism to review or monitor events should be implemented.

The output/results of the risk management process should be reviewed to take into account new knowledge and experience. Once a quality risk management process has been initiated, that process should continue to be utilized for events that might impact the original quality risk management decision, whether these events are planned (e.g. results of product review, inspections, audits, change control) or unplanned (e.g. root cause from failure investigations, recall). The frequency of any review should be based upon the level of risk. Risk review might include reconsideration of risk acceptance decisions (section 4.4).

## 5  Risk Management Methodology

Quality risk management supports a scientific and practical approach to decision-making. It provides documented, transparent and reproducible methods to accomplish steps of the quality risk management process based on current knowledge about assessing the probability, severity and sometimes detectability of the risk.

Traditionally, risks to quality have been assessed and managed in a variety of informal ways (empirical and/ or internal procedures) based on, for example, compilation of observations, trends and other information. Such approaches continue to provide useful information that might support topics such as handling of complaints, quality defects, deviations and allocation of resources.

Additionally, the pharmaceutical industry and regulators can assess and manage risk using recognized risk management tools and/ or internal procedures (e.g., standard operating procedures). Below is a non-exhaustive list of some of these tools (further details in Annex 1 and chapter 8):

- Basic risk management facilitation methods (flowcharts, check sheets etc.)
- Failure Mode Effects Analysis (FMEA)
- Failure Mode, Effects and Criticality Analysis (FMECA)
- Fault Tree Analysis (FTA)
- Hazard Analysis and Critical Control Points (HACCP)
- Hazard Operability Analysis (HAZOP)
- Preliminary Hazard Analysis (PHA)
- Risk ranking and filtering
- Supporting statistical tools

It might be appropriate to adapt these tools for use in specific areas pertaining to drug substance and drug (medicinal) product quality. Quality risk management methods and the supporting statistical tools can be used in combination (e.g. Probabilistic Risk Assessment). Combined use provides flexibility that can facilitate the application of quality risk management principles.

The degree of rigor and formality of quality risk management should reflect available knowledge and be commensurate with the complexity and/ or criticality of the issue to be addressed.

## 6 Integration of Quality Risk Management into Industry and Regulatory Operations

Quality risk management is a process that supports science-based and practical decisions when integrated into quality systems (see Annex II). As outlined in the introduction, appropriate use of quality risk management does not obviate industry's obligation to comply with regulatory requirements. However, effective quality risk management can facilitate better and more informed decisions, can provide regulators with greater assurance of a company's ability to deal with potential risks, and might affect the extent and level of direct regulatory oversight. In addition, quality risk management can facilitate better use of resources by all parties.

Training of both industry and regulatory personnel in quality risk management processes provides for greater understanding of decision-making processes and builds confidence in quality risk management outcomes.

Quality risk management should be integrated into existing operations and documented appropriately. Annex II provides examples of situations in which the use of the quality risk management process might provide information that could then be used in a variety of pharmaceutical operations. These examples are provided for illustrative purposes only and should not be considered a definitive or exhaustive list. These examples are not intended to create any new expectations beyond the requirements laid out in the current regulations.

Examples for industry and regulatory operations (see Annex II):

- Quality management

Examples for industry operations and activities (see Annex II):

- Development
- Facility, equipment and utilities
- Materials management
- Production
- Laboratory control and stability testing
- Packaging and labelling

Examples for regulatory operations (see Annex II):

- Inspection and assessment activities

While regulatory decisions will continue to be taken on a regional basis, a common understanding and application of quality risk management principles could facilitate mutual confidence and promote more consistent decisions among regulators on the basis of the same information. This collaboration could be important in the development of policies and guidelines that integrate and support quality risk management practices.

## 7 Definitions

*Decision maker(s)* – Person(s) with the competence and authority to make appropriate and timely quality risk management decisions

*Detectability* – the ability to discover or determine the existence, presence, or fact of a hazard

*Harm* – damage to health, including the damage that can occur from loss of product quality or availability

*Hazard* – the potential source of harm (ISO/IEC Guide 51)

*Product Lifecycle* – all phases in the life of the product from the initial development through marketing until the product's discontinuation

*Quality* – the degree to which a set of inherent properties of a product, system or process fulfils requirements (see ICH Q6a definition specifically for "quality" of drug substance and drug (medicinal) products.)

*Quality risk management* – a systematic process for the assessment, control, communication and review of risks to the quality of the drug (medicinal) product across the product lifecycle

*Quality system* – the sum of all aspects of a system that implements quality policy and ensures that quality objectives are met

*Requirements* – the explicit or implicit needs or expectations of the patients or their surrogates (e.g. health care professionals, regulators and legislators). In this document, "requirements" refers not only to statutory, legislative, or regulatory requirements, but also to such needs and expectations.

*Risk* – the combination of the probability of occurrence of harm and the severity of that harm (ISO/IEC Guide 51)

*Risk acceptance* – the decision to accept risk (ISO Guide 73)

*Risk analysis* – the estimation of the risk associated with the identified hazards

*Risk assessment* – a systematic process of organizing information to support a risk decision to be made within a risk management process. It consists of the identification of hazards and the analysis and evaluation of risks associated with exposure to those hazards.

*Risk communication* – the sharing of information about risk and risk management between the decision maker and other stakeholders

*Risk control* – actions implementing risk management decisions (ISO Guide 73)

*Risk evaluation* – the comparison of the estimated risk to given risk criteria using a quantitative or qualitative scale to determine the significance of the risk

*Risk identification* – the systematic use of information to identify potential sources of harm (hazards) referring to the risk question or problem description

*Risk management* – the systematic application of quality management policies, procedures, and practices to the tasks of assessing, controlling, communicating and reviewing risk

*Risk reduction* – actions taken to lessen the probability of occurrence of harm and the severity of that harm

*Risk review* – review or monitoring of output/results of the risk management process considering (if appropriate) new knowledge and experience about the risk

*Severity* – a measure of the possible consequences of a hazard

*Stakeholder* – any individual, group or organization that can affect, be affected by, or perceive itself to be affected by a risk. Decision makers might also be stakeholders. For the purposes of this guideline, the primary stakeholders are the patient, healthcare professional, regulatory authority, and industry

*Trend* – a statistical term referring to the direction or rate of change of a variable(s)

## 8 References

ICH Q8 Pharmaceutical development.

ISO/IEC Guide 73:2002 – Risk Management – Vocabulary – Guidelines for use in Standards.

ISO/IEC Guide 51:1999 – Safety Aspects – Guideline for their inclusion in standards.

*Process Mapping by the American Productivity & Quality Center* 2002, ISBN 1928593739.

IEC 61025 – Fault Tree Analysis (FTA)

IEC 60812 Analysis Techniques for system reliability—Procedures for failure mode and effects analysis (FMEA)

*Failure Mode and Effect Analysis, FMEA from Theory to Execution*, 2nd Edition 2003, D. H. Stamatis, ISBN 0873895983

*Guidelines for Failure Modes and Effects Analysis (FMEA)* for Medical Devices, 2003 Dyadem Press ISBN 0849319102

*The Basics of FMEA*, Robin McDermott, Raymond J. Mikulak, Michael R. Beauregard 1996 ISBN 0527763209

WHO Technical Report Series No 908, 2003 Annex 7 *Application of Hazard Analysis and Critical Control Point (HACCP) methodology to pharmaceuticals.*

IEC 61882 – Hazard Operability Analysis (HAZOP)

ISO 14971:2000 – Application of Risk Management to Medical Devices

ISO 7870:1993 – Control Charts

ISO 7871:1997 – Cumulative Sum Charts

ISO 7966:1993 – Acceptance Control Charts

ISO 8258:1991 – Shewhart Control Charts

*What is Total Quality Control?; The Japanese Way*, Kaoru Ishikawa (Translated by David J. Liu, 1985, ISBN 0139524339).

## ANNEX I RISK MANAGEMENT METHODS AND TOOLS

The purpose of this annex is to provide a general overview of and references for some of the primary tools that might be used in quality risk management by industry and regulators. The references are included as an aid to gain more knowledge and detail about the particular tool. This is not an exhaustive list. It is important to note that no one tool or set of tools is applicable to every situation in which a quality risk management procedure is used.

### I.1    Basic risk management facilitation methods

Some of the simple techniques that are commonly used to structure risk management by organizing data and facilitating decision-making are:

● Flowcharts
● Check Sheets
● Process Mapping
● Cause and Effect Diagrams (also called an Ishikawa diagram or fish bone diagram)

### I.2    Failure Mode Effects Analysis (FMEA)

FMEA (see IEC 60812) provides for an evaluation of potential failure modes for processes and their likely effect on outcomes and/or product performance. Once failure modes are established, risk reduction can be used to eliminate, contain, reduce or control the potential failures. FMEA relies on product and process understanding. FMEA methodically breaks down the analysis of complex processes into manageable steps. It is a powerful tool for summarizing the important modes of failure, factors causing these failures and the likely effects of these failures.

POTENTIAL AREAS OF USE(S)

FMEA can be used to prioritize risks and monitor the effectiveness of risk control activities.

FMEA can be applied to equipment and facilities and might be used to analyze a manufacturing operation and its effect on product or process. It identifies elements/operations within the system that render it vulnerable. The output/ results of FMEA can be used as a basis for design or further analysis or to guide resource deployment.

### I.3 Failure Mode, Effects and Criticality Analysis (FMECA)

FMEA might be extended to incorporate an investigation of the degree of severity of the consequences, their respective probabilities of occurrence, and their detectability, thereby becoming a Failure Mode Effect and Criticality Analysis (FMECA; see IEC 60812). In order for such an analysis to be performed, the product or process specifications should be established. FMECA can identify places where additional preventive actions might be appropriate to minimize risks.

POTENTIAL AREAS OF USE(S)

FMECA application in the pharmaceutical industry should mostly be utilized for failures and risks associated with manufacturing processes; however, it is not limited to this application. The output of an FMECA is a relative risk "score" for each failure mode, which is used to rank the modes on a relative risk basis.

### I.4 Fault Tree Analysis (FTA)

The FTA tool (see IEC 61025) is an approach that assumes failure of the functionality of a product or process. This tool evaluates system (or sub-system) failures one at a time but can combine multiple causes of failure by identifying causal chains. The results are represented pictorially in the form of a tree of fault modes. At each level in the tree, combinations of fault modes are described with logical operators (AND, OR, etc.). FTA relies on the experts' process understanding to identify causal factors.

POTENTIAL AREAS OF USE(S)

FTA can be used to establish the pathway to the root cause of the failure. FTA can be used to investigate complaints or deviations in order to fully understand their root cause and to ensure that intended improvements will fully resolve the issue and not lead to other issues (i.e. solve one problem yet cause a different problem). Fault Tree Analysis is an effective tool for evaluating how multiple factors affect a given issue. The output of an FTA includes a visual representation of failure modes. It is useful both for risk assessment and in developing monitoring programs.

### I.5 Hazard Analysis and Critical Control Points (HACCP)

HACCP is a systematic, proactive, and preventive tool for assuring product quality, reliability, and safety (see WHO Technical Report Series No 908, 2003 Annex 7). It is a structured approach that applies technical and scientific principles to analyze, evaluate, prevent, and control the risk or adverse consequence(s) of hazard(s) due to the design, development, production, and use of products.

HACCP consists of the following seven steps:

(1)  conduct a hazard analysis and identify preventive measures for each step of the process;
(2)  determine the critical control points;
(3)  establish critical limits;
(4)  establish a system to monitor the critical control points;
(5)  establish the corrective action to be taken when monitoring indicates that the critical control points are not in a state of control;
(6)  establish system to verify that the HACCP system is working effectively;
(7)  establish a record-keeping system.

## POTENTIAL AREAS OF USE(S)

HACCP might be used to identify and manage risks associated with physical, chemical and biological hazards (including microbiological contamination). HACCP is most useful when product and process understanding is sufficiently comprehensive to support identification of critical control points. The output of a HACCP analysis is risk management information that facilitates monitoring of critical points not only in the manufacturing process but also in other life cycle phases.

## I.6   Hazard Operability Analysis (HAZOP)

HAZOP (see IEC 61882) is based on a theory that assumes that risk events are caused by deviations from the design or operating intentions. It is a systematic brainstorming technique for identifying hazards using so-called "guide-words". "Guide-words" (e.g., No, More, Other Than, Part of, etc.) are applied to relevant parameters (e.g., contamination, temperature) to help identify potential deviations from normal use or design intentions. It often uses a team of people with expertise covering the design of the process or product and its application.

## POTENTIAL AREAS OF USE(S)

HAZOP can be applied to manufacturing processes, including outsourced production and formulation as well as the upstream suppliers, equipment and facilities for drug substances and drug (medicinal) products. It has also been used primarily in the pharmaceutical industry for evaluating process safety hazards. As is the case with HACCP, the output of a HAZOP analysis is a list of critical operations for risk management. This facilitates regular monitoring of critical points in the manufacturing process.

## I.7 Preliminary Hazard Analysis (PHA)

PHA is a tool of analysis based on applying prior experience or knowledge of a hazard or failure to identify future hazards, hazardous situations and events that might cause harm, as well as to estimate their probability of occurrence for a given activity, facility, product or system. The tool consists of: 1) the identification of the possibilities that the risk event happens, 2) the qualitative evaluation of the extent of possible injury or damage to health that could result and 3) a relative ranking of the hazard using a combination of severity and likelihood of occurrence, and 4) the identification of possible remedial measures

### POTENTIAL AREAS OF USE(S)

PHA might be useful when analyzing existing systems or prioritizing hazards where circumstances prevent a more extensive technique from being used. It can be used for product, process and facility design as well as to evaluate the types of hazards for the general product type, then the product class, and finally the specific product. PHA is most commonly used early in the development of a project when there is little information on design details or operating procedures; thus, it will often be a precursor to further studies. Typically, hazards identified in the PHA are further assessed with other risk management tools such as those in this section.

## I.8 Risk ranking and filtering

Risk ranking and filtering is a tool for comparing and ranking risks. Risk ranking of complex systems typically requires evaluation of multiple diverse quantitative and qualitative factors for each risk. The tool involves breaking down a basic risk question into as many components as needed to capture factors involved in the risk. These factors are combined into a single relative risk score that can then be used for ranking risks. "Filters," in the form of weighting factors or cut-offs for risk scores, can be used to scale or fit the risk ranking to management or policy objectives.

### POTENTIAL AREAS OF USE(S)

Risk ranking and filtering can be used to prioritize manufacturing sites for inspection/audit by regulators or industry. Risk ranking methods are particularly helpful in situations in which the portfolio of risks and the underlying consequences to be managed are diverse and difficult to compare using a single tool. Risk ranking is useful when management needs to evaluate both quantitatively-assessed and qualitatively-assessed risks within the same organizational framework.

## I.9  Supporting statistical tools

Statistical tools can support and facilitate quality risk management. They can enable effective data assessment, aid in determining the significance of the data set(s), and facilitate more reliable decision making. A listing of some of the principal statistical tools commonly used in the pharmaceutical industry is provided:

- Control charts, for example:
  - Acceptance control charts (see ISO 7966)
  - Control charts with arithmetic average and warning limits (see ISO 7873)
  - Cumulative sum charts (see ISO 7871)
  - Shewhart control charts (see ISO 8258)
  - Weighted moving average
- Design of Experiments (DOE)
- Histograms
- Pareto charts
- Process capability analysis

## ANNEX II POTENTIAL APPLICATIONS FOR QUALITY RISK MANAGEMENT

This annex is intended to identify potential uses of quality risk management principles and tools by industry and regulators. However, the selection of particular risk management tools is completely dependent upon specific facts and circumstances.

These examples are provided for illustrative purposes and only suggest potential uses of quality risk management. This Annex is not intended to create any new expectations beyond the current regulatory requirements.

### II.1   Quality risk management as part of integrated quality management

#### DOCUMENTATION

To review current interpretations and application of regulatory expectations

To determine the desirability of and/or develop the content for SOPs, guidelines, etc.

#### TRAINING AND EDUCATION

To determine the appropriateness of initial and/or ongoing training sessions based on education, experience and working habits of staff, as well as on a periodic assessment of previous training (e.g., its effectiveness)

To identify the training, experience, qualifications and physical abilities that allow personnel to perform an operation reliably and with no adverse impact on the quality of the product

#### QUALITY DEFECTS

To provide the basis for identifying, evaluating, and communicating the potential quality impact of a suspected quality defect, complaint, trend, deviation, investigation, out of specification result, etc.

To facilitate risk communications and determine appropriate action to address significant product defects, in conjunction with regulatory authorities (e.g., recall)

#### AUDITING / INSPECTION

To define the frequency and scope of audits, both internal and external, taking into account factors such as:

- Existing legal requirements
- Overall compliance status and history of the company or facility
- Robustness of a company's quality risk management activities
- Complexity of the site

- Complexity of the manufacturing process
- Complexity of the product and its therapeutic significance
- Number and significance of quality defects (e.g, recall)
- Results of previous audits/inspections
- Major changes of building, equipment, processes, key personnel
- Experience with manufacturing of a product (e.g. frequency, volume, number of batches)
- Test results of official control laboratories

## PERIODIC REVIEW

To select, evaluate and interpret trend results of data within the product quality review

To interpret monitoring data (e.g., to support an assessment of the appropriateness of revalidation or changes in sampling)

## CHANGE MANAGEMENT / CHANGE CONTROL

To manage changes based on knowledge and information accumulated in pharmaceutical development and during manufacturing

To evaluate the impact of the changes on the availability of the final product

To evaluate the impact on product quality of changes to the facility, equipment, material, manufacturing process or technical transfers

To determine appropriate actions preceding the implementation of a change, e.g., additional testing, (re)qualification, (re)validation or communication with regulators

## CONTINUAL IMPROVEMENT

To facilitate continual improvement in processes throughout the product lifecycle

## II.2   Quality risk management as part of regulatory operations

### INSPECTION AND ASSESSMENT ACTIVITIES

To assist with resource allocation including, for example, inspection planning and frequency, and inspection and assessment intensity (see "Auditing" section in Annex II.1)

To evaluate the significance of, for example, quality defects, potential recalls and inspectional findings To determine the appropriateness and type of post-inspection regulatory follow-up

To evaluate information submitted by industry including pharmaceutical development information

To evaluate impact of proposed variations or changes

To identify risks which should be communicated between inspectors and assessors to facilitate better understanding of how risks can be or are controlled (e.g., parametric release, Process Analytical Technology (PAT)).

## II.3　Quality risk management as part of development

To design a quality product and its manufacturing process to consistently deliver the intended performance of the product (see ICH Q8)

To enhance knowledge of product performance over a wide range of material attributes (e.g. particle size distribution, moisture content, flow properties), processing options and process parameters

To assess the critical attributes of raw materials, solvents, Active Pharmaceutical Ingredient (API) starting materials, APIs, excipients, or packaging materials

To establish appropriate specifications, identify critical process parameters and establish manufacturing controls (e.g., using information from pharmaceutical development studies regarding the clinical significance of quality attributes and the ability to control them during processing)

To decrease variability of quality attributes:

● reduce product and material defects
● reduce manufacturing defects

To assess the need for additional studies (e.g., bioequivalence, stability) relating to scale up and technology transfer

To make use of the "design space" concept (see ICH Q8)

## II.4　Quality risk management for facilities, equipment and utilities

DESIGN OF FACILITY / EQUIPMENT

To determine appropriate zones when designing buildings and facilities, e.g.,

● flow of material and personnel
● minimize contamination
● pest control measures
● prevention of mix-ups
● open versus closed equipment
● clean rooms versus isolator technologies
● dedicated or segregated facilities / equipment

To determine appropriate product contact materials for equipment and containers (e.g., selection of stainless steel grade, gaskets, lubricants)

To determine appropriate utilities (e.g., steam, gases, power source, compressed air, heating, ventilation and air conditioning (HVAC), water)

## PRODUCT REALISATION

Achievement of a product with the quality attributes appropriate to meet the needs of patients, health care professionals, and regulatory authorities (including compliance with marketing authorisation) and internal customers' requirements. (ICH Q10)

## QUALITY

The degree to which a set of inherent properties of a product, system or process fulfils requirements. (ICH Q9)

## QUALITY MANUAL

Document specifying the quality management system of an organisation. (ISO 9000:2005)

## QUALITY OBJECTIVES

A means to translate the quality policy and strategies into measurable activities. (ICH Q10)

## QUALITY PLANNING

Part of quality management focused on setting quality objectives and specifying necessary operational processes and related resources to fulfill the quality objectives. (ISO 9000:2005)

## QUALITY POLICY

Overall intentions and direction of an organisation related to quality as formally expressed by senior management. (ISO 9000:2005)

## QUALITY RISK MANAGEMENT

A systematic process for the assessment, control, communication and review of risks to the quality of the drug (medicinal) product across the product lifecycle. (ICH Q9)

## SENIOR MANAGEMENT

Person(s) who direct and control a company or site at the highest levels with the authority and responsibility to mobilise resources within the company or site. (ICH Q10 based in part on ISO 9000:2005)

## STATE OF CONTROL

A condition in which the set of controls consistently provides assurance of continued process performance and product quality. (ICH Q10)

# ANNEX 1 POTENTIAL OPPORTUNITIES TO ENHANCE SCIENCE AND RISK BASED REGULATORY APPROACHES*

| Scenario | Potential opportunity |
| --- | --- |
| 1. Comply with GMPs | Compliance – status quo |
| 2. Demonstrate effective pharmaceutical quality system, including effective use of quality risk management principles (e.g., ICH Q9 and ICH Q10). | Opportunity to:<br>• increase use of risk based approaches for regulatory inspections. |
| 3. Demonstrate product and process understanding, including effective use of quality risk management principles (e.g., ICH Q8 and ICH Q9). | Opportunity to:<br>• facilitate science based pharmaceutical quality assessment;<br>• enable innovative approaches to process validation;<br>• establish real-time release mechanisms. |
| 4. Demonstrate effective pharmaceutical quality system and product and process understanding, including the use of quality risk management principles (e.g., ICH Q8, ICH Q9 and ICH Q10). | Opportunity to:<br>• increase use of risk based approaches for regulatory inspections;<br>• facilitate science based pharmaceutical quality assessment;<br>• optimise science and risk based post-approval change processes to maximise benefits from innovation and continual improvement;<br>• enable innovative approaches to process validation;<br>• establish real-time release mechanisms. |

*Note: This annex reflects potential opportunities to enhance regulatory approaches. The actual regulatory process will be determined by region.

(11) **Certificate of GMP Compliance of all sites listed under 10 or, if available, EudraGMP reference number**
Certificate numbers and/or EudraGMP reference numbers should be listed under this item.

(12) **Results of analysis.**
Should include the authorised specifications, all results obtained and refer to the methods used (may refer to a separate certificate of analysis which must be dated, signed and attached).

(13) **Comments/remarks**
Any additional information that can be of value to the importer and/or inspector verifying the compliance of the batch certificate (e.g. specific storage or transportation conditions).

(14) **Certification statement.**
This statement should cover the fabrication/manufacturing, including packaging/labelling and quality control. The following text should be used: "I hereby certify that the above information is authentic and accurate. This batch of product has been manufactured, including packaging/labelling and quality control at the above mentioned site(s) in full compliance with the GMP requirements of the local Regulatory Authority and with the specifications in the Marketing Authorisation of the importing country or product specification file for Investigational Medicinal Products. The batch processing, packaging and analysis records were reviewed and found to be in compliance with GMP".

(15) **Name and position/title of person authorising the batch release**
Including the name and address, if more than one site is mentioned under item 10.

(16) **Signature of person authorising the batch release**

(17) **Date of signature**

## GLOSSARY OF EQUIVALENT TERMS USED IN THE CERTIFICATE TEMPLATE (NON-EXHAUSTIVE)

active substances = active pharmaceutical ingredients/constituents
batch = lot
dosage form = pharmaceutical form
manufacturer = fabricator
manufacturing/manufacture = fabrication
manufacturing authorisation = establishment licence
medicinal product = pharmaceutical product = drug product
quality control = testing

## TEMPLATE FOR THE 'WRITTEN CONFIRMATION' FOR ACTIVE SUBSTANCES EXPORTED TO THE EUROPEAN UNION FOR MEDICINAL PRODUCTS FOR HUMAN USE, IN ACCORDANCE WITH ARTICLE 46B(2)(B) OF DIRECTIVE 2001/83/EC

(1) Directive 2011/62/EU of the European Parliament and of the Council of 8 June 2011 amending Directive 2001/83/EC on the Community code relating to medicinal products for human use, as regards the prevention of the entry into the legal supply chain of falsified medicinal products (OJ L 174, 1.7.2011, p. 74) introduces EU-wide rules for the importation of active substances: According to Article 46b(2) of Directive 2001/83/EC, active substances shall only be imported if, *inter alia*, the active substances are accompanied by a **written confirmation** from the competent authority of the exporting third country which, as regards the plant manufacturing the exported active substance, confirms that the standards of good manufacturing practice and control of the plant are equivalent to those in the Union.

(2) The template for this written confirmation is set out in *annex*.

ANNEX

*Letterhead of the issuing regulatory authority*

**Written confirmation for active substances exported to the European Union (EU) for medicinal products for human use, in accordance with Article 46b(2) (b) of Directive 2001/83/EC**

*Confirmation no. (given by the issuing regulatory authority):*
..............................................................................................
*1. Name and address of site (including building number, where applicable):*
..............................................................................................
*2. Manufacturer's licence number(s):*[1]
..............................................................................................

**Regarding the Manufacturing Plant under (1) of the Following Active Substance (s) Exported to the Eu for Medicinal Products for Human Use**

| Active substance(s):[2] | Activity(ies):[3] |
| --- | --- |
|  |  |

## The Issuing Regulatory Authority Hereby Confirms That:

The standards of good manufacturing practice (GMP) applicable to this manufacturing plant are at least equivalent to those laid down in the EU (= GMP of WHO/ICH Q7);

The manufacturing plant is subject to regular, strict and transparent controls and to the effective enforcement of good manufacturing practice, including repeated and unannounced inspections, so as to ensure a protection of public health at least equivalent to that in the EU; and

In the event of findings relating to non-compliance, information on such findings is supplied by the exporting third country without delay to the EU. [4]

*Date of inspection of the plant under (1). Name of inspecting authority if different from the issuing regulatory authority:*

................................................................................................

This written confirmation remains valid until

................................................................................................

The authenticity of this written confirmation may be verified with the issuing regulatory authority.

This written confirmation is without prejudice to theresponsibilities of the manufacturer to ensure the quality of the medicinal product in accordance with Directive 2001/83/EC.

*Address of the issuing regulatory authority:*

................................................................................................

*Name and function of responsible person:*

................................................................................................

*E-mail, Telephone no., and Fax no.:*

................................................................................................

*Signature          Stamp of the authority and date*

---

[1] Where the regulatory authority issues a licence for the site. Record 'not applicable' in case where there is no legal framework for issuing of a licence.

[2] Identification of the specific active substances through an internationally-agreed terminology (preferably international nonproprietary name).

[3] For example, 'Chemical synthesis', 'Extraction from natural sources', 'Biological processes', 'Finishing steps'.

[4] qdefect@ema.europa.eu.

# Guidance on Manufacture and Importation

# UK Guidance on Manufacture

## Contents

## The Application and Inspection Process "What to Expect"

### Application

Application forms for a manufacturer's licence (MIA) or for a manufacturer's "specials" licence (MS) are available from MHRA's website.[1]

An application for a manufacturer's licence or for a manufacturer's "specials" licence should be accompanied by a Site Master File (SMF). This should contain specific and factual information about the production and/or control of the pharmaceutical operations to be carried out. Guidance on what information should be included in the Site Master File; a worked

---

[1]  http://www.mhra.gov.uk/Howweregulate/Medicines/Licensingofmedicines/
Informationforlicenceapplicants/Licenceapplicationforms/Wholesaledealers
licencesapplicationforms/index.htm

example for reference purposes can be obtained on request from the GMP Inspectorate.

MHRA acting as the licensing authority will only issue a manufacturer's licence or manufacturer's "specials" licence when it is satisfied, following an inspection of the site, that the information contained in the application is accurate and in compliance with the requirements of the legislation.

When appropriate, MHRA may refuse to grant the licence or may grant a licence otherwise than as applied for. In such cases the licensing authority will notify the applicant of its proposals. The notification will set out the reasons for its proposals and give the applicant a period of not less than 28 days to respond.

Once granted, any changes to the information shown on the licence must be submitted to the licensing authority for prior approval. This should be done by submitting a variation application. Variation application forms can be found on MHRA's website[1].

## Planning

A general Good Manufacturing Practice (GMP) inspection is carried out to assess the degree of conformity to prescribed standards of GMP and to assess compliance with the relevant regulatory requirements, for example the licence provisions.

In accordance with the GMP risk-based inspection process, sites will be required to complete a Compliance Report in advance of inspection. Further information and guidance can be found in the section on Risk-based inspections.

## Notification

Advance notice of inspection is normally given to a company, unless circumstances require that an unannounced inspection should take place. The timing of the inspection would normally be discussed by telephone with the licence holder and details confirmed in writing. In accordance with the GMP risk-based inspection process, sites will be required to complete a Compliance Report in advance of inspection.

The scope of the inspection may vary depending on the type of inspection and site size. For smaller sites, all regulated activities would normally be inspected at each visit. For large complex sites, all regulated activities would normally be inspected over a period of two years. For an overseas site, the inspection will focus on those activities associated with products licensed for supply in the UK, or in the case of inspections relating to Centralised Applications those products detailed in the inspection contract with the EMA. However, the company will be asked to confirm all products supplied to the EEA and the inspection scope may be extended in consultation with other authorities to ensure adequate coverage of these products. The intent is to minimise as far as possible the number of inspections performed in third countries.

## Conduct

The major stages of the inspection process are:

- the introductory or opening meeting;
- the detailed inspection; and
- the summary or closing meeting.

### INTRODUCTORY OR OPENING MEETING

The purpose of the meeting is for the inspector to meet with the appropriate key personnel from the company to discuss the arrangements for the inspection. The inspector would typically confirm the purpose and scope of the inspection, areas to be visited and indicate any documentation which may be required.

### SITE INSPECTION

The purpose of the site inspection is to determine the degree of conformity of the operations to requirements of good practice and to assess compliance with the terms and conditions of licences issued under the appropriate legislation or with details submitted in support of an application for a licence.

The inspection schedule is, therefore, determined by the type of inspection planned. The inspection will typically involve visits to operational areas, interviews with key personnel and documentation review. Any observations, recommendations and deficiencies noted during the inspection would normally be discussed with the company representatives at the time.

During inspections of manufacturing operations, samples of starting materials, work in progress and finished products may be taken for testing if an inspector considers that this might assist in the detection of quality deficiencies. Occasionally samples may be taken, when these cannot be obtained from other sources, for routine surveillance purposes.

### SUMMARY OR CLOSING MEETING

The purpose of the meeting is for the inspector to provide the company with a verbal summary of the inspection findings and to allow the company to correct at this stage any misconceptions. The inspector would typically summarise the definition and classification of deficiencies they propose to report and the company is encouraged to give an undertaking to resolve the deficiencies and to agree a provisional timetable for corrective action. The inspector would also describe the arrangements for the formal notification of the deficiencies to the company (the post-inspection letter) and what is expected as a response.

The choice of company representatives at the meeting is primarily for the company to decide, but should normally include the senior staff who were present during the inspection, technical management and the QPs.

## Definition of deficiencies

All deficiencies are classified as **critical, major** or **other.** A reference to the relevant sections of the GMP legislation or guidelines will be given for those deficiencies classified as critical or major. The definitions used are as per the EU Community Report format:

- **critical deficiency:**
  a deficiency which has produced, or leads to a significant risk of producing either a product which is harmful to the human or veterinary patient or a product which could result in a harmful residue in a food producing animal;
- **major deficiency:**
  a non-critical deficiency
  – that has produced, or may produce a product, which does not comply with its marketing authorisation, or
  – which indicates a major deviation from EU GMP, or
  – (within EU) which indicates a major deviation from the terms of the manufacturing authorisation, or
  – which indicates a failure to carry out satisfactory procedures for release of batches or (within EU) a failure of the QP to fulfil his legal duties, or
  – a combination of several 'other' deficiencies, none of which on their own may be major but which may together represent a major deficiency and should be explained and reported as such;
- **other deficiency:**
  a deficiency which cannot be classified as either critical or major but which indicates a departure from GMP (a deficiency may be 'other' either because it is judged as minor or because there is insufficient information to classify it as major or critical).

Several related major or other deficiencies may be taken together to constitute a critical or major deficiency (respectively) and will be reported as such.

All critical and major deficiencies found will be reported even if remedial action has been taken before the end of the inspection.

## Post-inspection letter

A post-inspection letter is sent to provide written confirmation of the deficiencies noted and reported verbally during the closing meeting.

Depending upon the inspection findings and the response from the company during and following the inspection, the inspector may take one of a number of actions ranging from:

- sending a GMP certificate or letter confirming essential compliance with GMP; to
- recommending to IAG consideration for adverse licensing action against a manufacturer's licence, manufacturer's "specials" licence or marketing authorisation.

## Company responses

The inspected site is expected to provide a written response to the post-inspection letter within the required timeframe. The response should consider the context of the deficiency within the overall quality system rather than just the specific issue identified. The response should include proposals for dealing with the deficiencies, together with a timetable for their implementation. It is helpful for the response to be structured as follows:

- restate the deficiency number;
- state the proposed corrective action;
- state the proposed target date for the completion of the corrective action(s);
- include any comment the company considers appropriate; and
- provide an electronic version via email.

## Inspection report

Once the inspector is satisfied that any necessary remedial action has been taken or is in hand and that the site is essentially in compliance with GMP, an inspection report and GMP certificate or close-out letter are finalised.

## Risk-based Inspection Programme

## Introduction

MHRA has been incorporating elements of risk management into its inspection programme for a number of years. A formal risk-based inspection programme was implemented on 1 April 2009, following public consultation MLX 345. The risk-based inspection programme covers all aspects of good practices associated with the inspection of clinical, pre-clinical and quality control laboratories, clinical trials, manufacturers, wholesalers and pharmacovigilance systems. The primary aim of the programme is to enable inspectorate resources to focus on areas that maximise protection of public health while reducing the overall administrative and economic burden to stakeholders.

## Sentinel risk information module

Working with technology partners Accenture, MHRA established its Sentinel IT system in 2005 which is used by most agency business areas to manage business processes for:

- marketing authorisations;
- pharmacovigilance;
- clinical trials;
- manufacturer's and wholesale dealer's licences;
- inspections; and
- issuing GMP and GDP certificates and automatic loading of these into the EMA's EudraGMDP database.

In February 2013, a newly developed Sentinel risk information module was deployed to expand upon the paper-based risk-based inspection system initiated in 2009.

The Risk Estimation Tool uses the intelligence data collected on regulated companies, their respective sites and previous inspection results across all GxP areas to predict a risk score as "likely next inspection result". This score is calculated for every site and can be interpreted as a weighted sum of inspection findings. Companies/sites are ranked based on predicted risk and business rules are applied to suggest a next inspection date.

A planning step allows inspectors to accept or reject the suggested date taking into account other information which may not be included in the statistical calculation. For estimation of the risk score, the tool uses a logistic regression statistical model incorporating all data elements for all companies and sites. The model is fit (i.e. recomputed) monthly based on the most recent data extracted from Sentinel. The Empirica algorithm software was designed by Oracle Health Services to provide detailed analysis of the risk information. MHRA first used Empirica software in 2006 for pharmacovigilance signal detection and management.

The model estimates the association between inspection findings and other covariates (events) observed in data. The algorithm makes a global estimate on how these events affect inspection score within a GxP and then applies this when these events are recorded in the future. As a result, those factors which are statistically most relevant to risk will receive the highest weighting and this will be continuously updated as more events are

UK GUIDANCE ON MANUFACTURE

recorded. The model looks at events over a five year period but applies greater significance to more recent data.

## Current implementation status

A number of aspects of the algorithm are being validated including:

- the risk score;
- the weighting of inspection outcomes;
- the weighting of the risk events;
- the generation of proposed inspection dates from the risk score; and
- inclusion of all appropriate risk events.

The algorithm is being assessed on an individual GxP basis as well as across the GxPs. The algorithm output is being compared against the existing risk-based inspection processes within the GxPs. Until the algorithm has been successfully validated, the existing risk-based inspection scheduling processes will remain in place.

## GMP risk-based inspection programme

The GMP risk-based inspection process commenced for all participating sites on 1 April 2009. Participating sites are those UK sites that hold a manufacturing authorisation (MIA, MS, MIA [IMP]) and third country sites that are named on a UK marketing authorisation or where UK has been the Reference Member State on a decentralised procedure.

## Compliance report and interim update

Sites are required to complete a Compliance Report in advance of inspection, this will be prompted by the inspector. A guidance document and example reports are also available to assist completion. The Compliance Report should be returned to the inspector prior to the inspection.

Following a site's first inspection after 1 April 2009, it is expected that relevant changes affecting the site will be advised to MHRA on a Compliance Report Interim Assessment.

## Risk rating process

Inspectors use the inspection outputs along with a number of other factors to identify a risk rating for the site which equates to a future inspection frequency. As this process is not concluded until the inspection is closed, the risk ratings **will not** be discussed at the closing meeting. However a copy of the full inspection report, which includes the full risk rating rationale, is provided to sites once the inspection has been closed.

The issue of a certificate of GMP compliance and/or support of the site on the relevant licence is an indication of meeting the minimum level of GMP compliance. Risk ratings identify the degree of surveillance required within the licensing and inspection programme. There is no intention that sites be rated against each other as a result of risk ratings assigned by MHRA. Risk ratings can change following inspection, resulting in either increased or decreased risk. Inspection risk ratings will not be published by MHRA.

There will be no formal process of appeal against risk ratings and future inspection frequency. However, any rating that results in an increased inspection frequency from the previous standard will be peer reviewed before conclusion by a GMP operations manager or a GMP expert inspector. MHRA does have a formal complaints process if sites wish to log an issue; however, any concerns regarding the inspection process should be raised with the inspector in the first instance.

## Conditions for Manufacturer's Licence

The holder of a manufacturer's licence must comply with certain conditions in relation to the manufacture, assembly and importation of medicinal products. These conditions are set out in regulations 37 to 41 of the Human Medicines Regulations 2012 [SI 2012 No. 1916]. They require that the licence holder shall:

- comply with the principles and guidelines for GMP including insofar as they relate to the import of medicinal products;
- only use active starting materials which have been manufactured in accordance with the principles and guidelines for good manufacturing practice for active substances and have been distributed in accordance with the guidelines on good distribution practice for active substances, unless they are for use or used in an exempt medicinal product (special medicinal product);
- verify that:
  - the manufacturer or distributor of an active substance that they have used has complied with the requirements of good manufacturing practice and good distribution practice for active substances by means of an audit performed directly by themselves or by a person acting on their behalf, and
  - unless the active substance is imported from a third country, any manufacturers, importers or distributors supplying them with the active substances are registered with the competent authority of a Member State in which they are established

- ensure the authenticity and quality of the active substance;
- ensure:
  - excipients are suitable for use in a medicinal product by ascertaining what the appropriate good manufacturing practice is,
  - that the ascertained good manufacturing practice is applied,
  - that the suitability of the excipient is ascertained on the basis of a formalised risk assessment as described in paragraph 5 of Article 47 of the Directive 2001/83/EC and the assessment takes account of the source requirements under other quality systems, intended use of the excipients, and previous instances of quality defects,
  - the authenticity and quality of any excipient used is verified, and
  - the measures taken under this paragraph are documented by the licence holder;
- maintain such staff, premises, equipment and facilities necessary to conduct the manufacture and assembly of medicinal products in accordance with the requirements of their manufacturer's licence and the appropriate authorisation of the medicinal product being manufactured;
- maintain such staff, premises, equipment and facilities for the handling, control, storage and distribution of the medicinal products manufactured or assembled in accordance with their manufacturer's licence as necessary to maintain the quality of those medicinal products;
- ensure that any arrangements made for the control, storage and distribution of the medicinal products are adequate to maintain the quality of those products;
- not carry out any manufacture or assembly of medicinal products other than in accordance with their manufacturer's licence and at the premises specified in the licence;
- not use any premises for the handling, control, storage or distribution of medicinal products other than those named on their manufacturer's licence which have been approved by the licensing authority for that purpose;
- inform the licensing authority before making any material alteration to the premises or facilities used under their manufacturer's licence, or in the operations for which they are used;
- inform the licensing authority of any proposed changes to any personnel named in their manufacturer's licence as responsible for quality control, including the person named as the qualified person;
- permit the licensing authority to carry out inspections, take samples or copies of documentation as necessary to enable the licensing authority to ascertain whether there are any grounds for suspending, revoking or terminating the manufacturer's licence or to verifying any statement contained in an application for a licence;

- ensure that any blood or blood component that they import into the UK and use as a starting material or raw material in the manufacture of a medicinal product meets equivalent standards of quality and safety to those laid down in Commission Directive 2004/33/EC, implementing Directive 2002/98/EC of the European Parliament and of the Council as regards certain technical requirements for blood and blood components; and
- ensure that they have at all times at their disposal the services of at least one Qualified Person who is responsible for carrying out, in relation to the medicinal products being manufactured or assembled, the duties specified in Article 51 of the Directive 2001/83/EC.

Where the manufacturer's licence holder distributes the medicinal product manufactured or assembled in accordance with the manufacturer's licence they shall:

- comply with the principles of good distribution practice;
- ensure the appropriate and continued supply of the medicinal product that they manufacture or assemble;
- sell only, or offer for sale or supply, the medicinal product in accordance and conformity with a marketing authorisation unless it is an exempt medicinal product or is distributed to another Member State where it can be legally used as an unlicensed medicinal product in the Member State concerned;
- distribute only their medicinal products to a holder of a wholesale dealer's licence relating to those products; a holder of an authorisation granted by the competent authority of another EEA State authorising the supply of those products by way of wholesale dealing; any person who may lawfully sell those products by retail or who may lawfully supply them in circumstances corresponding to retail sale; or any person who may lawfully administer those products;
- where the medicinal product is supplied to a person for retail sale or supply, the manufacturer's licence holder must enclose with the product a document which makes it possible to ascertain the date on which the supply took place; the name and pharmaceutical form of the product supplied; the quantity of product supplied; and the names and addresses of the person or persons from whom the products were supplied.

The manufacturer's licence holder must immediately inform the competent authority of a Member State and, where applicable, the marketing authorisation holder, of medicinal products which come within the scope of their manufacturing authorisation which the licence holder knows or suspects or has reasonable grounds for knowing or suspecting to be falsified.

The Standard Provisions are incorporated into all manufacturer's licences in the form set out in Schedule 4 of the Human Medicines Regulations 2012, that is, those provisions which may be included in all licences unless an individual licence provides variations to them. They require that the manufacturer's licence holder shall:

- place their quality control system referred to in Article 11(1) of Commission Directive 2003/94/EC under the authority of the head of the Quality Control (QC);
- provide information about the products being manufactured or assembled under their manufacturer's licence and about the operations being conducted in relation to such manufacture or assembly as may be requested by the licensing authority;
- inform the licensing authority of any proposed changes to be made to any personnel named on their licence, responsible for supervising the production operations; in charge of the animals from which are derived any substances used in the production of the medicinal products being manufactured or assembled; or responsible for the culture of any living tissues used in the manufacture of the medicinal products being manufactured or assembled;
- keep readily available for inspection by a person authorised by the licensing authority the batch documentation referred to in Article 9(1) of Commission Directive 2003/94/EC, and permit that person to take copies or make extracts from such documentation;
- keep readily available for examination by a person authorised by the licensing authority, samples of each batch of finished medicinal product referred to in Article 11(4) of Commission Directive 2003/94/EC;
- withhold any batch of any medicinal product from sale or export so far as may be reasonably practicable for up to 6 weeks when informed that it does not comply with its licence specifications or with the provisions of the Human Medicines Regulations 2012;
- ensure that any tests for determining conformity with the standards and specifications applying to any particular product used in the manufacture of a medicinal product shall, except so far as the conditions of the product specification for that product otherwise provide, be applied to samples taken from the medicinal product after all manufacturing processes have been completed, or at such earlier stage in the manufacture as may be approved by the licensing authority;
- where the manufacturer's licence relates to the assembly of any medicinal product or class of product, and the licence holder supplies that medicinal product at such a stage of assembly that does not fully comply with the provisions of the product specification that relate to labelling, the licence holder shall communicate the particulars of those provisions to the person to whom that product has been so supplied;

- where the manufacturer's licence relates to the assembly of a medicinal product; and that medicinal product is not manufactured by the licence holder; and particulars as to the name and address of the manufacturer of, or of the person who imports, that medicinal product have been given by the licence holder to the licensing authority, the licence holder shall forthwith notify the licensing authority in writing of any changes in such particulars;
- keep readily available for examination by a person authorised by the licensing authority durable records of the details of manufacture of any intermediate products held by them which are for use in the manufacture of biological medicinal products for human use and shall be in such form as to ensure that the manufacturer's licence holder has a comprehensive record of all matters that are relevant to an evaluation of the safety, quality and efficacy of any finished biological medicinal product for human use which they manufacture using those intermediate products. The records shall not be destroyed without the consent of the licensing authority until the records of the details of manufacture of any finished medicinal products which were or may be manufactured using those intermediate products may be destroyed in accordance with the requirements of these Regulations;
- arrange for animals which are used in the production of any medicinal products to be housed in premises of such a nature, and be managed in such a manner, as to facilitate compliance with the provisions relating to them in the relevant marketing authorisations;
- take all reasonable precautions and exercise all due diligence to ensure that any information they provide to the licensing authority which is relevant to an evaluation of the safety, quality or efficacy of any medicinal product for human use which they manufacture or assemble; or any starting materials or intermediate products that they hold which are for use in the manufacture of medicinal products, is not false or misleading in any material particular.

The manufacturer's licence holder may use a contract laboratory pursuant to Article 11(2) of Commission Directive 2003/94/EC if operated by a person approved by the licensing authority, i.e. if not on the manufacturer's licence a contract laboratory will not be acceptable.[2]

The Standard Provisions require the manufacturer's licence holder that imports medicinal products from a state other than an EEA State to:

- provide such information as may be requested by the licensing authority concerning the type and quantity of any medicinal products which the licence holder imports;

---

[2] A contract laboratory is required to be named on the manufacturer's licence.

- withhold the batch of imported product from distribution, so far as reasonably practicable, for up to six weeks when told that the strength, quality or purity of a batch of a medicinal product to which the licence relates has been found not to conform with the specification of the medicinal product in question; or those provisions of the Regulations that are applicable to the medicinal product;
- ensure that any tests for determining conformity with the standards and specifications applying to any ingredient used in the manufacture of a medicinal product must, except so far as the conditions of the product specification for that ingredient otherwise provide, be applied to samples taken from the medicinal product after all manufacturing processes have been completed, or at such earlier stage in the manufacture as may be approved by the licensing authority;
- take all reasonable precautions and exercise due diligence to ensure that any information provided to the licensing authority which is relevant to an evaluation of the safety, quality or efficacy of a medicinal product for human use which is imported from a state other than an EEA State, handled, stored or distributed under the licence is not false or misleading in a material particular.

The Standard Provisions also require the holder of a manufacturer's licence relating to the manufacture and assembly of exempt advanced therapy medicinal products to ensure that:

- the immediate packaging of an exempt advanced therapy medicinal product is labelled to show the following particulars:
  - the name of the exempt advanced therapy medicinal product,
  - the expiry date in clear terms including the year and month and, if applicable, the day;
  - a description of the active substance, expressed qualitatively and quantitatively;
  - where the product contains cells or tissues of human or animal origin:
    - a statement that the product contains such cells or tissues, and
    - a short description of the cells or tissues and of their specific origin;
  - the pharmaceutical form and the contents by weight, volume or number of doses of the product;
  - a list of excipients, including preservative systems;
  - the method of use, application, administration or implantation and, if appropriate, the route of administration, with space provided for the prescribed dose to be indicated;
  - any special storage precautions;
  - specific precautions relating to the disposal of the unused product or waste derived from the product and, where appropriate, reference to any appropriate collection system;
  - the name and address of the holder of the manufacturer's licence;

– the manufacturer's licence number;

– the manufacturer's batch number;

– the unique donation code referred to in Article 8(2) of Directive 2004/23/EC; and

– where the exempt advanced therapy medicinal product is for autologous use, the unique patient identifier and the words "for autologous use only".

● the package leaflet of the exempt advanced therapy medicinal product shall include the following particulars:

– the name of the exempt advanced therapy medicinal product;

– the intended effect of the medicinal product if correctly used, applied, administered or implanted;

– where the product contains cells or tissues of human or animal origin:

• a statement that the product contains such cells or tissues, and

• a short description of the cells or tissues and, where such cells or tissues are of animal origin, their specific origin;

● where the product contains a medical device or an active implantable medical device, a description of that device and, where that device contains cells or tissues of animal origin, their specific origin;

● any necessary instructions for use, including:

– the posology,

– the method of use, application, administration or implantation and, if appropriate, the route of administration,

– a description of symptoms of overdose,

– action to be taken in the event of overdose, including any emergency procedures,

– action to be taken if one or more doses have been missed, and

– a recommendation to consult the doctor or pharmacist for any clarification on the use of the product;

● where adverse reactions are known, a description of those which may occur under recommended conditions of use of the product and, if appropriate, an indication of action to be taken in such a case;

● an instruction that the patient report any adverse reaction not specified in the package leaflet to the doctor or pharmacist;

● the expiry date in clear terms and a warning against using the product after that date;

● any special storage precautions;

● a description of any visible signs of deterioration;

● a complete qualitative and quantitative composition;

● the name and address of the holder of the manufacturer's licence; and

● the date on which the package leaflet was last revised.

The licence holder must keep data to trace the exempt advanced therapy medicinal through the sourcing, manufacturing, packaging, storage, transport and delivery to the establishment where the product is used, for longer than 30 years.

## Qualified Persons

### General

All holders of a manufacturer's licence for licensed products, including for the purposes of import, are required to have available the services of at least one Qualified Person (QP), who must be named on the licence. When considering a nomination, the licensing authority (MHRA) routinely takes into account the assessment of the nominee's eligibility made by the joint assessment panel of the Society of Biology, the Royal Pharmaceutical Society and the Royal Society of Chemistry. Exceptionally, MHRA will assess a nominee directly if he or she is not a member of any of these professional bodies.

Title IV of Directive 2001/83/EC as amended lays down the requirements for QPs in relation to products for human use. Article 51 defines the duties of the QP; Articles 49 and 50 define the requirements for eligibility under the permanent and transitional arrangements respectively, and Article 52 requires Member States to ensure that the duties of QPs are fulfilled, either through administrative measures or by making such persons subject to a professional code of conduct. Title IV of Directive 2001/82/EC as amended lays down equivalent requirements in relation to veterinary products. Guidance on the duties of QPs is given in the EU Guide to GMP and in particular in its Annex 16.

By inspection and other means, the licensing authority routinely assesses whether or not QPs are fulfilling their duties. In making this assessment, reference is made to the *Code of Practice for Qualified Persons* produced jointly by the Society of Biology, the Royal Pharmaceutical Society and the Royal Society of Chemistry in collaboration with MHRA and the Veterinary Medicines Directorate. This reference is made whether or not the QP in question is a member of one or more of these bodies (see next section).

All QPs should be guided in fulfilling their duties by the Code of Practice, although the references in Sections 11.1 and 12.4 to the disciplinary machinery of the professional bodies, and in Section 11.6 to the advice which professional bodies can give, would not be relevant in the case of a QP who is not a member of one of these bodies. The European Industrial Pharmacists Group adopted a similar code[1] in 1995 for the guidance of its members.

---

[1] European Industrial Pharmacists Group (est. June 1966). Code of Practice for Qualified Persons. Available from the Industrial Pharmacists Group of the Royal Pharmaceutical Society.

## Code of Practice for Qualified Persons

### 1.0  Introduction

**1.1**  The concept of the Qualified Person (QP), first established in 1975, is a unique regulatory requirement that applies only within the European Union (EU). The only comparable situation exists within Member States of the European Economic Area (EEA) with whom the EU has reciprocal agreements.

**1.2**  Each holder of an Authorisation to Manufacture products for use in a Clinical Trial or products subject to Marketing Authorisations, within Member States of the EU, must name a person or persons who are eligible to act in the capacity of QP.

**1.3**  The requirement for QP covers both Human and Veterinary Medicinal Products including those intended for export.

**1.4**  Particular conditions for formal qualifications and practical experience for eligibility to act as a QP are specified in the relevant EU Council Directives (see 2.0 below). Ensuring compliance with these conditions is the responsibility of the Competent Authorities of the Member States.

**1.5**  The primary legal responsibility of the QP is to certify batches of Medicinal Product prior to use in a Clinical Trial (Human Medicinal Products only) or prior to release for sale and placing on the market (Human and Veterinary Medicinal Products). However, the wider technical, ethical and professional obligations in terms of patient safety, quality and efficacy must also be considered. Hence this professional Code of Practice, which is designed to take account of these issues.

### 2.0  Regulatory basis for the Qualified Person

For ease of reference the key regulatory documents concerning the QP are as follows:

(i)  Directive 2003/94/EC – Principles and Guidelines of Good Manufacturing Practice for Medicinal Products for Human Use – **Article 7.**

(ii)  Directive 91/412/EEC – Principles and Guidelines of Good Manufacturing Practice for Veterinary Medicinal Products – **Article 7.**

(iii)  Directive 2001/20/EC – Good Clinical Practice in the Conduct of Clinical Trials on Medicinal Products for Human Use – **Article 13**.

(iv)  Directive 2001/82/EC – Community Code Relating to Veterinary Medicinal Products – **Title IV – Manufacture and Imports – Articles**

UK GUIDANCE ON MANUFACTURE

44-57 (NB Articles 44, 50, 51, 53, 54 and 55 have been amended by Directive 2004/28/EC).

(v)   Directive 2001/83/EC – Community Code Relating to Medicinal Products for Human Use – **Title IV – Manufacture and Importation – Articles 40-53** (NB Articles 46, 47, 49, 50 and 51 have been amended by Directive 2004/27/EC).

(vi)   EudraLex Volume 4 – Good Manufacturing Practices

**Annex 13 – Manufacture of Investigational Medicinal Products**
**Annex 16 – Certification by a Qualified Person and Batch Release**

## 3.0   Purpose of the Code

**3.1**   The legal functions of the Qualified Person (QP) are stated in Article 51 of Directive 2001/83/EC or Article 55 of Directive 2001/82/EC and reproduced in the preface to the UK Joint Professional Bodies' Study Guide.

**3.2**   The aims and objectives of the Code of Practice are to provide operational guidelines for carrying out the functions of the Qualified Person within a professional code of conduct in accordance with Article 56 of Council Directive 2001/82/EC and/or Article 52 of Council Directive 2001/83/EC.

**3.3**   The Code is in the interests of Qualified Persons, their employers, patients and the Competent Authorities of the Member States.

## 4.0   Application of the Code

**4.1**   The Code is equally applicable to Qualified Persons who have achieved that status under the transitional arrangements, and under the permanent provisions.

**4.2**   Qualified Persons have a professional duty to decline to act as Qualified Persons in the release of product types for which they do not possess the relevant experience and knowledge.

**4.3**   It should be noted that Qualified Persons are eligible to certify batches of medicinal product as follows:

(i)   those who have achieved Qualified Person status under the permanent provisions, or under the transitional provisions of 2001/83/EC, are eligible to certify batches of human or veterinary medicinal products in any member state within the European Union (EU);

(ii)   those who have achieved Qualified Person status under the transitional arrangements for veterinary medicines are only eligible to certify batches of veterinary medicinal products, and such certification is restricted to acting in the UK although such products, once certified, can legally be sold or supplied throughout the EU;

(iii) those who have achieved Qualified Person status under the transitional arrangements for investigational medicinal products (2001/20/EC) are only eligible to certify batches of investigational medicinal products;

(iv) those who have achieved Qualified Person status under the transitional arrangements for traditional herbal medicinal products (2001/24/EC) are only eligible to certify batches of traditional herbal medicinal products.

**4.4**  The Code applies equally to Qualified Persons involved in human and/or veterinary medicines.

**4.5**  The Licensing Authority may refer to this Code in connection with disciplinary proceedings against a Qualified Person under Article 52 of Directive 2001/83/EC or Article 56 of Directive 2001/82/EC.

## 5.0  Terminology

**5.1**  The terminology used in this Code of Practice corresponds with that used in the current versions of the EC directives on Good Pharmaceutical Manufacturing Practice (GMP) and the Guide to Good Pharmaceutical Manufacturing Practice.

**5.2**  Within the EU the terms Marketing Authorisation, Manufacturing Authorisation and Investigational Medicinal Products Authorisation are generally used and shall henceforth be referred to throughout this Code.

## 6.0  General principles

**6.1**  Pharmaceutical Manufacturers and the Competent Authorities of the Member States have a duty to ensure that patients are properly protected and that medicinal products meet appropriate requirements for safety, quality and efficacy.

**6.2**  The legal framework is provided by the European Directives and "The Rules Governing Medicinal Products in the European Union", which are implemented by individual Member States' national legislation.

**6.3**  An operational framework is provided in the current Volume 4 of the Rules Governing Medical Products in the European Union 'Good Manufacturing Practices'. In Chapter 1 of the Guidelines, Quality Management, it states that:

> *"The holder of a Manufacturing Authorisation must manufacture medicinal products so as to ensure that they are fit for their intended use, comply with the requirements of the Marketing Authorisation*

*and do not place patients at risk due to inadequate safety, quality or efficacy. The attainment of this quality objective is the responsibility of senior management and requires the participation and commitment by staff in many different departments and at all levels within the company, the company's suppliers and the distributors.*

*To achieve the quality objective reliably there must be a comprehensively designed and correctly implemented system of Quality Assurance incorporating Good Manufacturing Practice and thus Quality Control. It should be fully documented and its effectiveness monitored. All parts of the Quality Assurance system should be adequately resourced with competent personnel, and suitable and sufficient premises, equipment and facilities. There are additional legal responsibilities for the holder of the Manufacturing Authorisation and for the Qualified Person(s).*

*The basic concepts of Quality Assurance, Good Manufacturing Practice and Quality Control are inter-related. They are described here in order to emphasise their relationships and their fundamental importance to the production and control of medicinal products".*

6.4    Qualified Persons should be aware that whilst Quality Management applies to full-scale manufacture, it also extends to original product design, development, formulation and manufacture of medicinal products for use in clinical trials. This includes the establishment of well-defined manufacturing processes, sampling programmes and analytical tests methods and appropriate specifications for ingredients, printed and unprinted packaging components and finished dosage forms.

## 7.0    Routine duties of a Qualified Person

Qualified Persons have routine duties, some of which may be delegated (see later), in line with the above general principles. Before certifying a batch prior to release the Qualified Person doing so should always **ensure** that the following requirements have been met:

*The meaning of the word **ensure** in this context is that the Qualified Person must be confident that various actions, which may not be under his/her direct control, have in fact been taken. See also Section 8.*

7.1    The Marketing Authorisation and Manufacturing Authorisation or Investigational Medicinal Products Authorisation requirements for the Medicinal Products have been met for the batch concerned.

**7.2** The principles and guidelines of GMP as stated in Directive 2003/94/EC (Human) or Directive 91/412/EEC (Veterinary) and as interpreted in the EU Guide to GMP have been followed.

**7.3** The principal manufacturing and testing processes have been validated.

**7.4** All the necessary quality control checks and tests have been performed, and account taken of the manufacturing and packaging conditions including a review of batch records. *The EU Guide to GMP suggests that the Head of Production and the Head of Quality Control assume line management responsibilities for these activities.*

**7.5** Any changes or deviations in manufacturing, packaging or quality control have been notified in accordance with a well-defined reporting system before any product batch is released. Such changes may need notification to and approval by the Competent Authorities of the Member States.

**7.6** Any additional sampling, inspection, tests and checks have been carried out or initiated, as appropriate, to cover changes or deviations.

**7.7** All necessary manufacturing, packaging and associated documentation has been completed and endorsed by suitably authorised staff trained in the concept of Quality Assurance and Good Manufacturing Practices.

**7.8** Regular audits, self-inspections and spot checks are being carried out by experienced staff.

**7.9** All relevant factors have been considered including any not specifically associated with the output batch directly under review (e.g. calibration and maintenance records, environmental monitoring).

**7.10** The legal requirements regarding imported products have been fully met. *For products imported from outside the EU or EEA the Qualified Person should ensure testing within the EU/EEA to the requirements of the Marketing Authorisation and any other tests to assure quality of the products, unless a mutual recognition agreement between the EU and the third country concerned allows the acceptance of manufacturer's batch certification in lieu.*

*The Qualified Person should also be satisfied that the medicinal products have been manufactured in accordance with GMP standards which are equivalent to those of the EU or EEA.*

**7.11** The Qualified Person should also recognise the need to consult other company experts in the various areas of the Study Guide to reinforce his/her knowledge on appropriate points when a doubtful situation arises *(e.g. stability, unusual analytical results, process or equipment changes, potential environmental or microbiological risks, re-labelling, abnormal yields, cross contamination risks etc.).*

**7.12** To maintain a register (or equivalent document) as a record of product batches certified by the Qualified Person prior to batch release.

**7.13** To retain reference samples of each product batch at the site of manufacture for a period of time in compliance with EU regulations and the Licensing Authority's requirements.

**7.14** In considering how to perform the above duties, 7.1 to 7.13, the Qualified Person will have to take account of the nature and size of the operations being performed. For example, in a very small company with a limited range of products it may be possible that the Qualified Person can take direct responsibility for some or all of the tasks outlined above. In larger organisations, the Qualified Person will be dependent upon the knowledge and expertise of his/her colleagues in undertaking some or all of the tasks.

*However, it is of paramount importance that the Qualified Person takes steps, within a well-planned Quality Management System, to assure himself or herself that the tasks allocated are in fact being performed satisfactorily. Hence the routine duties of the Qualified Person depend very much upon a team effort wherein the individuals concerned realise the position and responsibility of the Qualified Person and provide every support.*

*What cannot be over emphasised in this context is the Qualified Person's commitment to meet regularly with professional colleagues in all functional groups and to understand their contribution and impact upon quality.*

*The certification of a batch prior to release must be performed by a Qualified Person.*

## 8.0  Performance of duties and regulatory compliance

**8.1** Management, as a requirement of Quality Assurance, should clearly define the areas of work and the method of operating in the absence of the regular Qualified Person.

*In the absence of one Qualified Person, the task of certifying batches can only be delegated to another Qualified Person nominated on the Manufacturing Authorisation and who is knowledgeable and experienced with regard to the medicinal products under review.*

**8.2** Whilst each Qualified Person has a personal and professional responsibility for being certain that the various checks and tests have been carried out, the detail of this work is described in the EU Guide to GMP as normally the responsibility of the Head of Production and the Head of Quality Control who must ensure that appropriately trained and experienced staff are available.

*Ultimately the Qualified Person must be satisfied either directly or, more usually, by the proper operation of quality systems, which include appropriate approvals, audits, self-inspections and spot checks that manufacturing, packaging and quality control testing have complied with relevant requirements.*

**Batch certification without such adequate steps may be regarded as professional misconduct.**

**8.3** It must be recognised that the Qualified Person depends upon many of his/her working colleagues for the achievement of quality and regulatory compliance in the manufacture of medicinal products. It is therefore of paramount importance that he or she achieves a good working relationship with other persons in positions of responsibility. These are likely to include those responsible for:

- *processing and packing operations*
- *quality control laboratories*
- *validation*
- *application and maintenance of Manufacturing and Marketing Authorisations*
- *provision of engineering services*
- *procurement of starting and packaging materials*
- *storage, transport and distribution*
- *contract services*

**8.4** It is recommended that the company and the Qualified Person take the necessary steps to appraise other functional groups, and the responsible people who belong to them, of the role of the Qualified Person within the company and how they should give proper support.

**8.5** Ensuring compliance with the conditions of the Marketing Authorisation is a primary duty of the Qualified Person. It is, therefore, essential that the Qualified Person has access at all times to the dossiers upon which Marketing Authorisations have been granted, including any variations affecting such approval. The control of change needs to be rigorously monitored by the Qualified Person especially where there are implications for compliance, quality and patient safety. Particular attention needs to be paid to this when the manufacturer is making products for a Marketing Authorisation holder in a different company.

**8.6** The Qualified Person should be present at the manufacturing site for a sufficient proportion of the working time in order to discharge the legal and professional obligations outlined in this Code and to ensure the proper operation of a Quality Management System including the control of any delegated duties.

UK GUIDANCE ON MANUFACTURE

**8.7** Manufacturing Authorisations contain the names of the persons responsible for Production, Quality Control, and the name(s) of the Qualified Person(s). The duties of these members of staff must be clear in their respective job descriptions and they must have the authority required under the relevant EC directives.

## 9.0 Number and location of Qualified Persons

**9.1** The provisions in Article 52 of Council Directive 2001/82/EC and/or Article 48 of Council Directive 2001/83/EC. and the principles outlined in the EU Guide to GMP for Medicinal Products only require a company or organisation to nominate one person on a Manufacturing Authorisation to carry out the duties of the Qualified Person provided that person is at the disposal of the company at all times and can carry out the required functions.

**9.2** Some organisations may have a complex structure, or operate at several locations, or both, which would make it necessary, where justified, to nominate several Qualified Persons on its Manufacturing Authorisation.

## 10.0 Contracted Qualified Persons

**10.1** In a number of cases, especially with smaller companies, a 'Contracted Qualified Person' provides the service. In such cases the duties and responsibilities of a 'Contracted Qualified Person' are the same as those Qualified Persons who are permanently employed by their company; the QP is not an employee of the company but provides his services under contract.
   *The term 'Contracted Qualified Person' is not a formal title and is used only in the sense of a Qualified Person providing an independent service under contract to a company.*

**10.2** In addition to compliance with the provisions applicable to all QPs including all the routine duties outlined in this Code of Practice, Contracted Qualified Persons should observe the following:-

- have a clear written contract, which delineates the duties and responsibilities of the Qualified Person – as agreed between the company and the 'Contracted Qualified Person'. Both should sign and retain a copy of the contract;
- be readily available to the staff of the company for advice and discussion, and also be present during regulatory inspections and involved in communications with the inspectors;
- ensure that the company to whom the services are provided will allow free access to any people, information, documentation, premises, procedures etc. which are relevant to the decision-making processes

when certifying batches for sale. In addition the company should inform the Qualified Person of any deviations which need to be considered in relation to batch certification. Such deviations should be provided to the Qualified Person promptly and in writing;

- ensure that sufficient spot checks, inspections, and audits of the company (whether in the EU or overseas) are carried out. In particular the 'Contracted Qualified Person' should satisfy himself/herself that an effective pharmaceutical Quality Management System is being operated.

10.3    Particularly for smaller companies, the person acting as contracted QP may agree with the company to provide some of the necessary services such as, for example, staff training, internal audits and maintenance of authorisations, personally in addition to performing strictly QP duties.

10.4    If any doubt exists concerning the duties and responsibilities between the Qualified Person and the company who requires his/her services, it is recommended that he or she should contact their local Regulatory Inspector or their professional body for advice.

10.5    **This Code of Practice should be brought to the attention of the Chief Executive Officer of the company who wishes to have the services of a 'Contracted Qualified Person'.**

## 11.0    Contract manufacture and/or testing

11.1    Where products are manufactured and/or packed under contract there should be a clearly written technical agreement between the contract giver and the contract acceptor. Such an agreement should be reviewed and approved by the Qualified Person engaged by the contract giver and acceptor. The agreement should clearly delineate the areas and responsibilities of both Qualified Persons.

11.2    The contract acceptor, who normally will be required to hold a manufacturing authorisation, may accept full responsibility for batch certification provided that the Qualified Person has all the appropriate information (including access to relevant details in the Marketing Authorisation(s)) and authority to fulfil these duties. Nevertheless the decision concerning responsibility for batch certification remains a matter between contract giver and acceptor depending on the circumstances.

11.3    The provisions in 11.1 apply equally to the testing of samples under contract. The contract testing laboratory may not hold its own manufacturing authorisation but in this case must be authorised on the contract giver's authorisation.

## 12.0  Continuing Professional Development

**12.1**  Qualified Persons have a personal and professional duty to keep their knowledge and experience up to date (Annex 16, 8.3, EU Guide to GMP, Volume 4 of the "The Rules Governing Medicinal Products in the European Union"). It is expected that this would cover the current state of pharmaceutical quality management, regulatory aspects and GMP guideline standards, product manufacturing and control technology, and general work practices.

**12.2**  Records of Continuing Professional Development (CPD) should be kept to reflect this important longer-term aspect of the Qualified Person's continued performance of professional duties.

**12.3**  Attention is drawn to the individual Member State's statements on CPD, which underline the importance of this aspect of a Qualified Person's performance of duties. These statements appear as Appendix 1 to this Code, and they will also be of value to those Qualified Persons who are not members of any of the three professional bodies.

**12.4**  In the event of a Qualified Person making a major change in job responsibilities, for example from a company making only sterile dosage forms to one with a wider range of products including solid dose forms, the Qualified Person and the senior management of the company involved should recognise the need for additional education and training and take adequate steps to demonstrate that proper provision is made for this. Such extra training should be undertaken before the Qualified Person acts in a new situation.

## 13.0  Professional conduct

**13.1**  Qualified Persons are subject to the overall jurisdiction of the Bye-laws, Charters and Regulations, Codes of Conduct, Disciplinary Regulations and any general guidelines of their own professional body, and should have access to them.

**13.2**  Qualified Persons have duties not only to their employer but also to the Competent Authorities of the Member States and its inspection service. They must ensure that appropriate senior company executives are made fully aware of any manufacturing and/or testing difficulties which may cast doubt on the certification of batches or post facto might require a product recall.

**13.3**  If there is any aspect of the Quality Assurance system which is not in accordance with the Directives and Guidelines for Good Manufacturing Practice then the Qualified Person has a duty to bring this to the attention of Senior Management and ensure that appropriate corrective measures are taken.

13.4 Qualified Persons should establish a good working relationship with Regulatory Inspectors and as far as possible provide information on request during site inspections.

*NB. There may be situations outside of site inspections where the Qualified Person may wish to consult with the local Regulatory Inspector for advice or clarification in particular circumstances with which the Qualified Person is faced.*

13.5 The following assumption is made by the professional bodies acting jointly when certifying the eligibility of a Qualified Person:

- in co-operation with their employers, Qualified Persons will undertake Continuing Professional Development to maintain and extend their technical and professional competence. (See also Section 12.0 above.)

13.6 The following assumptions are made, firstly by the professional bodies acting jointly when certifying the eligibility of a Qualified Person and, secondly, by the Competent Authority when accepting an eligible Qualified Person for nomination on a Manufacturing Authorisation:

- in cases where undue pressures to depart from professional obligations cannot be counterbalanced by reference to this and other relevant Codes of Practice, Qualified Persons, preferably having informed their employer first, should consult the appropriate professional body for confidential advice.
- management has a duty to provide Qualified Persons with appropriate resources and to ensure that Quality Management Systems and communications are working effectively. Therefore, Qualified Persons also have a duty to make representations to management, if necessary in writing, whenever standards appear to be falling short of Good Manufacturing Practice(s). This duty should be reflected by appropriate wording in the Qualified Person's job description.

## 14.0 Disciplinary procedures

14.1 Article 56 of Council Directive 2001/82/EC and Article 52 of Council Directive 2001/83/EC read inter alia:

"Member States shall ensure that the duties of Qualified Persons … are fulfilled, either by means of appropriate administrative measures or by making such persons subject to a professional Code of Conduct.

Member states may provide for the temporary suspension of such a person upon the commencement of administrative or disciplinary procedures against him for failure to fulfil his obligations."

**If it were found that a QP had certified in a register or equivalent document a product batch as fit for sale without ensuring that the relevant tests and checks had been carried out, this failure might be a matter for consideration by the appropriate professional body to which he/she might belong as a matter of professional misconduct.**

14.2    The UK professional bodies have established disciplinary procedures to deal with cases of possible misconduct. One of the powers is to remove the name of an individual from the appropriate register or registers and they will act together as appropriate in the case of a Qualified Person who is a member of two or three of the Societies. In such cases, professional bodies will inform the Competent Authority.

14.3    The Member State Competent Authority is the body with the power to delete the Qualified Person's name from the Manufacturing Authorisation.

## Appendix 1: UK Statements on CPD

### Royal Pharmaceutical Society

Continuing Professional Development (CPD) ensures that you are keeping up-to-date and empowers you to do your job effectively and practice safely. CPD is more than continuing education and requires you to reflect and consider the impact of your learning on your day to day practice.

The Royal Pharmaceutical Society is the dedicated professional body for pharmacists and pharmacy in England, Scotland and Wales providing leadership, support and development for its members. RPS recognises that not everyone working in the pharmaceutical arena is a registered pharmacist and its membership categories include a category for pharmaceutical scientists. Career-long learning is important for everyone working as a pharmaceutical professional.

The General Pharmaceutical Council (GPhC) is the statutory organisation responsible for the regulation of pharmacy professionals, including pharmacists, in Great Britain. The Royal Pharmaceutical Society encourages members who are Qualified Persons to retain their registration as a pharmacist. The GPhC ensures that all pharmacists maintain their competence to practice by completing Continuing Professional Development through an ongoing process of reflection, planning, action and evaluation. Further details on the GPhC's regulatory CPD standards and framework can be found at www.pharmacyregulation.org.

Individuals who are not registered with the GPhC are not mandated by them to comply with their CPD requirements. However, all Qualified Persons are required to keep their knowledge and experience up-to-date (Annex 16, 8.3, EU Guide to GMP, Volume 4 of the "The Rules Governing Medicinal Products in the European Union") [see also section 12 above]. Records of Continuing Professional Development (CPD) should be kept and you should provide evidence of recording when required.

The Royal Pharmaceutical Society provides CPD support via the website, events, through RPS mentors, its library of accredited and endorsed training initiatives, resources via the Pharmaceutical Journal, other publications, networks, and a dedicated member support service. Support is available to all members and will also be of value to individuals who are not registered as pharmacists. Members access CPD and career support at a local level through their Local Practice Forums (LPFs). The RPS provides guidance on recording CPD, suitable CPD activities, submitting records to the GPhC, and maintaining a learning portfolio. Ongoing developments relating to professional recognition and CPD will be announced on our website. Further advice and CPD support can be found at http://www.rpharms.com/development/continuing-professional-development.asp (members-area).

## Royal Society of Chemistry

Continuing Professional Development (CPD) has been defined by the RSC as:

> "the responsibility of individuals for the systematic maintenance, improvement and broadening of knowledge and skills to ensure continuing competence as a professional throughout their career."

In today's world, professionals are required to demonstrate that their knowledge and professional skills are being kept up to date. Advances in the chemical sciences and the increasing need to use a variety of skills particularly when working at the interfaces with different scientific areas requires members to develop and maintain a range of skills. This will ensure that they are able to meet the needs of evolving employment requirements.

QP registrants are invited periodically to submit a summary CPD record to the RSC. The RSC will review your return to determine whether you have demonstrated that you are keeping your knowledge and skills up to date. If you send an appropriate return, the date will be noted in the QP Register.

You can find further information about the RSC CPD scheme on the RSC website at www.rsc.org/qp and www.rsc.org/cpd.

## Society of Biology

Continuing Professional Development Statement

In common with many other professional biologists, Qualified Persons work in a changing scientific, commercial and regulatory environment. This requires individuals to commit themselves to updating their knowledge and skills, in order to maintain their competence to do the job.

Increasingly, there is a demand from employees undertaking such development to have it recognised, and for employers to be able to demonstrate the competence of their employees to regulatory bodies, their customers and the general public. Continuing Professional Development (CPD) emphasises quality and confers a competitive edge.

The Society of Biology has therefore placed a high priority on the development of a Continuing Professional Development scheme, to ensure that chartered biologists keep up to date and maintain their competence. The Society of Biology's framework for CPD is based on a learning cycle of 'think, plan, do, review'. Individuals take charge of their own learning and can establish CPD objectives relevant to their needs by considering their present situation and identifying goals. The CPD scheme has been designed as a benefit and to support members in advancing self-education whilst also underpinning professional competence.

The scheme focuses on the demonstration of work place competence maintained by informal and formal activities, such as reading, conference attendance and short courses. For more information visit our website on www.societyofbiology.org/development/cpd.

## Import from Third Countries

For medicinal products imported into the EU from third countries (i.e. countries other than the EEA Member States), the provisions of Articles 51 and 55, respectively, of Directive 2001/83/EC as amended are required to be applied. This includes the full qualitative and quantitative analysis of at least all the active substances and all the other tests or checks necessary to ensure the quality of the medicinal products is in accordance with the requirements of the marketing authorisation. It is the Qualified Person of the importer who is responsible for ensuring that these requirements are met.

## ACAA

**Protocol to the Euro-Mediterranean Agreement establishing an association between the European Communities and their Member States, of the one part, and the State of Israel, of the other part on an agreement between the European Community and the State of Israel on the conformity assessment and acceptance of industrial products (ACAA) on Good Manufacturing Practice (GMP) and Manufacturing Authorisation**

The Agreement on Conformity Assessment and Acceptance of Industrial Products (ACAA) between the EU and Israel came into effect on 19 January 2013.

The ACAA with the State of Israel includes medicinal products, active substances and excipients used in the manufacture of both human medicines and veterinary medicines. This also includes chemical and biological pharmaceuticals, immunologicals, radiopharmaceuticals and herbal medicinal products. It does not cover medicinal products derived from human blood or human plasma, advanced therapy medicinal products, investigational medicinal products, homeopathic medicinal products, medical gases and veterinary immunologicals.

For finished medicinal products imported into the EU there is no requirement for re-control (re-testing) but they must be received by the holder of an MIA authorised for importation activities and that batch certification by a European QP is required as for other MRAs. This is based on obligation 2(c) from "Section IV" of the GMP Annex of the ACAA which provides:

> "Certification of the conformity of each batch to its specifications by either the manufacturer established in one of the Parties, or the importer, shall be recognised by the other Party without re-control at import from one Party to the other. However, the additional responsibilities of the qualified person or the responsible pharmacist of the importer in each Party, with respect to the certification of each batch as set out in Section I above, remain in accordance with the provisions of the EU and Israeli national laws set out in Section I."

The provisions of this obligation is extended to:

> "...finished or intermediate medicinal products imported from a third country and further exported to the other Party, only (1) if each batch of the medicinal product has been subject to re-control by either the importer from a third country or a manufacturer located in one of the Parties and (2) if the manufacturer in the third country has been subject to an inspection by the competent authority of either Party of which the outcome has been that for the product or product

UK GUIDANCE ON MANUFACTURE

category the manufacturer complies with Good Manufacturing Practice." *Obligation 2(d)*

However the obligation does not apply to:

"...products imported from a third country, that have exclusively been tested in and inspected by a competent authority of that or another third country. Any derogation from this provision on the basis of an agreement by one Party similar in effect to this Protocol, or any unilateral concessions by one Party to a third country or party having a similar effect to an agreement of this type shall be subject to the consent of the other Party." *Obligation 2(e)*

## Mutual Recognition Agreements on Good Manufacturing Practice (GMP) and Manufacturing Authorisation

The European Community has Mutual Recognition Agreements (MRAs) with several third countries with which it has substantial trade. The pharmaceutical or GMP sectors of these MRAs provide benefit to exporters and importers of medicinal products in the EU trading with these countries.

The basis for an MRA concerning medicinal products is equivalence of the principles and guidelines of GMP, the inspection systems and, in most cases, the arrangements for authorising manufacturers between both parties. An MRA only becomes operational after a mutual agreement of equivalence. The benefits of an MRA when in operation include:

* authority for an importer to accept a manufacturer's batch certification of compliance with GMP, the relevant marketing authorisation and certificate of analysis. The Qualified Person (QP) of the importer in the EU may certify an imported batch on the basis of such a certificate in place of full testing within the EU, in accordance with Article 51.2 of Directive 2001/83/EC as amended. Importers and exporters who wish to benefit from a MRA should use this certificate. The format of the certificate is provided in Part III of the EU Guide on GMP;
* normal acceptance between competent authorities of inspection reports and certification of authorisation and GMP compliance of a manufacturer.

MRAs that include a medicinal products sector have been negotiated between the EC and the following countries:

* Australia
* Canada
* Japan
* New Zealand
* Switzerland.

The MRA between the EC and United States is not in operation. The transitional period ended November 2001 but no decision on a formal extension has been taken. The two-way alert systems remain in operation.

The operational status and scope of individual MRAs at any given time may be checked on the Commission's website or with MHRA.

## UK Guidance on Certificates of Analysis

In certain circumstances a Certificate of Analysis from a third party may be used as part of a system to ensure the quality of materials. For such a certificate to be considered acceptable the following conditions should apply.

(a) The person responsible for Quality Control (QC) in the purchasing company must assure himself that the organisation issuing the certificate is competent to do so, whether that organisation is part of the supplying company or is independent of it (e.g. is a contract analytical service).

(b) The Certificate must:

  (i)   Identify the organisation issuing it. If Certificates are reproduced (e.g. when obtaining starting materials from an Agent, repacker or reprocessor), these Certificates must identify the name and address of the original manufacturer and the original batch Certificate reference number, a copy of which should be attached.

  (ii)  Be authorised by a person competent to do so, and state his qualifications and position. "Authorisation" may be by signature or acceptable electronic means (please refer to the guidance given on electronic signatures, see paragraph 14 of Annex 11 to the EC Guide to GMP).

  (iii) Name the material to which it refers and identify it by a batch number. For materials with an expiry or retest date, this should be listed on the Certificate.

  (iv)  State that the material has been tested, by whom and when this was done. In situations where some or all tests have been performed by a contract analytical service, this should be clearly identified, stating the name and address of the laboratory that performed the analysis.

  (v)   State the specification (e.g. Ph Eur) and methods against which, and by which, the tests were performed.

  (vi)  Give the test results obtained, or declare that the results obtained showed compliance with the stated specification.

Certificates which merely carry such statements as "a typical analysis is…", or state that the material is of a particular quality with no supporting evidence, are not acceptable.

Possession of a Certificate of Analysis does not eliminate the need to confirm the identity of the material supplied, its supply chain, or other relevant factors such as Transmissible Spongiform Encephalopathy status.

Possession of a Certificate of Analysis does not absolve the purchaser from ultimate responsibility for the correctness of the material to which it refers.

The above paragraphs, whilst particularly relevant to the certification of starting materials, also apply as appropriate to other materials and products.

*Note that the Certificate of Analysis described above is* not *the Manufacturer's Batch Certificate used within the context of a Mutual Recognition Agreement, Agreements on Conformity Assessment and Acceptance of Industrial Products (ACAA) or other appropriate arrangements on GMP with the European Union* (see Mutual Recognition Agreement section above).

## GMP for Starting Materials

(To be read in conjunction with Part II of the EC Guide to GMP.)

From 30 October 2005, Community requirements obliged manufacturing authorisation holders to use as starting materials only active substances that have been manufactured in accordance with GMP.

This includes both total and partial manufacture, as well as any repackaging or re-labelling activities carried out by a distributor or broker. Herb APIs used as active substances for traditional herbal medicinal products as defined in Directive 2004/24/EC are also required to comply with these requirements.

The Community legislation gives powers to the competent authorities in Member States to carry out inspections at the premises of manufacturers of such materials, the marketing authorisation (MA) holder and any laboratories employed by the MA holder. These inspections which are conducted by the competent authority, may be unannounced and may be carried out at the request of an API manufacturer, another Member State, the Commission, or the European Medicines Agency (EMA). The competent authority is empowered to inspect premises, take samples and examine documents.

A report will be provided to the manufacturer or MA holder who has undergone the inspection and, where relevant, a certificate of GMP compliance issued. Certificates will be entered on a central Community database, as will any failures in compliance.

In order to ensure the reliability of the supply chain and to respond to the increasing threat of falsified medicines entering the supply chain, Community medicines legislation has been further amended by Directive 2011/62/EU which requires that the particulars and documents required for a marketing authorisation now include the written confirmation that the finished product manufacturer has verified that the active substance is manufactured according to EU GMP.

Community legislation is also amended to provide further obligations on the finished product manufacturer to use only active substances, that have not only been manufactured in accordance with good manufacturing practices for active substances, but which have also been distributed in accordance with good distribution practices for active substances and verify compliance by the manufacturer and distributors of active substances with good manufacturing practice and good distribution practices by conducting audits at the manufacturing and distribution sites of the manufacturer and distributors of active substances.

The holder of the manufacturing authorisation has to verify such compliance either himself or, through an entity acting on his behalf under a contract.

The primary means by which EU regulatory authorities will supervise compliance with the requirement for active substances to be manufactured in accordance with GMP will be through review of audit reports during inspections of manufacturing authorisation holders.

Audits of active substance manufacturers should be performed by suitably trained auditors. During inspections the competence of auditors will be assessed and if not deemed appropriate this will be raised as an issue.

The holder of the manufacturing authorisation must also ensure that the excipients are suitable for use in medicinal products by ascertaining what the appropriate good manufacturing practice is. This shall be ascertained on the basis of a formalised risk assessment in accordance with the applicable guidelines to be adopted by the Commission under Community legislation. Such risk assessment shall take into account requirements under other appropriate quality systems as well as the source and intended use of the excipients and previous instances of quality defects.

The holder of the manufacturing authorisation must ensure that the appropriate good manufacturing practice so ascertained, is applied and document the measures that have been taken.

The new Community requirements also require manufacturers, importers and distributors to be registered with their competent authority.

**UK GUIDANCE ON MANUFACTURE**

## Guidance for UK Manufacturer's Licence and Manufacturing Authorisation (for Investigational Medicinal Products) Holders on the use of UK Stand Alone Contract Laboratories

### Introduction

This section:

- is applicable to all manufacturer's licence holders, i.e. import, export, herbals and specials;

- provides an update and details changes to the June 2010 published guidance;
- outlines MHRA's criteria for inspection of UK contract laboratories;
- provides guidance[1] as to when a UK contract laboratory must be named on a manufacturer's licence for medicinal products for human use[2] and/or a manufacturing authorisation for investigational medicinal products;
- provides guidance as to when a UK contract laboratory is not required to be named on a manufacturer's licence or manufacturing authorisation;
- outlines MHRA's expectations of the manufacturer's licence, manufacturing authorisation holders and UK stand alone contract laboratories; and
- outlines the inspection process for UK contract laboratories.

It is acknowledged that there are a number of manufacturer's licence and manufacturing authorisation holders that can also offer contract quality control testing to GMP. The inspection of these quality control testing activities is included within the scope of their routine GMP inspections. In this situation, the licence holder who is performing the testing and acts as the contract acceptor should be named as a contract laboratory on the contract giver's licence.

The criteria for inspection has been changed such that any stand alone contract laboratories that are only involved in microbiological testing of raw materials and/or environmental monitoring (for non-sterile manufacture) will no longer meet the criteria to be inspected. Therefore, these laboratories are no longer required to be named on manufacturer's licences or manufacturing authorisations. Laboratories performing environmental monitoring and/or process simulation (media fill) work for sterile product manufacturers will continue to meet the criteria for inspection.

Responsibility for oversight of any laboratories involved in raw material testing lies with the manufacturing site using those raw materials and with the certifying Qualified Person to ensure there is an acceptable level of GMP compliance.

Contract laboratories that no longer meet the criteria for inspection will be removed from any manufacturer's licences or manufacturing

---

[1] This section is for guidance and it is acknowledged that there may be some specific situations where the actual requirements may vary. In the case of contract laboratories supporting manufacture of biological products, the requirement for inspection will be made on a case by case basis, taking into account the guidance on application of GMP described in Annex 2 of the GMP Guide.

[2] Responsibility for veterinary only licences lies with the Veterinary Medicines Directorate.

authorisations by the licensing office, and the GMP certificates held by these contract laboratories will be allowed to lapse.

## Criteria for inspection of contract laboratories by MHRA

In accordance with MHRA's risk-based approach to inspections; fee-bearing inspections of stand alone contract quality control testing laboratories will be conducted against EU GMP if the laboratory is undertaking the following testing of a medicinal product or an investigational medicinal product for human use:

- microbiological, biological and chemical/physical testing of finished medicinal products, i.e. final testing prior to Qualified Person certification for the purposes of batch release;
- stability testing of finished marketed medicinal products;
- environmental monitoring and or process simulation (media fill) work for sterile product manufacturer; or
- biological testing if it is required to be conducted in accordance with the GMP Guide as described in Annex 2.

## When contract laboratories must be named on manufacturer's licences/manufacturing authorisations

Contract laboratories that meet the criteria for inspection must be named on manufacturer's licences or manufacturing authorisations, irrespective of the quantity or frequency of testing. This also includes any UK stand alone contract laboratory subcontracted by another stand alone contract laboratory.

Stand alone contract laboratories that are testing finished products on import into the EU must be named on manufacturer's licences and marketing authorisations.

## When contract laboratories should not be named on manufacturer's licences/manufacturing authorisations

Stand alone contract laboratories that conduct all other testing (e.g. raw material and API testing) or produce data for research where the products are not intended to be released onto the market or used in a clinical trial do not need to be named on a manufacturing licence or manufacturing authorisations.

## MHRA expectations of manufacturer's licence holders, manufacturing authorisation holders and stand alone contract laboratories

Manufacturer's licence and or manufacturing authorisation holders (contract givers) that wish to use a contract laboratory (contract acceptor) must:

- Have a system in place to assess the suitability, competency and GMP compliance of proposed contract laboratories prior to their use, whether the contract laboratory meets the criteria for a MHRA GMP inspection or not.
- Ensure that the contract laboratories used, irrespective of their location or whether they meet the criteria for inspection, are visible within the manufacturer's quality management system and listed in their Site Master File.
- Update their respective licences/authorisations to name the contract laboratory if the contract laboratory meets the criteria for a MHRA GMP inspection.
- Ensure that a written Technical Agreement which describes the GMP responsibilities of each party, and also refers to the scope of testing and type of tests covered by the agreement, has been put in place.
- Have a system of on-going supervision for contract laboratories, including arrangements to periodically formally re-assess compliance, based on risk.
- Ensure that contract laboratories meeting the criteria for inspection have a valid GMP certificate in place prior to data generated by the laboratory being used by the contract giver for batch disposition decisions.

The presence of an EU GMP certificate may be used as information to support the use of a contract laboratory; however, the scope of any certificate should be confirmed to be relevant to the work to be performed. The certificate may form part of the contract giver's wider assessment process but should not be used exclusively as a substitute for a formal assessment by a prospective contract giver.

A laboratory used on an 'ad hoc' basis to perform specialist testing in support of investigations is not expected to be approved prospectively on the manufacturer's licence and or manufacturer's authorisation, in order to facilitate timely investigation of unplanned events. Contract givers are encouraged to implement a process by which minimum expectations can be assessed in a timely manner, for instance by the use of a basic questionnaire, and/or by listing key compliance expectations as part of the written request for analysis that is then issued to the contract laboratory.

Contract laboratories involved in quality control testing of medicinal products or investigational products for human use must do so in accordance with the marketing authorisation, product specification file and EU GMP.

## Inspection process

Inspections of new laboratories are triggered by the submission of a variation to the manufacturer's licence and/or manufacturing authorisation to name the laboratory.

The scope of the inspection of a stand alone contract laboratory will be to assess their quality system for compliance with EU GMP, along with the specific activities they perform, e.g. chemical/physical analysis, microbiological testing, biological testing.

Within the UK there is no requirement for a stand alone contract laboratory to hold their own manufacturer's licence or manufacturing authorisation; however, a GMP certificate will be issued to the contract laboratory following a satisfactory inspection outcome.

Confirmation of the compliance status of a stand alone contract laboratory will be communicated directly to the laboratory on completion of the inspection process. The contract laboratory must notify the contract giver in writing of any data generated prior to receipt of a GMP certificate and any data generated by the laboratory must not be used by the contract giver for batch disposition purposes until a certificate of GMP compliance has been issued.

Stand alone contract laboratory details will be added to MHRA's list of inspected laboratories, which can be found on MHRA's website. This list will be updated at least annually.

## GMP non-compliance

GMP non-compliance may be managed via inspectorate Compliance Escalation or consideration of regulatory action by the Inspection Action Group (IAG).

Compliance Escalation is a non-statutory process to take action in response to poor compliance which does not yet meet the threshold for consideration of adverse regulatory action. The main aim of the Compliance Escalation process is to direct companies towards a state of compliance, thus avoiding the need for regulatory action and the potential adverse impact to patient health through lack of availability of medicines.

Actions may include close monitoring of compliance improvement work through inspection, meetings and correspondence with company senior management, alerting them to the compliance concerns and clearly outlining the consequences of continued non-compliance. Upon satisfactory conclusion of the remediation work, the company will be returned to the routine risk-based inspection programme; however, referral for consideration of regulatory action may still occur if the required improvements are not achieved in a timely manner.

In the event of serious non-compliance issues, a referral may be made to IAG. The final outcome of the IAG process may result in:

- the laboratory being removed from the licence and/or authorisation;
- the laboratory being issued with a statement of non-compliance with GMP; or
- the laboratory having their GMP certificate either withdrawn or replaced by a conditioned GMP certificate that only allows specific testing to be performed.

These actions may prevent the use of the laboratory for GMP testing until a satisfactory re-inspection has taken place.

## Good Laboratory Practice (GLP) and Good Manufacturing Practice (GMP)

The term Good Laboratory Practice (GLP) is a generic term that causes confusion when used to describe the quality control testing of medicinal products. Compliance with the OECD principles of GLP is a regulatory requirement when conducting non-clinical, safety studies of new chemical or biological substances. There is no legal requirement for the quality control testing of medicinal products to be conducted in accordance with the OECD principles of GLP and there is no requirement for laboratories involved in quality control testing of medicinal products to be members of the UK GLP Compliance Monitoring Programme.

## Reference

Eudralex volume 4 - Medicinal Products for Human and Veterinary Use: Good Manufacturing Practice.

## Manufacture and Importation of Unlicensed Medicines for Human Use

### Introduction

UK medicines legislation provides certain exemptions for the supply and use of unlicensed medicine for human use. Two of the more important exemptions are outlined here: the manufacture and supply of unlicensed medicinal products for individual patients ("specials") and the importation and supply of unlicensed medicinal products for individual patients.

A "medicinal product" is one to which the requirements of Directive 2001/83/EC as amended apply unless subject to an exemption in that Directive.

## Manufacture and supply of unlicensed medicinal products for individual patients ("specials")

The Human Medicines Regulations 2012 [SI 2012 No. 1916] require that medicinal products are licensed before they are marketed in the UK. However some patients may have special clinical needs that cannot be met by licensed medicinal products. So that these special needs may be met, the law allows manufacture and supply of unlicensed medicinal products (commonly known as "specials"), subject to certain conditions.

The conditions, laid down in regulation 167 of the Regulations, are that there is a bona fide unsolicited order, the product is formulated in accordance with the requirement of a doctor or dentist nurse independent prescriber, pharmacist independent prescriber or supplementary prescriber registered in the UK and the product is for use by one of their individual patients (on the basis of "special need") on the practitioner's direct personal responsibility. If a "special" is manufactured in the UK, the manufacturer must hold a Manufacturer's (Specials) Licence issued by MHRA. A "special" may not be advertised and may not be supplied if an equivalent licensed product is available which could meet the patient's clinical needs. Essential records must be kept and serious adverse drug reactions reported to MHRA. MHRA Guidance Note 14 *The supply of unlicensed medicinal products ("Specials")* provides guidance to manufacturers about the conditions under which they may manufacture and supply "specials" and their legal obligations.

## Importation and supply of unlicensed medicinal products for individual patients

An unlicensed medicinal product may only be imported in accordance with the Human Medicines Regulations 2012 [SI 2012 No. 1916]. An importer must hold the appropriate wholesale dealer's licence or manufacturer's (specials) licence (for further information see MHRA Guidance Notes 5 and 6: *Notes for applicants and holders of a manufacturer's/wholesale dealer's licence or brokering registration*) and must comply with the conditions of their licence. Wholesale dealers and importers from third countries licence conditions include the requirement that they must notify MHRA on each occasion that they intend to import such a product. Importation may proceed unless the importer has been informed by MHRA within 28 days of notification that it objects to importation. MHRA may object and prevent importation because it has concerns about the safety or quality of the product or because there is an equivalent licensed medicinal product available and it is not satisfied that there is a "special need" for the supply to an individual patient.

An imported unlicensed medicinal product may only be supplied in accordance with regulation 167 of the Regulations. Regulation 167 exempts, under defined conditions (discussed in the previous section on "specials") such a product when it is supplied to meet the "special need" of an individual patient. MHRA Guidance Note 14 provides guidance to importers about the conditions under which they may import and supply unlicensed medicinal products and their legal obligations.

Where a "special" is imported from a country outside of the EEA, the importer of the medicinal product must also be able to demonstrate compliance with the European Commission's *Notes for guidance on minimising the risk of transmitting animal spongiform encephalopathy agents via medicinal products* and future updates, in accordance with The Unlicensed Medicinal Products for Human Use (Transmissible Spongiform Encephalopathies) (Safety) Regulations 2003 [SI 2003/1680]. (See the MHRA's interim guidance: *Minimising the risk of Transmission of Transmissible Spongiform Encephalopathies via Unlicensed Medicinal Products for Human Use*, available from MHRA's website www.mhra. gov.uk).

## Contact

For further information about notification of intention to import, please contact the:

Unlicensed Imports Section
151 Buckingham Palace Road, Victoria, London SW1W 9SZ
Telephone: 020 3080 6625
Email: imports@mhra.gsi.gov.uk

## Manufacture and Supply of Unlicensed Advanced Therapy Medicinal Products for Individual Patients ("Hospital Exemption")

The Advanced Therapy Medicinal Products Regulation (No 1394/2007) came into force on 30 December 2007 (ATMP Regulation). The provisions of the Regulation applied from 30 December 2008.

An Advanced Therapy Medicinal Product (ATMP) is a medicinal product as defined in Directive 2001/83/EC as amended (the Directive). Specifically, an ATMP is a medicinal product which is either:

- a gene therapy medicinal product as defined in Part IV of Annex 1 to Directive 2001/83/EC;
- a somatic cell therapy medicinal product as defined in Part IV of Annex 1 to Directive 2001/83/EC;

- a tissue engineered product as defined in Article 2 1 (b) of the ATMP Regulation.

Under the ATMP Regulation, those medicinal products which come within the scope of Directive 2001/83/EC and are categorised as ATMPs are to be regulated under the centralised European procedure. Under this procedure, a centralised European marketing authorisation is granted by the European Commission following assessment by the European Medicines Agency (EMA).

Under Article 3 (7) of 2001/83/EC, there is an exemption from central authorisation for ATMPs which are prepared on a non routine basis and used within the same Member State in a hospital in accordance with a medical prescription for an individual patient. The exemption was included in the Regulation in recognition of the small scale and developmental nature of activity carried out in some hospitals, which argued for a degree of flexibility over the nature of regulatory requirements. Member States are required to implement this Community requirement for a hospital exemption by putting in place arrangements at national level to meet the specific requirements set out in the Regulation. MHRA is responsible for the regulatory arrangements under the exemption in the UK.

The UK's legislation for implementing the Regulation and the requirements that apply under the hospital exemption scheme has been consolidated in the Human Medicines Regulation 2012 [SI 2012/1916].

## Contact

Contact points for specific enquiries in relation to ATMPs are as follows:

- Borderline/product classification – ATMPadviceform@mhra.gsi.gov.uk
- Manufacturing and exemptions – gmpinspectorate@mhra.gsi.gov.uk
- Prelicensing and scientific guidance – biologicalsandbiotechnology@mhra.gsi.gov.uk
- Clinical trials – clintrialhelpline@mhra.gsi.gov.uk
- Patient information – patient.information@mhra.gsi.gov.uk
- Pharmacovigilance – info@mhra.gsi.gov.uk
- Medical device related aspects of combination ATMPs – info@mhra.gsi.gov.uk
- Coordination of UK legislation/guidance – info@mhra.gsi.gov.uk
- For queries not covered by other MHRA contact points – info@mhra.gsi.gov.uk

**4**

# UK Guidance on the Manufacture, Importation and Distribution of Active Substances

## Introduction

EU Directive 2001/83/EC lays down the rules for the manufacture, import, marketing and supply of medicinal products and ensures the functioning of the internal market for medicinal products while safeguarding a high level of protection of public health in the EU.

The falsification of medicinal products is a global problem, requiring effective and enhanced international coordination and cooperation in order to ensure that anti-falsification strategies are more effective, in particular as regards sale of such products via the Internet. To that end, the Commission and Member States are cooperating closely and supporting ongoing work in international fora on this subject, such as the Council of Europe, Europol and the United Nations. In addition, the Commission, working closely with Member States, is cooperating with the competent authorities of third countries with a view to effectively combating the trade in falsified medicinal products at a global level.

Active substances are those substances which give a medicinal product its therapeutic effect. They are the Active Pharmaceutical Ingredient (API).

Falsified active substances and active substances that do not comply with applicable requirements of Directive 2001/83/EC pose serious risks to public health.

The Falsified Medicines Directive 2011/62/EU amends Directive 2001/83/EC in order to facilitate the enforcement of and control of compliance with Union rules relating to active substances. It makes a number of significant changes to the controls on active substances intended for use in the manufacture of a medicinal product for human use.

A number of new terms have been introduced into the 2001 Directive by the Falsified Medicines Directive, including "falsified medicinal product" and "active substance". The aim of this is to ensure that other amendments introduced by the Falsified Medicines Directive are consistently interpreted and applied across the EU.

The 2001 Directive has been amended to permit the European Commission to adopt the following:

- the principles and guidelines of good manufacturing practice for active substances, by means of a delegated act; and
- the principles of good distribution practice for active substances, by means of adopted guidelines.

## Registration

To provide a greater level of control, and transparency of supply, for active substances within the European Community manufacturers, importers and distributors of active substances have to notify the relevant competent authorities of their activities and provide certain details. In the UK this will be MHRA. The competent authority has an obligation to enter these details into a Community Database (EudraGMDP) following the determination of a successful application for registration. The competent authority may then conduct inspections against the requirements of the relevant good practices before permitting such businesses to start trading. Manufacturers, importers and distributors of active substances will not only be subject to inspection on the basis of suspicions of non-compliance, but also on the basis of risk-analysis.

Authorised manufacturers of medicinal products who also manufacture and/or import active substances, either for use in their own products or products manufactured by other companies, are not exempt from the requirement to register.

Persons who are requested to import an active substance from a non-EEA country that provide facilities solely for transporting the active substance, or where they are acting as an import agent, imports the active substance solely to the order of another person who holds a certificate of good manufacturing practice issued by the licensing authority, are not required to register.

The registration regime for manufacturers, importers and distributors of active substances will be subject to an application procedure, followed by a determination procedure completed by MHRA.

The person applying for registration must notify MHRA immediately of any changes which have taken place as regards to the information in the registration form, where such changes may have an impact on quality or safety of the active substances that are manufactured, imported or distributed. These changes shall be treated as incorporated in the application form.

MHRA must grant or refuse an application for registration within 60 working days beginning immediately after the day on which a valid application is received.

MHRA will notify the applicant within 60 days of receipt of a valid application for registration whether they intend to undertake an inspection.

The applicant may not undertake any activity before either:

- 60 days have elapsed and the applicant has not been notified of the Agency's intention to inspect, or
- following inspection the Agency has notified the applicant that they may commence their activities.

After inspection MHRA will prepare a report and communicate that report to the applicant. The applicant will have the opportunity to respond to the report. Within 90 days of an inspection MHRA shall issue an appropriate good practice certificate to the applicant, indicating that the applicant complies with the requirements of the relevant good practices. Where an applicant is found to be non-compliant with the requisite standards, a statement of non-compliance will be issued by MHRA.

If after 60 days of the receipt of the application form MHRA has not notified the applicant of their intention to carry out an inspection, the applicant may commence their business activity and regard themselves as registered. MHRA will issue a certificate to the applicant and enter the details into the Community Database.

This Community Database which is publicly available will enable competent authorities in other EEA Member States or other legal entities, to establish the bona fides and compliance of manufacturers, importers and distributors of active substances established in the UK and those in other EEA territories. MHRA will investigate concerns with regards to UK registrations of non-compliance and reciprocal arrangements will apply with other EEA Member States.

# Registration requirements for UK companies involved in the sourcing and supply of active substances (ASs) to be used in the manufacture of licensed human medicines.

This flowchart may be used to determine the appropriate registration required for UK companies. Where more than one activity is carried out, the company should register for all activities that apply.

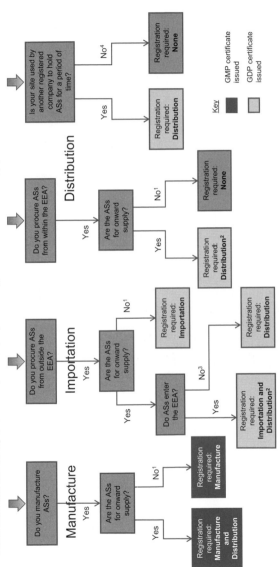

1. Site holds a manufacturer's licence and uses the ASs in the manufacture of the finished dose form.
2. Where the registration holder contracts out the physical handling of the AS, the company that physically handles the product should be named as a 3rd party site on the registration if they hold the ASs and this takes place in the UK.
   In addition, the company should hold its own registration. If the company are based in another EEA State, they should be registered with the competent authority in that State.
3. ASs procured from outside the EEA are supplied directly to customers based outside the EEA.
4. ASs are not held (stored) for any length of time and the company are simply contracted to transport the ASs.

**Figure 4.1** Registration requirements for UK companies involved in the sourcing and supply of active substances (ASs) to be used in the manufacture of licensed human medicines.

## Conditions of Registration as a Manufacturer, Importer or Distributor of an Active Substance

A person in the UK may not import, manufacture or distribute, an active substance for use in a licensed human medicine unless they are registered with MHRA in accordance with the Human Medicines Regulations 2012 and the respective conditions of those Regulations are met.

Registration holders must submit to MHRA an annual update of any changes to the information provided in the application. Any changes which may have an impact on the quality or safety of the active substance which the registrant is permitted to handle must be notified to the Agency immediately.

An annual compliance report will need to be submitted:

- in relation to any application made before 31 March 2013, the date of application; and
- in relation to each subsequent reporting year, 30 April following the end of that year.

Where the Commission has adopted principles and guidelines of good manufacturing practice under the third paragraph of Article 47[1] of Directive 2001/83/EC which applies to an active substance manufactured in the UK, the registered manufacturer must comply with good manufacturing practice in relation to that active substance.

Where the Commission has adopted principles and guidelines of good distribution practice under the fourth paragraph of Article 47 of Directive 2001/83/EC which applies to an active substance distributed in the UK, the registered distributor must comply with good distribution practice in relation to that active substance.

Where the Commission has adopted principles and guidelines of good manufacturing practice under the third paragraph of Article 47 of Directive 2001/83/EC which applies to an active substance imported into the UK and where an active substance is imported from a third country the registered importer must comply with good distribution practice in relation to the active substance.

Under such circumstances the active substances must have been manufactured in accordance with standards which are at least equivalent to EU good manufacturing practice and when imported must be accompanied by a written confirmation from the competent authority of the exporting third country unless a waiver exists.

---

[1] Article 47 was amended by Directive 2011/62/EU of the European Parliament and of the Council (OJ No L 174, 1.7.2011, p. 74).

## GMP for Active Substances

Directive 2001/83/EC has been amended to include a new definition of "active substance" which means any substance or mixture of substances intended to be used in the manufacture of a medicinal product and that, when used in its production, becomes an active ingredient of that product intended to exert a pharmacological, immunological or metabolic action with a view to restoring, correcting or modifying physiological functions or to make a medical diagnosis.

The manufacture of active substances should be subject to good manufacturing practice regardless of whether those active substances are manufactured in the Union or imported. Where active substances are manufactured in third countries it should be ensured that such substances have been manufactured to the relevant European standards of good manufacturing practice (GMP), so as to provide a level of protection of public health equivalent to that provided for by EU law.

A manufacturer or assembler of an active substance will have to comply with the principles and guidelines for GMP for active substances. Manufacture, in relation to an active substance, includes any process carried out in the course of making the substance and the various processes of dividing up, packaging, and presentation of the active substance. Assemble, in relation to an active substance, includes the various processes of dividing up, packaging and presentation of the substance, and "assembly" has a corresponding meaning. These activities will be the subject of a GMP certificate.

Importers of an active substance from a third country have to comply with the guidelines for Good Distribution Practice (GDP) in relation to the active substance. This activity will be the subject of a GDP certificate.

Distributors of an active substance within the UK which has been sourced from a manufacturer or an importer within the EU will have to comply with the guidelines for GDP for active substances. This activity will be the subject of a GDP certificate.

The 2001 Directive has been amended to permit the European Commission to adopt the following:

- the principles and guidelines of good manufacturing practice for active substances, by means of a delegated act; and
- the principles of good distribution practice for active substances, by means of adopted guidelines.

GMP for active substances is contained in Part II of the EU guidelines on Good Manufacturing Practice.

## GDP for Active Substances

In February 2013 the European Commission consulted on its draft "Guidelines on the principles of good distribution practices for active substances for medicinal products for human use".

The draft text sets out the quality system elements for the procuring, importing, holding, supplying or exporting active substances. However the scope of the proposed text excludes activities consisting of re-packaging, re-labelling or dividing up of active substances which are manufacturing activities and as such are subject to the guidelines on GMP of active substances. The draft text of the guidelines covers:

- Quality System
- Personnel
- Documentation
- Orders
- Procedures
- Records
- Premises and Equipment
- Receipt
- Storage
- Deliveries to Customers
- Transfer of Information
- Returns
- Complaints and Recalls
- Self-inspections.

## Written Confirmation

The Falsified Medicines Directive modifies EU Medicines Directive 2001/83/EC and from 2 July 2013 introduces new requirements for active substances imported into the EEA for use in the manufacture of authorised medicinal products.

The Falsified Medicines Directive requires importers of active substances to obtain written confirmations from competent authorities in non-EEA countries ("third countries") that the standards of manufacture of active substances at manufacturing sites on their territory are equivalent to EU good manufacturing practice (EU GMP). These confirmations are required before importation of active substances into the EU.

Each shipment of active substance received should be accompanied by a written confirmation from the competent authority of the exporting third country, stating that the active substance has been:

- manufactured to GMP standards at least equivalent to those laid down in the European Union;
- the third country manufacturing plant is subject to regular, strict and transparent inspections, and effective enforcement of GMP;
- in the event of non-conformance of the manufacturing site on inspection, such findings will be communicated to the European Union without delay.

The template for the written confirmation has been published in Part III of EudraLex, Volume 4 and is included in Chapter 2 of the Orange Guide.

## Waiver from Written Confirmation

The Falsified Medicines Directive provides two waivers if written confirmations are not provided. The first is where the regulatory framework applicable to active substances in those third countries has been assessed by the European Commission (EC) as providing an equivalent level of protection of public health over active substance manufacture and distribution to those applied in the EU. This assessment follows a request from the exporting third country's competent authority, and considers the regulatory framework for active substance manufacture and control and its equivalence to EU standards. Only if the exporting country is on the EC's ("white") list is the requirement for a written confirmation from that country's competent authority removed.

The second waiver is where the third country active substance manufacturing site has been inspected by an EU Member State, has issued a certificate of compliance with EU-GMP and that it remains within its period of validity. This is an exceptional waiver intended to apply where it is necessary to ensure the availability of medicinal products. Member States using this waiver should communicate this fact to the European Commission in accordance with the legislation (Article 46b(4)). MHRA has notified the European Commission of its intent to use this waiver should that be necessary.

## Procedure for Active Substance Importation

A summary of the overall active substance import process has been developed to promote a common expectation and common approaches by Member States and is available on the Heads of Medicines Agencies, website: http://www.hma.eu/43.html. The flow chart is reproduced here:

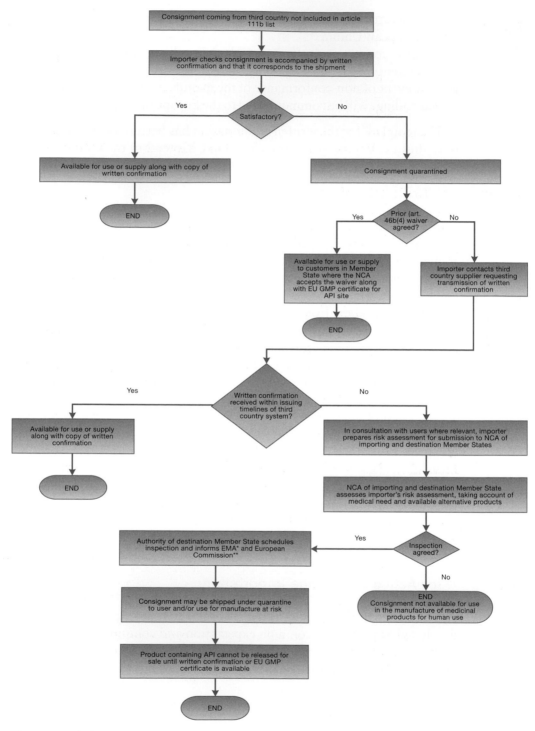

**Figure 4.2** A flowchart of the overall active substance import process

*GMPINS@ema.europa.eu

**sanco-pharmaceuticals-d6@ec.europa.eu

## Procedure for Waiver from Written Confirmation

UK based companies (registered importers and manufacturers who also import directly) who wish to import active substances under the second waiver should apply to gmpinspectorate@mhra.gsi.gov.uk using the form provided below which is available on the MHRA website.

Application Form for a waiver from the requirement to supply Written Confirmation with consignments of an imported Active Substance on the basis of a GMP certification of the Active Substance Manufacturer by an EEA Member State

**A. Details of Third Country Manufacturing Site**

Name of Active Substance :_____

*(Note: Only one active substance permitted per Waiver application. Use INN nomenclature)*

Name of Active Substance Manufacturer :_____
Address of Active Substance Manufacturer :_____
_____
_____
_____

Country :_____
Third Country Competent Authority :_____
site / facility reference number (if known)

**B. Reason for Application for this Waiver**

The manufacturer / importer should attach a document explaining the reason for requesting this waiver. It should be noted that if the active substance is being sourced from a third country where the authority there is known to issue Written Confirmations then under normal circumstances it would be expected that a Written Confirmation would be the basis for importation of active substances from that country.

**C. Details of GMP Certification**

Any differences between the name and address supplied above and those details supplied on the GMP certificate must be justified in order to ensure efficient processing of the application.

Name of authority which issued the GMP certificate :_____
Inspection Date Referenced on GMP certificate :_____
Period of validity of GMP certificate* (if stated) :_____
(*this is 3 years unless there is a statement to the contrary)
Please attach a copy of the GMP certificate to this application form.

**D. Details of Waiver Applicant**

The Waiver Application may be submitted either by a site which has been registered with the MHRA for importation activities in the UK relating to active substances or by an authorised manufacturer / importer of human medicines in the UK which is using the imported active substance for manufacture of medicines for human use (excludes Investigational Medicinal Products) at its manufacturing address. If the importation activities (purchase of the active substance from a third country site or acting as the direct site of physical importation of the active substance) are being carried out directly by an authorised manufacturer of human medicines then both sections D1 and D2 below should be completed.

D1. Active Substance Importer
Active Substance Importers Registration No.:_____
Importation activity carried out for this active substance
(tick all that apply)   ☐ Procurement (Purchasing)   ☐ Site of physical importation
Registered Name of Importer :_____

Registered Address of Importer  :_____

_____

_____

Country                         UK

D2. Authorised Manufacturer of Human Medicines using Imported Active Substance

Manufacturer's / Importers Authorisation No.  : _____

Name of Authorised Manufacturer            : _____

Manufacturing Site Address                 : _____

_____

_____

Country                         UK

E. Signature of Waiver Applicant

Signature      :_____  Date:_____

Name (Print) :_____

Position       :_____

---

**F. Decision by MHRA on Waiver**

Waiver Number:_____

Waiver approved (Yes / No):_____

Signature:_____  Date:_____

Name (Print):_____

Position:_____

---

## National Contingency Guidance

MHRA acknowledges that the introduction of these additional requirements may in some instance make the sourcing of active substances from some third countries difficult in the short term following 2 July 2013. MHRA has therefore developed contingency plans that would allow the Agency, in cases where there is an overriding need to ensure continued supply of specific active substances after 2 July 2013, to provide an opinion on the importation of the active substance to permit manufacture, QP certification and supply of finished medicinal products. The aim of these contingency plans is to ensure, as per the aims of the Falsified Medicines Directive, the continued supply of active substances of appropriate quality and maintain the responsibility for the quality of the authorised medicinal products with the manufacturer, as is the case under the current legislation in force. Where these supply difficulties exist, please contact the GMP inspectorate at GMPinspectorate@mhra.gsi.gov.uk.

Therefore for the short term only and where:

(a) the third country active substance manufacturing site is not covered by a written confirmation; and

(b) the exporting country has not been assessed by the EC as having standards equivalent to EU GMP; and

(c) the third country active substance manufacturing site is not the subject, following inspection, of a current certificate of compliance with EU GMP,

MHRA is actively seeking further information from impacted UK manufacturing sites identified through the active substance mapping exercise. Where UK Manufacturing Authorisation Holders ("MIA Holder") have determined that their third country active substance sources are at risk and have not been contacted by MHRA they should provide evidence in a submission / declaration template that:

(a) the active substance manufacturing site has been audited in the last three years either by himself or by a third party acting on his behalf and found to be operating in compliance with EU GMP for active substances; and

(b) the third country active substance manufacturing site is the subject, following inspection, of a current certificate of compliance with GMP issued by a recognised national authority or international organisation e.g. US-FDA, EU-MRA partners, EU-ACCA partners, PIC/S member states and the WHO.

UK based companies (registered importers and manufacturers who also import directly) who wish to import active substances under this guidance should apply to GMPinspectorate@mhra.gsi.gov.uk using the form provided at the end of this section which is available on the MHRA website.

Where the MIA Holder can make the first declaration but cannot declare that the third country active substance manufacturing site is the subject, following inspection, of a current certificate of compliance with GMP issued by a recognised national authority or international organisation then MHRA intends to enter details of the third country active substance manufacturing site onto a database of pending GMP inspection of a third country active substance manufacturing site.

UK GUIDANCE ON THE MANUFACTURE, IMPORTATION AND DISTRIBUTION

MHRA will conduct further assessment of the data supplied in the submission(s) at the next routine reinspection of these finished product manufacturing sites.

The entry on the database will be removed if the active substance manufacturing site and the AS subsequently become the subject of a written confirmation, the third country has been assessed as having standards equivalent to GMP, or the AS manufacturing site, following inspection has been issued with a certificate of compliance with EU GMP. The pending-inspection database will only be available as long as this is required as a contingency measure.

Importers of active substances are also asked to note that where the sourcing of active substances from some third countries is difficult because it is not covered by a written confirmation, the exporting country has not been assessed as equivalent and the active substance manufacturing site is not the subject of a valid GMP certificate, these circumstances are subject to on-going review coordinated at an EU level. A key element of this review is the gathering of further data from EU-based finished product manufacturers for active substance import risk assessment and, where required, the EU level coordination of third country active substance manufacturer inspections.

## National Contingency Guidance Submission Template

### PART A: Finished Product Manufacturer to which this declaration applies

| Name and address of MIA holder | Authorisation number |
|---|---|
| | |

### PART B: Concerned Third Country Active Substance Manufacturing Site

| Name and Address of Active Substance Manufacturing Site |
|---|
| |
| **Name of Active Substances manufactured at this site** |
| |
| |
| |
| |
| |
| |
| |
| |

## PART C: Basis of declaration in lieu of full compliance with Article 46b(2)

Please tick to confirm that an on-site audit of the active substance manufacturer has been conducted by the MIA holder or by a third party on their behalf

(i)    ☐    On-site audit of the active substance manufacturer(s) conducted by MIA holder or by a third party on their behalf:

An on site audit of the active substance(s) manufactured at the site listed in PART B has been completed either by the MIAH(s) listed below or by a third party auditing body i.e. contract acceptor(s) on behalf of the MIAH i.e. contract giver(s) as listed:

| MIAH (or contract giver) | Auditing body (contract acceptor) | Site audited | Date of audit[1] |
|---|---|---|---|
|  |  |  |  |
|  |  |  |  |
|  |  |  |  |
|  |  |  |  |

[1]The date of the last audit should not exceed 3 years.

(ii)    Availability of a current[2] certificate of compliance with GMP issued by a recognised national authority or international organisation e.g. EDQM-CEP, US-FDA, EU-MRA partners, EU-ACCA partners, PIC/S member states and the WHO.

   ☐    A current certificate for the site named in Section B of compliance with GMP issued by a recognised national authority or international organisation **is** available.

   ☐    A current certificate for the site named in Section B of compliance with GMP issued by a recognised national authority or international organisation **is not** available.

| Inspection Authority | Date of inspection |
|---|---|
|  |  |
|  |  |
|  |  |
|  |  |

[2]The date of the last inspection should not exceed 3 years.

(iii)  **Supplementary supportive information (optional):**

For the active substance manufacturing site listed, results of inspection report(s) or GMP certificate(s) issued by recognised national authorities or international organisations together with other supporting information are attached.

| Summary of supporting information provided |
| --- |
| |

## PART D: Declaration

I declare that:
QP Responsibility

- I am a QP with specific responsibility for GMP compliance of the active substance manufactured at the sites listed in Part B and am authorised to make this declaration.
- That the audit report(s) and all the other documentation relating to this declaration of GMP compliance of the active substance manufacturer(s) will be made available for inspection by the competent authorities, if requested.

## GMP Compliance

- The manufacture of the named active substance(s) at the site given in Part B is in accordance with the detailed guideline on good manufacturing practice for active substances used as starting materials as required by Article 46(f) of Directive 2001/83/EC as amended.
- This is based upon an on-site audit of the active substance manufacturer.
- That the outcome of the audit confirms that the active substance manufacturer complies with the principles and guidelines of good manufacturing practice.

## Audit

- In the case of third party audit(s), I have evaluated each of the named contract acceptor(s) give in Part C and that technical contractual arrangements are in place and that any measures taken by the contract giver(s) are documented e.g. signed undertakings by the auditor(s).
- In all cases, the audit(s) was/were conducted by properly qualified and trained staff, in accordance with approved procedures.

## Inspection, of the third country AS manufacturing site by a recognised national authority or international organisation

- Where available results of inspection report(s) or GMP certificate(s) issued by recognised national authorities or international organisations are within their period of validity and are attached together with other supporting information.

## Part E: Name and Signature of QP responsible for this Declaration

This declaration is submitted by:

Signatory _____

Status (job title)
_____

Print name _____

MIAH name:
_____

Date _____

MIAH number:
_____

# Legislation on Manufacture and Importation

# 5

# EU Legislation on Manufacture and Importation

## Contents

# DIRECTIVE 2001/83/EC, TITLE IV, MANUFACTURE AND IMPORTATION

## Directive 2001/83/EC of the European Parliament and of the Council of 6 November 2001 on the Community code relating to medicinal products for human use

### Title IV: Manufacture and Importation

**Editor's note**    Title IV of this directive is reproduced below. Reference should be made to the full Directive for the preamble, definitions and the general and final provisions.

## Article 40

1 Member States shall take all appropriate measures to ensure that the manufacture of the medicinal products within their territory is subject to the holding of an authorization. This manufacturing authorization shall be required notwithstanding that the medicinal products manufactured are intended for export.

2 The authorization referred to in paragraph 1 shall be required for both total and partial manufacture, and for the various processes of dividing up, packaging or presentation. However, such authorization shall not be required for preparation, dividing up, changes in packaging or presentation where these processes are carried out, solely for retail supply, by pharmacists in dispensing pharmacies or by persons legally authorized in the Member States to carry out such processes.

3 Authorization referred to in paragraph 1 shall also be required for imports coming from third countries into a Member State; this Title and Article 118 shall have corresponding application to such imports as they have to manufacture.

4 Member States shall enter the information relating to the authorisation referred to in paragraph 1 of this Article in the Union database referred to in Article 111(6).

The holder of the manufacturing authorisation shall ensure that the excipients are suitable for use in medicinal products by ascertaining what the appropriate good manufacturing practice is. This shall be ascertained on the basis of a formalised risk assessment in accordance with the applicable guidelines referred to in the fifth paragraph of Article 47. Such risk assessment shall take into account requirements under other appropriate quality systems as well as the source and intended use of the excipients and previous instances of quality defects. The holder of the manufacturing authorisation shall ensure that the appropriate good manufacturing practice so ascertained, is applied. The holder of the manufacturing authorisation shall document the measures taken under this paragraph;

(g) to inform the competent authority and the marketing authorisation holder immediately if he obtains information that medicinal products which come under the scope of his manufacturing authorisation are, or are suspected of being, falsified irrespective of whether those medicinal products were distributed within the legal supply chain or by illegal means, including illegal sale by means of information society services;

(h) to verify that the manufacturers, importers or distributors from whom he obtains active substances are registered with the competent authority of the Member State in which they are established;

(i) to verify the authenticity and quality of the active substances and the excipients.

## Article 46a

1    For the purposes of this Directive, manufacture of active substances used as starting materials shall include both total and partial manufacture or import of an active substance used as a starting material as defined in Part I, point 3.2.1.1 (b) Annex I, and the various processes of dividing up, packaging or presentation prior to its incorporation into a medicinal product, including repackaging or relabelling, such as are carried out by a distributor of starting materials.

2    The Commission shall be empowered to adapt paragraph 1 to take account of scientific and technical progress. That measure, designed to amend non-essential elements of this Directive, shall be adopted in accordance with the regulatory procedure with scrutiny referred to in Article 121(2a).

## Article 46b

1    Member States shall take appropriate measures to ensure that the manufacture, import and distribution on their territory of active

substances, including active substances that are intended for export, comply with good manufacturing practice and good distribution practices for active substances.

2    Active substances shall only be imported if the following conditions are fulfilled:

(a) the active substances have been manufactured in accordance with standards of good manufacturing practice at least equivalent to those laid down by the Union pursuant to the third paragraph of Article 47; and

(b) the active substances are accompanied by a written confirmation from the competent authority of the exporting third country of the following:
  (i)    the standards of good manufacturing practice applicable to the plant manufacturing the exported active substance are at least equivalent to those laid down by the Union pursuant to the third paragraph of Article 47;
  (ii)   the manufacturing plant concerned is subject to regular, strict and transparent controls and to the effective enforcement of good manufacturing practice, including repeated and unannounced inspections, so as to ensure a protection of public health at least equivalent to that in the Union; and
  (iii)  in the event of findings relating to non-compliance, information on such findings is supplied by the exporting third country to the Union without any delay.

This written confirmation shall be without prejudice to the obligations set out in Article 8 and in point (f) of Article 46.

3    The requirement set out in point (b) of paragraph 2 of this Article shall not apply if the exporting country is included in the list referred to in Article 111b.

4    Exceptionally and where necessary to ensure the availability of medicinal products, when a plant manufacturing an active substance for export has been inspected by a Member State and was found to comply with the principles and guidelines of good manufacturing practice laid down pursuant to the third paragraph of Article 47, the requirement set out in point (b) of paragraph 2 of this Article may be waived by any Member State for a period not exceeding the validity of the certificate of Good Manufacturing Practice. Member States that make use of the possibility of such waiver, shall communicate this to the Commission.

## Article 47

The principles and guidelines of good manufacturing practices for medicinal products referred to in Article 46(f) shall be adopted in the form of a directive. That measure, designed to amend non-essential elements of this Directive by supplementing it, shall be adopted in accordance with the regulatory procedure with scrutiny referred to in Article 121(2a).

Detailed guidelines in line with those principles will be published by the Commission and revised necessary to take account of technical and scientific progress.

The Commission shall adopt, by means of delegated acts in accordance with Article 121a and subject to the conditions laid down in Articles 121b and 121c, the principles and guidelines of good manufacturing practice for active substances referred to in the first paragraph of point (f) of Article 46 and in Article 46b.

The principles of good distribution practices for active substances referred to in the first paragraph of point (f) of Article 46 shall be adopted by the Commission in the form of guidelines.

The Commission shall adopt guidelines on the formalised risk assessment for ascertaining the appropriate good manufacturing practice for excipients referred to in the second paragraph of point (f) of Article 46.

## Article 47a

1  The safety features referred to in point (o) of Article 54 shall not be removed or covered, either fully or partially, unless the following conditions are fulfilled:

(a) the manufacturing authorisation holder verifies, prior to partly or fully removing or covering those safety features, that the medicinal product concerned is authentic and that it has not been tampered with;

(b) the manufacturing authorisation holder complies with point (o) of Article 54 by replacing those safety features with safety features which are equivalent as regards the possibility to verify the authenticity, identification and to provide evidence of tampering of the medicinal product. Such replacement shall be conducted without opening the immediate packaging as defined in point 23 of Article 1.

Safety features shall be considered equivalent if they:

(i)  comply with the requirements set out in the delegated acts adopted pursuant to Article 54a(2); and

    (ii)    are equally effective in enabling the verification of authenticity and identification of medicinal products and in providing evidence of tampering with medicinal products;

(c) the replacement of the safety features is conducted in accordance with applicable good manufacturing practice for medicinal products; and

(d) the replacement of the safety features is subject to supervision by the competent authority.

2    Manufacturing authorisation holders, including those performing the activities referred to in paragraph 1 of this Article, shall be regarded as producers and therefore held liable for damages in the cases and under the conditions set forth in Directive 85/374/EEC.

## Article 48

1    Member States shall take all appropriate measures to ensure that the holder of the manufacturing authorization has permanently and continuously at his disposal the services of at least one qualified person, in accordance with the conditions laid down in Article 49, responsible in particular for carrying out the duties specified in Article 51.

2    If he personally fulfils the conditions laid down in Article 49, the holder of the authorization may himself assume the responsibility referred to in paragraph 1.

## Article 49

1    Member States shall ensure that the qualified person referred to in Article 48 fulfils the conditions of qualification set out in paragraphs 2 and 3.

2    A qualified person shall be in possession of a diploma, certificate or other evidence of formal qualifications awarded on completion of a university course of study, or a course recognized as equivalent by the Member State concerned, extending over a period of at least four years of theoretical and practical study in one of the following scientific disciplines: pharmacy, medicine, veterinary medicine, chemistry, pharmaceutical chemistry and technology, biology.

    However, the minimum duration of the university course may be three and a half years where the course is followed by a period of theoretical and practical training of a minimum duration of one year and including a training period of at least six months in a pharmacy open to the public, corroborated by an examination at university level.

    Where two university courses or two courses recognized by the State as equivalent co-exist in a Member State and where one of these extends over four years and the other over three years, the three-year course leading to a diploma, certificate or other evidence of formal qualifications awarded on completion of a university course or its recognized equivalent shall be considered to fulfil the condition of duration referred to in the second subparagraph in so far as the diplomas, certificates or other evidence of formal qualifications awarded on completion of both courses are recognized as equivalent by the State in question.

The course shall include theoretical and practical study bearing upon at least the following basic subjects:

- Experimental physics
- General and inorganic chemistry
- Organic chemistry
- Analytical chemistry
- Pharmaceutical chemistry, including analysis of medicinal products
- General and applied biochemistry (medical)
- Physiology
- Microbiology
- Pharmacology
- Pharmaceutical technology
- Toxicology
- Pharmacognosy (study of the composition and effects of the natural active substances of plant and animal origin).

Studies in these subjects should be so balanced as to enable the person concerned to fulfil the obligations specified in Article 51.

In so far as certain diplomas, certificates or other evidence of formal qualifications mentioned in the first subparagraph do not fulfil the criteria laid down in this paragraph, the competent authority of the Member State shall ensure that the person concerned provides evidence of adequate knowledge of the subjects involved.

3   The qualified person shall have acquired practical experience over at least two years, in one or more undertakings which are authorized to manufacture medicinal products, in the activities of qualitative analysis of medicinal products, of quantitative analysis of active substances and of the testing and checking necessary to ensure the quality of medicinal products.

The duration of practical experience may be reduced by one year where a university course lasts for at least five years and by a year and a half where the course lasts for at least six years.

## Article 50

1   A person engaging in the activities of the person referred to in Article 48 from the time of the application of Directive 75/319/EEC, in a Member

State without complying with the provisions of Article 49 shall be eligible to continue to engage in those activities within the Community.

2   The holder of a diploma, certificate or other evidence of formal qualifications awarded on completion of a university course or a course recognized as equivalent by the Member State concerned in a scientific discipline allowing him to engage in the activities of the person referred to in Article 48 in accordance with the laws of that State may – if he began his course prior to 21 May 1975 – be considered as qualified to carry out in that State the duties of the person referred to in Article 48 provided that he has previously engaged in the following activities for at least two years before 21 May 1985 following notification of this directive in one or more undertakings authorized to manufacture: production supervision and/or qualitative and quantitative analysis of active substances, and the necessary testing and checking under the direct authority of the person referred to in Article 48 to ensure the quality of the medicinal products.

If the person concerned has acquired the practical experience referred to in the first subparagraph before 21 May 1965, a further one year's practical experience in accordance with the conditions referred to in the first subparagraph will be required to be completed immediately before he engages in such activities.

## Article 51

1   Member States shall take all appropriate measures to ensure that the qualified person referred to in Article 48, without prejudice to his relationship with the holder of the manufacturing authorization, is responsible, in the context of the procedures referred to in Article 52, for securing:

(a) in the case of medicinal products manufactured within the Member States concerned, that each batch of medicinal products has been manufactured and checked in compliance with the laws in force in that Member State and in accordance with the requirements of the marketing authorization.

(b) in the case of medicinal products coming from third countries, irrespective of whether the product has been manufactured in the Community, that each production batch has undergone in a Member State a full qualitative analysis, a quantitative analysis of at least all the active substances and all the other tests or checks necessary to ensure the quality of medicinal products in accordance with the requirements of the marketing authorisation.

The qualified person referred to in Article 48 shall in the case of medicinal products intended to be placed on the market in the Union, ensure that the safety features referred to in point (o) of Article 54 have been affixed on the packaging.

The batches of medicinal products which have undergone such controls in a Member State shall be exempt from the controls if they are marketed in another Member State, accompanied by the control reports signed by the qualified person.

2   In the case of medicinal products imported from a third country, where appropriate arrangements have been made by the Community with the exporting country to ensure that the manufacturer of the medicinal product applies standards of good manufacturing practice at least equivalent to those laid down by the Community, and to ensure that the controls referred to under point (b) of the first subparagraph of paragraph 1 have been carried out in the exporting country, the qualified person may be relieved of responsibility for carrying out those controls.

3   In all cases and particularly where the medicinal products are released for sale, the qualified person must certify in a register or equivalent document provided for that purpose, that each production batch satisfies the provisions of this Article; the said register or equivalent document must be kept up to date as operations are carried out and must remain at the disposal of the agents of the competent authority for the period specified in the provisions of the Member State concerned and in any event for at least five years.

## Article 52

Member States shall ensure that the duties of qualified persons referred to in Article 48 are fulfilled, either by means of appropriate administrative measures or by making such persons subject to a professional code of conduct. Member States may provide for the temporary suspension of such a person upon the commencement of administrative or disciplinary procedures against him for failure to fulfil his obligations.

## Article 52a

1   Importers, manufacturers and distributors of active substances who are established in the Union shall register their activity with the competent authority of the Member State in which they are established.

2   The registration form shall include, at least, the following information:

(i)    name or corporate name and permanent address;
(ii)   the active substances which are to be imported, manufactured or distributed;

(iii)   particulars regarding the premises and the technical equipment for their activity.

3    The persons referred to in paragraph 1 shall submit the registration form to the competent authority at least 60 days prior to the intended commencement of their activity.

4    The competent authority may, based on a risk assessment, decide to carry out an inspection. If the competent authority notifies the applicant within 60 days of the receipt of the registration form that an inspection will be carried out, the activity shall not begin before the competent authority has notified the applicant that he may commence the activity. If within 60 days of the receipt of the registration form the competent authority has not notified the applicant that an inspection will be carried out, the applicant may commence the activity.

5    The persons referred to in paragraph 1 shall communicate annually to the competent authority an inventory of the changes which have taken place as regards the information provided in the registration form. Any changes that may have an impact on the quality or safety of the active substances that are manufactured, imported or distributed must be notified immediately.

6    Persons referred to in paragraph 1 who had commenced their activity before 2 January 2013 shall submit the registration form to the competent authority by 2 March 2013.

7    Member States shall enter the information provided in accordance with paragraph 2 of this Article in the Union database referred to in Article 111(6).

8    This Article shall be without prejudice to Article 111.

## Article 52b

1    Notwithstanding Article 2(1), and without prejudice to Title VII, Member States shall take the necessary measures in order to prevent medicinal products that are introduced into the Union, but are not intended to be placed on the market of the Union, from entering into circulation if there are sufficient grounds to suspect that those products are falsified.

2    In order to establish what the necessary measures referred to in paragraph 1 of this Article are, the Commission may adopt, by means of delegated acts in accordance with Article 121a, and subject to the conditions laid down in Articles 121b and 121c, measures supplementing paragraph 1 of this Article as regards the criteria to be considered and the verifications to be made when assessing the potential falsified character of medicinal

products introduced into the Union but not intended to be placed on the market.

## Article 53

The provisions of this Title shall also apply to homeopathic medicinal products.

## DIRECTIVE 2003/94/EC, LAYING DOWN THE PRINCIPLES AND GUIDELINES OF GOOD MANUFACTURING PRACTICE FOR HUMAN MEDICINES

**Directive 2003/94/EC, laying down the principles and guidelines of good manufacturing practice in respect of medicinal products for human use and investigational medicinal products for human use**

> **Editor's note**   The Articles of this Directive are reproduced below. Reference should be made to the full Directive for the preambles.

## Article 1

SCOPE

This Directive lays down the principles and guidelines of good manufacturing practice in respect of medicinal products for human use whose manufacture requires the authorisation referred to in Article 40 of Directive 2001/83/EC and in respect of investigational medicinal products for human use whose manufacture requires the authorisation referred to in Article 13 of Directive 2001/20/EC.

## Article 2

DEFINITIONS

For the purposes of this Directive, the following definitions shall apply:

(1) "medicinal product" means any product as defined in Article 1(2) of Directive 2001/83/EC;

(2) "investigational medicinal product" means any product as defined in Article 2(d) of Directive 2001/20/EC;

(3) "manufacturer" means any person engaged in activities for which the authorisation referred to in Article 40(1) and (3) of Directive 2001/83/EC or the authorisation referred to in Article 13(1) of Directive 2001/20/EC is required;

(4) "qualified person" means the person referred to in Article 48 of Directive 2001/83/EC or in Article 13(2) of Directive 2001/20/EC;

(5) "pharmaceutical quality assurance" means the total sum of the organised arrangements made with the object of ensuring that medicinal products or investigational medicinal products are of the quality required for their intended use;

(6) "good manufacturing practice" means the part of quality assurance which ensures that products are consistently produced and controlled in accordance with the quality standards appropriate to their intended use;

(7) "blinding" means the deliberate disguising of the identity of an investigational medicinal product in accordance with the instructions of the sponsor;

(8) "unblinding" means the disclosure of the identity of a blinded product.

## Article 3

INSPECTIONS

1 By means of the repeated inspections referred to in Article 111(1) of Directive 2001/83/EC and by means of the inspections referred to in Article 15(1) of Directive 2001/20/EC, the Member States shall ensure that manufacturers respect the principles and guidelines of good manufacturing practice laid down by this Directive. Member States shall also take into account the compilation, published by the Commission, of Community procedures on inspections and exchange of information.

2 For the interpretation of the principles and guidelines of good manufacturing practice, the manufacturers and the competent authorities shall take into account the detailed guidelines referred to in the second paragraph of Article 47 of Directive 2001/83/EC, published by the Commission in the "Guide to good manufacturing practice for medicinal products and for investigational medicinal products".

## Article 4

CONFORMITY WITH GOOD MANUFACTURING PRACTICE

1 The manufacturer shall ensure that manufacturing operations are carried out in accordance with good manufacturing practice and with the manufacturing authorisation. This provision shall also apply to medicinal products intended only for export.

2 For medicinal products and investigational medicinal products imported from third countries, the importer shall ensure that the products have been manufactured in accordance with standards which are at least equivalent to the good manufacturing practice standards laid down by the Community.

In addition, an importer of medicinal products shall ensure that such products have been manufactured by manufacturers duly authorised to do so. An importer of investigational medicinal products shall ensure that such products have been manufactured by a manufacturer notified to the competent authorities and accepted by them for that purpose.

## Article 5

### COMPLIANCE WITH MARKETING AUTHORISATION

1   The manufacturer shall ensure that all manufacturing operations for medicinal products subject to a marketing authorisation are carried out in accordance with the information provided in the application for marketing authorisation as accepted by the competent authorities.

In the case of investigational medicinal products, the manufacturer shall ensure that all manufacturing operations are carried out in accordance with the information provided by the sponsor pursuant to Article 9(2) of Directive 2001/20/EC as accepted by the competent authorities.

2   The manufacturer shall regularly review his manufacturing methods in the light of scientific and technical progress and the development of the investigational medicinal product.

If a variation to the marketing authorisation dossier or an amendment to the request referred to in Article 9(2) of Directive 2001/20/EC is necessary, the application for modification shall be submitted to the competent authorities.

## Article 6

### QUALITY ASSURANCE SYSTEM

The manufacturer shall establish and implement an effective pharma-ceutical quality assurance system, involving the active participation of the management and personnel of the different departments.

## Article 7

### PERSONNEL

1   At each manufacturing site, the manufacturer shall have a sufficient number of competent and appropriately qualified personnel at his disposal to achieve the pharmaceutical quality assurance objective.

2   The duties of the managerial and supervisory staff, including the qualified persons, responsible for implementing and operating good manufacturing practice, shall be defined in job descriptions. Their hierarchical relationships shall be defined in an organisation chart. Organisation charts

and job descriptions shall be approved in accordance with the manufacturer's internal procedures.

3   The staff referred to in paragraph 2 shall be given sufficient authority to discharge their responsibility correctly.

4   The personnel shall receive initial and ongoing training, the effectiveness of which shall be verified, covering in particular the theory and application of the concept of quality assurance and good manufacturing practice, and, where appropriate, the particular requirements for the manufacture of investigational medicinal products.

5   Hygiene programmes adapted to the activities to be carried out shall be established and observed. These programmes shall, in particular, include procedures relating to health, hygiene practice and clothing of personnel.

# Article 8

## PREMISES AND EQUIPMENT

1   Premises and manufacturing equipment shall be located, designed, constructed, adapted and maintained to suit the intended operations.

2   Premises and manufacturing equipment shall be laid out, designed and operated in such a way as to minimise the risk of error and to permit effective cleaning and maintenance in order to avoid contamination, cross-contamination and, in general, any adverse effect on the quality of the product.

3   Premises and equipment to be used for manufacturing operations, which are critical to the quality of the products, shall be subjected to appropriate qualification and validation.

# Article 9

## DOCUMENTATION

1   The manufacturer shall establish and maintain a documentation system based upon specifications, manufacturing formulae and processing and packaging instructions, procedures and records covering the various manufacturing operations performed. Documents shall be clear, free from error and kept up to date. Pre-established procedures for general manufacturing operations and conditions shall be kept available, together with specific documents for the manufacture of each batch. That set of documents shall enable the history of the manufacture of each batch and the changes introduced during the development of an investigational medicinal product to be traced.

For a medicinal product, the batch documentation shall be retained for at least one year after the expiry date of the batches to which it relates or at least five years after the certification referred to in Article 51(3) of Directive 2001/83/EC, whichever is the longer period.

For an investigational medicinal product, the batch documentation shall be retained for at least five years after the completion or formal discontinuation of the last clinical trial in which the batch was used. The sponsor or marketing authorisation holder, if different, shall be responsible for ensuring that records are retained as required for marketing authorisation in accordance with the Annex I to Directive 2001/83/EC, if required for a subsequent marketing authorisation.

2   When electronic, photographic or other data processing systems are used instead of written documents, the manufacturer shall first validate the systems by showing that the data will be appropriately stored during the anticipated period of storage. Data stored by those systems shall be made readily available in legible form and shall be provided to the competent authorities at their request. The electronically stored data shall be protected, by methods such as duplication or back-up and transfer on to another storage system, against loss or damage of data, and audit trails shall be maintained.

## Article 10

PRODUCTION

1   The different production operations shall be carried out in accordance with pre-established instructions and procedures and in accordance with good manufacturing practice. Adequate and sufficient resources shall be made available for the in-process controls. All process deviations and product defects shall be documented and thoroughly investigated.

2   Appropriate technical or organisational measures shall be taken to avoid cross-contamination and mix-ups. In the case of investigational medicinal products, particular attention shall be paid to the handling of products during and after any blinding operation.

3   For medicinal products, any new manufacture or important modification of a manufacturing process of a medicinal product shall be validated. Critical phases of manufacturing processes shall be regularly re-validated.

4   For investigational medicinal products, the manufacturing process shall be validated in its entirety in so far as is appropriate, taking into account the stage of product development. At least the critical process steps, such as sterilisation, shall be validated. All steps in the design and development of the manufacturing process shall be fully documented.

# Article 11

## QUALITY CONTROL

1  The manufacturer shall establish and maintain a quality control system placed under the authority of a person who has the requisite qualifications and is independent of production. That person shall have at his disposal, or shall have access to, one or more quality control laboratories appropriately staffed and equipped to carry out the necessary examination and testing of the starting materials and packaging materials and the testing of intermediate and finished products.

2  For medicinal products, including those imported from third countries, contract laboratories may be used if authorised in accordance with Article 12 of this Directive and point (b) of Article 20 of Directive 2001/83/EC.

   For investigational medicinal products, the sponsor shall ensure that the contract laboratory complies with the content of the request referred to in Article 9(2) of Directive 2001/20/EC, as accepted by the competent authority. When the products are imported from third countries, analytical control shall not be mandatory.

3  During the final control of the finished product before its release for sale or distribution or for use in clinical trials, the quality control system shall take into account, in addition to analytical results, essential information such as the production conditions, the results of in-process controls, the examination of the manufacturing documents and the conformity of the product to its specifications, including the final finished pack.

4  Samples of each batch of finished medicinal product shall be retained for at least one year after the expiry date. For an investigational medicinal product, sufficient samples of each batch of bulk formulated product and of key packaging components used for each finished product batch shall be retained for at least two years after completion or formal discontinuation of the last clinical trial in which the batch was used, whichever period is the longer.

   Unless a longer period is required under the law of the Member State of manufacture, samples of starting materials, other than solvents, gases or water, used in the manufacturing process shall be retained for at least two years after the release of product. That period may be shortened if the period of stability of the material, as indicated in the relevant specification, is shorter. All those samples shall be maintained at the disposal of the competent authorities. Other conditions may be defined, by agreement with the competent authority, for the sampling and retaining of starting materials and certain products manufactured individually or in small quantities, or when their storage could raise special problems.

## Article 12

WORK CONTRACTED OUT

1   Any manufacturing operation or operation linked thereto which is carried out under contract shall be the subject of a written contract.

2   The contract shall clearly define the responsibilities of each party and shall define, in particular, the observance of good manufacturing practice to be followed by the contract acceptor and the manner in which the qualified person responsible for certifying each batch is to discharge his responsibilities.

3   The contract-acceptor shall not subcontract any of the work entrusted to him under the contract without written authorisation from the contract-giver.

4   The contract-acceptor shall comply with the principles and guidelines of good manufacturing practice and shall submit to inspections carried out by the competent authorities pursuant to Article 111 of Directive 2001/83/EC and Article 15 of Directive 2001/20/EC.

## Article 13

COMPLAINTS, PRODUCT RECALL AND EMERGENCY UNBLINDING

1   In the case of medicinal products, the manufacturer shall implement a system for recording and reviewing complaints together with an effective system for recalling, promptly and at any time, medicinal products in the distribution network. Any complaint concerning a defect shall be recorded and investigated by the manufacturer. The manufacturer shall inform the competent authority of any defect that could result in a recall or abnormal restriction on supply and, in so far as is possible, indicate the countries of destination. Any recall shall be made in accordance with the requirements referred to in Article 123 of Directive 2001/83/EC.

2   In the case of investigational medicinal products, the manufacturer shall, in cooperation with the sponsor, implement a system for recording and reviewing complaints together with an effective system for recalling promptly and at any time investigational medicinal products which have already entered the distribution network. The manufacturer shall record and investigate any complaint concerning a defect and shall inform the competent authority of any defect that could result in a recall or abnormal restriction on supply.

In the case of investigational medicinal products, all trial sites shall be identified and, in so far as is possible, the countries of destination shall be indicated.

In the case of an investigational medicinal product for which a marketing authorisation has been issued, the manufacturer of the investigational medicinal product shall, in cooperation with the sponsor, inform the marketing authorisation holder of any defect that could be related to the authorised medicinal product.

3  The sponsor shall implement a procedure for the rapid unblinding of blinded products, where this is necessary for a prompt recall as referred to in paragraph 2. The sponsor shall ensure that the procedure discloses the identity of the blinded product only in so far as is necessary.

## Article 14

SELF-INSPECTION

The manufacturer shall conduct repeated self-inspections as part of the quality assurance system in order to monitor the implementation and respect of good manufacturing practice and to propose any necessary corrective measures. Records shall be maintained of such self-inspections and any corrective action subsequently taken.

## Article 15

LABELLING

In the case of an investigational medicinal product, labelling shall be such as to ensure protection of the subject and traceability, to enable identification of the product and trial, and to facilitate proper use of the investigational medicinal product.

## Article 16

REPEAL OF DIRECTIVE 91/356/EEC

Directive 91/356/EEC is repealed. References to the repealed Directive shall be construed as references to this Directive.

## Article 17

TRANSPOSITION

1  Member States shall bring into force the laws, regulations and administrative provisions necessary to comply with this Directive by 30 April 2004 at the latest. They shall forthwith communicate to the Commission the text of the provisions and correlation table between those provisions and the provisions of this Directive.

When Member States adopt those provisions, they shall contain a reference to this Directive or be accompanied by such a reference on the occasion of their official publication. The Member States shall determine how such reference is to be made.

2 Member States shall communicate to the Commission the text of the main provisions of national law which they adopt in the field covered by this Directive.

## Article 18

ENTRY INTO FORCE

This Directive shall enter into force on the 20th day following that of its publication in the *Official Journal of the European Union*.

## Article 19

ADDRESSEES

This Directive is addressed to the Member States.

# UK Legislation on Manufacture and Importation

## Contents

## The Human Medicines Regulations 2012 (SI 2012/1916)

**Editor's note**    These extracts from the Human Medicines Regulations 2012 [SI 2012/1916] as amended by the Human Medicines (Amendment) Regulations 2013 [SI 2013/1855] are presented for the reader's convenience. Reproduction is with the permission of HMSO and the Queen's Printer for Scotland. For any definitive information reference must be made to the original Regulations.

The numbering and content within this section corresponds with the regulations set out in the published Statutory Instrument 2012 No. 1916.

## Citation and commencement

1    (1) These Regulations may be cited as the Human Medicines Regulations 2012.

       (2) These Regulations come into force on 14th August 2012.

## General interpretation

8    (1) In these Regulations (unless the context otherwise requires):

"the 2001 Directive" means Directive 2001/83/EC of the European Parliament and of the Council on the Community Code relating to medicinal products for human use;

"active substance" means any substance or mixture of substances intended to be used in the manufacture of a medicinal product and that, when used in its production, becomes an active ingredient of that product intended to exert a pharmacological, immunological or metabolic action with a view to restoring, correcting or modifying physiological functions or to make a medical diagnosis;

"Article 126a authorisation" means an authorisation granted by the licensing authority under Part 8 of these Regulations;

"assemble", in relation to a medicinal product or an active substance, includes the various processes of dividing up, packaging and presentation of the product or substance, and "assembly" has a corresponding meaning;

"biological medicinal product" and "biological substance" have the meaning given in the third indent of paragraph 3.2.1.1.(b) of Annex I to the 2001 Directive;

"blood component" means any of the following:

(a) red cells;

(b) white cells;

(c) platelets; and

(d) plasma;

"the British Pharmacopoeia" means the British Pharmacopoeia referred to in regulation 317;

"Directive 2002/98/EC" means Directive 2002/98/EC of the European Parliament and of the Council of 27 January 2003 setting standards of quality and safety for the collection, testing, processing, storage and distribution of human blood and blood components and amending Directive 2001/83/EC;

"Directive 2004/23/EC" means Directive 2004/23/EC of the European Parliament and of the Council of 31 March 2004 on setting standards of quality and safety for the donation, procurement, testing, processing, preservation, storage and distribution of human tissues and cells;

"electronic communication" means a communication transmitted (whether from one person to another, from one device to another or from a person to a device or vice versa):

(a) by means of an electronic communications network within the meaning of section 32(1) of the Communications Act 2003; or

(b) by other means but while in an electronic form;

"EU marketing authorisation" means a marketing authorisation granted or renewed by the European Commission under Regulation (EC) No 726/2004;

"European Economic Area" or "EEA" means the European Economic Area created by the EEA agreement;

"excipient" means any constituent of a medicinal product other than the active substance and the packaging material;

"exempt advanced therapy medicinal product" has the meaning given in regulation 171;

"the Good Manufacturing Practice Directive" means Commission Directive 2003/94/EC of 8 October 2003 laying down the principles and guidelines of good manufacturing practice in respect of medicinal products for human use and investigational medicinal products for human use;

"export" means export, or attempt to export, from the UK, whether by land, sea or air;

"falsified medicinal product" means any medicinal product with a false representation of:

(a) its identity, including its packaging and labelling, its name or its composition (other than any unintentional quality defect) as regards any of its ingredients including excipients and the strength of those ingredients;

(b) its source, including its manufacturer, its country of manufacturing, its country of origin or its marketing authorisation holder; or

(c) its history, including the records and documents relating to the distribution channels used;

"Fees Regulations" means the Medicines (Products for Human Use) (Fees) Regulations 2013;[1]

"herbal medicinal product" means a medicinal product whose only active ingredients are herbal substances or herbal preparations (or both);

"herbal preparation" means a preparation obtained by subjecting herbal substances to processes such as extraction, distillation, expression, fractionation, purification, concentration or fermentation, and includes a comminuted or powdered herbal substance, a tincture, an extract, an essential oil, an expressed juice or a processed exudate;

"herbal substance" means a plant or part of a plant, algae, fungi or lichen, or an unprocessed exudate of a plant, defined by the plant part used and the botanical name of the plant, either fresh or dried, but otherwise unprocessed;

"homoeopathic medicinal product" means a medicinal product prepared from homoeopathic stocks in accordance with a homoeopathic manufacturing procedure described by:

(a) the European Pharmacopoeia; or

(b) in the absence of such a description in the European Pharmacopoeia, in any pharmacopoeia used officially in an EEA State;

"import" means import, or attempt to import, into the UK, whether by land, sea or air;

"inspector" means a person authorised in writing by an enforcement authority for the purposes of Part 16 (enforcement) (and references to "the enforcement authority", in relation to an inspector, are to the enforcement authority by whom the inspector is so authorised);

"the licensing authority" has the meaning given by regulation 6(2);

"manufacture", in relation to a medicinal product, includes any process carried out in the course of making the product, but does not include dissolving or dispersing the product in, or diluting or mixing it with, a substance used as a vehicle for the purpose of administering it;

"manufacturer's licence" has the meaning given by regulation 17(1);

"marketing authorisation" means:

---

[1] S.I. 2013/532

(a) a UK marketing authorisation; or

(b) an EU marketing authorisation;

"outer packaging" in relation to a medicinal product means any packaging into which the immediate packaging of the medicinal product is placed;

"package" in relation to a medicinal product, includes:

(a) a container of the product;

(b) any box, packet or other article in which one or more containers of the product are or are to be enclosed; and

(c) any box, packet or other article in which a box, packet or other article mentioned in paragraph (b) or this paragraph is or is to be enclosed;

"qualified person", except in relation to the expression "appropriately qualified person", means:

(a) a person who satisfies the requirements specified in Part 1 or 2 of Schedule 7; or

(b) where an application for a licence is made before 30th April 2013, in so far as the application relates to activities in respect of traditional herbal medicinal products, a person who has been engaged in activities in respect of traditional herbal medicinal products equivalent to those in Part 3 of Schedule 7 on or before 30th April 2011 and continues to be so engaged at the time when the application is made;

"Regulation (EC) No 726/2004" means Regulation (EC) No 726/2004 of the European Parliament and of the Council of 31 March 2004 laying down Community procedures for the authorisation and supervision of medicinal products for human and veterinary use and establishing a European Medicines Agency;

"Regulation (EC) No 1394/2007" means Regulation (EC) No 1394/2007 of the European Parliament and of the Council of 13 November 2007 on advanced therapy medicinal products and amending Directive 2001/83/EC and Regulation (EC) No 726/2004;

"Regulation (EC) No 1234/2008" means Commission Regulation (EC) No 1234/2008 of 24 November 2008 concerning the examination of variations to the terms of marketing authorisations for medicinal products for human use and veterinary medicinal products;

"the relevant EU provisions" means the provisions of legislation of the European Union relating to medicinal products for human use, except to the extent that any other enactment provides for any function in relation to any such provision to be exercised otherwise than by the licensing authority;

"third country" means a country or territory outside the EEA.

## Standard provisions of licences

24   (1)  The standard provisions set out in Schedule 4 may be incorporated by the licensing authority in a licence under this Part granted on or after the date on which these Regulations come into force.

     (2)  The standard provisions may be incorporated in a licence with or without modifications and either generally or in relation to medicinal products of a particular class.

## Conditions for manufacturer's licence

36   (1)  Regulations 37 to 41 apply to the holder of a manufacturer's licence (referred to in those regulations as "the licence holder") and have effect as if they were provisions of the licence (but the provisions specified in paragraph (2) do not apply to the holder of a manufacturer's licence insofar as the licence relates to the manufacture or assembly of exempt advanced therapy medicinal products).

     (2)  Those provisions are regulations 37(3), 38, 39(6)(a) and (8), 40 and 41.

     (3)  The requirements of Part 1 of Schedule 6 apply to the holder of a manufacturer's licence insofar as the licence relates to the manufacture or assembly of exempt advanced therapy medicinal products, and have effect as if they were provisions of the licence.

## Manufacturing and assembly

37   (1)  This regulation applies in relation to a manufacturer's licence relating to the manufacture or assembly of medicinal products.

     (2)  The licence holder must comply with the principles and guidelines for good manufacturing practice set out in the Good Manufacturing Practice Directive.

     (3)  Unless paragraph (10) applies, the licence holder shall use active substances as starting materials only if:

        (a)  those substances have been manufactured in accordance with good manufacturing practice for active substances; and

        (b)  those substances have been distributed in accordance with the guidelines on good distribution practice for active substances.

     (4)  The licence holder shall verify:

        (a)  that the manufacturer or distributor of an active substance used by the licence holder has complied with the requirements of good manufacturing practice and good distribution practice for active substances by means of audits performed:

(i) directly by the licence holder, or

(ii) by a person acting on behalf of the licence holder under a contract;

(b) that unless the active substance is imported from a third country, any manufacturers, importers or distributors supplying active substances to the licence holder are registered with the competent authority of a member State in which they are established; and

(c) the authenticity and quality of the active substance.

(5) The licence holder shall ensure that:

(a) excipients are suitable for use in a medicinal product by:

(i) ascertaining what the appropriate good manufacturing practice is, and

(ii) ensuring that the ascertained good manufacturing practice is applied;

(b) the suitability of the excipient is ascertained on the basis of a formalised risk assessment as described in paragraph 5 of Article 47[2] of the 2001 Directive;

(c) the assessment under sub-paragraph (b) takes account of:

(i) the source,

(ii) requirements under other quality systems,

(iii) intended use of the excipients, and

(iv) previous instances of quality defects;

(d) the authenticity and quality of any excipient used is verified; and

(e) the measures taken under this paragraph are documented by the licence holder.

(6) The licence holder must maintain such staff, premises and equipment as are necessary for the stages of manufacture and assembly of medicinal products undertaken by the licence holder in accordance with:

(a) the manufacturer's licence; and

(b) the marketing authorisations, Article 126a authorisations, certificates of registration or traditional herbal registrations applying to the medicinal products.

(7) The licence holder must not manufacture or assemble medicinal products, or classes of medicinal products, other than those specified in the licence.

(8) The licence holder must not manufacture or assemble medicinal products on premises other than those specified in the licence as approved by the licensing authority for the purpose.

---

[2] Paragraph 5 of Article 47 was inserted by Directive 2011/62/EU of the European Parliament and of the Council (OJ No L 174, 1.7.2011, p. 74).

(9) The licence holder must ensure that blood, or blood components, imported into the United Kingdom and used as a starting material or raw material in the manufacture of a medicinal product meet:

(a) the standards of quality and safety specified in Commission Directive 2004/33/EC of 22 March 2004 implementing Directive 2002/98/EC of the European Parliament and of the Council as regards certain technical requirements for blood and blood components;[3] or

(b) equivalent standards.

(10) The requirements in paragraphs (3) to (5) do not apply in relation to the manufacture or assembly of special medicinal product to which regulation 167 (supply to fulfil special needs) applies.

(11) The licence holder must immediately inform the competent authority of a member State and, where applicable, the marketing authorisation holder, of medicinal products which come within the scope of manufacturing authorisation which the licence holder:

(a) knows or suspects; or

(b) has reasonable grounds for knowing or suspecting,
    to be falsified.

## Imports from states other than EEA States

38 (1) This regulation applies in relation to a manufacturer's licence relating to the import of medicinal products.

(2) The licence holder must comply with the conditions set out in this regulation in relation to the import of medicinal products from a state other than an EEA State.

(3) The licence holder must:

(a) comply with the principles and guidelines on good manufacturing practice in the Good Manufacturing Practice Directive in so far as they are relevant to the import of medicinal products; and

(b) ensure that active substances have been used as starting materials in the manufacture of medicinal products, other than special medicinal products, imported from a state other than an EEA State only if those substances have been manufactured or assembled in accordance with the principles and guidelines mentioned in paragraph (a), in so far as those principles and guidelines relate to starting materials.

---

[3] OJ No L 91, 30.3.2004, p. 25; relevant amending instrument is Commission Implementing Directive 2011/38/EU (OJ No L 97, 12.4.2011, p. 28).

## Further requirements for manufacturer's licence

**39** (1) This regulation applies in relation to any manufacturer's licence.

(2) The licence holder must maintain such staff, premises, equipment and facilities for the handling, control, storage and distribution of medicinal products under the licence as are appropriate in order to maintain the quality of the medicinal products.

(3) The licence holder must ensure that any arrangements made for the handling, control, storage and distribution of medicinal products are adequate to maintain the quality of the products.

(4) The licence holder must not handle, control, store or distribute medicinal products on any premises other than those specified in the licence as approved by the licensing authority for the purpose.

(5) The licence holder must inform the licensing authority before making a material alteration to the premises or facilities used under the licence, or to the purposes for which those premises or facilities are used.

(6) The licence holder must inform the licensing authority of any proposed change to:

(a) the qualified person; and

(b) any person named in the licence as having responsibility for quality control.

(7) For the purposes of enabling the licensing authority to determine whether there are grounds for suspending, revoking or varying the licence, the licence holder must permit a person authorised in writing by the licensing authority to do anything that the licensing authority could have done for the purposes of verifying a statement made in an application for a licence.

(8) In distributing a medicinal product by way of wholesale dealing, the licence holder must comply with regulations 43(1), (2) and (5) and 44 (4) and (6) as if the licence holder were the holder of a wholesale dealer's licence.

## Obligation to provide information relating to control methods

**40** (1) This regulation applies in relation to any manufacturer's licence.

(2) The licensing authority may require the licence holder to provide the authority with proof of the control methods employed by the holder in relation to a medicinal product.

## Requirements as to qualified persons

**41** (1) This regulation applies in relation to any manufacturer's licence.

(2) The licence holder must ensure that there is at the disposal of the holder at all times at least one qualified person who is responsible for

carrying out, in relation to medicinal products manufactured, assembled or imported under the licence, the duties specified in Part 3 of Schedule 7.

(3) If the licence holder satisfies the requirements of Part 1 or 2 of Schedule 7 the licence holder may act as a qualified person.

(4) A qualified person may be treated by the licence holder as satisfying the requirements of Part 1 or 2 of Schedule 7 if that person produces evidence that he or she:

(a) is a member of a body specified in paragraph (5); and

(b) is regarded by that body as satisfying those requirements.

(5) Those bodies are:

(a) the Society of Biology;

(b) the Royal Pharmaceutical Society;

(c) the Pharmaceutical Society of Northern Ireland;

(d) the Royal Society of Chemistry; and

(e) such other body as may be specified by the licensing authority for the purpose of this paragraph.

(6) Where the qualified person changes, the licence holder must give the licensing authority advance notification of:

(a) that change; and

(b) the name, address and qualifications of the new qualified person.

(7) The licence holder must not permit any person to act as a qualified person other than the person named in the licence or another person notified to the licensing authority under paragraph (6).

(8) Paragraph (9) applies if the licensing authority thinks, after giving the licence holder and a person acting as a qualified person the opportunity to make representations (orally or in writing), that the person:

(a) does not satisfy the requirements of Part 1 or 2 of Schedule 7 in relation to qualifications or experience;

(b) does not satisfy paragraph (b) of the definition of "qualified person" in regulation 8; or

(c) is failing to carry out the duties referred to in paragraph (2) adequately or at all.

(9) Where this paragraph applies, the licensing authority must notify the licence holder in writing that the person is not permitted to act as a qualified person.

(10) The licence holder must at all times provide and maintain such staff, premises and equipment as are necessary to enable the qualified person to carry out the duties referred to in paragraph (2).

(11) The licence holder is not obliged to meet the requirements of this regulation in relation to any activity under the licence which relates to special medicinal products or to products authorised on a

temporary basis under regulation 174 (supply in response to spread of pathogenic agents etc).

## Schedule 4 Standard Provisions of Licences

### PART 1 Manufacturer's licence relating to manufacture and assembly

1   The provisions of this Part are standard provisions of a manufacturer's licence relating to the manufacture or assembly of medicinal products.

2   The licence holder must place the quality control system referred to in Article 11(1) of the Good Manufacturing Practice Directive under the authority of the person notified to the licensing authority in accordance with paragraph 1(2)(g) of Schedule 3.

3   The licence holder may use a contract laboratory pursuant to Article 11(2) of the Good Manufacturing Practice Directive if the laboratory is operated by a person approved by the licensing authority.

4   The licence holder must provide such information as may be requested by the licensing authority:

   (a) about the products currently being manufactured or assembled by the licence holder; and

   (b) about the operations being carried out in relation to such manufacture or assembly.

5   The licence holder must inform the licensing authority of any change that the licence holder proposes to make to a person named in the licence as:

   (a) the person whose duty it is to supervise the manufacturing or assembling operations;

   (b) in charge of the animals from which are derived substances used in the production of the medicinal products being manufactured or assembled; or

   (c) responsible for the culture of living tissues used in the manufacture of the medicinal products being manufactured or assembled.

6   The licence holder must:

   (a) keep readily available for inspection by a person authorised by the licensing authority the batch documentation referred to in Article 9(1) of the Good Manufacturing Practice Directive; and

   (b) permit the authorised person to take copies or make extracts from such documentation.

7   The licence holder must keep readily available for examination by a person authorised by the licensing authority the samples in each batch of finished

medicinal product referred to in Article 11(4) of the Good Manufacturing Practice Directive.

8    Where the licence holder has been informed by the licensing authority that the strength, quality or purity of a batch of a medicinal product to which the licence relates has been found not to conform with:

(a) the specification for the finished product; or
(b) the provisions of these Regulations applicable to the medicinal product,

the holder must, if so directed, withhold the batch from distribution, so far as reasonably practicable, for a period (not exceeding six weeks) specified by the licensing authority.

9    The licence holder must ensure that tests for determining conformity with the standards and specifications applying to a product used in the manufacture of a medicinal product must, except so far as the conditions of the product specification for that product otherwise provide, be applied to samples taken from the medicinal product after all manufacturing processes have been completed, or at such earlier stage of the manufacture as may be approved by the licensing authority.

10   Where the manufacturer's licence relates to the assembly of a medicinal product or class of product, and the licence holder supplies the product at such a stage of assembly that does not fully comply with the provisions of the product specification which relate to labelling, the licence holder must communicate the particulars of those provisions to the person to whom that product has been supplied.

11   Where:

(a) the manufacturer's licence relates to the assembly of a medicinal product;
(b) the medicinal product is not manufactured by the licence holder; and
(c) particulars of the name and address of the manufacturer of the product, or the person who imports the product, have been given by the licence holder to the licensing authority,

the licence holder must immediately notify the licensing authority in writing of any changes in the particulars.

12   The licence holder must keep readily available for examination by a person authorised by the licensing authority durable records of the details of the manufacture of intermediate products held by the licence holder for use in the manufacture of biological medicinal products, and the records must:

(a) be in such form as to ensure that the licence holder has a comprehensive record of all matters that are relevant to an evaluation of the safety, quality and efficacy of a finished biological medicinal product manufactured using those intermediate products; and

(b) not be destroyed without the consent of the licensing authority until the records of the details of manufacture of finished medicinal products which were or may be manufactured using those intermediate products may be destroyed in accordance with the requirements of these Regulations.

13   Where:

(a) animals are used in the production of medicinal products; and
(b) a marketing authorisation, Article 126a authorisation, certificate of registration or traditional herbal registration contains provisions relating to them,

the manufacturer's licence holder must arrange for the animals to be housed in such premises, and managed in such a manner, as facilitates compliance with those provisions.

14   The licence holder must take all reasonable precautions and exercise all due diligence to ensure that any information provided to the licensing authority is not false or misleading in any material particular if:

(a) it relates to a medicinal product which the licence holder manufactures or assembles; or
(b) it relates to any starting materials or intermediate products held by the licence holder which are for use in the manufacture of medicinal products.

## PART 2 Manufacturer's licence relating to the import of medicinal products from a state other than an EEA State

15   The provisions of this Part are standard provisions of a manufacturer's licence relating to the import of medicinal products from a state other than an EEA State.

16   The licence holder must place the quality control system referred to in Article 11(1) of the Good Manufacturing Practice Directive under the authority of the person notified to the licensing authority in accordance with paragraph 2(2)(h) of Schedule 3.

17   The licence holder may use a contract laboratory pursuant to Article 11(2) of the Good Manufacturing Practice Directive if operated by a person approved by the licensing authority.

18    The licence holder must provide such information as may be requested by the licensing authority concerning the type and quantity of any medicinal products which the licence holder imports.

19    The licence holder must:

(a) keep readily available for inspection by a person authorised by the licensing authority the batch documentation referred to in Article 9(1) of the Good Manufacturing Practice Directive; and

(b) permit the person authorised to take copies or make extracts from such documentation.

20    Where the licence holder has been informed by the licensing authority that the strength, quality or purity of a batch of a medicinal product to which the licence relates has been found not to conform with:

(a) the specification of the medicinal product in question; or

(b) those provisions of these Regulations that are applicable to the medicinal product,

the licence holder must, if so directed, withhold the batch from distribution, so far as reasonably practicable, for such a period (not exceeding six weeks) as may be specified by the licensing authority.

21    The licence holder must ensure that any tests for determining conformity with the standards and specifications applying to any ingredient used in the manufacture of a medicinal product must, except so far as the conditions of the product specification for that ingredient otherwise provide, be applied to samples taken from the medicinal product after all manufacturing processes have been completed, or at such earlier stage in the manufacture as may be approved by the licensing authority.

22    (1) Where and in so far as the licence relates to special medicinal products, the licence holder may only import such products from a state other than an EEA State:

(a) in response to an order which satisfies the requirements of regulation 167 (supply to fulfil special patient needs); and

(b) where the conditions set out in sub-paragraphs (2) to (9) are complied with.

(2) No later than 28 days before the day on which each importation of a special medicinal product takes place, the licence holder must give written notice to the licensing authority stating the intention to import the product and stating the following particulars:

(a) the brand name, common name or scientific name of the medicinal product and (if different) any name under which the medicinal product is to be sold or supplied in the United Kingdom;

(b) any trademark or the name of the manufacturer of the medicinal product;

(c) in respect of each active constituent of the medicinal product, any international non-proprietary name or the British approved name or the monograph name, or where that constituent does not have any of those, the accepted scientific name or any other name descriptive of the true nature of the constituent;

(d) the quantity of medicinal product to be imported, which must not exceed the quantity specified in sub-paragraph (6); and

(e) the name and address of the manufacturer or assembler of the medicinal product in the form in which it is to be imported and, if the person who will supply the medicinal product for importation is not the manufacturer or assembler, the name and address of the supplier.

(3) The licence holder may not import the special medicinal product if, before the end of 28 days beginning immediately after the date on which the licensing authority sends or gives the licence holder an acknowledgement in writing by the licensing authority that it has received the notice referred to in sub-paragraph (2), the licensing authority has notified the licence holder in writing that the product should not be imported.

(4) The licence holder may import the special medicinal product referred to in the notice where the licence holder has been notified in writing by the licensing authority, before the end of the 28-day period referred to in sub-paragraph (3) that the product may be imported.

(5) Where the licence holder sells or supplies special medicinal products, the licence holder must, in addition to any other records which are required by the provisions of the licence, make and maintain written records relating to:

(a) the batch number of the batch of the product from which the sale or supply was made; and

(b) details of any adverse reaction to the product sold or supplied of which the licence holder becomes aware.

(6) The licence holder must not, on any one occasion, import more than such amount as is sufficient for 25 single administrations, or for 25 courses of treatment where the amount imported is sufficient for a maximum of three months' treatment, and must not, on any one occasion, import more than the quantity notified to the licensing authority under sub-paragraph (2)(d).

(7) The licence holder must not publish any advertisement, catalogue or circular relating to a special medicinal product or make any representations in respect of that product.

(8) The licence holder must inform the licensing authority immediately of any matter coming to the licence holder's attention which might

reasonably cause the licensing authority to believe that a special medicinal product imported in accordance with this paragraph can no longer be regarded as a product which can safely be administered to human beings or as a product which is of satisfactory quality for such administration.

(9) The licence holder must cease importing or supplying a special medicinal product if the licence holder receives a notice in writing from the licensing authority directing that, from a date specified in the notice, a particular product or class of products may no longer be imported or supplied.

(10) In this paragraph:

"British approved name" means the name which appears in the current edition of the list prepared by the British Pharmacopoeia Commission under regulation 318 (British Pharmacopoeia: lists of names);

"international non-proprietary name" means a name which has been selected by the World Health Organisation as a recommended international non-proprietary name and in respect of which the Director-General of the World Health Organisation has given notice to that effect in the World Health Organisation Chronicle; and

"monograph name" means the name or approved synonym which appears at the head of a monograph in the current edition of the British Pharmacopoeia, the European Pharmacopoeia or a foreign or international compendium of standards and "current" in this definition means current at the time the notice is sent to the licensing authority.

23    The licence holder must take all reasonable precautions and exercise due diligence to ensure that any information provided to the licensing authority which is relevant to an evaluation of the safety, quality or efficacy of a medicinal product for human use which is imported from a state other than an EEA State, handled, stored or distributed under the licence is not false or misleading in a material particular.

## PART 3 Manufacturer's licence relating to exempt advanced therapy medicinal products

24    The provisions of paragraphs 25 to 27 are incorporated as additional standard provisions of a manufacturer's licence relating to the manufacture and assembly of exempt advanced therapy medicinal products.

25    The licence holder must ensure that the immediate packaging of an exempt advanced therapy medicinal product is labelled to show the following particulars:

(a) the name of the exempt advanced therapy medicinal product;

(b) the expiry date in clear terms including the year and month and, if applicable, the day;

(c) a description of the active substance, expressed qualitatively and quantitatively;

(d) where the product contains cells or tissues of human or animal origin:

(i) a statement that the product contains such cells or tissues, and

(ii) a short description of the cells or tissues and of their specific origin;

(e) the pharmaceutical form and the contents by weight, volume or number of doses of the product;

(f) a list of excipients, including preservative systems;

(g) the method of use, application, administration or implantation and, if appropriate, the route of administration, with space provided for the prescribed dose to be indicated;

(h) any special storage precautions;

(i) specific precautions relating to the disposal of the unused product or waste derived from the product and, where appropriate, reference to any appropriate collection system;

(j) the name and address of the holder of the manufacturer's licence;

(k) the manufacturer's licence number;

(l) the manufacturer's batch number;

(m) the unique donation code referred to in Article 8(2) of Directive 2004/23/EC; and

(n) where the exempt advanced therapy medicinal product is for autologous use, the unique patient identifier and the words "for autologous use only".

26    The licence holder must ensure that the package leaflet of the exempt advanced therapy medicinal product shall include the following particulars:

(a) the name of the exempt advanced therapy medicinal product;

(b) the intended effect of the medicinal product if correctly used, applied, administered or implanted;

(c) where the product contains cells or tissues of human or animal origin:

(i) a statement that the product contains such cells or tissues, and

(ii) a short description of the cells or tissues and, where such cells or tissues are of animal origin, their specific origin;

(d) where the product contains a medical device or an active implantable medical device, a description of that device and, where that device contains cells or tissues of animal origin, their specific origin;

(e) any necessary instructions for use, including:

(i) the posology,

(ii) the method of use, application, administration or implantation and, if appropriate, the route of administration,

(iii) a description of symptoms of overdose,

(iv) action to be taken in the event of overdose, including any emergency procedures,

(v) action to be taken if one or more doses have been missed, and

(vi) a recommendation to consult the doctor or pharmacist for any clarification on the use of the product;

(f) where adverse reactions are known, a description of those which may occur under recommended conditions of use of the product and, if appropriate, an indication of action to be taken in such a case;

(g) an instruction that the patient report any adverse reaction not specified in the package leaflet to the doctor or pharmacist;

(h) the expiry date in clear terms and a warning against using the product after that date;

(i) any special storage precautions;

(j) a description of any visible signs of deterioration;

(k) a complete qualitative and quantitative composition;

(l) the name and address of the holder of the manufacturer's licence; and

(m) the date on which the package leaflet was last revised.

27 The licence holder must keep the data referred to in paragraph 8 of Schedule 6 for such period, being a period of longer than 30 years, as may be specified by the licensing authority.

## Schedule 6 Manufacturer's and Wholesale Dealer's Licences for Exempt Advanced Therapy Medicinal Products

## PART 1 Manufacturer's licences

1 The requirements in paragraphs 2 to 12 apply to a manufacturer's licence insofar as it relates to the manufacture and assembly of exempt advanced therapy medicinal products.

2 The licence holder must inform the licensing authority of any adverse reaction or suspected adverse reaction of which the holder is aware within the period of 15 days beginning on the day following the first day on which the holder knew about the reaction.

3 The licence holder must ensure, if using human cells or tissues in an exempt advanced therapy medicinal product, that the donation, procurement and testing of those cells or tissues is in accordance with Directive 2004/23/EC.

4 The licence holder must ensure that any human tissue or cell component imported into the United Kingdom and used by the holder as a starting material or raw material in the manufacture of an exempt advanced therapy medicinal product shall meet equivalent standards of quality and safety to those laid down in:

(a) Commission Directive 2006/17/EC of 8 February 2006 implementing Directive 2004/23/EC of the European Parliament and of the Council as regards certain technical requirements for the donation, procurement and testing of human tissues and cells[4]; and

(b) Commission Directive 2006/86/EC of 24 October 2006 implementing Directive 2004/23/EC of the European Parliament and of the Council as regards traceability requirements, notification of serious adverse reactions and events and certain technical requirements for the coding, processing, preservation, storage and distribution of human tissues and cells[5].

**5**   The licence holder must ensure that any blood or blood component imported into the United Kingdom and used by the manufacturer's licence holder as a starting material or raw material in the manufacture of an exempt advanced therapy medicinal product meets equivalent standards of quality and safety to those laid down in Commission Directive 2004/33/EC of 22 March 2004 implementing Directive 2002/98/EC of the European Parliament and of the Council as regards certain technical requirements for blood and blood components[6].

**6**   Where the holder of a manufacturer's licence distributes by way of wholesale dealing any exempt advanced therapy medicinal product manufactured or assembled pursuant to the licence that person must comply with:

(a) the requirements of paragraphs 15, 16, 18 and 19; and

(b) the guidelines on good distribution practice published by the European Commission in accordance with Article 84 of the 2001 Directive;

as if that person were the holder of a wholesale dealer's licence.

**7**   The licence holder must, at the written request of the licensing authority, set up a risk management system designed to identify, characterise, prevent or minimise risks related to the exempt advanced therapy medicinal product.

**8**   The licence holder must establish and maintain a system ensuring that the exempt advanced therapy medicinal product and its starting and raw materials, including all substances coming into contact with the cells or tissues it may contain, can be traced through the sourcing, manufacturing, packaging, storage, transport and delivery to the establishment where the product is used.

---

[4]  OJ No L 38, 9.2.2006, p. 40.

[5]  OJ No L 294, 25.10.2006, p. 32.

[6]  OJ No L 91, 30.3.2004, p. 25, as amended by Commission Directive 2011/38/EU, OJ No L 94, 12.4.2011, p. 28.

9    The licence holder must, subject to paragraph 27 of Schedule 4, keep the data referred to in paragraph 8 for a minimum of 30 years after the expiry date of the exempt advanced therapy medicinal product.

10   The licence holder must secure that the data referred to in paragraph 8 will, in the event that:

(a) the licence is suspended, revoked or withdrawn; or
(b) the licence holder becomes bankrupt or insolvent,

be held available to the licensing authority by the holder of a manufacturer's licence for the period described in paragraph 9 or such longer period as may be required pursuant to paragraph 27 of Schedule 4.

11   The licence holder must, where an exempt advanced therapy medicinal product contains human cells or tissues, ensure that the traceability system established in accordance with paragraph 8 is complementary to and compatible with the requirements laid down in:

(a) Articles 8 and 14 of Directive 2004/23/EC as regards human cells and tissues other than blood cells, and
(b) as regards human blood cells, Articles 14 and 24 of Directive 2002/98/EC.

12   The licence holder must not import or export any exempt advanced therapy medicinal product.

## Schedule 7 Qualified Persons

### PART 1 Qualification requirements for qualified person

1    A person must satisfy the requirements in paragraphs 2 and 8 or, alternatively, the requirements in paragraphs 7 and 8, of this Schedule before acting as a qualified person (but this is subject to Part 2).

2    The person must have a degree, diploma or other formal qualification which satisfies the requirements of this Part, in one of the following subjects:

(a) pharmacy;
(b) medicine;
(c) veterinary medicine;
(d) chemistry;
(e) pharmaceutical chemistry and technology; or
(f) biology,

but this paragraph is subject to paragraph 7.

**3** A qualification satisfies the requirements of this Part if it is awarded on completion of a university course of study, or a course recognised as equivalent by the member State in which it is studied, which:

(a) satisfies the minimum requirements specified in paragraph 4; and
(b) extends over a period of at least four years of theoretical and practical study of a subject specified in paragraph 2 (but this is subject to paragraphs 5 and 6).

**4** (1) A course should include at least the following core subjects:
(a) experimental physics;
(b) general and inorganic chemistry;
(c) organic chemistry;
(d) analytical chemistry;
(e) pharmaceutical chemistry, including analysis of medicinal products;
(f) general and applied medical biochemistry;
(g) physiology;
(h) microbiology;
(i) pharmacology;
(j) pharmaceutical technology;
(k) toxicology; and
(l) pharmacognosy.
(2) The subjects mentioned in sub-paragraph (1) should be balanced in such a way as to enable the person to fulfil the obligations specified in Part 3 of this Schedule.

**5** If the course referred to in paragraph 3 is followed by a period of theoretical and practical training of at least one year, including a training period of at least six months in a pharmacy open to the public and a final examination at university level, the minimum duration of the course is three and a half years.

**6** If two university courses, or courses recognised as of university equivalent standard, co-exist, one of which extends over four years and the other over three years, the three-year course is to be treated as fulfilling the condition as to the duration of the course in paragraph 3, provided that the member State in which the courses take place recognises the formal qualifications gained from each course as being equivalent.

**7** If the person's formal qualifications do not satisfy the requirements of this Part, the person may act as a qualified person if the licensing authority is satisfied, on the production of evidence, that the person has adequate knowledge of the subjects specified in paragraph 4(1).

8  (1)  The person must (subject to sub-paragraph (2)) have at least two years' practical experience in an undertaking authorised to manufacture medicinal products of:
   (a)  qualitative analysis of medicinal products;
   (b)  quantitative analysis of active substances; and
   (c)  the testing and checking necessary to ensure the quality of medicinal products.

   (2)  But:
   (a)  if the person has completed a university course lasting at least five years, the minimum period of practical experience under this paragraph is one year; and
   (b)  if the person has completed a university course lasting at least six years, the minimum period of practical experience under this paragraph is six months.

## PART 2 Qualified persons with long experience

9  (1)  This paragraph applies to a person who has acted as a qualified person since the coming into force of Directive 75/319/EEC of 20 May 1975 on the approximation of provisions laid down by law, regulation or administrative action relating to proprietary medicinal products[7].

   (2)  A person to whom this paragraph applies may continue to act as a qualified person.

10  (1)  This paragraph applies to a person who:
   (a)  holds a degree, diploma or other formal qualification in a scientific discipline awarded on completion of a university course or course recognised as equivalent; and
   (b)  began the course before 21 May 1975.

   (2)  A person to whom this paragraph applies may act as a qualified person provided that sub-paragraph (3) (and, where applicable, paragraph 11) is satisfied.

   (3)  This sub-paragraph is satisfied if, for at least two years before 21 May 1985, the person has carried out one of the following activities in an undertaking authorised to manufacture medicinal products:
   (a)  production supervision;
   (b)  qualitative and quantitative analysis of active substances; or
   (c)  testing and checking, under the direct supervision of the qualified person in respect of the undertaking, to ensure the quality of the medicinal products.

---

[7] OJ No L 147, 9.6.1975, p. 13, no longer in force.

11    If a person to whom paragraph 10 applies acquired the practical experience mentioned in paragraph 10(3) before 21 May 1965, the person must complete a further one year's practical experience of the kind specified in that paragraph immediately before the person may act as a qualified person.

## PART 3 Obligations of qualified person

12    The qualified person is responsible for securing:

(a) that each batch of medicinal products manufactured in the United Kingdom has been manufactured and checked in accordance with these Regulations and the requirements of the marketing authorisation, Article 126a authorisation, certificate of registration or traditional herbal registration relating to those products; and

(b) in the case of medicinal products imported from a non-EEA State, irrespective of whether the products have been manufactured in an EEA State, that each batch has undergone:

(i)   a full qualitative analysis,

(ii)  a quantitative analysis of all the active substances, and

(iii) all other tests or checks necessary to ensure the quality of medicinal products in accordance with the requirements of the marketing authorisation, Article 126a authorisation, certificate of registration or traditional herbal registration relating to those products.

13  (1)  This paragraph applies where:

(a) a medicinal product which has undergone the controls referred to in paragraph 12 in another member State is imported to the United Kingdom; and

(b) each batch of the product is accompanied by control reports signed by another qualified person in respect of the medicinal product.

(2)  Where this paragraph applies, the qualified person is not responsible for carrying out the controls referred to in paragraph 12.

14  (1)  This paragraph applies where:

(a) medicinal products are imported from a country other than an EEA State; and

(b) appropriate arrangements have been made by the European Union with that country to ensure that:

(i)   the manufacturer of the medicinal products applies standards of good manufacturing practice at least equivalent to those laid down by the European Union, and

(ii)  the controls referred to in paragraph 12(b) have been carried out in that country.

(2)   Where this paragraph applies, the qualified person is not responsible for carrying out the controls referred to in paragraph 12.

15   (1)   The qualified person is responsible for ensuring, in relation to a medicinal product, that documentary evidence is produced that each batch of the product satisfies the requirements of paragraph 12.

    (2)   The documentary evidence referred to in sub-paragraph (1) must be kept up to date and must be available for inspection by the licensing authority for a period of at least five years.

## Prescribed Conditions for Manufacturer's Undertakings for Imported Products

### Accompanying material

50   (1)   An applicant for the grant of a UK marketing authorisation for a relevant medicinal product must provide the material specified in Schedule 8 in relation to the product.

    (2)   An applicant for the grant of a UK marketing authorisation for a radionuclide generator must, in addition, provide:
    (a)   a general description of the system together with a detailed description of the components of the system which may affect the composition or quality of the daughter nucleid preparation; and
    (b)   qualitative and quantitative particulars of the eluate or the sublimate.

    (3)   The applicant must also, if requested by the licensing authority to do so, provide the licensing authority with material or information that the licensing authority reasonably considers necessary for dealing with the application.

    (4)   If any of the medicinal products to which the application relates is liable to be imported from a country other than an EEA State, the material or information referred to in paragraph (3) may include an undertaking from the manufacturer of the product to comply with the matters set out in Schedule 9.

    (5)   Material that is submitted under this regulation must be submitted in accordance with the applicable provisions of Annex I to the 2001 Directive.

    (6)   This regulation is subject to:
    (a)   regulation 51 (applications relating to generic medicinal products);
    (b)   regulation 52 (applications relating to certain medicinal products that do not qualify as generic etc);

(c) regulation 53 (applications relating to certain biological medicinal products);

(d) regulation 54 (applications relating to products in well-established medicinal use);

(e) regulation 55 (applications relating to new combinations of active substances);

(f) regulation 56 (applications containing information supplied in relation to another medicinal product with consent); and

(g) Schedule 10 (applications relating to national homoeopathic products).

## Schedule 9 Undertakings by non-EEA Manufacturers

1   The manufacturer must provide and maintain such staff, premises and plant as are necessary for the carrying out in accordance with the marketing authorisation of such stages of the manufacture and assembly of the medicinal products to which the authorisation relates as are undertaken by the manufacturer.

2   The manufacturer must provide and maintain such staff, premises, equipment and facilities for the handling, storage and distribution of the medicinal products to which the marketing authorisation relates and which the manufacturer handles, stores or distributes as are necessary to avoid deterioration of the medicinal products.

3   The manufacturer must provide and maintain a designated quality control department having authority in relation to quality control and being independent of all other departments.

4   The manufacturer must conduct all manufacture and assembly operations in such a way as to ensure that the medicinal products to which the marketing authorisation relates conform with the standards of strength, quality and purity applicable to them under the marketing authorisation.

5   The manufacturer must maintain an effective pharmaceutical quality assurance system involving the active participation of the management and personnel of the different services involved.

6   Where animals are used in the production of any medicinal product and the marketing authorisation contains provisions relating to them the manufacturer must arrange for the animals to be housed in premises of such a nature and to be managed in such a way as will facilitate compliance with such provisions.

7   The manufacturer must make such adequate and suitable arrangements as are necessary for carrying out in accordance with the marketing

authorisation any tests of the strength, quality or purity of the medicinal products to which the marketing authorisation relates.

8    The manufacturer must inform the holder of the marketing authorisation of any material alteration in the premises or plant used in connection with the manufacture or assembly of the medicinal products to which the marketing authorisation relates or in the operations for which such premises or plant are so used, and of any change since the granting of the relevant marketing authorisation in respect of any person:

(a) responsible for supervising the production operations;
(b) responsible for quality control of the medicinal products to which the marketing authorisation relates;
(c) in charge of the animals from which are derived any substance used in the production of the medicinal products to which the marketing authorisation relates; or
(d) responsible for the culture of any living tissues used in the manufacture of the medicinal products to which the marketing authorisation relates.

9    (1) The manufacturer shall keep readily available for inspection by a person authorised by the licensing authority durable records of:
        (a) the details of manufacture and assembly of each batch of the medicinal product to which the marketing authorisation relates; and
        (b) the tests carried out on the product,
in such a form that the records will be easily identifiable from the number of the batch as shown on each container in which the medicinal product is exported from the country where it has been manufactured or assembled.
    (2) The manufacturer shall permit the person authorised to take copies of or make extracts from such records.
    (3) Such records shall not be destroyed for a period of five years from the date of release of the batch concerned, or one year after the expiry date of the batch, whichever is the later.

10   The manufacturer must keep readily available for examination by a person authorised by the licensing authority samples of:

(a) each batch of finished products for at least a period of one year after their expiry date; and
(b) starting materials (other than solvents, gases or water) for at least a period of two years after release of the medicinal product of which those materials formed part,

except where the manufacturer is authorised by the licensing authority to destroy such samples earlier.

**11** **(1)** The manufacturer must implement a system for recording and reviewing complaints in relation to medicinal products to which a marketing authorisation relates, together with an effective system for recalling promptly and at any time the medicinal products in the distribution network.

**(2)** The manufacturer must record and investigate all complaints described in sub-paragraph (1) and must immediately inform the licensing authority of any defect which could result in a recall from sale, supply or export or in an abnormal restriction on such sale, supply or export.

**12** The manufacturer must inform the holder of the marketing authorisation of any material change since the day upon which the authorisation was granted in respect of:

**(a)** the facilities and equipment available at each of the premises of the manufacturer for carrying out any stage of the manufacture or assembly of the medicinal products to which the marketing authorisation relates;

**(b)** the facilities and equipment available at each of the premises of the manufacturer for the storage of the medicinal products to which the marketing authorisation relates on, and the distribution of the products from or between, such premises;

**(c)** any manufacturing operations, not being operations in relation to the medicinal products to which the marketing authorisation relates, which are carried on by the manufacturer on or near any of the premises on which medicinal products to which the marketing authorisation relates are manufactured or assembled, and the substances or articles in respect of which such operations are carried on;

**(d)** the arrangements for the identification and storage of materials and ingredients before and during manufacture or assembly of the medicinal products to which the marketing authorisation relates and the arrangements for the storage of the products after they have been manufactured or assembled;

**(e)** the arrangements for ensuring a satisfactory turnover of stocks of medicinal products to which the marketing authorisation relates;

**(f)** the arrangements for maintaining production records and records of analytical and other testing procedures applied in the course of manufacture or assembly of the medicinal products to which the marketing authorisation relates; or

**(g)** the arrangements for keeping reference samples of materials used in the manufacture of the medicinal products to which the marketing authorisation relates and reference samples of the medicinal products themselves.

# UK Legislation on the Manufacture, Importation and Distribution of Active Substances

## Contents

## The Human Medicines Regulations 2012 (SI 2012/1916)

| | |
|---|---|
| Editor's note | These extracts from the Human Medicines Regulations 2012 [SI 2012/1916] as amended by the Human Medicines (Amendment) Regulations 2013 [SI 2013/1855] are presented for the reader's convenience. Reproduction is with the permission of HMSO and the Queen's Printer for Scotland. For any definitive information reference must be made to the original Regulations. The numbering and content within this section corresponds with the regulations set out in the published Statutory Instrument (SI 2012 No. 1916) as amended. |

## Citation and commencement

1   (1)   These Regulations may be cited as the Human Medicines Regulations 2012.

   (2)   These Regulations come into force on 14th August 2012.

## General interpretation

8　(1)　In these Regulations (unless the context otherwise requires)-

"active substance" means any substance or mixture of substances intended to be used in the manufacture of a medicinal product and that, when used in its production, becomes an active ingredient of that product intended to exert a pharmacological, immunological or metabolic action with a view to restoring, correcting or modifying physiological functions or to make a medical diagnosis;

"assemble", in relation to a medicinal product or an active substance, includes the various processes of dividing up, packaging and presentation of the product or substance, and "assembly" has a corresponding meaning;

"excipient" means any constituent of a medicinal product other than the active substance and the packaging material;

"export" means export, or attempt to export, from the United Kingdom, whether by land, sea or air;

"falsified medicinal product" means any medicinal product with a false representation of:

(a) its identity, including its packaging and labelling, its name or its composition (other than any unintentional quality defect) as regards any of its ingredients including excipients and the strength of those ingredients;

(b) its source, including its manufacturer, its country of manufacturing, its country of origin or its marketing authorisation holder; or

(c) its history, including the records and documents relating to the distribution channels used;

"import" means import, or attempt to import, into the United Kingdom, whether by land, sea or air;

(8)　References in these Regulations to:

(a) good manufacturing practice for active substances relate to the principles and guidelines for good manufacturing practice adopted by the European Commission under the third paragraph of Article 47[1] of the 2001 Directive;

(b) good distribution practice for active substances relate to the guidelines on good distribution practices for active substances adopted by the European Commission under the fourth paragraph of Article 47 of the 2001 Directive.

---

[1] Paragraphs 3 and 4 of Article 47 were substituted by Directive 2011/62/EU of the European Parliament and of the Council (OJ No L 174, 1.7.2011, p74).

## Chapter 1 Manufacture and distribution of medicinal products and active substances

INTERPRETATION

**A17.** In this Part "manufacture", in relation to an active substance, includes any process carried out in the course of making the substance and the various processes of dividing up, packaging, and presentation of the active substance.

## Chapter 4 Importation, manufacture and distribution of active substances

CRITERIA FOR IMPORTATION, MANUFACTURE OR DISTRIBUTION OF ACTIVE SUBSTANCES

**45M.** (1) A person may not:
(a) import;
(b) manufacture; or
(c) distribute,
an active substance unless that person is registered with the licensing authority in accordance with regulation 45N and the requirements in regulation 45O are met.

(2) Paragraph (1) applies in relation to an active substance which is to be used in an investigational medicinal product only:
(a) if the product has a marketing authorisation, Article 126a authorisation, certificate of registration or traditional herbal registration; and
(b) to the extent that the manufacture of the active substance is in accordance with the terms and conditions of that authorisation, certificate or registration.

(3) Paragraph (1)(a) does not apply to a person who, in connection with the importation of an active substance from a state other than an EEA state:
(a) provides facilities solely for transporting the active substance; or
(b) acting as an import agent, imports the active substance solely to the order of another person who holds a certificate of good manufacturing practice issued by the licensing authority.

## Registration in relation to active substances

**45N.** (1) For registration in relation to active substances, the licensing authority must have received a valid registration form from the applicant for import, manufacture or, as the case may be, distribution of the active substance and:

(a) 60 days have elapsed since receipt and the licensing authority have not notified the applicant that an inspection will be carried out; or

(b) the licensing authority:

    (i) notified the applicant within 60 days of receipt of a registration form that an inspection will be carried out; and

    (ii) within 90 days of that inspection the licensing authority have issued that person with a certificate of good manufacturing practice or, as the case may be, of good distribution practice; and

(c) that person has not instructed the licensing authority to end that person's registration.

(2) The person applying for registration under paragraph (1) must notify the licensing authority of any changes which have taken place as regards the information in the registration form:

(a) immediately where such changes may have an impact on quality or safety of the active substances that are manufactured, imported or distributed;

(b) in any other case, on each anniversary of the receipt of the application form by the licensing authority.

(3) For the purpose of paragraph (2), changes which are notified in accordance with that paragraph shall be treated as incorporated in the application form.

(4) Any notification to the licensing authority under paragraph (2) must be accompanied by the appropriate fee in accordance with the Fees Regulations.

(5) A registration form is valid for the purpose of paragraph (1) if:

(a) it is provided to the licensing authority; and

(b) is completed in the way and form specified in Schedule 7A.

(6) Paragraph (1) does not apply until 20th October 2013 in relation to a person who had, before 20th August 2013, commenced the activity for which the person would, apart from this provision, need to send a registration form to the licensing authority.

## Requirements for registration as an importer, manufacturer or distributor of an active substance

**45O.** (1) Where the Commission has adopted principles and guidelines of good manufacturing practice under the third paragraph of Article 47[2] of the 2001 Directive which applies to an active substance manufactured in the UK, the manufacturer must comply with good manufacturing practice in relation to that active substance.

---

[2] Article 47 was amended by Directive 2011/62/EU of the European Parliament and of the Council (OJ No L 174, 1.7.2011, p74).

(2)   Where the Commission has adopted principles and guidelines of good distribution practice under the fourth paragraph of Article 47 of the 2001 Directive which applies to an active substance distributed in the United Kingdom, the distributor must comply with good distribution practice in relation to that active substance.

(3)   Without prejudice to regulation 37(4) (manufacture and assembly in relation to active substances) and paragraph 9A of Schedule 8 (material to accompany an application for a UK marketing authorisation in relation to an active substance), where the Commission has adopted principles and guidelines of good manufacturing practice under the third paragraph of Article 47 of the 2001 Directive which applies to an active substance imported into the UK and where an active substance is imported from a third country:

   (a)  the importer must comply with good manufacturing practice and good distribution practice in relation to the active substance;

   (b)  the active substances must have been manufactured in accordance with standards which are at least equivalent to good manufacturing practice; and

   (c)  the active substances must be accompanied by a written confirmation from the competent authority of the exporting third country of the following:

      (i)   the standards of manufacturing practice applicable to the plant manufacturing the exported active substance are at least equivalent to good manufacturing practice,

      (ii)  the manufacturing plant concerned is subject to regular, strict and transparent controls and to the effective enforcement of standards of manufacturing practice at least equivalent to good manufacturing practice, including repeated and unannounced inspections, so as to ensure a protection of public health at least equivalent to that in the Union, and

      (iii) in the event of findings relating to non-compliance, information on such findings is supplied by the exporting third country to the Union without any delay.

(4)   Paragraph (3)(c) does not apply:

   (a)  where the country from where the active substance is exported is included in the list referred to in Article 111b of the 2001 Directive; or

   (b)  for a period not exceeding the validity of the certificate of good manufacturing practice, where:

      (i)   in relation to a plant where active substances are manufactured where the competent authority of a member State has found, upon inspection, that a plant complies with the principles and guidelines of good manufacturing practice, and

       (ii) the licensing authority is of the opinion that it is necessary to waive the requirement to ensure availability of the active substance.

(5) The criteria in this regulation apply regardless of whether an active substance is intended for export.

## Provision of information

45P. (1) In this regulation:

"R" means a person who is, or has applied to the licensing authority to become, a registered importer, manufacturer or distributor of active substances;

"reporting year" means a period of twelve months ending on 31st March.

(2) On or before the date specified in paragraph (3), R must submit a report to the licensing authority which:

    (a) includes a declaration that R has in place an appropriate system to ensure compliance with regulations 45N, 45O and this regulation; and

    (b) details the system which R has in place to ensure such compliance.

(3) The date specified for the purposes of this paragraph is:

    (a) in relation to any application made before 31st March 2014, the date of the application; and

    (b) in relation to each subsequent reporting year, 30th April following the end of that year.

(4) R must without delay notify the licensing authority of any changes to the matters in respect of which evidence has been supplied in relation to paragraph (2) which might affect compliance with the requirements of this Chapter.

(5) Any report or notification to the licensing authority under paragraph (2) or (4) must be accompanied by the appropriate fee in accordance with the Fees Regulations.

(6) The licensing authority may give a notice to R, requiring R to provide information of a kind specified in the notice within the period specified in the notice.

(7) A notice under paragraph (6) may not be given to R unless it appears to the licensing authority that it is necessary for the licensing authority to consider whether the registration should be varied, suspended or removed from the active substance register.

(8) A notice under paragraph (6) may specify information which the licensing authority thinks necessary for considering whether the registration should be varied, suspended or removed from the active substance register.

UK LEGISLATION ON ACTIVE SUBSTANCES

## Schedule 7A - Information to be provided for registration as an importer, manufacturer or distributor of active substances

(1) The name and address of the applicant.

(2) The name and address of the person (if any) making the application on the applicant's behalf.

(3) The address of each of the premises where any operations to which the registration relates are to be carried out.

(4) The address of any premises not mentioned by virtue of the above requirement, where:

(a) the applicant proposes to keep any living animals, from which substance(s) used in the production of the active substance(s) to which the application relates are to be derived;

(b) materials of animal origin from which an active substance is to be derived, as mentioned in the above sub-paragraph, are to be kept.

(5) The address of each of the premises where active substances are to be stored, or from which active substances are to be distributed.

(6) The address of each of the premises where any testing associated with the manufacture or assembly of active substances to which the registration relates.

(7) The name, address, qualifications and experience of the person whose duty it will be to supervise any manufacturing operations, and the name and job title of the person to whom they report.

(8) The name, address, qualifications and experience of the person who will have responsibility for the quality control of active substances, and the name and job title of the person to whom they report.

(9) The name, address, qualifications and experience of the person whose duty it will be to supervise any importation, storage or distribution operations, and the name and job title of the person to whom they report.

(10) The name, address and qualifications of the person to be responsible for any animals kept as mentioned in paragraph 4(a).

(11) The name, address and qualifications of the person to be responsible for the culture of any living tissue for use in the manufacture of an active substance.

(12) For each active substance to be manufactured, imported, or distributed:

(a) the CAS registration number[3] assigned to that active substance by the Chemical Abstracts Service, a division of the American Chemical Society;

---

[3] Further information is available from the website of the Chemical Abstracts Service at www.cas.org.

(b) where applicable, the Anatomical Therapeutic Category code[4] assigned to that active substance under the Anatomical Therapeutic Chemical Classification System used for the classification of drugs by the World Health Organisation's Collaborating Centre for Drug Statistics Methodology;

(c) either:
    (i) the International Union of Pure and Applied Chemistry nomenclature, or
    (ii) the common name; and

(d) the intended quantities of each active substance to be manufactured, imported or distributed.

(13) Details of the operations to which the registration relates, including a statement of whether they include:
(a) the manufacture of active substances;
(b) the importation of active substances from third countries;
(c) the storage of active substances; or
(d) the distribution of active substances.

(14) A statement of the facilities and equipment available at each of the premises where active substances are to be manufactured, stored or distributed.

(15) A statement as to whether the particular active substances are intended for:
(a) use in a medicinal product with an EU marketing authorisation;
(b) use in a special medicinal product; or
(c) export to a third country.

(16) A separate statement in respect of each of the premises mentioned in the application of:
(a) the manufacturing, storage or distribution operations carried out at those sites, and the specific active substances to which those activities relate; and
(b) the equipment available at those premises for carrying out those activities.

(17) A statement of the authority conferred on the person responsible for quality control to reject unsatisfactory active substances.

(18) A description of the arrangements for the identification and storage of materials before and during the manufacture of active substances.

(19) A description of the arrangements for the identification and storage of active substances.

(20) A description of the arrangements at each of the premises where the applicant proposes to store active substances for ensuring, as far as practicable, the turn-over of stocks of active substances.

---

[4] Further information is available from the website of the WHO Collaborating Centre for Drug Statistics Methodology at www.whocc.no.

(**21**) A description of the arrangements for maintaining:
- (**a**) production records, including records of manufacture and assembly;
- (**b**) records of analytical and other tests used in the course of manufacture or assembly for ensuring compliance of materials used in manufacture, or of active substances, with the specification for such materials or active substances;
- (**c**) records of importation;
- (**d**) records of storage and distribution.

(**22**) A description of the arrangements for keeping reference samples of:
- (**a**) materials used in the manufacture of active substances; and
- (**b**) active substances.

(**23**) Where the application relates to active substances intended for use in an advanced therapy medicinal product, an outline of the arrangements for maintaining records to allow traceability containing sufficient detail to enable the linking of an active substance to the advanced therapy medicinal product it was used in the manufacture of and vice versa.

(**24**) Details of:
- (**a**) any manufacturing, importation, storage or distribution operations, other than those to which the application for registration relates, carried on by the applicant on or near each of the premises, and
- (**b**) the substances or articles to which those operations relate.

# Guidance on Wholesale Distribution Practice and Brokering Medicines

# Guidelines on Good Distribution Practice of Medicinal Products for Human Use (2013/C 343/01)

## Contents

## Guidelines on Good Distribution Practice of Medicinal Products for Human Use (2013/C 343/01)

These Guidelines are based on Article 84 and Article 85b(3) of Directive 2001/83/EC[1].

The Commission has published EU Guidelines on Good Distribution Practice (GDP) in 1994[2]. Revised guidelines were published in March 2013[3] in order to take into account recent advances in practices for appropriate storage and distribution of medicinal products in the European Union, as well as new requirements introduced by Directive 2011/62/EU[4].

This version corrects factual mistakes identified in subchapters 5.5 and 6.3 of the revised guidelines. It also gives more explanations on the rationale for the revision as well as a date of coming into operation.

It replaces the guidelines on GDP published in March 2013.

The wholesale distribution of medicinal products is an important activity in integrated supply chain management. Today's distribution network for medicinal products is increasingly complex and involves many players. These Guidelines lay down appropriate tools to assist wholesale distributors in conducting their activities and to prevent falsified medicines from entering the legal supply chain. Compliance with these Guidelines will ensure control of the distribution chain and consequently maintain the quality and the integrity of medicinal products.

According to Article 1(17) of Directive 2001/83/EC, wholesale distribution of medicinal products is 'all activities consisting of procuring, holding, supplying or exporting medicinal products, apart from supplying medicinal products to the public. Such activities are carried out with manufacturers or their depositories, importers, other wholesale distributors or with pharmacists and persons authorized or entitled to supply medicinal products to the public in the Member State concerned'.

Any person acting as a wholesale distributor has to hold a wholesale distribution authorisation. Article 80(g) of Directive 2001/83/EC provides that distributors must comply with the principle of and guidelines for GDP.

[1] Directive 2001/83/EC of the European Parliament and of the Council of 6 November 2001 on the Community code relating to medicinal products for human use, OJ L 311, 28.11.2001, p. 67.

[2] Guidelines on Good Distribution Practice of medicinal products for human use, OJ C 63, 1.3.1994, p. 4.

[3] Guidelines of 7 March 2013 on Good Distribution Practice of medicinal products for human use, OJ C 68, 8.3.2013, p. 1.

[4] Directive 2011/62/EU of the European Parliament and of the Council amending Directive 2001/83/EC as regards the prevention of the entry into the legal supply chain of falsified medicinal products, OJ L 174, 1.7.2011, p. 74.

Possession of a manufacturing authorisation includes authorisation to distribute the medicinal products covered by the authorisation. Manufacturers performing any distribution activities with their own products must therefore comply with GDP.

The definition of wholesale distribution does not depend on whether that distributor is established or operating in specific customs areas, such as in free zones or in free warehouses. All obligations related to wholesale distribution activities (such as exporting, holding or supplying) also apply to these distributors. Relevant sections of these Guidelines should also be adhered to by other actors involved in the distribution of medicinal products.

Other actors such as brokers may also play a role in the distribution channel for medicinal products. According to Article 85(b) of Directive 2001/83/EC, persons brokering medicinal products must be subject to certain provisions applicable to wholesale distributors, as well as specific provisions on brokering.

## Chapter 1 − Quality Management

### 1.1 Principle

Wholesale distributors must maintain a quality system setting out responsibilities, processes and risk management principles in relation to their activities[1]. All distribution activities should be clearly defined and systematically reviewed. All critical steps of distribution processes and significant changes should be justified and where relevant validated. The quality system is the responsibility of the organisation's management and requires their leadership and active participation and should be supported by staff commitment.

### 1.2 Quality system

The system for managing quality should encompass the organisational structure, procedures, processes and resources, as well as activities necessary to ensure confidence that the product delivered maintains its quality and integrity and remains within the legal supply chain during storage and/or transportation.

The quality system should be fully documented and its effectiveness monitored. All quality system-related activities should be defined and documented. A quality manual or equivalent documentation approach should be established.

EU GDP CHAPTER 1
QUALITY MANAGEMENT

---

[1] Article 80(h) of Directive 2001/83/EC.

A responsible person should be appointed by the management, who should have clearly specified authority and responsibility for ensuring that a quality system is implemented and maintained.

The management of the distributor should ensure that all parts of the quality system are adequately resourced with competent personnel, and suitable and sufficient premises, equipment and facilities.

The size, structure and complexity of distributor's activities should be taken into consideration when developing or modifying the quality system.

A change control system should be in place. This system should incorporate quality risk management principles, and be proportionate and effective.

The quality system should ensure that:

(i)     medicinal products are procured, held, supplied or exported in a way that is compliant with the requirements of GDP;
(ii)    management responsibilities are clearly specified;
(iii)   products are delivered to the right recipients within a satisfactory time period;
(iv)    records are made contemporaneously;
(v)     deviations from established procedures are documented and investigated;
(vi)    appropriate corrective and preventive actions (commonly known as 'CAPA') are taken to correct deviations and prevent them in line with the principles of quality risk management.

## 1.3   Management of outsourced activities

The quality system should extend to the control and review of any outsourced activities related to the procurement, holding, supply or export of medicinal products. These processes should incorporate quality risk management and include:

(i)     assessing the suitability and competence of the contract acceptor to carry out the activity and checking authorisation status, if required;
(ii)    defining the responsibilities and communication processes for the quality-related activities of the parties involved;
(iii)   monitoring and review of the performance of the contract acceptor, and the identification and implementation of any required improvements on a regular basis.

## 1.4   Management review and monitoring

The management should have a formal process for reviewing the quality system on a periodic basis. The review should include:

(i)    measurement of the achievement of quality system objectives;

(ii)   assessment of performance indicators that can be used to monitor the effectiveness of processes within the quality system, such as complaints, deviations, CAPA, changes to processes; feedback on outsourced activities; self-assessment processes including risk assessments and audits; and external assessments such as inspections, findings and customer audits;

(iii)  emerging regulations, guidance and quality issues that can impact the quality management system;

(iv)   innovations that might enhance the quality system;

(v)    changes in business environment and objectives.

The outcome of each management review of the quality system should be documented in a timely manner and effectively communicated internally.

## 1.5    Quality risk management

Quality risk management is a systematic process for the assessment, control, communication and review of risks to the quality of medicinal products. It can be applied both proactively and retrospectively.

Quality risk management should ensure that the evaluation of the risk to quality is based on scientific knowledge, experience with the process and ultimately links to the protection of the patient. The level of effort, formality and documentation of the process should be commensurate with the level of risk. Examples of the processes and applications of quality risk management can be found in guideline Q9 of the International Conference on Harmonisation ('ICH').

## Chapter 2 – Personnel

### 2.1    Principle

The correct distribution of medicinal products relies upon people. For this reason, there must be sufficient competent personnel to carry out all the tasks for which the wholesale distributor is responsible. Individual responsibilities should be clearly understood by the staff and be recorded.

### 2.2    Responsible person

The wholesale distributor must designate a person as responsible person. The responsible person should meet the qualifications and all conditions provided for by the legislation of the Member State concerned[1]. A degree in

---

[1]  Article 79(b) of Directive 2001/83/EC.

EU GDP CHAPTER 2
PERSONNEL

pharmacy is desirable. The responsible person should have appropriate competence and experience as well as knowledge of and training in GDP.

The responsible person should fulfil their responsibilities personally and should be continuously contactable. The responsible person may delegate duties but not responsibilities.

The written job description of the responsible person should define their authority to take decisions with regard to their responsibilities. The wholesale distributor should give the responsible person the defined authority, resources and responsibility needed to fulfil their duties.

The responsible person should carry out their duties in such a way as to ensure that the wholesale distributor can demonstrate GDP compliance and that public service obligations are met.

The responsibilities of the responsible person include:

(i)   ensuring that a quality management system is implemented and maintained;
(ii)  focusing on the management of authorised activities and the accuracy and quality of records;
(iii) ensuring that initial and continuous training programmes are implemented and maintained;
(iv)  coordinating and promptly performing any recall operations for medicinal products;
(v)   ensuring that relevant customer complaints are dealt with effectively;
(vi)  ensuring that suppliers and customers are approved;
(vii) approving any subcontracted activities which may impact on GDP;
(viii) ensuring that self-inspections are performed at appropriate regular intervals following a prearranged programme and necessary corrective measures are put in place;
(ix)  keeping appropriate records of any delegated duties;
(x)   deciding on the final disposition of returned, rejected, recalled or falsified products;
(xi)  approving any returns to saleable stock;
(xii) ensuring that any additional requirements imposed on certain products by national law are adhered to[2].

## 2.3   Other personnel

There should be an adequate number of competent personnel involved in all stages of the wholesale distribution activities of medicinal products. The number of personnel required will depend on the volume and scope of activities.

---

[2] Article 83 of Directive 2001/83/EC.

The organisational structure of the wholesale distributor should be set out in an organisation chart. The role, responsibilities, and interrelationships of all personnel should be clearly indicated.

The role and responsibilities of employees working in key positions should be set out in written job descriptions, along with any arrangements for deputising.

## 2.4   Training

All personnel involved in wholesale distribution activities should be trained on the requirements of GDP. They should have the appropriate competence and experience prior to commencing their tasks.

Personnel should receive initial and continuing training relevant to their role, based on written procedures and in accordance with a written training programme. The responsible person should also maintain their competence in GDP through regular training.

In addition, training should include aspects of product identification and avoidance of falsified medicines entering the supply chain.

Personnel dealing with any products which require more stringent handling conditions should receive specific training. Examples of such products include hazardous products, radioactive materials, products presenting special risks of abuse (including narcotic and psychotropic substances), and temperature-sensitive products.

A record of all training should be kept, and the effectiveness of training should be periodically assessed and documented.

## 2.5   Hygiene

Appropriate procedures relating to personnel hygiene, relevant to the activities being carried out, should be established and observed. Such procedures should cover health, hygiene and clothing.

## Chapter 3 – Premises and Equipment

### 3.1   Principle

Wholesale distributors must have suitable and adequate premises, installations and equipment[1], so as to ensure proper storage and distribution of medicinal products. In particular, the premises should be clean, dry and maintained within acceptable temperature limits.

---

[1]  Article 79(a) of Directive 2001/83/EC.

EU GDP CHAPTER 3 PREMISES AND EQUIPMENT

## 3.2  Premises

The premises should be designed or adapted to ensure that the required storage conditions are maintained. They should be suitably secure, structurally sound and of sufficient capacity to allow safe storage and handling of the medicinal products. Storage areas should be provided with adequate lighting to enable all operations to be carried out accurately and safely.

Where premises are not directly operated by the wholesale distributor, a contract should be in place. The contracted premises should be covered by a separate wholesale distribution authorisation.

Medicinal products should be stored in segregated areas which are clearly marked and have access restricted to authorised personnel. Any system replacing physical segregation, such as electronic segregation based on a computerised system, should provide equivalent security and should be validated.

Products pending a decision as to their disposition or products that have been removed from saleable stock should be segregated either physically or through an equivalent electronic system. This includes, for example, any product suspected of falsification and returned products. Medicinal products received from a third country but not intended for the Union market should also be physically segregated. Any falsified medicinal products, expired products, recalled products and rejected products found in the supply chain should be immediately physically segregated and stored in a dedicated area away from all other medicinal products. The appropriate degree of security should be applied in these areas to ensure that such items remain separate from saleable stock. These areas should be clearly identified.

Special attention should be paid to the storage of products with specific handling instructions as specified in national law. Special storage conditions (and special authorisations) may be required for such products (e.g. narcotics and psychotropic substances).

Radioactive materials and other hazardous products, as well as products presenting special safety risks of fire or explosion (e.g. medicinal gases, combustibles, flammable liquids and solids), should be stored in one or more dedicated areas subject to local legislation and appropriate safety and security measures.

Receiving and dispatch bays should protect products from prevailing weather conditions. There should be adequate separation between the receipt and dispatch and storage areas. Procedures should be in place to maintain control of inbound/outbound goods. Reception areas where deliveries are examined following receipt should be designated and suitably equipped.

Unauthorised access to all areas of the authorised premises should be prevented. Prevention measures would usually include a monitored intruder alarm system and appropriate access control. Visitors should be accompanied.

Premises and storage facilities should be clean and free from litter and dust. Cleaning programmes, instructions and records should be in place. Appropriate cleaning equipment and cleaning agents should be chosen and used so as not to present a source of contamination.

Premises should be designed and equipped so as to afford protection against the entry of insects, rodents or other animals. A preventive pest control programme should be in place.

Rest, wash and refreshment rooms for employees should be adequately separated from the storage areas. The presence of food, drink, smoking material or medicinal products for personal use should be prohibited in the storage areas.

### 3.2.1. TEMPERATURE AND ENVIRONMENT CONTROL

Suitable equipment and procedures should be in place to check the environment where medicinal products are stored. Environmental factors to be considered include temperature, light, humidity and cleanliness of the premises.

An initial temperature mapping exercise should be carried out on the storage area before use, under representative conditions. Temperature monitoring equipment should be located according to the results of the mapping exercise, ensuring that monitoring devices are positioned in the areas that experience the extremes of fluctuations. The mapping exercise should be repeated according to the results of a risk assessment exercise or whenever significant modifications are made to the facility or the temperature controlling equipment. For small premises of a few square meters which are at room temperature, an assessment of potential risks (e.g. heaters) should be conducted and temperature monitors placed accordingly.

## 3.3  Equipment

All equipment impacting on storage and distribution of medicinal products should be designed, located and maintained to a standard which suits its intended purpose. Planned maintenance should be in place for key equipment vital to the functionality of the operation.

Equipment used to control or to monitor the environment where the medicinal products are stored should be calibrated at defined intervals based on a risk and reliability assessment.

Calibration of equipment should be traceable to a national or international measurement standard. Appropriate alarm systems should be in place to provide alerts when there are excursions from pre-defined storage conditions. Alarm levels should be appropriately set and alarms should be regularly tested to ensure adequate functionality.

Equipment repair, maintenance and calibration operations should be carried out in such a way that the integrity of the medicinal products is not compromised.

Adequate records of repair, maintenance and calibration activities for key equipment should be made and the results should be retained. Key equipment would include for example cold stores, monitored intruder alarm and access control systems, refrigerators, thermo hygrometers, or other temperature and humidity recording devices, air handling units and any equipment used in conjunction with the onward supply chain.

## 3.3.1. COMPUTERISED SYSTEMS

Before a computerised system is brought into use, it should be demonstrated, through appropriate validation or verification studies, that the system is capable of achieving the desired results accurately, consistently and reproducibly.

A written, detailed description of the system should be available (including diagrams where appropriate). This should be kept up to date. The document should describe principles, objectives, security measures, system scope and main features, how the computerised system is used and the way it interacts with other systems.

Data should only be entered into the computerised system or amended by persons authorised to do so.

Data should be secured by physical or electronic means and protected against accidental or unauthorised modifications. Stored data should be checked periodically for accessibility. Data should be protected by backing up at regular intervals. Back up data should be retained for the period stated in national legislation but at least five years at a separate and secure location.

Procedures to be followed if the system fails or breaks down should be defined. This should include systems for the restoration of data.

## 3.3.2. QUALIFICATION AND VALIDATION

Wholesale distributors should identify what key equipment qualification and/or key process validation is necessary to ensure correct installation and operation. The scope and extent of such qualification and/or validation activities (such as storage, pick and pack processes) should be determined using a documented risk assessment approach.

Equipment and processes should be respectively qualified and/or validated before commencing use and after any significant changes e.g. repair or maintenance.

Validation and qualification reports should be prepared summarising the results obtained and commenting on any observed deviations. Deviations from established procedures should be documented and further actions decided to correct deviations and avoid their reoccurrence (corrective and preventive actions). The principles of CAPA should be applied where necessary. Evidence of satisfactory validation and acceptance of a process or piece of equipment should be produced and approved by appropriate personnel.

## Chapter 4 – Documentation

### 4.1 Principle

Good documentation constitutes an essential part of the quality system. Written documentation should prevent errors from spoken communication and permits the tracking of relevant operations during the distribution of medicinal products.

### 4.2 General

Documentation comprises all written procedures, instructions, contracts, records and data, in paper or in electronic form. Documentation should be readily available/retrievable.

With regard to the processing of personal data of employees, complainants or any other natural person, Directive 95/46/EC[1] on the protection of individuals applies to the processing of personal data and to the free movement of such data.

Documentation should be sufficiently comprehensive with respect to the scope of the wholesale distributor's activities and in a language understood by personnel. It should be written in clear, unambiguous language and be free from errors.

Procedure should be approved signed and dated by the responsible person. Documentation should be approved, signed and dated by appropriate authorised persons, as required. It should not be hand-written; although, where it is necessary, sufficient space should be provided for such entries.

EU GDP CHAPTER 4
DOCUMENTATION

---

[1] OJ L 281, 23.11.1995, p. 31.

Any alteration made in the documentation should be signed and dated; the alteration should permit the reading of the original information. Where appropriate, the reason for the alteration should be recorded.

Documents should be retained for the period stated in national legislation but at least five years. Personal data should be deleted or anonymised as soon as their storage is no longer than necessary for the purpose of distribution activities.

Each employee should have ready access to all necessary documentation for the tasks executed.

Attention should be paid to using valid and approved procedures. Documents should have unambiguous content; title, nature and purpose should be clearly stated. Documents should be reviewed regularly and kept up to date. Version control should be applied to procedures. After revision of a document a system should exist to prevent inadvertent use of the superseded version. Superseded or obsolete procedures should be removed from workstations and archived.

Records must be kept either in the form of purchase/sales invoices, delivery slips, or on computer or any other form, for any transaction in medicinal products received, supplied or brokered.

Records must include at least the following information: date; name of the medicinal product; quantity received, supplied or brokered; name and address of the supplier, customer, broker or consignee, as appropriate; and batch number at least for medicinal product bearing the safety features[2].

Records should be made at the time each operation is undertaken.

## Chapter 5 — Operations

### 5.1 Principle

All actions taken by wholesale distributors should ensure that the identity of the medicinal product is not lost and that the wholesale distribution of medicinal products is performed according to the information on the outer packaging. The wholesale distributor should use all means available to minimise the risk of falsified medicinal products entering the legal supply chain.

All medicinal products distributed in the EU by a wholesale distributor must be covered by a marketing authorisation granted by the EU or by a Member State[3].

Any distributor, other than the marketing authorisation holder, who imports a medicinal product from another Member State must notify the marketing authorisation holder and the competent authority in the

---

[2] Articles 80(e) and 82 of Directive 2001/83/EC.
[3] Articles 76(1) and (2) of Directive 2001/83/EC.

Member State to which the medicinal product will be imported of their intention to import that product[4]. All key operations described below should be fully described in the quality system in appropriate documentation.

## 5.2  Qualification of suppliers

Wholesale distributors must obtain their supplies of medicinal products only from persons who are themselves in possession of a wholesale distribution authorisation, or who are in possession of a manufacturing authorisation which covers the product in question[5].

Wholesale distributors receiving medicinal products from third countries for the purpose of importation, i.e. for the purpose of placing these products on the EU market, must hold a manufacturing authorisation[6].

Where medicinal products are obtained from another wholesale distributor the receiving wholesale distributor must verify that the supplier complies with the principles and guidelines of good distribution practices and that they hold an authorisation for example by using the Union database. If the medicinal product is obtained through brokering, the wholesale distributor must verify that the broker is registered and complies with the requirements in Chapter 10[1].

Appropriate qualification and approval of suppliers should be performed prior to any procurement of medicinal products. This should be controlled by a procedure and the results documented and periodically rechecked.

When entering into a new contract with new suppliers the wholesale distributor should carry out 'due diligence' checks in order to assess the suitability, competence and reliability of the other party. Attention should be paid to:

(i)    the reputation or reliability of the supplier;
(ii)   offers of medicinal products more likely to be falsified;
(iii)  large offers of medicinal products which are generally only available in limited quantities; and
(iv)  out-of-range prices.

---

[4]  Article 76(3) of Directive 2001/83/EC.
[5]  Article 80(b) of Directive 2001/83/EC.
[6]  Article 40, third paragraph of Directive 2001/83/EC.
[1]  Article 80, fourth paragraph of Directive 2001/83/EC.

## 5.3  Qualification of customers

Wholesale distributors must ensure they supply medicinal products only to persons who are themselves in possession of a wholesale distribution authorisation or who are authorised or entitled to supply medicinal products to the public.

Checks and periodic rechecks may include: requesting copies of customer's authorisations according to national law, verifying status on an authority website, requesting evidence of qualifications or entitlement according to national legislation.

Wholesale distributors should monitor their transactions and investigate any irregularity in the sales patterns of narcotics, psychotropic substances or other dangerous substances. Unusual sales patterns that may constitute diversion or misuse of medicinal product should be investigated and reported to competent authorities where necessary. Steps should be taken to ensure fulfilment of any public service obligation imposed upon them.

## 5.4  Receipt of medicinal products

The purpose of the receiving function is to ensure that the arriving consignment is correct, that the medicinal products originate from approved suppliers and that they have not been visibly damaged during transport.

Medicinal products requiring special storage or security measures should be prioritised and once appropriate checks have been conducted they should be immediately transferred to appropriate storage facilities.

Batches of medicinal products intended for the EU and EEA countries should not be transferred to saleable stock before assurance has been obtained in accordance with written procedures, that they are authorised for sale. For batches coming from another Member State, prior to their transfer to saleable stock, the control report referred to in Article 51(1) of Directive 2001/83/EC or another proof of release to the market in question based on an equivalent system should be carefully checked by appropriately trained personnel.

## 5.5  Storage

Medicinal products and, if necessary, healthcare products should be stored separately from other products likely to alter them and should be protected from the harmful effects of light, temperature, moisture and other external factors. Particular attention should be paid to products requiring specific storage conditions.

Incoming containers of medicinal products should be cleaned, if necessary, before storage.

Warehousing operations must ensure appropriate storage conditions are maintained and allow for appropriate security of stocks.

Stock should be rotated according to the 'first expiry, first out' (FEFO) principle. Exceptions should be documented.

Medicinal products should be handled and stored in such a manner as to prevent spillage, breakage, contamination and mix-ups. Medicinal products should not be stored directly on the floor unless the package is designed to allow such storage (such as for some medicinal gas cylinders).

Medicinal products that are nearing their expiry date/shelf life should be withdrawn immediately from saleable stock either physically or through other equivalent electronic segregation.

Stock inventories should be performed regularly taking into account national legislation requirements. Stock irregularities should be investigated and documented.

## 5.6   Destruction of obsolete goods

Medicinal products intended for destruction should be appropriately identified, held separately and handled in accordance with a written procedure.

Destruction of medicinal products should be in accordance with national or international requirements for handling, transport and disposal of such products.

Records of all destroyed medicinal products should be retained for a defined period.

## 5.7   Picking

Controls should be in place to ensure the correct product is picked. The product should have an appropriate remaining shelf life when it is picked.

## 5.8   Supply

For all supplies, a document (e.g. delivery note) must be enclosed stating the date; name and pharmaceutical form of the medicinal product, batch number at least for products bearing the safety features; quantity supplied; name and address of the supplier, name and delivery address of the consignee[1] (actual physical storage premises, if different) and applicable transport and storage conditions. Records should be kept so that the actual location of the product can be known.

[1]   Article 82 of Directive 2001/83/EC.

## 5.9    Export to third countries

The export of medicinal products falls within the definition of 'wholesale distribution'[2]. A person exporting medicinal products must hold a wholesale distribution authorisation or a manufacturing authorisation. This is also the case if the exporting wholesale distributor is operating from a free zone.

The rules for wholesale distribution apply in their entirety in the case of export of medicinal products. However, where medicinal products are exported, they do not need to be covered by a marketing authorisation of the Union or a Member State[3]. Wholesalers should take the appropriate measures in order to prevent these medicinal products reaching the Union market. Where wholesale distributors supply medicinal products to persons in third countries, they shall ensure that such supplies are only made to persons who are authorised or entitled to receive medicinal products for wholesale distribution or supply to the public in accordance with the applicable legal and administrative provisions of the country concerned.

# Chapter 6 – Complaints, Returns, Suspected Falsified Medicinal Products and Medicinal Product Recalls

## 6.1    Principle

All complaints, returns, suspected falsified medicinal products and recalls must be recorded and handled carefully according to written procedures. Records should be made available to the competent authorities. An assessment of returned medicinal products should be performed before any approval for resale. A consistent approach by all partners in the supply chain is required in order to be successful in the fight against falsified medicinal products.

## 6.2    Complaints

Complaints should be recorded with all the original details. A distinction should be made between complaints related to the quality of a medicinal product and those related to distribution. In the event of a complaint about the quality of a medicinal product and a potential product defect, the manufacturer and/or marketing authorisation holder should be informed without delay. Any product distribution complaint should be thoroughly investigated to identify the origin of or reason for the complaint.

---

[2]  Article 1(17) of Directive 2001/83/EC.
[3]  Article 85(a) of Directive 2001/83/EC.

A person should be appointed to handle complaints and allocated sufficient support personnel.

If necessary, appropriate follow-up actions (including CAPA) should be taken after investigation and evaluation of the complaint, including where required notification to the national competent authorities.

## 6.3  Returned medicinal products

Returned products must be handled according to a written, risk-based process taking into account the product concerned, any specific storage requirements and the time elapsed since the medicinal product was originally dispatched. Returns should be conducted in accordance with national law and contractual arrangements between the parties.

Medicinal products which have left the premises of the distributor should only be returned to saleable stock if all of the following are confirmed:

(i)     the medicinal products are in their unopened and undamaged secondary packaging and are in good condition; have not expired and have not been recalled;

(ii)    medicinal products returned from a customer not holding a wholesale distribution authorisation or from pharmacies authorised to supply medicinal products to the public should only be returned to saleable stock if they are returned within an acceptable time limit, for example 10 days.

(iii)   it has been demonstrated by the customer that the medicinal products have been transported, stored and handled in compliance with their specific storage requirements;

(iv)    they have been examined and assessed by a sufficiently trained and competent person authorised to do so;

(v)     the distributor has reasonable evidence that the product was supplied to that customer (via copies of the original delivery note or by referencing invoice numbers, etc.) and the batch number for products bearing the safety features is known, and that there is no reason to believe that the product has been falsified.

Moreover, for medicinal products requiring specific temperature storage conditions such as low temperature, returns to saleable stock can only be made if there is documented evidence that the product has been stored under the authorised storage conditions throughout the entire time. If any deviation has occurred a risk assessment has to be performed, on which basis the integrity of the product can be demonstrated. The evidence should cover:

(i)     delivery to customer;

(ii)   examination of the product;
(iii)  opening of the transport packaging;
(iv)  return of the product to the packaging;
(v)   collection and return to the distributor;
(vi)  return to the distribution site refrigerator.

Products returned to saleable stock should be placed such that the 'first expired first out' (FEFO) system operates effectively.

Stolen products that have been recovered cannot be returned to saleable stock and sold to customers.

## 6.4   Falsified medicinal products

Wholesale distributors must immediately inform the competent authority and the marketing authorisation holder of any medicinal products they identify as falsified or suspect to be falsified[1]. A procedure should be in place to this effect. It should be recorded with all the original details and investigated.

Any falsified medicinal products found in the supply chain should immediately be physically segregated and stored in a dedicated area away from all other medicinal products. All relevant activities in relation to such products should be documented and records retained.

## 6.5   Medicinal product recalls

The effectiveness of the arrangements for product recall should be evaluated regularly (at least annually).

Recall operations should be capable of being initiated promptly and at any time.

The distributor must follow the instructions of a recall message, which should be approved, if required, by the competent authorities.

Any recall operation should be recorded at the time it is carried out. Records should be made readily available to the competent authorities.

The distribution records should be readily accessible to the person(s) responsible for the recall, and should contain sufficient information on distributors and directly supplied customers (with addresses, phone and/or fax numbers inside and outside working hours, batch numbers at least for medicinal products bearing safety features as required by legislation and quantities delivered), including those for exported products and medicinal product samples.

The progress of the recall process should be recorded for a final report.

---

[1] Article 80(i) of Directive 2001/83/EC.

## Chapter 7 – Outsourced Activities

### 7.1 Principle

Any activity covered by the GDP guide that is outsourced should be correctly defined, agreed and controlled in order to avoid misunderstandings which could affect the integrity of the product. There must be a written contract between the contract giver and the contract acceptor which clearly establishes the duties of each party.

### 7.2 Contract giver

The contract giver is responsible for the activities contracted out.

The contract giver is responsible for assessing the competence of the contract acceptor to successfully carry out the work required and for ensuring by means of the contract and through audits that the principles and guidelines of GDP are followed. An audit of the contract acceptor should be performed before commencement of, and whenever there has been a change to, the outsourced activities. The frequency of audit should be defined based on risk depending on the nature of the outsourced activities. Audits should be permitted at any time.

The contract giver should provide the contract acceptor with all the information necessary to carry out the contracted operations in accordance with the specific product requirements and any other relevant requirements.

### 7.3 Contract acceptor

The contract acceptor should have adequate premises and equipment, procedures, knowledge and experience, and competent personnel to carry out the work ordered by the contract giver.

The contract acceptor should not pass to a third party any of the work entrusted to him under the contract without the contract giver's prior evaluation and approval of the arrangements and an audit of the third party by the contract giver or the contract acceptor. Arrangements made between the contract acceptor and any third party should ensure that the wholesale distribution information is made available in the same way as between the original contract giver and contract acceptor.

The contract acceptor should refrain from any activity which may adversely affect the quality of the product(s) handled for the contract giver.

The contract acceptor must forward any information that can influence the quality of the product(s) to the contract giver in accordance with the requirement of the contract.

## Chapter 8 – Self-inspections

### 8.1  Principle

Self-inspections should be conducted in order to monitor implementation and compliance with GDP principles and to propose necessary corrective measures.

### 8.2  Self-inspections

A self-inspection programme should be implemented covering all aspects of GDP and compliance with the regulations, guidelines and procedures within a defined time frame. Self-inspections may be divided into several individual self-inspections of limited scope.

Self-inspections should be conducted in an impartial and detailed way by designated competent company personnel. Audits by independent external experts may also be useful but may not be used as a substitute for self-inspection.

All self-inspections should be recorded. Reports should contain all the observations made during the inspection. A copy of the report should be provided to the management and other relevant persons. In the event that irregularities and/or deficiencies are observed, their cause should be determined and the corrective and preventive actions (CAPA) should be documented and followed up.

## Chapter 9 – Transportation

### 9.1  Principle

It is the responsibility of the supplying wholesale distributor to protect medicinal products against breakage, adulteration and theft, and to ensure that temperature conditions are maintained within acceptable limits during transport.

Regardless of the mode of transport, it should be possible to demonstrate that the medicines have not been exposed to conditions that may compromise their quality and integrity. A risk-based approach should be utilised when planning transportation.

## 9.2   Transportation

The required storage conditions for medicinal products should be maintained during transportation within the defined limits as described by the manufacturers or on the outer packaging.

If a deviation such as temperature excursion or product damage has occurred during transportation, this should be reported to the distributor and recipient of the affected medicinal products. A procedure should also be in place for investigating and handling temperature excursions.

It is the responsibility of the wholesale distributor to ensure that vehicles and equipment used to distribute, store or handle medicinal products are suitable for their use and appropriately equipped to prevent exposure of the products to conditions that could affect their quality and packaging integrity.

There should be written procedures in place for the operation and maintenance of all vehicles and equipment involved in the distribution process, including cleaning and safety precautions.

Risk assessment of delivery routes should be used to determine where temperature controls are required. Equipment used for temperature monitoring during transport within vehicles and/or containers, should be maintained and calibrated at regular intervals at least once a year.

Dedicated vehicles and equipment should be used, where possible, when handling medicinal products. Where non-dedicated vehicles and equipment are used procedures should be in place to ensure that the quality of the medicinal product will not be compromised.

Deliveries should be made to the address stated on the delivery note and into the care or the premises of the consignee. Medicinal products should not be left on alternative premises.

For emergency deliveries outside normal business hours, persons should be designated and written procedures should be available.

Where transportation is performed by a third party, the contract in place should encompass the requirements of Chapter 7. Transportation providers should be made aware by the wholesale distributor of the relevant transport conditions applicable to the consignment. Where the transportation route includes unloading and reloading or transit storage at a transportation hub, particular attention should be paid to temperature monitoring, cleanliness and the security of any intermediate storage facilities.

Provision should be made to minimise the duration of temporary storage while awaiting the next stage of the transportation route.

EU GDP CHAPTER 9
TRANSPORTATION

## 9.3    Containers, packaging and labelling

Medicinal products should be transported in containers that have no adverse effect on the quality of the products, and that offer adequate protection from external influences, including contamination.

Selection of a container and packaging should be based on the storage and transportation requirements of the medicinal products; the space required for the amount of medicines; the anticipated external temperature extremes; the estimated maximum time for transportation including transit storage at customs; the qualification status of the packaging and the validation status of the shipping containers.

Containers should bear labels providing sufficient information on handling and storage requirements and precautions to ensure that the products are properly handled and secured at all times. The containers should enable identification of the contents of the containers and the source.

## 9.4    Products requiring special conditions

In relation to deliveries containing medicinal products requiring special conditions such as narcotics or psychotropic substances, the wholesale distributor should maintain a safe and secure supply chain for these products in accordance with requirements laid down by the Member States concerned. There should be additional control systems in place for delivery of these products. There should be a protocol to address the occurrence of any theft.

Medicinal products comprising highly active and radioactive materials should be transported in safe, dedicated and secure containers and vehicles. The relevant safety measures should be in accordance with international agreements and national legislation.

For temperature-sensitive products, qualified equipment (e.g. thermal packaging, temperature-controlled containers or temperature controlled vehicles) should be used to ensure correct transport conditions are maintained between the manufacturer, wholesale distributor and customer.

If temperature-controlled vehicles are used, the temperature monitoring equipment used during transport should be maintained and calibrated at regular intervals. Temperature mapping under representative conditions should be carried out and should take into account seasonal variations.

If requested, customers should be provided with information to demonstrate that products have complied with the temperature storage conditions.

If cool packs are used in insulated boxes, they need to be located such that the product does not come in direct contact with the cool pack. Staff must be trained on the procedures for assembly of the insulated boxes (seasonal configurations) and on the re-use of cool packs.

There should be a system in place to control the re-use of cool packs to ensure that incompletely cooled packs are not used in error. There should be adequate physical segregation between frozen and chilled ice packs.

The process for delivery of sensitive products and control of seasonal temperature variations should be described in a written procedure.

## Chapter 10 – Specific Provisions for Brokers[1]

### 10.1 Principle

A 'broker' is a person involved in activities in relation to the sale or purchase of medicinal products, except for wholesale distribution, that do not include physical handling and that consist of negotiating independently and on behalf of another legal or natural person.[2]

Brokers are subject to a registration requirement. They must have a permanent address and contact details in the Member State where they are registered[3]. They must notify the competent authority of any changes to those details without unnecessary delay.

By definition, brokers do not procure, supply or hold medicines. Therefore, requirements for premises, installations and equipment as set out in Directive 2001/83/EC do not apply. However, all other rules in Directive 2001/83/EC that apply to wholesale distributors also apply to brokers.

### 10.2 Quality system

The quality system of a broker should be defined in writing, approved and kept up to date. It should set out responsibilities, processes and risk management in relation to their activities.

The quality system should include an emergency plan which ensures effective recall of medicinal products from the market ordered by the manufacturer or the competent authorities or carried out in cooperation with the manufacturer or marketing authorisation holder for the medicinal product concerned[4]. The competent authorities must be immediately informed of any suspected falsified medicines offered in the supply chain[5].

EU GDP CHAPTER 10
SPECIFIC PROVISIONS
FOR BROKERS

---

[1]  Article 85b(3) of Directive 2001/83/EC.
[2]  Article 1(17a) of Directive 2001/83/EC.
[3]  Article 85b of Directive 2001/83/EC.
[4]  Article 80(d) of Directive 2001/83/EC.
[5]  Article 85b(1), third paragraph of Directive 2001/83/EC.

## 10.3   Personnel

Any member of personnel involved in the brokering activities should be trained in the applicable EU and national legislation and in the issues concerning falsified medicinal products.

## 10.4   Documentation

The general provisions on documentation in Chapter 4 apply.

In addition, at least the following procedures and instructions, along with the corresponding records of execution, should be in place:

(i)     procedure for complaints handling;

(ii)    procedure for informing competent authorities and marketing authorisation holders of suspected falsified medicinal products;

(iii)   procedure for supporting recalls;

(iv)   procedure for ensuring that medicinal products brokered have a marketing authorisation;

(v)    procedure for verifying that their supplying wholesale distributors hold a distribution authorisation, their supplying manufacturers or importers hold a manufacturing authorisation and their customers are authorised to supply medicinal products in the Member State concerned;

(vi)   records should be kept either in the form of purchase/sales invoices or on computer, or in any other form for any transaction in medicinal products brokered and should contain at least the following information: date; name of the medicinal product; quantity brokered; name and address of the supplier and the customer; and batch number at least for products bearing the safety features.

Records should be made available to the competent authorities, for inspection purposes, for the period stated in national legislation but at least five years.

## Chapter 11 − Final Provisions

These Guidelines replace the Guidelines on Good Distribution Practice of medicinal products for human use, published on 1 March 1994[1] and the Guidelines of 7 March 2013 on Good Distribution Practice of medicinal products for human use[2].

These Guidelines will be applied from the first day following their publication in the *Official Journal of the European Union*. EN C 343/12 Official Journal of the European Union 23.11.2013.

---

[1]  OJ C 63, 1.3.1994, p. 4.

[2]  OJ C 68, 8.3.2013, p. 1.

# ANNEX

## Glossary of terms

| Term | Definition |
| --- | --- |
| Good Distribution Practice (GDP) | GDP is that part of quality assurance which ensures that the quality of medicinal products is maintained throughout all stages of the supply chain from the site of manufacturer to the pharmacy or person authorised or entitled to supply medicinal products to the public. |
| Export procedure | Export procedure: allow Community goods to leave the customs territory of the Union. For the purpose of these guidelines, the supply of medicines from EU Member State to a contracting State of the European Economic Area is not considered as export. |
| Falsified medicinal product[1] | Any medicinal product with a false representation of: (a) its identity, including its packaging and labelling, its name or its composition as regards any of the ingredients including excipients and the strength of those ingredients; (b) its source, including its manufacturer, its country of manufacturing, its country of origin or its marketing authorisation holder; or (c) its history, including the records and documents relating to the distribution channels used. |
| Free zones and free warehouses[2] | Free zones and free warehouses are parts of the customs territory of the Community or premises situated in that territory and separated from the rest of it in which: (a) Community goods are considered, for the purpose of import duties and commercial policy import measures, as not being on Community customs territory, provided they are not released for free circulation or placed under another customs procedure or used or consumed under conditions other than those provided for in customs regulations; (b) Community goods for which such provision is made under Community legislation governing specific fields qualify, by virtue of being placed in a free zone or free warehouse, for measures normally attaching to the export of goods. |

*(Continued)*

EU GDP ANNEX

## Glossary of terms (*Continued*)

| Term | Definition |
|---|---|
| Holding | Storing medicinal products. |
| Transport | Moving medicinal products between two locations without storing them for unjustified periods of time. |
| Procuring | Obtaining, acquiring, purchasing or buying medicinal products from manufacturers, importers or other wholesale distributors. |
| Qualification | Action of proving that any equipment works correctly and actually leads to the expected results. The word 'validation' is sometimes widened to incorporate the concept of qualification. (Defined in EudraLex Volume 4 Glossary to the GMP Guidelines). |
| Supplying | All activities of providing, selling, donating medicinal products to wholesalers, pharmacists, or persons authorised or entitled to supply medicinal products to the public. |
| Quality risk management | A systematic process for the assessment, control, communication and review of risks to the quality of the drug (medicinal) product across the product lifecycle. |
| Quality system | The sum of all aspects of a system that implements quality policy and ensures that quality objectives are met. (International Conference on Harmonisation of Technical Requirements for Registration of Pharmaceuticals for Human Use, Q9). |
| Validation | Action of proving that any procedure, process, equipment, material, activity or system actually leads to the expected results (see also 'qualification'). (Defined in EudraLex Volume 4 Glossary to the GMP Guidelines) |

[1] Article 1(33) of Directive 2001/83/EC.

[2] Articles 166 to Article 181 of Council Regulation (EEC) No 2913/92 of 12 October 1992 establishing the Community Customs Code, (OJ L 302, 19.10.1992, p. 1).

# UK Guidance on Wholesale Distribution Practice

## Contents

## Conditions of Holding a Wholesale Dealer's Licence

The holder of a wholesale dealer's licence must comply with certain conditions in relation to the wholesale distribution of medicinal products. These conditions are set out in regulations 43 – 45 of the Human Medicines Regulations 2012 [SI 2012/1916] ("the Regulations"). They require that the licence holder shall:

- comply with the guidelines on Good Distribution Practice (GDP);[1]
- ensure, within the limits of their responsibility as a distributor of medicinal products, the appropriate and continued supply of such medicinal

---

[1]  Guidelines on Good Distribution Practice of Medicinal Products for Human Use (2013/C 343/01) http://eur-lex.europa.eu/LexUriServ/LexUriServ.do?uri=OJ: C:2013:343:0001:0014:EN:PDF.

products to pharmacies and persons who may lawfully sell such products by retail or who may lawfully supply them in circumstances corresponding to retail sale, so that the needs of patients in the UK are met;

- provide and maintain such staff, premises, equipment and facilities for the handling, storage and distribution of the medicinal products under the licence as are necessary to maintain the quality of, and ensure proper distribution of the medicinal products;
- inform the licensing authority of any proposed structural alteration to, or discontinued use of, premises to which the licence relates or premises which have been approved by the licensing authority;
- inform the licensing authority of any change to the Responsible Person;
- not sell or offer for sale or supply any medicinal product unless there is a marketing authorisation, Article 126a authorisation, certificate of registration or traditional herbal registration ("an authorisation") for the time being in force in respect of that product; and the sale or offer for sale is in accordance with the provisions of that authorisation. This restriction on the holder of a wholesale dealer's licence shall not apply to:
  - the sale or offer for sale of a special medicinal product; and
  - the export to an EEA State, or supply for the purposes of such export, of a medicinal product which may be placed on the market in that State without a marketing authorisation, Article 126a authorisation, certificate of registration or traditional herbal registration by virtue of legislation adopted by that State under Article 5(1) of the 2001 Directive; or
  - the sale or supply, or offer for sale or supply, of an unauthorised medicinal product where the Secretary of State has temporarily authorised the distribution of the product under regulation 174 of the Regulations.

The holder of a wholesale dealer's licence shall:

- keep such documents relating to the sale of medicinal products to which their licence relates as will facilitate the withdrawal or recall from sale of medicinal products in accordance with an emergency plan referred to below;
- have in place an emergency plan which will ensure effective implementation of the recall from the market of any relevant medicinal products where such recall is:
  - ordered by the licensing authority or by the competent authority of any other EEA State, or
  - carried out in co-operation with the manufacturer of, or the holder of the marketing authorisation for, the product in question;
- keep records in relation to the receipt, dispatch or brokering of medicinal products, of the date of receipt, the date of despatch, the date of brokering, the name of the medicinal product, the quantity of the product received, dispatched or brokered, the name and address of the

person from whom the products were received or to whom they are dispatched, and the batch number of medicinal products bearing safety features referred to in point (o) of Article 54 of the 2001 Directive.[2]

Where the holder of a wholesale dealer's licence imports from another EEA State for which they are not the holder of the marketing authorisation, Article 126a authorisation, certificate of registration or a traditional herbal registration of the product, then they shall notify the holder of that authorisation of their intention to import that product. In the case where the product is the subject of a marketing authorisation granted under Regulation (EC) No 726/2004, the holder of the wholesale dealer's licence shall notify the EMA or for any other authorisation they shall notify the licensing authority. In both cases they will be required to pay a fee to the EMA in accordance with Article 76(4) of the 2001 Directive[3] or the licensing authority as the case may be, in accordance with the Fees Regulations. These requirements will not apply in relation to the wholesale distribution of medicinal products to a person in a non-EEA country.

The licence holder, for the purposes of enabling the licensing authority to determine whether there are grounds for suspending, revoking or varying the licence, must permit a person authorised in writing by the licensing authority, on production of identification, to carry out any inspection, or to take any samples or copies, which an inspector could carry out or take under Part 16 (enforcement) of the Regulations.

The holder of a wholesale dealer's licence must verify that any medicinal products they receive which are required by Article 54a of the Directive[4] to bear safety features are not falsified. This does not apply in relation to the distribution of medicinal products received from a third country by a person for supply to a person in a third country. Any verification is carried out by checking the safety features on the outer packaging, in accordance with the requirements laid down in the delegated acts adopted under Article 54a(2) of the 2001 Directive.

The licence holder must maintain a quality system setting out responsibilities, processes and risk management measures in relation to their activities.

The licence holder must also immediately inform the licensing authority and, where applicable, the marketing authorisation holder, of medicinal products which the licence holder receives or is offered which the licence holder knows or suspects, or has reasonable grounds for knowing or suspecting, to be falsified.

---

[2] Point (o) of Article 54 was inserted by Directive 2011/62/EU of the European Parliament and of the Council (OJ No L 174, 1.7.2011, p74).

[3] Article 76(4) was inserted by Directive 2011/62/EU of the European Parliament and of the Council (OJ No L 174, 1.7.2011, p74).

[4] Article 54a was inserted by Directive 2011/62/EU of the European Parliament and of the Council (OJ No L 174, 1.7.2011, p74).

Where the medicinal product is obtained through brokering, the licence holder must verify that the broker involved fulfils the requirements set out in the Regulations.

The licence holder must not obtain supplies of medicinal products from anyone except the holder of a manufacturer's licence or wholesale dealer's licence in relation to products of that description or the person who holds an authorisation granted by another EEA State authorising the manufacture of products of the description or their distribution by way of wholesale dealing. The supply must be in accordance with the principles and guidelines of good distribution practice. This does not apply in relation to the distribution of medicinal products directly received from a non-EEA country but not imported into the EU.

From 28th October 2013, where the medicinal product is directly received from a non-EEA country for export to a non-EEA country, the licensed wholesale dealer must check that the supplier of the medicinal product in the exporting non-EEA country is authorised or entitled to supply such medicinal products in accordance with the legal and administrative provisions in that country.

The holder of a wholesale dealer's licence must verify that the wholesale dealer who supplies the product complies with the principles and guidelines of good distribution practices; or the manufacturer or importer who supplies the product holds a manufacturing authorisation.

The holder of a wholesale dealer's licence may distribute medicinal products by way of wholesale dealing only to the holder of a wholesale dealer's licence relating to those products, the holder of an authorisation granted by the competent authority of another EEA State authorising the supply of those products by way of wholesale dealing, a person who may lawfully sell those products by retail or may lawfully supply them in circumstances corresponding to retail sale; or a person who may lawfully administer those products. This does not apply in relation to medicinal products which are distributed by way of wholesale dealing to a person in a non-EEA country.

From 28th October 2013, where the medicinal product is supplied directly to persons in a non-EEA country the licensed wholesale dealer must check that the person that receives it is authorised or entitled to receive medicinal products for wholesale distribution or supply to the public in accordance with the applicable legal and administrative provisions of the non-EEA country concerned.

Where any medicinal product is supplied to any person who may lawfully sell those products by retail or who may lawfully supply them in circumstances corresponding to retail sale, the licence holder shall enclose with the product a document which makes it possible to ascertain:

- the date on which the supply took place;
- the name and pharmaceutical form of the product supplied;

- the quantity of product supplied;
- the names and addresses of the person or persons from whom the products were supplied to the licence holder; and
- the batch number of the medicinal products bearing the safety features referred to in point (o) of Article 54 of the 2001 Directive.

The holder of a wholesale dealer's licence shall keep a record of the information supplied where any medicinal product is supplied to any person who may lawfully sell those products by retail or who may lawfully supply them in circumstance corresponding to retail sale for a minimum period of five years after the date on which it is supplied and ensure, during that period, that that record is available to the licensing authority for inspection.

The wholesale dealer's licence holder shall at all times have at their disposal the services of a responsible person who, in the opinion of the licensing authority has knowledge of the activities to be carried out and of the procedures to be performed under the licence which is adequate for performing the functions of responsible person; and has experience in those procedures and activities which is adequate for those purposes.

The functions of the responsible person shall be to ensure, in relation to medicinal products, that the conditions under which the licence has been granted have been, and are being, complied with and the quality of medicinal products which are being handled by the wholesale dealer's licence holder are being maintained in accordance with the requirements of the marketing authorisations, Article 126a authorisations, certificates of registration or traditional herbal registrations applicable to those products.

The standard provisions for wholesale dealer's licences, that is, those provisions which may be included in all licences unless the licence specifically provides otherwise, insofar as those licences relate to relevant medicinal products, shall be those provisions set out in Part 4 of Schedule 4 of the Regulations.

The licence holder shall not use any premises for the purpose of the handling, storage or distribution of relevant medicinal products other than those specified in their licence or notified to the licensing authority by them and approved by the licensing authority.

The licence holder shall provide such information as may be requested by the licensing authority concerning the type and quantity of any relevant medicinal products which they handle, store or distribute.

Where and insofar as the licence relates to special medicinal products to which regulation 167 of the Regulations apply which do not have a UK or EMA authorisation and are commonly known as "specials" (refer to Guidance Note 14), the licence holder shall only import such products from another EEA State in response to an order which satisfies the requirements of regulation 167 of the Regulations; and where the following conditions are complied with:

- No later than 28 days prior to each importation of a special medicinal product, the licence holder shall give written notice to the licensing authority stating their intention to import that special medicinal product and stating the following particulars:
  - the name of the medicinal product, being the brand name or the common name, or the scientific name, and any name, if different, under which the medicinal product is to be sold or supplied in the United Kingdom,
  - any trademark or name of the manufacturer of the medicinal product,
  - in respect of each active constituent of the medicinal product, any international non-proprietary name or the British approved name or the monograph name or, where that constituent does not have an international non-proprietary name, a British approved name or a monograph name, the accepted scientific name or any other name descriptive of the true nature of that constituent,
  - the quantity of medicinal product which is to be imported which shall not exceed more, on any one occasion, than such amount as is sufficient for 25 single administrations, or for 25 courses of treatment where the amount imported is sufficient for a maximum of three months' treatment, and
  - the name and address of the manufacturer or assembler of that medicinal product in the form in which it is to be imported and, if the person who will supply that medicinal product for importation is not the manufacturer or assembler, the name and address of such supplier.
- Subject to the next bullet point below, the licence holder shall not import the special medicinal product if, before the end of 28 days from the date on which the licensing authority sends or gives the licence holder an acknowledgement in writing by the licensing authority that they have received the notice referred to in the bullet point above, the licensing authority have notified them in writing that the product should not be imported.
- The licence holder may import the special medicinal product referred to in the notice where they have been notified in writing by the licensing authority, before the end of the 28 day period referred to in the bullet point above, that the special medicinal product may be imported.
- Where the licence holder sells or supplies special medicinal products, they shall, in addition to any other records which they are required to make by the provisions of their licence, make and maintain written records relating to the batch number of the batch of the product from which the sale or supply was made and details of any adverse reaction to the product so sold or supplied of which they become aware.
- The licence holder shall import no more on any one occasion than such amount as is sufficient for 25 single administrations, or for 25 courses of treatment where the amount imported is sufficient for a maximum of three months' treatment, and on any such occasion shall not import more

than the quantity notified to the licensing authority in the notification of intention to import.

- The licence holder shall inform the licensing authority forthwith of any matter coming to their attention which might reasonably cause the licensing authority to believe that the medicinal product can no longer be regarded either as a product which can safely be administered to human beings or as a product which is of satisfactory quality for such administration.
- The licence holder shall not issue any advertisement, catalogue or circular relating to the special medicinal product or make any representations in respect of that product.
- The licence holder shall cease importing or supplying a special medicinal product if they have received a notice in writing from the licensing authority directing that, as from a date specified in that notice, a particular product or class of products shall no longer be imported or supplied.

The licence holder shall take all reasonable precautions and exercise all due diligence to ensure that any information they provide to the licensing authority which is relevant to an evaluation of the safety, quality or efficacy of any medicinal product for human use which they handle, store or distribute is not false or misleading in a material particular.

Where a wholesale dealer's licence relates to exempt advanced therapy medicinal products the licence holder shall keep the data for the system for the traceability of the advanced therapy medicinal products for such period, being a period of longer than 30 years, as may be specified by the licensing authority.

The Standard Provisions also require the holder of a wholesale dealer's licence that relates to exempt advanced therapy medicinal products to obtain supplies of exempt advanced therapy medicinal products only from the holder of a manufacturer's licence in respect of those products or the holder of a wholesale dealer's licence in respect of those products.

The licence holder must:

- distribute an exempt advanced therapy medicinal product by way of wholesale dealing only to the holder of a wholesale dealer's licence in respect of those products; or a person who may lawfully administer those products, and solicited the product for an individual patient;
- establish and maintain a system ensuring that the exempt advanced therapy medicinal product and its starting and raw materials, including all substances coming into contact with the cells or tissues it may contain, can be traced through the sourcing, manufacturing, packaging, storage, transport and delivery to the establishment where the product is used;
- inform the licensing authority of any adverse reaction to any exempt advanced therapy medicinal product supplied by the holder of the wholesale dealer's licence of which the holder is aware;

- keep the data for ensuring traceability for a minimum of 30 years after the expiry date of the exempt advanced therapy medicinal product or longer as specified by the licensing authority;
- ensure that the data for ensuring traceability will, in the event that the licence is suspended, revoked or withdrawn or the licence holder becomes bankrupt or insolvent, be held available to the licensing authority by the holder of a wholesale dealer's licence for the same period that the data has to be kept; and
- not import or export any exempt advanced therapy medicinal product.

## Appointment and Duties of the Responsible Person

Title VII of the Directive on the Community code relating to medicinal products for human use (Directive 2001/83/EC) obliges holders of a distribution authorisation to have a "qualified person designated as responsible". Regulation 45 of the Human Medicines Regulations 2012 [SI 2012/1916] state the requirement for a Responsible Person (RP) within the UK.

The RP is responsible for safeguarding product users against potential hazards arising from poor distribution practices as a result, for example, of purchasing suspect products, poor storage or failure to establish the bona fides of purchasers. The duties of a RP include:

- to ensure that the provisions of the licence are observed
- to ensure that the guidelines on Good Distribution Practice (GDP) are complied with
- to ensure that the operations do not compromise the quality of medicines
- to ensure that an adequate quality system is established and maintained
- to oversee audit of the quality system and to carry out independent audits
- to ensure that adequate records are maintained
- to ensure that all personnel are trained
- to ensure full and prompt cooperation with marketing authorisation holders in the event of recalls.

In order to carry out his duties, the RP should be resident in the UK and have a clear reporting line to the licence holder or MD. The RP should have personal knowledge of the products traded under the licence and the conditions necessary for their safe storage and distribution. The RP should have access to all areas, sites, stores and records which relate to the licensable activities and regularly review and monitor all such areas, etc. and the standards achieved.

If the RP is not adequately carrying out those duties, the licensing authority may consider the suspension of the licence, withdrawal of acceptance of the RP on that licence and the acceptability on any other licence.

The RP does not have to be an employee of the licence holder but must be available to the licence holder when required. Where the RP is not an employee, there should be a written contract specifying responsibilities, duties, authority and so on.

In the case of small companies, the licensing authority may accept the licence holder as the nominated RP. In larger companies, however, this is not desirable.

There is no statutory requirement for the RP to be a pharmacist.

The RP should have access to pharmaceutical knowledge and advice when it is required, and have personal knowledge of:

- The relevant provisions of the Human Medicines Regulations 2012 [SI 2012/1916].
- Directive 2001/83/EC as amended on the wholesale distribution of medicinal products for human use.
- The EU Guidelines on Good Distribution Practice of Medicinal Products for Human Use (2013/C 343/01).
- The conditions of the wholesale dealer's licence for which nominated.
- The products traded under the licence and the conditions necessary for their safe storage and distribution.
- The categories of persons to whom products may be distributed.

Where the RP is not a pharmacist or eligible to act as a Qualified Person (QP) (as defined in Directive 2001/83/EC as amended), the RP should have at least one year's practical experience in both or either of the following areas:

- Handling, storage and distribution of medicinal products.
- Transactions in or selling or procuring medicinal products.
  In addition, the RP should have at least one year's managerial experience in controlling and directing the wholesale distribution of medicinal products on a scale, and of a kind, appropriate to the licence for which nominated.

To carry out responsibilities, the RP should:

- Have a clear reporting line to either the licence holder or the Managing Director.
- Have access to all areas, sites, stores, staff and records relating to the licensable activities being carried out.
- Demonstrate regular review and monitoring of all such areas, sites and staff etc. or have delegated arrangements whereby the RP receives written reports that such delegated actions have been carried out on behalf of the RP in compliance with standard operating procedures and GDP.
  Where arrangements are delegated, the RP remains responsible and should personally carry out the delegated functions at least once a year.
- Focus on the management of licensable activities, the accuracy and quality of records, compliance with standard operating procedures and GDP, the quality of handling and storage equipment and facilities, and the standards achieved.

● Keep appropriate records relating to the discharge of the RP responsibilities.

Where the licence covers a number of sites, the RP may have a nominated deputy with appropriate reporting and delegating arrangements. However, the RP should be able to demonstrate to the licensing authority that the necessary controls and checks are in place.

The licence holder should ensure that there is a written standard operating procedure for receiving advice and comment from the RP and recording the consequent action taken as may be necessary.

Should it prove impossible to resolve a disagreement between the licence holder and the RP, the licensing authority should be consulted.

Whilst a joint referral is clearly to be preferred, either party may approach the licensing authority independently. If an RP finds difficulty over performing statutory responsibilities or the activities being carried out under the licence, the licensing authority should be consulted in strict confidence.

## The Responsible Person Gold Standard

The Human Medicines Regulations 2012 require holders of a wholesale dealer's licence to designate and ensure that there is available at all times at least one person, referred to in the regulations as the "responsible person", who in the opinion of the licensing authority:

(a) has knowledge of the activities to be carried out and of the procedures to be performed under the licence; and

(b) has adequate experience relating to those activities and procedures.

Guidance on the role and responsibilities of the Responsible Person (RP) is set out in Chapter 2 of the EU Good Distribution Practice Guide and these remain the same irrespective of whether the RP is a permanent or contracted employee of a company.

The RP plays a vital part in ensuring the quality and the integrity of medicinal products are maintained throughout the distribution chain and it is essential that they have the right knowledge, demonstrate competence and deploy the right skills so that patients and healthcare professionals have the confidence and trust to use medicines.

In order to facilitate this and to standardise the requirements for individuals operating as, or aspiring to be, a RP, Cogent (the national skills body for the science industries) has, following extensive discussion with pharmaceutical companies and MHRA, published a new Gold Standard role profile for the RP[1].

---

[1] http://www.mhra.gov.uk/Howweregulate/Medicines/Inspectionandstandards/GoodManufacturingPractice/News/CON421310.

# Responsible Person
# Medicinal Products

*The Human Medicines Regulations require a distributor to designate a Responsible Person(s), named on the applicable licence. Regulation 45 and the EU GDP Guide set out the requirements and the responsibilities.*

*Where the RP is contracted to a company, the duties remain the same as for those of the permanently employed RP. The responsibilities should be covered in a contract.*

| Compliance | **The Gold Standard**<br>Job Role skills, knowledge and behaviours |
|---|---|
| | *the individual should understand:*<br>• *the role of MHRA in the licensing of medicines and as the competent authority including the risk-based inspection process, the role of the enforcement group, the Inspection Action Group (IAG), and resulting actions that can be taken due to non-compliance*<br>• *the UK regulations in relation to Wholesale Distribution*<br>• *the European Pharmaceutical Directive related to Wholesale Distribution of Medicinal Products*<br>• *Good Distribution Practice (GDP)*<br>• *the importance of a clear reporting line to the wholesale distribution authorisation holder, senior manager and/or CEO*<br><br>*the individual shall:*<br>• *employ due diligence in the discharge of their duties, maintaining full compliance to procedures and appropriate regulations*<br>• *report to senior management, the Marketing Authorisation holder and the MHRA any suspicious events of which they become aware*<br><br>*in addition, the individual also has knowledge of:*<br>• *the role of the professional bodies and organisations that regulate those supplying medicinal products to the public e.g. GPhC*<br>• *the role of the Home Office in relation to the handling of Controlled Drugs*<br>• *the role of the Veterinary Medicines Directorate (VMD) in relation to veterinary medicines*<br>• *the role of the European Medicines Agency (EMA) and use of EUDRAGMDP*<br>• *the Falsified Medicines Directive*<br>• *the Principles and Guidelines of Good Manufacturing Practice and how the principles of GDP maintain product quality throughout the distribution chain* |
| **Knowledge** | **The Gold Standard**<br>Job Role skills, knowledge and behaviours |
| | *the individual should have:*<br><br>• *the prior relevant knowledge and experience related to the distribution of medicinal products*<br>• *access to pharmaceutical knowledge and advice when it is required*<br>• *knowledge of the products traded under the licence*<br>• *if not a pharmacist or QP, one year's relevant practical and managerial experience of medicinal products* |

UK GUIDANCE ON WHOLESALE DISTRIBUTION PRACTICE

Supported by MHRA

cogent | Skills for Science Based Industries

# Responsible Person
# Medicinal Products

| Technical Competence | The Gold Standard<br>Job Role skills, knowledge and behaviours |
|---|---|
| | *the individual is able to perform duties including:*<br><br>**Quality Management**<br>*the individual shall ensure that a quality management system proportionate to the distributor's activities is implemented and maintained including:*<br>• *Quality Risk Management*<br>• *Corrective and Preventative Actions (CAPA) to address deviations*<br>• *Change Control*<br>• *Measurement of performance indicators and management review*<br><br>**Personnel**<br>*The Responsible Person is required to:*<br>• *understand their own responsibilities*<br>• *carry out all duties in such a way as to ensure that the wholesale distributor can demonstrate GDP compliance*<br>• *define personal and staff roles, responsibilities and accountabilities and record all delegated duties*<br>• *ensure that initial and continuous training programmes are implemented and maintained*<br>• *ensure all personnel are trained in GDP, their own duties, product identification, the risks of falsified medicines and specific training for products requiring more stringent handling*<br>• *maintain training records for self and others and ensure training is periodically assessed*<br><br>**Premises & Equipment**<br>• *ensure that appropriate standards of GDP are maintained for own premises and contracted storage premises*<br>• *identify medicinal products, legal categories, storage conditions and different Marketing Authorisation types*<br>• *maintain the safety and security of medicinal products within the appropriate environments, including product integrity and product storage*<br>• *use the appropriate systems to segregate, store and distribute medicinal products*<br>• *maintain records for the repair, maintenance, calibration and validation of equipment including computerised systems*<br>• *ensure storage areas are temperature mapped, qualified and validated*<br><br>**Documentation**<br>*The individual shall focus on:*<br>• *the accuracy and quality of records*<br>• *contemporaneous records*<br>• *records storage*<br>• *maintaining comprehensive written procedures that are understood and followed*<br>• *ensure procedures are valid and version controlled* |

Supported by MHRA

cogent | Skills for Science Based Industries

# Responsible Person
# Medicinal Products

*Operations*
- carry out due diligence checks and ensure that suppliers and customers are qualified
- ensure all necessary checks are carried out and that medicinal products are authorised for sale
- manage authorised activities to ensure operations do not compromise the quality of medicines and can demonstrate compliance with GDP
- demonstrate the application of activities and provisions in accordance with the wholesale distribution authorisation and of company processes and procedures
- ensure that any additional requirements imposed on certain products by national law are adhered to e.g. specials, unlicensed imports & Controlled Drugs

*Complaints, returns, suspected falsified medicinal products and medicinal product recalls*
- ensure relevant customer complaints are dealt with effectively, informing the manufacturer and/or marketing authorisation holder of any product quality/product defect issues
- decide on the final disposition of returned, rejected, recalled or falsified products
- approve any returns to saleable stock
- coordinate and promptly perform any recall operations for medicinal products
- co-operate with marketing authorisation holders and national competent authorities in the event of recalls
- have an awareness of the issues surrounding falsified medicines

*Outsourced Activities*
- approve any subcontracted activities which may impact on GDP

*Self-Inspection*
- ensure that self-inspections are performed at appropriate regular intervals following a prearranged programme and necessary corrective measures are put in place

*Transportation*
- apply the appropriate transport requirements and methods for cold chain, ambient and hazardous product
- ensure all transport equipment is appropriately qualified

*Brokers*
- ensure that transactions are only made with brokers who are registered
- ensure that any broker activities performed are registered

| Business Improvement | **The Gold Standard** Job Role skills, knowledge and behaviours |
|---|---|
| | the individual should: • practise continuous improvement practices and utilise appropriate tools and techniques to solve problems |

UK GUIDANCE ON WHOLESALE DISTRIBUTION PRACTICE

# Responsible Person
# Medicinal Products

| Functional & Behavioural | The Gold Standard<br>Job Role skills, knowledge and behaviours |
|---|---|
|  | *the individual has:*<br>• *relevant skills in:*<br>   o *English (level 2)*<br>   o *Mathematics (level 2)*<br>   o *ICT*<br><br>*the individual can demonstrate relevant personal qualities in:*<br>  *Autonomy*<br>   o *take responsibility for planning and developing courses of action, including responsibility for the work of others*<br>   o *exercise autonomy and judgement within broad but generally well-defined parameters*<br>• *Management & Leadership*<br>   o *develop and implement operational plans for their area of responsibility*<br>   o *manage diversity & discrimination issues*<br>   o *provide leadership for their team*<br><br>• *Working with others*<br>   o *ensure effective delegation whilst retaining ownership of the outcome*<br>   o *develop and maintain productive working relationships with colleagues and stakeholders*<br>   o *monitor the progress and quality of work within their area of responsibility*<br><br>• *Personal development*<br>   o *manage their professional development by setting targets and planning how they will be met*<br>   o *review progress towards targets and establish evidence of achievements*<br><br>• *Communication*<br>   o *put across ideas in clear and concise manner and present a well-structured case*<br>   o *communicate complex information to others*<br><br>• *Business*<br>   o *understands the business environment in which the company operates*<br>   o *has an appreciation of the industry sector and competitors*<br><br>• *Customers*<br>   o *understands the customer base and is aware of customer requirements* |
| *For more information on how to achieve the Gold Standard contact us on 0845 607 014* | |
| *Version 2 July 2014* | |

Supported by MHRA

This sets out an industry-agreed framework that identifies the skills required in four competency areas and includes not only traditional qualifications and technical requirements but also the behavioural skills necessary to do the job to a high standard.

## Best Practice Temperature Monitoring

### Why control and monitor temperature?

1   Manufacturers subject their products to stability studies that are used to determine appropriate storage conditions including those for temperature. These conditions are therefore specific for each product, and wholesalers should refer to manufacturers' information when deciding the storage conditions to use.

   Medicinal products experiencing an adverse temperature may undergo physical, chemical or microbiological degradation. In the most serious of cases this may lead to conversion of the medicine to ineffective or harmful forms. The ability to detect these changes may not appear until the medicine is consumed, and it is therefore essential that appropriate temperature conditions are controlled and monitored throughout each step of the supply chain.

### Control and monitoring of storage areas

2   Where medicines are stored that may be required in an emergency then contingency measures should be put in place such as linking essential equipment in a large warehouse to a source of emergency power. These emergency measures should be routinely tested, such as the confirmation of restoration of stored data and settings when emergency power supply is activated and after normal power is resumed. For these products there should be a system in place to ensure that on-call personnel are notified in the event of power failure or temperature alarms being triggered including notification outside of normal working hours.

3   The application of Mean Kinetic Temperature (MKT) to temperature monitoring of wholesale products is only appropriate where an acceptable MKT value is provided by the MA holder for a specific product, and the recording of temperature can be confirmed to be consistent and complete from the moment of leaving the manufacturer's premises. In practice the application of MKT fails where a complete chain of temperature recording cannot be allocated to a specific consignment of a product. Attempts to apply MKT have been proposed by wholesalers as an alternative to having adequate temperature control within their warehouses as well as attempting to downgrade the impact of temperature excursions. The use

of MKT in the wholesale environment without robust supporting information and methodology is therefore discouraged.

## SMALL REFRIGERATORS

4   Refrigerators used to store pharmaceuticals should be demonstrated to be fit for purpose. In the simplest of cases a new off-the–shelf refrigerator installed according to the manufacturer's instructions and temperature monitored with an appropriate device may be considered appropriately qualified for storing cold chain product that is shown to be unaffected by minor temperature excursions. A refrigerator used for holding more susceptible stock such as biological products will require more extensive qualification.

5   In addition to temperature mapping and monitoring there should be safeguards to preserve appropriate storage conditions. Some small refrigerators are purported to be medical or pharmaceutical refrigerators but this on its own does not automatically render them suitable for wholesale use. The refrigerator should be capable of restoring the temperature quickly after the door has been opened and without danger of overshooting to extreme cold. This could be assisted by an internal fan and good shelf design which enables an efficient air flow. There should be no internal ice box and no internal temperature dials capable of being inadvertently knocked and adjusted.

6   Storage practices for using small refrigerators should include consideration of segregation of stock with different status, e.g. incoming, quarantine, returned and outgoing stock. Sufficient space should be maintained to permit adequate air circulation and product should not be stored in contact with the walls or on the floor of the refrigerator. If the refrigerator is filled to capacity the effect on temperature distribution should be investigated. Where non-refrigerated items are introduced to the refrigerator, such as non-conditioned gel packs, the impact of introducing these items should be assessed regarding the increase in temperature they cause.

## LARGE COMMERCIAL REFRIGERATORS AND WALK-IN COLD ROOMS

7   These should be of appropriate design, suitably sited and be constructed with appropriate materials. The design should ensure general principles of GDP can be maintained, such as segregation of stock. Condensate from chillers should not be collected inside the unit and there should be a capability to carry out routine maintenance and service activities as much as possible from outside the unit. The temperature should be monitored with an electronic temperature-recording device that measures load temperature in one or more locations depending on the size of the unit,

and alarms should be fitted to indicate power outages and temperature excursions.

## FREEZERS

8  The same general principles apply to freezers as apply to other cold chain storage units above. Walk-in freezers pose a significant operator health and safety risk, and the impact of ways of working should be reviewed with consideration of risk to causing temperature excursions.

## Calibration of temperature monitoring devices

9  In order to have confidence in temperature readings monitoring devices should be calibrated to demonstrate they have appropriate accuracy and precision. Temperate storage thermometers should be capable of reading $\pm1°$C, and cold chain devices capable of reading $\pm0.5°$C. Calibration should extend across the whole of the working range, so for a temperate storage range of 15°C to 25°C the calibration range may be 10°C to 30°C to allow the thermometer to be used in assessing temperature excursions or to be used in temperature mapping exercises. Results of the calibration exercise should be presented in a report or calibration certificate approved by the calibrator and demonstrated to be appropriate for use by the wholesaler. The certificate should include the following details:

- Serial number of the calibrated instrument
- Serial numbers of test instruments
- Traceability to national or international calibration standards
- Calibration test method used
- ISO or equivalent registration details of calibration laboratory
- Date of calibration
- Calibration results
- Unique certificate number
- Approval of results by calibrator.

Where a temperature monitoring device reads temperature from a main monitoring unit plus a remote probe it should be clear from the calibration certificate which part of the device the calibration refers to. Calibration should be carried out annually, and where adjustments are made to the equipment as part of calibration an assessment of accuracy and precision should be made prior to adjustment in addition to following adjustment. On completion a suitable representative from the wholesaler should approve the calibration indicating its suitability for use.

## Qualification of Customers and Suppliers

Before commencing wholesale dealing activities with a customer or supplier (trading partners), wholesale dealers should ensure that their proposed trading partners are entitled to trade with them. Checks should demonstrate that trading partners either hold the required manufacturing and wholesale dealer's licence where necessary or that they are entitled to receive medicines for the purpose of retail supply or for use in the course of their business.

Wholesale dealers should request those trading partners that wholesale or manufacture human medicines to supply a copy of their licence before trading commences.

Subsequent and continuing bona fides checks can be made by checking against the Register of licence holders on MHRA's website.

## Qualification of suppliers

Maintaining the integrity of the supply chain is one of the most important aspects of wholesale distribution. A robust fully documented system to ensure medicines are sourced appropriately must be in place and subjected to regular review. Wholesalers must ensure their suppliers are appropriately licenced to supply medicines. The qualification of suppliers requires the following steps to be fully complaint.

- The licence of the supplier should be viewed, either a copy obtained from the company or the details can be viewed on the MHRA's website that has registers of wholesalers and manufacturers.[1] Whilst MHRA registers are updated regularly they must not be relied on as a sole means of qualifying suppliers' authority to supply.
- The EudraGMDP website has daily updates from the MHRA and contains all current live licences. The EudraGMDP website does not however contain all the information on a WDA(H) that companies need to fully qualify suppliers and must not be relied on as a sole means of qualifying suppliers' authority to supply.[2]
- For supplies from other EEA member states the same checks should be made on EudraGMDP and via licences that have been translated. The translated licences should be translated and authenticated as such by a notary.

---

[1] http://www.mhra.gov.uk/Howweregulate/Medicines/Licensingofmedicines/Manufacturersandwholesaledealerslicences/index.htm

[2] http://eudragmdp.ema.europa.eu/inspections/logonGeneralPublic.do

## Compliance with GDP

Wholesalers must verify that wholesale suppliers comply with the principles and guidelines of good distribution practices.

● The GDP certificate of the wholesaler should be viewed on the EudraGMDP website. The date of the certificate expiry should be noted.

● If there is no GDP certificate available then other evidence of GDP compliance by the wholesale supplier should be obtained, such as a copy of the inspection close out letter confirming GDP compliance.

## Routine re-qualification

Wholesalers must be aware of issues that could affect their suppliers' continued authority to supply. The following should be carried out:

● Regular checks at least twice a month of MHRA's list of suspended licence holders.

● Regular checks on EudraGMDP website for issued GMP and GDP statements of non-compliance.

● At least annually, a documented full re-qualification of suppliers.

## Due diligence

When entering into a new contract with new suppliers, the wholesale distributor should carry out 'due diligence' checks in order to assess the suitability, competence and reliability of the other party. This could include checking the financial status of the supplier.

## Falsified Medicines

A "falsified medicinal product" means any medicinal product with a false representation of:

(a) its identity, including its packaging and labelling, its name or its composition (other than any unintentional quality defect) as regards any of its ingredients including excipients and the strength of those ingredients;

(b) its source, including its manufacturer, its country of manufacturing, its country of origin or its marketing authorisation holder; or

(c) its history, including the records and documents relating to the distribution channels used.

The supply of falsified medicines is a global phenomenon and one which MHRA takes very seriously. Falsified medicines represent a threat to the legitimate UK supply chain and to patient safety. They are fraudulent and may be deliberately misrepresented with respect to identity, composition and/or source. Falsification can apply to both innovator and generic products, prescription and self-medication, as well as to traditional herbal remedies. Falsified medicines may include products with the correct ingredients but fake packaging, with the wrong ingredients, without active ingredients or with insufficient active ingredients, and may even contain harmful or poisonous substances.

The supply and distribution of medicines is tightly controlled within the European Community.

All licensed wholesalers must comply with the Community's agreed standards of good distribution practice (GDP) and there exist strict licensing and regulatory requirements in UK domestic legislation to safeguard patients against potential hazards arising from poor distribution practices: for example, purchasing suspect or falsified products, failing to establish the "bona fides" of suppliers and purchasers, inadequate record keeping, and so on.

Section 6.4 of the EU Guide to GDP is of principal importance to wholesale dealers. This states:

> "Wholesale distributors must immediately inform the competent authority and the marketing authorisation holder of any medicinal products they identify as falsified or suspect to be falsified[6]. A procedure should be in place to this effect. It should be recorded with all the original details and investigated.
>
> Any falsified medicinal products found in the supply chain should immediately be physically segregated and stored in a dedicated area away from all other medicinal products. All relevant activities in relation to such products should be documented and records retained."

Wholesale dealers in particular should maintain a high level of vigilance against the procurement or supply of potentially falsified product. Such product may be offered for sale below the established market price so rigorous checks should be made on the bona fides of the supplier and the origin of the product. It is known that some wholesalers are themselves developing good practice strategies – such as conducting rigorous physical inspections of packs when grey market purchases are made – and this is encouraged. Any suspicious activity should be reported to:

---

[6] Article 80(i) of Directive 2001/83/EC.

Email: casereferrals@mhra.gsi.gov.uk
Telephone: +44 (0)20 3080 6330

To report suspected counterfeit medicines or medical devices:
Email: counterfeit@mhra.gsi.gov.uk
Website: www.mhra.gov.uk
Telephone: +44 (0)20 3080 6701

## Regulatory Action

The competent authority will take regulatory action where breaches of legislation are identified; this may take the form of adverse licensing action e.g. make a variation to an existing licence, suspension or revocation of a licence and/or the instigation of criminal proceedings.

## Diverted Medicines

Diversion is the term used for the fraudulent activity where medicines destined for non-EU markets re-enter the EU and are placed back on to the European market at a higher price.

The diversion of medicines involves medicinal products being offered at preferential prices and exported to specific markets (normally third countries) outside the EU. Diversion occurs when unscrupulous traders, on receipt of the medicines, re-export the products back to the EU – with the consequence that patients for whom these preferentially-priced medicines were intended, are denied access to them. Such products appearing on the EU market are then known as "diverted" from their intended market. This represents not only a corrupt diversion for profit, but such activity also poses the risk of inappropriate or unlicensed use, and the risk that the product may also be compromised due to poor storage and transportation.

As with counterfeit products, wholesale dealers in particular should maintain a high level of vigilance against the procurement or supply of potentially diverted product. Diverted products may be offered for sale below the established market value, therefore appropriate checks should be made on the bona fides of the supplier and the origin of the product should be ascertained.

## Parallel Distribution

Parallel distribution embodies two fundamental principles of the European Community's founding Treaty (of Rome): the free movement of goods and Community-wide exhaustion of intellectual property rights. It is also referred to as parallel trade and also, less correctly (since the EEA[7] is a single market with no internal borders), as parallel import or export.

Parallel distribution exists in the absence of price harmonisation of pharmaceutical products within the European Union, i.e. when there are significant price differences between countries; this is the case in the European Union, where prices of medicines are not governed by free competition laws, but are generally fixed by the government.

It involves the transfer of genuine, original branded products, authorised in accordance with Community legislation, marketed in one Member State of the EEA at a lower price (the source country) to another EEA member state (the country of destination) by a parallel distributor, and placed on the market in competition with a therapeutically identical product already marketed there at a higher price by or under licence from the owner of the brand.

The pharmaceutical products which are distributed in this way are identical in all respects to the branded version marketed by the originator in the country into which it is imported. They are not copies; they do not vary in any respect from the original; and they are manufactured normally by the originator or by the licensee to the approved product specification. All such products require a Product Licence for Parallel Import (PLPI) which is a "piggy-back" authorisation granted by the competent regulatory authority (MHRA in the UK), after extensive checks to ensure that the imported drug is therapeutically the same as the domestic version.

Parallel distributors operating in the UK are subject to a system of licensing and inspection, which ensures that licensed medicinal products conform to internationally agreed standards, and that those medicines are stored and distributed in compliance with the required regulatory standards. Distributors are required to hold a wholesale dealer's licence, in accordance with Article 77 of Directive 2001/83/EC, as amended. The only exception is if a manufacturing authorisation includes provision for wholesale dealing. In accordance with the wholesaling authorisation, parallel distributors are obliged to follow GDP guidelines in accordance with Article 84 of the Directive, employ a Responsible Person and are subject to periodic inspection by the competent (licensing) authority.

In addition, parallel distributors in the country of destination (the receiving country) involved in repackaging or relabelling of product must employ at least one Qualified Person (QP), who has received the relevant education and training (in accordance with Article 48 of the Directive), with responsibility to ensure that a quality system is implemented and maintained. A Manufacturing (assembly) Authorisation is also required. Regular GMP inspections are undertaken at parallel assemblers and

---

[7] The member states of the European Union plus Iceland, Norway and Liechtenstein.

distributors (performing relabelling/repacking activities) by the competent authority in the Member State concerned to ensure that GMP is adhered to.

Parallel distributors are required to have effective recall procedures in place. MHRA has systems in place to receive and investigate reports of packaging and labelling problems with medicines, including parallel traded products.

## Relabelling/Repackaging

The goods should remain in their original packaging as long as possible. However, once the received product is approved for processing, relabelling may be undertaken in accordance with the national simplified marketing authorisation of the parallel-distributed product, under conditions of GMP, i.e. exactly the same procedures as those followed by all pharmaceutical manufacturers.

This either involves replacement of the original outer carton with a brand new one or over-stickering the original outer carton, with both providing the approved label text in the language of the country of destination. In all cases, the existing package leaflet is removed and replaced by a new one originated by the parallel distributor in accordance with the simplified marketing authorisation in the language of the country of destination. In addition to the requirements of the PLPI marketing authorisation it may be necessary, as part of any repackaging specifications, for the applicant to address any trademark concerns that might arise. This may involve technical and commercial discussions between the trademark holder and the PLPI applicant.

Both the original cartons – if these are replaced – and the original leaflets must be destroyed. No handling of the actual product (e.g. open units of tablets or capsules) within its immediate packaging (e.g. blister or foil packs) should take place during replacement of the original carton and it is important to maintain the audit trail back to the origin.

As with any other pharmaceutical manufacturer, parallel distributor operators involved in relabelling and/or repackaging should be given regular training in GMP. Batch documentation should be retained for each batch.

## Maintenance of the integrity of the supply chain

Parallel distributors should only purchase medicinal products with marketing authorisations from authorised wholesalers or manufacturers in other EEA countries. The supplying wholesaler should make available before sale a copy of its wholesale authorisation and provide assurance that the supplies were obtained from the original manufacturer and/or an authorised wholesaler within the EEA.

Parallel distributors should also only sell or supply medicinal products with marketing authorisations to authorised wholesalers, registered pharmacies or other persons entitled to sell medicinal products to the general public. A copy of the authorisation should be requested if there is any doubt.

## Continued Supply

Under Article 23a of Directive 2001/83/EC, as inserted by Article 1(22) of Directive 2004/27/EC, the marketing authorisation holder is required to notify the competent authority (MHRA in the UK) of the date of actual marketing of the medicinal product, taking account of the various presentations authorised, and to notify the competent authority if the product ceases to be placed on the market either temporarily or permanently. Except in exceptional circumstances, the notification must be made no less than two months before the interruption.

Any authorisation which within three years of granting is not placed on the market will cease to be valid. In respect of generic medicinal products, the three year period will start on the grant of the authorisation, or at the end of the period of market exclusivity or patent protection of the reference product, whichever is the later date. If a product is placed on the market after authorisation, but subsequently ceases to be available on the market in the UK for a period of three consecutive years, it will also cease to be valid. In these circumstances MHRA will, however, when it is aware of the imminent expiry of the three year period, notify the marketing authorisation holder in advance that their marketing authorisation will cease to be valid. In exceptional circumstances, and on public health grounds, MHRA may grant an exemption from the invalidation of the marketing authorisation after three years. Whether there are exceptional circumstances and public health grounds for an exemption will be assessed on a case by case basis. When assessing such cases, MHRA will, in particular, consider the implications for patients and public health more generally of a marketing authorisation no longer being valid.

MHRA has received requests for advice on implications for maintaining the harmonisation of an authorisation across Member States if a presentation of a product is withdrawn from the market of the Reference Member State (RMS) and remains unavailable on that market for three years. Discussions on applying the sunset clause provision in such circumstances continue at EU level. In the meantime the MHRA will address the implications of this issue on a case by case basis.

Those provisions are implemented in the UK by Part 5 of the Human Medicines Regulations 2012.

In accordance with MHRA's interpretation of the expression "placing on the market" when used elsewhere in the Directive, MHRA's view is that a product is "placed on the market" at the first transaction by which the product enters the distribution chain in the UK. The marketing authorisation holder must, therefore, notify MHRA when a product with a new marketing authorisation is first placed into the distribution chain, rather than the first date it becomes available to individual patients. MHRA requests that you notify us of this first "placing on the market" within one calendar month. In order to ensure that a marketing authorisation continues to be valid, the marketing authorisation holder must ensure that at least one packaging presentation (e.g. bottle or blister pack) of the product, which can include own label supplies, authorised under that marketing authorisation is present on the market.

The marketing authorisation holder must report all cessations/interruptions to MHRA. However, MHRA does not need to be notified of the following:

(a) normal seasonal changes in manufacturing and/or distribution schedules (such as cold and flu remedies);
(b) short-term temporary interruptions in placing on the market that will not affect normal availability to distributors.

If you are in doubt about whether or not you need to notify an interruption in supply, you should err on the side of caution and report it to MHRA in the normal way. You must notify MHRA if any of the presentations authorised under a single marketing authorisation cease to be placed on the market either temporarily or permanently, but, as stated above, the absence of availability of one or more presentations – as long as one presentation of the product authorised under the single marketing authorisation remains on the market – will not invalidate the marketing authorisation. Problems relating to manufacturing or assembly should also be discussed with the appropriate GMP Inspector and issues of availability of medicines relating to suspected or confirmed product defects should be directly notified to, and discussed with, the Defective Medicines Reporting Centre (Tel: 020 3080 6574).

The Department of Health (DH) also has an interest in the availability of products for supply to the NHS, and together with the Association of the British Pharmaceutical Industry (ABPI) and the British Generics Manufacturers Association (BGMA), has developed best practice guidelines for notifying medicine shortages. These guidelines, together with DH/ABPI guidelines "Ensuring Best Practice in the Notification of Product Discontinuations" complement the statutory requirements under the European legislation and may be found (in PDF format) on the

DH website (www.dh.gov.uk). Marketing authorisation holders should, therefore, continue to notify the Department of Health about interruptions and cessations of marketing in accordance with these guidelines.

In this context, your attention is also drawn to Article 81 of Directive 2001/83/EC as substituted by Article 1(57) of Directive 2004/27/EC, under which the marketing authorisation holder and the distributors of a medicinal product actually placed on the market shall, within the limits of their responsibilities, ensure appropriate and continued supplies of that medicinal product to pharmacies and persons authorised to supply medicinal products so that the needs of patients in the Member State in question are covered. Failure by a marketing authorisation holder to comply with this obligation is a criminal offence, unless the marketing authorisation holder took all reasonable precautions and exercised all due diligence to avoid such a failure.

## Product Recall/Withdrawal

Manufacturers, importers and distributors are obliged to inform the MHRA of any suspected quality defect in a medicinal product that could or would result in a recall, or restriction on supply.

A defective medicinal product is one whose quality does not conform to the requirements of its marketing authorisation, specification or for some other reason of quality is potentially hazardous. A defective product may be suspected because of a visible defect or contamination or as a result of tests performed on it, or because it has caused untoward reactions in a patient or for other reasons involving poor manufacturing or distribution practice. Falsified medicines are considered as defective products.

The Human Medicines Regulations 2012 [SI 2012/1916] imposes certain obligations on licence holders with regard to withdrawal and recall from sale. The aim of the Defective Medicines Report Centre (DMRC) within MHRA is to minimise the hazard to patients arising from the distribution of defective (human) medicinal products by providing an emergency assessment and communications system between the suppliers (manufacturers and distributors), the regulatory authorities and the end user. The DMRC achieves this by receiving reports of suspected defective (human) medicinal products; monitoring and, as far as is necessary, directing and advising actions by the relevant licence holder(s) and communicating the details of this action with the appropriate urgency and distribution to users of the products. The communication normally used is a "Drug Alert".

Immediately a hazard is identified from any source, it will be necessary to evaluate the level of danger, and the category of recall, if required. Where the reported defect is a confirmed defect, the DMRC will then take one of the following courses of action and obtain a report from the manufacturer on the nature of the defect, their handling of the defect and action to be taken to prevent its recurrence.

## Issue a "Recall"

Under normal circumstances a recall is always required where a defect is confirmed unless the defect is shown to be of a trivial nature and/or there are unlikely to be significant amounts of the affected product remaining in the market.

It is the licence holder's responsibility to recall products from customers, in a manner agreed with the DMRC. The company should provide copies of draft recall letters for agreement with the DMRC. If the company (licence holder) does not agree to a recall voluntarily, MHRA, as licensing authority, may be obliged to take compulsory action.

## Issue a "Drug Alert"

Recall and withdrawal of product from the market is normally the responsibility of the licence holder. However, where a product has been distributed widely and/or there is a serious risk to health from the defect, MHRA can opt to issue a Drug Alert letter. The Drug Alert cascade mechanism ensures rapid communication of safety information; it is not a substitute for, but complementary to, any action taken by the licence holder. The text of the Alert should be agreed between MHRA and the company concerned.

In some cases, where a product has been supplied to a small number of known customers, MHRA may decide that notification will be adequate and a Drug Alert is not needed.

The DMRC may also request companies to insert notification in the professional press in certain cases.

## Management of the recall

The company should directly contact wholesalers, hospitals, retail pharmacies and overseas distributors supplied. The DMRC is likely to take the lead in notifying Regional Contacts for NHS Trusts and Provider Units and Health Authorities, special and Government hospitals and overseas regulatory authorities.

The DMRC will liaise with the company and discuss arrangements for the recall, requesting the dates that supply started and ceased and a copy of any letters sent out by that company concerning the recall. Again, it is desirable that the text of the notices sent via the company and by the DMRC should be mutually agreed.

## Follow-up action

The DMRC will monitor the conduct and success of the recall by the manufacturer or distributor. As follow-up action, it may be necessary to consider any or all of the following:

- arrange a visit to the licence holder/manufacturer/distributor;
- arrange a visit to the point of discovery of the defect;
- refer to the Inspectorate to arrange an inspection;
- seek special surveillance of adverse reaction reports;
- refer the matter for adverse licensing and/or enforcement action.

## Reporting a suspected defect

Suspected defects can be reported by telephone, e-mail or letter or using our online form:

**Address:**
DMRC, 151 Buckingham Palace Road, London, SW1W 9SZ, UK.
**Telephone:** +44 (0)20 3080 6574 (08:45 – 16:45 Monday to Friday)
**Telephone:** +44 (0)7795 641532 (urgent calls outside working hours, at weekends or on public holidays)
**E-mail:** dmrc@mhra.gsi.gov.uk
**Online form:** www.mhra.gov.uk
http://www.mhra.gov.uk/Safetyinformation/Reportingsafetyproblems/
Reportingsuspecteddefectsinmedicines/Suspecteddefectonlineform/index.
htm

# CHAPTER 10

# UK Guidance on Brokering Medicines

## Introduction

Persons procuring, holding, storing, supplying or exporting medicinal products are required to hold a wholesale distribution authorisation in accordance with Directive 2001/83/EC which lays down the rules for the wholesale distribution of medicinal products in the Union.

However, the distribution network for medicinal products may involve operators who are not necessarily authorised wholesale distributors. To ensure the reliability of the supply chain, Directive 2011/62/EU, the Falsified Medicines Directive extends medicine legislation to the entire supply chain. This now includes not only wholesale distributors, whether or not they physically handle the medicinal products, but also brokers who are involved in the sale or purchase of medicinal products without selling or purchasing those products themselves, and without owning and physically handling the medicinal products.

## Brokering in Medicinal Products

Brokering of medicinal products is defined in the Falsified Medicines Directive and means:

*All activities in relation to the sale or purchase of medicinal products, except for wholesale distribution, that do not include physical handling and that consist of negotiating independently and on behalf of another legal or natural person.*

To accord with the Directive brokers may only broker medicinal products that are the subject of an authorisation granted by the European Commission or a National Competent Authority.

Brokers should be established at a permanent address and have contact details in the EU and may only operate following registration of these details with the National Competent Authority. In the UK this is MHRA. A broker must provide required details for registration which will include their name, corporate name and permanent address. They must also notify any changes without unnecessary delay. This is to ensure the brokers accurate identification, location, communication and supervision of their activities by the National Competent Authorities.

Brokers can negotiate between the manufacturer and a wholesaler, or one wholesaler and another wholesaler, or the manufacturer or wholesale dealer with a person who may lawfully sell those products by retail or may lawfully supply them in circumstances corresponding to retail sale or a person who may lawfully administer those products.

Brokers are not virtual wholesale dealers; the definition of "Brokering medicinal products" specifically excludes the activity of "wholesale dealing". Wholesale dealing and brokering of medicinal products are separate activities. Therefore wholesale dealers who wish to broker will require a separate registration, because:

- EU legislation defines wholesale distribution and brokering a medicinal product separately;
- wholesale dealers are licensed;
- the brokering of medicinal products is subject to registration.

## Registration

UK based companies that broker medicinal products and are involved in the sale or purchase of medicinal products without selling or purchasing those products themselves, and without owning and physically handling the medicinal products are considered to be brokers and will have to register with MHRA.

In order to register in the UK, brokers will have a permanent address and contact details in the UK and will only be allowed to operate as a bona fide broker following their successful registration with MHRA.

## Application for Brokering Registration

The registration regime for UK brokers is subject to an application procedure, followed by a determination procedure completed by MHRA. The application procedure will include:

- making an application for registration;
- assessment by MHRA of the application;

- providing specific evidence to check bona fides;
- advising an applicant of the decision.

UK brokers may be subject to inspection at their registered premises. This will be under a risk-based inspection programme. Once registered a broker's registration will be recognised by other Member States and will allow the broker to broker across the EEA. UK medicines legislation in respect of brokering will also recognise registered brokers in other EEA Member States in the same way.

MHRA has an obligation to enter the information on a publicly accessible UK register following the determination of successful application for registration.

This publicly available UK register is required to enable National Competent Authorities in other EEA Member States to establish the bona fides and compliance of brokers established in the UK where they are involved in the sale or purchase of medicines on their territories and the UK will investigate complaints of non-compliance. Reciprocal arrangements will apply for brokers established in other Member States involved in the sale or purchase of medicines to and from the UK.

## Criteria of Broker's Registration

A person may not broker a medicinal product unless that product is covered by an authorisation granted under Regulation (EC) No 726/2004 or by a competent authority of an EEA Member State and that person is validly registered as a broker with a competent authority of an EEA Member State.

A broker is not validly registered if the broker's permanent address is not entered into a register of brokers kept by a competent authority of a member State or the registration is suspended or the broker has notified the competent authority of an EEA Member State to remove them from the register.

Brokers must satisfy all the conditions of brokering and:

- have a permanent address in the UK;
- have an emergency plan which ensures effective implementation of any recall from the market ordered by the competent authorities or carried out in cooperation with the manufacturer or marketing authorisation holder for the medicinal product concerned;
- keep records either in the form of purchase/sales invoices or on computer, or in any other form, giving for any transaction in medicinal products brokered at least the following information:
  - date on which the sale or purchase of the product is brokered;
  - name of the medicinal product;

- quantity brokered;
- name and address of the supplier or consignee, as appropriate;
- batch number of the medicinal products at least for products bearing the safety features referred to in point (o) of Article 54 of Directive 2001/83/EC;

● keep the records available to the competent authorities, for inspection purposes, for a period of five years;

● comply with the principles and guidelines of good distribution practice for medicinal products as laid down in Article 84 of Directive 2001/83/EC;

● maintain a quality system setting out responsibilities, processes and risk management measures in relation to their activities.

Where the address at which the plan or records necessary to comply with the provisions of brokering are kept is different from the address notified in accordance with the application, the broker must ensure that the plan or records are kept at an address in the UK and inform the licensing authority of the address at which the plan or records are kept.

The broker must provide such information as may be requested by MHRA concerning the type and quantity of medicinal products brokered within the period specified by MHRA.

The broker must take all reasonable precautions and exercise all due diligence to ensure that any information provided by that broker to MHRA is not false or misleading.

For the purposes of enabling MHRA to determine whether there are grounds for suspending, revoking or varying the registration, the broker must permit a person authorised in writing by MHRA, on production of identification, to carry out any inspection, or to take any copies, which an inspector may carry out or take under the provisions of the Human Medicines Regulations 2012 [SI 2012/1916].

## Provision of Information

Once registered, a broker will have to notify MHRA of any changes to the details for registration which might affect compliance with the requirements of the legislation in respect of brokering without unnecessary delay. This notification will be subject to a variation procedure. Responsibility for notifying MHRA of any changes lies with the person responsible for management of the brokering activities.

The person responsible for management of the brokering activities shall be required to submit a report which shall include:

● a declaration that the broker has in place appropriate systems to ensure compliance with the requirements for brokering;

● provide the details of the systems which it has in place to ensure such compliance.

An annual compliance report will need to be submitted in relation to any application made before 31st March 2014, the date of the application and in relation to each subsequent reporting year, by the 30th April following the end of that year. The annual compliance report will be subject to a variation procedure so that the broker can change the original details provided.

The broker must without delay notify the licensing authority of any changes to the matters in respect of which evidence has been supplied in relation to the compliance report which might affect compliance with the requirements of brokering.

The broker must immediately inform MHRA and the marketing authorisation holder, of medicinal products they are offered which they identify as falsified or suspect to be falsified.

## Good Distribution Practice

The Commission's guidelines on good distribution practice, referred to in Article 84 of Directive 2001/83/EC have been updated to include specific provisions for brokering, see Chapter 8.

# Legislation on Wholesale Distribution and Brokering Medicines

# EU Legislation on Wholesale Distribution and Brokering Medicines

## Contents

## DIRECTIVE 2001/83/EC, AS AMENDED, TITLE VII, WHOLESALE DISTRIBUTION AND BROKERING MEDICINES

Directive 2001/83/EC of the European Parliament and of the Council of 6 November 2001 on the Community code relating to medicinal products for human use as amended.

## Title VII: Wholesale Distribution and Brokering of Medicinal Products

**Editor's note**  Title VII of this Directive is reproduced below. Title VII has been amended by Directive 2011/62/EU and Directive 2012/26/EU. A new article 85a extends the need for a Wholesale Dealer's Licence for the export of medicine to a non-EEA country and to "introduced" medicines that are imported from a non-EEA country for the purpose of export back to a non-EEA country. A new article 85b introduces measures for persons brokering medicinal products. Reference should be made to the full Directive 2001/83/EU as amended for the preamble, definitions and the general and final provisions.

## Article 76

1   Without prejudice to Article 6, Member States shall take all appropriate action to ensure that only medicinal products in respect of which a marketing authorization has been granted in accordance with Community law are distributed on their territory.

2   In the case of wholesale distribution and storage, medicinal products shall be covered by a marketing authorisation granted pursuant to Regulation (EC) No. 726/2004 or by the competent authorities of a Member State in accordance with this Directive.

3   Any distributor, not being the marketing authorisation holder, who imports a medicinal product from another Member State shall notify the marketing authorisation holder and the competent authority in the Member State to which the medicinal product will be imported of his intention to import that product. In the case of medicinal products which have not been granted an authorisation pursuant to Regulation (EC) No 726/2004, the notification to the competent authority shall be without prejudice to additional procedures provided for in the legislation of that Member State and to fees payable to the competent authority for examining the notification.

4   In the case of medicinal products which have been granted an authorisation pursuant to Regulation (EC) No 726/2004, the distributor shall submit the notification in accordance with paragraph 3 of this Article to the marketing authorisation holder and the Agency. A fee shall be payable to the Agency for checking that the conditions laid down in Union legislation on medicinal products and in the marketing authorisations are observed.

## Article 77

1 Member States shall take all appropriate measures to ensure that the wholesale distribution of medicinal products is subject to the possession of an authorisation to engage in activity as a wholesaler in medicinal products, stating the premises located on their territory for which it is valid.

2 Where persons authorized or entitled to supply medicinal products to the public may also, under national law, engage in wholesale business, such persons shall be subject to the authorization provided for in paragraph 1.

3 Possession of a manufacturing authorization shall include authorization to distribute by wholesale the medicinal products covered by that authorization. Possession of an authorization to engage in activity as a wholesaler in medicinal products shall not give dispensation from the obligation to possess a manufacturing authorization and to comply with the conditions set out in that respect, even where the manufacturing or import business is secondary.

4 Member States shall enter the information relating to the authorisations referred to in paragraph 1 of this Article in the Union database referred to in Article 111(6). At the request of the Commission or any Member State, Member States shall provide all appropriate information concerning the individual authorisations which they have granted under paragraph 1 of this Article.

5 Checks on the persons authorised to engage in activity as a wholesaler in medicinal products, and the inspection of their premises, shall be carried out under the responsibility of the Member State which granted the authorisation for premises located on its territory.

6 The Member State which granted the authorization referred to in paragraph 1 shall suspend or revoke that authorization if the conditions of authorization cease to be met. It shall forthwith inform the other Member States and the Commission thereof.

7 Should a Member State consider that, in respect of a person holding an authorization granted by another Member State under the terms of paragraph 1, the conditions of authorization are not, or are no longer met, it shall forthwith inform the Commission and the other Member State involved. The latter shall take the measures necessary and shall inform the Commission and the first Member State of the decisions taken and the reasons for those decisions.

## Article 78

Member States shall ensure that the time taken for the procedure for examining the application for the distribution authorization does not exceed 90 days from the day on which the competent authority of the Member State concerned receives the application.

The competent authority may, if need be, require the applicant to supply all necessary information concerning the conditions of authorization. Where the authority exercises this option, the period laid down in the first paragraph shall be suspended until the requisite additional data have been supplied.

## Article 79

In order to obtain the distribution authorization, applicants must fulfil the following minimum requirements:

(a) they must have suitable and adequate premises, installations and equipment, so as to ensure proper conservation and distribution of the medicinal products;

(b) they must have staff, and in particular, a qualified person designated as responsible, meeting the conditions provided for by the legislation of the Member State concerned;

(c) they must undertake to fulfil the obligations incumbent on them under the terms of Article 80.

## Article 80

Holders of the distribution authorization must fulfil the following minimum requirements:

(a) they must make the premises, installations and equipment referred to in Article 79(a) accessible at all times to the persons responsible for inspecting them;

(b) they must obtain their supplies of medicinal products only from persons who are themselves in possession of the distribution authorization or who are exempt from obtaining such authorization under the terms of Article 77(3);

(c) they must supply medicinal products only to persons who are themselves in possession of the distribution authorization or who are authorized or entitled to supply medicinal products to the public in the Member State concerned;

(ca) they must verify that the medicinal products received are not falsified by checking the safety features on the outer packaging, in accordance with the requirements laid down in the delegated acts referred to in Article 54a(2);

(d) they must have an emergency plan which ensures effective implementation of any recall from the market ordered by the competent authorities or carried out in cooperation with the manufacturer or marketing authorization holder for the medicinal product concerned;

(e) they must keep records either in the form of purchase/sales invoices or on computer, or in any other form, giving for any transaction in medicinal products received, dispatched or brokered at least the following information:
  - date,
  - name of the medicinal product,
  - quantity received, supplied or brokered,
  - name and address of the supplier or consignee, as appropriate,
  - batch number of the medicinal products at least for products bearing the safety features referred to in point (o) of Article 54;

(f) they must keep the records referred to under (e) available to the competent authorities, for inspection purposes, for a period of five years;

(g) they must comply with the principles and guidelines of good distribution practice for medicinal products as laid down in Article 84.

(h) they must maintain a quality system setting out responsibilities, processes and risk management measures in relation to their activities;

(i) they must immediately inform the competent authority and, where applicable, the marketing authorisation holder, of medicinal products they receive or are offered which they identify as falsified or suspect to be falsified.

For the purposes of point (b), where the medicinal product is obtained from another wholesale distributor, wholesale distribution authorisation holders must verify compliance with the principles and guidelines of good distribution practices by the supplying wholesale distributor. This includes verifying whether the supplying wholesale distributor holds a wholesale distribution authorisation.

Where the medicinal product is obtained from the manufacturer or importer, wholesale distribution authorisation holders must verify that the manufacturer or importer holds a manufacturing authorisation.

Where the medicinal product is obtained through brokering, the wholesale distribution authorisation holders must verify that the broker involved fulfils the requirements set out in this Directive.

## Article 81

With regard to the supply of medicinal products to pharmacists and persons authorised or entitled to supply medicinal products to the public, Member States shall not impose upon the holder of a distribution authorisation which has been granted by another Member State any obligation, in particular public service obligations, more stringent than those they impose on persons whom they have themselves authorised to engage in equivalent activities.

The holder of a marketing authorisation for a medicinal product and the distributors of the said medicinal product actually placed on the market in a Member State shall, within the limits of their responsibilities, ensure appropriate and continued supplies of that medicinal product to pharmacies and persons authorised to supply medicinal products so that the needs of patients in the Member State in question are covered.

The arrangements for implementing this Article should, moreover, be justified on grounds of public health protection and be proportionate in relation to the objective of such protection, in compliance with the Treaty rules, particularly those concerning the free movement of goods and competition.

## Article 82

For all supplies of medicinal products to a person authorized or entitled to supply medicinal products to the public in the Member State concerned, the authorized wholesaler must enclose a document that makes it possible to ascertain:

- batch number of the medicinal products at least for products bearing the safety features referred to in point (o) of Article 54;
- the date;
- the name and pharmaceutical form of the medicinal product;
- the quantity supplied;
- the name and address of the supplier and consignor.

Member States shall take all appropriate measures to ensure that persons authorized or entitled to supply medicinal products to the public are able to provide information that makes it possible to trace the distribution path of every medicinal product.

## Article 83

The provisions of this Title shall not prevent the application of more stringent requirements laid down by Member States in respect of the wholesale distribution of:

- narcotic or psychotropic substances within their territory;
- medicinal products derived from blood;
- immunological medicinal products;
- radiopharmaceuticals.

## Article 84

The Commission shall publish guidelines on good distribution practice. To this end, it shall consult the Committee for Medicinal Products for Human Use and the Pharmaceutical Committee established by Council Decision 75/320/EEC.[1]

## Article 85

This Title shall apply to homeopathic medicinal products.

## Article 85a

In the case of wholesale distribution of medicinal products to third countries, Article 76 and point (c) of the first paragraph of Article 80 shall not apply. Moreover, points (b) and (ca) of the first paragraph of Article 80 shall not apply where a product is directly received from a third country but not imported. However, in that case wholesale distributors shall ensure that the medicinal products are obtained only from persons who are authorised or entitled to supply medicinal products in accordance with the applicable legal and administrative provisions of the third country concerned. Where wholesale distributors supply medicinal products to persons in third countries, they shall ensure that such supplies are only made to persons who are authorised or entitled to receive medicinal products for wholesale distribution or supply to the public in accordance with the applicable legal and administrative provisions of the third country concerned. The requirements set out in Article 82 shall apply to the supply of medicinal products to persons in third countries authorised or entitled to supply medicinal products to the public.

---

[1] OJ L 147, 9.6.1975, p. 23.

## Article 85b

1   Persons brokering medicinal products shall ensure that the brokered medicinal products are covered by a marketing authorisation granted pursuant to Regulation (EC) No 726/2004 or by the competent authorities of a Member State in accordance with this Directive.

Persons brokering medicinal products shall have a permanent address and contact details in the Union, so as to ensure accurate identification, location, communication and supervision of their activities by competent authorities.

The requirements set out in points (d) to (i) of Article 80 shall apply *mutatis mutandis* to the brokering of medicinal products.

2   Persons may only broker medicinal products if they are registered with the competent authority of the Member State of their permanent address referred to in paragraph 1. Those persons shall submit, at least, their name, corporate name and permanent address in order to register. They shall notify the competent authority of any changes thereof without unnecessary delay.

Persons brokering medicinal products who had commenced their activity before 2 January 2013 shall register with the competent authority by 2 March 2013.

The competent authority shall enter the information referred to in the first subparagraph in a register that shall be publicly accessible.

3   The guidelines referred to in Article 84 shall include specific provisions for brokering.

4   This Article shall be without prejudice to Article 111. Inspections referred to in Article 111 shall be carried out under the responsibility of the Member State where the person brokering medicinal products is registered.

If a person brokering medicinal products does not comply with the requirements set out in this Article, the competent authority may decide to remove that person from the register referred to in paragraph 2. The competent authority shall notify that person thereof.

# UK Legislation on Wholesale Distribution

## Contents

## The Human Medicines Regulations 2012 [SI 2012/1916]

Editor's note   These extracts from the Regulations and Standard Provisions of the Human Medicines Regulations 2012 [SI 2012/1916] are presented for the reader's convenience. Reproduction is with the permission of HMSO and the Queen's Printer for Scotland. For any definitive information reference must be made to the original Regulations. The numbering and content within this section corresponds with the regulations set out in the published Statutory Instrument (SI 2012 No.1916).

## Citation and commencement

1   (1)   These Regulations may be cited as the Human Medicines Regulations 2012.

(2)   These Regulations come into force on 14th August 2012.

## General interpretation

8  (1)  In these Regulations (unless the context otherwise requires):

"the 2001 Directive" means Directive 2001/83/EC of the European Parliament and of the Council on the Community Code relating to medicinal products for human use;

"Article 126a authorisation" means an authorisation granted by the licensing authority under Part 8 of these Regulations;

"brokering" means all activities in relation to the sale or purchase of medicinal products, except for wholesale distribution, that do not include physical handling and that consist of negotiating independently and on behalf of another legal or natural person;

"Directive 2002/98/EC" means Directive 2002/98/EC of the European Parliament and of the Council of 27 January 2003 setting standards of quality and safety for the collection, testing, processing, storage and distribution of human blood and blood components and amending Directive 2001/83/EC;

"Directive 2004/23/EC" means Directive 2004/23/EC of the European Parliament and of the Council of 31 March 2004 on setting standards of quality and safety for the donation, procurement, testing, processing, preservation, storage and distribution of human tissues and cells;

"electronic communication" means a communication transmitted (whether from one person to another, from one device to another or from a person to a device or vice versa):

(a) by means of an electronic communications network within the meaning of section 32(1) of the Communications Act 2003; or

(b) by other means but while in an electronic form;

"EU marketing authorisation" means a marketing authorisation granted or renewed by the European Commission under Regulation (EC) No 726/2004;

"European Economic Area" or "EEA" means the European Economic Area created by the EEA agreement;

"exempt advanced therapy medicinal product" has the meaning given in regulation 171;

"export" means export, or attempt to export, from the United Kingdom, whether by land, sea or air;

"falsified medicinal product" means any medicinal product with a false representation of:

(a) its identity, including its packaging and labelling, its name or its composition (other than any unintentional quality defect) as regards any of its ingredients including excipients and the strength of those ingredients;

(b) its source, including its manufacturer, its country of manufacturing, its country of origin or its marketing authorisation holder; or

(c) its history, including the records and documents relating to the distribution channels used;

"Fees Regulations" means the Medicines (Products for Human Use) (Fees) Regulations 2013[1];

"herbal medicinal product" means a medicinal product whose only active ingredients are herbal substances or herbal preparations (or both);

"herbal preparation" means a preparation obtained by subjecting herbal substances to processes such as extraction, distillation, expression, fractionation, purification, concentration or fermentation, and includes a comminuted or powdered herbal substance, a tincture, an extract, an essential oil, an expressed juice or a processed exudate;

"herbal substance" means a plant or part of a plant, algae, fungi or lichen, or an unprocessed exudate of a plant, defined by the plant part used and the botanical name of the plant, either fresh or dried, but otherwise unprocessed;

"homoeopathic medicinal product" means a medicinal product prepared from homoeopathic stocks in accordance with a homoeopathic manufacturing procedure described by:

(a) the European Pharmacopoeia; or

(b) in the absence of such a description in the European Pharmacopoeia, in any pharmacopoeia used officially in an EEA State;

"import" means import, or attempt to import, into the UK, whether by land, sea or air;

"inspector" means a person authorised in writing by an enforcement authority for the purposes of Part 16 (enforcement) (and references to "the enforcement authority", in relation to an inspector, are to the enforcement authority by whom the inspector is so authorised);

"the licensing authority" has the meaning given by regulation 6(2);

"manufacturer's licence" has the meaning given by regulation 17(1);

"marketing authorisation" means:

(a) a UK marketing authorisation; or

(b) an EU marketing authorisation;

"medicinal product subject to general sale" has the meaning given in regulation 5(1) (classification of medicinal products);

---

[1] S.I. 2013/532.

"Regulation (EC) No 726/2004" means Regulation (EC) No 726/2004 of the European Parliament and of the Council of 31 March 2004 laying down Community procedures for the authorisation and supervision of medicinal products for human and veterinary use and establishing a European Medicines Agency;

"Regulation (EC) No 1394/2007" means Regulation (EC) No 1394/2007 of the European Parliament and of the Council of 13 November 2007 on advanced therapy medicinal products and amending Directive 2001/83/EC and Regulation (EC) No 726/2004;

"Regulation (EC) No 1234/2008" means Commission Regulation (EC) No 1234/2008 of 24 November 2008 concerning the examination of variations to the terms of marketing authorisations for medicinal products for human use and veterinary medicinal products;

"the relevant EU provisions" means the provisions of legislation of the European Union relating to medicinal products for human use, except to the extent that any other enactment provides for any function in relation to any such provision to be exercised otherwise than by the licensing authority;

"relevant European State" means an EEA State or Switzerland;

"relevant medicinal product" has the meaning given by regulation 48;

"special medicinal product" means a product within the meaning of regulation 167 or any equivalent legislation in an EEA State other than the UK;

"third country" means a country or territory outside the EEA:

"traditional herbal medicinal product" means a herbal medicinal product to which regulation 125 applies;

"traditional herbal registration" means a traditional herbal registration granted by the licensing authority under these Regulations;

"UK marketing authorisation" means a marketing authorisation granted by the licensing authority under:

(a) Part 5 of these Regulations; or

(b) Chapter 4 of Title III to the 2001 Directive (mutual recognition and decentralised procedure);

"wholesale dealer's licence" has the meaning given by regulation 18(1).

(2) In these Regulations, references to distribution of a product by way of wholesale dealing are to be construed in accordance with regulation 18(7) and (8).

(3) In these Regulations, references to selling by retail, or to retail sale, are references to selling a product to a person who buys it otherwise than for a purpose specified in regulation 18(8).

(4) In these Regulations, references to supplying anything in circumstances corresponding to retail sale are references to supplying it,

otherwise than by way of sale, to a person who receives it otherwise than for a purpose specified in regulation 18(8);

## Conditions for wholesale dealer's licence

42 (1) Regulations 43 to 45 apply to the holder of a wholesale dealer's licence (referred to in those regulations as "the licence holder") and have effect as if they were provisions of the licence (but the provisions specified in paragraph (2) do not apply to the holder of a wholesale dealer's licence insofar as the licence relates to exempt advanced therapy medicinal products).

(2) Those provisions are regulations 43(2) and (8) and 44.

(3) The requirements in Part 2 of Schedule 6 apply to the holder of a wholesale dealer's licence insofar as the licence relates to exempt advanced therapy medicinal products, and have effect as if they were provisions of the licence.

## Obligations of licence holder

43 (1) The licence holder must comply with the guidelines on good distribution practice published by the European Commission in accordance with Article 84 of the 2001 Directive.

(2) The licence holder must ensure, within the limits of the holder's responsibility, the continued supply of medicinal products to pharmacies, and other persons who may lawfully sell medicinal products by retail or supply them in circumstances corresponding to retail sale, so that the needs of patients in the United Kingdom are met.

(3) The licence holder must provide and maintain such staff, premises, equipment and facilities for the handling, storage and distribution of medicinal products under the licence as are necessary:
(a) to maintain the quality of the products; and
(b) to ensure their proper distribution.

(4) The licence holder must inform the licensing authority of any proposed structural alteration to, or discontinuance of use of, premises to which the licence relates or which have otherwise been approved by the licensing authority.

(5) Subject to paragraph (6), the licence holder must not sell or supply a medicinal product, or offer it for sale or supply, unless:
(a) there is a marketing authorisation, Article 126a authorisation, certificate of registration or traditional herbal registration (an "authorisation") in force in relation to the product; and

(b) the sale or supply, or offer for sale or supply, is in accordance with the authorisation.

(6) The restriction in paragraph (5) does not apply to:

(a) the sale or supply, or offer for sale or supply, of a special medicinal product;

(b) the export to an EEA State, or supply for the purposes of such export, of a medicinal product which may be placed on the market in that State without a marketing authorisation, Article 126a authorisation, certificate of registration or traditional herbal registration by virtue of legislation adopted by that State under Article 5(1) of the 2001 Directive; or

(c) the sale or supply, or offer for sale or supply, of an unauthorised medicinal product where the Secretary of State has temporarily authorised the distribution of the product under regulation 174.

(7) The licence holder must:

(a) keep documents relating to the sale or supply of medicinal products under the licence which may facilitate the withdrawal or recall from sale of medicinal products in accordance with paragraph (b);

(b) maintain an emergency plan to ensure effective implementation of the recall from the market of a medicinal product where recall is:

(i) ordered by the licensing authority or by the competent authority of any EEA State, or

(ii) carried out in co-operation with the manufacturer of, or the holder of the marketing authorisation, Article 126a authorisation, certificate of registration or traditional herbal registration for, the product; and

(c) keep records in relation to the receipt, dispatch or brokering of medicinal products, of:

(i) the date of receipt,

(ii) the date of despatch,

(iii) the date of brokering,

(iv) the name of the medicinal product,

(v) the quantity of the product received, dispatched or brokered,

(vi) the name and address of the person from whom the products were received or to whom they are dispatched,

(vii) the batch number of medicinal products bearing safety features referred to in point (o) of Article $54^2$ of the 2001 Directive.

(8) A licence holder ("L") who imports from another EEA State a medicinal product in relation to which L is not the holder of a

[2] Point (o) of Article 54a was inserted by Directive 2011/62/EU of the European Parliament and of the Council (OJ No L 174, 1.7.2011, p74).

marketing authorisation, Article 126a authorisation, certificate of registration or a traditional herbal registration shall:

(a) notify the intention to import that product to the holder of the authorisation and:

   (i)   in the case of a product which has been granted a marketing authorisation under Regulation (EC) No 726/2004, to the EMA; or

   (ii)  in any other case, the licensing authority; and

(b) pay a fee to the EMA in accordance with Article 76(4)[3] of the 2001 Directive or the licensing authority as the case may be, in accordance with the Fees Regulations, but this paragraph does not apply in relation to the wholesale distribution of medicinal products to a person in a third country.

(9) For the purposes of enabling the licensing authority to determine whether there are grounds for suspending, revoking or varying the licence, the licence holder must permit a person authorised in writing by the licensing authority, on production of identification, to carry out any inspection, or to take any samples or copies, which an inspector could carry out or take under Part 16 (enforcement).

(10) The holder ("L") must verify in accordance with paragraph (11) that any medicinal products received by L that are required by Article 54a[4] of the Directive to bear safety features are not falsified but this paragraph does not apply in relation to the distribution of medicinal products received from a third country by a person to a person in a third country.

(11) Verification under this paragraph is carried out by checking the safety features on the outer packaging, in accordance with the requirements laid down in the delegated acts adopted under Article 54a(2) of the 2001 Directive.

(12) The licence holder must maintain a quality system setting out responsibilities, processes and risk management measures in relation to their activities.

(13) The licence holder must immediately inform the licensing authority and, where applicable, the marketing authorisation holder, of medicinal products which the licence holder receives or is offered which the licence holder:

(a) knows or suspects; or

(b) has reasonable grounds for knowing or suspecting, to be falsified.

---

[3] Article 76(4) was inserted by Directive 2011/62/EU of the European Parliament and of the Council (OJ No L 174, 1.7.2011, p74).

[4] Article 54a was inserted by Directive 2011/62/EU of the European Parliament and of the Council (OJ No L 174, 1.7.2011, p74).

(14) Where the medicinal product is obtained through brokering, the licence holder must verify that the broker involved fulfils the requirements set out in regulation 45A(1)(b).

(15) In this regulation, "marketing authorisation" means:
   (a) a marketing authorisation issued by a competent authority in accordance with the 2001 Directive; or
   (b) an EU marketing authorisation.

## Requirement that wholesale dealers to deal only with specified persons

44  (1) Unless paragraph (2) applies, the licence holder must not obtain supplies of medicinal products from anyone except:
   (a) the holder of a manufacturer's licence or wholesale dealer's licence in relation to products of that description;
   (b) the person who holds an authorisation granted by another EEA State authorising the manufacture of products of the description or their distribution by way of wholesale dealing; or
   (c) where the supplier is not the holder of a manufacturer's licence, where the supply is in accordance with the principles and guidelines of good distribution practice,

   but this paragraph does not apply in relation to the distribution of medicinal products directly received from a third country but not imported into the EU.

   (2) From 28th October 2013 the licence holder must not obtain supplies of medicinal products from anyone except:
   (a) the holder of a manufacturer's licence or wholesale dealer's licence in relation to products of that description;
   (b) the person who holds an authorisation granted by another EEA State authorising the manufacture of products of the description or their distribution by way of wholesale dealing;
   (c) where the medicinal product is directly received from a third country ("A") for export to a third country ("B"), the supplier of the medicinal product in country A is a person who is authorised or entitled to supply such medicinal products in accordance with the legal and administrative provisions in country A; or
   (d) where the supplier is not the holder of a manufacturer's licence, where the supply is in accordance with the principles and guidelines of good distribution practice.

   (3) Where a medicinal product is obtained in accordance with paragraph (1), (2)(a) or (b), the licence holder must verify that:
   (a) the wholesale dealer who supplies the product complies with the principles and guidelines of good distribution practices; or

(b) the manufacturer or importer who supplies the product holds a manufacturing authorisation.

(4) Unless paragraph (5) applies, the licence holder may distribute medicinal products by way of wholesale dealing only to:

(a) the holder of a wholesale dealer's licence relating to those products;

(b) the holder of an authorisation granted by the competent authority of another EEA State authorising the supply of those products by way of wholesale dealing;

(c) a person who may lawfully sell those products by retail or may lawfully supply them in circumstances corresponding to retail sale; or

(d) a person who may lawfully administer those products,

but this paragraph does not apply in relation to medicinal products which are distributed by way of wholesale dealing to a person in a third country.

(5) From 28th October 2013, the licence holder may distribute medicinal products by way of wholesale dealing only to:

(a) the holder of a wholesale dealer's licence relating to those products;

(b) the holder of an authorisation granted by the competent authority of another EEA State authorising the supply of those products by way of wholesale dealing;

(c) a person who may lawfully sell those products by retail or may lawfully supply them in circumstances corresponding to retail sale;

(d) a person who may lawfully administer those products; or

(e) in relation to supply to persons in third countries, a person who is authorised or entitled to receive medicinal products for wholesale distribution or supply to the public in accordance with the applicable legal and administrative provisions of the third country concerned.

(6) Where a medicinal product is supplied to a person who is authorised or entitled to supply medicinal products to the public in accordance with paragraph (4)(c), (5)(c) or (e), the licence holder must enclose with the product a document stating the:

(a) date on which the supply took place;

(b) name and pharmaceutical form of the product supplied;

(c) quantity of product supplied;

(d) name and address of the licence holder; and

(e) batch number of the medicinal products bearing the safety features referred to in point (o) of Article 54 of the 2001 Directive.

(7)  The licence holder must:
   (a) keep a record of information supplied in accordance with paragraph (6) for at least five years beginning immediately after the date on which the information is supplied; and
   (b) ensure that the record is available to the licensing authority for inspection.

## Requirement as to responsible persons

45  (1)  The licence holder must ensure that there is available at all times at least one person (referred to in this regulation as the "responsible person") who in the opinion of the licensing authority:
   (a) has knowledge of the activities to be carried out and of the procedures to be performed under the licence which is adequate to carry out the functions mentioned in paragraph (2); and
   (b) has adequate experience relating to those activities and procedures.

(2)  Those functions are:
   (a) ensuring that the conditions under which the licence was granted have been, and are being, complied with; and
   (b) ensuring that the quality of medicinal products handled by the licence holder is being maintained in accordance with the requirements of the marketing authorisations, Article 126a authorisations, certificates of registration or traditional herbal registrations applicable to those products.

(3)  The licence holder must notify the licensing authority of:
   (a) any change to the responsible person; and
   (b) the name, address, qualifications and experience of the responsible person.

(4)  The licence holder must not permit any person to act as a responsible person other than the person named in the licence or another person notified to the licensing authority under paragraph (3).

(5)  Paragraph (6) applies if, after giving the licence holder and a person acting as a responsible person the opportunity to make representations (orally or in writing), the licensing authority thinks that the person:
   (a) does not satisfy the requirements of paragraph (1) in relation to qualifications or experience; or
   (b) is failing to carry out the functions referred to in paragraph (2) adequately or at all.

(6)  Where this paragraph applies, the licensing authority must notify the licence holder in writing that the person is not permitted to act as a responsible person.

## Standard provisions of licences

24   (1)   The standard provisions set out in Schedule 4 may be incorporated by the licensing authority in a licence under this Part granted on or after the date on which these Regulations come into force.

     (2)   The standard provisions may be incorporated in a licence with or without modifications and either generally or in relation to medicinal products of a particular class.

## Schedule 4 Standard provisions of licences

PART 4 WHOLESALE DEALER'S LICENCE

All wholesale dealer's licences

28   The provisions of this Part are standard provisions of a wholesale dealer's licence.

29   The licence holder must not use any premises for the handling, storage or distribution of medicinal products other than those specified in the licence or notified to the licensing authority from time to time and approved by the licensing authority.

30   The licence holder must provide such information as may be requested by the licensing authority concerning the type and quantity of medicinal products which the licence holder handles, stores or distributes.

31   The licence holder must take all reasonable precautions and exercise all due diligence to ensure that any information provided by the licence holder to the licensing authority which is relevant to an evaluation of the safety, quality or efficacy of a medicinal product which the licence holder handles, stores or distributes is not false or misleading.

Wholesale dealer's licence relating to special medicinal products

32   The provisions of paragraphs 33 to 42 are incorporated as additional standard provisions of a wholesale dealer's licence relating to special medicinal products.

33   Where and in so far as the licence relates to special medicinal products, the licence holder may only import such products from another EEA State:

    (a) in response to an order which satisfies the requirements of regulation 167, and

    (b) where the conditions set out in paragraphs 34 to 41 are complied with.

34  No later than 28 days prior to each importation of a special medicinal product, the licence holder must give written notice to the licensing authority stating the intention to import the product and stating the following particulars:

(a) the brand name, common name or scientific name of the medicinal product and (if different) any name under which the medicinal product is to be sold or supplied in the United Kingdom;

(b) any trademark or the name of the manufacturer of the medicinal product;

(c) in respect of each active constituent of the medicinal product, any international non-proprietary name or the British approved name or the monograph name, or where that constituent does not have any of those, the accepted scientific name or any other name descriptive of the true nature of the constituent;

(d) the quantity of medicinal product to be imported, which must not exceed the quantity specified in paragraph 38; and

(e) the name and address of the manufacturer or assembler of the medicinal product in the form in which it is to be imported and, if the person who will supply the medicinal product for importation is not the manufacturer or assembler, the name and address of the supplier.

35  The licence holder may not import the special medicinal product if, before the end of 28 days beginning immediately after the date on which the licensing authority sends or gives the licence holder an acknowledgement in writing by the licensing authority that it has received the notice referred to in paragraph 34, the licensing authority has notified the licence holder in writing that the product should not be imported.

36  The licence holder may import the special medicinal product referred to in the notice where the licence holder has been notified in writing by the licensing authority, before the end of the 28-day period referred to in paragraph 35, that the product may be imported.

37  Where the licence holder sells or supplies special medicinal products, the licence holder must, in addition to any other records which are required by the provisions of the licence, make and maintain written records relating to:

(a) the batch number of the batch of the product from which the sale or supply was made; and

(b) details of any adverse reaction to the product sold or supplied of which the licence holder becomes aware.

38  The licence holder must not, on any one occasion, import more than such amount as is sufficient for 25 single administrations, or for 25 courses of

treatment where the amount imported is sufficient for a maximum of three months' treatment, and must not, on any one occasion, import more than the quantity notified to the licensing authority under paragraph 34(d).

39    The licence holder must inform the licensing authority immediately of any matter coming to the licence holder's attention which might reasonably cause the licensing authority to believe that a special medicinal product imported in accordance with this paragraph can no longer be regarded as a product which can safely be administered to human beings or as a product which is of satisfactory quality for such administration.

40    The licence holder must not publish any advertisement, catalogue, or circular relating to a special medicinal product or make any representations in respect of that product.

41    The licence holder must cease importing or supplying a special medicinal product if the licence holder receives a notice in writing from the licensing authority directing that, from a date specified in the notice, a particular product or class of products may no longer be imported or supplied.

42    In this Part:

"British approved name" means the name which appears in the current edition of the list prepared by the British Pharmacopoeia Commission under regulation 318 (British Pharmacopoeia- lists of names);

"international non-proprietary name" means a name which has been selected by the World Health Organisation as a recommended international non-proprietary name and in respect of which the Director-General of the World Health Organisation has given notice to that effect in the World Health Organisation Chronicle; and

"monograph name" means the name or approved synonym which appears at the head of a monograph in the current edition of the British Pharmacopoeia, the European Pharmacopoeia or a foreign or international compendium of standards, and "current" in this definition means current at the time the notice is sent to the licensing authority.

## Wholesale dealer's licence relating to exempt advanced therapy medicinal products

43    The provisions of paragraph 44 are incorporated as additional standard provisions of a wholesale dealer's licence relating to exempt advanced therapy medicinal products.

44    The licence holder shall keep the data referred to in paragraph 16 of Schedule 6 for such period, being a period of longer than 30 years, as may be specified by the licensing authority.

## Schedule 6 Manufacturer's and wholesale dealer's licences for exempt advanced therapy medicinal products

### PART 2 WHOLESALE DEALER'S LICENCES

13    The requirements in paragraphs 14 to 20 apply to a wholesale dealer's licence insofar as it relates to exempt advanced therapy medicinal products.

14    The licence holder must obtain supplies of exempt advanced therapy medicinal products only from:

(a) the holder of a manufacturer's licence in respect of those products; or
(b) the holder of a wholesale dealer's licence in respect of those products.

15    The licence holder must distribute an exempt advanced therapy medicinal product by way of wholesale dealing only to:

(a) the holder of a wholesale dealer's licence in respect of those products; or
(b) a person who:
    (i)    may lawfully administer those products, and
    (ii)   solicited the product for an individual patient.

16    The licence holder must establish and maintain a system ensuring that the exempt advanced therapy medicinal product and its starting and raw materials, including all substances coming into contact with the cells or tissues it may contain, can be traced through the sourcing, manufacturing, packaging, storage, transport and delivery to the establishment where the product is used.

17    The licence holder must inform the licensing authority of any adverse reaction to any exempt advanced therapy medicinal product supplied by the holder of the wholesale dealer's licence of which the holder is aware.

18    The licence holder must, subject to paragraph 44 of Schedule 4, keep the data referred to in paragraph 16 for a minimum of 30 years after the expiry date of the exempt advanced therapy medicinal product.

19    The licence holder must secure that the data referred to in paragraph 16 will, in the event that:

(a) the licence is suspended, revoked or withdrawn; or
(b) the licence holder becomes bankrupt or insolvent,

be held available to the licensing authority by the holder of a wholesale dealer's licence for the period described in paragraph 18 or such longer period as may be required pursuant to paragraph 44 of Schedule 4.

20    The licence holder must not import or export any exempt advanced therapy medicinal product.

# UK Legislation on Brokering Medicines

## Contents

## The Human Medicines Regulations 2012 [SI 2012/1916]

> **Editor's note**  These extracts from the Human Medicines Regulations 2012 [SI 2012/1916] as amended by the Human Medicines (Amendment) Regulations 2013 [SI 2013/1855] are presented for the reader's convenience. Reproduction is with the permission of HMSO and the Queen's Printer for Scotland. For any definitive information reference must be made to the original amending Regulations. The numbering and content within this section corresponds with the regulations set out in the published Statutory Instrument (SI 2012 No. 1916) as amended.

## Citation and commencement

1   (1) These Regulations may be cited as the Human Medicines Regulations 2012.

(2) These Regulations come into force on 14th August 2012.

## General interpretation

8   (1) In these Regulations (unless the context otherwise requires)-
"brokering" means all activities in relation to the sale or purchase of medicinal products, except for wholesale distribution, that do not

include physical handling and that consist of negotiating independently and on behalf of another legal or natural person;

"falsified medicinal product" means any medicinal product with a false representation of:

(a) its identity, including its packaging and labelling, its name or its composition (other than any unintentional quality defect) as regards any of its ingredients including excipients and the strength of those ingredients;

(b) its source, including its manufacturer, its country of manufacturing, its country of origin or its marketing authorisation holder; or

(c) its history, including the records and documents relating to the distribution channels used.

## Brokering in medicinal products

**45A.** (1) A person may not broker a medicinal product unless:

(a) that product is covered by an authorisation granted:

(i) under Regulation (EC) No 726/2004; or

(ii) by a competent authority of a member State; and

(b) that person:

(i) is validly registered as a broker with a competent authority of a member State,

(ii) except where the person is validly registered with the competent authority of another EEA state, has a permanent address in the United Kingdom, and

(iii) complies with the guidelines on good distribution practice published by the European Commission in accordance with Article 84 of the 2001 Directive insofar as those guidelines apply to brokers.

(2) A person is not validly registered for the purpose of paragraph (1)(b) if:

(a) the person's permanent address is not entered into a register of brokers kept by a competent authority of a member State;

(b) the registration is suspended; or

(c) the person has notified the competent authority of a member State to remove that person from the register.

(3) Paragraph (1)(b)(i) does not apply until 20th October 2013 in relation to a person who brokered any medicinal product before 20th August 2013.

## Application for brokering registration

45B. (1) The licensing authority may not register a person as a broker unless paragraphs (2) to (7) are complied with.

(2) An application for registration must be made containing:

(a) the name of the person to be registered;

(b) the name under which that person is trading (if different to the name of that person);

(c) that person's:
   (i) permanent address in the United Kingdom,
   (ii) e-mail address, and
   (iii) telephone number;

(d) a statement of whether the medicinal products to be brokered are:
   (i) prescription only medicines,
   (ii) pharmacy medicines, or
   (iii) medicines subject to general sale;

(e) an indication of the range of medicinal products to be brokered;

(f) evidence that that person can comply with regulations 45A(1)(b)(iii), 45E(3)(a) to (f) and 45F(1); and

(g) any fee payable in connection with the application in accordance with the Fees Regulations.

(3) Where the address at which the emergency plan, documents or record necessary to comply with regulation 45E(3)(b) to (d) are kept is different from the address notified in accordance with sub-paragraph (2)(c)(i), the application must contain:

(a) that address where the plan or records are to be kept;

(b) the name of a person who can provide access to that address for the purpose of regulation 325 (rights of entry); and

(c) that person's:
   (i) address,
   (ii) e-mail address, and
   (iii) telephone number.

(4) Unless paragraph (6) applies, the application for registration must:

(a) be in English; and

(b) be signed by the person seeking a brokering registration.

(5) The pages of the application must be serially numbered.

(6) Where the application is made on behalf of the person seeking a brokering registration by another person ("A"), the application must:

(a) contain the name and address of A; and

(b) be signed by A.

## Criteria of broker's registration

**45E.** **(1)** Registration of a broker is conditional on that broker:

(a) complying with regulation 45A(1); and

(b) satisfying:

    (i)  the criteria in paragraphs (3), (4) and (7), and

    (ii) such other criteria as the licensing authority considers appropriate and notifies the broker of.

**(2)** The criteria referred to in paragraph (1)(b)(ii) may include (but are not limited to) the criteria specified in paragraphs (5) and (6).

**(3)** The broker must:

(a) have a permanent address in the United Kingdom;

(b) maintain an emergency plan to ensure effective implementation of the recall from the market of a medicinal product where recall is:

    (i)  ordered by the licensing authority or by the competent authority of any EEA State, or

    (ii) carried out in co-operation with the manufacturer of, or the holder of the marketing authorisation, for the product;

(c) keep documents relating to the sale or supply of medicinal products under the licence which may facilitate the withdrawal or recall from sale of medicinal products in accordance with sub-paragraph (b);

(d) record in relation to the brokering of each medicinal product:

    (i)  the name of the medicinal product,

    (ii) the quantity of the product brokered,

    (iii) the batch number of the medicinal product bearing the safety features referred to in point (o) of Article 54 of the 2001 Directive,

    (iv) the name and address of the:

        (aa) supplier, or

        (bb) consignee, and

    (v) the date on which the sale or purchase of the product is brokered;

(e) maintain a quality system setting out responsibilities, processes and risk management measures in relation to their activities; and

(f) keep the documents or record required by sub-paragraph (c) or (d) available to the licensing authority for a period of five years; and

(g) comply with regulation 45F(1), (2) and (4).

**(4)** Where the address at which the plan or records necessary to comply with paragraph (3)(b) to (d) are kept is different from the address notified in accordance with regulation 45B(2)(c)(i), the broker must:

(a) ensure that the plan or records are kept at an address in the United Kingdom; and

(b) inform the licensing authority of the address at which the plan or records are kept.

(5) The broker must provide such information as may be requested by the licensing authority concerning the type and quantity of medicinal products brokered within the period specified by the licensing authority.

(6) The broker must take all reasonable precautions and exercise all due diligence to ensure that any information provided by that broker to the licensing authority in accordance with regulation 45F is not false or misleading.

(7) For the purposes of enabling the licensing authority to determine whether there are grounds for suspending, revoking or varying the registration, the broker must permit a person authorised in writing by the licensing authority, on production of identification, to carry out any inspection, or to take any copies, which an inspector may carry out or take under regulations 325 (rights of entry) and 327 (powers of inspection, sampling and seizure).

## Provision of information

45F.  (1) A broker registered in the UK must immediately inform:
    (a) the licensing authority; and
    (b) where applicable, the marketing authorisation holder, of medicinal products which the broker identifies as, suspects to be, or has reasonable grounds for knowing or suspecting to be, falsified.

(2) On or before the date specified in paragraph (3), a broker who is, or has applied to the licensing authority to become, a registered broker in the United Kingdom must submit a report to the licensing authority, which:
    (a) includes a declaration that the broker has in place an appropriate system to ensure compliance with regulations 45A, 45B and this regulation; and
    (b) details the system which the broker has in place to ensure such compliance.

(3) The date specified for the purposes of this paragraph is:
    (a) in relation to any application made before 31st March 2014, the date of the application; and
    (b) in relation to each subsequent reporting year, 30th April following the end of that year.

(4) The broker must without delay notify the licensing authority of any changes to the matters in respect of which evidence has been supplied in relation to paragraph (2) which might affect compliance with the requirements of this Chapter.

(5) Any report or notification to the licensing authority under paragraph (2) or (4) must be accompanied by the appropriate fee in accordance with the Fees Regulations.

(6) The licensing authority may give a notice to a registered broker requiring that broker to provide information of a kind specified in the notice within the period specified in the notice.

(7) A notice under paragraph (6) may not be given to a registered broker unless it appears to the licensing authority that it is necessary for the licensing authority to consider whether the registration should be varied, suspended or revoked.

(8) A notice under paragraph (6) may specify information which the licensing authority thinks necessary for considering whether the registration should be varied, suspended or revoked.

(9) In paragraph (3)(b), "reporting year" means a period of twelve months ending on 31st March.

# Glossary of Legislation

## Contents

## European Legislation

**Council Directive 2001/83/EC on the Community code relating to medicinal products for human use**

This legislation regulates the licensing, manufacture of and wholesale dealing in medicinal products and registration, brokering of medicinal products and manufacture, importation and distribution of active substances within the European Community.

**Council Directive 2003/94/EC laying down the principles and guidelines of good manufacturing practice in respect of medicinal products for human use and investigational medicinal products**

This Directive lays down the principles and guidelines of good manufacturing practice in respect of medicinal products for human use whose manufacture requires an authorisation.

## UK Legislation

**The Human Medicines Regulations 2012 (SI 2012/1916)**

The Regulations set out a comprehensive regime for the authorisation of medicinal products for human use; for the manufacture, import, distribution, sale and supply of those products; for their labelling and advertising; and for pharmacovigilance.

For the most part the Regulations implement Directive 2001/83/EC of the European Parliament and of the Council of 6 November 2001 on the community code relating to medicinal products for human use (as amended). They also provide for the enforcement in the United Kingdom of Regulation (EC) No 726/2004 laying down Community procedures for the authorisation and supervision of medicinal products for human and veterinary use and establishing a European Medicines Agency.

These Regulations consolidate the 1968 Medicines Act and its supporting regulations including:

- **The Medicines (Applications for Manufacturer's and Wholesale Dealer's Licences) Regulations 1971 (SI 1971 No. 974), as amended**
- **Medicines (Manufacturer's Undertakings for Imported Products) Regulations 1977 (SI 1977 No. 1038), as amended**
- **Medicines for Human Use (Marketing Authorisations Etc.) Regulations 1994 (SI 1994 No. 3144), as amended**
- **Prescription Only Medicines (Human Use) Order 1997 (as amended) (SI 1997 No. 1830), as amended**

## The Medicines (Products for Human Use) (Fees) Regulations 2013 (2013 No. 532)

These Regulations make provision for the fees payable under the Medicines Act 1971 in respect of marketing authorizations, licences and certificates relating to medicinal products for human use.

## The Medicines for Human Use (Clinical Trials) Regulations 2004 (SI 2004 No. 1031) as amended

These Regulations implement Directive 2001/20/EC on the approximation of laws, regulations and administrative provisions of the Member States relating to the implementation of good clinical practice in the conduct of clinical trials on medicinal products for human use.

## The Unlicensed Medicinal Products for Human Use (Transmissible Spongiform Encephalopathies) (Safety) Regulations 2003 (SI 2003 No. 1680)

Regulates the importation and marketing of unlicensed medicinal products for human use in order to minimise the risk of the transmission of Transmissible Spongiform Encephalopathies via those products.

# Appendix

# Appendix

## Human and Veterinary Medicines Authorities in Europe

### Austria

Austrian Medicines and Medical Devices
Agency - Austrian Federal Office for Safety in
Health Care
Traisengasse 5
A-1200 Vienna
Austria
Phone +43 50 555 36111
Email  BASG-AGESMedizinmarktaufsicht
@ages.at
Website(s) http://www.basg.gv.at

### Belgium

DG Enterprise and Industry - F/2 BREY 10/073
Avenue d'Auderghem 45
B - 1049 Brussels
Belgium

Federal Agency for Medicines and Health
Products
EUROSTATION
Victor Horta
40 40
1060 Brussels
Belgium
Email welcome@fagg-afmps.be
Website(s) http://www.fagg-afmps.be/en/

### Bulgaria

Bulgarian Drug Agency
8, Damyan Gruev Str
1303 Sofia
Bulgaria
Phone +359 2 8903 555
Fax +359 2 8903 434
Email bda@bda.bg
Website(s) http://www.bda.bg

National Veterinary Service
15A, Pencho Slaveiko Blvd
1606 Sofia
Bulgaria
Phone +359 2 915 98 20
Fax +359 2 954 95 93
Email cvo@nvms.government.bg
Website(s) http://www.nvms.government.bg

### Croatia

Croatian Agency for Medicinal Products and
Medical Devices
Ksaverska c.4
10000 Zagreb
Croatia
Phone +385 1 4884 100
Fax +385 1 4884 110
Email halmed@halmed.hr
Website(s) http://www.halmed.hr

Ministry of Agriculture, Veterinary and Food
Safety Directorate
Planinska Street 2a
10000 Zagreb
Croatia
Phone +385 6443 540
Fax +385 6443 899
Email veterinarstvo@mps.hr
Website(s) http://www.veterinarstvo.hr

### Cyprus

Ministry of Health Pharmaceutical Services
7 Larnacos Ave
CY - 1475 Nicosia
Cyprus
Website(s) http://www.moh.gov.cy

## Czech Republic

**State Institute for Drug Control**
Srobárova 48
CZ - 100 41 Praha 10
Czech Republic
Phone + 420 272 185 111
Fax + 420 271 732 377
Email posta@sukl.cz
Website(s) http://www.sukl.eu

**Institute for State Control of Veterinary Biologicals and Medicaments**
Hudcova Str. 56A
CZ-621 00 Brno-Medlánky
Czech Republic
Phone +420 541 518 211
Fax +420 541 210 026
Email uskvbl@uskvbl.cz
Website(s) http://www.uskvbl.cz/

## Denmark

**Danish Health and Medicines Agency**
Axel Heides Gade 1
DK–2300 København S
Denmark
Phone +45 72 22 74 00
Fax +45 44 88 95 99
Email sst@sst.dk
Website(s) http://www.dkma.dk

## European Commission

**DG Enterprise F2 Pharmaceuticals**
Rue de la Loi 200
B-1049 Brussels
Belgium

**DG Health and Consumers: Unit D6: Medicinal Products - Quality, Safety and Efficacy; Unit D5: Medicinal Products - Authorisations, European Medicines Agency**
Rue de la Loi 200
B-1049 Brussels
Belgium
Phone +32 2 299 11 11
Email: sanco-pharmaceuticals-d5@ec.europa.eu; sanco-pharmaceuticals-d6@ec.europa.eu
Website(s) http://ec.europa.eu/health/human-use/index_en.htm

## European Medicines Agency (EMA)
7 Westferry Circus
London E14 4HB
United Kingdom
Phone +44 20 74 18 84 00
Fax +44 20 74 18 84 16
Email info@ema.europa.eu
Website(s) http://www.ema.europa.eu/

## Estonia

**State Agency of Medicines**
1 Nooruse St
EE-50411 Tartu
Estonia
Phone +372 737 41 40
Fax +372 737 41 42
Email sam@sam.ee
Website(s) http://www.sam.ee/

## Finland

**Finnish Medicines Agency**
PO Box 55
FI-00034 Fimea
Finland
Phone +358 29 522 3341
Fax +358 29 522 3001
Website(s) http://www.fimea.fi/

## France

**French National Agency for Medicines and Health Products Safety (ANSM)**
143-147 bd
Anatole France
FR-93285 Saint Denis Cedex
France
Email ANSM@ansm.sante.fr
Website(s) http://www.ansm.sante.fr

**Agence Nationale du Médicament Vétérinaire, Agence nationale de sécurité sanitaire de l'alimentation, de l'environnement et du travail (ANMV)**
8 rue Claude Bourgelat, Parc d'Activités de la Grande Marche, Javené BP
CS 70611 - 35306 Fougères
France
Phone +33 (0) 2 99 94 78 71

Email sylvie.goby@anses.fr
Website(s) http://www.anses.fr

## Germany

**Federal Institute for Drugs and Medical Devices (BfArM)**
Kurt-Georg-Kiesinger-Allee 3
53175 Bonn
Germany
Phone +49 (0)228-207-30
Fax +49 (0)228-207-5207
Email poststelle@bfarm.de
Website(s) http://www.bfarm.de

**Federal Office of Consumer Protection and Food Safety**
Mauerstraße 39-42
D-10117 Berlin
Germany
Phone +49 30 1 84 44-000
Fax +49 30 1 84 44-89 999
Email poststelle@bvl.bund.de
Website(s) http://www.bvl.bund.de
(pharmaceuticals)

**Paul-Ehrlich Institut (Federal Institute for Vaccines and Biomedicines)**
Paul-Ehrlich-Straße 51-59
63225 Langen
Germany
Phone +49 6103 77 0
Fax +49 6103 77 1234
Email pei@pei.de
Website(s) http://www.pei.de
(vaccines, blood products, sera)

## Greece

**National Organization for Medicines**
Messogion Avenue 284
GR - 15562 Athens
Greece
Phone +30 210 6507200
Fax +30 210 6545535
Email relation@eof.gr
Website(s) http://www.eof.gr/
(pharmaceuticals and immunologicals)

## Hungary

**National Institute of Pharmacy**
Zrínyi U. 3
H-1051 Budapest
Hungary
Website(s) http://www.ogyi.hu/

**National Food Chain Safety Office, Directorate of Veterinary Medicinal Products**
Szállás utca 8
H-1107 Budapest 10.Pf. 318
Hungary
Phone +36 1 433 03 30
Fax +36 1 262 28 39
Email info.aogyti@oai.hu
Website(s) http://www.nebih.gov.hu/en/specialities/veterinary

## Iceland

**Icelandic Medicines Agency**
Vinlandsleid 14
IS - 113 Reykjavik
Iceland
Phone +354 520 2100
Fax +354 561 2170
Email ima@ima.is
Website(s) http://www.ima.is

## Ireland

**Health Products Regulatory Agency**
Kevin O'Malley House
Earlsfort Centre
Earlsfort Terrace
IRL - Dublin 2
Ireland
Phone +353 1 676 4971
Fax +353 1 676 7836
Email info@hpra.ie
Website(s) http://www.hpra.ie

**Department of Agriculture and Food**
Kildare St
Dublin
Ireland
Phone +353 1 607 20 00
Fax +353 1 661 62 63
Email info@agriculture.gov.ie
Website(s) http://www.agriculture.gov.ie

## Italy

**Italian Medicines Agency**
Via del Tritone, 181
I-00187 Rome
Italy
Phone +39 6 5978401
Website(s) http://www.agenziafarmaco.it/

**Laboratorio di Medicina Veterinaria, Istituto Superiore di Sanità**
Viale Regina Elena 299
I - 00161 Rome
Italy
Phone +39 6 49 38 70 76
Fax +39 6 49 38 70 77

**Ministero della Salute, Direzione Generale della Sanità Pubblica Veterinaria, degli Allimenti e della Nutrizione, Uff. XI**
Piazzale G. Marconi 25
I - 00144 Rome
Italy
Phone +39 06 59 94 65 84
Fax +39 06 59 94 69 49
Website(s) http://www.ministerosalute.it/

## Latvia

**State Agency of Medicines of Latvia**
15 Jersikas Street
LV - 1003 Riga
Latvia
Phone +371-7078424
Fax +371-7078428
Email info@zva.gov.lv
Website(s) http://www.zva.gov.lv/

**Food and Veterinary Service**
Peldu St 30
LV - 1050 Riga
Latvia
Phone +371 67095271
Fax +371 67095270
Email nrd@pvd.gov.lv
Website(s) http://www.pvd.gov.lv

## Liechtenstein

**Office of Health/Medicinal Products Control Agency**
Äulestr 512
FL - 9490 Vaduz

Liechtenstein
Email pharminfo@llv.li
Website(s) www.llv.li/

## Lithuania

**State Medicines Control Agency**
Žirmūnų str. 139A
LT-09120 Vilnius
Lithuania
Phone +370 5 263 92 64
Fax +370 5 263 92 65
Email vvkt@vvkt.lt
Website(s) http://www.vvkt.lt/

**National Food and Veterinary Risk Assessment Institute**
J. Kairiukscio str. 10
LT-08409 Vilnius
Lithuania
Phone +370 5 2780470
Fax +370 5 2780471
Email nmvrvi@vet.lt
Website(s) http://www.nmvrvi.lt

**State Food and Veterinary Service**
Siesiku str. 19
LT-07170 Vilnius
Lithuania
Email vvt@vet.lt
Website(s) http://www.vet.lt

## Luxembourg

**Ministry of Health**
Allée Marconi
L - 2120 Luxembourg
Luxembourg
Phone +352 24785593
Fax +352 24795615
Email jacqueline.genoux-hames@ms.etat.lu
Website(s) http://www.ms.etat.lu

## Malta

**Medicines Authority**
203, Level 3, Rue D'Argens
GZR 1368 Gzira
Malta

Phone +356 23439000
Fax +356 23439161
Email info.medicinesauthority@gov.mt
Website(s) http://www.medicinesauthority.gov.mt

**Veterinary Medicines and Animal Nutrition Section**
Abattoir Square
Albert Town
MRS 1123 Marsa
Malta
Phone + 356 22925375
Email vafd.msdec@gov.mt
Website(s) http://vafd.gov.mt/approved-vet-pharmaceaticals-in-malta

## Netherlands

**Medicines Evaluation Board**
Graadt van Roggenweg 500
NL - 3531 AH Utrecht
The Netherlands
Phone +31 (0) 88 - 224 80 00
Fax +31 (0) 88 - 224 80 01
Website(s) http://www.cbg-meb.nl/

## Norway

**Norwegian Medicines Agency (NOMA)**
Sven Oftedalsvei 6
N - 0950 Oslo
Norway
Phone +47 22 89 77 00
Fax +47 22 89 77 99
Email post@legemiddelverket.no
Website(s) http://www.legemiddelverket.no

## Poland

**Office for Registration of Medicinal Products, Medical Devices and Biocidal Products**
41 Zabkowska Str
03-736 Warsaw
Poland
Phone +48 (22) 492 11 00
Fax +48 (22) 492 11 09
Website(s) http://bip.urpl.gov.pl

## Portugal

**INFARMED - National Authority of Medicines and Health Products, IP**
Av. do Brasil 53
P - 1749-004 Lisbon
Portugal
Phone +351 217987100
Fax +351 217987316
Email infarmed@infarmed.pt
Website(s) http://www.infarmed.pt/portal/page/portal/INFARMED

**Food and Veterinary Directorate General**
Largo da Academia Nacional de Belas Artes, n. 2
1294-105 Lisbon
Portugal
Phone +351 21 323 95 00
Fax +351 21 346 35 18
Email dirgeral@dgav.pt
Website(s) http://www.dgav.pt

## Romania

**National Agency for Medicines and Medical Devices**
48, Av. Sanatescu
011478 Bucharest
Romania
Phone +4021 3171100
Fax +4021 3163497
Website(s) http://www.anm.ro/en/home.html

**Institute for Control of Biological Products and Veterinary Medicines**
Str. Dudului 37, sector 6
060603 Bucharest
Romania
Phone +40 21 220 21 12
Fax +40 21 221 31 71
Email icbmv@icbmv.ro
Website(s) http://www.icbmv.ro/

## Slovakia

**State Institute for Drug Control**
Kvetná 11
SK-825 08 Bratislava 26
Slovakia
Phone +421 2 5070 1111
Fax +421 2 5556 4127

Email sukl@sukl.sk
Website(s) http://www.sukl.sk/

**Institute for State Control of Veterinary Biologicals and Medicaments**
Biovetská 34
PO Box 52c
SK-949 01 Nitra
Slovakia
Phone +421 37 6515506
Fax +421 37 6517915
Email uskvbl@uskvbl.sk
Website(s) http://www.uskvbl.sk/

## Slovenia

**Javna agencija Republike Slovenije za zdravila in medicinske pripomočke**
Ptujska ulica 21
Sl-1000 Ljubljana
Slovenia
Phone + 38 6 8 2000 500
Fax + 38 6 8 2000 510
Email info@jazmp.si
Website(s) http://www.jazmp.si

## Spain

**Spanish Agency of Medicines and Medical Devices**
Parque Empresarial Las
Mercedes Edificio 8C/
Campezo, 1
E - 28022 Madrid
Spain
Phone +34 91 8225997
Fax +34 91 8225128

Email internacional@aemps.es
Website(s) www.agemed.es

## Sweden

**Medical Products Agency**
Dag Hammarskjölds väg 42 / Box 26
SE - 751 03 Uppsala
Sweden
Phone +46 (0) 18 17 46 00
Fax +46 (0) 18 54 85 66
Email registrator@mpa.se
Website(s) www.lakemedelsverket.se

## United Kingdom

**Medicines and Healthcare Products Regulatory Agency**
151 Buckingham Palace Road
Victoria
London
SW1W 9SZ
United Kingdom
Phone +44 (0)20 3080 6000
Fax +44 (0)203 118 9803
Website(s) www.mhra.gov.uk

**Veterinary Medicines Directorate (VMD)**
Woodham Lane
New Haw
Addlestone
KT15 3LS
United Kingdom
Phone +44 1932 33 69 11
Fax +44 1932 33 66 18
Email postmaster@vmd.defra.gsi.gov.uk
Website(s) www.vmd.defra.gov.uk

# Index